THE CHINA SEA DIRECTORY.
VOL. IV. 1873.

THE
CHINA SEA DIRECTORY,

VOL. IV.

COMPRISING THE

COASTS OF KOREA, RUSSIAN TARTARY, THE JAPAN ISLANDS, GULFS OF TARTARY AND AMÚR, AND THE SEA OF OKHOTSK;

ALSO THE

MEIACO, LIU-KIU, LINSCHOTEN, MARIANA, BONIN, SAGHALIN, AND KURIL ISLANDS.

COMPILED FROM VARIOUS SOURCES

By Navigating Lieutenant FREDERICK W. JARRAD, R.N.

PUBLISHED BY ORDER OF THE LORDS COMMISSIONERS OF THE ADMIRALTY.

LONDON:
PRINTED FOR THE HYDROGRAPHIC OFFICE, ADMIRALTY;
AND SOLD BY
J. D. POTTER, *Agent for the Admiralty Charts,*
31, POULTRY, AND 11, KING STREET, TOWER HILL.
1873.

Price Six Shillings.

A Short Glossary of Japanese Words used in the Charts and Sailing Directions.

Japanese.	English.	Japanese.	English.
Chisai	Little, small.	Minami	South.
Ko, as a prefix	"	Higashi	East.
Oki	Large, great.	Nishi	West.
Ō, as a prefix		Kaze	Wind.
Daibo	Fort.	Ame	Rain.
Kuchi, makes Guchi in the compound, as	Mouth.	Yuki	Snow.
		Kumo	Clouds.
		Midzu	Water.
		Hi	Fire.
Kawa guchi	The river's mouth.	Tsŭki	Moon.
Kawa, makes Gawa in the compound	River.	Ō Hi	Sun.
		Ki	Tree.
		Michi	Road.
		Machi	Street.
Yama	Mountain.	Iye	House.
Kuni	Country.	Hiroi	Wide.
Nada	A sea.	Hoso	Narrow.
Umi	The sea.	Nagai, pronounced in Yedo Nangai	Long.
Seto	Strait.		
Hana	Point.		
Saki	Cape.	Mijikai	Short.
Misaki	A prominent cape.	No (possessive pron.)	Of.
Ura	Bay.		
Minato	Harbour.	Wa (the definite art.)	The.
Mura	Village.		
Sima, in the Yedo dialect pronounced Shima, and sometimes forms in the compound Jima, as	Island.	Wo, the objective case.	
		Ga (the indefinite art.)	A or any.
		Kane, makes in the compound Gane	Metal.
Awa jima	Awa island.	Aki-gane (red metal)	Copper.
Hama	Coast, shore.		
Tei-haku	Anchorage.	Kin	Gold.
Siwo, pronounced in Yedo Shiwo	Tide.	Gin	Silver.
		Tetsŭ	Iron.
		Tomio	Lighthouse.
Ō shiwo, or siwo	Spring tide.	Se	A shoal.
Ko shiwo "	Neap tide.	Fukai	Deep.
Michi shiwo "	Flood tide.	Asai	Shallow.
Hiki shiwo "	Ebb tide.	Takai	High, lofty, tall.
Iwa	Rock.	Tera	Temple.
Ishi	Stone.	Fune	Boat.
Kita	North.	Joki sen	Steamer.

GLOSSARY OF JAPANESE WORDS.

Japanese.	English.	Japanese.	English.
Ho bune	Sailing vessel.	Aki	Autumn.
Kuroi	Black.	Fuyu	Winter.
Shiroi	White.	Hama	Sand.
Hana iro	Blue.	Doro	Mud.
Ki iro	Yellow.	Hashi	Bridge.
Hatoba	Wharf, landing place.	Sibansho	Guard house.
		Gunkan	Man-of-war.
Gake	Cliff.	Hata	Flag.
Take	Hill.	Gats	Month.
Ikari	Anchor.	Nichi	Day.
Uma	Horse.	Omo kaji	Starboard.
Imo	Potatoes.	Tori kaji	Port.
Mame	Beans.	Ushi	Bull.
Kochira ni asai ka	Is it shoal here?	Niwatori	Fowl.
„ fukai „	Is it deep here?	Tamago	Egg.
Nin or jin	Man.	Kamo	Duck.
Onna	Woman.	Karo	Magistrate.
Kodomo	Child.	Shikwan	Officer.
Uchi	In, inside.	Daimio	Noble.
Haru	Spring.	Joki sha	Railway.
Natsŭ	Summer.	Oka	Land.
Unjosho	Custom house.	Midzu umi	Lake.

Note.—The vowels are sounded as in the continental pronunciation of Latin; or as in the following English words;—*a*, as *a* in father; *e*, as *ay* in say; *i*, as *ee* in meet; *o*, as *o* in more; and *u*, as *oo* in fool. *i* and *u* are often almost inaudible; in such cases they are written ĭ, ŭ; *au, ou,* and *oo* are written ō (long). The consonants are pronounced as in English.*

---

* This method of writing Japanese names has been carried out in the body of this work, and it is requested that officers contributing information will follow the same rule in this respect.

ADVERTISEMENT.

The China Sea Directory, Vol. IV., comprises Sailing Directions for the coasts of Korea, Russian Tartary, and Kamchatka; for the seas of Japan and Okhotsk; for the Liu-kiu, Linschoten, Japan, Saghalin, and Kuril islands; and for the off-lying islands and dangers between the parallels of 12° N. and 35° N., and the meridians of 130° E. and 180°.

These Directions were formerly contained in the fourth edition of the China Pilot, which has since been revised, and is now published in two parts under the title of "The China Sea Directory, Vols. III. and IV." The information contained in this volume has been obtained from the following sources:—

The description of the west and south coasts of Korea, which are not yet completely surveyed, is from the voyages of the *Alceste* and *Lyra* in the year 1816, the ship *Lord Amherst*, 1832; H.M. ships *Blonde* and *Pylades*, 1840; the French frigate *Virginie*, 1856; H.M. surveying vessels *Actæon*, *Dove* and *Swallow*, 1859–63; and from the published remarks of Officers of the United States Navy in 1868.

The east coast of Korea, from Tsau-liang-hai (discovered by Capt. Broughton in 1797) to Tumen ula, is principally from the voyage of the Russian frigate *Pallas* in 1854, and of the French frigate *Virginie*, 1856. From Posiette harbour to the river Amúr, from the report of the Russian survey in 1861, and from the observations of various Officers of H.M. ships.

Descriptive information of the coasts of Japan and of the intricate parts of the Inland sea has been obtained from the surveys and remarks of Commanders Ward, Bullock, Brooker, and St. John, of Staff Commanders J. Richards and E. Wilds, of Navigating Lieutenant W. F. Maxwell, and other Officers of H.M. Navy.

The coast line of the island of Yezo has been lately in part examined by H.M. surveying vessel *Sylvia*. The description of the off-lying islands and dangers are from various sources; but chiefly from Krusenstern, 1804; Basil Hall, 1816; Beechey, 1827; Seibold, 1828; Belcher, 1845; Cecille, 1846; the American Expedition to Japan under Commodore Perry in 1853–4; and Don E. Sanchez y Zaya, 1865; and from documents in Hydrographic Office, including the Anuario de la direction Hidrographia, and Annuale Hydrographique.

This volume must, of necessity, be considered incomplete, as it comprises the description of a large extent of coast, and of numerous islands and dangers which have been imperfectly explored. Under these circumstances it is hoped that, with a view to the general benefit of the mariner, Officers both of the Royal Navy and Mercantile Marine will transmit to the Secretary of the Admiralty notice of errors or omissions which may come under their observation, and also of any fresh information they may obtain.

G. H. R.

Hydrographic Office, Admiralty, London,
March 1873.

CONTENTS.

CHAPTER I.

GENERAL REMARKS.—CLIMATE, PREVAILING WINDS AND WEATHER, FOGS, STORMS, GALES, TYPHOONS, AND CURRENTS; AND REMARKS ON MAKING PASSAGES.

	Page
Winds and currents on the west coast of Korea	1, 2
——————————, Sea of Japan and east coast of Korea	2–5
——————————, Gulf of Tartary, sea of Okhotsk, and S.E. coast of Kamchatka	5–9
——————————, Mariana and Bonin islands	9–11
——————————, Meiaco sima, Liu-Kiu, and Linschoten islands	11, 12
——————————, Japan islands; south and east coasts	12–15
——————————, Straits of Tsugar and La Pérouse, Yezo and Kuril islands	15–19
Typhoons	19–22
Currents.—Japan stream, Kamchatka current, and Oya Siwo	23–26
Remarks on making passages	26–30

CHAPTER II.

WEST, SOUTH-WEST, AND SOUTH COASTS OF KOREA; AND KOREA STRAIT.

West coast of Korea.—Ping Yang inlet, Sir James Hall group, Joachim, Caroline, and Deception bays; Marjoribanks harbour; Shoal gulf and Korean archipelago	31–48
South-west coast of Korea.—Bate group; Quelpart island	48–54
South coast of Korea.—Kuper harbour; Chrichton and Nan How groups; Peel group; Sentinel island; Tsau-liang-hai harbour; Tsu sima and Korea strait	54–74

CHAPTER III.

SEA OF JAPAN.—EAST COAST OF KOREA AND RUSSIAN TARTARY.—GULF OF TARTARY AND RIVER AMÚR.—TARTARY STRAIT.—SEA OF OKHOTSK, AND KAMCHATKA.

East coast of Korea.—Unkofsky bay; Ping hai harbour; Port Lazaref; cape Bruat; Goshkevich bay; the Tumen river	75–86

viii   CONTENTS.

	Page
Russian Tartary.—Posiette bay; Expedition bay; Nov-gorod harbour; the Eastern Bosphorus; America bay; Siau Wuhu bay; Olga bay; St. Vladmir bay	86–99
Gulf of Tartary.—Barracouta harbour; Castries bay; gulf of Amúr; river Amúr	100–107
Sea of Okhotsk.—Shantarski islands; port Aian; Okhotsk harbour	108–111
S.E. coast of Kamchatka.—Avatcha bay; Petropaulski	111–115

CHAPTER IV.

MARIANA OR LADRONE ISLANDS; ISLANDS SOUTH-EAST OF JAPAN; MEIACO SIMA, LIU-KIU, AND LINSCHOTEN GROUPS.

Mariana islands.—Guam; Port San Luis d'Apra; Rota island; Aguijan island; Tinian island; Saipan island; Magicienne bay; Anatajan island; Zelandia breakers; Agrigan; Assumption; Urracas; Farallon de Pajaros	116–127
Islands in the Western Pacific.—Weeks island; Euphrosyne reef; Parece vela; Britomart reef; Lindsay island; Volcano islands; the Malabrigos; Bonin islands; Borodino islands; Rasa island	128–135
Meiaco sima group.—Koumi island; Port Broughton; Port Haddington; Ty-pin-san group; Pinnacle, Craig, and Agincourt islands; Raleigh rock	135–142
Liu-Kiu islands.—Okinawa sima; Napha-Kiang; Port Oonting; Montgomery group; Germantown reef; Sandon rocks	143–154
Linschoten islands.—Colnett strait; Tanega sima; Taka sima; Kowose; Kuro sima; Van Diemen strait	155–158

CHAPTER V.

THE JAPAN ISLANDS, COMPRISING THE SOUTH AND EAST COASTS OF KIUSIU, SIKOK, AND NIPON, AND THE ISLANDS LYING SOUTH OF YEDO GULF.

South and East coasts of Kiusiu and Sikok.—Satano misaki; Nelly rock; Nomi; Su saki; Ura no utsi; Kotsi inlet	160, 161
S.E. coast of Nipon.—Ō sima; Owasi bay; Goza harbour; cape Sima; Matoya harbour; Owari bay; Lady Inglis rock; Portsmouth breakers; gulf of Suruga; Mikomoto; Simoda harbour; Odawara bay; Joka sima	161–178
Gulf of Yedo.—Cape Sagami; Kaneda bay; Yokoska harbour; Treaty point; Yokohama; Yedo; Futsu saki; Tati-yama bay; Mela head	179–191
Islands south of Yedo Gulf.—Lots Wife; Fatsizio; Redfield rocks; Kosu sima; Utone; Vries island	192–196
E. coast of Nipon.—Sendai bay; Yamada harbour; Miyako; cape de Vries; Siriya saki	196–200

CONTENTS.

CHAPTER VI.

THE SETO UCHI, OR INLAND SEA, AND ITS APPROACHES.

	Page
The Boungo channel.—Okino sima; Euryalus rock; Takanaba	201, 202
The Kii Channel.—I sima; Naruto passage; Yura; Yura no uchi; Hino misaki; Tanabe bay; Siwo misaki	202–216
Isumi nada.—Isumi strait; Ōsaka; Hiogo; Kobe; Akashi strait	218–224
Harima nada.—Awadji sima; Sozu sima; St. Vincent channel	225–234
Bingo nada.—Takaikami; Kurusima strait; the Northern route	235–252
Misima nada.—Nokona; Mosuki; Kosii sima; cape Simonamba	235–254
Iyo nada.—Yuri island; Hime sima	255
Suwo nada.—Cape Imagawa; I saki; Moto yama; Simonoseki strait	256–265

CHAPTER VII.

JAPAN ISLANDS.—THE GOTO ISLANDS, AND THE WEST COASTS OF KIUSIU AND NIPON.

The Goto islands; Pallas rocks; Meac sima; Kosiki islands; Pioneer rocks, and Udsi sima	266–271
West coast of Kiusiu.—Kagosima gulf; Nagasaki harbour; Hirado no seto; Imari gulf, and Hakosaki bay	271–312
West coast of Nipon.—Oki islands; Tsuruga bay; Nanao harbour; Niegata; Sado island; Awa sima, and Bittern rocks	312–324

CHAPTER VIII.

JAPAN ISLANDS.—TSUGAR STRAIT, NORTH COAST OF NIPON, YEZO ISLAND; SAGHALIN AND KURIL ISLANDS.

Tsugar strait.—Awomori bay; Toriwi saki; Hakodate, and cape Yesan	325–337
West coast of Yezo.—Iwani; Oterranai; cape Nossyab, and Endermo harbour	337–341
East coast of Yezo.—Akishi; Hamanaki; cape Noyshap, and islands off cape Noyshap	341–346
Yezo strait, &c.—Notske spit; cape Sirotoko; Abashira; Risiri island; Refunsiri island	346–349
La Pérouse strait.—Dangerous rock; Aniwa bay; Tobootchi bay	349–354
E. and W. coasts of Saghalin.—Dui; Jonquière bay; cape Patience; cape Elizabeth, and cape Mary	354–360
Kuril islands.—Kunashir; Skotan; Port Tavano; Paramushir; Kuril, and Little Kuril straits	360–365
TABLE OF POSITIONS	366–372
TIDE TABLE	373
INDEX	374–386

IN THIS WORK THE BEARINGS, INCLUDING THE DIRECTION
OF WINDS AND CURRENTS, ARE ALL MAGNETIC,
EXCEPT WHERE MARKED AS TRUE.

THE DISTANCES ARE EXPRESSED IN SEA MILES OF
60 TO A DEGREE OF LATITUDE.

A CABLE'S LENGTH IS THE TENTH PART OF A MILE, OR 101·26
FATHOMS, BUT ASSUMED TO BE EQUAL TO 100 FATHOMS.

THE CHINA SEA DIRECTORY,

Vol. IV.

CHAPTER I.

GENERAL REMARKS—CLIMATE, PREVAILING WINDS AND WEATHER, FOGS, STORMS AND GALES, TYPHOONS—CURRENTS—MAKING PASSAGES.*

THE KOREA, KOREA STRAIT, COAST OF TARTARY, SEA OF JAPAN, GULF OF TARTARY, SEA OF OKHOTSK AND KAMCHATKA.

THE KOREA.—This large peninsula, separated from China, on the West by the Yalu kiang, and from Russian Tartary on the East by the Tumen ula, has been but little visited. The numerous groups of islands lying contiguous to its western shores were visited by Captain Basil Hall in 1816, and Captain Belcher, in 1845, and their positions have been laid down with tolerable accuracy; but few vessels have visited this coast since,† and little has been added to our knowledge of it; so that of the climate of the Korea, or of the prevailing winds and weather, there are but limited observations from which to deduce positive information.

On the west coast however, and in the Yellow sea, the following seem to be the usual changes of weather, and the prevailing winds at the different seasons:

Winds.—From January to March, inclusive, N.W. winds prevail, and in January stormy lasting gales from North and N.W. are frequent. On the western shores of the Yellow sea, the wind follows the trend of the coast, and is more to the north and north-eastward.

From April to June, inclusive, N.E. and easterly winds prevail, which moderate, as they haul to the northward and are accompanied by drizzle; occasionally however it blows hard from the N.E. quarter. On the

---

* *See* Admiralty Atlas:—Wind and current charts for Pacific, Atlantic, and Indian Oceans. October 1872.

† French frigate *Virginie* in 1856. H.M.S. *Nimrod* in 1860. H.M.S. *Dove* in 1859 and 1861.

mainland of the Korea the wind is very variable, S.W. winds bringing fine weather, and those from the southward being accompanied by fog.

From July to September, inclusive, the wind is variable, but south-easterly winds prevail, and are generally accompanied by fine weather, sudden heavy squalls and thunder storms being occasionally experienced; the latter end of August and the month of September, are very unsettled, being the season when the monsoon changes in the China sea, when northerly winds prevail with rain and very stormy weather.

From October to December, inclusive, winds from N.W., North, (and N.N.E., on the coast of China) prevail, and in December frequent and heavy gales from the North and N.W. are experienced.

In the Korea strait and on the south coast of the Korea, from January to March, inclusive, northerly and north-easterly winds prevail, sometimes north-westerly; they are generally stormy, and North and N.W. gales are of frequent occurrence bringing (in January), snow and sleet.

From April to June, inclusive, northerly, north-easterly, and easterly winds prevail, and are fresh, sometimes increasing to a gale, when from the northward. South-westerly winds sometimes intervene, they are, however, generally light; in the middle of May rain commences and continues in the ratio of two days rain to one without rain, until the end of June.

Fogs are of frequent occurrence in June.

From July to September, inclusive, north-westerly winds prevail in the strait; they, however, become light and variable, with frequent calms on nearing the coast. Thunder storms are frequent and are very heavy, and Typhoons not uncommon.

From October to December, inclusive, north and north-westerly winds prevail, and are generally fresh; gales may also be expected from the same quarters, bringing snow and sleet, in November and December.

The finest weather is from the middle of August to the middle of November.

SEA OF JAPAN AND EAST COAST OF KOREA.—There exists at present but little information regarding the meteorology of this sea, especially of the East coast of the Korea.

The Russians have surveyed the coast of their newly acquired territory from the river Amùr to the Tumen ula, but of the prevailing winds and weather in that part of the sea of Japan very little is known. The winds appear very variable, and from the scarcity of observations, and also from the fact that those are somewhat conflicting, the following remarks give only a very general idea of the winds and weather which appear to prevail at the different seasons.

Winds.—According to Krusenstern " North and N.E. winds blow for ten months in the year on the East coast of the Korea, and if sometimes they change to the South during this time, which is rare, it is only for a short time;" this seems to be nearly correct, as N.W., North, and N.E. winds, undoubtedly prevail during the greater part of the year on this coast, following the trend in its direction, and blowing through the Korea strait from the north-eastward.

From January to March, inclusive, northerly winds prevail on the Korean coast, hauling to the westward, in the middle of the Japan sea; on the coast of Tartary southerly and south-westerly winds prevail, and on the East coast of the Japan sea westerly and north-westerly winds and calms are experienced.

From April to June, inclusive, the winds are variable, but light southerly winds prevail with frequent calms, and fine weather, especially between the parallels of 40° and 45° N.; the wind hauls to the eastward on the coast of Japan, and is accompanied by mist, it, however, sometimes freshens to a stormy breeze, with squalls, from the north-eastward; the weather however is generally fine.

Fogs prevail during the whole of this season (April to June inclusive) all over the sea of Japan, especially on the northern coast of Korea and coast of Tartary, and are most dense in June; they are however generally dispersed by S.W. winds.

Rain falls in May and June on the Japan coast.

From July to September, inclusive, on the Korean coast moderate northerly winds prevail, with fine weather, in September; on the coast of Tartary southerly and easterly winds with calms are experienced and during the whole of this season, between the parallels of 40° and 45° N., calms are most frequent. In the northern part of the sea, fogs and rain last until August, the former generally being dispersed by S.W. winds, and decrease in density as the summer advances. Gales occur at the equinoxes, generally commencing at S.E. on the coast of Japan, and veering to the southward and westward, excepting when they are associated with a Typhoon, the centers of which as a rule pass south of Japan, when the wind veers from South to S.E., East, and North, generally clearing up at N.W. These latter gales are generally very heavy, and have been known to last three days; these however are rare.

From October to December, inclusive, north-westerly winds prevail, and heavy gales are sometimes experienced, generally commencing at South, veering to West, and ceasing at N.W., they are fierce and of short duration; the weather is generally fine, but easterly wind brings rain and snow; gales of the same description as those occurring from July to September, being the outer limit of a Typhoon, sometimes occur in October, but they are apparently rare.*

---

* H.M.S. *Barracouta*.   H.M.S. *Scylla*, 1866.

Gales.—During the prosecution of the Russian survey of the coast of Tartary in 1860, the winds were in the months of July and August mostly southerly and easterly, moderate, with clear weather; S.W. winds were rare, as was stormy weather or rain, what little was experienced being of short duration. The temperature was very uniform, and even at an extreme range did not exceed 86° Fahr. In the middle of September the weather changed, the thermometer shewing 37° Fahr. in St. Vladmir bay. From the beginning of September the wind blew from N.W. and S.W., and the weather was foggy.*

It may be remarked that fogs, mist, or hazy weather generally accompany N.E., East, or S.E. winds, and that winds from N.W., West, or S.W. are certain precursors of fine weather. About the autumnal equinox, the weather breaks up between the parallels of 40° and 46° N., and gales at that period are of frequent occurrence; they are generally found to be cyclones the path of whose centres is to the south-eastward of the Japan islands; their features here, however, are only partially cyclonic, the wind seldom veering over more than 8 points. The sea of Japan is subject to sudden strong gales from March until November, but more especially from July to October, inclusive; they are apparently not at all arbitrary in their direction, and may blow from almost any quarter. From the middle of September to the middle of November 1859, there occurred thirteen gales, eleven of which were cyclones and two "blue north-westers," their force from 7 to 10, and their duration two to four days, with intervals of seldom more than two or three days between them.

During the months of September, October, and November 1859, H.M.S. *Actæon*, whilst surveying on the north-west coast of Japan, encountered a succession of heavy gales, sometimes reaching force 10; nearly the whole of these gales had the same features, commencing with a freshening breeze from the southward with a clear blue sky and a low barometer, but sometimes at S.E. or N.E., the latter bringing the heaviest weather, the wind gradually veering to the westward, and the sky becoming overcast, followed by rain or snow. A rapid rise of the barometer ushered in the full force of the gale, which generally expended itself to the north-westward.

The *Actæon* and *Dove* encountered a heavy gale from the N.E. whilst at anchor in St. Vladmir bay, on the coast of Tartary. The sea was so heavy as to cause one continuous roller to break across from Low point to Roudanoffski point, and circling round the former caused both vessels to roll heavily. The beach after this gale was literally piled with fish. The barometer stood steadily at 29·89 during the height of the gale, falling to 28·96 on the third day; this fall of the barometer was followed by the wind veering to the northward, and on shifting to

---

* Russian Naval Magazine, May 1862.

N.W. the weather cleared; this gale was felt as a typhoon in the China sea, and to the south-eastward of the Japan islands, where it raged furiously, committing great ravages on the South and East coasts of Japan.

GULF OF TARTARY.—From cape Disappointment, in lat. 45° 40½′ N., the coast of Tartary trends to the north-east, and forms with the west coast of the island of Saghalin, a long channel named the gulf of Tartary, which communicates with the gulf of Amùr to the northward by the strait of Tartary.

The Climate of the northern part of the sea of Japan is in winter very severe, January and February are the coldest months, the thermometer standing at 17° below freezing point in lat. 47° N. The temperature in April and May ranged between 30° and 50° and during June and July 45° to 60° in Castries bay, and in the latter end of October it was seldom above freezing point and sometimes as low as 18°. The barometer in May, June, and July 1853, ranged between 29·65 and 30·28, falling once to 29·0 in a heavy south-easterly gale.

Winds.—From January to March inclusive, northerly winds are said to prevail, veering from N.E. to N.W. with frequent gales and snow storms. In March the wind hauls to eastward and fogs set in. From April to June, inclusive, the wind is from the southward and eastward, and occasionally E.N.E., these easterly winds bringing very foggy weather; S.S.W. winds at times intervene, they are moderate and bring fine clear weather; sometimes the S.E. wind is high and squally, and occasionally in May a furious south-easterly gale and snow storm, lasting ten or twelve hours, has been experienced; they may be expected with a previously freshening breeze from the East and S.E., and sometimes a rapidly falling barometer; the wind in these storms rises suddenly and falls equally so, and will most probably veer to the South, S.W., West, and perhaps N.W.

In July S.E. winds prevail, and in July and September the winds are variable, north-easterly winds being the most prevalent and generally blowing from that quarter round to the N.W., West, and S.W., with fine clear weather after the middle of August, when the fogs which are almost continuous from March until that time disappear; they are most prevalent and dense in June, a S.W. wind generally dispersing them. About the time of the equinox unsettled weather is experienced and gales are frequent.

In September 1866 a heavy gale was experienced in Castries bay of a revolving character; this gale was the margin of a furious typhoon which was felt as far west as Shanghai, and raged with great violence in the northern part of the China sea, doing great damage at Nagasaki, Yokohama, and Hakodate; these revolving storms however are rarely felt as far north as the gulf of Tartary.

From October to December inclusive the wind prevails from North and N.W. sometimes N.E. with frequent snow storms; the summer breaking up and winter setting in in the month of October, this change generally taking place suddenly. Ice begins to form at that time, and continues until May, and the season for sailing vessels to be in the gulf on ordinary occasions must be considered as having terminated; gales from the N.E. to N.W. are frequent, and are sometimes very heavy.

Currents.—A branch of the Japan stream (Kuro Siwo) enters the Japan sea through the Korea strait (see p. 23), and continues its course in a north-easterly direction; it has been found to set at a rate of from 2 to 2½ knots an hour in the strait, and as far as the parallel of 38° N., northward of which it is generally found to be weaker, gradually lessening in force until the strait of Tsugar is approached, when it splits, one branch increasing in strength sets to the eastward towards the strait, through which it flows with great velocity (p. 16), the other branch continues its north-easterly course with greatly diminished strength, along the west coast of the island of Yezo, and flows into the Pacific through the strait of La Pérouse (p. 18); this current however is very variable both in direction and force, and appears to be greatly influenced by the prevailing winds, attaining its greatest force during the season of the south-west monsoon in the China sea, slackening and becoming variable at the change of the monsoons in the months of April and October, and setting to the southward during the winter months, or season of the north-east monsoon in the China sea.

On the 4th June 1855 the Russian frigate *Constantine*, proceeding from Korea strait to the strait of Tsugar, experienced a current of 36 miles a day, setting to the E.N.E., in lat. 36° 48′ N., long. 131° 52′ E., while on the following days, the rate varied from 6 to 9 miles, and the direction was from N. by E. to E. by N., until near the parallel of Tsugar strait, when its rate was 11 miles a day to the N. ½ E. During the whole of this passage the weather was fine and the winds light from West to South; two days only they were from South to East, with cloudy showery weather.

In November 1855, the same vessel proceeding from Tsugar strait to that of Korea experienced a current setting E. by N. 28 miles a day on the parallel of the strait; to the S. by E. 7 miles in 40° N. and 138° E.; to the S. ½ E. in 39° N.; and the day following E. by S. 41 miles in 38° N. During all this time, the winds were from N.W. and N.N.W. and the weather fine; but on the wind changing to East and E.N.E. accompanied by rain, the current set N.N.E. ½ E. 26 miles.

In June 1859 H.M. Surveying vessel *Dove*, after passing the north point of Tsu sima, lost the Japan stream, and in a strong northerly wind found the current East, but the wind veering to East with a moderate gale, the current ran to the N.N.E. at the rate of 2 knots per hour as far as Matu sima. From this island to Peter the Great bay the currents were weak and irregular, but they were found running at the rate of one knot an hour to the S.W. along the coast of Tartary.

From May to July 1856, H.M.S. *Hornet* had little or no current either in this sea or in Korea strait; but in the latter end of July and the month of August it ran strong to the N.E., on one occasion as much as 48 miles in twenty-four hours; it, however, gradually decreased as the vessel proceeded to the northward. These currents were evidently much influenced by the wind, for on one occasion, in the vicinity of the Liancourt rocks, she was set 1½ miles an hour to the S.E.

On the west side of the sea of Japan along the coasts of Korea and Tartary the currents are very uncertain both in direction and force; as a rule, however, they are very feeble, and only attain to any strength off the abrupt points of the coast.

Capt. Broughton, who in October 1797 passed along this coast, notices a current setting to S.S.W. at the rate of one mile an hour. The French frigate *Virginie* in July 1856, and the Russian Surveying vessel *Vostok* in the same month in 1860 and two following months, found the current setting to the northward at from one-half to three-quarters knot an hour. Along the coast of Korea and Tartary it does not however appear to set in one direction, but is governed by the direction of the winds; also with the growth of their force the rapidity of the current increases.*

In the gulf of Tartary, north of La Pérouse strait, there is scarcely any current, the waters in that locality being subjected to tidal influence. The great body of water flowing into it from the Amùr river causes a general set to the southward in the middle of the gulf, but it is scarcely perceptible south of the parallel of 50°; with strong northerly winds, however, it is materially increased, and again with winds from the South it is not appreciable.

SEA OF OKHOTSK.—This sea is bounded on the North by Russian Tartary, on the West by the island of Saghalin, on the East by the peninsula of Kamchatka, and on the South by the Kuril islands, and, like the sea of Japan, it may be considered land-locked; it is but seldom visited, except by the Russians, who have settlements at various places on its shores; and very little is known of its navigation.

Winds.†—The prevailing winds on its northern and western shores during June, July, and August are from the southward and eastward, and seldom from any other quarter, moderate, with either fog or rain.

---

* Supplement to Russian Naval Magazine, May 1862.
† Observations at Okhotsk by M. Tessan.

In September, about sunset, the wind, which during the day is from the southward, veers to the westward or north-westward, and remains fresh from that quarter during the night; at about 10 a.m. it moderates, shifting back again to the southward. About the beginning or middle of September southerly gales are said to be experienced, but this month has in other respects finer weather than August.

From the middle of October to December stormy weather and gales may be expected, with winds from East and S.E.; when the wind is North and N.W. fine weather follows.

From December to April the wind is from North to N.E., fresh, with a clear sky, bringing snow if it hauls to the eastward.

In April and May the winds are moderate, from North during the night and South in the day. Fogs are nearly constant, they are most dense with S.E. or easterly winds; winds off-shore disperse them.

On the south-west coast of Kamchatka westerly winds prevail from September to May, and light easterly winds, variable between N.E. and S.E., and frequent calms are experienced during the summer. In the winter months the westerly winds are frequently very stormy, but in the summer they are generally accompanied by fine weather, while winds from the eastward bring snow and rain. Near the Kuril islands the winds during the summer months are said to be variable, and it is difficult to determine which are the prevalent quarters; with winds from S.S.E. to S.S.W. the weather is usually foggy, but the haze being dry the sun is often visible through the fog; East and N.E. winds bring rain and bad weather; with the wind from N.N.E. to N.N.W. the weather clears and the temperature is cold; it is also cold with the wind from N.N.W. to W.S.W., and the air is dry and hazy. With the wind between S.S.W. and W.S.W. the sky is clear and fogs are rare. The open season is of shorter duration in the neighbourhood of the Shantarski islands than at port Aian, the ice about the former in July preventing an approach within some miles.

Currents.—The direction of the currents in this sea is uncertain; they are found to increase in strength, as the land is approached. Near cape Elizabeth on the north-east coast of Saghalin, and approaching the gulf of Amùr heavy overfalls and ripples occur which appear to be produced by shallow surface currents, and often render a vessel quite unmanageable. This may be naturally expected as the immense body of water from the Amùr river, meeting with the obstruction caused by Saghalin island, effects its escape through the largest outlet or gulf of Amùr, and following the line of coast round the north end of Saghalin island causes, especially with easterly or south-easterly winds, a very dangerous race, to form off cape Elizabeth, extending 3 or 4 miles off shore. The current sets strong to the southward along the east coast of Saghalin island, where the sea for some distance off shore is discoloured by it, and joining the easterly current through La Pérouse strait off cape Siretoko it passes into the Pacific to the S.E. through the various passages between the Kuril islands; it especially sets with great velocity to the southward through the Yezo strait between Kunashir island and Yezo.

The shores of the sea to a considerable distance are covered with ice from November to April, but the main entrance continues open throughout the year.

SOUTH EAST COAST OF KAMCHATKA.—The weather is generally fine at Petropaulski up to the 15th October, but after this period it is wet, and the land begins to be covered with snow which becomes permanent, and lasting through the winter does not disappear until May or June. In November, December, and January violent storms are experienced. In fine weather the morning breeze is from North to N.N.W., lasting until about 9 a.m., sometimes until 11 a.m., then shifting to the West and South it sinks altogether in the afternoon, about one or two o'clock; the breeze from the offing sets in, varying from South to East.

During the winter the cold is severe; snow falls in abundance, and frequently rises as high as the houses; but whatever may be the intensity of the cold, it is rarely the roadstead is entirely frozen over, the ice does not generally extend more than a cable's length off shore, and after bad weather, occasioned by winds from seaward, as well as those from West and North, it becomes detached from the land, and is carried out into the road. In ordinary winters, the coves, bays, and rivers are only blocked up with ice, and then not often too thick to prevent a passage by breaking or cutting.

Currents.—Along the S.E. coast of Kamchatka, the cold waters of the Arctic seas set to the southward, along the eastern shores of the Kuril islands and the island of Yezo, forming a cold belt between the Kuro Siwo or Japan stream and these islands (p. 25).

MARIANA ISLANDS, BONIN ISLANDS, MEIACO-SIMA, LIU-KIU AND LINSCHOTEN ISLANDS.

MARIANA OR LADRONE ISLANDS lie in the region of the northeast trade wind: this trade wind prevails over the group, but between October and June it may be said to incorporate itself with and become a part of the north-east monsoon, which blows during this season westward of the Mariana islands. The south-west monsoon is however felt as far East as the 147° meridian, and these islands may be therefore said to lie in the boundary between the monsoon region of the China sea and the trade wind region of the Pacific ocean.

From January to March, inclusive, east-north-easterly winds prevail with variable weather in January and February, but in March it becomes fine.

From April to June, inclusive, the wind is from the eastward, variable between N.E. and S.E. About the middle of June, the wind hauls to the southward.

From July to September, inclusive, the Mariana islands are under the influence of the south-west monsoon, causing variable winds to prevail. At this season the north-east trade wind and the south-west monsoon may be said to contend for the ascendancy. Southerly winds variable between S.E. and West, with frequent calms are experienced. Strong winds and heavy gales from any quarter are frequent, principally West in August and September, and in July and August it rains heavily at intervals, and thunder storms are of frequent occurrence.

About the middle of October the wind hauls to the eastward, and continues from between East and N.E. until the end of December. The weather during the last month is variable, and sometimes heavy gales are experienced; from July to October, inclusive, may be said to be the season of bad weather, storms, thunder, and rain, whilst from March to June, inclusive, and November are the fine months.

Earthquakes are of frequent occurrence in these islands.

Currents.—In the vicinity of the Mariana islands the currents are variable, and are greatly influenced by the prevailing winds. The group however as a rule lie in the drift current, resulting from the N.E. trade wind, and the general set is to the N.W. and West, from one to two knots an hour, but they have been experienced as setting to the N.E. in the face of a wind from that quarter.

THE BONIN ISLANDS lie northward of the region of the north-east trade winds, and eastward of the monsoon region; the climate is said to be remarkably fine. From January to March, inclusive, westerly winds prevail, variable between North and South, with occasional calms, the latter month being showery. In January and February the N.W. and westerly winds often freshen into gales. From April to June easterly winds prevail, variable between N.E. and S.E. with occasional calms. The change from the westerly winds occurs in April, during which month the wind is variable, with showers; gales are sometimes experienced in May, generally from S.E. veering to South and West, they are not however of frequent occurrence; the weather is fine, but the heat is oppressive, and the atmosphere very damp; winds from the south-west sometimes intervene, especially in June.

Fogs are frequent in June; and are especially dense to windward of the islands. In July they are less frequent.

From July to September easterly winds prevail, variable round to South and sometimes S.W. with occasional calms. In July the weather is frequently foggy, and in July and August it rains heavily.

From October to December northerly winds prevail, variable between N.E. and N.W., and sometimes hauling more to the East or West; in December gales are experienced from N.W. and West.

Typhoons occur in the neighbourhood of these islands from July to October, but more frequently in the latter month, and are then very severe.

Currents.—Very little information has been obtained as to the currents in the vicinity of these islands; they appear to lie between the north-east trade drift current and the Kuro Siwo, in a region of little or no current; the Bonin islands, however, probably lie within the limits of the Kuro Siwo during the season of the south-west monsoon in the China sea, when a general set to the eastward and S.E. may be experienced.

MEIACO SIMA GROUP lies in the monsoon region of the China sea, the south-west monsoon blowing from April to September, and the north-east monsoon from October to March.

From January to March, inclusive, N.E. winds prevail, variable between North and East, strong, with haze and rain; in March the monsoon moderates, and occasional calms are experienced.

In April the wind is variable between South and S.E. with unsettled weather.

In May and June S.W. winds prevail, variable round to South.

From July to September S.W. winds prevail, variable round to South and sometimes south-east. In September the monsoon changes, and unsettled weather is experienced during that month; strong variable winds, with squalls and rain.

From October to December, inclusive, strong winds from North and N.E., with haze or rain.

Typhoons are experienced from July to October, inclusive, and sometimes November.

LIU-KIU (LU-CHU) and LINSCHOTEN ISLANDS lie on the edge of the north-east monsoon, but within the limits of the south-west; the climate is mild, the heat and cold being never excessive, and fresh breezes blow all the year round.

From January to March, inclusive, northerly winds prevail, variable between N.W. and N.E; in March the winds are moderate and variable, and occasional calms are experienced.

In April the wind is variable from the southward and eastward; in May and June the south-west monsoon is steady, moderate, with fine weather.

From July to September, inclusive, south-westerly and southerly winds prevail, sometimes S.E. with squalls and rain. In September the monsoon changes and the weather is unsettled, and strong winds, squalls, and rain are experienced.

From October to December, inclusive, northerly winds prevail, interrupted occasionally by fresh gales from the N.W. or North, with heavy rain.

* During the visit of the United States squadron, in 1854, the south-west monsoon prevailed steadily in May and June, and veered to the southward and eastward in July. In August the wind was changeable and blew at times quite strong, with squalls and rain. The monsoon changed about the 1st of September.

Typhoons may be experienced from July to October, and sometimes in November.

Currents.—Very little information has been obtained as to the set of the currents in the vicinity of and amongst the Liu-kiu islands, the channels between which are said to be under tidal influence; during the season of the south-west monsoon in the China sea it has been noticed that within 12 miles of, and in the channels between, these islands the influence of the Kuro Siwo is felt in a much less degree.

JAPAN ISLANDS, STRAITS OF TSUGAR AND LA PÉROUSE, YEZO AND KURIL ISLANDS.

JAPAN, SOUTH and EAST COASTS.—THE CLIMATE of Japan varies considerably between its southern and northern extremes, the former enjoying almost a tropical climate, the latter condemned to a Siberian. At Nagasaki, in the island of Kiusiu, the weather is very changeable. The average temperature in January was 35°, and in August it ranged to 98° Fahr. In December and January the ground is covered with hoar frost, and occasionally with snow, except in very mild winters.

The extremes of temperature are never very great, the cold blast of winter being tempered by the Japan stream, and the high range of the thermometer in summer being compensated by the refreshing sea breeze which blows nearly every day up the entire length of the harbour.†
Up to the end of June the range of the thermometer is 62° to 78°. Later, the heat is greater and on calm days excessive, the surface water on one occasion having been registered at 90°. August brings unsettled weather on the coast, with short gales from various quarters, squalls, rain, and

---

* Perry's Japan Expeditions.

† At Nagasaki, in August, a north-easterly breeze blows from about 2 A.M. till 9 A.M., followed generally by a calm or light airs from north-west until about 3 P.M., when a south-westerly wind sets in and lasts until about 9 P.M.—F. Darbishire, Nav. Lieut., H.M.S. *Osprey*, 1865.

frequent calms; November brings the north-west wind, which prevails in the Korea strait and Japan sea during the winter months. There is little actual winter in the south, though occasional snow-storms fetch home to the coast in the north-westers. It is a healthy climate for Europeans, sickness being rare. Small-pox is, however, very prevalent amongst the Japanese.

At Simoda, on the south-east coast of Nipon, the climate is more or less variable in the winter and spring. The presence of snow upon the lofty peaks, although there is seldom frost or snow at Simoda itself, and the not unfrequent rains and fogs, give an occasional humidity and rareness to the atmosphere which must be productive of occasional inflammatory diseases. The change of wind alternates often between the warm sea breezes from the south, and the cold blasts from the snow-capped mountains inland. In summer it is occasionally very hot in the daytime, but the nights are refreshed by the sea breezes. The peak of Fusi yama is only clear of snow during September, and not always then.

At Yedo, January and February are the coldest months, and the mean temperature in February is about 46° Fahr.; about the middle of the latter month, the weather which has been fine but gradually becoming colder during the winter breaks with rain and snow, and east winds swelling into gales of two or three days' duration succeed. In March, April, and the middle of May (when the rains commence) the climate is delightful, as it is also in autumn. In summer the maximum temperature in the shade is 86°, ordinarily 80° at noon, and the evenings are cool and pleasant. In the months of July and August, which are the hottest, south winds with a little westing, sea breezes are prevalent in the gulf, being often very fresh off Yedo, and sometimes lasting during the entire night.

Earthquakes.—The whole region of the Japanese islands is volcanic, and many of the eruptions are fraught with extreme danger to ships. At Yedo, one occurred in August 1783, exceeding in its horrors and wide-spread desolation that of Lisbon. Another occurred at Yedo on the 10th November 1855 which is said to have caused the destruction of 100,000 dwellings and 54 temples, and the death of 30,000 persons.

In 1854, the town of Simoda was reduced to ruins, and the Russian frigate *Diana* nearly wrecked in the harbour, being whirled many times round her anchors, at one time aground, at another in many fathoms depth. She was then greatly injured and was subsequently lost in an inexplicable submarine tonardo, whilst in tow of a multitude of Japanese boats which deserted her suddenly at some (to them) well known warning.

Simabara, in Kiusiu, is also a locality of terrible earthquakes, one of which is said to have altered the whole feature and coast-line of the neighbouring province.

Rain is frequent at all seasons, but from the middle of May to the end of June may be considered the rainy season in the south of Japan. The rains generally set in at Nagasaki towards the end of May. They are heavy and continue about six weeks. The rainy days alternate with dry days, which as the season advances become extremely hot, the proportion of rainy days, according to the meteorological record kept at Desima for ten years, being as two to one.

Fogs are very prevalent on the coasts of Japan, especially in the northern parts. In June and July, they occur frequently in the Korea strait, and on the East coast in July and August.

Winds.—Near the coast of Japan by far the average wind throughout the year is from the northward, variable between N.E. and N.W., or off the land, the average wind being N.E.

From January to March inclusive, winds from the northward and westward prevail, shifting occasionally to the north or north-eastward, bringing snow and sleet in January and the beginning of February.

From April to June the winds are light and variable, principally from the northward round to West and sometimes S.W., with frequent calms; the latter end of May and the whole of June is the rainy season on the south and east coasts, the winds are then variable, but haul to the southward towards the middle of June.

From July to October, southerly winds, variable between S.E. and S.W. prevail, winds from S.E. being more prevalent during August and September than in any other months. The weather is unsettled about the period of the autumnal equinox, and the wind becomes variable, continuing so until the middle of October, but gradually settling to the north-westward, and becomes tolerably steady from that quarter about the latter part of that month. In July thunder-storms are of frequent occurrence.

From October to December, inclusive, northerly winds, from N.W. to N.E., prevail, moderate, with fine weather; a bright day with a clear sky being generally a sign of a strong N.W. wind; when they freshen from N.E. rain or snow falls, the latter only in December, but occasionally the N.E. wind freshens into a gale. November is usually a wet month on the east coast, and rain falls at intervals throughout the winter months. From November until May local gales blow down the numerous channels and gulfs, especially in the Boungo and Kii channels, and the gulfs of Owari, Suruga, and Yedo: these winds blow fiercely for from 3 to 36 hours, frequently lulling or altogether subsiding at the sun's or moon's setting. During the winter, winds from the N.E. most frequently bring rain, from the N.W. bright clear weather, and from S.E., South, or S.W., a cloudy sky, and often rain.

In the Seto Uchi (Inland sea) little rain falls, the high land of the island of Sikok and the almost as mountainous country of Nipon forming a great barrier to rain and bad weather generally.

North-westerly winds prevail throughout the winter months, and in the summer months light variable winds, principally from the N.E. and S.W., with frequent calms are experienced. In the winter the north-westerly winds, which are fresh throughout the day, often lull at sunset. An easterly wind at this season is generally accompanied by rain.

* During the spring and summer months in the gulf of Yedo, very violent and sudden squalls from the north come on frequently without any warning, from almost a calm or perhaps a light air from the S.W. Vessels passing between Yokohama and Hakodate report having experienced the same at this season, and have met with loss of spars and sails in consequence.

In the spring and summer months westerly winds are generally experienced between Siwo misaki (at entrance to the Kii channel) and Mikomoto (Rock island), on passing which, the westerly wind falls, and a N.E. wind is often found blowing strong down the gulf of Yedo.

" In the early part of July fogs enveloped the whole coast, accompanying calms and light east winds (chiefly from the southward of East), but the fogs were not generally found so thick in-shore as to render the navigation dangerous, nor to prevent the recognition of the land. Within one or two miles of the shore the fog frequently lifted and the land was visible.

" In the latter part of July fogs were only experienced between lat. 36° N. and lat. 37° N.; fine weather with land and sea breezes prevailing. Northward of 38° N. stiff breezes from west lasted a few hours.

" On the south-east coast the weather appeared to be quite different. The fogs became modified when in contiguity with the warm water of the Japan stream, and formed into detached banks or clouds which hung over sea and land, obscuring the hills almost to their bases. A strong S.W. wind may here also be met with when a light east wind or calm is prevailing on the east coast." †

Gales.—Ordinary gales occur frequently throughout the year, they spring up sometimes very suddenly, their prevailing direction being from the southward between S.E. and S.W. (from seaward). In the winter months, near the coast, gales from N.E., S.W., and West, are often experienced.

The barometer generally rises previous to a gale from the northward, and if it falls after a strong N.E. wind has set in, bad weather will follow. Before a southerly gale the barometer falls. Very frequently a long heavy swell rolls in from the southward some time before any wind is

---

* Capt. C. S. Stanhope, H.M.S. *Ocean*, 1868.
† Commander C. Bullock, R.N.

felt. Such a swell with a falling barometer is a certain prognostication of a coming gale.*

Typhoons occur from June to October, inclusive, and commit great ravages all over Japan, they have been known to occur in May, but from the middle of August to the middle of October they prevail most frequently. (See Typhoons, pages 19 to 22.)

STRAIT OF TSUGAR.—Strong N.W. winds prevail in this strait during the winter months, accompanied by snow and rain, and the weather is very boisterous. In April the wind hauls to the westward, with heavy squalls from the S.W. In May the wind is from the southward, variable between S.W. and S.E., sometimes more easterly or westerly, and fine weather commences, lasting until the middle of September when the weather becomes unsettled and summer commences to break up with frequent gales; winter fairly setting in in October.

During H.M.S. *Saracen's* survey of the strait of Tsugar, May, June, July, and August 1855, the prevailing winds were from the South, with much fine clear weather. The wind was less frequent from the N.W. than any other quarter.

Fogs.—Dense fogs prevailed in May and June; after that period they are comparatively rare.

The wind in shifting usually followed the course of the sun. After a few days of light southerly wind and fine weather it freshened, and veered to the westward, accompanied by fine clear and cold weather. At N.W. it usually died away, or flew round suddenly to the eastward; in the latter case it was always followed by a dense fog or a gale; the weather getting fine again as the wind veered to the southward.

Current.—Through the middle of Tsugar strait the current sets constantly to the north-eastward, but its breadth varies considerably according to the state of the wind and weather; its usual rate is from 2 to 2¼ knots per hour, but with westerly or south-westerly winds it increases greatly in velocity and expands filling up two-thirds of the channel; under these circumstances it often attains a rate of from 4 to 5 knots an hour. With strong winds from East or N.E. it diminishes greatly both in strength and dimensions. The shores of the strait are subject to tidal influence, the flood making to the eastward and the ebb to the westward; the velocity of the whole stream, on the flood tide being thus considerably augmented; whilst on the ebb it is diminished.

---

* Off Yedo, in February 1863, H.M.S. *Swallow* experienced a sharp short gale of ten hours' duration, with little or no warning. The sky was very clear, with steady falling barometer, and in two hours the ship was reduced to close-reefed main topsail, &c. In the months of August and September 1858, H.M.S. *Furious* experienced heavy gales from E.N.E. shifting round to the southward and westward.

YEZO ISLAND.—The climate of Yezo is severe (almost Siberian*), the winter commencing about the middle of September, when snow appears on the tops of the mountains reaching the lower ground in October and lasting until the end of May in the south, and until the first week in June in the northern parts of the island. There appears to be no spring, the summer coming immediately on the disappearance of the snow, and the country is green in a few days, so sudden is the transition that it seems almost incredible. Fogs now make their appearance, increasing in density and duration until August, about the latter part of which month they gradually disappear. Towards the middle of September the summer begins to break and soon disappears. Frosts set in, and snow falls on the higher ranges about the end of the month, and ice forms in large patches in Yezo strait by December.

The western shores of the island are washed by the warm waters of the Kuro Siwo flowing northward through the Korea strait; whilst the eastern coast comes in contact with the cold arctic stream from the North (see page 25); the temperature of the former in the month of May being over 50°, whilst that of the latter is 37°; this naturally causes a great difference in the fertility of these coasts, the western shores being well-wooded, and the soil favourable for cultivation, whilst the eastern coast from the increased severity of its climate and longer duration of winter renders the soil unfit for agricultural purposes, and causes the wood to be comparatively stunted in its growth.

In April the maximum temperature is 67°, and the minimum 28°. In May the max. 71°, min. 30°. In June max. 87°, min. 37°. In July, max. 87°, min. 54°. In August, max. 90°, min. 52°.

Rain appears to fall at intervals throughout the year.

Winds.—From January to March the wind is westerly from North to S.W., but strong N.W. winds prevail, and the ground is covered with snow. April is very unsettled, N.W. winds prevail, and snow still lies on the ground, and falls frequently until the middle of May when the wind hauls to the southward, and it rapidly disappears. Southerly winds, variable between West and East, with occasional calms, prevail until the end of June, and gales are not unfrequent. In July and August, light variable winds from the southward between S.W. and S.E., with occasional calms and fine weather, are experienced. In September the weather becomes unsettled, and gales are of frequent occurrence.

During the winter months westerly and north-westerly winds are said to blow almost continually, and usually with great violence.

---

* Sir R. Alcock.

On the South and East coasts winds from S.W. round seawards to N.E. bring fog almost without exception, whilst those off the land or from West to N.E. are accompanied by fine weather.*

The following is a translation of notes on weather, &c. made by the governor of Nemero during three years residence there:—

"It begins to snow at the end of October, is two feet deep all over the ground during the winter, and disappears by May.

The ground is frozen hard to a depth of two feet, and remains so up to June, and the sea freezes a long way out.

The Japanese never can wear summer clothes.

Fog is constant all the summer, so much so in June, July, and August that the sun is not seen for frequently three weeks at a time."

LA PÉROUSE STRAIT.—The winds at the different seasons in this strait are in their general conditions identical with those experienced in the gulf of Tartary, (p. 5); there is no information regarding any local particulars, except that during the autumn months (September and October) heavy gales from the westward are of frequent occurrence.

Current.—In the middle of the strait the current is found to set to the south-eastward about 1½ knots an hour, and sometimes from 2 to 3 knots; near the shore it is regulated by and united with the tides, and consequently varies both in direction and force. The flood stream sets to the eastward through the straits at which time the whole stream in the strait sets in that direction, and is considerably augmented in its rate; it is also much influenced by prevailing winds.

H.M.S. *Actæon*, in September 1859, while engaged in surveying the islands Risiri and Rifunsiri, was blown by a W.S.W. gale through the strait of La Pérouse. The atmosphere was so laden with spray as to render it impossible to determine the ship's position.

During the strength of this gale, a strong current was experienced running to the S.E. at the rate of 3 knots an hour; but its strength decreased as the gale abated.

KURIL ISLANDS (PACIFIC COAST).—Little is known of the climate or meteorology of this locality, the islands are however said to be constantly enveloped in fog, rendering the navigation in their vicinity extremely dangerous. From January to March northerly and north-westerly winds are said to prevail, and throughout the winter much heavy weather with frequent strong gales accompanied by snow and sleet are experienced.

---

* These remarks have been compiled principally from Capt. H. C. St. John's report on the climate, &c. of Yezo, during H.M.S. *Sylvia's* visit in 1871.

From April to June, inclusive, south-easterly winds prevail with frequent calms. From July to September, winds from the southward variable between West and East prevail, with occasional calms.

Fogs prevail throughout the year, and are most dense in July and August.

Westerly winds set in in September and prevail principally from North-west, from which quarter they blow violently throughout the winter months, accompanied frequently by snow and sleet.

Currents.—In the strait of Yezo (between Yezo island and Kunashir) the current sets constantly to the southward with great velocity, adding considerably to the already numerous dangers experienced in the navigation of this strait. Russian vessels of war always pass through the Pico channel, between the islands of Kunashir and Iturup: from this fact it may be inferred that it is less influenced by currents,* and that its navigation is easy; but little is known, however, of the different channels between the numerous islands forming the Kuril group, though violent currents are said to be experienced in all of them.

TYPHOONS.†—The whole of the western portion of the North Pacific ocean between the parallels of 10° N. and 45° N., together with the China sea, is subject to violent storms, termed typhoons, which, between the parallels of 20° N. and 45° N., are experienced from June to November, inclusive, more particularly about the autumnal equinox, especially if the perigee or change of the moon coincide with the equinox.

The paths which the centres of these storms describe during their progress, usually lie to the South and East of the Japan islands, which are commonly visited by typhoons when pursuing a north-easterly course after having recurved; they are, however, sometimes experienced when they are travelling from south-east to north-west, as also when pursuing a direct northerly course; but these latter occur less frequently. The paths of the centres of these storms rarely appear to reach to the north-west of Japan, but sometimes sweep over the southern portion of the Japan islands causing immense damage from the great amount of rain which falls, and often sweeps houses, trees, and soil completely away.‡

These storms have not only a progressive motion, but also one that is cyclonical or rotatory, (*i.e.* they gyrate or blow in a circle of greater or less diameter) and, having their origin on the eastern edge of the south-west monsoon, where that monsoon meets with the north-east trade wind,

---

* Commander H. C. St. John.—H.M. Surveying vessel *Sylvia*, 1871.
† See Remarks on Revolving Storms—published by the Admiralty—price 6*d.*
‡ See notes, and paths of Typhoons on Wind Charts in Admiralty Atlas.

they travel from south-east to north-west, but as the south-west monsoon retires and the north-east monsoon sets in, (in September and October,) these storms, on nearing the China coast, recurve on the southern edge of the advancing monsoon, and travel from south-west to north-east; it is when pursuing this course that they extend over the greatest area.

In the tropics where the barometer varies so slightly under ordinary circumstances that any fall greater than ·15 in. is a sure sign of an atmospheric disturbance, the prognostics are more evident; but in more temperate latitudes where the barometer varies considerably with no apparent atmospheric change, the prognostics are less certain. In Japan, the barometer during the months of September and October, varies from 29·90 in. to 30·0 in., but when it stands exceptionally high with an increase of oppressive heat above the mean temperature, and accompanied by a threatening aspect of the sky; such as a misty halo round the sun or moon, lurid clouds tufted in shape and a heavy bank of leaden-coloured clouds in the horizon, then a typhoon may be confidently expected.

When the barometer falls slowly and regularly, the southerly current has reached the ship's position, and she is within the limits of the storm; under these circumstances it is necessary to ascertain first the position of the ship with regard to the centre of the storm, and then the direction in which the storm is advancing.

The rotation of the wind in the northern hemisphere is "against the hands of a watch," hence different portions of the storm have each their own peculiar winds; from this fact a simple rule is deduced by which the bearing of the storm's centre from the ship may be determined, viz. :— Note the direction of the wind at the commencement of the storm, the centre of which (in the northern hemisphere) will then bear 8 points to the right; for instance, the direction of the wind at the ship being S.E., the centre will bear from the ship S.W.

The region in which the cyclone rotates, is divided by the path, its axis describes as it progresses into two semicircles, and if the observer face the direction in which the storm is advancing, one semicircle will lie on the right of the path, and the other on the left, the shift of wind as observed at a stationary point in the one being in the reverse direction to that in the other. In the right hand semicircle (or when the centre of the storm passes to the left of the ship) it veers "with the hands of a watch," viz., S.→W.→N.→E., whilst in the left hand semicircle (or when the centre of the storm passes to the right of the ship) it veers "against the hands of a watch," viz.;—S.→E.→N.→W. By observing, therefore, the direction in which the wind veers, the position of the ship in the storm is readily known (*i.e.* in which semicircle), this together with the already determined bearing of the centre will show the direction in which the storm is progressing, thus,—when the ships position has been ascertained to lie in the right hand semicircle, and the bearing of the centre of the storm shifts from S.W. by West, to N.W. and North the storm is travelling to the north-eastward, but if the bearing of the centre shift from N.E. by East, to S.E. and South, the storm is travelling to the north-westward. If it has been determined that she lie in the left-hand semicircle, and the bearing of the storms centre shift from S.W., by South to S.E. and East, the storm is progressing to the north-eastward; if, however, it should shift through N.E., by North, to N.W. and West, the storm is travelling to the north-westward.

For a correct deduction, it is essential that the ship's position be as nearly as possible stationary; for if a ship advance somewhat faster than, and in the same direction as, an approaching storm, having the wind also in the same direction (ship running), the wind may shift in a direction exactly opposite to that which would have been observed had the ship been stationary, and an erroneous conclusion as to her position in the storm would be drawn. The advisibility of heaving-to on the first approach of a typhoon cannot therefore be too strongly urged.

We have now to consider how a ship should be handled when overtaken by a typhoon, so as to escape from its path as quickly as possible. Remembering that the wind rotates in opposite directions on either side of the path of the storm's centre, it is essential that if the ship be hove-to she should be placed on that tack on which she would come up as the wind shifts, if she is not she will be in constant danger of being taken aback; therefore, when the ship is in the right-hand semicircle she should be hove-to on the starboard tack, and if in the left-hand semicircle, on the port tack.

If a line is drawn through the centre of the storm, perpendicular to its path and dividing its area into quadrants, it will be seen that (still facing the direction in which the storm is progressing) the right-hand quadrant will be that in which the ship cannot get farther from the storm by sailing on; she must therefore when in this position in the storm be invariably hove-to on the starboard tack.

In the left-hand quadrant the ship may however get farther away by running before the wind, or being placed on the port tack.

If the wind be found to continue long in the same direction, and increase in violence, it may be presumed that the ship lies in the direct path of the storm's centre, if this be succeeded by a short interval of calm, (the barometer having been at its lowest, now commencing to rise very slowly) followed by a sudden and violent wind from the opposite quarter, the centre of the storm has passed over the ship.

The quadrants lying behind the storm's centre are not dangerous as the storm is momentarily increasing its distance from the ship.

The following table, taken from Professor Dove's Law of Storms, gives in detail how a ship should be handled under any circumstances in a typhoon in the Northern hemisphere.

	Direction of wind at the beginning of storm.	Bearing of the centre from the Ship.	Shift of wind.	Corresponding course to be held.		Shift of wind.	Course to be held.	
1	N.W.	N.E.	N.W. towards W.	S.E.		N.W. towards N.		
2	N.W. by N.	N.E. by E.	N.W.byN. ,, W.	S.E. by S.		N.W.byN. ,, N.		
3	N.N.W.	E.N.E.	N.N.W. ,, W.	S.S.E.		N.N.W. ,, N.		
4	N. by W.	E. by N.	N. by W. ,, W.	S. by E.		N.by W. ,, N.		
5	North	East	North ,, W.	South		North ,, E.		Ship to be hove-to on the starboard tack.
6	N. by E.	E. by S.	N. by E. ,, N.	S. by W.		N. by E. ,, E.		
7	N.N.E.	E.S.E.	N.N.E. ,, N.	S.S.W.		N.N.E. ,, E.		
8	N.E. by N.	S.E. by E.	N.E.byN.,, N.	S.W. by S.	Or heave-to on the port tack.	N.E.byN.,, E.		
9	N.E.	S.E.	N.E. ,, N.	S.W.		N.E. ,, E.		
10	N.E. by E.	S.E. by S.	N.E.byE. ,, N.	S.W. by W.		N.E.byE.,, E.		
11	E.N.E.	S.S.E.	E.N.E. ,, N.	W.S.W.		E.N.E. ,, E.		
12	E. by N.	S. by E.	E. by N. ,, N.	W. by S.		E. by N. ,, E.		
13	East	South	East ,, N.	West		East ,, S.		
14	E. by S.	S. by W.	E. by S. ,, E.	W. by N.		E. by S. ,, S.		
15	E.S.E.	S.S.W.	E.S.E. ,, E.	W.N.W.		E.S.E. ,, S.		
16	S.E. by E.	S.W. by S.	S.E.byE.,, E.	N.W. by W.		S.E.byE.,, S.		
17	S.E.	S.W.	S.E. ,, E.	N.W.		S.E. ,, S.		
18	S.E. by S.	S.W. by W.	S.E.byS. ,, E.	N.W. by N.		S.E.byS. ,, S.		
19	S.S.E.	W.S.W.	S.S.E. ,, E.	N.N.W.		S.S.E. ,, S.		
20	S. by E.	W. by S.	S. by E ,, E.	N. by W.		S. by E.,, S.		
21	South	West	South ,, E.	North		South ,, W.		
22	S. by W.	W. by N.	S. by W. ,, S.	N. by E.		S.byW. ,, W.		
23	S.S.W.	W.N.W.	S.S.W. ,, S.	N.N.E.		S.S.W. ,, W.		
24	S.W. by S.	N.W. by W.	S.W.byS.,, S.	N.E. by N.		S.W.byS. ,, W.		
25	S.W.	N.W.	S.W. ,, S.	N.E.		S.W. ,, W.		

Vessels when near the Japan coast will, as above mentioned, be usually therefore in the left-hand semicircle, and will consequently experience winds from E. through North to West. It has, however, been observed that the wind near the coast is principally from the eastward, that is, it blows from that quarter longest.

It will be observed that vessels under these circumstances if hove-to on the port tack (the ship being in the left-hand semicircle and the storm travelling to the north-eastward) will be heading off shore, and as the wind veers the coast becomes a weather shore. It would, however, be prudent if in such a position to make for one of the numerous harbours on the south coast of Nipon on the first indication of an approaching typhoon, as the atmosphere soon becomes thick and obscures the land; this circumstance, combined with the strong current experienced in this locality (Kuro Siwo) will render the ship's position very precarious.

JAPAN STREAM (KURO SIWO).* The north-east trade drift current of the Pacific, which flows to the westward between the parallels of 9° N. and 20° N., on reaching the eastern shores of the Philippine islands is deflected to the northward, forming in latitude 21° N., between the meridian of 125° E. and the east coast of Formosa, the commencement of the great oceanic current known as the Kuro Siwo, or Japan stream, the limits and velocity of which are considerably influenced by the monsoons of the China sea and the prevailing winds in the Yellow and Japan seas.†

During the north-east monsoon a part of the Pacific drift-current continues its course to the westward through the Bashee and Balintang channels, joining the monsoon drift current which sets strong to the south-westward at this season, through the Formosa channel and China sea.‡

During the south-west monsoon the drift-current which flows to the northward in the China sea and Formosa channel, joins the Kuro Siwo, and extends the western limit of its stream to a line joining the island of Tung-Ying (on the coast of China) to Tsu sima (in the Korea strait); this limit is very perceptible, the waters of the Japan stream being of a dark blue colour whilst that of the colder water is of a pale green, the difference in temperature of the two streams is also very marked.

The main body of the Kuro Siwo is joined at this season by the monsoon drift-current of the China sea, which also sets to the north-east through the Bashee and Balintang channels, and, being augmented in force, flows rapidly to the northward along the east coast of Formosa, passing between the north end of that island and the Meiaco sima group, as far as the parallel of 26° N., where it turns to the eastward and continues in a north-easterly direction to the westward of the Liu-Kiu islands until it reaches the southern point of Japan; here an off-shoot of the main stream passes to the northward through the Korea strait into the Japan sea (*see* page 6); the body of the stream, however, continues its course and trending still more to the eastward, flows in an east-north-east direction through Van Diemen strait, the numerous channels between the islands north of the Linschoten group and along the southern shores of the islands of Kiusiu and Sikok, forming (especially along its margin near the shore where it meets with an opposing tide) races and tide rips often resembling heavy breakers on reefs or shoals, and attaining its greatest velocity when abreast the latter island, where it has been known to set 100 miles in 24 hours, its usual velocity in this locality, however, being from 2 to 3 knots an hour.

---

* Black stream or tide, so called from its black appearance.

† *See* Chart; Stream and drift currents of Pacific, Atlantic, and Indian Oceans, No. 2,640. October 1872.

‡ *See* also page 25 for further information relating to the velocity and temperature during this monsoon.

Continuing its course along the south coast of the island of Nipon, past the gulf of Yedo, the Kuro Siwo flows through the chain of islands lying south of that gulf, in the numerous channels between which its direction is found to be variable and under tidal influence,* thus forming many tide rips and whirlpools; still continuing in an east-north-east direction as far as latitude 36½° N., its northern edge then leaves the coast of Nipon (which takes a sudden trend to the northward from about Inaboye saki) and allows a cold arctic current, setting to the southward along the shores of Kamchatka and the Kuril islands, to intervene between the Kuro Siwo and the north-eastern shores of Nipon and Yezo (see page 25); continuing to the northward, the Kuro Siwo begins to expand, and diminishes greatly in velocity after passing the meridian of 145° E.

At about the meridian of 150° E. it divides, one stream flowing to the northward and, taking the name of the Kamchatka current, is felt as far as the Aleutian islands and Behring strait (see page 25), whilst the greater portion of the stream continues in an easterly direction, between the parallels of 32° N., and 41° N. as far as the meridian of 160° E., where it is deflected to the south-eastward as far as the meridian of 180°, there losing its identity in the drift-currents of the North Pacific ocean which flow to the north and north-eastward.

The maximum temperature of the stream during the south-west monsoon is 86°, and its north-western edge is strongly marked by a sudden thermal change in the water of from 12° to 20°; but the southern and eastern limits at this season extending to the Bonin islands are much less distinctly marked.

It has been thought that the Kuro Siwo and the Gulf stream present features that are analogous in the constant high temperature of their waters, but from recent numerous observations of temperature in the former it appears they do not.

In the summer months, viz., from May to September inclusive, the mean temperature of the stream is 82°, or 7° higher than the mean temperature of the ocean, due to its latitude; it is during these months that the flow of tropical waters from the equatorial and drift-currents of the Pacific, together with the monsoon drifts of the China sea, join to swell the stream and raise the temperature of the Kuro Siwo.

In the months of April and October hot and cold belts are found alternating in the stream, the temperatures of which belts differ from 7° to 10°; whilst during the winter months, viz., from November to March, the tem-

---

* In a boat anchored in 10 fathoms close off the south-west point of Fatsizio, the flood, according to time of high water at Susaki (Tatiyama), set to the S.S.E. 3 to 4 knots, and changed at the ebb to the N.N.W. Between Fatsizio and Mikura, the ebb stream (by the shore) was found by H.M.S. *Actæon* setting to the N.N.W. 2 to 3 knots; also to the N. by W. 3 to 4 knots near the Broughton rocks; and, near the Redfield rocks, the flood (by the shore) set to the S.W. 2 to 3 knots.—Lieutenant C. J. Bullock, R.N., Commanding H.M. surveying vessel *Dove*, 1861.

perature of the stream, attaining in the latitude of Formosa a mean of 74° (which is rather higher than the temperature of the ocean, due to its latitude), falls on reaching the shores of Japan to 63°, or below the temperature of the ocean at the same season: this may be accounted for by the fact that during these months the great body of water which lies to the westward of the Liu-Kiu islands between the parallels of 26° N. and 28½° N., and which during the summer season flowed to the north-east, from 20 to 30 miles a day, bringing warm water from the China sea to join the Kuro Siwo, is now quiescent, no perceptible current being experienced within its limits; whilst further to the north of this still water a cold current, forced down by the prevailing northerly winds in the Japan and Yellow seas and setting strong to the eastward between the parallels 29° N. and 31° N., flows through Van Diemen strait and joins the Kuro Siwo, the temperature of which is thus considerably lowered; at the same time the stream is contracted to an average width of 250 miles in the meridian of 142° E., and its velocity is diminished to a mean rate of 2 knots an hour in consequence of the cessation of the supply of tropical waters.

The Kuro Siwo is however undoubtedly a warm current, its waters being always of a higher temperature than the surrounding atmosphere.

There is a floating seaweed found in the stream resembling the *fucus natans* of the Gulf stream.*

THE KAMCHATKA CURRENT is a branch of the Kuro Siwo, from which it separates in the parallel of 40° N. on the meridian of 150° E., and flows at an average rate of 18 miles a day (with a breadth of about 200 miles) to the north-eastward as far as 51° N., where it deflects to the eastward towards the Aleutian islands; between the parallels of 51° N. and 60° N.† there is a difficulty in tracing it, but beyond 60° N. it is again found setting to the north-east and, passing west of St. Mathew island and east of St. Lawrence island, it flows along the American coast through Behring strait into the Arctic ocean; in the strait the mean temperature of its waters (52°) is 15 degrees higher than that of the waters along the Asiatic shore, and which is entirely blocked in with ice until July, when from the higher temperature of this stream the coast of America is entirely free of it in the month of April.‡

THE OYA SIWO.—A counter current of cold water called the Oya Siwo sets to the southward, along the south-east coast of Kamchatka and

---

* The remarks on the temperature of the Kuro Siwo are deduced from the observations taken by the U.S. expedition to Japan, 1854, the remark books of H.M. ships, documents in the Hydrographic Department of the Admiralty, notes by Commander St. John in H.M. surveying vessel *Sylvia*, and the observations of Captain J. O. Hopkins, H.M.S. *Liverpool*.

† Observations in this locality are few and imperfect.

‡ Remarks of Dr. John Simpson, R.N., H.M.S. *Plover*, 1852.

the Kuril islands, and, flowing along the east coast of Yezo island and north-east coast of Nipon is felt as far south as Inaboye saki. It has an average breadth of 200 miles, but varies in velocity and extent in the different seasons, being much stronger in the winter than in the summer.

Except between the Kuril islands, through the straits, and past cape Noyshap, the force of the cold stream is about 18 miles a day; through these narrows however it sweeps occasionally with great speed, particularly during or after a strong north-easterly wind. Whirls, eddies, and tide rips take place off cape Noyshap.

During the spring (April), great quantities of floating ice are frequently brought down from the Kuril islands and the northward, and are left grounded along the Yezo coast from cape Yerimo eastward to cape Noyshap.*

Its temperature varies, according to the season, from 10° to 15° lower than that of the Kuro Siwo. This counter current is shown in Japanese itineraries, where the junk course is drawn well off shore, so as to avoid it by passing outside and getting into the Kamchatka current. The average temperature of the Oya Siwo in May was 37° (10° below that of the surrounding atmosphere). It was 66° in July between 10 and 30 miles from the shore; when the temperature rose to 70°, or where it bordered on the Kamchatka current flowing to the northward, this current was not perceptible. After passing westward round Inaboye saki, the temperature of the sea water rose from 66° to 79° where the Kuro Siwo was setting N.E. by E. 2 knots an hour. The Oya Siwo is not felt close to the shore, but is merged in the tides.

MAKING PASSAGES.

DURING the NORTH-EAST MONSOON.—HONG KONG TO YEDO.— A vessel bound from Hong Kong to Yedo at this season should work up the coast of China as far as Breaker point, taking care to be always under the land at nightfall, the wind during the night always hauling to the northward (off the land), when she may make a long tack off, standing in again in the morning when the wind shifts to the north-east, and frequently more easterly still. From Breaker point the vessel may then stand across with the wind free for the south end of Formosa, experiencing a southerly set whilst in the Formosa channel, but on nearing the island she will lose it, and, on passing South cape fall in with the Kuro Siwo setting strong to the north-east. Ships following this route (which is usually taken) from March to June inclusive, but more especially in March and April during brisk north-east winds and a strong westerly current, frequently take a week beating along shore to reach Breaker point before standing off.

---

* Commander H. C. St. John, R.N., H.M.S. *Sylvia*, 1871.

* Whereas, it has been found that, had vessels after clearing the Lema channel stood off on a wind clean full to the south-east, they would soon have got out of the westerly current, and on nearing Luzon would experience the wind more from the eastward and sometimes from southeast, enabling them to tack to the N.N.E. with a strong current in their favour, and thus would probably get to the eastward of Formosa in less time than it would have taken to reach Breaker point by keeping along the coast of China.

Having passed South cape Formosa, the vessel may work up the coast of that island, passing between it and the Meiaco Sima group, and to the westward of the Liu-Kiu islands, having the current with her as far as the parallel of 26° N., beyond which parallel she will experience no current until 30° N., where a strong current will be found setting to the eastward, the wind also being more from the North and West. She may then pass through any of the channels between the islands lying off the south point of Japan, after which keeping at about from 50 to 80 miles from the land, in the strength of the Kuro Siwo, she may make the lights at Ō sima (entrance of the Kii channel) and passing them at a distance of from 5 to 10 miles, may steer to pass just outside Mikomoto (Rock island). (For directions for the gulf of Yedo, see page 189–191.)

From Yedo to Hong Kong.—On leaving the gulf of Yedo, stand to the south-westward as far as 28° S. and 135° E., whence a course may be shaped to pass northward of Kakirouma, one of the Liu-Kiu group, thus avoiding the influence of the Kuro Siwo. After passing Iwo sima a straight course may be steered for Tung Ying, on making which island stand down the China coast for Hong Kong.

From Shanghae to Nagasaki.—At this season if the wind is to the eastward of North, it would be well on leaving the Yang-tse to stand to the north-westward on the starboard tack, and when the wind hauls round to the north-westward, which it will as the ship advances northward, tack, and steer a straight course for Nagasaki, making allowance for the south-easterly and easterly set from the Yellow sea and Korea strait, otherwise the ship may be swept to the eastward through Van Diemen strait. During the periodic easterly winds (variable between E.N.E. and S.E.) which prevail on the China coast in the vicinity of the Yang-tse, from March to June inclusive, with a sailing vessel, every opportunity must be taken to make easting, even with a fair wind, which it may be almost surely inferred will be but of short duration. In May and June, however, the set of the current will be changed, and will be found running to the north-eastward; under these circumstances there is a probability that a

---

* Meteorological Department of the Board of Trade.

vessel kept on the starboard tack would be set over to the Korean archipelago. With these considerations the navigator must act on his own judgment, there being only difficulty in making the passage, when baffling winds and thick, rainy, and squally weather are met with in the vicinity of the Meac sima, the Pallas, or the Goto islands, or they are passed on dark nights. If not, therefore, sure of the vessel's position, it would be well to make them in the daytime, unless the nights are moderately fine.

Hakodate through Korea strait.—If bound on to Hakodate at the same season or even as late as the end of June, it will be found difficult with a sailing vessel to make easting at all along the west coast of Nipon. It will be advantageous in April, May, and June, to pass well east of Tsu sima in the strength of the Japan stream which sets N.E. by N. through the Korea strait, attaining at times, although not constant, a velocity of 2 knots an hour. Should a S.W. wind occur at this season, it may be expected to last only 24 hours, unless it follow an easterly gale with depressed barometer. During the winter, gales from North and N.W. are very frequent in the Korea strait, lasting three or four days, and are sometimes violent. A rapidly falling barometer indicates their approach, the wind increasing in force after the mercury commences to rise, and not attaining its height until 24 hours after. In such weather, if making for Nagasaki on the port tack, beware of being blown to leeward into Van Diemen strait, for if set through by the Japan stream, it will take a long time to regain the lost ground against the current, (one vessel having been nearly three weeks endeavouring to beat round cape Chichakoff); and if on the starboard tack, there is probability of being set up the Korea strait to the northward of Ose saki. As both cases have happened to vessels, it is recommended that they should endeavour to make the land in daylight, and find anchorage, or secure a knowledge of their position.

In winter, when north-west and west winds prevail, a direct course should be steered from the Korea strait when bound to Hakodate; but if bound from Hakodate southward, it is necessary to endeavour to make westing when possible, and keep a long offing, for the coast of Nipon is a lee shore. After passing Korea strait as well to windward as possible, the winds will be found more liable to change when arrived at lat. 32° N., long. 125° E., but sometimes they continue so steadily between N.W. and W.S.W., as to set a vessel to leeward of the Yang-tse.

Shanghae to Yedo.—On leaving the Yang-tse the wind will be rarely found as far to the eastward as N.E., it is best, therefore, to keep the ship on the starboard tack, remembering that she will be set to the eastward towards Van Diemen strait, after passing which pursue the same route as directed in the passage from Hong Kong.

DURING the SOUTH-WEST MONSOON.—HONG KONG TO YEDO.— A vessel bound from Hong Kong to Yedo should run up the China coast as far as Tung Ying, then shape a course for Akusi sima, one of the Linschoten group; on passing the meridian of 125° E. the set will be strong to the north-eastward. Pass through any of the channels between the islands south of Japan in preference to Van Diemen strait, as the dense fogs which hang over the coast at this season render the navigation of this strait difficult, whilst farther seaward when in the warm stream of the Kuro Siwo the atmosphere is bright and clear. After passing the channel steer to make the lights at Ō sima, remembering the current sets along the coast of Japan to the north-eastward at this season from 2 to $4\frac{1}{2}$ knots an hour. After passing Ō sima at a distance of from 5 to 10 miles steer for Mikomoto (Rock island) light. If bound from Hong Kong to Nagasaki after leaving Tung Ying steer for Meac sima, passing between which group and the Pallas rocks a course E.N.E. 80 miles will place the ship off the lighthouse on Signal head (the North point of Iwo sima) at the entrance to Nagasaki harbour, on nearing which it should not be brought to bear northward of N.N.E.

From Yedo to Hong Kong.—This passage is so seldom made by sailing vessels that very little is known of the best route to be pursued, the following, however, is recommended :—

On leaving the gulf of Yedo shape a course to the south-eastward to cross the parallel of 30° N. in about 145° E., and passing East of St. Margaret's island cross the meridian of 140° E. in lat. 21° N., thence steer (with a favourable current) for the north-east point of Luzon, on passing which enter the China sea, when a direct course may be shaped for Hong Kong, taking care to allow for the drift-current setting to the north-east at this season. It may here be remarked that this route lies directly across the paths of the typhoons, which are prevalent in the tropics at this period.

This voyage is rarely made as sailing vessels so take advantage of the monsoons that they leave Hong Kong for the northern ports and Japan at the commencement of the south-west monsoon, and, remaining at the ports of the latter islands until the monsoon takes off, leave for the South at the commencement of the north-east monsoon.

Steamers, however, run at all times between the two places, and at this season usually on leaving Yedo gulf, and passing Mikomoto keep well in shore to Ō sima (*see* page 179), passing which they keep up the Kii channel through Isumi strait and the Inland sea. On passing Simonoseki strait, if not bound to Nagasaki, they keep to westward of the Goto islands, and making the Saddle islands off the Yang-tse keep close to the shore, and from thence pursue the same course to the southward as vessels bound from Shanghae to Hong Kong.*

From Shanghae to Nagasaki.—On leaving the Yang-tse steer to pass between the Pallas rocks and Meac sima (Asses Ears), which last is visible in clear weather at a distance of 30 miles. The current will be found setting to the north-eastward through Korea straits (*see* page 6), care must be taken therefore to avoid being set to the northward of Ose saki, the south point of the Goto islands, as the current during the south-west monsoon is often strong in this locality. Passing the Amherst rocks a course E. ¾ N. 390 miles will lead midway between the Pallas rocks and Ose saki (cape Goto).

FROM SYDNEY TO YEDO.—Vessels bound from Sydney to Japan should pursue, as far as lat. 8° N. and long. 160° E., the same course as those bound for Hong Kong; from that position a course should be shaped to pass to the northward of the Mariana islands and to the south-westward of the Volcano islands, after passing which steer to make Ō sima lights, remembering that the ship must pass the strength of the Kuro Siwo, and will, when in its stream, be set to the north-eastward from 2 to 3 knots an hour.

---

* *See* China Sea Directory, Vol. III.

CHAPTER II.

WEST, SOUTH-WEST, AND SOUTH COASTS OF KOREA; AND KOREA STRAIT.

VARIATION 4° 0′ West in 1872.

THE KOREA* is separated from China on the north-west by the Yalu kiang, the estuary of which river is in about lat. 39° 50′ N., long. 124° 10′ E.

The coast eastward of the Yalu kiang † appears to trend to the south-east as far as Ping Yang inlet, and is skirted by numerous islands, the whole of which are as yet unexplored. Banks with shoal water on them extend a long distance to seaward of these islands, and vessels navigating in this locality should use great caution, as banks of rock and sand rise precipitously from the water.

PYLADES SHOAL, in lat. 38° 55′ N., long. 124° 39′ E., is a shoal bank, which appears to be joined to the group of lofty islands lying about 12 miles to the south-east of this position.

PING YANG INLET, situated at the mouth of the Ping Yang river, is difficult of approach owing to the numerous shoals which encumber its entrance. A good anchorage may be had in 9 fathoms mud, with Station island bearing N. by W., and Cowies point W. by N. Station island is in lat. 38° 42½′ N., long. 125° 10′ E.‡ The coast from Ping Yang inlet trends to the south-west to Humbug point, off which lies the island of Douchen, between which and the mainland is a channel, 1¼ miles wide, carrying a depth of 10 fathoms. From Humbug point the coast takes a south-west direction for 17 miles as far as Phelans point, and midway between these points lies Choda island, forming a channel 4 miles wide, with deep water between it and the mainland.

CHODA ISLAND, separated from the mainland of the Korea by Febigers channel, is well wooded and cultivated, and on its southern shore in a small bight are two villages and a harbour for junks. About a mile southward of the west point of the island, near which is a small islet, is the

---

* The description of the west coast of Korea, north of the Conference group, and of the south-west coast between Mackau and Aberdeen islands, is partly from Admiral Guérin's report of the voyage of the French frigate *Virginie* in 1855–56.

† *See* Charts: Gulfs of Pe-chili and Liau-tung, No. 1,256; Japan and Korea, No. 2,347, scale $m = 0 \cdot 04$ of an inch; and Korean Archipelago, No. 104.

‡ *See* Chart: Ping Yang inlet, No. 1,257, scale $m = 1 \cdot 12$ inch, by Commander S. C. Febiger, U. S. N. 1868.

beginning of an extensive shoal bank projecting to the south-westward for 5 or 6 miles; its exact extent, however, has not been determined.

ANCHORAGE may be found in the channel between the north end of the bank and the small islet in 8 and 10 fathoms, quite sheltered by Choda to the north-east, and by the bank to the west. The shore around this bight is studded with villages and well cultivated.

TIDES.—On the 3rd and 4th September 1856 (three and four days after the change of moon), it was high water in the bay on the south side of Choda at 8h. 40m., and the tide rose 10 feet; the approximate establishment, full and change, may be assumed at 6h. 20m., and the rise 11 to 12 feet.

From Phelans point to the entrance to the Ta-Tong river the coast trends to the S.S.W. for 17 miles, forming the promontory of Chwang-shan; this coast was visited by the ship *Amherst** in 1832, and received the name of Daniel island; it is, however, evidently part of the mainland of Korea, but has not yet been surveyed. The land is clothed with luxuriant vegetation and high trees; the lower part near the sea was cleared and cultivated, and numerous cattle and several villages were seen.

TA-TONG RIVER.†—From Chwang-shan promontory the coast trends to the eastward, forming a deep bight, into which flows the Ta-Tong river. On entering this bight pass the north point of Peh Leng Tao (the northern island of Sir James Hall group) within 1½ miles, and steer a N.E. by E. course until in mid-channel between the mainland and the island of Yne Nae Tau, after passing which the chart will be found sufficient guide. The Ta-Tong river is reported by the natives to be only navigable for junks and boats. The north point of Peh Leng Tao will be recognised by its perpendicular sides of basaltic rock, and the sharp detached rock lying off it.

TIDES.—At Neu To island the ebb generally sets to the eastward, and the flood to the westward, they are, however, irregular both in force and direction.

SIR JAMES HALL GROUP, consisting of three islands, lying nearly north and south, about 18 miles to the south-westward of the Ping Yang inlet, was discovered by H.M. ships *Alceste* and *Lyra*, 1st September 1816. The rock off the north-west end of the northern island, by Captain Basil Hall, is in long. 124° 44½' E.‡

---

* From the voyage of the ship *Amherst* to the northern ports of China, Gutzlaff's third voyage in 1832.

† See Chart: Approach to Ta-Tong river, No. 1,257, scale $m = \cdot 05$ inch, by Commander R. W. Shufeldt, U. S. N., 1867.

‡ The position of this rock on the charts, 37° 57' 30" N., 124° 34' 30" E., is given on the authority of a survey of the entrance of Ta-Tong river, by Commander Schufeldt, of the United States Navy, 1867.

PEH LENG TAO, the northern and largest of the group, is fronted on the north-west point by bold perpendicular cliffs about 300 feet high, at the extreme of which is an off-lying needle or finger-shaped rock about 150 feet high.

Along the north-west side of the island, a few detached rocks extend a cable off shore.

Off the south point of the island there is a remarkable rocky islet, with a large wedge-shaped hole through its north side. About $1\frac{1}{4}$ miles to the southward of this perforated islet is a sharp rock 50 feet in height, with a ledge of rocks extending one-third of a mile from its north side; two of these rocks are always uncovered. At a quarter of a mile south of the 50 feet rock is broken water, having the appearance of a rock nearly awash at low water.

About three-quarters of a mile to the east-south-east of the perforated islet are some detached rocks, the outermost of which is 20 feet high. Between these and the ledge of rocks to the north of the 50 feet rock, is a channel carrying from 7 to 8 fathoms.

H.M.S. *Ringdove* anchored off a small village in a bay near the south-west point of the island, about three quarters of a mile from the shore, in 12 fathoms hard mud. From the anchorage, the perforated islet, which is off the east point of the bay (south point of Peh Leng Tao), bore E. by S. $\frac{1}{2}$ S.; the 50 feet rock S.S.E. $\frac{1}{2}$ E.; and a clump of trees in the valley behind the village N. $\frac{1}{4}$ E.

The hills at the back are smooth-topped and covered with grass, and can easily be distinguished when standing in from the south-eastward.

TA CHENG TAO is the middle island of the group; it has a conspicuous hill or peak about 900 feet high, which appears conical in form when seen from the westward. A small islet, 170 feet high, lies about one mile off the west side.

On the south-east side of the island is a bay with a shingle beach, in which the *Ringdove* anchored in 8 fathoms, sand, off a small village, with the east point of the bay bearing N. by E. $\frac{1}{4}$ E., and centre of village S.W. by W. $\frac{3}{4}$ W. The anchorage is protected from S.S.W. round by west to N. by E., and is also sheltered from heavy seas from the southward by Sho Cheng Tao; it is therefore preferable to the anchorage in the south bay of that island.

SHO CHENG TAO has off its south-west point a dangerous reef (with some of the rocks always uncovered), extending in a south-west direction for about a mile; 19 fathoms, sand and mud, was obtained at a distance of nearly 2 miles off the south-west point of the island.

The south-east point is remarkable from its being fronted with white cliffs. A sharp conical rock lies about a quarter of a mile to the east-south-east of the point.

Detached rocks, as also the appearance of shoal water, extend for half a mile from the east side of the island: soundings in from 10 to 13 fathoms were obtained at a distance of about 1½ miles from the shore.

H.M.S. *Ringdove* anchored in a bay, in which are two villages, on the south side of the island, in 9 fathoms, sand. This bay affords shelter from W.S.W. round by north, to E. by N., but is entirely open to the southward. Vessels on entering this bay from the westward should not approach the south-west point of the island nearer than 2 miles until the centre of the bay bears N.N.W., when they may steer in, and anchor in 8 fathoms.

With the conical rock off the south-east point of the island bearing E. by N., and the centre of the western village N.W. ¾ N., there is a depth of 7 fathoms.

In the channel between Ta Cheng Tao and Peh Leng Tao, broken water was seen in several places, particularly off the north side of Ta Cheng Tao island; in many cases this appearance was probably occasioned by the tide, but from soundings having been suddenly struck in 7 fathoms after a depth of 13 fathoms, it is inferred there is an irregular bottom, and that caution is necessary in using the channel.

No rocks were observed above water in the channel between Sho Cheng Tao and Ta Cheng Tao.

TIDES. Between the islands, the flood-stream sets to the west, and the ebb-stream to the east.

Off the west side of Peh Leng Tao, the flood-stream sets north, and the ebb-stream south, from 1½ to 2 knots an hour. Off its north-west point the time of high water at full and change was approximately considered to be 4h. 30m.

By observation the *Ringdove's* anchorage is in lat. 37° 55′ N., long. 124° 45′ E.* *Variation 3° 20′ W. in 1871.*†

THE COAST from Ta Tong river to Tsia Tung island, at the northern entrance to the Séoul river, a distance of about 45 miles has not yet been surveyed.

PRINCE IMPÉRIAL ARCHIPELAGO.‡—Southward of the above anchorage are the numberless isles of the Prince Impérial archipelago, and to the south-east the shores of Prince Jérôme gulf. In the latter

---

* This position would place the Finger rock off the N.W. point of Peh Leng Tao in 37° 58′ N., 124° 42′ 30″ E., which agrees nearly with that given by Capt. Basil Hall, but differs 8′ with Commander Shufeldt's survey.

† The description of the Sir James Hall group is by Nav. Lieut. J. Cole, R.N., H.M.S. *Ringdove*, 1871.

‡ The description of the Prince Impérial archipelago and of the approaches to Séoul are from the remarks of Lieut. Commander H. F. Picking, U. S. N. *See* Chart: Approaches to Séoul, No. 1,258.

direction, to within 1½ miles of the coast, is a channel of 11 fathoms, breaking off suddenly into irregular depths.

To the S.E. by S. is an indentation of the land about 10 miles deep, with an average width of one mile. At that distance the shores approach each other, and there were all the signs of a considerable river; many populous villages were seen, the soil was well cultivated, and junks were at anchor in all the creeks.

ISLES FERRIERES.—Is comprised of a group of four islets. North-west island has the appearance of two, but its parts are joined by a rocky ledge which is uncovered at low water. The western part is rocky and irregular, the other quite regular and steep-to; the height of the latter, ascertained by measurement, is 98 feet, the former not quite so high. North-east island, the middle one, is very regular and of greater extent, it is 179 feet high. South island is regular, and rises gradually in cone shape to about 113 feet. All are of small extent, and are neither cultivated nor inhabited.

A rock has been reported as lying about one mile S.W. from South island.

TIDES.—The flood tide commences from N.W., and gradually flows around by the west to about south. The ebb commences from the N.E., and goes by the east to south; at the rate of about two knots per hour. Rise and fall of spring tide is about 20 feet.

POUNG TO (Fernande) is about three-quarters of a mile in its greatest length, and rises gradually to a height of 729 feet. It has some cultivation on the eastern side and a small village on the north-east end.

THE OLIVIER GROUP consists of six small islands, the largest being about half a mile long, the one to the south-east being simply a rock. They vary in height, the most elevated being 189 feet, and the rock 60 feet high. The northernmost has a rock off its north point, which rises perpendicularly from the sea to a height of about 40 feet. The middle island of the group is the largest, and has a small settlement with a little cultivation.

AUGUSTE ISLAND, which has a peak about 345 feet high, is apparently large.

Eugénie Island extends north and south about one mile, and is about one-third of a mile wide. At its northern end there is a separation extending nearly to the water, almost forming another small island. This portion rises directly from the water, very steep-to, and about 100 feet high. The highest peak of Eugénie island is 339 feet. The surface of the island is irregular; it has no inhabitants and no appearance of cultivation. There is a rocky bank along its western coast, on which is only about 3 feet at low water at about one-quarter of a mile from the beach.

LE FRÈRE, a rock about 15 feet above high water, lies half a mile to the north-westward of the northern point of Eugénie island.

TORI (Ilot Fournier) rises almost perpendicularly on its western side to about 153 feet. It is of small extent, and has a yellow sandy appearance, and is surrounded by rocks which are covered at high water.

Cape Chanoine is an island separated from the mainland by a narrow passage which is nearly dry at low water.

The passage indicated on the chart between Lebarbier de Tinan and the mainland is impracticable even for junks. At low water a mud flat nearly connects the island with the mainland, leaving only a small channel. The southern point of Lebarbier de Tinan is a steep bluff rising to about 70 feet. The island is of considerable extent, its surface irregular, is inhabited, and seems well cultivated. Landing here is impracticable, the coast being skirted by a rocky ledge. The "Arbre remarquable" is an excellent landmark, and being large and standing alone, it is noticed at some distance.

In the channel between Kien Chan and Lebarbier de Tinan lie the islands Coupée du Rona. There is deep water in the channel, but the approaches at either end being impracticable render it useless.

KIEN CHAN ISLAND is about 500 feet high, is irregular in shape and steep on its north-western side. It appears well cultivated; water seems abundant, as a small stream was seen on one of the hills, coming apparently from a spring. There is a large village on the western side.

The bank of 4 fathoms marked to the southward of Kien Chan does not extend quite so far from the land, and apparently shoals gradually.

Between Cape Chanoine and Ilot Fournier is shallow and rocky, the most water being 2 fathoms; the approach, however, being regular. Between Ilot Fournier and Ile Eugénie the soundings are regular, running from 16 fathoms in mid-channel to 6 fathoms close to each island. Between Ile Eugénie and the Olivier group the soundings were very irregular, varying from 1½ to 16 fathoms. A rocky ledge runs from Henri island toward the small island of the Olivier group. A number of sunken rocks appear about the islands of the Olivier group.

LE CHAPEAU at low water looks very much like a cocked hat. It is of very small extent, and about 42 feet high.

HUMANN ISLAND extends in a N.E. and S.W. direction for about a mile; is irregular and hilly, and has no appearance of inhabitants or cultivation. The highest part of the island has about 250 feet elevation.

ROCHE CONIQUE is recognisable from its shape, is small in extent, and rises out of the sea to an elevation of 63 feet.

LES TAS DE POIX are easily recognized as two rocky islets close together, the eastern one being the smaller. The height of Grivel is 147 feet. Edmond island is reported awash at high water. Philippe island, lying to the southward of Richy, is 102 feet high. It has a single peak of regular shape. The height of Louis island is 168 feet.

LA TACHE BLANCHE is a rocky ledge of small extent lying nearly in the channel, serving as a very good mark; the tops of the rocks being white are easily recognized, and are just visible at high water.

THE LAGUERRE GROUP consists of three uninhabited and uncultivated islands of small extent, together with several outlying rocks.

LE CHAT rises directly out of the sea to a height of about 179 feet, and is of small extent. There is apparently a good passage between it and Brisant du Chat.

BRISANT DU CHAT is just awash at high water neap tides; at high water spring tides it is very dangerous and should be given a good berth.

Between Ile Ronde and the Vedette du Nord there are 2½ and 3-fathom spots.

In Roze Roads the greatest velocity of the current is about 2 knots an hour. The tide rises about 30 feet setting easterly on the flood and westerly on the ebb. The prevailing wind in May and June is from S.W., and blows strong for several days at a time. The barometer veering between 29.70 and 29.80.

DIRECTIONS.—With South island bearing North, steer E.N.E. to pass about a mile from So Pai Oul, this course clears the Chasseriau bank, and leads up in mid-channel between Sou Heng and Pong To. South island appears very different on this bearing, being almost divided by a narrow gorge which reaches nearly to the water's edge, forming a very good mark for changing the course, as it opens very suddenly. The soundings are regular, after passing South island, for about 10 miles, but when So Pai Oul bears N.W. there is a sudden shoaling from 42 to 21 fathoms. This course leads between Mêquet island and Fernande island, after passing which steer E. by N. for Brisant du Chat. The soundings are regular.

ANCHORAGE may be had in 11 fathoms, with the following bearings, viz., Le Frère, S. by E. ½ E.; Ilot Fournier, S.E., by E. ¾ E., and Le Chapeau, N.W. by W. The bottom is very hard, and apparently of a rocky formation, but about half a mile more to the northward there is soft bottom and very good holding ground.

CHASSERIAU BANK.—The south point of which is in lat. 36° 59′ 20″ N., long. 126° 12′ E., follows from thence the trend of the coast as far as lat. 37° 6½′ N., in long. 126° 32′ E. It is about three-quarters to a quarter of a mile wide, and the soundings over it irregular on all parts. There are only 6 to 9 feet on its two extremes, but both its sides appeared steep-to, as the depth is 12 to 15 fathoms near its western, and 11 to 12 fathoms near its eastern edge. It shelters both Caroline and Deception bays, and forms with the coast a long channel about 2 miles wide, in which the depth is more than 12 fathoms, and the anchorage secure in every part.

DIRECTIONS. — BOISÉE ANCHORAGE. — Having Le Chat bearing W. by S., and the western tangent of Kien Chan N. by E., steer up north to pass between La Tache Blanche and Kien Chan. The former may be passed quite close in 10 fathoms, from which continue the same course until the northern tangent of Marolles bears west, when alter course to N.E. ¼ N., which leads up to the Vedette du Nord, bearing west; steer N.E. by E. ¼ E. to pass between it and Ile Ronde. When the latter bears west steer N.E. for Roze island. A good mark for this channel is to bring the eastern end of Ile Ronde just clear of the western end of Kien Chan, and when Bouquet Zoé, a clump of trees on the high peak on the mainland bears east, change the course to N. by E., which leads between Bochet island, Boisée island, and Roze island. Pass in mid-channel and anchor in 13 fathoms water on the following bearings: Guerrière island, N.E. ½ E.; Primauguet island, N. ½ W.; Boisée island, S.W. ½ W., and Roze island, S. ½ E.

Ile Ronde is 213 feet in height, its ascent is regular, there is no cultivation, and but one small house on its eastern side.

Roze island is easily recognised. It rises very gradually to an elevation of about 400 feet, and has on the highest part a clump of trees. The slope on the western side is more gradual than on the eastern, and it has a long low building, apparently of stone, which looks like a barracks. There is a small fishing village on the eastern side where a few junks are generally seen. There is a passage at high water for junks between this island and the mainland.

Bochet island is joined to Ieung Tjong by a mud flat uncovered at low water, and also appears to be connected by a causeway which is always dry; the island is about 100 feet high, the highest part being on the western end, and is of a yellowish or sandy appearance. There is a wall about 6 feet high running nearly the whole length of the island, and is probably for the protection of the large village on the north-eastern end.

Boisée island is thickly wooded, and from this circumstance can be recognised at some distance as it is the only wooded land seen. It is about 100 feet high, and has a wall about 4 feet high running for some distance along the top.

IEUNG TJONG is a large island, irregular in shape and height, the highest peak reaching an elevation of upward of 1,000 feet, and has on its top a clump of trees. It is cultivated, and has several small villages on it.

GUERRIERE ISLAND is about half a mile in length and about 300 feet high, a ridge extending nearly its whole length, the northern end of which is perpendicular, with a gradual slope toward the southern end. The highest peak is nearly in the middle of the island, and has a clump of trees on it. There is a separation at its northern end which leaves a small portion of the island detached at high water.

The high bluff rock-formed islands, rising out of a mud bank, which are seen detached from the land at high water, are connected at low water by extensive mud flats on which it is possible to walk without much difficulty.

There is a ledge of rocks running from Boisée in the direction of Roze island, and also a ledge from Roze island in the direction of Boisée. Apparently there is deep water in mid-channel.

TIDES.—The greatest rise of water at spring tides is 33 feet, and its maximum velocity at flood $3\frac{1}{2}$ knots, and at ebb $3\frac{1}{3}$ knots. The eastern end of Boisée is in lat. 37° 29′ 30″ N., long. 126° 34′ 9″ E. A rock about 20 feet above high water, lies to the westward of Le Chat. A small island regular in shape, with steep bluffs, which rises to an elevation of 96 feet, lies to the westward.

MEQUET ISLAND is about 228 feet high, and extends about half a mile east and west. The highest peak is near the middle of the island.

ADOLPHE ISLAND, more to the northward, is of greater extent and has on the western end a peak about 300 feet high; this island is inhabited.

To the westward of Adolphe lies the island of Guérin, which is about $1\frac{1}{2}$ miles long east and west, and has two peaks, the higher 600 feet. Ernest lies directly to the southward of Guérin, is of small extent and about 200 feet high. Jouan lies beeween the two former. Its height was not determined, but is apparently not higher than Ernest, and very little greater in extent. Rigault de Genonilly is irregular, having several peaks, the highest of which is 816 feet; the southern end of this island is steep-to. A rock, which uncovers at low water, lies S. by E., about 1 mile from the south end of the island. Chasseloup Laubat has two high peaks, the northern one being about 500 feet, and the southern one 513 feet high. It is very irregular, uncultivated, and uninhabited. Off the south-eastern end there are a number of detached rocks. The islands to the northward appear to be of the same general character—high, barren, and uninhabited.

DECEPTION BAY, where the *Virginie* anchored after some difficult navigation between the land and the Chassériau bank, is (the entrance) in lat. 37° 3′ N., long. 126° 33′ E. It owes its name to the deceitful indications of a river which seems to open into the deep and narrow channel terminating it to the south, and in which the depth is about 5½ fathoms.

There is excellent sheltered anchorage off the entrance of this channel, but the outer passages to it present great difficulty of approach from being in the midst of islands and surrounded by banks; the greatest obstacle is the strength of the current, which in the inner channel runs 5 knots The last of the summits of the Table chain overlook the shores of Deception bay and those of Prince Jérôme gulf.

CAROLINE BAY, the west point of entrance to which is in lat. 37° 1½′ N., long. 126° 25′ E., has a safe outer roadstead, carrying about 9 fathoms water, between Alfred peninsula and the Cormorandière rock, lying off the west point of the bay. There are numerous villages on the coast. The tide rises about 26 feet.

The entrance to this bay, little more than a mile wide, is much contracted by a tongue of sand which uncovers, and beginning at the eastern point of the bay extends three-quarters of a mile westward across the channel; but between the western extreme and the opposite shore there is a channel of 11 fathoms water, which leads to a large lagoon.

JOACHIM BAY.—In steering for this bay, the *Virginie* passed 3 miles north of Tas-de-Foin or Haycock islet, off the entrance of Shoal gulf, and had 11 fathoms in the middle of the central islands of the archipelago. Between the Clifford islands, lat. 36° 44′ N., long. 125° 44′ E., and the coast the depth was 33 fathoms. The frigate anchored in 9 fathoms about one mile off the west point of entrance of Joachim bay.

This bay, in lat. 36° 53½′ N., long. 126° 17¾′ E., is a large bight which extends to the south-east, and looks from a distance as if it afforded excellent anchorage; but part of its entrance is barred by two reefs, the summits of which are never covered. Having passed eastward of these reefs, through a channel carrying 16 feet at low water, a sheltered anchorage was found in 7 to 9 fathoms soft mud, abreast a village containing about 4,000 inhabitants.

From hence the remainder of the bight is nothing but a large lagoon, forming to the south-east and east two bays 4 or 5 miles deep, having not more than 3 feet in them at low water.

MARJORIBANKS HARBOUR.—The *Amherst* left her anchorage under Chwang-shan, and steered to the southward; after passing numerous islands, she anchored under the the Loktaou islands, about 2 miles from a large village built on the brow of a steep hill, westward of Table mountain. From the Loktaou she steered N.E. 7 miles for another group, and then N.E. towards a passage among numerous islands, where she found sheltered and convenient anchorage near a large village. This anchorage was named Marjoribanks harbour.*

The approaches to Marjoribanks harbour are well pointed out by Table mountain, 3,280 feet high, which rises E. by N. ¾ N. from the anchorage, but they are studded with islets and rocks, amongst which it is difficult to navigate.

The harbour is described as fronting the mouth of the channel leading into Shoal gulf, and is formed by three islands of moderate size; one to the north-west (Chang-kon-yam), one to the north-east (Ko-tian), and one to the south, and by a small islet Mauzac surrounded by reefs to the west. The depth is 8 to 12 fathoms at low water, in the middle of the harbour, abreast the south point of Ko-tian; but north of this, and in line with Mauzac islet, lying off the south point of Chang-kon-yam, the water shoals rapidly to 20 and 12 feet near some rocks awash, which seem to encumber the north side of the harbour. To the southward the depth decreases less rapidly; there are 12½, 6, and 5 fathoms as far as the line which joins the northern point of the south island to the rock above water, which lies one mile W.N.W. of this point. Mauzac islet is in lat. 36° 26¾' N., long. 126° 28. E.

There is a valley in a bay with a sand beach on the middle of the west coast of Chang-kon-yam, and another village on the north-west coast of Ko-tian. One mile eastward of this latter island is a large island named Roussin, on which there are three villages; it occupies nearly all the entrance of Shoal gulf. The channel which it forms with the south end of Lindsay island is 2 miles long and 1½ miles wide, but it is difficult to navigate, being encumbered with islets and rocks.

A party proceeded to the northward to explore a deep and wide gulf, which was named Shoal gulf.† The western side of the gulf was studded with numerous beautiful verdant islets, mostly cultivated and inhabited, and thickly wooded with fine fir timber, many of the trees of which were fit for spars, and the wood of the best quality, close grained, and full of turpentine. In advancing up the gulf it became much wider, at the entrance 5 miles, and 10 miles up nearly double that breadth; the soundings were variable, but 8 to 12 fathoms were carried in the fair channel. The island to the eastward was 2 miles in length, fertile, and with several large villages on it. Having proceeded about 6 miles farther, and the head of

---

* After Mr. Marjoribanks, late President of the Select Committee of Supercargoes at Canton.

† There is a discrepancy between the chart of the *Amherst's* voyage by Capt. Rees, her commander, and the account of her voyage by Mr. Gutzlaff and Mr. Lindsay. Marjoribanks harbour of the chart is called Gankeang in Gutzlaff's Voyages, page 330; and Shoal gulf of the chart is named Marjoribanks harbour in Lindsay's Report, 2nd Edition, p. 240.

the gulf appearing at a great distance, they abandoned the idea of reaching its extremity, and landed on an island which was named Lindsay island.*

On ascending a high hill, the open sea was seen to the westward, and Lindsay island was observed to be separated from the mainland by a narrow passage. The head of the gulf was divided into two parts, the western of which extended about 7 or 8 miles to the northward, but the termination of the eastern one, which trends to the N.N.E. could not be seen. A cluster of islands lie in the centre of the gulf, about 10 miles from the entrance.

Marjoribanks harbour and Shoal gulf were also visited by the French frigate *Virginie* in 1856.

SHOAL GULF is described as extending 30 miles in a northerly direction from its entrance. Although its name implies that it is shallow, yet there is an average depth of about 11 fathoms to 25 miles north of Roussin island, which forms the western part of its mouth. All the western part of the gulf, as far as the Mathilde group, in lat. 36° 44′ N. was sounded over by the boats of the *Virginie*, the depth varying from 6 to 10 fathoms. In the bay north of the group, the soundings were 4 and 5 fathoms, and in the bay E.N.E. of the group 22 to 26 feet near the shore.

The water in the gulf rises about 26 feet. The tides produce strong eddies, which, although they favour the junks, would no doubt be an obstacle in its navigation by a sailing vessel of large draught, particularly with the variable winds of these latitudes. The coasting trade is considerable, and its importance to the Koreans is pointed out by beacons, which are kept up with great care on all the points, and on the shoals which cover at high water.

The general aspect of the shores of the gulf is uniform. Lindsay island is a long range of wooded summits united by chains of rocks, covered at high water. In all the creeks are hamlets and villages, the principal of which are on Roussin island and at port Lourmel. The eastern coast of the gulf, on the contrary, is an uninterrupted series of bare hills, with abrupt declivities, throwing out into the sea their granite bases. Behind these hills are the high mountains of the Table chain, which run in a N.W. and S.E. direction. There are only two or three villages on this coast, but there appeared to be a large population in the interior.

Three channels lead into the gulf. The two westward of Roussin island are only practicable for junks. The third must be sought for to the southward of the Marjoribanks islands, Chang-kon-yam, Ko-tian, and another, and which, bounding them to the east, carries 6½ to 22 fathoms water, as far as the south-east point of Roussin, where a circular bay,

---

* After Mr. Lindsay, the H.E.I. Company's supercargo in the *Amherst*.

formed by this point and Bouët island, offers good anchorage. All the southern part of the gulf between the Parseval group, Roussin island, and the mainland, affords fair anchorage near the shore, especially to the south of Penaud island, where the current runs with less strength than in the gulf. The Parseval are 3 miles north, the Penaud 1½ miles north-east of the east end of Roussin.

In proceeding up the gulf the soundings were 9 to 16 fathoms, sand and shells, as far as the Dénudées islands, which lie 10 miles within the entrance. At a mile southward of the centre island of this group, in 8 fathoms, sand, a convenient shelter may be found abreast a creek, where the junks await the change of tide. At 1½ miles N.N.W. of the Dénudées is a flat 4 cables in extent, and carrying 26 feet water, which must be left to the westward, and the channel taken between it and Lindsay island.

The Mathilde group will now be seen at 6 miles to the N. by E. They divide the head of the gulf into two deep bays, one trending to the north, the other to the north-east. At half a mile south of the most southerly island of this group is a small islet, distinguished by a large white pagoda covered with tiles standing in the midst of trees. At 3 miles S.W. by W. of this islet, and at the same distance from the nearest point of Lindsay island, is another flat of less extent than the former, but carrying the same depth, 26 feet; in proceeding north this also must be left to the eastward, so as to keep in the channel.

From thence, steering towards the north part of Lindsay island, a bight, named port Lourmel, about 1½ miles deep, will be seen to the W. by N., and a large village on the declivity of a steep hill. This is one of the most commercial points of the gulf. A channel, carrying 6½ to 9 fathoms, leads to it and forms a sheltered roadstead, the only inconvenience being the currents, which set strongly from a lagoon leading to the westward. This lagoon is only navigable at high tides to the junks, which penetrate some distance into the interior.

Port Lourmel is the limit of the deep soundings, for as soon as the small islet to the north is passed, the depths are irregular, the channel becomes contracted, and not more than 26 feet will be carried for 6 or 7 miles. Here one of the most remarkable mountains of the coast is to be seen; remarkable, inasmuch as it may be recognized in all directions, and that it rises from the centre of three large bays. Its peak is conical, and has three little paps on its summit.

To the eastward of port Lourmel is the entrance of the north-east bay of the gulf, which is open to the south-west. Its high shores seemed to announce deep soundings; not more, however than 32 feet were found, and at low water a bank, more than 1½ miles in extent, was left dry surrounding Great Mandarin point.

TIDES.—At Marjoribanks harbour, it is high water, full and change, at 3h. 30m., and springs rise 29 feet. In Shoal gulf the rise is 26 feet.

DIRECTIONS.—In running for the harbour, the *Virginie* had 27 fathoms water at 2½ miles south of Guérin island, 951 feet high, in lat 36° 7′ N., long. 126° 1′ E.; from thence she steered to pass 4 miles east of Wai-ian-do island, elevated 1,050 feet, the soundings being 14 and 16 fathoms. After sailing 7 miles eastward of this position she steered to the northward, passing some distance east of Camille, Pellion, and Charner islands, in soundings of 8 and 10 fathoms, until abreast of Tas-de-Foin islet, in lat. 36° 24½′ N., long. 126° 24′ E., and from thence to Marjoribanks harbour.

BASIL OR CHU-YING BAY, discovered by the *Alceste* and *Lyra*, 4th September 1816, is formed on the east side of a curved tongue of land, on which is a peaked hill. The south end of this tongue, by Capt. Basil Hall, is in lat. 36° 7′ 38″ N., long. 126° 42½′ E. The bay is about 4 miles wide, but it is open to the south, and has not water enough to allow vessels of moderate draught to enter, there being only 2½ to 3 fathoms inside the points. The *Alceste* and *Lyra* anchored outside in 5 fathoms.

To the south-west, 5 miles, of the west point of entrance, is a peaked islet named Helens island, 930 feet high, which forms a good mark to lead to the bay. The bay is skirted by large villages, ornamented with trees, and surrounded by cultivation, both on the mainland and on many of the neighbouring islands, which form a part of the Korean archipelago.

TIDES.—In Basil bay, September 4th, 1816, the rise of tide, 2½ days before full moon, was 15½ feet ; low water at 8h. p.m., and high water at 2h. 30m. a.m., showing an approximate establishment of 4h. 15m., and a rise of 17 to 18 feet at springs.

KOREAN ARCHIPELAGO.—From Basil bay the *Alceste* and *Lyra* proceeded southward among the Korean archipelago, carrying soundings of 7 to 17 fathoms, and usually anchored at night. On 8th September they came to in 11 fathoms, soft bottom, in Murray sound, about 2 cables off the east side of Thistle island, in lat. 34° 22′ 39″ N., long. 126° 3′ E. The islands here are so situated as to form a capacious and secure anchorage, with passages among them in all directions. The tides ran at the rate of 3½ knots at springs ; the flood to the north-east; the rise and fall was 15 feet. From the summit of a high peak, elevated 800 feet, of an island to the south-east, upwards of two hundred islands were counted, many large and high, and almost all cultivated.

THE KOKOUN-TAU GROUP are the only islands tolerably known in the interior of this archipelago. They are high, mountainous, and 9 miles in extent, east and west, and about the same north and south, if Peak islet be included. They are separated by narrow channels, and form a mass of bare peaks and arid cliffs. The sea breaks with violence on their rocky points during S.W. gales, and the flood stream runs violently into the passage between the islets. In the interior the parts are less abrupt and covered with trees; there are some sandy beaches between the rocky ground, and at the foot of the hills many houses surrounded by cultivated fields.

Camp islet, the easternmost and largest of the group, is 2 miles long, east and west, and 1 mile wide. Its eastern point, in lat. 35° 48' 8" N., long. 126° 31' E., is high, and covered with stunted trees; it falls towards the west, were it terminates in broken rocks, and is low; it is not inhabited. On a shingle beach, between two points of rock forming a small bay, the crews of the French ships *Gloire* and *Victorieuse* disembarked on the 11th of August 1847. These vessels found the anchorage on its south side safe during the northern monsoon, sheltered as it is by the lofty mountains of the mainland; but in a S.W. gale, the swell must be heavy, and the anchors would perhaps drag on account of the slope of the bottom from south to north.

The resources of these islands are trifling. The inhabitants are poor; they live on the product of their fishing, and some little barley and rice that they gather in; and they are very mistrustful of strangers. Ships can obtain good and abundant water at about 2 miles from the anchorage.

TIDES.—It is high water, full and change, at Camp islet at 2h. 25m.; the tide rises 20 feet at equinoctial springs, and the range is 10 feet at neaps. The streams follow the direction of the channel, and average perhaps 3 knots an hour.

Saddle island has a peak at either end, which, seen from the offing, nearly join and give it the appearance of the hollow of a saddle. It may also be known by an islet lying $1\frac{1}{2}$ miles from its north side. In passing the north or south side of the island, the two peaks separate, leaving between them a hollow, which has the appearance of a Turkish saddle. The west peak is in lat. 35° 36' 50" N., long. 126° 6' E. About 10 miles farther east are two islets lying close to each other.

DIRECTIONS.—When bound towards the Kokoun-tau group from the westward, it will be necessary first to sight Saddle island, and when 5 miles north of that island and steering east, Peak islet will be seen ahead, and to the north the islands of the Kokoun-tau group will rise one after the other. The flood runs strongly to the northward, and must be allowed for. The soundings will vary from 10 to $3\frac{1}{4}$ fathoms. At 4 miles north of Peak islet is a point remarkable for a hole pierced in the rock a few feet above water, and which, when approached from the westward, will be easily perceived. When between Roche Percée and Peak islet steer N.E. by E., or for the east point of Camp islet, and anchor in 9 fathoms, over a bottom of soft mud, at one mile off shore the middle of Peak islet bearing S. by W. ¼ W., and the eastern end of Camp islet N.E. If working in, which can only be done with the tide, care must be taken when approaching the east bank off the mainland, for the soundings vary suddenly from 6 to 3 fathoms.

BARREN ISLANDS are a desolate looking group of three islands with several islets about them extending 5 miles in a north-east direction, in lat. 35° 21′ N., long. 125° 58′ E. On the centre and largest is a conical hill 600 feet high; on the southern are three or four hills, the highest 500 feet; and the northern island is 300 feet high, with cliffs on its north side and two islets off its south-east point.

It would not be prudent to pass between any of these islands in bad weather; the northern passage is broad, but there are two small islets at the northern, and a rock awash off the southern entrance to it. This rock which uncovers at a quarter ebb, lies 1½ miles N.E. ½ E. of the south-east point (a steep head) of the large island. At half a mile west or S.W. of this point is the best anchorage, should a vessel be driven over to this coast by north or north-west winds, in 12 fathoms, sand and shells; closer to the point the water is deeper than 14 fathoms. In December 1861 H.M. gunboat *Dove* found fair shelter from a N.W. gale with good holding ground, but much swell.* She passed round the north island at half a mile, which appeared bold-to. There is a great rise and fall of tide.

An islet 20 feet high, and a rock 10 feet high, a mile apart, lie N.W. of the group, the latter at 1½ miles distance; there is also a small rock between these, and another two cables S.E. by S. of the 10 feet rock. About 3 miles E.S.E. of these rocks are two islets, the northern 50 feet and the southern 100 feet high, with several rocks about them of jagged appearance; the *Dove* passed 2 to 3 cables west of these. There appeared to be no other islands or rocks within 8 or 10 miles of the group. To the north-eastward the soundings decreased suddenly to 5 fathoms, mud, where there was a heavy ground swell, so that the *Dove* was obliged to tack off shore.

MODESTE ISLAND lies at the north-west extreme of the southern group of the archipelago. It is 3 miles long, N.N.E. and S.S.W., and has two peaks, of which the northern and higher, which attains an elevation of 1,228 feet, is in lat. 34° 42½′ N., long. 125° 16′ E.

MACKAU ISLAND, 8 miles eastward of Modeste, is 6 miles long north and south, 1,457 feet high, and its centre is in lat. 34° 40′ 5″ N.,

---

* Several small Korean boats (? fishing boats) were riding out the gale at a mile from the shore, under the lee of the islands; probably the water is shallow there.

long. 125° 28½' E. Between Modeste and Mackau, the soundings were 51 fathoms.

VENANCOURT ROCK, lying N.E. ¾ N., 4 miles from the north island of Hydrographer's group, is round-topped and about 50 feet high.

HYDROGRAPHERS GROUP, consisting of three long looking islands of nearly uniform height, 200 to 300 feet, with two smaller ones off their north end, lie in a curved line, 5 miles in length, the eastern points of the north and south islands being in a N. ¼ W. direction. Between the southern island, which is the largest and highest, and the other four which are all connected by reefs, there appeared to be a clear passage.

The north extreme of the group, is a bluff, and N.W. ¼ W. of it, and N. by E. ¾ E. of the west extreme of the group, is a small rock (whether connected with the shore or not is unknown, but breakers were seen).* It appeared to be about 5 feet high. Both bluff and rock may be passed safely to the north-eastward at a mile.

TIDES.—The westerly stream set strongly across the northern extreme of the group. The *Dove*, steering a N.W. by N. course, had to haul up North to clear the bluff and reef.

REILLE ROCK, lying 4⅓ miles S.W. ¼ S. of the south point of the same group, is round with steep sides, and there is a small rock close to the north of it. There is also a rock, about 80 feet high, and similar in shape to the above two, at 16 or 17 miles eastward of the Venancourt.

MAURY GROUP, in lat. 34° 12' N., long. 125° 30' E., consists of three islands, the summits of which are generally seen from a long distance, the western being about half the height of the others, and the north-eastern, about 700 feet, the highest. This peak bears about E.N.E. of the summit of Ross island, from which it is distant 20 miles. The islands rise abruptly from the sea and appear bold-to, but along their north-eastern side, at the distance of 1 to 2 miles, are four large rocks, the three eastern nearly in line, bearing N. ¾ E. of the eastern island, 1¼, 1¾, and 2¼ miles respectively; the middle of the three is a sharp double pointed rock, the higher part of which is 60 feet above the sea. One mile W.N.W. of this rock and the same distance N.N.E. of the north-west island, is the fourth rock with a flattish top; no others were seen. Some islets lie close off the western side of the group.

ROSS ISLAND, also called Alceste, in about lat. 34° 6' N., long. 125° 7' E., marks the south-west limit of the archipelago. It has a peak, 1,920 feet high, at one-third from its north-western end. The island is 3 miles in extent N.W. and S.E., and its north-west and south-east points have high bluffs; the western shore is also steep. Two villages stand on

---

* The *Dove* passed this rock at dusk, Nov. 29th 1861.

its southern slopes, the eastern being the larger, but they are very difficult to discern.

The soundings were 48 fathoms, broken shells, at 5 miles north of the island; 51 fathoms, sand and mud, at the same distance west; and 40 fathoms, soft mud, a mile south.

Three large rocks, extending in a line nearly a mile East, lie at 1½ miles north of the north-western head of the island. The centre one, which is the largest, and is 150 feet in height, is visible upwards of 25 miles. A rock was seen between these and the shore, from which extended a large reef.

CRAIG HARRIET, in lat. 34° 12′ N., long. 125° 51′ E., is an island bearing E. ½ S. 12 miles from the Maury group. It is 2½ miles in extent, and somewhat flat; its central hill about 500 feet high. On either side of it, nearly east and west, are two large peaked rocks or islets, the eastern of which is three-quarters of a mile off, and very conspicuous at a distance of 23 miles from the south-west, and marking the south entrance of Murray sound. Nearly in mid-channel, between this islet and Craig Harriet, lies Salamis reef. The western rock is scarcely less conspicuous, and is nearly 2 miles from the island.

LYRA GROUP, in lat. 34° 8′ N., long. 125° 56′ E., and 4 miles south-east of Craig Harriet, consists of two islands, about 500 feet high, lying close together, the opening between them being only visible from the south-west, and looking, when first seen from that direction, like two large boulders. They have a remarkable appearance, no other island in the locality bearing any resemblance to them, being rugged, craggy, with vertical cliffs, and somewhat resembling a cock's comb.

MURRAY SOUND is about 15 miles northward of the Craig Harriet and Lyra islands, and Thistle island, in lat. 34° 22′ 39″ N., long. about 125° 57′ E.,* bounds it on the west. The *Lyra* (page 44) passed round the northern end of this island (to avoid some reefs seen off its southern point) in 17 to 10 and 11 fathoms with one cast of 9 fathoms, and anchored at 2 cables from the middle of its east side in 11 fathoms soft bottom. Montreal island, 3 miles to the south-eastward, has a high peak.

The numerous islands of Murray sound are so situated as to form a capacious and secure anchorage; many of them are large and high; almost all are cultivated, and their forms present an endless diversity.† Their general appearance is somewhat low, and very irregular in outline, the islands being generally covered with small hills, with (except Lyra) no striking characteristics. There are, however, two prominent peaks

---

* Lieut. Bullock, H.M.S. *Dove,* 1861.
† Capt. Basil Hall, R.N., of H.M.S. *Lyra,* 1816.

marking the eastern part of the sound; Lagravière peak, which makes like a hunch inclining to the westward; and 14½ miles to the south-west of it, Maxwell peak, which has a very sharp summit, and which is N.E. ¼ E. 7 miles from Lyra. The eastern island of the group (Virginie island) is in lat. 34° 13′ N., long. 126° 9′ E., making as a flat saddle when first seen at 20 miles to the south-west.

LEVEN REEF.—A dangerous sunken reef, on which the sea breaks heavily, appearing to be about half a mile in extent east and west; lies E. by S. ¾ S., distant about 11½ miles from the Lyra group, in the fairway of navigation between those islands and the Bate group.

The SOUTH-WEST COAST of KOREA,[*] and the islands lying off it are but little known, with the exception of those above described. The passages between the islands have been traversed by many vessels,[†] and all the outer groups fixed with tolerable precision. H.M.S. *Lyra* passed southward along the inner groups, rounded Windsor Castle, a remarkable peak resembling a tower or tall chimney, and stood to the south-eastward into Murray sound. H.M.S. *Nimrod* passed 2½ miles eastward of Modeste island, and from thence steered S.E., but a thick fog coming on, she endeavoured to find anchorage under a cluster of islands (Craig Harriet), but was unable to obtain less than 19 fathoms water, coarse sand and shells, close to the shore and in an exposed position. She therefore steered for another group (Nimrod islands), distant about 8 miles to the N.E., and anchored in a bay formed by the junction of two islands open to the S.W., with a channel apparently safe but narrow to the N.E.; Lyra island bearing from the anchorage S. by W. about 7 miles.

The *Nimrod* here anchored in 14 fathoms, over a bottom of sand and shells, with rocky patches, and rode out a gale from the E.S.E., which lasted nearly two days. There were several villages in the bay, and the inhabitants were civil and obliging. On the west side of the bay are two smaller bays, where tolerable shelter for small vessels may be found in 5 fathoms, muddy bottom. Good water was obtained, and fish by hauling the seine.

This anchorage cannot be recommended as secure, but may be preferred to the risk of navigating among these islands at night or in thick weather.

TIDES.—The flood tide sets to the N.E., the ebb to the S.W. High water, full and change, about 8h. 30m.

The French frigate *Virginie* vainly tried to penetrate the archipelago to the northward of Murray sound. On the 2nd of August she sailed from the Port Hamilton group, and sought a passage to the N.W. towards

---

[*] See Chart: Korean Archipelago (Preliminary), No. 104.

[†] H.M.S. *Alceste* and *Lyra* in 1816; H.M.S. *Modeste* in 1840; the French frigate *Virginie* in 1856; H.M.S. *Nimrod* in 1860; H.M.S. *Dove* in 1859 and 1861.

the continent. Strong and opposing currents retarded rather than aided her progress; the winds were also variable and light. In 34° 11′ N., and 126° 27½′ E., it was hoped that a passage was found across a gulf (Washington gulf) that seemed to belong to the mainland. The bottom was regular, the depth more than 16 fathoms, and the frigate had nearly reached the end when she was brought up in lat. 34° 32′ N., long. 126° E., by a bank stretching ahead from N.W. to the land. The boats could find no passage, and the vessel was obliged to return. In returning to the southward she passed eastward of Virginie island, and then stood to the westward between the Lyra and Nimrod islands. The *Nimrod* also passed through the latter channel.

WASHINGTON GULF is bounded on the west by Lagravière peak, 1,506 feet high, which will be recognised by the peculiar hooked nose shape it presents when viewed from the south and eastward. The peak is in lat. 34° 24′ N., long. 126° 16′ E., and 4 miles N.E. from it is Needle hill, the sharp pointed summit of which, 1,381 feet high, shows out very distinctly. At half a mile westward of the Needle summit is another mountain 1,641 feet high.

Smooth Top hill, on the southern part of the eastern shore of the gulf, is 349 feet high, and distant 12 miles E. by S. ¼ S. from Lagravière peak. Off its south side, and separated from it by a narrow channel, is an island of nearly the same height. From Smooth Top the eastern shore trends in a northerly direction for 10 miles to the head of the gulf, which is 4 miles wide. There is little wood on either shore, excepting on an island, not yet surveyed, lying under Lagravière peak.

South Double island, about 250 feet high, and bearing W.N.W. 4 miles from Bluff cliff, may be said to be the southern island in the gulf. N. by W. ¼ W. 3¼ miles from Bluff cliff, and N.E. by E. ½ E. 3 miles from South Double, is a rock 6 feet above high water, and with 11 and 15 fathoms on either side.

The Deserted islands lie in the entrance of the gulf, the highest and southern, 258 feet high, bearing S.E. ¼ S. 5 miles from Lagravière peak. There is a good boat harbour formed by it and the island off its north side.

The Family group are on the west shore of the gulf, N.E. ¾ N. 6 miles from the Deserted islands. The northern, largest, and highest island is elevated 303 feet. On the eastern side are 5 and 6 fathoms, but to the westward the water suddenly shoals.

The Green islands, five in number, extend 3 miles in a N.N.W. and S.S.E. direction in the middle of the upper part of the gulf. The southern or highest has on the eastern side a summit 186 feet high.

ANCHORAGE.—There is no shelter in the middle of Washington gulf with southerly winds between S.W. and S.E., but with those from the northward, between West and East, excellent shelter will be found in 5 to 7 fathoms good holding ground. The *Swallow*, during her fortnight's stay, anchored at one-third of a mile off the eastern shore of the Green islands in 3 fathoms, with only room to swing clear of a 2-fathom bank of large extent lying to the eastward.

Water can be obtained in boats under the hill, 675 feet high, bearing East from the north extreme of the Green islands; also on the west extreme of Thornton island, Bate group.

TIDES.—It is high water, full and change, at the Green islands, Washington gulf, at 11h.; springs rise 12 feet, neaps 8¾ feet. About the Bate group the streams attain a velocity of 5 knots at springs, and near the islands the overfalls are very dangerous for boats. The flood sets to the westward, the ebb to the eastward.* Approaching Washington gulf the streams somewhat slacken, the rate being 3 to 4 knots between Josling island and Craig Nicoll. In the gulf the flood sets in a north, the ebb in a south direction, but the rate seldom exceeds 2 knots.

LONG ISLAND GROUP consists of five small islands, the northern and highest of which, 276 feet high, lies 4 miles W. ¾ N. from Josling island, off the western entrance of Kuper harbour. A short distance off the north-east end of this island is a small islet, between which and the point terminating the Saw Tooth range is a channel of 15 fathoms water. The other four islands of the group greatly resemble each other.

The TWINS are two rocks about 15 feet high, from which the highest part of the northern island of the Long island group bears N.E. by E. ¾ E. distant 3 miles.

BLUFF CLIFF ISLAND, 225 feet high, is the centre of a small group, and bears N.W. by N. 8 miles from Race point, the south-west extreme of the Crichton group, and W. by S. ½ S. the same distance from Josling island. A little more than a mile West of it is a similar island, 280 feet high; and to the eastward the same distance is a low flat island with two detached high-water rocks off it to the south-east.

BATE GROUP,* consisting of small islands, islets, and rocks, (about 20 in number,) may be said to lie within a square, the sides of which are about nine miles in extent. The summit, 517 feet high, of Thornton island, the largest, highest, and central island of the group is in lat. 33° 57′ N., long. 126° 18′ E.

Sober island, 470 feet high, and the second largest of the group is separated from the west extreme of Thornton by a narrow channel.

The Nine Pin rock, 149 feet high, is distant 5 miles in a S. ¼ W. direc-

---

* From the remarks of Nav. Lieut. G. Stanley, R.N.

tion from the summit of Thornton. There are 44 fathoms water within a mile of its north-eastern side.

The Bott rock is 3 miles S. by E. ½ E. from the summit of Thornton. Its northern part being 404 feet high and falling perpendicular to the sea, gives this islet a most striking appearance, and makes it the indicating feature of the Bate group.

The South Black rock, 61 feet high, is 4 miles S.E. by E. from the summit of Thornton. A vessel can approach its northern side to half a mile when standing for the anchorage off the northern shore of Thornton.

Whale island is the northern boundary of the group. It is a little more than a mile long, east and west, a quarter of a mile broad, and off its east and west ends are detached high-water rocks. Its most elevated part, 487 feet high, is on the eastern end.

Ripple island, 317 feet high, is the westernmost of the group. Nearly midway between it and Whale island is a rock awash at high water.

The Swallow rock, with only 6 feet on it at low water, lies about one-third of a mile off the western part of the north shore of Thornton, and from it the summit of that island bears S.E. by S. distant one mile, and the summit of Sober island W. ¼ S. one mile.

It is recommended not to pass amongst these rocks and islands unless pressed for shelter, for large clusters of rocks and reefs lie on their eastern side, and encumber the channels.

The tides run strongly by the northern island, upon which both eastern and western streams seem to press. At half flood the stream was setting strong to the E.S.E. The northern island should be passed if close by, on an East or West course. From the eastward the islands appear all in a row, stretching north and south with the largest island in the middle.

ANCHORAGE.—A vessel seeking shelter amongst the Bate group, would in all probability anchor about half a mile off the north shore of Thornton island, at about one-third of a mile eastward of the Swallow rock, with the summit of the island bearing South. This anchorage cannot be called good, as the water is deep, 12 and 14 fathoms, over rocky bottom. Steering for it from the westward, pass between Ripple and Sober islands; from the eastward, pass south of the north-east islet (about 150 feet high) of the group, or north of North Black rock, or north of South Black rock.

FLOWER ISLAND, 203 feet high, bears N.E. 4 miles from Sea rock, and may be distinguished from it by the flat top which it assumes from all views. The least depth obtained in the passage between these islets was 35 fathoms, mud.

SEA ROCK, the southernmost islet of the Korean archipelago, is in lat. 33° 42′ N., long. 126° 19¾′ E.,* and distant about 13 miles in a north

---

* These longitudes depend on Richard's Longitude of Port Hamilton, 127° 20′ 34″ E.

direction from Roberton point, Quelpart island. It is 160 feet high, pinnacle shaped, rises abruptly from the sea, and the water is deep, 50 and 70 fathoms, close around it.

QUELPART ISLAND, about 40 miles long E.N.E. and W.S.W. and 17 miles wide, is of considerable height, and detached from the islands which face the south-west coast of Korea. Its general outline* is that of an oval, with few deep indentations to affect its regularity. Its general appearance, as viewed from the sea, is inviting, there being a pleasing variety of hill and dale, and on the northern and eastern sides much cleared land, cultivation rising probably to the level of 2,000 feet. Above this all appears to be buried in thick forests of pines and other northern trees, even to the highest peak, mount Auckland, 6,558 feet above the level of the sea. Towards the northern and eastern parts some of the cones, 500 to 800 feet high, are so smooth and circular, that, with their little batteries or watch towers on the summit, they appear almost to be the work of art. This probably results from their method of cultivating the sides, as all the furrows appear to be made horizontally, which in process of time, by the constant falling down of the ridges, would effect such a regular outline.

The space on which the city stands is a broad valley, situated about the centre of the northern coast of the island, having a conspicuous flat eminence on its eastern side, and a small river or copious stream on the western; the country immediately surrounding it on all sides being barren. The city wall, on the sea face, occupies a line of about 500 yards, containing seven bastions, apparently with embrasures throughout, but no guns were noticed.

The manners of the population, excluding the superior class, are filthy in person and habit. Their fishing vessels are few, and of the most miserable construction. It is highly probable that Quelpart occupies the position of one of the penal settlements of Korea, and viewing it in this light, accounts for the gross manners complained of, and it will readily account for the variety in the races of beings which were found assembled, and for the low state of cultivation.

The eastern extreme of Quelpart is a peninsular promontory, named cape Dundas, 2 miles north of which is Beaufort island. Between this island and the city on the north coast, the depths in-shore vary from 6 to 27 fathoms. A second city stands nearly opposite the former, on the south shore of the island, with a small bay on its west side, fronted by two small islands, named Hooper and Burnet, the latter being outside the former. West of Burnet is Richardson island, and east of it the islands of Mahon and Barrow, the latter surrounded by a reef. These four islands occupy a

---

* The description is by Captain Sir E. Belcher, H.M.S. *Samarang*, whose officers surveyed it in 1845.

space of about 8 miles in an east and west direction parallel with the coast and not more than one or two miles distant from it. Towards the west end of Quelpart, on its south shore, there is a projecting promontory named Loney bluff, on the east side of which is a deep bay, with an island in it, Marryat island, surrounded by a reef, lying about 2 miles N.E. of the bluff.

Barlow and Giffard islands lie south of the bluff above mentioned, at the respective distances of one and 4 miles from it; they are both low and flat, and the former is surrounded by a reef.

Samarang rock lies W. b. N. about 2 miles from Barlow, and S.W. about the same distance from Loney bluff.

Naboska rock, a sunken rock, on which the Russian ship *Naboska* was wrecked, about 500 feet long with deep water around, and on which the sea does not always break, is said to lie about 13 miles from the main land of Quelpart, bearing nearly South from the west end of the island, in lat. 32° 59′ N., long. 126° 13′ E.

A strong N.E. current sometimes sets past the south side of Quelpart; the *Dove*, in a gale between S.E. and East, was set 30 miles in 24 hours in May 1861.

Supplies.—The productions of Quelpart are in very small variety. Rice, wheat, barley, sweet potatoe, large Russian radish, maize, and small garden produce, comprise all that was noticed, either in the grounds, under cultivation, or among the people. This does not appear the result of any deficiency in land fit for cultivation, but rather in the poor nature of the soil.

Water appears to abound on the southern side of Quelpart, but only on Hooper island could it be procured easily. It can be easily obtained on Barlow island, but there is not safe and convenient anchorage near it. Wood was purchased from the authorities, but in very small quantities; it is, however, abundant on the mountains, and on two of the off-lying islets it can be obtained by slight labour.

ANCHORAGE.—Quelpart, throughout its extent, has but one safe anchorage, and that is at its east end off the southern bay of Beaufort island, which here forms a channel with Quelpart, about 2 miles wide, and through which the current sets strong to the southward. The second temporary roadstead is off the city on the northern shore of the island, but a vessel would be compelled to seek an offing at the first symptom of a N.W. breeze.

The third anchorage, at the western extreme of Quelpart, within Eden island, affords shelter from North (round east) to N.W., and offers an escape to leeward if requisite. A fourth temporary but dangerous anchorage is off Hooper island, near the city on the southern shore; but this is open from West to S.E., and is too confined to admit of beating out, should wind and sea come in suddenly.

SOUTH COAST OF KOREA.—Off the south coast of Korea, between Maisonneuve island and Kuper harbour on the west, and Castle islands and Herschel island on the east, are about 100 conspicuous islands, from 300 to upwards of 2,000 feet in height, more than two-thirds of which are inhabited; and including the smaller islands, the whole number, more than 200, are contained in a space of between 1,500 and 2,000 square miles. Speaking generally of this archipelago, it is bold, presenting very few hidden dangers. All these off-lying islands have been examined, but the mainland of the south coast of Korea is yet unsurveyed. In its south-east part the temperature in June averaged 75°, only a range of 3° between night and day; in July 80°. The climate is damp and humid, and although not excessively hot, very enervating. In spring and summer there are local variable breezes of small extent.

KUPER HARBOUR is formed by Josling and Hunter islands on the south, and the Saw Tooth range on the north. The observatory spot on the north-east extreme of Josling, is in lat. 34° 17′ 20″ N., long. 126° 35′ 28″ E. To a stranger the Saw Tooth range, 1,323 to 1,643 feet high, will easily point out the harbour, as the range extends upwards of 2 miles, N. by E. and S. by W. with great irregularity. Entering the harbour from the eastward between Josling and Hunter island, steer for an anchorage in 5 fathoms, with the extremes of Hunter E. by N. ¾ N. and S.S.E. ¼ E. out of the influence of the tides, which run strong about this cluster, attaining sometimes a velocity of 5 or 6 knots at springs.

CRICHTON GROUP is the next cluster to the southward of Josling, from which it is separated by a channel 1½ miles wide carrying 17 to 21 fathoms water. This group consists of four large conspicuous islands with numerous smaller ones attached.

Craig Nicoll.—The northern of the four islands is 656 feet high, and presents from the eastward a flat ridge, with the southern part very irregular and falling in a precipitous cliff about 400 feet; it is unmistakable, nothing in the vicinity having the least resemblance to it.

Pa-oon.—The eastern island is 5 miles long north and south, and almost divided into two parts by a narrow neck of land. The eastern extreme of the northern part rises to a summit 1,080 feet high, which extends to the westward in a regular ridge, elevated 919 feet. Harford peak, 1,148 feet high, the southern and highest part of the island, falls steep to the narrow neck, but extends in a regular ridge to the southward.

The central of the large islands is the lowest, its eastern and highest summit being only 520 feet high. On its south-east side are two bays, but at low water they dry out to their entrance points.

Montebello.—The south-western island is separated from the central island by a channel, in some places not more than 2 cables broad. Its southern part is thickly wooded, which makes it a striking contrast to the islands around it. When viewed from the south-eastward its high summit 1,466 feet high, which is immediately over Race point, its south-west extreme, shows out very prominently; from this an almost level ridge extends E.N.E. 2 miles, and a little farther eastward is a nipple 956 feet high.

Harbour Entrance Island, the southern of the Crichton group, is a mile long north and south, and a mile wide at its broadest or southern part. It is wooded, and its highest summit, 755 feet high, falls steep on the south side. The northern part of the island is 283 feet high and almost perpendicular.

CRICHTON HARBOUR, formed in the centre of the Crichton group, affords shelter from all winds. A vessel making for this harbour should if possible enter it from the southward between the eastern island of the group and Harbour Entrance island, both steep-to.

The northern entrance is between the north end of the eastern island and Green islet, 339 feet high, lying half a mile to the north-west; but there are two rocks awash at high water, one, the South Sister, lying close to the north end of the island, and the other, the North Sister, three-quarters of a mile to the northward. The channel, a quarter of a mile wide, is between Green islet and the South Sister. The islet may be approached on a westerly course to a cable, then bring it to bear N. by E. and steer to the southward mid-channel for an anchorage. A good berth is in 10 or 12 fathoms, good holding ground, with Craig Nicoll just open westward of Green islet, bearing North, and Harford peak S.E. by E. Here the *Swallow* rode out a heavy south-east gale without starting her anchor. It is high water, full and change, at 9h. 50m.; springs rise 12 feet.

SELBY ISLAND is 8 miles long S.E. and N.W., about 4 miles broad, and thickly wooded, with its two highest and central summits elevated 1,962 and 2,013 feet, the southern being the highest. At about half a mile south of the south-west point of the island, with the highest summit bearing North, is a rock which covers at high water. The island is separated from the west end of Mandarin island by a passage which appears free from danger; it has, however, not yet been examined.

MANDARIN ISLAND (Shun-he), lying eastward of Selby island, is 7 miles in extent, east and west, and 3 miles at its broadest part. The most striking feature is the high summit on its western end, which rises to 1,058 feet, and from seaward appears as an island, being only connected with the main part by a narrow neck of land.

SERRATED ISLAND.—At 4 miles eastward of the Crichton group, between it and Montressor island, are three islands, lying in a N. by E.

and S. by W. direction, of which the middle and largest, Serrated island, 756 feet high, receives its name from its very irregular summit.

Stanley, the northern island, is separated from the north end of Serrated by a passage half a mile wide, but it has not been sounded. At half a mile westward of the south point of Stanley is a rock which covers at high water.

Roberts, the southern island, is separated from the south end of Serrated by a passage 1½ miles wide, carrying 12 to 21 fathoms, mud. At a cable from the north point of the island is a rock which uncovers.

MONTRESSOR ISLAND, lying 6½ miles S.E. from the south-east point of Selby, is about 13 miles in circumference, and bold-to all round. One of the highest hills near its centre rises to the height of 1,187 feet, and on its south-east side is a summit 1,236 feet high. Two low islets lie off its north-west side, where in fine weather good anchorage may be obtained in 8 or 9 fathoms, with a rock 15 feet high bearing South distant one-third of a mile.

Boat and Barrett Islands are two small islands, the latter being 387 feet in height, and lie 4 miles to the northward of Montressor island, and 1½ miles southward of Mandarin island.

MAISONNEUVE, bearing S. by E. 11 miles from the Crichton group, is 314 feet high, and appears flat-topped from all views, with upright cliffs. There is deep water 28 and 30 fathoms on all sides.

MONTRAVEL, in lat. 33° 59′ N., long. 126° 55′ E., and 15 miles E. by N. from Maisonneuve, is 1,041 feet high, and covers an area of about a square mile. When seen from the westward it makes as a smooth round hill, with a long point or ridge running to the north-east. Its shores are bold, and on the north side is a bay and village containing about 300 inhabitants.

INSULT ISLAND (Kyo-ne), one mile northward of Mandarin island, has two summits, the easternmost of which, 1,108 feet high, is sharp and very conspicuous, and the westernmost, 1,275 feet high, generally appears as a long level range.

GOALEN ISLAND, 2¼ miles south-east of Insult island, is one of the most conspicuous in this archipelago. It has two distinct summits, the higher and more northern 1,537 feet high, and slightly flat; the lower, 1,146 feet high, generally appearing as two nipples. Ridges gradually fall from the tops to the water's edge on the eastern side of the island, but on the western side is a steep descent, appearing almost inaccessible. Three detached low islets lie off the south-east side. No anchorage can be recommended immediately under the island.

FISHERMAN ROCK, lying W.¼S. 1½ miles from the summit of Bowker island, is very dangerous, as it covers at high water, and has 16 fathoms close to. The Koreans have placed a perch on it, which, though small, indicates its position.

BOWKER ISLAND is separated from the north end of Douglas island by a channel 1½ cables wide, carrying 16 to 18 fathoms water.

The SOUTH and NORTH DOT GROUPS are a string of islets extending 4 miles in a N. by E. and S. by W. direction. The South Dot, averaging about 100 feet in height, extends 2 miles N. by E. from the southern islet, which is round and bears N. ¾ E. nearly 4 miles from the summit of Goalen island. On the west side the water gradually shoals from 13 to 5 fathoms. At one cable North of the north end of the northern islet is a low water rock.

The North Dot, consisting of four islets, is separated from the South Dot by a passage three-quarters of a mile wide; the highest and central islet is 140 feet high.

DOUGLAS ISLAND, 6 miles long E.S.E. and W.N.W., and more than 2 in breadth, is separated from the north-east side of Goalen island by an excellent channel about half a mile wide, and carrying 8 to 10 fathoms over mud bottom. The north-east side of Goalen island is bold, and may safely be approached, but on the south-west side of Douglas island is a muddy bay which dries out nearly a mile at low water, to the outer of the low rocky islets in it.

The sandy bays on the south-east side of Douglas island form one of its most conspicuous features, and cannot be mistaken for those of Auckland island (page 59), as its highest summit is only 794 feet high. Its south-west promontory falls steep to the westward from a height of 516 feet; its south-east point terminates in a hill 605 feet high.

SMALL GROUP is a cluster of six islands fronting the south-east side of Douglas island.

COIN ISLAND, 5 miles south-west of Small group, is 214 feet high, and about a cable off its east side is a rock which breaks at low water; and a shelving rock lies off its south-east end. There is also at a third of a mile W. by S. of the island a flat rock 10 feet above high water.

WEBSTER ISLAND, bearing South 1½ miles from Coin island, when viewed from east or west presents two distinct summits, the higher rising 435 feet above high water.

BIG and LITTLE BROTHER are two islands, 523 and 422 feet respectively in height, lying 1½ miles South of Webster island, and which bear a resemblance to each other, but are easily distinguished by the former being the larger. They are wooded, and present a darker appearance

CHAP. II.] DOT GROUPS.—KEPPEL AND HOOPER ISLANDS. 59

than the other islands in their vicinity. In passing southward of Big Brother it will be prudent to give it a berth of 2 miles, as detached rocks, 10 feet above high water, lie S. by W. one mile, and S.E. 1¼ miles, from its summit.

MOUSE ISLANDS are a small group which appear as one island, bearing S.E. 3¼ miles from the Brothers, and N.W. by W. ⅓ W. 18½ miles from Cone island. They have 18 and 20 fathoms close to, are inhabited by Koreans, and have on their east side a good boat harbour.

WEST, MIDDLE, and EAST DIRT ISLANDS, bearing respectively W. by S. ½ S. 12½ miles; W. by S. ½ S. 9½ miles; and W. by S. ¼ S. 6 miles from Haycock island; and 40, 30, and 10 feet above high water, can be passed close to, and have deep water between.

CLIFF ISLAND, about 300 feet high and bearing N.E. ½ N. distant nearly a mile from Middle Dirt, has lying off its east side a flat rock 6 feet above high water.

KEPPEL ISLAND has a level, ridgy top, and its summit, about 700 feet high, rises at 3 miles N.E. from the highest peak of Douglas island. Its north side terminates in a bold cliff. Between its south-east point and the east end of Douglas island are three islets, with 17 fathoms close to.

TRACY ISLAND, lying northward of Bowker and Keppel islands, is nearly 4 miles long, north and south, and nearly 2 broad. Its west side is marked by three distinct summits, the northern 624 feet high; the middle, and highest of the island, 765 feet; and the southern very sharp, 646 feet. Its north and east sides are precipitous cliffs, and the depths are 19 and 20 fathoms close in shore.

AUCKLAND ISLAND, the south-eastern face of which has only been examined, rises to an elevation of 1,881 feet, and being covered with trees from base to summit, presents a striking contrast to the almost bare appearance of mountains of equal height on Hope promontory. Sandy bays show out very conspicuously on its south-west side.

PRETTY ISLANDS, two in number, lie off the south-west end of Auckland island, and are so named from their appearance, being well cultivated and partially wooded. There are 19 fathoms between them.

HOOPER ISLAND (Si San) is 3 miles long in a S.E. by S. direction, of an average breadth of a mile, and its summit, 571 feet high, from every view appears almost round. It lies 1¾ miles S.E. of Island point, the south-east extreme of Auckland, and the passage between its north end and the islets off Island point is a mile wide and carries 10 or 11 fathoms, mud. On the east and west sides of the island the water shoals to 4 and 5 fathoms, mud.

TRIANGLE ISLAND, bearing W. by S. 3¼ miles from the summit of Hooper Island, is 300 feet high, and from all views presents a very sharp summit.

SHAPE ISLAND, about 250 feet high and with 11 fathoms close to, lies S.S.W. ¼ W. 4¼ miles from the south-east point of Hooper island.

MITRE ROCK bears W. ¾ N. 5 miles from the summit of Double Peak, and between it and the Peel group are several low islands, about 100 feet high, all having deep water close to.

HAYCOCK ISLAND, 4 miles to the north-west of Double Peak, is small, but rising to the height of 588 feet, presents from a southern view almost a perfect cone. It is bold all round.

SADDLE ISLAND, nearly 3 miles N. by W. ¾ W. from the centre of Double peak, is small, 223 feet high, and bold all round.

SON TSIX GROUP, of three islands, is easily distinguished by its easternmost island having a sharp double peak 1,066 feet high. The western island, 788 feet high, is nearly a mile westward of the eastern, and fronting the north entrance of the passage between is Middle island; 7 fathoms may be carried through the channel between Double Peaked and Middle, but the western channel between Middle, and the western island is narrow and has only two fathoms in it.

There is good shelter from northerly winds in 8 fathoms at half a mile southward of Middle island; and excellent shelter from southerly winds between S.E. and W.S.W., in 6 fathoms, in the bay on the north side of the western island. There is a large village in this bay, and good water can be obtained.

Black Foot rocks lie E. ¼ S., 2½ miles from Double Peak island.

BROOK ISLANDS, lying 3 miles south-east of Double Peak, are a cluster of five, the southern 516 feet high, inaccessible, and the central and largest inhabited. They are steep-to all round with passages between. There are 20 fathoms in the passage between the southern and central islands.

SURLEY ISLAND, so called from its forbidding appearance and opposition by the natives to the officers of *the Swallow* ascending the summit, lies N. by W. 12¼ miles of the Pinnacle group. The summit rises to the height of 714 feet, and about 400 feet from the top of its steep south side is a Korean village. The natives have built a landing place, but it is only available in the finest weather.

FARMER ISLAND, 635 feet high and lying N.N.E. ½ E. 7½ miles from the north point of Port Hamilton group, has off its north extreme a detached high water rock. The island is steep-to on all sides, covered with trees about 30 feet high, and easily recognized by its dark appearance.

SON TSIK GROUP.—NAN HOW GROUP.

NAN HOW GROUP.—PORT HAMILTON,* lying about N.N.E. ½ E. 38 miles from the north-east end of Quelpart, consists of two large islands, deeply indented, the northern points of which nearly meet, and which, with a third and smaller island, Observatory island, situated between their south-eastern points, form a spacious and well sheltered harbour, named port Hamilton, the main entrance to which is at the south-east part of the group. These islands may be readily distinguished from the numerous clumps of islets and rocks in the neighbourhood, by their greater size and massive bold appearance, as well as their peculiar position. Except at a great distance from the south-eastward, they invariably make as one island.

Supplies.—Within Observatory island a vessel may be safely hove down for repair. Wood is scarce—fresh water is plentiful and good, and easily embarked. Fish may be caught with the seine. Although the natives were friendly their supplies were too limited, and H.M. surveying vessel *Saracen* could not obtain fresh stock of any description in 1856. The crew roamed over the island as they pleased, but the inhabitants would not allow them to enter their houses. The largest village is in the north-west part of the harbour, and in 1859 it contained 250 inhabitants.

TIDES.—It is high water, full and change, in port Hamilton at 8h. 30m., and springs rise 11 feet; but the rise is very irregular, the water standing at a higher level by 2 or 3 feet with southerly winds than with those from the northward. The tide sets pretty strong, over the bridge, in the narrows, but in the harbour it is slack.

DIRECTIONS.—The Nan How group, so far as their examination went, is clear of danger on all sides, but is best approached from the south-east. On entering the port, the only danger that does not show is the Saracen rock, with 7 feet on it, lying at the entrance, 2 cables eastward of the east end of Observatory island. It is a small pinnacle, steep-to on the outside, but may be easily avoided by opening the Gap tree, on Aberdeen island, a little northward of Observatory island, before bringing Triangle peak in line with Nose point, bearing S.S.W. Vessels may anchor anywhere within the port; the holding ground is so good as to render it difficult to trip the anchor after a few days.

When working in, it should not be forgotten that the north shore of the entrance nearly up to Shoal point is as steep as a wall, and that the Observatory island shore is quite safe, although rather shelving. The 3 fathoms edge of soundings from Shoal point extends more than half way across towards the west point of Observatory island, and there are only 2 fathoms water for nearly one-third of this distance.

---

* See Plan of Port Hamilton, No. 1,280, scale *m* = 3 inches, with views; surveyed by Capt. E. Belcher, C.B., H.M.S. *Samarang*, 1845.

The narrows or northern entrance may be used in fine weather by vessels of light draught. It is but 2 cables wide, and farther narrowed to 250 yards, by a small half-tide rock on the western side and a reef off the eastern. A stony bridge here connects the islands, and the best water over it is nearly mid-channel, in 12 feet low water springs, rather away from the eastern side, which is the shoaler. With an off-shore wind a vessel under sail would be liable to be becalmed in the funnel shaped entrance outside the narrows.

The Samarang rock, which always shows (there are two at low water), lies N.N.E. ½ E. 7 cables from the eastern point of the northern entrance; at 7 cables farther out in the same direction the water deepens to 44 fathoms.

There is no difficulty in entering the port at night if the weather be not very thick.

CONE and MOSQUITO ISLANDS.—Cone island, lying E.N.E. 3 miles from the south entrance of port Hamilton, is three-quarters of a mile in extent, of triangular shape, and on the centre of its north-east face is a remarkable cone about 610 feet in height. The island has low steep cliffs on all sides and is very bold of approach. Midway between it and the entrance of the port is a cluster of steep islets, about 300 feet high, called the Mosquitos, which are equally safe of approach.

PEEL GROUP consists of four conspicuous islands lying in a N.E. by E. and S.W. by W. direction, each having off-lying islets. The central or largest island, named Zeyts-por, bears N.W. by W. 20½ miles from the highest of the Pinnacle group, and may be recognized by a peculiar long ridge rising to a summit 1,075 feet high, which when viewed from north and south assumes the appearance of a sharp peak. The two south-west islands are respectively 1½ and 2½ miles westward of the south end of Zeyts-por, and are well cultivated, the former rising to a summit 489 feet high and the latter with a flat top 559 feet, falling with steep sides. The northern of the four islands is 440 feet high, and the passage between it and Zeyts-por is half a mile wide and carries 16 fathoms water.

ANCHORAGE in 5 to 8 fathoms and sheltered from easterly winds, between N.E. and S.W., may be obtained at a half mile from the the west shore of Zeyts-por, with its highest summit bearing S.S.E.

HOPE PROMONTORY.—Dome island lies 7 miles W.S.W. of Harvey point, and the bays and indentations between, on the east side of Hope promontory, are studded with numerous small islands and high water rocks. No anchorages can be recommended, as the general depths are not more than 2 fathoms. A rock lies a third of a mile S. by E. from the south-east extreme of the little horse-shoe shaped island off the east side of Dome, but as it generally breaks it is easily avoided. The southern part of Dome is 646 feet high; its western face is over-hanging.

From Dome island the west side of Hope promontory trends 7 miles in a N.W. by N. direction, and the passage between it and Auckland island, 2 miles to the westward, may be boldly run for in the event of a vessel being caught in an easterly gale. To do this, after giving Dome and the islets northward of it a berth of a mile, steer to pass half a mile off Brereton point, the west extreme of Hope promontory, when Gull islet, 10 feet high, (the northern of a small cluster of islets) will easily be made out. Gull may be passed close to on its south side, as there are 7 fathoms within half a cable of it, when steer W. by N. about 1½ miles, or until Dome island summit is in line with the north-east end of Auckland island; the vessel will then be in a good sheltered anchorage in 14 fathoms.

HERSCHEL ISLAND.—At 23 miles N. by W. of the highest of the Pinnacle group, is Gage point, the south extreme of Herschel island, and immediately over it rises a wooded even range which runs 1½ miles to the northward to Herschel summit 1,381 feet high. At 1½ miles N. by W. ¾ W. of Gage point is Cooper promontory, and between is a bay about three-quarters of a mile deep, in which a vessel may anchor in 4 fathoms low water springs, close under the point with the south extreme of Bald rock touching the point; this, however, is an unsafe anchorage with the wind south of S.S.E. and west of N.N.W.

From Cooper promontory the west coast of Herschel island trends N.N.W. 4 miles to Harvey point, and is fronted at the distance of about half a mile by three islands, of which the largest and northernmost is Taylor island, 767 feet high. Between this island and the coast is Herschel cove, the entrance to which, a quarter of a mile wide, is between Taylor and the next island south of it. The cove affords nearly landlocked anchorage in 4 fathoms, low water, with the summit of Hooper island in line with the entrance, and the north-east extreme of Taylor island touching Harvey point.

BALD ROCK is 9 miles N.E. ½ N. from the centre of Double Peak. Between it and Herschel island there are 8 to 15 fathoms water.

WALKER ISLAND, lying 6¾ miles N.E. by E. ½ E. of Cone island (Nan How group) is a rugged lump of rock, 325 feet high, elongated a little in an east and west direction.

Powell rock lying 2½ miles farther in the same direction, are two pinnacle rocks close together, and about 20 feet above high water, with reefs one cable off their southern sides.

PINNACLE and CASTLE ISLANDS form each two groups of three islands lying in a N.W. by N. and S.E. by S. direction, and are unmistakable, their name from all points of view being an exact description. The Castle, lying East 14 miles from the entrance to port Hamilton, is the south-easternmost group on this part of the coast. The high land of the

Korea is well in sight from them in clear weather, but there are no islands to be seen to the eastward of a North bearing. From a distance they appear as three steep blocks, 300 feet high, in a north and south direction; there is an islet to the east of them, and one off their south point.

To the north-west of the Castle group, and separated from it by a channel a mile wide carrying 44 fathoms water, is the Pinnacle group of two islands, and an islet 60 feet high and perpendicular on all sides lying a mile to the eastward, but as their name implies they are of a different form. The southern of the two islands has a sharp conical peak, 333 feet high; its west face is perpendicular, and from its south end extends detached high water rocks half a mile to the south-east.

ANCHORAGE.—One of the best anchorages in this archipelago is in Long reach formed between Insult and Mandarin islands. Vessels steering for it should pass eastward of Perforated island, 200 feet high (lying half a mile off the east end of Mandarin island), rounding it close as there is deep water. Precaution should be taken not to shut the summit of Goalen island in with the north-east point of Mandarin, as a mud bank extends more than 2 cables off the Mandarin island shore. If thick weather and Goalen is obscured, the north-east point of Mandarin touching Perforated, and the highest summit of Insult island N.E. by N., is the best anchorage.

Supplies.—Water can be obtained at most of the inhabited islands. The natives were not allowed to barter, and had to obtain the permission of the most influential mandarin to make a present. In this manner a few bullocks, pigs, and fowls were obtained by the *Swallow*. Few fish were caught, although the seine was frequently hauled.

TIDES.—Amongst the islands off the south coast of Korea the time of high water, full and change, appears to be earlier at port Hamilton than at Kuper harbour, with an increasing regularity from east to west. At port Hamilton it is at 8h. 30m., Hooper island at 9h. 10m., Tracey island at 8h. 58m., Kuper harbour at 9h. 28m., and at Crichton harbour at 9h. 50m.; and springs rise $11\frac{1}{2}$ feet, neaps $8\frac{1}{4}$ feet. The flood stream sets to the westward, the ebb to the eastward, turning 2 hours after high and low water by the shore.

The time of high water in Crichton harbour was found to be very irregular, southerly winds causing an early flood, and a very late ebb. Between port Hamilton and Hope promontory the rate of the streams seldom exceeds 2 knots, but to the westward about the Crichton group, they sometimes run 6 knots, with dangerous overfalls among the islands.

The COAST from Herschel island trends to the north-eastward as far as Tsau-liang-hai (Chosan harbour) a distance of about 100 miles, forming three deep indentations, which have not yet been surveyed, viz., Willes gulf, Purvis inlet, and Shadwell gulf. Numerous islands skirt the shore, but only the off-lying ones have been examined.

Seen island lies about 13 miles to the eastward of Herschel island, its coast has not been surveyed and its position only approximately ascertained.

Bedwell island.—The position of this island is doubtful, it is however said to lie about 5½ miles to the eastward of Seen island; it is somewhat similar in form to Spindle islet but round topped, and was seen from that island 8 or 9 miles S.W. by W., and beyond it about the same distance what appeared to be the mainland.

SPINDLE ISLET, lying W. ¼ N., 18 miles from Sea rock, has two peculiar sharp rocks out of its summit when seen from the S.S.W. From the E.S.E. these rocks are in a line and resemble a blacksmith's punch. On its west side is a low flat shoulder; it is otherwise very steep and almost conical. It is thus minutely described, for in thick weather a vessel may be, owing to a strong N.E. current, from 20 to 30 miles out of her reckoning in 24 hours, and have some difficulty in ascertaining her position if any of the numerous islands of the archipelago are made.

SKEEN ISLAND, 400 feet high and W. by N. ¾ N. 13¾ miles from Sea rock, makes from the southward as a steep massive island not unlike the port Hamilton group, but less extensive, being only one-third the size. From the south-east it shows four summits, the south appearing nearly detached, and at a distance quite so. It appears bold-to, and may be passed on the west side at half a mile.

OBSERVATION ISLAND, 3 miles north-eastward of Skeen island, is 3½ miles in extent, and in outline resembles a star fish. It has five arms, on the east, west, and south, formed by ridges which run down from its peak (1,200 feet in height), which has a high shoulder to the north; there are deep bays between the arms. The headland at the extremity of the southern arm is 5½ miles N.W. by W. of the Broken group, and between them, scattered over the intervening space to the northward, and south of the south-eastern arm of Observation island and its two low off-lying islands, were seen five low rocks, some of which must cover. A long wooded island 2 miles in extent east and west (on the west end of which is a hill 300 feet high) lies 2 miles from the eastern arm of Observation island. The northern shores of these arms are unexplored. Observation island is densely wooded. The point of its western arm was found by observation (sea horizon) to be in lat. 34° 39′ N., long, 128° 14′ E.* The *Dove*, after bearing up for shelter in an easterly gale in May 1861, which lasted two days, anchored in the bay east of this point, finding 15 fathoms

---

* By *Dove's* track survey and true bearing of the south point of Tsu sima in 1861.

at 2 cables and 20 fathoms at 5 cables from the head of the bay—well sheltered except from westerly winds.

TIDES.—It is high water, full and change, in this bay at 9h. 15m.; the rise and fall being about 10 feet.

OPPOSITE ISLAND, 3 miles north-west of Observation island, is 1½ miles long, and very bold. Its peak is 1,500 feet high, from which it slopes very steeply to the water's edge. To the north of Observation island and E.S.E. of Opposite island, distant from each 1⅓ miles, there is another island, nearly 3 miles long east and west, with a low ridge of hills.

A small rock or islet lies 5 miles west of Observation island.

BROKEN ISLANDS are a small group of islands and rocks, a mile in extent in a north and south direction. The southern or highest island, elevated 330 feet, is 6¾ miles N.W. by W. of Sea rock; there is a hollow in its summit.

FALSE SENTINEL, a high brown rugged island, of which the northern part is 730 feet high, lies 3 miles N.N.W. of Sea rock, and 13 miles westward of Sentinel island, which it might be taken for from a distance from the south-west.

SEA ROCK, a small bold rock, flat topped, and 30 feet high, lying S.E. by S. 3 miles from False Sentinel, may be passed at three cables south in 34 fathoms water.

Two Rocks.—N.E. ½ N. of Sea rock, at 4½ and 5½ miles distance, are two high rocks; the south-western is nine-pin shaped, the other a broader islet.

SPLIT ISLAND.—N.E. by N., 9 miles from Sea rock, is an island somewhat flat, with a small peak in its centre, 500 feet high, which has a split or cleft in it.

INNER AND OUTER JUNK ISLETS.—West and S.E. 1¾ miles respectively of this peak are two groups of rocks, some of which appear like small junks.

SKETCH ISLAND.—North 8 miles from Sea rock is a small high island, nearly quoin shaped, about 700 feet high, the steep part being to the west; this island lies about 4 miles to the southward of a fine peak with a flattened summit, 960 feet in height (Flat Peak).

SENTINEL ISLAND, the outermost island of the group forming the eastern part of the Korean archipelago, is N.W. by W. ½ W. 28 miles from the entrance of Tsu sima sound and 12 miles from the nearest part of the Korea. It is isolated, bold, somewhat rugged with a spur on its north slope, and shows a double summit steeply sloping to the sea. It is only 3 cables in extent and rises to the height of about 400 feet. Its position is 34° 33′ N. 128° 40′ E.

The mountains of the Korea are plainly visible from this part of the strait, the nearest of which is a high dome-shaped mountain 1,860 feet in height, 13 miles N.N.W. of Sentinel. The coast then recedes far towards the west, bordered by an archipelago containing numerous rocks and islands, of which it is probable the above dome mountain is but one, and not the mainland.

BROUGHTON HEAD,* in lat. 34° 48′ N., long. 128° 44′ E., is a somewhat low but prominent headland, 15 miles N. ½ E. of Sentinel island. It forms the eastern extremity of the high land of the coast under the conspicuous dome-shaped mountain which rises to the height of 1,860 feet. The adjacent shores, which are of moderate elevation, receded from the head to the south-west, and to the north for a few miles, the country being hilly.

The COAST between Broughton head and Tsau-liang-hai harbour, which is 20 miles to the north-east, forms a large bay broken by two wide and extensive inlets separated by a narrow peninsula or perhaps island (it not having been closely examined); on this, in a southerly direction, runs an irregular chain of hills, the central peak of which (mount Borlase) is about 1,000 feet high, and very conspicuous, showing a remarkable spur on the south of its rocky summit. Brine point, the southern extremity of this peninsula, is low, but the northern, Brown hill, is a semi-detached headland 400 feet high, joined to the mainland by a low isthmus.

DOUGLAS and ASHBY INLETS.—Douglas inlet lies on the west of the above peninsula, its breadth at its entrance being 5 miles between Brine point and a notched peak on the coast to the westward. This inlet is as yet unexplored.

Ashby inlet on the east of the peninsula has been partially surveyed. It has an entrance of 7 miles in width east of Brine point, which, with the extension of a large valley for several miles to the northward, gives the inlet an appearance of great extent from seaward. From the summit of Brown hill it was seen to be nearly filled up with sandbanks within a line joining the hill with the opposite point of the entrance. One or more narrow channels appear to exist, the entrance to which passes close to Brown hill point. An extensive arm stretches away to the westward for a considerable distance; it is studded with islands, and is apparently shallow.

ANCHORAGE may be obtained, though it is very exposed, at the entrance to Ashby inlet in 6 to 7 fathoms, mud, with Brine point S.W. by W., and Brown hill point N.W. After shoaling to 5 fathoms, the sand

---

* The description of the coast from Broughton head to Tsau-liang-hai is by Commander C. Bullock, R.N., H.M.S. *Serpent*, 1866.

banks rise abruptly. A very conspicuous tree is seen nearly in the centre of the inlet when approaching.

Point island lies on the east point of the entrance to Ashby inlet.

TSAU-LIANG-HAI HARBOUR, discovered by Broughton and named by him Chosan in October 1797, is formed on the south-east coast of Korea in lat. 35° 6' N. The entrance is between cape Young on the north and cape Vashon on the south, which bear from each other N.N.E. ¼ E. and S.S.W. ½ W., and are 3 miles apart; from thence the harbour trends in a N.W. direction 4½ miles, and is from 1 to 2 miles wide. At 3 miles within the entrance there are some rocks always above water, one of which, the Channel rock, 6 feet high, lies nearly in mid-channel, and the passage on each side of it is much narrowed by foul ground extending from both shores; otherwise the harbour is clear of danger, and the soundings gradually decrease from 12 fathoms at entrance to 3 fathoms at its head.*

No perceptible trade is carried on in the harbour. A few boats were occasionally seen moving about, but their cargoes generally consisted of firewood and straw. The population varies according to the season of the year; in the summer, when probably only the regular inhabitants are met with, from 6,000 to 8,000 may occupy the four villages at the head of the harbour; but at the commencement of the fishing season, thousands from the interior press to the sea shore, and impromptu villages spring up by hundreds along the coast, composed of bamboos and mats, and all Korea appears, at this season, to be intent on catching, curing, and drying the ribbon fish.

The natives are very uncouth, noisy, and excessively filthy in their dress, persons, and dwellings, added to which they are most determined and dexterous thieves. The Japanese of the settlement or garrison, some 250 or 300 men, have but little intercourse with the natives, and apparently hold them in supreme contempt. They are all military men belonging to Tsu sima, and are relieved periodically from that island, where their wives and families reside.

The hills in the vicinity of Tsau-liang-hai, and in fact, excepting Deer island, all the country in this part of Tchao-sian (the native name for the eastern division of the Korea) is singularly destitute of wood. A few pines and firs are arranged in mathematical order around the cemeteries, but only in sufficient number to show, by contrast, how very bare the hills are. They are most of them conical, and covered with rank grass to the summit, giving them in summer a fresh green appearance, but in autumn and winter a brown and barren look, with the addition of large patches of rock and stones cropping out. These ranges reach from an

---

* See Plan of Tsau-liang-hai, No. 1,259, scale, $m = 2$ inches.

elevation of 800 to 2,000 feet, and are, generally speaking, nearly parallel with the coast line, having spurs running down to the shore, forming valleys, which are turned to account for the cultivation of rice and other grain crops by the natives (the female portion of them), but apparently only in sufficient quantities for their own immediate wants.

Supplies.—The *Actæon* obtained a few bullocks and chickens, and a very small quantity of vegetables, principally onions and leeks. A few pigs were seen, but no sheep or goats. In the month of June a large number of horses were grazing on Deer island, but they were not there in November.

At the latter end of November Deer island afforded remunerative pastime to the sportsman. Pheasants, quail, snipe, and water-fowl were abundant, and nine hog-deer were shot during the week. No fish was to be had in June, but in November and December immense quantities of the ribbon fish were being taken by the natives, and readily parted with for dollars. No wood, or fuel of any kind, is to be obtained from the mainland. The slopes of Deer island are covered with a quantity of scrub, composed of stunted oak, while numerous trees of a larger description crown the summit, and are found on the south-east part of the island. Water can be obtained at several places, in fact nearly every valley has its stream. The *Actæon* found every facility for watering at a stream situated at the north part of the island.

DIRECTIONS.—Approaching Tsau-liang-hai harbour from the southward, cape Vashon, the south-east point of Deer island, will be readily recognized; it is a fine bold head, 825 feet high, having a few detached rocks round it, but all within half a cable of the foot of the cliff. At a mile South of the cape is the Vashon rock, 120 feet high, and quite steep-to, and from being solitary, will, even in thick weather, be readily distinguished from the Black rocks which form a group half a mile South of cape Young, the north point of entrance. Mudge island, lying one mile North of cape Vashon, is 450 feet in height. Its north and east sides rise abruptly from the sea, and 7 to 9 fathoms will be found close to the rocks, but its south end, which is low, is connected with Deer island by a ledge, which in N.E. gales breaks heavily. Shallow water also extends a cable from the west shore of the island.

Vessels intending to make only a temporary stay will find excellent shelter in 4 to 6 fathoms, mud, on the west side of Mudge island, anchoring with the south-west extreme of the island touching cape Vashon, S.S.E., and the most southern of the Black rocks open its own width northward of the island, E. by N. ½ N.

To proceed to the best anchorage in the bay, that off the Japanese settlement;—after rounding cape Vashon and Mudge island, both of which may be passed close to, steer N.W. ¼ W., which, from 2 cables N.E. of Mudge island, will lead midway between the Channel rock, 6 feet high, and a rocky ledge extending 3 cables northward of Deer island, on which ledge some of the small rocks show.

Running up the harbour, the Japanese settlement, with its neat white houses, situated round the base of a small but well-wooded hill, will readily be recognized. Continue the N.W. ¼ W. course until the extreme rocky point of the Military station, or the southern jetty of the small camber, comes in line with the high peak (1,066 feet high) 1¼ miles W.S.W. of it, bearing W. by S. ¾ S. nearly, when the course may be altered for the jetty, and good anchorage found in 5 to 6 fathoms, black mud, at a quarter of a mile east of it. Should a nearer berth to Deer island be chosen, it will be necessary to moor, as the tides set along the shore of the island, and the anchor would probably soon be fouled.

Bound for Tsau-liang-hai from the north-eastward, Chaldron mountain, 2,040 feet high, and not quite 6 miles N. by E. of cape Young, will, in clear weather, be seen from a considerable distance, and forms a good landmark. Approaching the harbour, the cape will be readily recognized by the five Black rocks, the highest of which, 90 feet high, is half a mile south of it; the outer four forming a group lying north and south, with an isolated one inshore, 1½ cables from the cape. There is a very narrow channel of 10 fathoms water between the outer group and the inner rock.

If intending to use the anchorage at Mudge island, having rounded the Black rocks, which have no hidden danger near them, steer W. by S., and giving the island a berth of 2 cables, anchor on the bearings before given.

If proceeding up the harbour, from 2 cables south of the Black rocks, a W.N.W. course leads up, passing 2 cables south of Magnetic head,* a bold headland, 565 feet high, and not less than that distance from any known danger. On passing Channel rock, use the precautions already recommended for clearing Deer island ledge, and anchor as before directed.

Working in for the anchorage at the head of the bay, long boards may be made until the first rock, 8 feet high, west of Magnetic head is passed, when the channel becomes narrowed by the ledge off Deer island. The Channel rock may be passed on either side, but not so any of the other rocks which show in the harbour.

The bay immediately west of Magnetic head is not to be recommended even as a temporary anchorage, as even a light S.E. wind sends in a most unpleasant sea; it is shallow, so that small vessels cannot get sufficiently close in to find shelter from the head, and they would find a difficulty in working out.

---

* Named so by Broughton from its affecting his compasses. His vessel anchored in the bay on its west side.

CHAP. II.]   TSAU-LIANG-HAI HARBOUR.—THE COVE.   71

Inner Entrance.—Steam or sailing vessels with a *leading* and commanding wind, coming from the southward and drawing under 14 feet, will find a good but narrow channel between the west side of Deer island and the mainland. From a mile east of Blakeney island, which, however, may be passed on either side, steer N. by E. ½ E., and having run about 5 miles, the south-east point of Deer island will bear E. by S. ½ S., and the wooded hill of the Japanese station, seen over the low point of Deer island, N. ¼ E. From thence steer North, gradually closing the north-west point of Deer island, which is nearly a flat terminating in a shingly spit; round the point at less than a cable's distance from it, being careful to use a quick helm, especially with the flood stream, which sets through with considerable strength, and catching a vessel on the bow, might force her over on the flat, extending out from the Japanese settlement a full cable's length from the shore; should a long vessel be caught by the stream, and unable quickly to recover herself, an anchor should be immediately let go. To avoid this flat, when the shingly point bears South, steer East until the opening into the camber bears North, and then for the anchorage.

The Cove.—The coast for some considerable distance south-west of Tsau-liang-hai is much broken up by small bays and other sinuosities, but few of them appear to be of any value to the mariner. At 5¼ miles west of cape Vashon and 4 miles north of Blakeney island, is a bay on the west side of which is a small bight named the Cove. The bay is well marked by an island rather larger than Blakeney, 295 feet high, having three other rocks in its neighbourhood, on the west side of the entrance. One of these rocks, 95 feet high, has a rocky spur running out to the northward one cable. Running up the bay, the entrance to the Cove will open out, and anchorage close to the rocky point on its north side may be obtained in 3 or 4 fathoms, well sheltered and landlocked.

In making for the Cove from the southward, take care not to run into Open bay, immediately eastward of it, as it forms a cul-de-sac into which a heavy sea rolls with southerly winds, and a vessel might experience a difficulty, if once embayed, in working out.

Blakeney Island, bearing from cape Vashon S.W. ½ W., distant 7 miles, is a small rocky islet, 156 feet high, 3½ cables long, N.E. and S.W., and a cable broad at its widest part; at two cables eastward of it is a detached cluster of rocks, the highest being 25 feet above water.

Craigie and Aunt Islets lie south of Blakeney island directly in line between Sentinel island and Tsau-liang-hai harbour at from 6 to 11 miles from the coast.

Craigie islet.—The southern, is N.N.E. ¾ E., 23 miles from Sentinel island, and 6 miles S.S.W. of Blakeney island; it has steep sides with a wooded summit 70 feet in height. A small reef extends off from its western side.

Aunt islets, midway between Craigie islet and Blakeney island, are two islets very similar in appearance, forming in three hummocks from 40 to 60 feet in height, and lie east and west, their bases being joined. A reef extends one cable from their western side.

Neither of these groups should be passed too closely; no dangers were observed near them from elevated positions on the neighbouring coast.

TSU SIMA (Japanese, originally Korean), is situated at the entrance to the sea of Japan, in the Korea strait, which it separates into two channels. The island is 37 miles in length N.N.E. and S.S.W., and except close in shore, is free of hidden danger. Some reefs and rocks off Mame saki its south-west end, and Tayo saki its north end show; a berth, however, of 1½ miles will clear everything.*

At high water Tsu sima becomes a double island, a deep Sound dividing it into two parts. The southern portion is mountainous (2,126 feet high), and on the north of its range is a double sharp peak (1,700 feet high), named Uyama, forming like asses ears when bearing S.E. The northern portion is much lower, and somewhat level in appearance, except at one third from its north-east extreme, where it rises into a flat topped mountain, which has a double peak on the east. For vessels of large draught there is but one navigable channel into this Sound, the western one, that on the east side being only available for boats and small craft at high water.

The centre of the western entrance is 5 miles northward of Uyama peak, which cannot, if seen, be mistaken, and will, from a considerable distance, guide to the entrance; but when close to the channel it becomes shut in by the high land of Osaki.

TATE MURA (Tsu sima sound).—The entrance is 1½ miles wide, and, although the bottom is very uneven, the only danger, except from the detached rocks which closely fringe the shore, is a sunken rock lying off the southern shore at two-thirds of a cable from the north side of Strata islet, which is a low mass of slate stone, somewhat wedge-shaped, dipping to the southward. To clear this danger, do not bring the two low rocks, lying off South head, the south point of entrance, to the northward of W.½N. until Flat islet, 56 feet high, bears S.E.; or, should Flat islet not be readily recognized until the conspicuous islet, Usi sima, lying off the north point of entrance bears N.N.W., when a course may be shaped for any part of the Sound.

Tsu sima sound possesses a large number of small harbours and basins quite landlocked and sheltered from all winds; they are arms branching

---

* See Plan of Tsu sima Sound, No. 2,710; scale, $m = 3$ inches.

off from the main body of the Sound, and all of them have deep water. The sides of these little havens are so steep, that vessels may moor to the rocks and trees, and lie as quiet as if they were in a dock; the only thing to move them being the rise and fall of tide.

Creasy creek, Water basin, Mussel cove, and Oyster sound, are all on the south side of the western portion of the sound and may be safely entered. Of these, Oyster sound and Mussel cove are the largest and most eastern; there is some foul rocky ground between Steep island, or Mioban sima, which marks the entrance to them, and the island to the south-west of it. Vessels intending to occupy an anchorage in either of these two harbours, must therefore pass eastward of Steep island, from the east point of which the mid-entrance to Oyster sound bears S.E. $\frac{1}{2}$ E., distant two-thirds of a mile, and that of Mussel cove S. by W. $\frac{3}{4}$ W. half a mile. Creasy creek and Water basin are close together, in the S.S.W. corner of the Sound, and are, for steamers, easy of access; the latter possesses a stream of excellent water, in which is a number of small trout.

If desirous of proceeding beyond the anchorages afforded by the west portion of the Sound, from the centre of the western entrance, steer E. by S. $\frac{1}{2}$ S.; this course leads northward of Ino saki, to the eastward of which is a peninsula with a square block end looking like an island. The channels on each side of this peninsula are deep, the southern one particularly so, and lead into an almost endless variety of friths and deep-water inlets, sufficient to afford accommodation to a large fleet, where they would be quite sheltered and free from the observation of passers by.

The *Actæon* anchored in 9 fathoms in Ima-haru bay, about 2 cables south of Observatory rock, which may be known by its being the southernmost of two small rocks, connected with the mainland at low water; the northern one has a small shrine on it. This is a convenient anchorage for sailing ships, or if only intending a short stay; under other circumstances one of the others should be sought. Vessels damaged so as to require to be hove down, would find Tsu sima sound well adapted to careening purposes.

Supplies.—There are three small villages on the shores of Ima-haru bay. Wood, water, and vegetables were abundant, but, owing to the interference of the officials, very scantily supplied. Some hundred head of horned cattle were seen, and two were procured, also a small quantity of poultry. Sheep are not known. A few pigs were seen, and the corn-fields swarmed with pheasants.

The seine afforded but little fish, although the native boats each morning brought in large quantities. The rocks, however, in some places were covered with oysters and mussels, some of them of a most extraordinary size.

TIDES.—It is high water, full and change, in Tsu sima sound at 8h. 30m., and the rise is 8 feet. Both flood and ebb are rather strong at entrance.

KOREA STRAIT* divides the south-east coast of Korea from the south-west coasts of the Japan islands; it is split into two channels by Tsu sima.

The Western channel is 34 miles wide, between Sentinel island and the south point of Tsu sima, narrowing to 25 miles between the north point of that island and Tsau-liang-hai; its greatest depth is 90 fathoms near the west coast of Tsu sima. H.M.S. *Dove* in crossing the Korea strait from the Goto islands in 1861, after decreasing the soundings from 83 to 53 fathoms in 15 miles on the parallel of 33° N., obtained a sounding of 23 fathoms in long. 127° 38′ E. On sounding again one mile N.N.E. of this position, there were 56 fathoms, deepening again to 81 fathoms at 11 miles in the same direction.

The Eastern channel is 25 miles wide at its narrowest part, between the south point of Tsu sima and Iki island; its greatest depth is 65 fathoms.

---

* *See* Chart : Japan-Korea strait, No. 358.

CHAPTER III.

SEA OF JAPAN;—EAST COAST OF KOREA, AND RUSSIAN TARTARY—GULF OF TARTARY AND RIVER AMÚR—TARTARY STRAIT—SEA OF OKHOTSK, AND KAMCHATKA.

VARIATION in 1872.

East Coast of Korea 5° W. | Coast of Tartary 6° W.
Sea of Okhotsk from 2° W. to 1° E.

The SEA of JAPAN, bounded on the east and south by the Japan islands, and on the west and north-west by the coasts of Korea and Russian Tartary is about 900 miles long, N.N.E. and S.S.W., and 600 miles East and West, at its broadest part. Surrounded by land on all sides, this sea is only accessible by the following narrow passages:—To the south by the Korea strait, which connects it with the China sea; to the east by La Pérouse and Tsugar straits, by which it communicates with the Pacific; and to the north by the gulf of Tartary, through which it communicates with the sea of Okhotsk by the gulf of Amúr; this sea is, as far as is known, clear of rocks or dangers with the following exceptions * :—

LIANCOURT ROCKS are named after the French ship *Liancourt*, which discovered them in 1849; they were also called Menalai and Olivutsa rocks by the Russian frigate *Pallas* in 1854, and Hornet islands by H.M.S. *Hornet* in 1855. Captain Forsyth, of the latter vessel, gives their position as lat. 37° 14′ N. long. 131° 55′ E., and describes them as being two barren rocky islets, covered with guano, which makes them appear white; they are about a mile in extent N.W. by W. and S.E. by E., a quarter of a mile apart, and apparently joined together by a reef. The western islet, elevated about 410 feet above the sea, has a sugar-loaf form; the easternmost is much lower and flat-topped. The water appeared deep close-to, but they are dangerous from their position, being directly in the track of vessels steering up the sea of Japan for Hakodate.

MATU SIMA (Dagelet island) is a collection of sharp conical hills, well clothed with wood, supporting an imposing peak in the centre, in lat. 37° 30′ N., long. 130° 53′ E. It is 18 miles in circumference, and in

---

* *See* Chart of Japan, Japan islands, and part of Korea, No. 2,347.

shape approximates a semicircle, the northern side, its diameter, running nearly E. by N. and W. by S. 6¼ miles. From each end the coast trends rather abruptly to the southward, curving gradually to the east and west, with several slight sinuosities until meeting at Seal point, the south extreme of the island, off which is a small rock.

There are several detached rocks along its shores, principally, however, on the north and east sides, some reaching an elevation of 400 to 500 feet. They are all, like the island, steep-to, and the lead affords no warning, but none of them are more than a quarter of a mile from the cliffs, except the Boussole rock, the largest, which is 7 cables from the east shore of the island. Hole rock on the north shore is remarkable, from having a large hole, or rather a natural archway through it, while nearly abreast it on the shore is a smooth but very steep sugar-loaf hill, apparently of bare granite, about 800 feet high.

The sides of the island are so steep, that soundings could only be obtained by the *Actæon's* boats, almost at the base of the cliffs, while in the ship at 4 miles to the southward no bottom could be found at 400 fathoms, and 2¼ miles north none at 366 fathoms. Landing may be effected in fine weather, with difficulty, on some small shingly beaches which occur at intervals, but the greater part of the island is inaccessible.

During the spring and summer months some Koreans reside on the island, and build junks, which they take across to the mainland; they also collect and dry large quantities of shell-fish. Except a few iron clamps, their boats are all wood-fastened, and they do not appear to appreciate the value of seasoned timber, as they invariably use quite green wood.

WAYWODA ROCK is said[*] to have been discovered by the Russian corvette, Waywoda. It appeared to be 12 feet high, 70 feet broad, and its approximate position is lat. 42° 14½' N., long. 137° 17' E.

The EAST COAST of KOREA, unlike the western coast, is steep-to at a short distance from the shore. A running survey was made by the Russian frigate *Pallas* in 1854 of its whole extent for about 600 miles, from cape Young to lat. 42° 31' N., long. 131° 10' E. Port Lazaref, Napoléon road or Posiette harbour, and the Tumen river were surveyed by her boats.[†]

The frigate had steady fair winds, and kept from one to 4 miles off shore, approaching even nearer at some parts, and following its windings. The coast has a uniform appearance; sometimes, however, its character

---

[*] Renseignements Hydrographiques sur la Mer du Japon, &c., 2nd edition, page 124, 1860.

[†] The description of the east coast of Korea is chiefly from the voyage of the Russian frigate *Pallas* in 1854 and of the French frigate *Virginie* in 1855.

changes suddenly; from being mountainous and rocky it becomes low and sandy, assuming its former appearance after a short interval.

The COAST from Tsau-liang-hai trends in a N.N.E. direction 63 miles to cape Clonard and over the whole of this extent it preserves a uniformly mountainous and desert character. The space between the high mountain range, running in a parallel direction with the shore, is occupied by rows of sand hills which are detached from the range, and projecting towards the sea in abrupt points, form an unbroken series of little bays which give no shelter. Close to the southward of Tikmenef point there is an island of considerable size which appears to hide the mouth of a river or large bay.

CAPE CLONARD, in lat. 36° 5¾′ N., is the extremity of a rather low peninsula, which advances boldly towards the north-east, and is visible 18 or 20 miles off, and forms the easternmost point of this part of the Korea.

UNKOFSKY BAY.—Cape Clonard forms the south side of the bay of Unkofsky, the extent of which has not been determined; but which is 4 miles wide at its mouth, comprised between the peninsula and Crown point to the north-west. The trend of the bay is to the south-west; it has 17 to 12 fathoms at entrance, and 7 fathoms with good anchoring ground at 2 miles from its shores, but it is open to the prevalent autumnal winds, and those from the north-east in winter. It appears clear of danger throughout, but the north part of cape Clonard must be avoided, as foul ground extends a little distance from it.

The northern and southern shores of the bay have a marked difference in character. Those on the south are elevated, the hills of the main range here approaching the sea; they then retire at the centre of the bay, resuming their original direction parallel with the coast. The northern and western shores are of moderate height; the former consisting chiefly of abrupt or steep sandy cliffs of snowy whiteness, with hills of the same description. Several large settlements spread along the shores, the inhabitants being probably employed in fishing.

PING-HAI HARBOUR, in lat. 36° 36′ N., long. 129° 20′ E., is a small creek in the sandy coast surrounded by high hills. At its entrance is a conical-shaped island, which shelters the whole roadstead. On the side of the island is a large group of houses standing near the sea. The *Pallas* had 23 and 32 fathoms water within 1½ miles of the land; and the *Virginie*, which coasted it for 3 miles, had 27 fathoms. Moreover, the steep and rocky shores seem to show that they are steep-to; there was no apparent danger between the frigate and the shore, and the current averaged 10 miles to the north in twenty-four hours.

Three mountains rise to the south-west of Ping-hai, and three rounded summits of one sloping mountain at a little distance to the north. The mountains resemble each other; they are however so situate, N.E. and S.W., that their summits seem to rise one above the other.

The COAST from Unkofsky bay trends in a northerly direction to a large round headland slightly advanced, named by the *Virginie* cape Pélissier. Its less mountainous character does not, however, dispel the appearance of sterility, rows of round sand-hills occuring for a considerable distance inland. To the W. by N. of the cape is mount Popof, a high mountain of regular pyramidal form, and the loftiest of those that occur near the shore.

From cape Pélissier the coast changes its direction, and runs nearly in a straight line N.N.W. for 120 miles to cape Duroch. Between these two capes there is not a bay worth mentioning; the coast appears steep, and there are a few houses near the water's edge.

Beyond the parallel of 38° N., the land becomes gradually depressed. Groves of cedar trees cover the sides of the sloping mountains. The Sedlovaya, or Saddle-shaped mountain, is the most remarkable elevation along the coast. Its two blunt summits, 5,525 feet high with an arched slope between them, rise about 5 miles inland in lat. 38° $10\frac{1}{2}'$ N., the western summit being the highest. Several considerable mountains, having more or less pointed summits, surround this mountain on all sides, particularly on the north.

Several small islands occur near the coast north of mount Sedlovaya. They are mostly desolate and rocky, intermingled with high reefs. The bay, in lat. 38° 42' N., is a small indentation of the coast, about a mile wide, and less than a mile deep. Two islets lie half a mile west of its entrance, and they are connected with its high and rocky north extreme by a bed of rocks, some of which are uncovered. The islets at the south extreme of the bay are nothing but bare rocks, and serve as a refuge for innumerable seals and penguins.

CAPE DUROCH, or Peschurof, forming the south point of Broughton bay, is a massive cliff presenting to the north-east a front 8 miles long and bordered by rocks level with the water and close to the land. The depth was 104 fathoms at 5 miles to the east, and 23 fathoms at less than a mile north of the cape.

BROUGHTON BAY—(Korea gulf) is 93 miles wide between cape Duroch on the south and cape Petit Thouars on the north, and 55 miles deep, and Yung-hing bay and Port Lazaref at its head offer excellent shelter. The shores of the bay are winding and mostly low, and vessels can anchor in a moderate depth off them with safety.

The north and south shores of Broughton bay are commanded by lofty heights near the sea. The Belavenz mountains, about 15 miles southwest of cape Duroch, are respectively 6,092 and 5,884 feet above the sea; and to the north at 24 miles in the interior, W.N.W. of cape Petit Thouars, mount Hienfung reaches the height of 8,114 feet. The shores, although wooded and verdant, are varied occasionally by waste lands and rocky cliffs.

After passing cape Duroch, a moderate sized bay will open out with a low sandy shore, and it probably affords good anchoring ground during southerly winds, as in general all the bays examined on this coast invariably do. A group of small islands and sunken rocks lie in the middle and north-west parts of this bay, on several of which a few cedar trees are growing. From the north extreme of the bay the coast again becomes winding and rocky, and gradually falls towards Felény point.

Felény point, with the islands adjoining it, is the southern boundary of a shelving bay of moderate depth, 18 fathoms, at a distance of 3 or 4 miles from the coast, and 5 fathoms within a few cables of it. Mian-tsin-liang point, the north extreme of this bay, is high and abrupt, and at a distance appears as an island, being separated from the shores of the bay by low land. A rocky islet, named Observation island, lies in the centre of the bay, at $1\frac{1}{2}$ miles from the shore.

Mouchez island (or Khalezov of the Russian chart), lies 8 miles northeast of Observation island, and $7\frac{1}{4}$ miles off shore, the channel between being clear and safe. It is 476 feet high, and visible from a distance 24 miles. Coming from the southward, it is an excellent land-mark when bound for Yung-hing bay. A shoal extends about half a cable from its south-west point.

The COAST from Mian-tsin-liang point trends in a north-west direction 16 miles to Codrika point. On the north side of the low isthmus which connects Mian-tsin-liang point with the mainland, is a small circular-shaped bay, into which a clear rivulet flows, and on the shore of which is the large village of Lon. The shores of the bay contain much basalt; the rocks off its northern point consisting almost exclusively of basalt columns. From Lon bay, northward, the coast is indented by small inlets with high points.

CODRIKA POINT, on which is a large village, is 326 feet high, and steep-to. At three-quarters of a mile N.W. $\frac{1}{2}$ W. of the point is Basalt or Michaud islet, near which the depth is 6 to 8 fathoms. This islet has two remarkable grottos, the sides of which consist of perpendicular basalt columns about 40 feet high, in each of which boats can freely enter.

On the west side of Codrika point is a small bay sheltered from almost all except N.E. winds. The average soundings are 8 fathoms in the entrance, between the point and Basalt islet, and 11 fathoms in the bay. Two small rivulets flow to the west of a high point in the centre of the bay, and some isolated huts appear on their banks, forming together the village of Anbian.

YUNG-KING BAY,[*] comprised between Ilary or Périer point to the south, and Desfossés point to the north, has an area of about 10 square miles. The depths are moderate, 11 fathoms in the middle, and 7 or 8 fathoms at 2 or 3 cables from the shores of the bay, over good holding ground; but the best shelter will be found to the northward in port Lazaref, which is formed on the western side of Nakhimof peninsula, and has an area of 4 square miles. The entrance to the bay is fronted by the following group of islands and rocks, which protect the anchorages on their western sides from easterly winds.

Nikolski, the largest and southern outer island of this group, is of oblong form and 3 miles in circumference. It is high, and covered with hills or mounds overgrown with cedars, and has a village on its western side; a small islet lies near its north point, and another at half a mile from its south extreme.

The French corvette *Capricieuse* anchored in 7 fathoms about one mile south-west of this island; but this outer anchorage is of little value, being 8 miles from the chief villages on the coast. The safest channel into the bay is between the south-west point of Nikolski and Ilary point; it is about 3 miles wide, and carries a depth of 8 to 10 fathoms.

Kuprianof Island, lying 1¼ miles north of Nikolski, is somewhat smaller than the latter, also rounder and more desolate, forming, as it were, one sloping mountain. The channel between these two islands is apparently deep and safe, and convenient for vessels entering the bay.

Annenkof Island, at 3 miles west of Nikolski, is one mile long, east and west, and three-quarters of a mile wide. It consists of a series of hills crowned with cedars. The north side is steep and straight; the remaining shores though precipitous form little bays, at the head of one of which is a village.

Two small but high islands lie off the south-west face of Annenkof, and form with it a snug anchorage, carrying a depth of 10 fathoms. The channel between these islands and Muravief point to the south-west is three-quarters of a mile wide, and has 6 and 7 fathoms water in it; this point is the north extreme of a peninsula, which being connected with the main by low land, makes at a distance like an island.

Vishnevski Island, lying 2 miles north of Annenkof, is high and narrow, and about half a mile in extent N.E. and S.W. With the exception of its southern side, it is surrounded by a reef of sunken and dry rocks. Within the reef is another small islet or rock.

---

[*] This bay and Port Lazaref were partially surveyed by the Russian frigate *Pallas* in 1854, and the description is chiefly from the report of her voyage.

The channel between this island and Annenkof carries a depth of 16 fathoms in the middle, decreasing gradually on both sides to 10 fathoms, at a distance of one or two cables from the shore.

In addition to the foregoing chief islands of the group, there are several islets, which, with the exception of one, lie eastward of Vishnevski, between it and Kuprianof island. Of these, Cone islet is remarkable from its conical form; all the others are more or less alike. There are several rocks above water surrounded by reefs, between these islets, as also north of them off the south face of Nakhimof peninsula, of which Desfossés point is the south-east extreme: some of these rocks from their whiteness are visible from a considerable distance.

These dangers would offer some difficulties if attempting the channel between the islets and Desfossés point. The channel is half a mile wide between this point and the most northerly white rock, but a sailing vessel might have baffling or light winds when passing the south end of the peninsula.

PORT LAZAREF (Virginie bay of the French charts), the entrance to which is in the northern part of Yung-hing bay, is formed on the west side of Nakhimof peninsula, which shelters it from the eastward. It is 2 miles wide at entrance, from thence it trends about 6 miles in a northerly direction, and its breadth varies from $1\frac{3}{4}$ to $3\frac{1}{2}$ miles, and carries a depth of 7 to 10 fathoms, over a mud bottom. The peninsula is covered with high hills, from the centre of which rises a sloping mountain with two sharp summits W. by N. and E. by S. of each other. It is connected with the mainland by a narrow sand spit, on which are several elevations having the appearance of islands, the western side being indented with small bays, on the shores of which are villages. A sand spit extends a quarter of a mile from Aliman point, its south-west extreme.

In the northern part of the port are two islands, and in its north-west angle the mouth of the Dun-gan river. Butenef, the westernmost and the largest of these islands, is $3\frac{1}{2}$ miles in circumference, and all its shores are steep except the eastern, from which a long spit extends in that direction. The best anchorages are at $1\frac{1}{2}$ miles, and at 3 miles within the entrance. The first or outer anchorage is in 10 fathoms, mud, in the middle of the port, the water shoaling gradually to both shores. The other or inner anchorage is in 8 fathoms, mud, in the channel a mile wide between the south end of Butenef and the shore to the southward; the latter is a convenient position for merchant vessels receiving cargo.

From the inner anchorage towards the mouth of the river, the soundings gradually decrease to 7 fathoms; they then suddenly shoal to 5 and 3 fathoms to the banks which front the entrance. These banks approach very near the north-west end of Butenef island, and of Trifanof point to the south-west, leaving narrow channels between. The channel between the banks and the island is silted up at its northern part; that between the banks and the point leads into a wide though shallow bay.

This shallow bay extends westward 2 miles from Trifanof point. Its breadth at the entrance is about half a mile, becoming wider farther in. The shores are winding and varied in character, and there is an island at the north-west angle, and two islets in the middle of the bay. The whole of its northern part is occupied by a continuous reef, carrying only a few feet water which surrounds the two islets and extends to both the north and south shores of the bay. The bay is thus divided into two parts; one west, and the other east, of the meridian of the islets. The first or inner part is inaccessible from all sides; the other or outer part is connected with the north-west part of port Lazaref by the channel between the banks fronting the mouth of the river and Trifanof point, and may serve as an excellent shelter for small vessels during winter.

The Dun-gan* (Eastern river) falls into the north-west part of port Lazaref, and with its collateral branches, occupies the whole plain extending between two ranges of low hills. Winding along the plain, it approaches first one and then the other range which borders it. At its mouth, the river divides into several shallow channels, formed by a group of low marshy islands covered with villages. The breadth of the principal channel is about 3 cables, and the entrance to it is difficult, from its shallowness, and from its winding between the steep part of the banks before approaching the islands. The current of the river is weak, and the water for a considerable distance from its mouth is of a bad colour and taste.

Admiral Guérin, who visited this port in the *Virginie* in 1855, states that the surrounding land is well cultivated and populous, particularly at the river's mouth. On the marshy island at the termination of the left bank there is a large village, apparently the commercial emporium of a considerable town in the interior, and which the natives said was the chief city of the province; the information gathered from them only making the distance from Yung-hing to Séoul† (the capital of Korea) 30 miles, and establishing the possibility of going there by water; the river probably extends as far as Séoul.

The bar of the river had 10 feet over it at low water, a depth which seems to be the limit of the lowness of the river at this season (the height of summer). From thence the course of the river was to the north, the soundings gradually deepening to 5 fathoms to the distance of 6 miles

---

* River Aube of the French charts.

† Séoul is 115 miles from Port Lazaref: this information is therefore to be doubted.

from its mouth, when it divided into several branches and appeared to run to the westward through a large plain terminating in a chain of high parallel mountains, covered with houses, hamlets, and villages.

Supplies.—Fresh provisions, oxen, pigs, poultry, and vegetables, are plentiful both in Yung-hing bay and port Lazaref. Instead of procuring water from the Dun-gan river, it will be preferable to obtain it from the river Giffard, a clear and rapid stream in the south-west corner of the bay.

Tides.—The tidal streams are weak in Yung-hing bay; their influence being only felt in port Lazaref. High water, full and change, at 5h. 20m., and the rise is $2\frac{1}{2}$ feet.

Directions.—The approach to Yung-hing bay and port Lazaref is not accompanied with difficulty. Besides the mountain with the sharp summits on Nakhimof peninsula, the proximity of the bay may be recognised by the islands fronting it. As before stated, the channel into the bay between the south end of the peninsula and the rocks and islets fronting it, is narrow and intricate, and a sailing vessel might have light or baffling winds when passing Desfossés point.

The middle channel between the two outer large islands is apparently safe and convenient for vessels entering the bay. If entering by the southern channel between Nikolski island and Ilary point, and between Nikolski and Annenkof islands, do not stand towards the shore to less than 7 fathoms water. The channel between the two small islands lying off the south-west face of Annenkof and Muravief point, the southern inner point of the bay, although narrow, is clear and deep. The only danger to avoid in entering port Lazaref is the reef extending from Aliman point, the east point of entrance.

The Coast, after passing Nakhimof peninsula, trends to the North and N.E., 54 miles to cape Rouge (cape Goncharof of the Russian charts). As far as Trompeuse or Losef point, which is the eastern extreme of a high headland in lat. 39° 35' N., the shore is low and sandy, with several sloping hills rising at a little distance inland. Between this headland and Muséef point, 13 miles to the N. by E., the coast forms an extensive bay, the shores of which are low and sandy, and the soundings regular, 8 and 9 fathoms, over a bottom of fine sand. A round hill rises on the parallel of the centre of the bay, and may serve as a good landmark for vessels entering, as it stands detached on a plain at a distance from the adjacent hills and mountains.

Hodo island.—In the northern part of this bay is an island about 2 miles in circumference named Hodo (Flowery), with two islets off its eastern extreme, separated from it by a narrow rocky channel. The northern part of the island, as well as a portion of the western part, are sandy; the remainder is rocky and high. The channel between its northwest end and the main is about a mile wide, but it is partly blocked up by a shoal which extends nearly half way across it from the island towards the main. The other part of the channel is probably shallow; large fishing boats were, however, seen to pass through it.

At 3 miles S.E. of Hodo are two small isolated rocks. Leaving the bay with an easterly wind, the *Pallas* had 9 fathoms between these rocks and the coast, but in attempting to pass between them and the island, the depth decreased to 6 fathoms, which compelled her to go south of them. A river disembogues in the northern part of the bay.

The COAST from Muséef point trends to the north-east towards cape Petit Thouars, and is moderately high, and indented by bays with cliffy shores and points. Along its whole extent it is bordered by scattered rocks and some islands, the largest of which are, an island 3 miles in circumference, lying off the south side of Anjou point, and an island lying off cape Rouge. This latter has rocky shores, and is divided into two parts by a narrow creek, and forms with the coast a channel about half a mile wide, with an islet at its eastern end. This channel, providing there are no dangers in it, presents a good and apparently a safe harbour.

On the parallel of Muséef and Anjou points two high peaks show themselves inland. Anjou point is perpendicular and high. Cape Rouge, from its peculiar aspect, and having a high peak about 5 miles to the north-west of it, may be easily recognised. There are several villages hereabouts at the bottom of the creeks and bays, and traces of cultivation on the heights. Weirich point, on which a village is situated, lies to the north-east of this cape, and is a long narrow spit with three hills rising on it.

CAPE PETIT THOUARS, or Schwartz, seen from the south, makes in the form of a mamelon or small eminence, commanded by a conical but flat-topped hill a little west of it. The face of the cape is a large reddish cliff, 5 miles long, off which is a small pointed islet. To the W.N.W. of the cape, at 20 miles inland, the range of the Hienfung mountains, 8,114 feet high, is a conspicuous object. Between this cape and cape Rouge the soundings were 27 to 37 fathoms at 2 miles outside the points.

CAPE BRUAT, or Boltin, 60 miles farther to the north-east, is the eastern extreme of a chain of mountains, which presents two pointed summits 50 miles apart, the northern or mount Tao Kwang attains an elevation of 6,310 feet; the range slopes by a gradual declivity towards the east, where it terminates in a low cliff. Cape Bruat, 1,541 feet high, forms with cape Schlippenback, 27 miles to the south-west, a deep bay in which the soundings were 23 to 24 fathoms at above 2 miles off shore.

COCKS COMB ROCKS.—The approach to the above bay is well marked by some jagged white rocks in the form of a cock's comb, lying 10 miles from the coast in lat. 40° 41¼′ N. There is also a group of three islets, named Arevief isles, connected together by shoals, in the northern part of this bay, in front of and at 1¾ miles from a projecting hill. The *Pallas* passed inside these islets, between them and the coast, and found the channel deep, 16 fathoms, and clear of shoals.

The COAST from cape Bruat turns abruptly to the northward and takes a N. by E. trend for 31 miles to cape Kozakof. For the first 10 miles it is an inaccessible and perpendicular wall. The vegetation along its extent is very poor, not a tree or hovel being visible until near the cape, when villages again appear near the shore.

Cape Kozakof is a bluff rocky projection, about 2,615 feet high, and the limit of the high coast line; beyond it the coast turns to the N.W., and forms an extensive bay, 24 miles wide, north and south, and 6 miles deep, but open to the east. The depth was 40 fathoms in its northern part and no danger. Mount Stolovaya, a conspicuous object in this locality, rises 5 miles inland West of the cape. To the north of this elevation several detached hillocks and hills present themselves along the coast.

Kolokozev point, elevated 1,791 feet, and in lat. 41° 47′ 40″ N., is the north-east termination of a small bay formed between it and Urusof point to the south. From hence the coast curves to the north-east, assumes a more hilly appearance, and small islands and rocks lie off. To the northeast of Bougarel or Linden point the shore is indented by a series of small bays as far as the large bay of Goshkevich.

Avvakum islets.—A group of high, rocky, and desolate islets lie 7 miles N.E. of Bougarel point, and near the shore. The group consists of two large islets, about the same size, with some smaller ones; the soundings were 20 to 26 fathoms near them.

GOSHKEVICH BAY* is formed between a steep point to the north-east of the Avvakum group and Sisuro point or cape Casy, the south extreme of the Sisuro peninsula. In some of its nooks it has convenient anchoring ground protected nearly on all sides. A round island, rather remarkable for the regularity of its form, and a smaller one near it, lie at the head of the bay. An island with white cliffs, and surrounded by rocks, named Belaya Skala, lies in the middle of the entrance, at 3 miles S.W. of Sisuro point.

---

* *See* Chart; Tumen Ula to Strelok Bay, No. 2,432.

The northern shores of the bay are sloping, and the bay is connected to the north-east with a deep basin. This connexion is not visible from seaward. The basin was accidentally discovered during the survey of the shores of the Tumen river, and was not examined.

SISURO POINT.—Sisuro peninsula, the south-eastern extremity of this bay, is connected with the mainland by a very narrow isthmus; its sides, with the exception of the one facing the isthmus, are rocky. Sisuro village stands on the east side of the peninsula, on the shores of a small bay convenient of access for fishing boats; the village is large and surrounded by low stone walls. This small bay is formed by the peninsula and a small promontory, which, with the inconsiderable precipitous mountains to the north-east, are the principal landmarks for the mouth of the Tumen, without which there would be difficulty in finding it on the sandy coast. The limit of muddy water extends too far off shore to serve as a guide to the position of the river's mouth.

M. Rocquemaurel, captain of the French corvette *Capricieuse*, in his report says, "Sisuro point is only 153 feet high. At 10 or 12 miles off it resembles a large rock scarped and jagged like the profile of a Venetian fort. Completely isolated from the mountains which rise above it to the north, it appears severed from the shore, to which it is joined by a long low beach trending N.N.E. About 18 miles inland, to the west, mount Chienlong, rising 4,215 feet above the sea level, appears to form the north-eastern range of heights extending some 30 miles to the south-west, at about 10 miles inland."

"To the eastward of the river the range of mountains suddenly change their direction to the north-west, leaving a large valley between them. The remarkable structure of the ground consists generally in beds of gneiss or schist thrown up so to form cliffs or pointed hills, which rise abruptly from a low swampy shore; everything bears the stamp of a complete change in soil, climate, and people."

The TUMEN,* or Tsing-hing river, the position of which is vaguely marked on the charts of Lapérouse and Broughton, separates the Korea from the vast territory occupied by the Manchu Tartars; and by the Russo-Chinese treaty of 14th November 1860, it now forms the southern limit of the Russian territory on the shores of the sea of Japan. Its embouchure opens in the middle of a low plain, 4½ miles eastward of Sisuro point, in lat. 42° 18′ N., long. 130° 36′ E.

This river, which was examined for the first 10 miles from its entrance by the boats of the *Pallas* in 1854, not only serves as the northern boundary of the Korea, but is the limit of the mountainous coast line.

---

* *See* Plan, Tumen Ula, No. 2,407.

It is bounded on the west from its fall to the sea, a distance of 10 miles, by a high projection of the coast, on the west side of which is Goshkevich bay, and by a sloping depression of the land on the east.

From seaward the entrance is only observable on account of the elevation of its right bank. A long sand-spit, extending from the left bank, narrows the entrance, and forms a bar carrying 9 feet water. The channel is winding, the soundings irregular, from 3 to 1 fathoms, and even less, and it runs between numerous shoals and banks, several of which appear above water in the form of low islands. This renders the navigation difficult, and higher up from its mouth the river becomes so shallow as to be fordable.

The right bank of the Tumen is hilly, and terminates in steep sandy slopes; the left bank presents an extensive plain, covered with lakes, or rather marshes, filled with brackish water. The banks preserve this character for the 10 miles examined. As regards its course higher up, no positive information could be procured from the Koreans, who are in general taciturn.

POSIETTE BAY (D'Anville Gulf of the French charts) is comprised between Sisuro point to the south, and cape Gamov to the north, about 33 miles apart. This latter cape, rising 1,800 feet above the sea, is the end of a peninsula extending to the south, and is formed by a conical mountain sloping gently to the north, where, as in the south, it terminates in steep cliffs. It is visible 30 miles off, and coming from the north-east is a good landmark for this bay, as Sisuro point is from the south.

The land at the bottom of the bay is low, marshy, and broken by a range of steep bluffs, resembling at a little distance a group of islands. At the head of the bay are the anchorages, named Pallada road, Nov-gorod harbour, and Expedition bay.*

Yedo rock † lies in mid-channel at entrance to Pallada road with the middle of Furugelma island bearing south, and cape Gamov E. $\frac{1}{2}$ S. There is no discoloured water, nor any indications of a shoal; and it is believed to be a pyramidal rock steep-to on all sides.

Farugelma island, lying in the south-west part of Posiette bay, is 3 miles in circumference and 413 feet high. It forms a good mark for entering the bay, when distinguishable from the high lands to the north-

---

* The French corvette *Capricieuse* examined Posiette bay and the anchorages at its head in 1852. It was still farther examined by the Russian frigate *Pallas* in 1854, and it was here that her survey terminated. In 1855 a survey was made of Posiette bay, by F. H. May, Master of H.M.S. *Winchester*, and D. H. Wilder, Master of H.M.S. *Nankin*. See Plan of Peter the Great bay and Posiette bay, No. 2,432; scale, $m = 0.25$ of an inch.

† Reported by Mr. J. West, Master of the British ship *Yedo*.

west, with which it is generally blended when approaching from the southward. There are two villages on its west face. A reef of rocks extends more than half a mile from its south-west point, and another reef projects from its north-west point. At half and two-thirds of a mile N.N.E. ¼ E. and E. by N. ¾ N. respectively from its north-eastern point lie the Pilier and Buoy rocks near which no soundings have been made; the Pilier is about 8 feet in height, but the latter rock hardly shows at high water.

The channel between the island and the coast is 3½ miles wide, and carries 12 to 18 fathoms, but in the middle lies the Baliene or Whale rock 8 feet above high-water.

KALAVALA BAY (Moule Bay) is partly sheltered to the south-east by Farugelma island, and to the north-east by Bodisko peninsula, the summit of which, named mount Direction, is 820 feet high; the peninsula is joined to the coast by a low isthmus, on which is a village. The bay is 1¾ miles deep, north and south, and one mile wide at entrance, which is narrowed by a reef of rocks, awash, stretching nearly 2 cables off the west shore.

The depth, 8 fathoms, at the entrance of this bay, decreases gradually up to the sandy beach, near which there are 16 feet. The holding ground is not good, being composed of fine sand and gravel with but little clay. It is open from S.S.E. and E.S.E. but the force of the sea from the latter direction is expended on Patau point, the south-east end of the peninsula. With the wind from S.E. to S.S.E. a heavy swell sets in, and makes the anchorage unsafe. The highest tides observed rose about 3½ feet.

PALLADA ROAD, comprised between mount Direction to the south and Klaproth point to the north, is 5 miles deep N.W. and S.E., with a mean width of 3 miles. It affords fair anchorage within Balbi and Ostrano points, the inner points of the bay, in from 12 to 5 fathoms, over mud bottom. The best berth is in 7 fathoms, mud, upwards of a mile south of Porsic point; but as this bay is open to S.E. winds which throw in a heavy swell, it can only be considered as a temporary anchorage for vessels waiting to pass into Expedition bay or Nov-gorod harbour at its head.

DIRECTIONS.—Entering Pallada road it will be necessary for a vessel either to sight Sisuro or Gamov point, to make sure of her position; sighting Farugelma island must not be depended on, for it is often blended with the high lands towering over it to the north-west;* and great care must be taken to avoid the Yedo rock lying in mid-entrance.

---

* The remarks on Peter the Great bay are by Francis H. May, Master of H.M.S. *Winchester*, 1855.

If beating up against north-west winds, which are often fresh, a vessel should, when standing to the south-west towards the Pillier and Buoy rocks, go about when Ostrano and Bergasse points come in line bearing N.W. ¼ N.; the latter rock is nearly covered at high water.

EXPEDITION BAY is a good and secure harbour, and affords a safe retreat for vessels not wishing to ride out a south-easterly gale in Pallada road. The entrance to it (between Tchurkhoda, which is the northern termination of the sandy spit at the head of Pallada road, and Porsic point, the west extreme of Krabbeh peninsula) is nearly half a mile wide, but it is divided into two channels by a large bare rock named Tcherkarsky island, about 60 feet high, which appears white, from its being covered with guano. The eastern of these channels should on no account be taken, as the ground is rocky and uneven, with a depth of only 4½ fathoms in its centre. The other channel on the west side of Tcherkarsky must be entered with caution, for it is narrow, and a shoal extends nearly half way across from Tchurkhoda, so that it is advisable rather to close the former, as it is almost steep-to on its western side.

Entering the bay, take care to avoid a small knoll of 3½ fathoms water with 5 or 6 fathoms close to, which can be done by borrowing on the northern side of the fairway, as the knoll is directly or very nearly in the centre.

The observation spot on Tchurkhoda rock was found by the *Winchester* to be in lat. 42° 37′ 22″ N., long. 130° 44′ 10″ E.;† the meridian distance from Hakodadi being 0h. 39m. 43·8s. By the Russian chart it is in lat. 42° 37′ 50″ N., long. 130° 50′ 50″ E.

Water can be procured from the river in the north-east part of Expedition bay, but on account of the shallowness of the entrance none but small boats can go in except at high tide. The *Winchester* was a whole day procuring one turn of water with the boom boats, as the casks had to be rolled from the bar to about half a mile up the river to the fresh water, it being brackish at the entrance.

TIDES.—It is high water, full and change, at the entrance to Expedition bay, at 2h. 30m., and the rise is about 2½ feet.

NOV-GOROD HARBOUR.—After passing through the channel between Tchurkhoda and Tcherkarsky rocks, Nov-gorod harbour will open out to the eastward. There are no dangers after the harbour is open, and the spits off some of the points can be avoided by attention to the lead. Anchorage may be taken any where in mid-channel, with good holding ground, mud and sand, and land-locked. There is a Russian settlement

---

* See Chart, Tumen Ula to Strelok bay, No. 2,432.

on Mokhouvey peninsula, and telegraph communication with the other Russian posts on the coast.

A hard sandy spit runs across the upper part of the harbour, where several fine bullocks and horses were observed to cross at low water. Above this spit is a large lagoon, about $2\frac{1}{2}$ miles across each way, with irregular soundings in it, from $2\frac{1}{2}$ fathoms to 4 feet. The harbour abounds with fish.*

Supplies.—There are several small runs of good water, which are marked on the plan of the harbour, and one spring, from which about 10 tons per day might be collected, all close to the shore. There are also various beds of oysters, and one of large mussels. The hills are covered with long grass, and abound with pheasants, partridges, and foxes; and the low ground, which is swampy, with woodcock and snipe. Coal is found on Mokhouvey peninsula, and was supplied to Her Majesty's ship *Scylla* at three dollars per ton.

The only export is seaweed, which is sent to Chefoo.

AMUR BAY.—The *Winchester* left Expedition bay September 3rd, and rounding Gamov point passed between it and the Korsakov islands; from thence she proceeded to the north-east into Amur bay, 40 miles in extent, in which there are several good anchorages. The only danger seen was a rock awash, lying about N.W. $\frac{1}{2}$ W. three-quarters of a mile from the northernmost of the three small islets west of the Korsakov islands. To the north-west of these islets is a bay in which the *Styx* anchored in 8 fathoms sandy bottom, but it only affords shelter in northerly and westerly winds.

WHITE CLIFF BAY.—Passing between Red cliff island and the main, a bay, named White cliff, was observed, which apparently affords good shelter, but there was no opportunity of examining it. The south point, with rocks off it, should not be approached too near, as irregular soundings were obtained in its vicinity.

SLAVIANSKI BAY.—The *Winchester* passed eastward of the two islands fronting White Cliff bay (Antipanko and Sebereakov islands), near the northernmost of which there is a remarkable rock called the Ninepin. About 3 miles northward of these islands is a conspicuous cliffy point, which forms the south-east point of a secure and deep bight, named Slavianski bay.

This bay forms an excellent harbour and is well protected by the Eugénie archipelago, which fronts it, and forms a good breakwater in

---

* The description of Nov-gorod harbour is by David H. Wilder, Master, R.N., H.M.S. *Nankin*, 1854, and J. Jones, Master, H.M.S. *Scylla*, 1866. *See* Plan of Nov-gorod harbour on Chart No. 2432.

south-easterly winds. There is no difficulty in working in, as there are 10 fathoms close to Bruce point, the south point of entrance, and the same depth near the islands on its northern side. The soundings are regular, and a vessel may anchor near the head of the bay, where there is a small river, in 4 fathoms water, good holding ground. Fish and potatoes were procured from the natives, and they appear to be amply provided with those necessaries.

PESTCHANOI POINT (Sandy point).—When abreast Slavianski bay a high table hill will be seen to the north-eastward, with a tuft of trees on its summit, called mount Virginie, and another farther in the same direction named mount Winchester, the eastern slope of which terminates in a low sandy point, in lat. 43° 11' N., long. 131° 46' 30" E. The *Winchester* anchored in 6½ fathoms, mud, with this point bearing S. by W. ½ W.; Retchnoi islet N.N.E. ½ E.; Skrebtsoff islet E. ⅓ S., and Aube bluff, E. by N. ¼ N. This anchorage is good and quite land-locked.

There is an extensive bight in the north-east part of Amur bay, but the water in it is shallow.

Water.—The Sui-fun river at the head of Amur bay, is apparently of some extent, and good water can be procured about a mile from the entrance; but the same difficulty would be experienced in watering as at the one already alluded to in Expedition bay. The distance from Pestchanoi point to the entrance of the river is 7 miles. A vessel might anchor within 3 miles of the entrance, as the depths gradually shoal towards it.

Wood can be obtained on any part of the coast, the land being covered with trees and the beach with drift-wood.

EUGÉNIE ARCHIPELAGO is the chain of islands extending in a south-west direction from Murivief Amursky peninsula. There are some good harbours in it, named Novik bay,* Voevoda bay, and Boyarin bay, affording shelter for ships of the largest draught, and no doubt good water can be procured at these as well at every other part of this coast by digging wells; but no running streams of any size were seen.

There are two excellent outlets through the archipelago into Peter the Great bay, called Japanese strait and Currie channel.

The EASTERN BOSPHORUS, between the south end of Muravief Amursky peninsula and the islands forming the Eugénie archipelago, is 6 miles long, and about half a mile broad in its narrowest part. At its western entrance is a sand spit stretching half-way across the passage from the northern point, cape Tokarefsky; the spit is steep-to, having 28 fathoms water within a ship's length of it. When past the spit there is

---

* *See* Plan of Novik bay, No. 2,407; scale, m = 3½ inches.

no danger, and a vessel may run or work through, by paying common attention to the lead. The tidal stream flows through at the rate of about 2 knots an hour.

PORT VLADIVOSTOK—(Golden Horn Bay), on the northern side of the Eastern Bosphorus, is an excellent harbour, where a vessel may lie quite land-locked in 8 or 9 fathoms, mud bottom. The land is high, and for the most part thickly wooded. The Russians have established a settlement here (numbering in 1866 about 350 inhabitants), which is fast rising in importance; it possesses a dock 150 feet in length with 17 feet water over the sill, and a small steam factory sufficient to repair ships, engines, or boilers; and has telegraphic communication with St. Petersburgh.

OUSOURI BAY.—The *Winchester* anchored near the western entrance of the Eastern Bosphorus in 14 fathoms, mud, and afterwards the *Styx* proceeded through the strait, and steamed round an extensive inlet called Ousouri bay. The boats landed at its head, at the entrance of the river Ful-dsia, but nothing could be seen of the least indication of a good harbour, although it was thought there was one on its eastern side. The bay is about 30 miles deep and about 16 broad, abreast Eastern Bosphorus, and the land everywhere is bold, and resembles that of Amur bay.

AMERICA BAY (Hornet bay) is formed at the eastern extreme of Peter the Great bay, and Captain C. C. Forsyth, who discovered it in H.M.S. *Hornet* in July 1856, describes it as a spacious inlet, carrying a moderate depth up to its head, but open to southerly winds. There is snug anchorage on its western side, between the mainland and an islet, named Lisi island. The Sutchan, a river apparently of some magnitude, flows round the foot of a peculiar conical hill at the head of the bay; it is probably navigable for some distance. Vessels should not pass between Lisi island and the mainland as sunken rocks are found off the west shores of the island. Many villages and several herds of cattle were seen. The country is thickly populated, and the natives freely bartered their vegetables for old clothes, bottles, &c.

WRANGLE BAY, running in to the right shore of America bay in a S.E. direction, is a little over a half a mile wide at its entrance, and about $1\frac{1}{2}$ miles deep, perfectly sheltered from all winds. Two small rivers flow into the bay, but both have sand bars at their entrances. The tide rises 2 feet in Wrangle bay, and the variation in 1862 was 4° 10′ W.

NAKHODKA BAY indents the mainland on the western side of America bay, it is nearly a mile wide at its entrance and 2 miles deep, and is perfectly sheltered from all winds. There are a few natives settled on the eastern shore of the bay.

ANCHORAGE may be had in 4½ fathoms, soft mud. There is no perceptible rise and fall of tide.

The COAST* between America bay and that of St. Vladimir is intersected with mountain ranges, the slopes of which terminate in cliffs or shelve gradually towards the sea, and form sheltered bays and harbours. The woods spreading over this extent consist principally of oak suitable for building purposes; the cedar, ash, birch, lime, and cork tree likewise occur.

CAPE ZAMOK (Ostrovni or Island point)† is a fine bold rocky headland, between which and St. Vladimir bay the coast is remarkably clear of treacherous dangers, a fortunate circumstance where the navigator is so frequently enveloped in dense fogs. Its general trend is to the N.E., but it is broken occasionally by harbours and sandy bays. The coast line is usually a narrow fringe of large boulders and shingle, bordering steep cliffs and banks of from 200 to 400 feet high. A small rocky islet (Zamok) lies off the cape.

Proceeding to the north-eastward from cape Zamok, high ranges of hills, some reaching an altitude of 2,700 feet are seen, a mile or two inland, and occasionally large tracts of country, densely wooded. The valleys occurring at intervals, appear to be choked with undergrowth; no fields nor signs of cultivation meet the eye in any direction. Along the shore at short distances are met, in summer, villages of the migratory Chinese, sea-weed collectors; but these strike their tents in August, and proceed to the southward with the produce of their summer's work: no other sign of population was seen in passing.

Water.—As a general rule, along the coast of Russian Tartary, every valley which terminates on the sea-beach has its stream of excellent water, and generally in the summer months the sea is smooth enough to allow of boat-work. Drift-wood is generally to be found on the beaches, and there are but few portions of the coast where wood cannot be cut in the immediate vicinity of any beach where landing may be effected.

TCHENIYA BAY lies about 27 miles to the north-eastward of America bay; it is small, being only a mile in depth, and open to the southward. Yakimova point, on the western side of its entrance, is in lat. 42° 49′ 30″, long. 133° 30′ 0″ E. There is abundance of wood for fuel, and water may be obtained from the Talengoida river (on the north-west shore) on the right bank of which there is a settlement. There is

---

* See Chart, Strelok bay to St. Vladimir bay, No. 2,511.

† The coast between America bay and St. Vladimir bay was surveyed by the Russian schooner *Vostok* in 1861, and the description of this coast is principally from the report of her survey translated from the Russian Naval Magazine, May 1862. From cape Zamok to St. Vladimir bay was surveyed by H.M.S. *Actæon* and *Dove* in 1859.

another village in the north-east part of the bay; the rise and fall of tide is 2 feet.

Petrova and Beltzova islets.—At a distance of 5 miles from Ostrovni point, in a north-east direction, lie two rocky islands, situated three-quarters of a mile from each other at a little over $2\frac{1}{4}$ cables from the shore, to which they are both connected by reefs. The southern Petrova is the largest, and the reef connecting it with the main is covered. The northern is named Beltzova, and the reef between it and the shore is uncovered.

SIAU WUHU BAY.—The first anchorage to the north-eastward of Ostrovni point is a small but well sheltered one in Siau Wuhu bay (Preobrajenya). From the southward, a hill 2,720 feet high, the most elevated in the immediate neighbourhood, is a good mark to point out its position; it bears N.W. by N. $4\frac{1}{2}$ miles from Orekhof island which partly shelters the anchorage. Vessels requiring a refit would find the Inner harbour admirably adapted for the purpose, perhaps the most eligible place on the coast; but if it should be necessary to beach, it should be borne in mind that the rise and fall of tide is inconsiderable, and what little there is appears to be due to direction and force of wind.*

From a mile outside cape Zamok the course and distance to Orekhof island is N.E. $\frac{1}{2}$ N., 8 miles. This will lead clear of all danger, passing about a mile outside Petrova and Beltzova islands, both of which are connected by reefs with the mainland. Rounding Zamok island give it a berth of 2 cables, and do not approach the dangerous spit extending one cable northward from the centre of the island to within a less depth than 6 fathoms. When the east side of the island comes in line with the extreme outer point of the mainland bearing S. by E., this danger will be passed, and good anchorage may be found in 6 or 7 fathoms.

Should it be desirable to enter the Inner harbour, a mid-channel course is quite safe; and excellent shelter will be found half a mile inside the entrance points in 5 to 6 fathoms, mud bottom, sheltered from all winds. There is no perceptible rise and fall of the tide.

Supplies.—An extensive plain on the north side of the outer anchorage affords pasturage for cattle, which are, however, small, but the beef is excellent. The country in the vicinity abounds in deer, but they are very shy and not easily got at. Vegetables are plentiful and wild grapes grow in the valleys; wood is also plentiful. A few native families reside here permanently, they keep cattle and horses but demand high prices for them as well as other necessaries, accepting nothing but silver in payment.

---

* *See* Plan of Siau Wuhu bay, No. 2,716; scale, m = 4 inches.

Water may be obtained at a stream which flows into the north-east corner of the outer bay. The seine in the month of July afforded an abundant supply of salmon, a few small turbot, a large quantity of prawns, and a few other fish. Drift timber is plentiful along the beach, and any quantity of green wood may be had, by cutting it, and good hard-wood knees for boats.

CAPE CREASY.—Approaching Siau Wuhu bay from the north-eastward, cape Creasy, a bold rocky headland, the summit of which is 695 feet high, conspicuously marks the east side of entrance. Three small rocks, 5 feet high, will be seen off the cape, one immediately under the highest cliff, its most southern point, and two on the west side of the cape, but they all lie within a cable of the shore.

ST. VALENTINE BAY.— Situated 22 miles N.E. by E. of cape Creasy, is about a mile wide at its entrance between Silina point and Orlova point, is quite exposed to the southward and eastward, and can only be recommended as a temporary anchorage for steamers. A sailing vessel might find difficulty in working out. The position of the bay is marked by a hill 2,370 feet high $1\frac{1}{2}$ miles north of it; and its north-east side by four very conspicuous cliffs. The best anchorage is in 5 to 6 fathoms sand and mud inside a cliffy point on the south side. There is a village in the bay, but no supplies could be obtained, with the exception of timber, and the water from the rivulet at the head of the bay soon becomes unfit for use.

CASTLE POINT, N.E. by E. $\frac{1}{2}$ E. distant 15 miles from St. Valentine bay, is a remarkably fine-looking bluff, its yellow cliffs rising almost precipitously from the beach to an elevation of 1,060 feet, and sloping gradually inshore gives the idea of a large hill half cut off.

BROKEN HEAD is a fine rocky promontory $8\frac{1}{2}$ miles N.E. by E. $\frac{3}{4}$ E. of Castle point, and the termination of a range of hills, to the rear and northward of which is spread an extensive and well-watered plain covered with rank vegetation, but void of trees. Off the south-east face of Broken head is a high rock like a shark's fin.

From 8 to 9 miles N.E. of Broken head are a line of conspicuous white cliffs on the sea face of a wooded range, and 2 miles farther a good sized open bay, with anchorage in from 5 to 8 fathoms.

MOSQUITO RIVER entrance is $2\frac{1}{2}$ miles north of Broken Head, at the north-east extreme of a clean sandy beach, which, terminating in a rather steep bank, forms the west side of entrance, and a conspicuous rocky bluff the east side. Inside the entrance is a small basin of 3 to 5 fathoms water, quite sheltered from all winds, but too small to be available to any but small craft, as large vessels would not have room to swing. The bar at entrance has 13 feet on it (1859), but probably winter frosts alter the depths.

Supplies.—Drift wood may be obtained in small quantities along the beach, and there are some trees a considerable distance from the entrance of the river. Water can be pumped in alongside on the ebb, or brought by boats from the higher parts of the river.

ST. EUSTAPHIA BAY, N.E. ½ E. distant 13 miles from Broken head, is a small bay open to southerly winds; it is a little more than a mile wide at its entrance, and about the same depth. Anchorage may be had in from 4 to 5 fathoms, sandy bottom, but the anchorage is exposed.

The COAST from St. Eustaphia bay takes an E.N.E. direction for 7½ miles to Nizmenny and Low Table point. Along the coast the mountains slope gently to the sea, and are covered principally with leafy timber.

LOW TABLE POINT, at 20 miles N.E. by E. of Broken head, notwithstanding its appellation is 120 feet high, it bears the name given it probably on account of the perfectly level nature of the country in its immediate vicinity; it is bordered with a vertical cliff, extending 2 miles to the eastward from the base of a conspicuous round topped mountain about 1,200 feet above the sea. It is especially useful in making Olga bay from the southward, before Table point is risen; and being the only piece of tableland in the neighbourhood will readily be recognised. A few rocks are off it, but they are quite close inshore, and no dangers are known.

OLGA BAY, in lat. 43° 41′ N., 11 miles N.N.E. ½ E. from Low Table point was discovered by H.M.S. *Hornet*, July 1856, and named port Michael Seymour. It is open to the southward, but there is shelter from all winds in its northern part, in 10 fathoms, muddy bottom.

Brydone island (Chikachef), lying off cape Scott (the northern point of Olga bay) to which it is connected by a reef, is steep-to, and appears white from seaward; between this island and Manevski point (the south point) is 3 miles; from these points the bay narrows to 1 mile, between cape Peschurof and cape Sacken, after which it again widens and forms a bay 1½ miles in depth and about 1¼ miles in width.

A narrow passage, named Brown channel at its north-east part, leads into an inner harbour or estuary, named Tikaya, which is well adapted for careening purposes, as there is but little rise and fall, the water at all times smooth, and deep close to the southern bank; a river disembogues at its head. Brown channel has 4 fathoms water in it, deepening to 6 and 7 fathoms towards the inner harbour,* on the shores of which the Russians have a settlement.

---

* *See* Plan of Olga Bay, No. 2,511; scale, m = 2 inches.

Avakum river flows into the north-west angle of the port; its mouth is broad and shallow, with only 2½ feet on the bar, but soon deepens when crossed, and flows in the bed of a deep valley, with high mountains on either side; few places are void of vegetation, save some abrupt and precipitous crags, the valley itself consisting of marshy and turfy land, with flat islands in the course of the river. A few miles up, the river divides into branches, and becomes shallow and narrow; there are some native settlements on its banks.

Petrova rock, having 5 feet on it with 5 and 6 fathoms round it, lies 6 cables E.½ S. of cape Linden on the western coast at the entrance to Olga bay. A surf sometimes breaks on this rock, and large flocks of geese settle on it.

Supplies can be had in moderate quantities, and the seine will always procure an abundance of capital fish, such as salmon and trout, in any spot where it is possible to haul it, and particularly near a stream; a few fowls may also be procured, and a small supply of fresh beef. The watering stream runs through a valley on the eastern side of the port, near the ordinary anchorage. A thick growth of oaks, hazel, and willows completely hides it from view. Wood may be obtained in any quantity; also good oak knees for boats.

DIRECTIONS.—The positions of Olga bay may be easily known when approaching it from the northward by Brydone island, on the eastern side of entrance, and the only one on this part of the coast. The island is steep on its eastern side, sloping on its western, and is joined to the mainland by a reef of rocks; no bottom with 20 fathoms line was obtained within a quarter of a mile from its southern side, which appears to be free from danger. When within the entrance keep the starboard shore aboard, but not nearer than 1¼ cables distant, as it is fronted by a steep bank.

Approaching from the southward, the entrance will be recognised by the opening in the land. Brydone island is not distinguishable at any great distance, as, being only 325 feet high, it looks like a cliff of the high hill, 1,341 feet high, behind it. A vessel can pass between Petrova rock and the western shore of the bay in 13 fathoms; but it is advisable to keep to the eastward of the rock, *i.e.*, keep the eastern shore on board if intending to enter Tikhaya harbour, the narrow entrance to which (Brown channel) is only a cable wide; the eastern coast should be kept close to until within a short distance of the inner point off which there is only 9 feet.

A black cask buoy is placed on the extreme end of the shoal ground on the northern shore of Brown channel, and should be passed on the port hand.

ANCHORAGE may be had in the inner harbour in 5 fathoms muddy bottom.

TIDES.—In Olga bay it is high water, full and change, at 5h. 30m., and the rise is about 2 feet.

ST. VLADIMIR BAY, in lat. 43° 54′ N., was discovered by the Russian frigate *America*, in 1857. Its entrance, 1¼ miles wide, and open to the east, is formed between North Head or cape Ballouzek, 347 feet high, to the north, and South Head, or cape Watauski, 712 feet high, to the south, both of which, when approaching the bay from the east or north-east, appear like islands, each being connected with the mainland by low isthmuses. From thence the bay extends westward, and forms three arms, one to the north, one to the south, and the other, the smallest, to the west. The north and south arms are large circular basins separated from each other by a hilly and wooded peninsula, and both are surrounded and sheltered by adjacent high hills covered with wood. The depths are about 15 to 5 fathoms in both arms.*

The North bay is clear of all dangers, its eastern shore is, however, shoal, there being 5 fathoms half a mile from the shore. The northern bay forms an excellent harbour.

The West bay, between Kuzmina and Roudanoffski points, is comparatively shallow. A bank named Artsibasheva with only 2 feet on it lies in mid-channel at the entrance. Vessels entering this bay should close the northern shore, but it is recommended to anchor either in North or South bay in preference.

The South bay is well sheltered, but, as a slight swell is frequently experienced there, it can scarcely be recommended as a fit place for careening, especially with Olga bay in such close proximity, where there is a Russian settlement and every facility for repairs. To the south it communicates by a stream with a lake of 16 to 10 feet water, which with little trouble might be formed into a graving dock.

There is no fixed population in this bay, and from the report of other natives, it appears that these arms are only frozen over from the middle of December to the middle of February; the entrance of the bay remains in a great measure free from ice by the effect of the offing swell.

Supplies.—A few bullocks were seen, but their owners would not part with them for anything but sycee silver, refusing dollars. Some potatoes were obtained, and a quantity of wild onions. The seine gave a good supply of salmon (July and August), some small turbot, and prawns. Water can be obtained at three or four different places.

Drift-wood abounds on the beach, and any quantity of green wood can be had for the trouble of cutting. There is a species of dwarf oak, which furnishes excellent boats' knees.

---

* *See* Plan of St. Vladimir bay, No. 2,773; scale, m = 3 inches.

TIDES.—The tides are irregular in St. Vladimir bay. It is high water full and change, at 1h. 0m., and the range is about 2 feet.

DIRECTIONS.—Approaching St. Vladimir bay from the southward, the coast between Olga bay and it will present an almost uninterrupted line of steep cliffs, ranging from 250 to 400 feet high. Pinnacle and Chetyrek points are the only remarkable features on it; the former may be known by its having at its extreme a sharp single needle rock. Chetyrek point, which is 3¼ miles S.S.W. of the South head of the bay, is formed by three rocky summits, and will be readily distinguished. Deep soundings were carried very close inshore, there being 20 fathoms and upwards at a mile from the land; little warning, therefore, may be expected from the hand lead. No unseen dangers are known. A few detached rocks were met with, but all within a cable's length of the shore.

Having passed Chetyrek point, South head will be readily recognized, and may be rounded at a distance of 2 cables. If intending to anchor in the south arm, from the entrance steer for the south-east part of Roudanoffski point or rather peninsula; it appears like a cliff, and its summit is 205 feet high. Give Low point a berth of, at least, 3 cables, in rounding it, and pay particular attention to the lead, not approaching the point into less than six fathoms water, as the stony ledge extending off it is rather steep-to.

The most prudent plan to adopt is to steer for the south-east part of Roudanoffski point, until the extreme point of North head bears N.E.; then steer S.W., keeping that bearing on astern until Low point, which has a beacon on its extremity bears E. by S., when steer for the centre of the low isthmus connecting South head with the mainland, and anchor in 10 fathoms, with Low point bearing North, and the highest part of South head E. by N.

Approaching the bay from the east or north-east, North head being quite clear of all hidden danger, may be past at 2 cables distant, and the anchorage in the south arm steered for, using the same precaution on approaching the vicinity of Low point as before directed.

The COAST from America bay to St. Vladimir, a distance of 150 miles, embraces mountain ranges, which do not rise higher than 3,000 feet above the sea. The coast is bordered by forests, consisting of oak, ash, birch, alder, and lime, maple, and cork trees, the oak is suitable for ship building. Inland the trees are taller and thicker, and the mountain summits are clothed with coniferous trees. The formation of the coast is basalt, and is uniform along its whole line. It is thinly populated by the Tasa and Manza tribes, both of which are engaged in agriculture; they grow maize, millet, barley, and vegetables. During the summer they resort to the coast in great numbers, and collect seakale and shells; these natives are very communicative and obliging. From St. Vladimir bay the coast trends in a N.E. by N. direction to Barracouta harbour, in 49° 2′ N., then N. by E. to Castries bay, and is free from apparent danger. Its outline was but imperfectly known until 1855, when H.M. ships *Sybille* and *Barracouta* sailed along it, and determined the following points and anchorages.

SHELTER BAY, in 44° 30′ N., affords shelter from north-east winds. Good fresh water can be obtained in a river a cable wide, with a bar at its mouth, within which there is a depth of 9 feet, over a fine sandy bottom. The land is high to the northward of this bay, and its aspect is that of bluff and barren headlands.

SYBILLE BAY, in 44° 44′ N., affords shelter from S.S.E. winds; its entrance is remarkable from having on each side some prominent pinnacled rocks, high and isolated. The south side of the bay is high and rocky, with small deep valleys opening towards the sea; many large rocks lie along the beach. The north side consists of a series of hills, clay and sand. The bay is closed by a broad valley, through which some streams run and form a small river, which flows into the bay. The soundings become gradually shallow towards the valley; the bottom is rocky, and covered by a thick growth of seaweed.

PIQUE BAY, in lat. 44° 46′ N., affords good shelter from N.E. and easterly winds. The best anchorage is in 5 fathoms, with the point bearing S.E. by E. There is good water in a river, separated from the bay by a spit of sand, at the mouth of which is a bar. Cattle may be obtained at this anchorage.

BULLOCK BAY, in 45° 5′ N., affords but bad anchorage. Bullocks and fowls can be procured, but with difficulty, although they may be frequently seen near the beach; but it is necessary to search for the natives in the interior.

Luké point in 45° 19½′ N., is high, bluff, and woody. Cape Disappointment, in 45° 42′ N., has rocks extending a cable from it.

GULF OF TARTARY.—From cape Disappointment, in lat. 45° 42′ N., the coast of Tartary trends to the north-east, and forms with the west coast of Saghalin island a long channel named the Gulf of Tartary, which communicates with the gulf of Amúr to the northward by Tartary strait. This strait may be considered to begin on the parallel of about 51° N.; on the parallel of Castries bay the coasts of Tartary and Saghalin converge rapidly; and abreast cape Catherine, in 51° 57′ N., they are only 7 miles apart; 17 miles farther north, between capes Lazaref and Pogobi, they approach to within 3½ miles; and this is the gorge of the strait, and the entrance into the gulf of Amúr.

The only ports at present known in the gulf are Barracouta harbour and Castries bay on its western coast, and Jonquière bay on its eastern; there are, however, on both coasts many indentations, which may afford occasional shelter. The anchorage along the eastern coast is safe during the summer months, when easterly winds prevail; but a vessel must be prepared to weigh, should the wind veer to the west.

The coast on both sides of the gulf is high, and there are no particular land marks useful for seamen. On the eastern shore the country is everywhere thickly wooded, but in no way cultivated; towards the end of May or beginning of June, when the snow disappears, it has a most inviting appearance, and presents an agreeable variety of hill and dale with streams and torrents. It appears to be thinly inhabited by a simple-minded race of people of small stature and dark complexion, with features partaking of, but more developed than the Chinese character; they subsist chiefly upon fish, and consequently locate themselves on the sea shore. (For description of the west coast of Saghalin, see page 354.)

No dangers have as yet been observed off either coast of the gulf. The soundings decrease gradually towards its shores, though near the headlands, and where the coast looks bold, as may be expected, deep water is carried closer in, and the lead gives shorter warning of approach to land; a peculiarity, however, in the soundings has been noticed off some parts of the west coast of Saghalin, the water there being found to deepen when approaching within 3 or 4 miles of the land.

The soundings in Tartary strait, from 51° N. northward, vary from 46 to 26 fathoms, which latter is on the parallel of Castries bay, whence they rapidly decrease to 16, 10, 7, and 4 fathoms, in 51° 42′ N., abreast cape Chihachef, and which may be considered the bar of the strait, unless, indeed, there be deep water close under this cape or over towards Saghalin, which seems doubtful.* To the northward of this spot the water deepens to 8 and 10 fathoms, which depth, with few exceptions, is carried up to the gorge.

The navigation of the gulf would be simple enough, but the fogs render it dangerous, requiring the greatest caution to be observed. It has been remarked by former voyagers that on nearing the land in these seas a vessel will suddenly emerge from the fog or find it lift; this was found frequently to be the case by H.M. ships in 1855–56, but of course it would not be prudent to run for the land in full reliance on such an occurrence; the best method appears to be to stand in cautiously for the land in the daytime, when a clearance from fog, as just described, may be met with.

---

* It does not appear clearly whether Admiral Kusnetsof with his squadron in 1858 passed eastward or westward of this bar.

Supplies.—Wood and water can be procured in abundance, and with facility on all parts of the coast of the gulf, and coal of fair quality in any quantity at Dui, the next anchorage south of Jonquière bay (see page 355).

Fish and wild fowl are plentiful; very-fine codfish have been caught in soundings from 73 to 30 fathoms.

TIDES.—The tides in the gulf are regular close in shore, the flood stream setting to the northward, the ebb to the southward. The currents are uncertain and irregular.

SUFFREN BAY, formed by cape Suffren to the south, in lat. 47° 20′ N.,[*] is but an exposed anchorage, surrounded by vast forests which extend out of sight. Its shores are fringed by a low shingle beach, on which the sea constantly breaks. The cape is fronted by rocks, which stretch half a mile into the offing.

FISH RIVER, in 47° 55′ N., has anchorage off its entrance in 9 fathoms, at about a mile from the land sheltered from N.W. and westerly winds.

LOW CAPE, in 48° 28′ N., has high land behind it, and a depth of 8 fathoms was obtained a mile off shore.

From Low cape the coast line northward is irregular for 15 miles; its trend is then N. by E. 20 miles to Beechy head; it is steep-to, the lead giving 14 to 17 fathoms at 2 miles off shore. High snowy mountains are visible inland, and pine forests cover the ground to the coast, which is hilly, and in cliffs.

BARRACOUTA HARBOUR.—The entrance to this bay, in lat. 49° 2′ N., is between Freeman point on the north and Tullo island on the south, which bear N. by W. and S. by E. from each other, distant three-quarters of a mile. The general depths in the bay are 5 to 15 fathoms over a mud bottom. The entrance is open to the eastward, but within the bay are several inlets, which afford shelter for all classes of vessels.

Carr bank, with 1½ and 2 fathoms on it, extends a cable off shore on the north-west side of the entrance, one-third the distance between Sybille head and Freeman point.[†]

This bay remains frozen for about the same time as Castries bay. Its shores are covered with wood fit for building purposes, such as the larch, fir, and stone-pine.

ANCHORAGE may be had anywhere in the numerous creeks, but the best is in Pallas bay off the Russian settlement, where there is a wooden pier 250 feet in length for unloading at; the water here is nearly fresh alongside. The river to the westward of Pallas bay can be ascended for 7 miles in boats. Wild fowl and fish can be obtained in moderate quantities.[‡]

---

[*] The positions on this part of the coast are by H.M.S. *Barracouta* in 1856.
[†] *See* Plan of Barracouta Harbour, No. 2,508; scale, m = 3·0 inches.
[‡] Remarks of J. Jones, Nav. Lieut. *Scylla*, 1866.

DIRECTIONS.—Approaching Barracouta harbour from the northward, and having made Barren bluff, in lat. 49° 18½′ N., the three hills over Beechy head will be seen if the weather is clear, and by bringing the centre one S. by W. it will lead to the entrance. A beacon between 40 and 50 feet in height is erected about one mile north of Freeman point. At 3 miles N. by E. ½ E. from Freeman point the shore should not be approached within 2 cables, to avoid a rock on which the sea occasionally breaks; it lies about a cable off a point bare of trees, at 2 cables from which the depth is 12 fathoms, and thence to Freeman point 13 to 15 fathoms. Pass the latter point at a convenient distance, and avoiding Carr bank proceed into the harbour, where the best anchorage, with the exception of Pallas bay, is on its south side to the S.S.W. of Fortescue island.

Vessels bound into the harbour from the southward or south-east should make the land near Beechy head, which may readily be distinguished by some rocks above water, half a cable's length off its extremity. From Beechy head, which may be passed at a convenient distance, Tronson point, half a mile south of the harbour entrance, bears N.N.W. distant about 5 miles. This point is low, rugged, and devoid of trees, and should not be approached within 1½ cables; between it and Tullo island the shore is clear of danger. Give this island a berth of a cable, at which distance there are 12 or 13 fathoms water, and then proceed to an anchorage.

CAUTION.—Vessels approaching this harbour in foggy weather should not shoal their water under 40 or 35 fathoms, unless well assured of their position, and in all cases due allowance must be made for currents, which generally set along the coast to the southward in northerly winds, and to the northward in southerly winds. In strong breezes they have been found to run as much as 25 and 30 miles a day; they are sometimes, however, extremely variable.

TIDES.—In Barracouta harbour it is high water, full and change, at at 10h. 0m., and the rise is 3 to 4 feet.

The COAST from Beechy head trends in a northerly direction to Castries bay, and is steep-to, with 15 to 18 fathoms at 2 miles off shore; 25 and 30 fathoms have, however, been obtained at a cable's length off cape Byki, in lat. 49° 35′ N. The coast assumes a bolder aspect in proceeding northwards. From Beechy head to Barren bluff, the land, backed by high mountains, forms two ranges when seen from the offing; one of these mountains cone-shaped and covered with snow, is visible 50 miles off. The steep coast is undermined in some places by the sea; large masses of rock, which are detached from time to time, fall down, and form a dangerous rocky shore. The coast-line is irregular, but by keeping outside a line, joining the promontories of Beechy head and Barren bluff, all the intermediate points are cleared.

Barren bluff is a high perpendicular headland. Vessels will find shelter under it during winds from N.N.E. to N.W., in 5 or 6 fathoms water with its extreme point bearing N.E.

Cape Byki.—Before approaching cape Byki, there is a wide and low forest, extending for miles westward, backed by a high range of mountains. This cape is a bluff headland, bleak and rugged, with many traces of continual disintegration.

Cape Destitution, in 49° 46′ N., is bold, high land, having a bay on its north side, which affords good shelter from S.E. to S.W. in 9 or 10 fathoms, with the extreme of the cape, E.S.E., distant about one mile.

Cape Dent, in 50° 00′ N., declines to the eastward, and has a bay on its north side; at half a cable from its extremity, is the Gulf rock, of pinnacle shape, and about 20 feet high.

CASTRIES BAY* is used by vessels to procure a pilot, or to discharge their cargoes, when bound to the Amúr, as those above 12 feet draught cannot enter that river. Its entrance is 4 miles wide between Kloster-Camp, or Quoin point on the south, and Castries point on the north; Quoin point, is in lat. 51° 25′ N. Although the greater part of the bay is open to easterly winds, which throw in a heavy sea, yet vessels, if their draught will permit, will find shelter behind the islands in it, particularly at its head on the west of Observatory island. The bay is covered with ice from the middle of November or December to April, being open to navigation for 7 or 8 months in the year. The isthmus which separates it from the principal branch of the Amúr is not more than 40 miles across, and lake Kyzi is only 15 miles distant. At the head of the bay is the Russian settlement Alexandrovski, composed of five or six wooden houses inhabited by a guard of about 60 men. A number of torpedos were stored here in 1866, otherwise the bay was not fortified.

The general nature of the ground in this bay appears to be mud, but from many circumstances this is supposed to be a mere superficial covering to a rocky or otherwise treacherous bottom.

Vostok bank, upon which the sea occasionally breaks heavily, but which does not show in smooth water, lies in the middle of the entrance, with the western part of the promontory (the east extreme of which is Quoin point) in line with the bluff headland beyond, bearing about South. Its north end is marked by a white buoy, and its south end by a pole; the north end of Observatory island bearing West, leads well to the northward of it. A flat rocky bank with only 5 feet on it lies about midway between Oyster and South islands.

---

* *See* Plan of Castries bay, scale, $m = 0·7$ of an inch, on Chart of Kuril Islands, No. 2,405.

LIGHT.—A *fixed* white light, visible from seaward and in the bay when bearing from N.E. ⅓ E. (round by the north) to S.E. ⅓ S., is shown from a square wooden tower, 38 feet high, painted white with a gray lantern, on Quoin point, the south point of entrance to Castries bay. It is elevated 250 feet above the sea, and visible in clear weather at 18 miles.

Supplies.—Water may be obtained on the south shore opposite the beacons; fresh meat and vegetables are scarce. The river abounds in fish.

DIRECTIONS.—In making the bay from the southward two small high and barren islets will be seen near the coast, about 16 miles southward of Quoin point. In entering the bay and passing southward of Vostok bank; the reef which extends a considerable distance from the north end of Oyster island, the north end of which is marked by a white flag, must be guarded against, but that channel is in other respects clear. Two white beacons with triangular frames on Kikoff point in line (N. 73° W.) leads in mid-channel between these dangers.

ANCHORAGE should not be taken up in the bay South of Oyster island, the bottom being soft is not good holding ground and several vessels have been driven on the beach in westerly gales.

The best anchorage is with Castries point N.E. by E. ½ E. and St. Catherine point S.E. by E.

TIDES.—It is high water, full and change, in Castries bay at 10h. 30m., neaps rise 6 feet, springs rise 8½ feet.

The GULF of AMÚR or Saghalin, is 70 miles long, north and south, and 25 miles at its greatest breadth. The waters of the river Amúr, which flow into this vast basin with great rapidity, have formed banks of sand and mud, which cover almost its whole surface, barely leaving the shallow channels by which the stream flows on one side to the sea of Okhotsk and on the other to the strait of Tartary; this renders the entrance of this great river difficult and at times dangerous.*

The South channel.—Immediately north of cape Lazaref, at the south entrance of the gulf, the channel from the strait of Tartary divides into two branches. That which goes to the N.N.W., narrow and slightly winding, is called the South channel, and keeps close to the Tartary shore, passing the isles of Chomé and Hagemir; it bends abruptly around cape Prongé, and thence holds a N.W. course to Nikolaevsk, which is 65 miles from cape Lazaref. The channel varies from one quarter of a mile to 2 miles in width; the depths are generally small, but occasionally are as much as 14 fathoms. The least water is 2¼ fathoms, and a flat with this

---

* *See* Chart of Strait of Tartary and the entrance of the Amúr river, No. 2,650; scale, m = 0·25 of an inch.

depth extends for nearly 10 miles between Korsakof and Prongé points, and this may be considered the real bar of the river, and must be crossed to enter it. Beyond this bar the water deepens, and 11 fathoms are found abreast the town of Nikolaevsk, above which the river is said to be navigable for 1,500 miles.

Saghalin Fairway.—The N.N.E. branch or Saghalin Fairway is wider and deeper than the other, the least depth being 18 feet at low water, according to the Russian chart made between the years 1849 and 1854. It keeps along the Saghalin shore at about 5 miles distant, for nearly 60 miles, until just north of cape Halezof, where it almost touches the coast; and 20 miles farther north, between capes Golovachef and Menshikof, 16 miles apart, it opens out into the sea of Okhotsk.

The North channel.—A narrow gut, dignified with the name of North channel, leads close to cape Tabak, the north point of entrance of the Amúr, and then in a N.E. direction 30 miles to the sea of Okhotsk. The least water in it is 13 feet, until within one mile of the sea, where apparently there is a bar or flat of 6 feet (probably a closer examination would discover a deeper pass); but with a 6 feet rise of tide in the sea of Okhotsk, or with a northerly wind, in fine weather, vessels under 12 feet draught might, there is little doubt, pass over it.

The RIVER AMÚR or Saghalin ula is formed of the streams Shilka and Argun, which unite in lat. 53° 30′ N. on the frontiers of Russia and China. The former of these consists of the Ingoda and Onon; the latter being the main stream which rises south-east of lake Baikal, in the mountain chain called Khing-khan ula by the Chinese, and Yablonoi Krebit by the Russians.

The river flows east as far as Nertchinsk, here it is said to be 600 yards wide, and very deep; then north, then again east, when it receives the Argun which comes from the south near Baksanova. The united streams, under the name of Amúr, continue to the east and south-east, receiving from the south the affluents Sungari and Usúri, and reaching its southern limit in 47° 48′ N., whence it turns abruptly to the north-east and east, falling into the gulf of Amúr between capes Prongé and Tabak, which are 8 miles apart. The length of the Amúr, including all its windings, is about 2,500 miles; it is navigable for large vessels as far as Nertchinsk, 1,500 miles from its mouth, in the summer season; in the winter it is frozen over.

The fortress of Nikolaevsk is built on the left bank of the river, at an elevation of about 50 feet above the sea, and at 22 miles from the entrance; it contains about 5,000 inhabitants, principally exiles; and the town is surrounded and defended by batteries and strong advanced works. Abreast the town the river is about 2 miles in width. The channels leading from the gulf to the anchorage are frequently changing, owing to the great débris sent down by the strong current of the river, and with the constant fogs, frequent squalls, and gales, would render the approach to them both difficult and dangerous were it not for the admirable way in which they are buoyed and beaconed.*

Supplies and assistance in the way of repairs are difficult to be obtained at Nikolaevsk. Provisions even cannot be had. Timber is plentiful, and the forests extend as far as the eye can reach, but the export of wood is strictly forbidden.

Owing to the vicinity of the sea of Okhotsk, with its masses of ice, and the easterly winds prevailing during spring, the seasons at Nikolaevsk are much more inclement than higher up the Amúr. Even at the commencement of September continued rains set in. October brings snow and cold, and at the end of the month or commencement of November the mouth of the river is frozen over. November, and the first half of December, are mostly clear; the temperature is low, the minimum being 39° Fahrenheit. At the latter part of December, and during January, severe snow storms, with westerly winds, render the communication between the different houses difficult, and even dangerous. The temperature during that time rises often above freezing point. The river navigation does not open before May, while snow and ice are to be found in the forests and more sheltered bays as late as June.

LIGHT.—A square wooden tower, 29 feet high, painted white, with gray lantern is erected on the western part of the battery, at the east end of Constantine island, in the Amúr, abreast Nikolaevsk. It exhibits at 40 feet above high water a *fixed* white light of the sixth order, visible in clear weather at 7 miles.

DIRECTIONS.—A vessel entering the gulf of Amúr from the strait of Tartary, should proceed with great caution and have an anchor ready at a moment's notice.

A Russian steam squadron, under the command of Admiral Kusnetsof, visited this gulf in September 1858, but they found that it could not be navigated safely without being buoyed and beaconed, and also that many alterations had taken place in the South channel leading to Nikolaevsk since the survey of 1854. In 1860 this channel was buoyed, and conspicuous wooden beacons erected on the land to guide through the different bends. The beacon buoys which carry flags may be passed on either side.

The intricate navigation commences off cape Suschef which lies N.E. ¾ E. distant 14 miles from Castries point; here the strait between capes Suschef

---

* *See* Plan of Amur river, Nos. 861 and 862; scale, m = 1·7 inches.

and Liak narrows to 17 miles, and is divided by an extensive bank called Fox bank, (which lies in a N.N.E. and S.S.E. direction, and is about 13 miles in length,) into two channels which unite again off cape Catherine. The south end of the Fox bank is marked by a buoy. The eastern channel is generally used, it being both wider and deeper than the channel East of the Fox bank.

From the buoy (R.W.V.S.) which lies in 4 fathoms, a course N.N.E. leads up to cape Catherine, and N.N.E. easterly to cape Nevelskoi. A buoy carrying a flag marks the position of the 6-feet patch lying north of the latter cape; passing this a course should be shaped to clear the flag off cape Muravief, passing the two flags which mark the 3-feet patch north of the cape, steering for the village of Pogobi until Ogbi island is just seen touching cape Lazaref, when steer for it; this mark clears the north side of the flat which extends between capes Muravief and Lazaref.

A flag marks the position of the 12-feet patch opposite Ogbi island, and a buoy with a flag the bank to the southward.

From this buoy to the buoy carrying a flag to the north-east of Chakmut island, keep the centre of the island west of Chomé island, in line with the centre of a gap formed by two hills, one on either side of the Tymi river. The west side of the channel up to Korsakof point is buoyed to mark the extensive flat extending from the mainland outside Hagemir islands. By passing these buoys, leaving them close-to on the port hand, the ship may be taken up to Korsakof point, from whence through the South channel the services of a pilot becomes necessary.*

TIDES.—At cape Lazaref the tide flows twice in the 24 hours, the rise is 5 feet, and the ebb runs $3\frac{1}{2}$ to 4 knots. Abreast of Chomé island, the rise is 4 feet, and the water remains at its highest level about fifty minutes. From cape Djaoré to cape Prongé, there appeared to be no regularity in the tidal action, it being greatly influenced by the winds. It was high water only once in 24 hours and the tide rose one foot with a southerly and 3 feet with a northerly wind.

During the few days H.M. ships were off the northern entrance of the gulf of Amúr in 1855–56, the greatest rise of tide observed was 5 feet. The current from the Amúr set to the N.N.E. over the banks, sometimes 3 knots per hour. At cape Korsakof the tides meet, H.W. along the coast varying from 10. 30 a.m. to 2 p.m.

SEA OF OKHOTSK.—This sea, surrounded as it is on all its northern and western sides by the continent, and to the south-east by the Kuril islands, may be considered as completely land-locked. A large portion of its shores is comparatively unknown, for with the exception of its single

---

* From the remark book of Navg. Lieut. F. K. Taylor, R.N., H.M.S. *Salamis*, 1868.

important port, from which it derives its name, we have no accurate description of its details.*

Whaling vessels frequent this sea from the beginning of July to the beginning of October, few, if any, being in it by the 10th October. The shores are covered with ice from November to April, but the main expanse continues open throughout the year, and being generally deep without any apparent danger, its navigation is safe, notwithstanding the fogs and storms with which it is often visited.

The western coast of Kamchatka is uniformly low and sandy to the distance of about 25 to 30 miles inland, when the mountains commence; it produces only willow, alder, and mountain ash, with some scattered patches of stunted trees. The soundings are shallow for a considerable distance off shore; nor is there at the entrance into any of the rivers more than 6 feet at low water, with a considerable surf breaking on the sandy beach. Those vessels that navigate this coast endeavour not to lose sight of it, and in foggy weather judge their distance from the land by the soundings, allowing a fathom for a mile.

CAUTION.—Sailing vessels should not approach capes Elizabeth (the north point of Saghalin island) and Mary, within 20 miles, to avoid the current (they are occasionally swept helplessly round North bay, between these capes, towards cape Elizabeth), and the winds are generally light and variable inshore when strong in the offing; by standing over to the Tartary coast the current is less, soundings are regular, and depth of water moderate, affording safe anchorage in case of calm or fog.

Care must also be observed in approaching the coasts of Saghalin and the shores of the sea of Okhotsk, their longitude in connexion with that of parts better ascertained being most probably erroneous.

The navigation to the northward of the gulf of Amúr during the summer months in unsurveyed waters where strong currents exist and thick fogs are so universal, is less dangerous than would at first appear, anchorage being commonly found when near the land, for a vessel to await the clearance of fog to ascertain her position.

SHANTARSKI ISLANDS lie off the eastern coast of the sea of Okhotsk, and although the largest island is 35 miles long, east and west, and about the same distance broad, yet it does not appear to afford any port or shelter; but its south-west point projects to the S.W. so as to form a bay on the eastern side. Between this point and the nearest point of the continent, 14 miles distant to the south-west, are two islets surrounded by rocks and reefs. Soundings of 30 to 40 fathoms, stones, will be found at 8 to 10 miles to the eastward of the group. The tides run from $1\frac{1}{4}$ to 2 knots an hour.

---

* *See* Chart of Sea of Okhotsk, No. 2,388; scale, $d = 2$ inches.

To the southward of the south points of great Shantar island are some small islands which have not been examined. At the distance of 6 miles from its west side is Feklistoff island, 20 miles in extent, N.E. and S.W., and 10 miles wide, but it has no port nor shelter.

ST. JONA ISLAND, in lat. 56° 22½′ N., long. 143° 15¾′ E., is merely a bare rock, about 2 miles in circumference, and 1,200 feet high, surrounded on all sides, except the west, by detached rocks, against which the waves beat with great violence, and which probably extend a considerable distance under water. With the island bearing North, distant 12 miles, Krusenstern had 15 fathoms water, but when it bore West about 10 miles, no bottom with 120 fathoms.

PORT AIAN, on the western coast of the sea of Okhotsk, may be recognised from the southward by cape Vneshni or Outer cape, a high barren promontory with several craggy peaks upon it, at a mile eastward of its eastern point of entrance. The coast in the neighbourhood is high and bold, and at 3 miles in the offing the soundings are 35 and 40 fathoms, sand.*

The inner part of the port is from one quarter to half a mile wide, and three-quarters of a mile deep, and affords good shelter for small vessels in 2 to 4 fathoms, muddy bottom. The outer part of the port is exposed to S.W. and southerly winds, which send in a heavy sea; it has depths of 8 to 12 fathoms over good holding ground. On the west side of the entrance is a reef of rocks with 4 fathoms close-to, barely covered at high water; the eastern shore is steep, and may be closely approached.

The climate here is abominable, and fogs are uninterrupted; the ice breaks up in June, and snow does not always disappear before August. The port is frozen over in November.

Supplies are scarce in port Aian and difficult to be obtained. To the southward of the entrance is a sandy bay in which the soundings appear to be regular, and where water may be conveniently procured. Scurvy is common and fatal among the inhabitants, but the wild rhubarb growing close to the sea in most parts of the harbour is of great service as an anti-scorbutic.

DIRECTIONS.—Vessels approaching port Aian should make the land to the southward of cape Vneshni, which is remarkably prominent; from that direction only can the entrance be seen, and with northerly winds the fog frequently lifts from 2 or 3 miles off shore to leeward of that headland, when it remains thick elsewhere. The high land of the peninsula should be avoided, on account of the calm it occasions. In the event

---

* See Plan of Port Aian on Chart of Sea of Okhotsk, No. 2,388.

of falling in with the land to the northward of the cape, Malminsk island, if seen, will guide to the harbour; but to judge from the appearance of the coast in that direction, as seen from the heights of Aian, it is not to be approached too closely. The tides at this port have not been as yet correctly ascertained, but their rise appears to be about 12 feet. A current set strong to the eastward, out of the harbour.

OKHOTSK HARBOUR, on the north-west side of this sea, is its principal port, but the shallowness of the water a long distance from the entrance, and the violence and cross set of the tides at the harbour's mouth, preclude the possibility of its being easily accessible, except for vessels of small draught. The mouth of the river Okhota has only 9 feet water, and is only accessible from June to September, being blocked up with snow and ice the remainder of the year.

The town stands on a narrow tongue of land at the mouths of the rivers Okhota and Kuktúi. It possesses a shipbuilder's yard, an hospital, and large storehouses. The population in 1842 amounted to 800. Not a tree, and hardly even a blade of grass, is to be seen within miles of the town, and a more dreary scene can scarcely be conceived. Summer consists of three months of damp and chilly weather, succeeded by nine months of dreary winter, as raw as it is intense. The principal food of the inhabitants is fish, which is also the staple food of the cattle and poultry. The sea of Okhotsk yields as much as fourteen varieties of salmon alone. Scurvy, in particular, rages here during the winter.

The SOUTH-EAST COAST OF KAMCHATKA.—Very little is known of the shores of this peninsula; from cape Lopatka, its southern point, to cape Shipunski, a distance of 180 miles, the shores are bordered by lofty mountains, some attaining an altitude of nearly 20,000 feet.

The coast from cape Lopatka trends in a N.E. ½ E. direction, 95 miles, to cape Piratkoff with few indentations, and no known anchorages. From the latter cape the coast deflects to the northward, forming between it and cape Shipunski the large bay of Avatcha, in the middle of which is the Russian settlement of Petropaulski.

AVATCHA BAY is formed at the bottom of the large outer bay of the same name on the south-east coast of the peninsula of Kamchatka. It is the principal port of the peninsula, and so extensive and excellent that it would afford secure shelter for all the fleets in the world. The channel leading to this bay is 4 miles long and 1 mile broad, and there is anchorage throughout its whole extent. It trends in a N. by W. direction, and when the wind is fair vessels may sail through by keeping in mid-channel; but it frequently happens that they have to beat in, and as the narrowness of the channel renders it necessary to stand as close to the dangers as possible, in order to lessen the number of tacks, it will be requisite to attend strictly to the leading marks.*

The extensive outer bay of Avatcha is between capes Povorotnoï and Shipunski, which are the best landfalls for making the port; for should a vessel, when off either of these capes, be overtaken by thick fogs or strong East or S.E. winds, it is always possible to keep the sea; whereas should the port be made on its parallel, and the vessel surprised by any contrariety, her situation would be precarious, there being no soundings on the coast, nor any anchorage which could be taken under such circumstances.

PETROPAULSKI.—The harbour of Petropaulski, on the eastern side of Avatcha bay, is small, deep, well shut in, and a convenient place for a refit of any kind. The town stands at the head of the harbour, in an amphitheatre on the slopes of two hills, which form the valley, and is composed of a group of small wooden houses, covered with reeds and dry grass, and surrounded by courts and gardens, with palisades. At the lower part of the town, in the valley, is the church, which is remarkable for its fantastic construction, and for its roof, which, painted green, seems to add considerably to the effect of the picture, surrounded as it is by lofty mountains. Tareinski harbour, in the south-west part of the bay, is extensive and excellent, but as there is neither population nor commerce in it, it has been of no utility. Rakovya harbour also forms, to the southward of Petropaulski, an equally excellent port, but it is of less easy access than the foregoing, on account of the Rakovya shoal, lying in the middle of its entrance.

The weather is frequently fine at Petropaulski up to the 15th October; but after this period it is wet, and the land begins to be covered with snow, which becomes permanent, and does not disappear until May or June in the ensuing year. In November, December, and January, violent storms are experienced.

During winter the cold is severe; the snow falls in abundance far from common, and frequently rises as high as the houses, which thus become buried until the return of spring; but whatever may be the intensity of the cold, it is rare that the roadstead is entirely frozen over; the ice does not generally extend more than a cable's length off shore; and after bad weather, occasioned by winds from seaward, as well as those from West and North, it becomes detached from the land, and is carried out into the road. One of the most severe winters remembered was that of 1814, when the road was almost entirely blocked up. In ordinary winters the coves, bays, and rivers are only covered, and the ice is not always too thick to hinder a passage by breaking or cutting.

---

* *See* Charts: Sea of Okhotsk, No. 2,388, scale, $d = 2$ inches; Avatcha bay, with Plan of Petropaulski harbour, No. 1,040, scale, $m = 1$ inch; and Avatcha outer bay, No. 1,041, scale, $m = 0.2$ inch.

Supplies.—A vessel in need of repair will only find safe anchorage in Avatcha bay, and must depend on her own resources both for provisions and workmen; it is, however, possible to procure in urgent cases some slight aid from the government stores, and some workmen of the port; but these assistances, besides being limited, are precarious. Wood and water are easily obtained. A supply of fresh beef may be procured, and a little fresh butter, but it is difficult to get poultry or eggs. Fish is abundant in the bay in the season; it begins with cod and herrings, and is followed by salmon and salmon trout.

LIGHTS.—There are three *fixed* white lights exhibited at the entrance of Avatcha bay, at 449, 294, and 378 feet respectively above the level of the sea. The first, on the eastern point of entrance, is visible at 21 miles; the second, on the inner point on west side of entrance, at 9 miles; and the other, on the signal station, about half a mile south of the entrance to Rakovya harbour, is visible at 9 miles.

TIDES.—It is high water, full and change, in Petropaulski harbour at 3h. 30m.; springs rise $6\frac{3}{4}$ feet; neaps $4\frac{1}{4}$ feet.

DIRECTIONS.—A sailing vessel bound to Avatcha bay from the southward should make the coast well south of cape Povorotnoï, and round it as close as possible, as the wind will in all probability veer to the northward on passing it. If the weather be clear, two mountains will be seen to the west and north-west of the cape, and one far off to the northward and eastward. The eastern one of the two former, mount Villeuchinski, 7,372 feet high, is in lat. 52° 42′ N., long. 158° 20′ E., and peaked like a sugar-loaf. Mount Avatcha, the highest and most northern of the three, is 11,554 feet high, and may be seen in clear weather a very considerable distance. To the eastward of this peak, and close to it, is the Roselskoï volcano, but it emits but little smoke.

These peaks are the best guides to Avatcha bay, until near enough to distinguish the entrance, which will then appear to be between two perpendicular cliffs. Upon the eastern one of these, the lighthouse bluff, there are a hut and signal staff. If the entrance of the bay be open a large rock, called Baboushka, will be seen on the western side of the channel, and three others, named Brothers, on the eastern side.

The outer dangers are, a reef of rocks lying S.E., about 2 miles from the lighthouse bluff, and a reef lying off a bank which connects Stanitski point with the point to the southward of it. To avoid the lighthouse reef, do not shut in the land to the northward of the lighthouse bluff, unless certain of being $2\frac{1}{2}$ miles off shore, and when within three-quarters of a mile only, tack when the lighthouse bluff bears North, or N. $\frac{1}{2}$ E.; the Brothers rock in line with the lighthouse, leads close to the edge of the reef.

The first danger on the western shore has a rock above water upon it, and may be avoided by not opening Baboushka rock with the point beyond, with a flagstaff upon it. In standing towards this rock, take care that the ebb tide in particular does not set the vessel upon it. A good working mark for all this western shore is the Baboushka open with Direction bluff, the *last* hill on the *left* upon the low land at the head of Avatcha bay. The bay south of Stanitski point is filled with rocks and foul ground. The lighthouse reef is connected with the Brothers, and the lighthouse bluff must not be approached in any part within half a mile, nor the Brothers within a full cable's length. There are no good marks for the exact limit of this reef off the Brothers, and vessels must estimate that short distance; they must also, in beating through this channel, allow for shooting in stays, and for the tides, which ebb and flood, sweep over towards these rocks, running S.E. and N.E. Good way should also be kept on the vessel, as the eddy tides may otherwise prevent her staying.

To the northward of the Brothers, two-thirds of the distance between them and a ragged cape, named Pinnacle point, there are some rocks nearly awash; and off the point there is a small reef, one of the outer rocks of which dries at half-tide. These dangers can always be seen; their outer edges lie nearly in line, and they may be approached to one cable's length. If they are not seen, do not shut in the Rakovya signal bluff. There is deeper water outside the dangers off Pinnacle point than in mid-channel, and the soundings are irregular.

When northward of Stanitski point, the Baboushka rock may be opened to the eastward a little with the signal staff bluff, but be careful of a shoal which extends about 3 cables south of the Baboushka. The Baboushka has no danger to the eastward, at a greater distance than a cable's length; and when it is passed, there is nothing to fear on the western shore, until N.N.W. of the signal staff bluff, off which there is a long shoal with only 2 and $2\frac{1}{2}$ fathoms on it. The soundings shoal gradually towards it, and the helm may be safely put down in $4\frac{3}{4}$ fathoms; but a certain guide is not to open the west extreme of the Baboushka with Stanitski point.

When the vessel is one cable's length north of Pinnacle reef, she can stand into Ismennai bay, guided by the soundings, which are regular, taking care to avoid a 3-fathoms knoll, lying half-way between Pinnacle point and the second cliff north of it. This bay affords good anchorage, and it may be convenient to anchor in for a tide; there is no danger but the 3-fathoms knoll, and the Ismennai rock may be passed at a cable's length. This rock is connected with Ismennai point by a reef, and in standing towards it, Pinnacle point must be kept open of the light-house bluff (when in line the depth is only $3\frac{1}{2}$ fathoms); Rakovya signal staff in line with the bluff south of it, will place a vessel in 5 fathoms water close to the rocks.

A small reef extends a full cable's length from Ismennai point, and until this is passed do not shut in Pinnacle point with the lighthouse bluff; but to the northward of it a vessel may stand to about one cable's length of the bluffs.

Northward of Rakovya signal staff the only danger is the Rakovya shoal, upon the west part of which there is a buoy in summer, and to clear this keep the Brothers in sight. There is no good mark for determining when the vessel is northward of this rocky shoal, which has only $4\frac{1}{4}$ feet least water on it, and as the tides in their course up to Rakovya harbour will be apt to set her towards it, keep the Brothers open, until it is certain, by the distance, of having passed it (its northern edge is nearly 9 cables from Rakovya bluff), particularly as the vessel may now stretch well to the westward, and as there is nothing to obstruct her up to the anchorage. Rakovya harbour will afford good security to a vessel when running in from sea with a southerly gale, at which time she might find difficulty in bringing up at the usual anchorage. In this case the Rakovya shoal must be left to the northward; 5 and $5\frac{1}{2}$ fathoms will be close upon the edge of it, but the water must not be shoaled under 9 fathoms.

In entering Petropaulski harbour it is only necessary to guard against a near approach to the signal staff on the end of the peninsula on the western side of entrance, named Shackoff point. In approaching this point, on which there is a battery, a white buoy will be seen, marking the extremity of a bank, extending S.S.E. nearly a quarter of a mile from high-water mark, and having 3 fathoms on its extreme point.* Keep the south end of the cemetery N.E. until the church of Petropaulski appears in the centre of the valley; this mark leads to the southward of the shoal in 6 fathoms, or the buoy may be passed close to, leaving it to the westward, and from thence steer for the end of a low sandy point which projects at an angle of 45° from the direction of the coast, and nearly closes the bottom of the bay, forming it into an excellent natural harbour. This tongue of land, like an artificial causeway, is but little above the level of the sea, and is covered with huts raised on piles above the ground, serving to dry fish. This point may be passed close to.

A sailing vessel leaving the harbour with light winds and with the beginning of the ebb, must guard against being swept down upon the Rakovya shoal, and when past it upon the signal bluff. There are strong eddies all over this bay, and when the winds are light, vessels often become unmanageable. It will be better to weigh with the last drain of flood.

---

* Valentine G. Roberts, Master, R.N., H.M.S. *President*, 1855.

CHAPTER IV.

MARIANA OR LADRONE ISLANDS; ISLANDS SOUTH-EAST OF JAPAN.—MEIACO SIMA, LIU-KIU AND LINSCHOTEN GROUPS.

VARIATION IN 1872.

Mariana Islands 2° to 3° E. | Liu-kiu and Linschoten Islands 2° to 3° W.
Islands in the Western Pacific lying south-east of Japan, 1° E. to 1° W.

MARIANA or LADRONES ISLANDS.*—This archipelago is composed of a chain of volcanic islands, which extend in a north and south direction from lat. 13° 12′ N. to lat. 20° 32′ N. over a space of 420 miles. Magalhaens, the first circumnavigator, discovered them on March 6th 1521, but he only saw Saipan, Tinian, and Guam. The Spaniards, who colonized them, named them Ladrones, from the great propensity to thieving evinced by the natives, and this name they retained until 1668, when they received the name of Mariana, in honour of Maria Anna of Austria, the widow of Philip IV. King of Spain.

The whole archipelago is divided into three groups.

The southern consists of the islands of Guam, Rota, Aguigan, Tinian, and Saipan. These are the larger islands, and are of moderate height, but less mountainous than the remainder, and at present are the only inhabited islands of the Mariana group.

The central group consists of the Farallon de Medinilla, Anatajan, Sariguan, Guguan, and Pagan. These are a collection of large rocky islets rather than islands, in some of which the volcanoes are extinct; in the two latter, however, they are active.

The northern group consisting of Agrigan Assumption, Urracas, and Farallon de Pajaros, are merely volcanic cones, of which the last only is active.

GUAM (Guajan), the southernmost and largest as well as most populous island of the Mariana group, is about 29 miles long N.E. by N. and S.W. by S.; its greatest breadth is about 10 miles, narrowing to 3 miles near the centre. It is bordered throughout a greater part of its circuit by a chain of reefs, which are uncovered at times. It contained, in 1858,† a

---

* The description of these islands is principally from the Anuario de la Direccion de Hidrografia, año. 3, 1865. *See* chart:—Pacific Ocean, sheet 5, No. 2,463, scale $d = 0.5$ of an inch; and Islands between Formosa and Japan, No. 2,412; Mariana or Ladrone Islands, with plans, No. 1,101, scale various.

† Captain N. Vansittart, H.M.S. *Magicienne*, July 1858.

population of about 4,000 persons, and there was a plentiful supply of water and fresh provisions.

At a distance this island will appear flat and even. There is no anchorage on its east side, which is bordered with steep rocks, against which the sea dashes with great violence. The north side of the island is rather low, the small hill of Santa Rosa being the only elevation, but to the southward it is more mountainous. The west side is full of small sandy bays, divided with as many rocky points. The soil is reddish, dry, and indifferently fruitful. The produce is chiefly rice, pine-apples, water melons, oranges and limes, cocoa-nuts, and bread-fruit. The cocoa-nut trees grow on the western side in extensive groves, 3 or 4 miles long and 1 or 2 miles broad.

PAGO HARBOUR.—The eastern coast of Guam, as far southward as Tarofofo harbour in lat. 13° 18′ 12″ N., affords no shelter, and therefore ought to be avoided during the N.E. monsoon. The only openings are Pago harbour, in lat. 13° 24½′ N., accessible only for boats, and Ylic bay, 2 miles to the southward, and equally unimportant.

TAROFOFO HARBOUR, 4½ miles south of Ylic bay, is the only port, next to San Luis d'Apra, that will receive a vessel at all seasons of the year; there are no rocks in it, nor is there any danger. It is formed of two inlets, the northern of which, Tarofofo, about a third of a mile wide, is open to the east, in which direction it is 1½ miles long; the other is smaller, and called Paicpouc cove. The Tarofofo river, the most considerable in Guam, enters the head of the harbour, and the Madreporic hills, very steep, rise abruptly from both its sides; The Mahilouc, on the north side, are celebrated in the history of the country. There is no village near this locality.

HOUNLODGNA, YNARAJAN, and AGFAYAN BAYS.—From Tarofofo to Hounlodgna bay, 1¼ miles to the south-west, the land is low, with sandy beaches and rocky points; this bay is only fit for boats.

Ynarajan bay, at a mile farther to the south-west, is a quarter of a mile wide at entrance, and half a mile deep, but the reefs fringing the shore considerably contract the anchorage; this bay is open from East to South. A vessel would be quite safe in it during westerly winds, but not with winds from the opposite quarter. The town of Ynarajan stands on its south-west side, and at the head of the bay are several streams.

Agfayan bay, at three-quarters of a mile farther south-west, is much smaller than the latter bay; it may have good anchorage for vessels of less than 15 feet draught, but it is open to the E.N.E. At its head is a small brook, where boats can easily obtain water.

UMATA BAY, about 1¾ miles northward of the south-west point of Guam, is one-third of a mile deep, east and west, and three cables wide at its entrance. The bay is sheltered from North (round East) to South, but in the season of westerly winds, or from June to September, it would be imprudent, or perhaps impossible, to remain in it, on account of the heavy swell which sets on the shores.

Tougouéne point, the narrow, low, south point of entrance to this bay, has a reef projecting nearly 2 cables from it to the westward; a little north of this point is the fort of Neustra Señora de la Soledad. The north point of entrance is an isolated and picturesque rock with a fort (San Angel) on it, which is approached by steps cut in the rock. These fortresses are little more than ruins, and have no guns.

The south shore is mountainous to the head of the bay, where the river Umata or Saloupa enters the sea, and where a church is built at the foot of the mountains. The town (or what remains of it) stands on the north shore, which is low, and was destroyed by an earthquake on the 25th January 1849. The present village consists only of a few huts, a small church, and the Governor's house, and a mass of ruins. Behind the town the hills rise in an amphitheatre, and are neither high nor remarkable. Excellent water can be obtained from a rivulet which flows into the sea on the south shore, between mount Inago and the hill on which fort Soledad is situated.

The whole of the island is cleared and partly under cultivation, and wood is difficult to procure.

ANCHORAGE may be had in $7\frac{1}{2}$ fathoms (sand and shells) with fort San Angel bearing N.N.E .$\frac{1}{2}$ E., and fort Soledad S.E. by E. $\frac{1}{2}$ E.

PORT SAN LUIS D'APRA.—From Umata bay the west coast of Guam trends N.N.W. 3 miles to Facpi point, and has several sinuosities, the deepest of which is Cetti bay, as large as that of Umata. Facpi point is remarkable for being pointed, projecting, and terminating in an isolated rock joined to the shore by a reef uncovered at low water. From hence to Oroté point, 6 miles to the N.N.W., the coast falls back 2 miles, and forms a bay, in which are several coves and islets.*

Oroté point is the extremity of a narrow peninsula, projecting $3\frac{1}{2}$ miles N.W. by W. from the coast, and which cannot be traversed on account of the number of large rocks and precipices which cover it. A small islet lies close to the north side of the point, and from it the north coast of the peninsula trends E. by S. and S.E. by S. to the village of Apra, which is built on the isthmus connecting the peninsula to the main land. From thence it bends round to the East and North, forming a deep indentation, named port San Luis d'Apra, the opening to which is nearly closed by a long narrow island, named Apapa or Cabras, the Luminan reefs, and the Calalan bank.

---

* *See* Plan of Port San Luis D'Apra, on sheet No. 1,107; scale, $m = 2$ in.

This port is extensive and safe, but is much encumbered with numerous banks, rocks, and islets. The usual entrance is northward of the islet lying close to Oroté point, by a deep channel a third of a mile wide, between that islet and the west end of the Calalan bank; but this end of the bank must be given a wide berth, as a shoal spot named Spanish rock lies half a mile from the north point of Oroté island, which may be passed at about 2 cables. There is a channel, of $5\frac{1}{2}$ fathoms water, between the east end of this bank and the Luminan reefs, but it should not be used without buoys. In the centre of the port is a rock level with the water, on which fort Santa Cruz is built. The general anchorage is about 2 cables north of this fort, in a space carrying 5 to 15 fathoms, muddy bottom, surrounded by coral patches 2 or 3 feet below water. Some of the channels leading to this anchorage are narrow; the last before entering is not more than 120 yards wide; but the patches are steep-to, and may be approached almost to touching. Landing is very inconvenient, the shore being everywhere fringed with reefs which extend a considerable distance from it, alternating in rocky heads and deep holes. These islets and reefs are of coral formation.

The watering-place is at a small river which falls into the port at three-quarters of a mile from Santa Cruz fort. The casks are usually filled at low tide, and the boats sent at high water to bring them off.

The COAST from the east point of port San Luis d'Apra trends E.N.E. $1\frac{1}{2}$ miles to a perpendicular rocky point, named Acahi-Fanahi, near to which is Gapan islet. At $1\frac{1}{2}$ miles eastward of this islet is Adeloup point, better known to the inhabitants as Punta del Diablo, on account of the rapidity of the currents, which makes it difficult to be doubled. From hence a sandy beach commences, which trends to the east and north, forming Agaña bay,* in the middle of which is the harbour of Agaña, only fit for small craft.

From Agaña bay the north-west coast of Guam is of steep rocks. At $1\frac{1}{2}$ miles north-east of Agaña is Tumun bay, which appears filled with reefs, but there are several passages through them, where boats can reach the shore without difficulty. Near the middle of the coast of this bay is the village of Gnaton. From hence the coast is barren and uninhabited.

Point Ritidian.—A short distance inland from Ritidian point, the north extreme of Guam, the perpendicular hills form, scarcely without interruption, the circuit of the island. In the middle of the north face of the island, between Ritidian point and Patay North point, there is a bay, but it is fronted with coral reefs from the last-mentioned point as far as point Ritidian, where the coast is steep.

---

* See **Plan of Agaña bay**; scale, $m = 2\cdot 67$ inches on Sheet No. 1,107.

The eastern side of the island, southward of Patay East point (the north-east point of the island), is rugged and steep, and there is no shelter northward of port Tarofofo during the north-east monsoon.

Supplies.—Cattle, pigs, fowls, ducks, turkeys, and pea fowl are bred; and vegetables, fruit, and wild birds in great variety are plentiful, as is also fish.

SOUTH END of GUAM.—Ajayan point, the south-east extreme of Guam, forms the eastern side of Ajayan bay, which is so obstructed by reefs that it is dangerous of approach if there is much sea on. The south end of Guam is an uninterrupted sandy beach fronted by a reef, with two or three small islands on it. This reef, after encircling Bali and Cocos islands, lying $2\frac{1}{2}$ miles from the south-west extreme of Guam, trends the same distance to the northward to the south-west point of Guam, where is the small harbour of Merizo, only fit for boats.

Santa Rosa shoal (position doubtful), of which no description has ever been given, is said to be in lat. 12° 30′ N., long. 144° 15′ E. A Spanish galleon is said to have struck on it, and to have lost her rudder. Dampier, when approaching the south end of Guam, in 1686, sailed over a rocky shoal of 4 fathoms water.

Galvez bank (position doubtful).—Galvez also, in 1740, discovered a bank lying about 20 miles from the south-west end of Guam in lat. 13° N.; it is probably the same as the Santa Rosa. The *Narvaez* passed very close to its assigned position, but saw nothing of it. Great caution, however, should be observed when in this locality, as the uncertainty of the positions of these shoals renders it doubly necessary.

The Channel between Guam and Rota (the next island to the northward) is 30 miles in width, and clear of known dangers.

ROTA, bearing N.N.E. $\frac{1}{2}$ E., 30 miles from the north end of Guam, is 12 miles long (N.E. by E. and S.W. by W.), and $5\frac{1}{2}$ miles broad; its highest part is about 600 feet above the sea. Its east and centre portions are hilly, but the land becomes lower to the south-west, to a low sandy isthmus on which the villages of Sosanlago and Sosanhaya are built; they contain about eighty houses and huts. To the south-west of this isthmus is the south-west point, a hill terminating in a level and regular plateau. Some cattle, pigs, cocoa-nuts, bread-fruit, bananas, and a few other vegetables, constitute the entire riches of the island. Three wells furnish the inhabitants with water; two of them are artificial and the water bad; the third, which is natural, affords better, though it is brackish. On the east coast of the island, at 5 miles from the villages, there is a rivulet of very good water.

The mountain summit is said to be a volcanic crater, but it has not been active for several centuries, and is now covered with an impenetrable growth of bushes and underwood.

Numerous monuments of rudely cut stone mark the burial places of the original inhabitants of the island before the Chamorros occupied it.

The south-east end of the island is tolerably high and perpendicular on the sea shore, presenting thus a straight wall, and at its angles vertical fissures like the embrasures of a fort. In other parts the land descends gradually to the sea, terminating in long and low points. The portion of the island not inhabited is so encumbered with bushes that it is difficult to penetrate; on the north side there are some cocoa-nut trees.

Rota is nearly surrounded by reefs. Its north-east coast and the south-east side of the isthmus are bordered with numerous rocks, on which the sea breaks more or less, according to the direction of the wind.

Sosanhaya bay, 4 miles wide and 2 miles deep, is formed between the the south and south-west points of the island, in which vessels can find good shelter from northerly winds; but the bottom, being coral, is very foul. The shore cannot be approached, and if wishing to land it must be on the west side of the isthmus, where a sort of stage or jetty makes an easy access for boats.

ANCHORAGE may be had in Sosanlago bay, but it is very bad, in fact, the worst in the whole Mariana group; the depth is very irregular, the bottom being patches of sand and coral alternating, and the vessel when at anchor is so near the breakers as to render it very unsafe.

The channel through the reefs requires the assistance of a pilot, and extreme caution is necessary.

Supplies may be had in moderate quantities either in exchange for money or clothes, tools, nails, &c., &c.; there is a great deficiency of water.

AGUIJAN ISLAND, 44 miles N.N.E. from Rota, is not more than 3 miles long and 2 miles wide. At its north part are high, perpendicular, and nearly naked rocks, except at their summits, which are crowned with thick wood. The only points fit for landing are on the west and north-west sides, where there are some small creeks bordered by sandy beaches. The coasts of the island appear clear of danger, with the exception of a rock lying a mile off its south-west point. Goats are numerous, but it is uninhabited.

The channel between Aguijan and Rota is clear of known dangers.

TINIAN ISLAND, separated from Aguijan by a channel 5 miles wide, is 10 miles long, north and south, and 4½ miles broad. It was celebrated, in Anson's voyage in 1742; he arrived here with his crew suffering from scurvy, and spoke of its healthy and dry soil, the beauty of its meadows, and its diversified woods, lawns, valleys, and hills, abounding with herds of thousands of cattle, guanacoes, wild hogs, wild fowl, guavas, cocoa-nuts, limes, oranges, and bread-fruit. Later navigators have not given its description in such glowing colours. Instead of valleys and lawns, the trees were thick and almost impenetrable, the land overgrown with a stubborn reed or rush, the climate insufferably hot, the water scarce and bad, the plague of fleas intolerable, and swarms of scorpions, centipedes, large black ants, and other venomous insects without number; all the refreshments, however, mentioned above could be obtained. Not a long time previous to Anson's visit the island had been depopulated by the Spaniards. In 1819 there were not more than twenty inhabitants on it.

Sunharon roads is the only anchorage for large ships, and was formerly called Anson road; it is on the south-west shore of Tinian, abreast the village of Sunharon, which consists of half-a-dozen houses inhabited by about 20 persons who come periodically from Guam to kill the wild cattle, which are numerous. The village is in lat. 14° 59′ N., long. 145° 36′ E. This road, however, being open to the westward, and the bottom full of pointed coral rocks, cannot be recommended as an anchorage, particularly between the months of June and October, during the season of the western monsoon. From the middle of October to the middle of June the weather is settled and the road secure. H.M.S. *Centurion* anchored here, however, from 27th August till the end of October 1742, about 1½ miles off shore, abreast a sandy bay, in 22 fathoms, on a bottom of hard sand and coral, with the two extremes of the island bearing N.W.¼N. and S.E.¼E. the centre of Aguijan S.S.W., the peak of Saipan seen over the northern part of Tinian N.N.E.½E., and a reef of rocks lying between the vessel and the shore E. by S.¾S. The anchoring bank is shelving, and free from danger, except a reef lying about half a mile off shore, and affording a narrow passage into the small sandy bay, which is the only place the boats can land.*

Water may be obtained from an ancient well near the anchorage.

The channel between Tinian and Saipan is but little known, and should be used with great caution, if attempted at all.

SAIPAN ISLAND, three miles north-east of Tinian, may be recognised by its lofty peak, which has been estimated at 2,000 feet above the sea. This peak which is conical in form is an extinct volcano; about 2 or 3 miles northward of it is another extinct crater of considerable elevation. It is generally visited† annually by three or four whalers, which anchor off its north-west side, outside a long reef extending in a southerly direction from the north-west part of the island towards the north part of Tinian; there is, however, a passage through this reef off the north-west part of the island, near a small island, with anchorage inside for several vessels.

---

* See Plan of Tinian Bay, No. 1,102; scale, $m = 0·75$ of an inch.

† Captain N. Vansittart, C.B., and John W. H. Harvey, Master R.N., H.M.S. *Magicienne*, July 1858.

The inhabitants stated that there was no passage up inside the reef, although it extends a long distance off shore from the south-west end of Saipan; but that there is a ship channel between the north end of Tinian and the south end of Saipan and reef.

Garapan, the only village on Saipan, is on its north-west side. It is ruled by a man appointed from Guam, and inhabited by old and young settlers, and natives, and in 1864 contained in all about 400 persons. The natives for the most part are fine young men from the Caroline islands; they are quiet, and in a state of nudity, with the exception of a narrow slip of cotton round the lower part of their bodies. These people have cleared the greater part of the island, and have it well under cultivation; the men are also capital sailors and pilots.

ANCHORAGE.—During the season of the north-east trade winds, a vessel may lie at the anchorage off Garapan, but during the south-west monsoon she will be in considerable danger. The *Narvaez* anchored in 14 fathoms (rock and sand) Mañgasa islet, west point, N. 11° E., east point N. 14° E. The principal house in the village, N. 68° E., Tinian island (north-west point) S. 24° W.

A boat channel, which is buoyed with trunks of trees, leads through the reefs from the anchorage to the village.

TANAPAG HARBOUR, on the north-west coast of Saipan, between it and the island of Mañgasa, is formed by coral reefs, in the same manner as that of San Luis D'Apra, in Guam, which it approaches in size, but is free from the numerous shoals and reefs found at that port. It is sheltered from south-west winds, and appears free of danger; the channel leading in is narrow, and has several scattered rocky heads in it, but when in the harbour, is a snug and safe anchorage; it has not been examined closely, but is probably one of, if not the best anchorage in the whole of the Mariana islands.

MAGICIENNE BAY.—H.M.S. *Magicienne,* on her passage from the Sandwich islands to Hong Kong, July 1858, having lost the N.E. trades in long. 156° 38′ E., and being short of fuel, steered for Saipan island, and anchored on its south-east side in Magicienne bay, in lat. 15° 8½′ N., long. 145° 44′ E.*

This bay cannot be recommended to a sailing vessel, as the water is deep, and the anchorage so close to a coral reef bordering its shore, that with a southerly wind there would be no room to weigh. The depth is 30 fathoms, over coral with sandy patches, at only a third of a mile from the bluff at the head of the bay, decreasing rapidly to 3 fathoms close alongside the coral reef, which nearly dries at low water. The *Magicienne*

---

* See Sketch of Magicienne Bay on No. 1,101; scale, $m = 2\frac{1}{2}$ inches.

anchored in 18 fathoms, with the south-west point of the bay S. ½ E. about 2½ miles; the south-east point, which is a bluff, E.S.E. 1¼ miles; and a wooded bluff at the head of the bay, N.N.W. ½ W. nearly 3½ cables. When the vessel swung to the shore, there were 9 fathoms, coral patches, under her stern, and she was distant only 1 cable's length from the reef; at 1 cable southward of her anchor there was no bottom at 70 fathoms. The bay is well protected, being open only from E.S.E. to South. During the few days the vessel remained in it, the wind was light from the S.E. during the day, and at night a light air from the land between N.E. and N.W. The best place for landing is on the sandy beach eastward of the wooded bluff at the head of the bay.

Supplies.—There is no water at Saipan, except what is caught during the rains, and the rainy season in August, September, and October. Cocoa-nuts, bread-fruit, and limes are plentiful; there are also many wild pigs and bullocks—the latter belong to the Spanish government. Pigs, poultry, and fruit can be obtained at the village of Garapan.

Wood grows on the shores of Magicienne bay, sufficient to supply any number of vessels, being for the most part the thickness of a man's body, white when cut, and in substance something between a bad ash and a poplar. The crew of the *Magicienne* cut down and brought on board 172 fathoms in six days, the wood growing close to the beach, and easily carried to the boats, which could lie afloat close to the reef.

The wood soon dried, but being freshly cut, it was necessary to split and bark it on board before using it for steaming purposes, also to use a small quantity of coal with it; the bark was very sappy. The wood being free of resinous substances, did not give out so much heat as might have been expected; three and a half fathoms of it being only equal to one ton of good Welsh coal.

TIDES.—It was high water, full and change, in Magicienne bay, at 6h. 45m., and the rise was about 2½ feet.

FARALLON de MEDINILLA, or Bird island, is in lat. 15° 59½′ N., long. 146° 0½′ E., distant about 41 miles N.N.E. of the north end of Saipan. It is flat, barren, and with perpendicular sides, is 2 miles long (N.E. and S.W.), and its breadth is much less. It is of volcanic origin, and on its highest part there are vestiges of a crater, but the island is destitute of vegetation. On the south and west sides are some deep caverns or grottos. The south point is terminated by a small hill, which appeared to be joined to the island by a narrow neck of land.*

---

* The *Narvaez* passed along both sides of this island, and this hummock was carefully looked for but could not be seen; the connexion was entire at every point, and all of the same height.

ANATAJAN ISLAND, at 27 miles north-west of the Farallon de Medinilla, is about 5 miles long (east and west), and rather more than 1½ miles wide; it has two high and steep peaks, which are volcanic, and have been seen in clear weather upwards of 40 miles.

The coast is everywhere steep and precipitous except on the south side, where there is a small sandy beach, and some projecting rocks form a small creek. There is no safe anchorage owing to the great depth until close to the shore; there may, however, be anchorage in some other part, as the island was inhabited when it was discovered by the Spaniards. The island is covered with trees and bushes, amongst which is the cocoa-nut palm.

SARIGUAN ISLAND, to the N.N.E. and distant 18 miles from Anatajan, appears to be merely a high rock of the form of an upright cone, with nearly a circular base, 1½ miles in diameter. Its summit is rounded; is well covered with vegetation, and seems to be of volcanic origin. It is uninhabited.

ZEALANDIA BREAKERS* (Piedras de Torres), were reported by the ship *Zealandia*, December 1858, when steering to pass between Sariguan and Guguan, observed two patches of breakers right ahead, distant about three-quarters of a mile. At 4h. 20m. Sariguan bore S. by W. ½ W. about 11 or 12 miles, when the breakers were in line with the island, and distant half a mile from the ship; this would place them in about lat. 16° 50′ N., long. 145° 50′ E. The two patches, which at times broke heavily, lie N. by E. and S. by W. about a quarter of a mile apart, and have dark water between and around them. The wind was light and easterly, but the lateness of the day and the unsettled state of the weather did not permit a close examination. These rocks were on Espinosas' chart, but were expunged after the voyage of the *Uranie* in 1819, when Guguan was then mistaken for them and named Farallon de Torres, which name it retained until visited by the *Narvaez* in 1865. This shoal was not seen, but from information obtained from the natives its position is approximately correct. From the uncertainty of its position this reef should be passed with the utmost caution, for in fine weather it might not be seen until the ship was upon it.

GUGUAN ISLAND, lying northward about 36 miles from Sariguan, is a small island, 2½ miles long (N.N.E. and S.S.W.), about 1 mile broad, of moderate height, and much resembles the Farallon de Medinilla. Its north point is the lowest, but presents no facilities for landing, and it is perpendicular and unapproachable on all sides. The whole is covered with vegetation.

---

* Mercantile Marine Magazine, September 1859, p. 284.

ALAMAGAN, one of the highest islands in this archipelago, bears North, and is distant 16½ miles from Guguan. It is 2¼ miles long (north and south), and has two peaks, the highest of which is estimated to be about 2,000 feet above the sea. To the south and east the slope of the hills is extremely rapid, and the rock, which descends to the sea, is composed of lava and completely destitute of vegetation. On the north-east side of the island there is a large extinct crater, half a mile across; being on the slope of the mountain it is seen from seaward, and shows as a large elliptical opening below the north peak. When the island is seen, bearing between south and west, the interior of this immense extinct crater is fully exposed to view. The western side of the mountain is traversed from its summit to base by deep ravines, full of dark coloured vegetation, which is especially abundant in the lower parts of the ravines, causing the island when viewed from a distance to appear clothed in green in stripes. The north side is not quite so steep as the south. The highest point on the north side is a vast crater, from which large volumes of smoke have been seen to issue.

PAGAN ISLAND, about 25 miles North of Alamagan, is about 8 miles long (N.E. and S.W.), and 2½ miles wide. Its extremes being high, with a valley between, it appears when seen from a distance like two or three separate islands. Pagan has three active volcanoes on it, one on its north-west, the others on its south-west end. Tropical vegetation, in spite of the volcanoes, reaches nearly to the summit of the two latter, but the sides of the former are nearly destitute of any. This island is celebrated among the Marianas on account of the treasure which was supposed to be concealed there.

ANCHORAGE is bad, entirely rocky, with little or no shelter. The *Narvaez* anchored off the north-west coast, which, near the middle of the island, forms a small cove. There is a large rock on the beach, which when seen from seaward appears like an islet. Landing is very difficult, as the surf breaks heavily on the steep beach in the finest weather. The southern shores are still more exposed than the northern, but anchorage probably might be found near three high pinnacle rocks lying off the south-east point.

AGRIGAN ISLAND, N. by W. ½ W., 41 miles from Pagan, is about 6 miles long (N.W. and S.E.), and 2½ miles wide, and on it are two high peaks, estimated to be about 1,400 feet above the sea. Agrigan is of volcanic origin, but presents no signs of an extinct crater; the surface is covered with vegetation from the shores to summits, and the soil is very fertile.

ANCHORAGE may be found on the south-west side of this island in front of a small sandy beach, the only one in the island. The anchorage is very limited, as the rest of the coast is steep, to near this bank, and has from 16 to 11 fathoms sandy bottom, the former depth being obtained at about 4 cables from the shore. The *Narvaez* anchored in 11 fathoms with the following bearing, S.W. point of Agrigan N. 24° W.; South point of the same island S. 64° E. Landing is very difficult owing to the steepness of the beach and the heavy surf.

Supplies.—The *Narvaez* left on the island numerous animals of various kinds, and vessels will find furnished huts and outbuildings, domestic animals, &c., &c., besides pigs, goats, fowls, &c.

Cocoa-nuts, plantains, and other tropical fruit are in abundance.

ASSUMPTION ISLAND, called also Asuncion, is 54 miles N. by W. from Agrigan. It is a remarkable object, being a perfect volcanic cone rising abruptly from the sea to the height of about 2,600 feet. At its summit is a large crater, and it is probably not extinct; the sides of the mountain are covered with ashes a considerable distance down; the remainder is covered with lava, which has formed in its course steep ravines. These are bordered with a few stunted cocoa-nut trees very scattered, and thick impenetrable underwood.

ANCHORAGE.—La Pérouse anchored at this island in 30 fathoms, but the *Narvaez* could find no bottom at this depth anywhere round the island. In clear weather both this island and Agrigan can be seen about 45 miles off.

URRACAS ISLANDS are a rocky group lying N.N.W. ½ W. 22 miles from Assumption, in lat. 20° 7′ N., long. 145° 20′ E. They consist of three islets, of which the western is the largest, and that to the north-east the smallest; are tolerably high, very jagged, and form a circle of about 2 to 3 miles in diameter, enclosing a space of water not unlike that formed by a coral island. The group presents the appearance of being a conical volcano the summit of which has fallen in.

The line of the shores of these islands are as nearly as possible in the circumference of a circle, and the islets are joined by reefs, the outer face of the whole being steep-to, and presents no known danger outside them. The group is devoid of vegetation, excepting a little moss near the summit of the western islet.

FARALLON DE PAJAROS, the northernmost of the Mariana group, is 2 miles long (east and west), and 1½ miles wide, and lies about 24 miles N.N.W. from Urracas islands. Its summit forms in a conical mountain about 1,100 feet in height, and is an active volcano. The north, south, and east sides are perpendicular, with no known off-lying dangers. A large rock connected to the island lies on the south-east side, and farther southward are several smaller rocks, one of which is conspicuous. On the south-west side there is also a rock resembling that to the south-east. The island is precipitous on all sides except the west, where the mountain slopes more gradually, but there is no appearance of a bank off this side, and it may be approached within a mile. The island is barren except on the south shore, where there are a few trees and some scant vegetation. It is not known if anchorage may be obtained.

Los Jardines or Marshall islands.—Two small islands, in lat. 21° 40' N., long. 151° 35' E., were discovered by Captain Marshall of the ship *Scarborough* in 1788, and are thought to be the same as Los Jardines of Alvaro de Saavedra, in 1529. Nothing, however, is known of them beyond the most vague rumours.

Weeks Island was reported by Capt. Gelett in 1864, and by several later authorities. The island is about 5 miles long, low, sandy, and covered with trees and shrubs. A knoll near the centre rises about 200 feet above the sea, and a reef extends to the north of the island.* Its assumed position is lat. 24° 5' N., long. 154° 2' E. Weeks and Marcus islands are probably identical.

Mears and Congress islands, reported by whaling vessels, and placed on the charts, the former in lat. 23° 50' N., long. 147° 2' E., and the latter in lat. 23° 30' N., long. 147° 45' E., are otherwise unknown.

An Island and Valetta reef, reported by a whaling vessel, and placed on the chart, the former in lat. 22° 20' N., long. 145° 45' E., and the latter, in 21° 0' N., long. 143° 0' E., are otherwise unknown.

Peru or Three islands, reported by whaling vessels, and placed on the chart, in lat. 21° 12' N., long. 141° 40' E., are otherwise unknown.

Euphrosyne Reef † has been several times reported, and the positions assigned to it all agree so nearly as to leave little doubt of its existence, it is placed on the charts in lat. 21° 43' N., long. 140° 55' E., but this position requires to be verified.

Mears reef and a reef, the former placed on the charts in lat. 21° 0' N., long. 136° 38' E., and the latter, in lat. 21° 40' N., long. 138° 25' E., are otherwise unknown.

Parece Vela or Douglas Reef, discovered Sept. 1789, by Captain Douglas, is in about lat. 20° 31' N., long. 136° 6' E. It is described by Mr. Sproule, of the ship *Maria*,‡ who partially examined it in his boat, March 1848, as being a narrow perpendicular belt of coral, enclosing an oblong lagoon of water, with heavy breakers rolling over its north and north-east sides. The boat rowed under the lee of the reef, its whole

---

* From the report of Capt. Gelett of the ship *Morning Star*.

† *See* chart:—Pacific Ocean, sheet 5, No. 2,463, scale $d = 0.5$ of an inch; and Islands between Formosa and Japan, No. 2,412.

‡ Nautical Magazine, 1848, p. 242.

length, which is only two miles; and three-quarters of a mile wide at one-third from the eastern point. Sharp heads of coral appeared frequently through the surf, and one isolated rock, about 12 feet high and 15 feet long, rose from the smooth water lagoon near its western extreme. The rock when first seen from the vessel, about 3 miles off, appeared like a boat's tanned lug-sail. The reef, from its being visible only a short distance off, should be carefully approached, especially in dark and blowing weather. Sperm whale and fish of different descriptions were abundant. This reef should be approached with great caution as in the winter season when stormy weather prevails it can be seen only when at a short distance.

Two Reefs placed on the chart, one in lat. 22° 10′ N., the other in 22° 50′ N., and both in long. 142° 20′ E., are otherwise unknown.

Britomart reef, placed on the charts in lat. 19° 15′ N., long. 141° 35′ E., was reported by the ship *Britomart* in 1869, as being level with the water, and from 400 to 500 feet in length.

LINDSAY ISLAND was discovered by Mr. Lindsay, of the British schooner *Amelia*, December 1848, in lat. 19° 20′ N., long. 141° 15½′ E. It appeared about 40 feet high, 4 miles long, and very barren.*

VOLCANO ISLANDS, three in number, were discovered in 1543 by Bernard de Torres, and received their name from the volcano on the central island. There is no doubt of their being the same as the Sulphur islands of Captain King in 1779. They were also seen by Krusenstern in 1805. The southern island is named San Augustino, the centre Sulphur island, and the northern San Alessandro.

San Augustino, the summit of which is in lat. 24° 14′ N., long. 141° 20′ E., is a single hill of a square form, flat at the top, and 396 feet high.

Sulphur island is about 5 miles long N.N.E. and S.S.W., and its summit is in 24° 48′ N., 141° 13′ E.† The south point of the island is a high barren hill, flattish at the top, and when seen from the W.S.W., presents an evident volcanic crater. A low narrow neck of land connects this hill with the south end of the island, which spreads out into a circumference of 9 or 12 miles, and is of moderate height. The part near the isthmus has some bushes on it, and a green appearance, but that to the north-east is barren and full of detached rocks, many of which are white. Dangerous breakers extend 2½ miles to the east and 2 miles to the west from the middle part of the island.

---

* The *Britomart* reported having passed over the position assigned to Lindsay island without seeing it.

† King in Cook's Voyages, 1779; the longitude is probably 3 or 4 miles too much to the East.

San Alessandro, the northern island, is a single mountain of considerable height, and its peak, which is of a conical shape, is in 25° 14′ N. 141° 11′ E.

Forfana island, which has not been seen since its discovery by the ship *San Juan* in 1543, is said to be in lat. 25° 35′ N., long. 143° 00′ E.

SEBASTIAN LOBOS or Grampus Islands.—The Grampus group, discovered by Captain Meares, in April 1788, consists of three islands, two of which are close together, and the third to the south-west of them. The south-west island is assumed to be in 25° 10′ N., 146° 40′ E. The Sebastian Lobos, with which these are supposed to be identical, are nearly in this latitude. Meares does not give their position, but Krusenstern places them from his track in 25° 40′ N. Another island of this name is inserted on the chart in lat. 25° 40′ N., long 153° 55′ E., and is probably taken from the old Spanish charts. Its existence is exceedingly doubtful.

Tree island, placed on the charts in lat 26° N., long. 146° 15′ E., is not otherwise known.

The MALABRIGOS or Margaret islands, in lat. 27° 20′ N., long. 145° 45′ E., are a group of three islands seen in 1773 by Captain Magee They have been considered to be the Malabrigos islets (bad shelter) of Bernard de Torres in 1543, and their position required to be verified.

ARZOBISPO or BONIN ISLANDS were formally taken possession of by Captain F. W. Beechey, H.M.S, *Blossom*, in June 1827. They consist of three groups or clusters, viz., Bailey group to the south, Beechy group in the centre, and Parry group to the northward, the whole extending in a N. by E. direction from the parallel of 26° 30′ to 27° 50′ N. They had no signs of ever having been inhabited. The climate is excellent, and the soil productive. In 1853 there were a few whites and Sandwich islanders, 36 in all, settled on Peel island.

BAILEY GROUP were first visited by Mr. Coffin, in 1823; they were named by Captain Beechey in 1827. A reconnoissance of these islands was made in 1857.

HILLSBOROUGH ISLAND (the largest of the group) is 7½ miles long N.N.W. and S.S.E., 1¼ miles wide, 1,471 feet high, and the greater part hilly and rocky. There are some wild hogs upon it, fish is abundant, and turtle plenty in the season.

Off the north point and north-west points of the island, dangerous reefs and rocks extend to seaward some distance.

New-port on the south-west side of the island is 2 miles wide from the main to Plymouth island, which it fronts and partially shelters. The harbour is deep in the centre.

With the exception of New-port, in lat. 26° 36′ N., long. 142° 9′ E., and a small cove just northward of it, there is no place on the shores of any of the islands suitable for a coal depôt, nor can New-port or the cove be recommended as places suitable for such a purpose. They are both open from S.W. to N.W. and the holding ground is not good, being sand and rocks; vessels could, however, always get to sea on the approach of a gale. The *Plymouth* anchored in 14 fathoms about half a mile from the head of the port.

From the south-west point of the island a continuous line of reefs and islets (terminated by a narrow island) extend to a distance of 2½ miles.

KELLY island lies to the south-east 3 miles from Hillsborough, and is 1 mile long and half a mile wide.

PERRY ISLAND lies 2 miles to the westward, and is 1¼ miles long and half a mile wide: a rocky patch lies three-quarters of a mile to the south-eastward of Perry island.

Supplies.—Both wood and water may be procured, the latter from a small stream near the head of the cove to the northward of the anchorage.

TIDES.—It is high water at New-port, full and change, at 11h. 32m., and the rise of tide is 3½ feet.*

BEECHEY GROUP consists of three islands, of which Peel island, the largest and most southern, is 4¼ miles in length. The northern island is named Stapleton, and the centre one Buckland. This group is 9¼ miles in length, and is divided by two channels so narrow that they can only be seen when abreast of them. Neither of them is navigable; the northern on account of rocks, which render it impassable even for boats, and the other on account of rapid tides and currents, which, as there is no anchoring ground, would drift a ship on to the rocks.

PEEL ISLAND is 4½ miles long, and about 890 feet high; its origin evidently is volcanic, the hills being well wooded and watered: this island was first inhabited in 1830.

Knorr island lies off the south-west end of Peel island and has several rocks and islets in its vicinity.

Sail rocks, 60 feet high, lie to the northward of Knorr island.

PORT LLOYD.—The entrance to this harbour, on the western side of Peel island, is well defined, so that it can scarcely be mistaken. Before entering it would be well to place a boat on the shoal which extends South fully 2 cables from the eastern point of Square rock (260 feet high), lying off the northern point of entrance. The shoal can, however, be easily seen from aloft even when there is no swell on, and its centre is awash with a

---

* Lieut. Balch, U.S. ship *Plymouth*.

smooth sea. A coral rock, with 8 feet water on it, lies about a cable's length northward of the Southern head.*

Supplies.—Peel island, as well as those surrounding it, is chiefly visited by whale ships, and its products, therefore, are such as to suit their wants. Potatoes, yams, and other vegetables, fruits of various kinds, together with wild hogs and goats, can be procured from the few whites and Sandwich islanders settled at Port Lloyd. Wood is good, and plentiful; and water can be had, though in limited quantities, and slightly tainted by the coral rocks from which it springs. The best watering-place is in Ten-fathom Hole; but it will be necessary to be cautious of the sharks, which are very numerous.

DIRECTIONS.—Having ascertained the position of Port Lloyd, steer boldly in for the Southern head, taking care, when approaching from the southward, not to bring it northward of N.E. ¼ E., nor shut it in with two paps on the north-east side of the harbour, and which will be seen nearly in one with it on this bearing. In this position they are a safe leading mark; to the southward of this line there is broken ground.

In a sailing vessel, if the wind be from the southward, which is generally the case in the summer season, round the Southern head, at the distance of a long cable's length, close to the sunken rock, which will be distinctly seen in clear weather. Keep fresh way upon the vessel, in order that she may shoot through the eddy winds, which baffle under the lee of the head, and to prevent her coming round against her helm, which would be dangerous. She will at first break off, but will presently come up again; if not, be ready to go about, as the vessel will be close upon the reefs to the northward, and the helm must be put down before the south end of the island, off the port to the north-westward, comes on with the west side of Square rock.

If the vessel comes up, steer for a high Castle rock, at the eastern part of the port, until a pointed rock (white on top with bird's dung, and looks like an island) on the sandy neck eastward of the Southern head comes in one with a high sugar-loaf-shaped grassy hill southward of it; after which bear away for the anchorage, taking care not to open the sugar-loaf again to the westward of the Pointed rock. The best anchorage (Ten-fathom Hole excepted, which it will be necessary to warp into,) is at the northern part of the port, where the anchor is marked on the Admiralty plan.

---

* *See* Plan of Port Lloyd, No. 1,100; scale, *m* = 4 inches. In this plan the longitude of Ten-fathom Hole is given as 142° 11′ 30″ E. The Master of the U.S. ship *Susquehanna* gives the longitude 5′ farther East. In a meridian distance measured from Hong Kong with 5 chronometers, interval 33 days, Collinson, in 1852, made the longitude of Port Lloyd, 142° 15′ E., assuming Hong Kong as 114° 10 48″ E.

In anchoring, take care to avoid a spit extending off the south end of the small island near Ten-fathom Hole, and not to shoot so far over to the western reef as to bring a rock at the outer foot of the Southern head, in one with some *black* rocks, which will be seen a short distance to the south-westward. The depth will be 18 to 20 fathoms, clay and sand. The anchorage is fair, though open to the south-west.

If the wind be from the northward, turn to windward between the line of the before-mentioned sugar-loaf and Pointed rock, and a north and south line from the Castle rock. This rock, on the western side, as well as the bluff to the northward of it, may be passed close to, if necessary. The hand lead will be of little use in beating in, as the general depth is 20 or 24 fathoms.

ANCHORAGE.—Port Lloyd is easy of ingress and egress, and is safe and commodious although the water is deep, vessels usually anchoring in from 18 to 22 fathoms. The best position, Ten-fathom Hole excepted, is as high up the harbour as the vessel can go, so that she has room to swing and veer cable.

TIDES.—It is high water, full and change, at Port Lloyd at 6h. 8m., and springs rise 3 feet.

FITTON BAY, at the south-east angle of Peel island, is $1\frac{1}{4}$ miles deep and nearly a mile wide at its entrance, and is enclosed by perpendicular rocks; this bay affords good anchorage, but is open to the S.E., and as the winds from this quarter blow generally during summer, it will be prudent not to anchor there during that season. On the north side of the entrance there is a large islet connected with the north bluff of the bay by a reef, and to the southward of the entrance lie some sunken rocks; ships should therefore not close the land in that direction so as to shut in the paps (at the north-east angle of Port Lloyd) with the south bluff of the bay.

Goat island, in lat. 27° 7′ N., lies off the west entrance to the channel between Peel island and Buckland island (the centre of the Beechy group); it is about 300 feet high, and is surrounded by rocks and islets.

BUCKLAND ISLAND lies to the North of Peel island and is $3\frac{1}{2}$ miles long (N.W. and S.E.); it has off its south-west side a small sandy bight.

Walker bay, the sandy bight above mentioned, affords good anchorage, but vessels must be careful in bringing up to avoid being swept out of soundings by the current. An island connected to the main by a reef lies on the west side of this bay.

Little Goat island lies to the westward of Buckland island, and a little over half a mile to the north-west of the island above mentioned, and is connected to the main by a reef.

STAPLETON ISLAND, the most northern island of the Beechey group, is also of volcanic origin, its surface is hilly interspersed with large tracts of fertile land.

There is a small bay on the western side, which appears to be deep, surrounded by rocks, and the mountains here rise from 800 to 1,500 feet in height; a small promontory divides the bay, and on the land bordering the north part is a spring of capital water which issues from a rock.

Supplies.—There are a great many goats which have become wild, and the same supplies may be procured as at Peel island.

Kater island, in lat. 27° 30′ N., long. 142° 15′ E., lies in the channel between the Beechey and Parry groups. It is about 1½ miles long (N.W. and S.E.), and is surrounded by rocks in every direction.

PARRY GROUP.—The northern cluster is composed of small islands and pointed rocks, and has much broken ground about it, which renders caution necessary in approaching it. They extend 9 miles in a N.E. by N. and S.E. by S. direction.

CAUTION.—When in the vicinity of the Bonin islands, the navigator must exercise considerable caution, as the currents both in direction and force (especially between the islands) are uncertain. *See* page 10.

ROSARIO or Disappointment island, in lat. 27° 16′ N., long. 140° 51′ E., and about 70 miles W. by N. from Peel island (Bonin group), is small, being only about 1 mile long, east and west, and its highest part 148 feet above the level of the sea. It is rugged, apparently unsusceptible of cultivation, and surrounded by numerous isolated rocks. The surf breaks heavily all around it, and landing is impracticable.

Abreojos.—A shoal inserted on the charts, in lat. 22° 0′ N., long. 129° 15′ E., and which appears on the old Spanish charts, is not otherwise known. An island was reported by a whaling vessel as being near this position, but has not since been seen. It is however probable that the island or shoal exists, but its position is very uncertain.

RASA ISLAND, seen by the Spanish frigate *Magellan* in 1815, and by the French frigate *La Cannonière* in 1807, is in lat. 24° 27′ N., long. 131° 6′ E., about 4 miles long N.W. and S.E., low, its highest part being about 220 feet above the sea, covered with bushes, and surrounded with rocks.*

Dolores island, placed on the charts in lat. 24° 50′ N. long. 134° 15′ E. is in nearly the same position as an island reported and named Kendrick island, and described as being low and about 6 miles in length; it is not otherwise known.

---

* This island has been reported by numerous vessels, and the positions given by them agree very nearly.

Bishop rocks, in lat. 25° 20′ N., long. 131° 15′ E., were discovered by Captain Bishop, in the ship *Nautilus*, in 1796, but they do not appear to have since been seen.*

BORODINO ISLANDS.—These two islands lie in a N.N.E. and S.S.W. direction from each other, distant about 5 miles. The southernmost (the centre of which is in lat. 25° 52¾′ N., long. 131° 12¼′ E.) is the largest, about 4 miles in extent east and west, low, of coral formation, covered with vegetation, and has a reef extending along its south shore, affording no visible harbour. The north island is 3 miles in length, also flat, but has a rise near the north end gradually sloping towards the sea.

CAUTION.—The mariner, when navigating the space described between Formosa and the Mariana and Bonin islands, should use extreme caution when approaching the locality of many of the islands and shoals marked on the chart, especially at night, or during dark and hazy weather, for the existence, or at least the positions, assigned to some of them appear to be very doubtful. They would seem to have been inserted on the charts from the uncertain reckoning kept on board whaling vessels, or others, which, from the very nature of their pursuits, cannot be entitled to much confidence.

MEIACO SIMA, LIU-KIU, AND LINSCHOTEN GROUPS.

These groups form a chain of islands extending in an easterly and a north-easterly direction from Formosa to the southern extremity of Japan, and lie between the parallels of 24° N. and 31° N.

MEIACO SIMA GROUP.†—This group is the westernmost of the chain, and lies between the parallels of 24° 0′ N. and 25° 6′ N., and the meridians of 122° 55′ E. and 125° 30′ E.; it may be divided into two clusters, Pat-chung-san and Ty-pin-san, with the outlying islands of Koumi and Chung-chi. The whole group is clothed with vegetation, the soil is good, and horses and cattle are in abundance; the people, however, are not very enterprising. These islands are subject to the chief of the Liu-kiu group.

KOUMI ISLAND is composed of coralline limestone, all its ranges are capped with trees and brushwood, but excepting the pine fir, which contains a great portion of resin, none attain any size. There are four villages on the island, one on the west, and two on the north side, one of which is inland, in a basin-shaped valley. The principal town and port is on the north side, in which were several junks of about 50 tons riding at anchor; but the entrance from the sea is so narrow and shallow, that

---

* Lieut. Rodgers, U.S. Navy, passed over this position and saw nothing of these rocks.
† See Plan of the Meiaco-sima group, No. 2,105; scale, $m = 0.5$ in. The description of this group is from the voyage of H.M.S. *Samarang*, by Capt. Sir E. Belcher.

ingress and egress can only be effected at spring tides and with very smooth water. Temporary anchorage, in fine weather, may be found on a sandy ledge northward of the town.

Chung-chi island is a high uninhabited cluster of rocks, with dangerous patches extending between it and the south-west point of Ku-kien-san.

Boudrouet rocks, placed on the chart in lat. 24° 10′ N., long. 122° 33′ E., were reported by M. Boudrouet, of the French vessel *Roebur*, as being a group of rocks 65 feet high, perpendicular on all sides, broken in two or three places, their summits being of uniform height, the whole being about 100 yards in length.

A dangerous shoal,* 3 miles in extent, E. by N. and W. by S., is said to lie about 10 miles N.W. by W. from Koumi island.

Another shoal is inserted on the chart as lying S.W. by W. about the same distance from the same island; its existence is doubtful; but great caution should be used when in this vicinity, as the numerous patches between the Meiaco Sima group leaves still a probability of its existence.

PAT-CHUNG-SAN GROUP consists of ten islands, the nearest being 32 miles to the eastward of Koumi. Five only are at all mountainous, the remainder are flat, like the coral islands, and similarly belted with reefs, such as connect this group. The principal islands are Koo-kien-san and Pat-chung-san, which afford several commodious harbours, and are, with good charts, quite safe of approach. Port Haddington, on the west side of the latter island, would shelter a large fleet, but it abounds with coral patches, rising suddenly from 10 or 15 fathoms almost to the surface; in clear weather all those having as little as 5 fathoms are clearly discernible, and therefore easily avoided. Except on the northern side of Koo-kien-san and the latter port, watering is difficult, as reefs extend a great distance from the mouths of the streams. Seymour bay, at the south-west angle of Koo-kien-san, must, however, be excepted, for there a fine stream enters the sea in deep water, and a vessel might be moored sufficiently close to lead the hoses from the pumps into her without the intervention of boats and casks.

KOO-KIEN-SAN ISLAND is 15½ miles long and 12 miles wide, and is about 2,000 feet above the sea. A small island lies 2½ miles to the northward of Koo-kien-san, it is about 40 feet in height, and encircled by a reef.

With respect to the various harbours of Koo-kien-san, there are two or three adapted for shelter for small vessels, or even those drawing 18 feet, where a refit might be accomplished in still water in any monsoon, or where steam vessels might lie safely for the purpose of obtaining wood; and there are two other open bays, well sheltered in the N.E. monsoon,

---

* Reported by Mr. Whittingham, of the British ship *Helen Stewart*, 1843.

admirably adapted for watering; but there is not any other inducement to visit this island. All the dangers are well marked by the coral fringe which extends about a cable's length from the outline.

Ports Gage, Herbert, and Cockburn are on the west side of the island.

Seymour bay is on the south side.

HASYOKAN (Sandy Island) is 3 miles long, east and west, and has a few trees and huts on it. A reef extends about a mile off the south-west point, and there is no safe channel between this island and Chung-chi.

Koubah, Roberton, Baugh, Inglefield, and Loney islands are on the reef connecting Koo-kien-san with Bat-chung-san, the latter island being also connected, by numerous reefs, with Hasyokan.

PAT-CHUNG-SAN ISLAND is very irregular in outline; to the north-east is a narrow peninsula 11 miles in length, terminating in point Adam, the position of which is lat. 24° 38′ N., long. 124° 20′ E. Every part of the island is fringed by a coral reef, and it is connected to the above-mentioned islands by a plateau of coral. Its highest part near the centre of the peninsula is 1,700 feet, and there are two other peaks of 1,500 and 1,200 respectively, the last-mentioned being near Adams point. The two ports are Port Broughton on the south and Port Haddington on the west side of the island.

PORT BROUGHTON.—The only directions which will assist the seaman in finding this snug little anchorage (safe only, however, during the N.E. monsoon) are as follows:—

Approaching from the westward, as Chung-chi is neared, Hasyokan or Sandy island will soon be seen, and avoiding the space included northerly of a line between Chung-chi and it, a vessel may safely stand on, passing within one mile of the southern limit of Hasyokan, and work for the south-west angle of Pat-chung-san, avoiding the reefs, which extend from it in a direct line N.E. and S.W. to Hasyokan. A high rock, named South rock, will point out the outer reefs of Pat-chung-san. The dangers between it and Pat-chung-san must be avoided by eye, the shoals being visible in 5 or 6 fathoms, and breaking upon those of 2 and 3 fathoms. The opening in the reef is in the heart of a deep indentation just northward of the low south-west point of the island, and it has apparently a centre bar. The right-hand opening is the proper one.

From the eastward there are no dangers which are not clearly visible. After making the land, edge along the southern and eastern breakers until the abrupt turn of the breaker line is seen, at which moment the extreme south-west point of the bay will open. The breakers have regular soundings off them, but the course in will probably lead in 7, 8, or 9 fathoms, deepening to 14 or 15 off the inlet. As the breeze generally blows out, it will be advisable to send a boat to find clear ground off the opening, and shoot up and anchor; the vessel may then be warped in. If, however, the ship's stay is to be short, the outer anchorage appears good. Port Broughton is only useful as a port of refuge with still water in case of disaster, when a disabled vessel could not reach the more secure anchorage of Port Haddington.

Supplies.—Neither wood or water can be conveniently procured.

PORT HADDINGTON.—No safe anchorage is to be met with between port Broughton and port Haddington, which last is on the west side of Pat-chung-san; although during the S.W. monsoon there are several good bays on the northern side of the island, where anchorage might be found, but they are certainly not adapted for refitting.*

When rounding the north-eastern extremity of Pat-chung-san the two low coral islets of Mitsuna and Tarara ought to be avoided at night, but the dangers by day are clearly denoted by breakers. To the northward of these islets the ground is foul, and the *Samarang* was compelled to tack to the westward in 7 fathoms, at least 10 miles north of them.

Proceeding from port Broughton to port Haddington, after rounding the north-east end of the Pat-chung-san breakers, and running to the westward the length of the island, haul close round the north-west angle, and edge along southerly within about 1 mile of the breakers. The port will then open out, into which, with the prevailing breeze of the N.E. monsoon, it will be necessary to beat. Off Hamilton point, the north point of the port, will be seen a remarkable little rocky hummock upon which was left a large pile of stones. The bottom, for more than a mile off the point, is rocky and dangerous; but as all the dangers of this port are visible from aloft, there is no risk with a proper look out. The inner parts of the port have numerous shoals, but there is still abundance of excellent anchorage without, and where the vessel will be land-locked.† The *Samarang* anchored about a mile or less within Hamilton point, in 10 fathoms, clear bottom.

From the westward port Haddington may be sought and reached more expeditiously by working up on the north-west side of Koo-kien-san, rounding Isaac island and running down off the danger line from Melros point round the reef, which extends one mile off Hamilton point, and shoot into 15 fathoms. The chart exhibits several awkward patches, but a vessel which works decently can thread her way between them, if the sun be bright, as all the shoals may easily be traced from aloft.

---

* There is a passage from Port Haddington into Port Broughton, which was used by H.M. Ships *Lilly* and *Contest*, but it abounds with coral reefs.—*Commander J. W. Spencer, H.M. Sloop Contest*, 1852.

† Two rocks were reported by Lieut. Luard, R.N., but he gave no marks for determining their position.

CHAP. IV.] PAT-CHUNG-SAN ISLAND.—PORT HADDINGTON. 139

This is a most convenient port during the N.E. monsoon; it is land-locked, it is true, but there is a long fetch for the sea with a S.W. gale, and in that season Typhoons are said to be very violent about this region.

Hamilton point is in about lat. 24° 25′ N., long. 124° 6′½ E.

Supplies.—A convenient watering place was established by sinking a cask and suspending the suction hose over it, so as to prevent the sand from being sucked in. The stream from above was regulated by dams to ensure not more than a sufficient supply, by which means the water obtained was beautifully clear; the process however is difficult as the streams are difficult of approach at low water, and at high water they are brackish. Here wood is abundant, and the position is farther preferable by being so far from the villages as to prevent the authorities from feeling alarmed. Sufficient fire-wood was cut at Tamanu beach to fill the ship, and trees were obtained of pine and other woods adapted for plank.

Tarara and Mitsuna islands are situated between Pat-chung-san and Ty-pin-san, they are surrounded by reefs and are very dangerous; these reefs are said to be connected with the Providence reef.

TY-PIN-SAN GROUP.—The eastern cluster is composed of several islands, viz., Ty-pin-san, Ashu-mah, E-ra-bou, Coru-mah, and Hummock island,* all of which are connected to each other by extensive coral reefs. The reefs do not project far westward from Ashu-mah unless in patches unconnected with the main belt. Off E-ra-bou they extend 3 or 4 miles, but close towards its north-western angle a deep water channel admits vessels within the belt up to Hummock island, and into the main harbour of Ty-pin-san. The reefs again spit out on the south-west angle of Coru-mah, and sweep northerly as far as the eye can reach (from 100 feet elevation) round to east in a continuous line of breakers, edging in towards the south-east extremity of Hummock island; it was on this reef that H.M.S. *Providence*, Capt. Broughton, was wrecked in 1797. A high patch of rocks lies on the north-east angle of this outer belt, probably 10 miles from the northern point of Ty-pin-san.

ANCHORAGE.—Safe anchorage may be found during the south-west monsoon inside the reefs of Hummock island, and this position is also safe in the other monsoon, but the passage in or out at the latter season would be attended with risk, as sudden squalls and gales (besides the numerous patches of rocks) are of frequent occurrence. The southern coast, from the south-east breaker patch to the south-west anchorage, does not present many dangers, if a good look out be observed; the reefs not extending more than half a cable from the shore.

---

* These names are from Chart No. 2,412; Sir E. Belcher, in his Voyage of the *Samarang*, names them thus—Ty-pin-san, Ku-ri-mah, Yed-rap-boo, Ykima, and Ogame.

Supplies.—There can be no inducement for a vessel to visit Ty-pin-san. Neither wood, water, or any other necessaries could be procured excepting in the smallest quantity; and this would hardly warrant the risk on such a dangerous coast.

DIRECTIONS.—Great caution is requisite in approaching the Meiaco-Sima group from the north-east, or south, particularly with fresh breezes, and in the absence of the sun, by the aid of which reefs below water can be detected. They are, from their greenish hue, being covered with seaweed, less distinct than at other places, and therefore were not marked on the chart. It must not be presumed that the space is free from danger; the lead will not afford timely warning.

Approaching the group from the south-west, the island of Koo-kien-san from its great height will be first distinguished, presenting a round-backed summit closely clad with trees; knolls occur, elevated 2,000 feet above the sea, but as they seldom present the same appearance, owing to those nearer the coast eclipsing them, their accurate measurement could not be obtained; Adam peak, which may be noticed on the south-eastern outline, was determined to be 1,200 feet. As the island is neared, the high rocky basaltic island of Chung-chi will show out when the western limit of Koo-kien-san bears N.E. by N., and working for this islet no danger can be feared, and should night set in, all the space on the north-west of Koo-kien-san up to the island of Koumi is safe.

The *Samarang* entered the group from the westward, passing within 2 miles of the southern reefs or breakers off Hasyokan, and standing on close hauled to the eastward, intending to make Ykima, and beat up from it to Ty-pin-san. On the morning following, not seeing Ykima (which is supposed not to exist), and the weather being very boisterous, she stood on to the westward to get under the lee of Pat-chung-san, and endeavoured to reach some place of shelter. On nearing the latter island, she ran down the eastern and southern side, to the south-western extremity of its reef.

Here was a barrier of breakers as far as the eye could reach from the mast-head, and apparently connecting Hasyokan island with the group of larger islands. An opening, however, was found into the reef, and after due examination the vessel was shot up into 13 fathoms, into Port Broughton, and warped into a snug position, where she was moored with just sufficient room to swing, the depths up to the coral ledges varying from 13 to 7 fathoms.

PORT HADDINGTON to TY-PIN-SAN.—After quitting port Haddington the *Samarang* beat to the northward, and endeavoured to weather the two low coral islets, Mitsuna and Tarara. She had passed the breakers, leaving them about 5 miles under her lee, when finding the depths decrease to

7 fathoms, the vessel was immediately tacked, and stood to the S.W. Capt. Belcher strongly suspects that extensive banks or ledges of coral connect these islets (northerly) with Ty-pin-san; and a good reason for this offers in the fact of their being included by the natives in the Ty-pin-san group, when they are much closer by half the distance to Pat-chung-san.

Upon nearing the south-west part of Ty-pin-san, and having tacked twice, rather close to two off-lying patches, and obtaining soundings with 15 fathoms, a boat was sent ahead. Upon a given signal, for "danger discovered," the anchor was let go, and the vessel found to be in a secure berth in 12 fathoms, the boat being on the reefs. It is merely an indentation formed by the reefs connecting the western island Ashu-mah with Ty-pin-san, and is very unsafe, a heavy sea tumbling in with a southerly wind. The observatory at the south-west angle of Ty-pin-san (at the most convenient landing-place within the reefs and the last rocky point towards the long sandy bay) is in lat. 24° 43′ 35″ N., long. 125° 17′ 49″ E. Ty-pin-san should not be approached at all on its northern side.

Ykimah Island, with an islet to the north-east of it, and placed on the charts in lat. 24° 25½′ N., long. 125° 28′ E., 17 miles southward of Ty-pin-san is not otherwise known. It was not seen by Sir E. Belcher, who searched for it in 1844, or by the U.S. expedition to Japan under Commodore Perry, 1856.

PINNACLE, CRAIG, and AGINCOURT ISLANDS, lying north-eastward of the north end of Formosa, have often been sighted by passing vessels, but as yet no description has been given of them; their positions are as follows:—Pinnacle (about 200 feet in height), lat. 25° 27′ N., long. 121° 58′ E.; Craig, 25° 29′ N., 122° 9′ E; Agincourt, 25° 38′ N., 122° 8′ E.*

HOA-PIN-SU, PINNACLE, and TI-A-USU ISLANDS form a triangle, of which the hypothenuse, or distance between Hoa-pin-su and Ti-a-usu, extends about 15 miles, and that between Hoa-pin-su and the southern Pinnacle island about 2 miles. Within this space are several reefs; and although a safe channel exists between Hoa-pin-su and the Pinnacle islands, it ought not (on account of the strength of the current) to be attempted by sailing vessels if it can be avoided.

The extreme height of Hoa-pin-su is 1,181 feet, the island apparently being cut away vertically at this elevation, on the southern side, in a W.N.W. direction; the remaining portion sloping to the eastward, where the inclination furnished copious rills of excellent water. That this supply is not casual is proved by the existence of fresh-water fish found

---

* See Chart of the islands between Formosa and Japan, with the adjacent Coast of China, No. 2,412; scale, $m = 0.05$ of an inch.

in most of the natural cisterns, which are connected almost with the sea, and abound in weeds which shelter them. The north face of the island is in lat. 25° 47′ 7″ N., long. 123° 30½′ E. There are no traces of inhabitants, indeed the soil is insufficient for the maintenance of half a dozen persons.

The Pinnacle group, which is connected by a reef and bank of soundings with Hoa-pin-su, allowing a channel of about 12 fathoms water between it and the Channel rock, presents the appearance of an up-heaved and subsequently ruptured mass of compact gray columnar basalt, rising suddenly into needle-shaped pinnacles, which are apparently ready for disintegration by the first disturbing cause, either gales of wind or earthquake. On the summits of some of the flat rocks long grass was found, but no shrubs or trees. The rocks were everywhere whitened by the dung of marine birds, comprising the Booby, Frigate bird, and various Tern, the noise of which is almost deafening. The reef (as shown on the chart) on which these rocks are situated extends 6 miles to the eastward and 4 miles to the northward of Hoa-pin-su.

Ti-a-usu, about 15 miles to the north-eastward from Hoa-pin-su, appears to be composed of huge boulders of a greenish porphyritic stone. The top of this island from about 60 feet to its summit, which is 600 feet high, is covered with a loose brushwood, but no trees of any size. In addition to the sea birds mentioned on Pinnacle island, the Gigantic Petrel is found here. The centre of the island is in lat. 25° 58½′ N., long. 123° 40′ E.

RALEIGH ROCK, in lat. 25° 55′ N., long. 124° 34′ E., rises abruptly from a reef to a height of 270 feet above the sea, is perpendicular on all sides, and appears in the distance as a junk under sail. The existence of this rock was considered doubtful before July 1837, when it was seen by H.M.S. *Raleigh*. It was afterwards visited by Captain Belcher in 1845, and has since been several times reported. Owing to its lying in the Kuro Siwo or Japan stream, several very widely differing positions have been assigned to it.*

THE LIU-KIU GROUP† (Lu-chu), lies to the north-eastward of the Meiaco Sima's, about 120 miles from the northern island of the latter group to the southern island of the former. It consists of three large islands—Okinawa sima (Great Lu-chu), to the south-west; Kakirouma, in the centre; and Oho sima to the north-east, between which and in their vicinity are numerous smaller islands, some of which form clusters, the whole, with some outlying rocks, lying between the parallels of 26° N. and 28° 46′ N., and the meridians of 126° 42′ E. and 130° 16′ E.

---

* Recruit island, reported in 1861, and this rock are identical.
† See Plan, Liu-kiu group, No. 2,412.

OKINAWA SIMA (Great Lu-chu island), the largest of the group, is about 56 miles long, N.E. and S.W., preserves a tolerably uniform breadth of about 10 or 12 miles. The north end is high and bold, with wood on the tops of the hills; the north-east coast is also abrupt but quite barren, and the north-west side rugged and bare. The south-east side is low, with very little appearance of cultivation. The south, south-west, and western coasts, particularly the two former, are of moderate height, and present a scene of great fertility and high cultivation, and here the mass of the population reside.

There are two good harbours in the island, viz., Napha-Kiang and port Oonting or Melville, on the west and north-west side. Deep bay, on the same side, and Barrow bay, on the east coast, are not recommended. The inhabitants of the Liu-kiu islands are both friendly and hospitable; their chief resides at Sheudi, the capital, and formerly paid tribute both to China and to Satsuma, a powerful Japanese Daimio. They have but little commerce, except amongst the neighbouring islands of the group.

NAPHA-KIANG, on the south-west side of Okinawa sima, is the principal seaport of the island, and perhaps the only one possessing the privileges of a port of entry. The inner, or Junk harbour, carries a depth of 2 to 3 fathoms, and though small is sufficiently large to accommodate with ease the fifteen or twenty moderate-sized junks which are usually found moored in it. These are mostly Japanese, with a few Chinese and some small coasting craft, which seem to carry on a sluggish trade with the neighbouring islands. The outer harbour, or Napha-kiang road,* is protected to the eastward and southward by the mainland, whilst in other directions it is surrounded by merely a chain of coral reefs, which answer as a tolerable breakwater against a swell from the northward or westward, but afford, of course, no shelter from the wind. The holding ground is so good, however, that a well-found vessel could here ride out almost any gale in safety.

Abbey point, the south extremity of the road, may be known by its ragged outline, and by a small wooded eminence called Wood hill, about 1½ miles south of it. The mainland here falls back and forms a bay, which is sheltered by coral reefs extending northward from Abbey point; they are, however, disconnected, and between them and the point there is a channel sufficiently deep for the largest ship.

Nearly in the centre of this channel, outside withal, there is a coral bank named Blossom reef, with a good passage on each side. The south channel, between it and Abbey point, should be adopted with southerly winds and flood tides, and the Oar channel, between Blossom and Oar

---

* See Plan of Napha-kiang Road, with views, No. 990; scale, m = 3 inches.

reefs, with the reverse. A reef extends from Abbey point to the southwest, and also to the northward. When off Abbey point, Kumi head, a rocky headland, will be seen about 1½ miles north of the town; and upon the ridge of high land beyond it are three hummocks to the left of a cluster of trees. In the distance, a little to the left of these, is mount Onnodake, in lat. 26° 27′ N. A remarkable rock, which from its form has been named Capstan head, will next appear; and then to the northward of the town a rocky head, with a house upon its summit, called False Capstan head. At the back of Capstan head is Sheudi hill, upon which the upper town, the capital of Okinawa, is built.

Water.—An abundance of water can always be obtained at the fountains in Junk river, where there is excellent landing for boats. There is a good spring near the tombs at Kumi bluff; but unless the water is quite smooth the landing is impracticable, and under any circumstances it is inconvenient from the want of sufficient depth, except at high tide.

Buoys.* —A *black* spar-buoy is moored on Blossom reef half way between its eastern and western extreme; a *red* spar-buoy on the point of reef W.N.W. of Abbey point; and a *white* spar-buoy on the south-east extreme of Oar reef. Flags of corresponding colours are attached to all these buoys, and they afford good guides for the South and Oar channels. There are two large stakes on the reefs eastward and westward of the North channel, planted there by the natives, this being the channel mostly used by junks trading to the northward.

Tides.—It is high water, full and change, in Napha-kiang road, at 6h. 30m., and the rise is from 5 to 7½ feet; but this was very irregular during the *Blossom's* stay at this anchorage. The flood tide sets to the northward over Blossom reef, and the ebb to the southward.

Directions.†—Vessels bound from Hong Kong to the Liu-kiu islands during the S.W. monsoon, should pass through the Formosa channel, giving Pinnacle, Craig, and Agincourt islands, off the north end of Formosa, a safe berth. From thence a course should be shaped to pass northward of Hoa-pin-su, Ti-a-usu, and the Raleigh rock (*see* page 141), after which haul to the eastward to sight Komisang, and pass either northward or southward of it, and of Tunashee, and the small islet near the latter, but *not* between them, as reefs are said to have been seen there. If to the northward, give a good berth to Tu sima, a small rocky islet a quarter of a mile in extent, with a reef projecting 1½ miles to the northward and about 4 cables in other directions; it is about 80 feet high, much broken, and lies N. by E. ⅓ E., 13¼ miles from the northernmost peak of

---

* The spar-buoys may be displaced, or entirely removed by the heave of the sea, and should, therefore, not be implicitly relied on.

† Lieutenant H. K. Stevens, U.S. Surveying Expedition, 1857.

Kume sima, and W. ½ N. from the centre of Agunyeh. Pass southward of Agunyeh, which will be readily recognised by its bold south point and wedge-shaped appearance. The Amakirima group will be seen to the S.S.E., Okinawa sima, visible on the eastern horizon, and in a short time the Reef islets will heave in sight to the southward and eastward; these latter are low and sandy, slightly covered with vegetation, and surrounded by coral reefs.

During the N.E. monsoon, round the south end of Formosa, and with the strong current setting to the northward, beat to the northward and eastward along its eastern shore. Pass between Hoa-pin-su and the Meiaco Sima group, and either northward or southward of Komisang; if to the southward, a vessel may hug the northern shores of the Amakirima islands, as it is believed there are no hidden dangers near them.

During the Typhoon season, however, it is advisable to pass southward of the Meiaco Sima group, in order to have plenty of sea room, in the event of encountering one of these storms. The passage southward of the Amakirima islands is clear with the exception of the Heber reef and Halls reef.

Vessels bound into the road from the southward may pass close round cape Yakimu, the south extreme of Okinawa sima, and sail along the western coast at the distance of 3 or 3½ miles, leaving Heber and Halls reefs to the westward.

CHANNELS leading to NAPHA-KIANG.—There are three passages leading into Napha-Kiang road, viz., the South, the Oar, and the North channels. When sailing into this anchorage great care should be used to avoid the numerous reefs and rocky patches which surround it.

Through SOUTH CHANNEL.—To sail by this channel, between Blossom and Abbey reefs, having well opened Capstan head, haul towards Abbey reef, and bring the right-hand hummock about half a point eastward of Kumi head; this mark will lead through the South channel, in about 7 fathoms, over the tail of Blossom reef. A vessel may now round Abbey reef tolerably close and steer for the anchorage in 7 fathoms, about half a mile N.N.W. of False Capstan head. Should the wind veer to the eastward in the South channel, with the above mark on, do not stand to the northward, unless the outer cluster of trees near the extremity of Wood hill is in line with, or open westward of Table hill, a square rocky headland to the southward of it over Abbey point. This mark clears also the tongue of Oar reef.

Ingersoll patches.—Care must be taken to clear these patches, on which there is only one fathom water; they lie 8½ cables W. ¼ S. from Capstan head, and 7¼ cables N. by W. ¾ W. from South fort.

S.W. rock, having 2 fathoms on it, and lying 6 cables N. by E. ¾ E. from Abbey point and one mile W. by N. ¼ N. from False Capstan head, must also be avoided. These two reefs lie one on each side of the fairway through the South channel.

Lexington reef lies W. ½ S., 1¼ miles from Abbey point with 2½ fathoms on it, and another patch with 1½ fathoms on it lies W.S.W. 1¾ miles from the same point.

* The clearest approach to Napha-kiang road from the westward is by passing northward of the Amakirima islands and sighting Agunyeh island, which will be recognised by its wedge-shaped appearance; from thence steer a S.E. course for the road, passing on either side of the Reef islands; being careful, however, not to approach them too near on the western and southern sides, as the reefs below water in these directions are said to be more extensive than is shown on the chart.

After clearing the Reef islands, steer for Wood hill on a S.S.E bearing until getting upon the line of bearing for the South channel. This will lead well clear of Blossom reef, yet not so far off but that the white tomb and clump of trees or bushes southward of Kumi head can be easily distinguished. An E. by N. ¼ N. course now until Abbey point is in one with outer trees will clear S.W. rock, when haul up for Kumi head, and select a berth about half a mile northward and westward of False Capstan head. This channel, being quite straight, is more desirable for a stranger entering the harbour than the Oar channel, which, though wider, has the disadvantage of its being necessary for a vessel to alter course some four or five points, just when she is in the midst of reefs which are nearly all covered.

Through OAR CHANNEL.—If the wind be to the north-eastward it will be advisable to beat through the Oar channel, in preference to the South channel. To do this, bring False Capstan head in line with a flat cluster of trees on the ridge to the right of the first gap south of Sheudi. This will clear the north tongue of Blossom reef; but unless Table hill be open eastward of Wood hill, do not stand to the southward, but tack directly the water shoals to less than 12 fathoms, and endeavour to enter with the marks on. Having passed north-east of Blossom reef, which will be known by Wood hill being seen to the right of Table hill, stand towards Abbey point as close as convenient, and on nearing Oar reef take care of a tongue which extends to the eastward of it and of the S.W. rock, and be careful to tack immediately the outer trees of Wood point open with Abbey point. In entering at either of the western

---

* These directions are by Lieut. S. Bent, U.S.N., who surveyed this anchorage in 1853.

channels, remember that the flood sets northward, over Blossom reef, and the ebb southward.

A good mark to run through this channel is to bring the centre of the island in Junk harbour (known by the deep verdure of its vegetation) to fill the gap between the forts at the entrance of that harbour, and steer a S.E. ½ E. course, until Capstan head bears East, when haul up E.N.E., and anchor as before directed.

Through NORTH CHANNEL.—This channel is much contracted by a range of detached rocks extending from the reef on the west side, and should not under ordinary circumstances be attempted by a stranger, as at high water the reefs are almost entirely covered, and it is difficult to judge of the vessel's exact position unless familiar with the various localities and landmarks. To enter by this channel, bring a remarkable notch in the southern range of hills in line with a small hillock just eastward of False Capstan head, and stand in with this mark bearing S. by E. ½ E. until Kumi head bears E. ½ N., when open it a little to the southward, so as to give the reef to the eastward a berth, and select an anchorage.

ANCHORAGE.—The best anchorage is in Barnpool, at the north-east part of the road, in 7 fathoms, where a vessel may ride with great security. The outer anchorage would be dangerous with strong westerly gales. H.M.S. *Blossom* anchored there in 14 fathoms, muddy bottom, Abbey bluff bearing S.W. ¼ S., and Capstan head E. by S. ¼ S.

The entrance to Barnpool is between Barn head and the reef off Capstan head. In entering, do not approach Barn head nearer than to bring the north edge of Hole rock on with the before-mentioned flat clump of trees on the hill south of Sheudi, until the point of the burying ground (Cemetery point) is seen just clear of False Capstan head. Anchorage may be taken in any part of Barnpool.

The COAST from Napha-Kiang trends in a N.E. and then N.W. direction, forming a deep bight, of which nothing is known.

Gama Satchi (cape Broughton), off which there is a reef, is the northern extreme of this bight.

From Gama Satchi the coast takes an E.N.E. direction for 58 miles, and then W.N.W. for 26 miles to Suco island, between which and Gama Satchi there is a deep indentation named Deep bay.

DEEP BAY*—the observatory spot at the head of which is in lat. 26° 35′ 35″ N., long. 127° 59′ 42″ E.—is formed on the western side of Okinawa sima, and although open to the West and S.W. affords good anchorage off the town of Naguh, about half a mile from its head;

---

* From the remarks of Lieut. Whiting, U.S.N., 1854.

for winds from these quarters rarely blow home, and if they do they never raise a sea, as the latter is broken by the great depth of the bay.

The country around the head of this bay is fertile and populous, Motube and Naguh being the largest towns. At the town of Oon-sah there is a good ship and timber yard where junks are built; here also the natives were found more affable and sociable than on any other part of the coast. This part of Okinawa sima (extending to beyond Nacosi on the opposite coast) appears to be in a high state of cultivation; rice and sweet potatoes are the principal productions; but on the northern side of the peninsula, north of Deep bay, extensive fields of wheat were seen extending uninterruptedly for several miles. Cotton was observed also in many places, but the growth was small and the yield poor. Peas, beans, radishes, turnips, and sugar-cane were growing in considerable quantities, also mustard and ginger. On the Natchijen mountains, 1,488 feet high, cinnamon was growing wild, and there was also a fine growth of timber, which furnishes most of the spars for the native junks; Nakazuni cove, on the north side of the peninsula, being the principal depôt, whence they are transported to the other parts of the island.

SUCO or SETEI ISLAND,* lying about a quarter of mile from the north-west coast of Okinawa sima, to the northward of Deep bay, has excellent anchorage between its eastern side and the coast, protected from all winds; and wood, water, and fresh provisions can be easily procured. There is free egress to the northward and southward, and although the anchorage appears open to the southward, yet it is well sheltered in that direction by the reef extending S.S.E. nearly half a mile from the south end of Suco, and by the southern shore of Deep bay.

TUBOOTCH HARBOUR, a little to the north of Suco island, is 2 miles long and three-quarters of a mile wide; though open to the westward it is partially protected in that direction by a line of reefs, on which the sea breaks heavily, but the continuity of which is here and there interrupted by a narrow but tolerably deep channel. The north side of this bay is full of banks, but towards the centre there are safe spots with from $3\frac{3}{4}$ to 11 fathoms water; mud bottom. The best channel is that to the south, which is about two cables wide, with a depth of 7 fathoms.

Cape Niofa, the north-western point of Okinawa sima, is $2\frac{1}{2}$ miles to the north of Tubootch, between which and the latter are the small islands named Mina (to the southward) and Gibson (to the northward), with a deep channel between them and the shores of Okinawa.

Iye island lies to the westward of cape Niofa, between which and the island is a channel 2 miles in width, it is however encumbered with shoals.

---

* See Plan of Tubootch and Suco Harbours on sheet, No. 2,146; Liu-Kiu group.

Iye is 4½ miles in length (east and west) and about 1¾ miles wide, and has a sugar-loaf peak 575 feet above the sea.

The COAST from cape Niofa takes an easterly direction for 8½ miles to Kui island at the north side of the entrance to port Oonting.

PORT OONTING,[*] or Melville, is on the north-west part of Okinawa sima, and its entrance is between the western side of Kuï or Herbert island and the eastern side of the reef fronting the peninsula, and which projects 5 or 6 cables to the westward, having a small islet near its extremity. Iye sima, lying about 12 miles westward of the entrance, is a good guide for it.

Water.—Good water can be obtained at the village of Oonting.

TIDES.—In port Oonting it is high water, full and change, at 6h. 35m., and the rise is about 8 feet.

DIRECTIONS.—When bound to this port from the westward, passing to the northward of Iye sima, an E.S.E. course will lead to the entrance; here it will be advisable to heave-to, or anchor in 20 or 25 fathoms, until boats or buoys can be placed along the edges of the reefs bordering the channel; for without some such guides it will be difficult for a vessel of large draught to find her way in between the reefs, which contract, in places, to within a cable's length of each other, and are at all times covered.

In entering, steer for the western shore of Kuï island until Hele rock is in line with Double-topped mountain (a distant double-topped hill, the second highest of the range,) bearing S.E. ½ S. Steer in on this mark, until Chimney rock bears S. ¼ E.; then for Chimney rock until Rankin point bears S.W. ½ W.; then for that point until the port is entered, when anchor, giving the vessel room to swing clear of the reef extending northward of Rankin point, and she will be as snug as if lying in dock, with good holding ground, completely land-locked, and sheltered almost entirely from every wind.

SHAH BAY, about 8 miles E.S.E. of port Oonting, is a beautiful land-locked sheet of water, but the reef fronting the entrance prevents its being accessible to vessels of larger size than the junks which frequent it; within the entrance the water deepens to 12 and 8 fathoms, the bottom being soft mud. On the southern shore of the bay was found iron ore, mineral coal, and sulphur. The coal appeared of poor quality and mixed with earth, but good coal might perhaps be found by digging.

The COAST from Shah bay trends to the N.N.E. for 47 miles, and appears to be void of anchorage; it has not been minutely examined, but it is probable that it is very foul.

---

[*] *See* Plan of Port Oonting, with views, No. 2,436; scale, $m = 3\cdot4$ inches; and Shah Bay, on No. 2,416.

Cape Heto, the northern extremity of the island, is hilly, and from thence round the eastern shore of Okinawa, as far as Barrow bay, there appears to be no anchorage. A small island, named Sidmouth, surrounded by reefs, lies off the north-east side of the island.

BARROW BAY is a deep inlet, bounded by shoals, near the middle of the eastern coast of Okinawa. The following description is by Lieutenant G. B. Balch, of the U.S. ship *Plymouth* :—

"A reef, of coral formation and bold to approach, commences 5 miles from the south point of Okinawa, and extends in an unbroken chain, outside all the small islands, as far as the north-east point of Ichey island, with the exception of a narrow channel between the islet off the north-east end of Kudaka island, and the island of Taking. Ichey island forms the south-eastern point of Barrow bay, which is useless for all purposes of navigation, being exposed to the east winds and ocean swell. There is, however, secure anchorage in about 15 fathoms water on the western sides of Ichey, and of Hanadi, the next islet to the southward; this anchorage is the only place of shelter on the eastern coast of Okinawa."

Mathews bay, near the south-east end of the island, is of no practical utility, being filled with coral reefs, which skirt the shore.

Cape Yakimu, the south end of Okinawa, is hilly, and appears steep-to; it would, however, be advisable not to approach it within 2 or 3 miles, as it has not been closely examined.

Heber reef, reported as a rock about 5 feet above water, surrounded by reefs, lying 6 or 8 miles W.S.W. from cape Yakimu, has been inserted on the charts in lat. 26° 2′ N., long. 127° 34¾′ E. Its existence is doubtful, as its description agrees in every particular with Hall's reef.

HALL'S REEF is a large, circular, rocky patch, a part of which is above water; it lies 7 miles W. by N. ⅓ N. from the south-west point of Okinawa sima.

AMAKIRIMA GROUP lies to the westward of Napha-kiang, between lat. 26° 7′ N. and 26° 16′ N., and between long. 127° 15′ and 127° 29′ E. It consists of the Makirima islands, Koru sima (Saddle island), Toka shee, Assa island, Steven's island, Yakang island, Kupa sima, with many islets and rocks in their vicinity.

Makirima islands, the easternmost of the group consist of one island 540 feet in height, and two other islets to the northward; the northern (Cone islet), is in lat. 26° 14′ N., long. 127° 28½′ E., has a conspicuous detached rock off its south-west end, and must not be approached within a mile, as reefs surround it.

Koru sima (Saddle island), the most northern of the Amakirima group, is in lat. 25° 15′ N., long. 127° 25½′ E., is 459 feet above the sea; off its north-west end there are a few small islets and rocks, and a reef extends half a mile from its south and south-west ends.

Assa island, the north-western island of the group, is 3 miles long E.N.E. and W.S.W., very rugged and irregular of outline. In the centre, two deep bights one on each side, narrow the island to a low neck half a mile wide; the land on either side is comparatively high, the highest part being 540 feet above the sea.

Yakang island is of circular form, about a mile in diameter; the peak is 756 feet in height; it is bordered by a reef which stretches farthest to seaward, off the north end of the island, and has a detached rock at its extreme north end.

Kupa sima is the westernmost of the group; it is 916 feet above the sea, and has a reef with several detached rocks projecting from its north-west side, as also from the south point.

Steven's island consists of three islands with several islets and rocks, the whole lying in a N.N.W. and S.S.E. direction to the south of Assa and east of Yakang and Kupa sima. The northern island, which is the largest, is 641 feet in height.

Toka-shee, the centre island of the group, is the largest, being nearly 5 miles in length (north and south), and more than 1 mile in width. An islet with a reef, having detached rocks on it, extends 1½ miles from its north-east point, and a large rock (Chimney rock) with a similar reef projects from the southern point.

Mole and Whale reefs are rocky patches appearing above water; the former lies south-west 1½ miles, and the latter 2¼ miles from the south point of the most southern of the Steven's islands.

ANCHORAGE may be had to the south of Assa island opposite the bight before mentioned in that island. In approaching this anchorage from the northward, take care to avoid the patch lying off the eastern point. Several other patches exist, of which there is no description. Great caution should therefore be used when navigating in this locality.

REEF ISLANDS are four in number, lying 4 miles W.N.W. from the entrance to the channels leading to Nafa-kiang; the two easternmost are together on the same reef, and are low, sandy, slightly covered with vegetation, and surrounded by coral reefs.

TUNASHEE lies N.N.W. ¼ W. 9½ miles from Yakang; its northern peak is 492 feet in height, and that to the southward 603 feet above the sea. A reef extends to a considerable distance from its north and north-west sides.

Aghesinak (Flat island), lying about 2½ miles to the westward of the north peak of Tunashee, is merely a rock surrounded by a reef.

KOMISANG, is very irregular in shape, about 6 miles long, and the same in width; its northern peak is 1,108 feet in height, and that to the southward 1,028 feet; the western side of the island being fringed with reefs.

Elizabeth reef.—A very dangerous reef, extends 6 miles to the eastward of Komisang.

TU SIMA, in lat. 26° 35½′ N., long. 126° 51′ E., lies N. by E. ⅓ E., 13¼ miles from the north peak of Komisang. It is a rocky islet about 60 feet high, one quarter of a mile in extent, with a reef surrounding it.

MONTGOMERY GROUP consists of two large islands, with several islets and shoals near them. It lies north-west from cape Heto (the north point of Okinawa sima), forming a channel 15 to 16 miles in width.

Yebeya sima, the largest and northern island of the group, 963 feet in height, is 7 miles long (N.E. by N. and S.W. by W.); off its southern end a reef extends 2½ miles to the south-west, having an islet (Jabo islet) about a mile from the shore, and a rock awash at its extreme.

Isena sima, the southern island, is about 400 feet above the sea. Its south-east extreme, a conspicuous and prominent point, attains an elevation of 309 feet; there is a small detached rock about one mile east of the island.

Kusikawa, an islet surrounded by detached rocks, lies between Yebeya and Isena, S.E. by E. 1¼ miles from Jabo islet.

Yanagi islet, to the southward of Isena sima, is about 50 feet high, and has off its north-west side a reef with several rocks on it.

YORI SIMA, lying N.E. ½ N. 12 miles from the northern point of Okinawa sima, is 413 feet high, and is nearly surrounded by a reef which projects farthest off its north and east sides. The channel between it and Okinawa sima, as well as that between it and the Montgomery group, is apparently safe.

YERABU SIMA lies 18 miles northward of Yori sima, is 9½ miles long (N.E. and S.W.), and its southern peak is 687 feet in height, and in about lat. 27° 22½′ N., long. 128° 35′ E. The channel between it and Yori sima is safe.

KAKIROUMA, Tok sima of Siebold, or Crown island of Broughton, is 15 miles long (N. and S.) and 8 miles wide; the highest peak, which is near the centre on the east side, is in lat. 27° 45′ N., long. 128° 59′ E.; height, 2,207 feet. Its northern peak is 1,860 feet above the sea, with a village built on its north-west face.

Two small islets, named Tok-sima-utse, 166 feet high, lie 2 miles north of the north-east point of the island.

Yori sima, Yerabu sima, and Kakirouma are well wooded, and appear to be inhabited.

IWO SIMA, or Sulphur island, lies 34 miles west of the north-west point of Kakirouma. The channel between them is safe. The south peak, in lat. 27° 51′ N., long. 128° 14′ E. (128° 19′ E. by Collinson), is 541 feet high, and is a volcanic mountain still in action, the cliffs near the volcano being of a pale yellow interspersed with brown streaks; the ground is very rugged and broken, with here and there a thin coat of brown grass. The south end is of a deep blood colour, with occasional spots of bright green. The island is 1½ miles long (N.W. and S.E.), and is inaccessible.

OHO SIMA, or Harbour island, is the largest of the chain of islands lying between Okinawa sima or Great Lu-chu and Japan. It is about 30 miles in length (N.E. and S.W.), is high, well cultivated, and, from the number of villages seen along the coast, must contain a large population. There are two peaks on its south end, 1,674 and 1,420 feet respectively above the sea.

This island was partially surveyed by the American squadron in 1856, and by their chart the outline of its coasts appears much broken and deeply indented with numerous bights, most of which are very bold. Wood and water are good and plentiful, but refreshments scarce. The inhabitants are timid and harmless. The north end is high, and being connected with the main part of the island by a narrow low isthmus, it has the appearance on some bearings of being isolated. Foul ground appears to extend about 2½ miles N.E. by E. from the north end, and two rocks to rise from it, the northern of which is about 80 feet high. There are several open bays on the N.W. side of the island, and there is anchorage on its west side. Sima-u bay, on the east coast, also affords anchorage. North extreme of the island, lat. 28° 31′ 40″ N., long. 129° 42½′ 12″ E.; south extreme, lat. 28° 6′ 30″ N., long. 129° 24½′ E.

Katona sima.—The south end of the above island is separated from Katona sima by a narrow channel (Porpoise strait), in some places not more than half a mile wide. The *Vincennes* anchored at its western entrance, in Vincennes bay, a small bay formed at the north end of Katona sima. In entering an anchor should be ready to let go, in case of being set too near danger, for the entrance is narrow and the current strong.

TIDES.—By three days' observations in Vincennes bay, it was high water, full and change, at 7h. 30m.; and the rise and fall 5½ feet.

Yori sima and Uru sima are two small islands from 1½ to 2 miles southward of Katona sima; the former is 1,002 feet high, and the latter 1,356 feet. In the vicinity of Oho sima are many scattered islets and rocks, most of which are high and conspicuous.

KIKAI SIMA, lying about 15 miles south-east of the north end of Oho sima, is moderately high, about 7 miles in length, N.N.E. and S.S.W. and inhabited. The summit (867 feet high) is in lat. 28° 18′ N., long. 129° 57½′ E.*

GERMANTOWN REEF.†—The U.S. ship *Germantown* in 1859 struck on a coral reef said to lie in lat. 28° 16′ N., long. 129° 58′ E.‡ From the shoalest spot found, 6 feet, the highest terrace on Kikai sima bore N.E. ¼ E. 6 or 7 miles. The reef is about a mile long in a N.N.E. and S.S.W. direction, and half a mile wide.

Another shoal spot was found lying North 2 miles from the centre of this reef, with apparently a clear passage between. Reefs were also seen from aloft, extending from one to two miles from the south-west and south-east points of Kikai sima.

Marsh reef, placed on the charts in lat. 28° 14′ N., long. 129° 55′ E., was reported by Mr. Marsh in 1853 as lying 7 miles S.W. of Kikai sima, extending N.N.E. and S.S.W. about 3 miles, with 12 feet on it at high water.

ANCHORAGE.—The *Germantown* anchored at 1¼ miles from the shore in 25 fathoms, coral and shell, with the south-east point of Kikai sima bearing S.E. by E. ½ E., and the south-west point N. ½ E. The tides here set strong; the ebb from E.N.E. to N.E., and the flood from West to W.N.W. The strength was about 2 knots per hour, with an undertow of at least double that velocity.

Hesper island, placed on the charts in lat. 28° 9′ N., long. 130° 15′ E., was reported by Mr. James, commanding H.M.S. *Hesper*, as lying S.E. by S., 18 or 20 miles from Tabiyo saki, but it is doubtful if this latter island exists, at least in the position assigned to it; the position of Hesper island is therefore very uncertain.

SANDON ROCKS.—The highest rock is about 33 feet above the sea, with two low detached rocks to the westward, and a reef between them. At a quarter of a cable's length from their north-west side were 12 fathoms water, and at half a mile to the north-west 15 to 22 fathoms with overfalls over an uneven coral bottom. Their position is given as lat. 28° 45′ N. long. 129° 47¼′ E.

---

* From American chart, 1855. † Hong Kong Register, 26th April 1859.

‡ In the American chart Germantown reef is placed 2¼ miles S. by W. ¾ W. from the south-west extreme of Kikai sima, or in lat. 28° 14¾′ N., long. 129° 53′ E.; and there is another danger, named Marsh reef, 1½ miles southward of it.

The **LINSCHOTEN ISLANDS**,* or Cecille archipelago (so called in the French charts after Admiral Cecille, by whose directions the islands were examined), extend from lat. 28° 49′ N. to 30° 6′ N., and from long. 129° to 130° 3′ E. They consist of 12 islands and rocks, some of which are inhabited, and there appears to be many safe channels between them. The mariner is, however, cautioned not to place too much dependence either on their configurations or positions as shown on the chart of this part of the ocean, for they are by no means correct; they are from the Japanese as collated by Siebold, and from detached surveys and corrections by English, French, and American navigators. The French corvette *La Sabine* examined them in the year 1846; their positions, to which we have given the native names and restored those of former explorers,† appear on the chart of her track to be as follows:—

YOKO SIMA, rising to the height of 1,700 feet above the sea, is an extinct volcano, the highest part of which is in lat. 28° 48′ N., long. 129° 2′ E.

Kaminone, lies 1½ miles to the northward of Yoko sima, is 972 feet above the sea, and volcanic.

TOKARA SIMA, 860 feet above the sea, is in lat. 29° 8′ N., long. 129° 13½′ E. It is inhabited, and the north end is cultivated. Several rocks and islets lie off its S.W., East, and S.E. sides.

SIMAGO, are four small islets, the highest of which, 372 feet above the sea, is in lat. 29° 13′ N., long. 129° 20½′ E. The easternmost islet bears from it about E. ½ N. 3 miles.

AKUISI SIMA, 1,978 feet above the sea, is 4 miles long (E. and W.), in lat. 29° 28′ N., long. 129° 37½′ E. The shores are generally steep and inaccessible, except at one place, where there appears to be some cultivated land; the west end is bold and high and thickly wooded. A small islet lies off its north-west face.

SUWA SIMA is an active volcano, 2,706 feet high, in lat. 29° 38′ N., long. 129° 42′ E., and is about 5 miles long and 3 miles wide.

FIRA SIMA, in lat. 29° 41′ N., long. 129° 32½′ E., lies 8 miles W.N.W. of Suwa sima, is 812 feet high.

---

* *See* Chart of Islands between Formosa and Japan, No. 2,412.

† It is greatly to be regretted that navigators will not endeavour to ascertain the names of places as given by the natives; or, failing these, that they will not retain the names affixed to islands by the first discoverers. In the present case there are three and occasionally four names for each of the islands in this archipelago. So long as this practice is pursued our charts will remain a maze of confusion.

NAKA SIMA, in lat. 29° 52′ N., long. 129° 52½′ E., is 3,400 feet above the sea and is an active volcano. The island is 5 miles long (N.W. and S.E.) and 3 miles wide. Off its south and south-east sides are two islets respectively 87 and 86 feet high.

HEBI SIMA rises to the height of 1,687 feet above the sea, in lat. 29° 54′ N., long. 129° 33′ E. There is a small islet off its north-west face.

KOHEBI SIMA, 3½ miles to the south-eastward of Hebi sima, is 996 feet above the sea, in lat. 29° 53′ N., long. 129° 38′ E.

KUTSINO SIMA is 4 miles long N.N.W. and S.S.E.; its peak which is 2,230 feet above the sea, is in lat. 29° 59′ N., long. 129° 56′ E.

FIRASE, (Blake reef,) consists of several islets and rocks, extending about 3 miles in a N.E. and S.W. direction; the highest islet, 92 feet above the sea, is in lat. 30° 4′ N., long. 130° 3′ E.

Henty reef, on which the sea was seen breaking heavily, has been reported as lying N.W. ½ N. 3¾ miles from the north point of Kutsino sima, and about 10½ miles to the westward of Firase.

COLNETT STRAIT, which separates the Linschoten group from the group to the northward, appears preferable to Van Diemen strait for vessels bound from China to Japan; Yakuno sima, being lofty and steep-to, is an excellent mark; besides which better weather is generally experienced in this strait than in the latter.

Medusa reef,* reported as being indicated by discoloured water and high breakers, 2 miles in extent north and south, and lying 8 miles to the northward of Firase, is inserted on the chart in lat. 30° 13′ N., long. 130° 4′ E.; it has not since been noticed, but if it exists it is a dangerous impediment to the navigation of Colnett strait.

YAKUNO SIMA.—To the north-eastward of Firase, is the island of Yakuno, the highest peak of which, mount Motomi, 6,345 feet high, is in lat. 30° 20′ N., long 130° 31′ E., and shows double from the eastward. The island is about 15 miles long north and south, and 15 miles wide, and has several lofty peaks. The village of Muja ura lies on its north-east side at the head of a small bay. Off the south-west side of the island is an islet named Ko sima, and off the east side is White rock.

NAGAROBE, (Yerabu sima,) Julie island of the French, lies 7 miles to the north-westward of Yakuno sima. The island is 6 miles long, E.S.E. and W.N.W., and its greatest breadth is 3 miles; it is an active volcano, and the highest peak near the south-east end is 2,297 feet above the sea, and is in lat. 30° 26½′ N., long. 130° 14′ E.

---

* Reported by the Commander of the Dutch war steamer *Medusa*, and described in the Official Netherlands Magazine, 1864.

TANEGA SIMA, the most eastern of this group, is 32 miles long, N.N.E and S.S.W., and has not been minutely examined. Its northern part appears low with smooth round undulating hills; the centre and southern end is more elevated, the highest peak being 1,200 feet high, and the island generally, well wooded. The French chart shows the outline of a good harbour on its western side, and several towns or villages are noticed.

Off the south-east point of the island is a conspicuous detached rock, 80 feet in height, named S.E. rock.

A reef* of rocks showing above water, and a shoal about 2 miles S.S.E. from them, are reported as lying nearly 7 miles from the south-east point of Tanega sima. "When the south point of Tanega sima bore North about 8 miles, and the south point of Yakuno sima W. by N., struck soundings in 8 fathoms, rocky bottom; the following cast no bottom in 13 fathoms."†

To clear these dangers, the south point of Yakuno sima should not be brought westward of W. by N. until the high conspicuous rock off the south-east point of Tanega bears N. ¼ W.

This reef has been inserted on the charts 5 miles South of S.E. rock, in lat. 30° 15′ N., long. 131° 2½′ E., but its position is very uncertain.

VINCENNES STRAIT between Yakuno sima and Tanega sima is 10 miles wide in the narrowest part; caution is necessary in approaching the positions of the above-reported shoals.

SERIPHOS or Omuru rock is marked on the French charts as a rock under water; it is inserted on the charts in lat. 30° 49′ N., long. 130° 45′ E.

TAKE SIMA, (Apollos island,) in lat. 30° 48½′ N., long. 130° 26½′ E., is about 2 miles in circumference and 816 feet high.

A rocky spit extends 2½ cables from its east extremity, and a dangerous shoal has been reported a short distance north of the island.

IWOGA SIMA, (Volcano island on French chart,) is an active volcano; its highest peak, 2,469 feet above the sea, is in lat. 30° 47′ N., long. 130° 19′ E. Some rocks and reefs extend about three-quarters of a mile from the east and N.E. points of the island.

KOWOSE (Powhattan reef).—This dangerous reef, in lat. 30° 41′ N., long. 130° 19′ E., was discovered by the U.S. frigate *Powhattan* in January

---

* This shoal was reported by Mr. A. F. Boxer, Commanding H.M.S. *Hesper*, 1865. The bearings, however, do not at all agree with the estimated distance.

† A shoal has been reported nearly in this position by Mr. Mills, of the ship *Malvern*, 1872; from its assigned position the south point of Tanega sima bore N. ¼ E., and the south point of Yakuno sima West.

1860. From the centre rock, about 18 feet above the sea, the south-west point of Iwoga sima bore N.W.; the east point N. ½ W., and the east point of Take sima N.E. ¼ N.

Other rocks were seen awash, or a few feet above water, stretching out about three-quarters of a mile from the centre rock.

USE (Trio rocks) are three distinct islets of about an equal height; the centre islet, 206 feet above the sea, is in lat. 30° 45′ N., long. 130° 7′ E.

KURO SIMA, (St. Clair island on French chart,) is about 3 miles long (East and West). It is an active volcano,* and its peak rises to the height of 2,160 feet above the sea, and its centre is in lat. 30° 50′ N., long. 129° 56½′ E.

KUSAKI SIMA, (Ingersoll or Morrison rocks,) are eight in number, and extend N.E. and S.W. about 5½ miles; the highest, in the centre, 468 feet above the sea, is in lat. 30° 51′ N., long. 129° 26′ E., and visible in clear weather at 25 miles.

VAN DIEMEN STRAIT lies between Kiusiu island on the north, and Iwoga sima, Take sima, Make sima, and Tanega sima on the south-west and south; it is clear of dangers,† and consequently safe. Making this strait from the westward, mount Horner, on Kiusiu, 3,069 feet high, and the peak of Iwoga sima (2,469 feet high), form two conspicuous land marks. The only drawback to the navigation of this channel is the heavy weather and thick atmosphere usually met with off Satano misaki; the Japan stream setting strong through this strait at all times causes the latter to become a serious disadvantage, which is, however, somewhat lessened by the light now exhibited on the above cape (*see* page 160).

---

* J. Ryan, Navg. Lieut. H.M.S. *Leopard*, 1868.

† A shoal spot of 8 fathoms was reported about 2½ miles to the southward of Satano misaki, the south point of Kiusiu.

CHAPTER V.

THE JAPAN ISLANDS, COMPRISING THE SOUTH AND EAST COASTS OF KIUSIU, SIKOK, AND NIPON, AND THE ISLANDS LYING SOUTH OF YEDO GULF.

VARIATION, from 2° to 3° W. in 1872.

JAPAN ISLANDS.*—The empire of Japan is composed of four large islands, Kiusiu, Sikok, Nipon, and Yezo, and numerous smaller islands. Nipon, the largest and most important of these, and that which gives its name to the whole empire, is more than 700 miles in length N.E. and S.W., and its breadth varies from 50 to 150 miles. South of Nipon, and separated from it by a narrow channel, is Kiusiu, about 180 miles in length, north and south, and about 80 in average breadth.

Lying north-east of Kiusiu, and eastward of the south extreme of Nipon, is the island of Sikok, about 130 miles in length, N.E. and S.W., and 60 in breadth. It is separated from Kiusiu by the Boungo channel, and with Kiusiu and the western part of Nipon forms a basin or inland sea named Seto Uchi. This sea communicates with the Pacific ocean by the Kii channel to the east of Sikok, and by the Boungo channel to the west of it, and with the Japan sea by the strait of Simonoseki. North of Nipon, and separated from it by the strait of Tsugar, is the large island of Yezo, a conquest and colony of Japan. Its form is that of an irregular triangle, and its area is computed at 30,000 square miles. The southern portion of the island of Saghalin, which is separated from Yezo by La Pérouse strait, and the three southernmost of the Kuril islands—Kunashir, Iturup, and Urup—belong to Japan.

The Japanese islands are exceedingly broken and mountainous, with numerous peaks, the highest of which, Fusi yama, in lat. 35° 21′ 5″ N., long. 138° 43½′ E., attains an elevation of 12,450 feet above the level of the sea, and is an excellent landmark for vessels approaching the gulf of Yedo.

Treaty ports.—The following are the ports opened to British subjects by treaty, between Her Majesty the Queen of Great Britain and Ireland and the Mikado of Japan:—Kanagawa,† in the gulf of Yedo; Nagasaki,

---

* See Chart of Nipon Island, Kiusiu and Sikok, and part of the Coast of Korea, No. 2,347, scale $d = 2 \cdot 3$ inches; corrected to August 1872.

† This port includes Yedo and Yokohama.

on the west coast of Kiusiu; Hiogo and Ōosaka, in the Isumi nada (eastern part of the inland sea); Niegata, on the north-west coast of Nipon; and Hakodate, on the south coast of the island of Yezo.

SOUTH AND EAST COASTS OF KIUSIU AND SIKOK.

SATANO MISAKI (cape Chichakoff), the southern point of Kiusiu and of the Japanese empire, is situated in lat. 30° 58′ 45″ N., long. 130° 40′ 15″ E.; it is about 650 feet in height, the mountains at the back, from which it is a spur, rising to a considerable elevation, at some points between 2,000 and 3,000 feet. A small island and several small detached rocks lie off it. This cape is well known to vessels trading to Japan, and has attained celebrity from the fact that almost constant bad weather is experienced in its vicinity, violent gales with a thick murky atmosphere rendering the passage through Van Diemen strait at times somewhat perilous. At about 2½ miles S.S.W. from the cape, a shoal spot of 8 fathoms has been reported, and is the only known danger in Van Diemen strait. Heavy tide races occur off the cape.

LIGHT.—Situated on a small island about 300 yards from the cape, exhibits, at an elevation of 200 feet above the sea, a *fixed* white light of the first order, obscured landward between N.N.W. ⅛ W. to N.E. by E. ¾ E., and is visible in clear weather from a distance of 21 miles. The lighthouse is 35 feet in height, constructed of iron, octagonal shaped, and painted white, and is in lat. 30° 58′ 30″ N., long. 130° 40′ E.

The COAST for 140 miles to the north-eastward, comprising the whole of the east coast of Kiusiu, is comparatively unknown.

Nelly rock.—In 1863 the British barque *Nelly* discovered a sunken rock off the south-east coast of Kiusiu on the western side of entrance to the Boungo channel. Its position is given as lat. 31° 48′ N., long. 131° 37′ E., Oö sima bearing S.S.W. The bottom had a white appearance, with soundings of 8 and 5 fathoms close to the rock. This rock was searched for in vain in the position assigned to it, and even soundings of 24 fathoms were found in every direction, the bottom being rotten stone.*

The SOUTH COAST of SIKOK, from Isa saki at the eastern entrance to the Boungo channel to I. sima at the western entrance to the Kii channel, is also as yet unsurveyed. This coast is about 150 miles in extent, and is divided by the projecting peninsula, of which Murato saki is the extreme point, into two bights, that to the westward being the deepest. The chart originally compiled from the Japanese manuscript † represents it as very

---

* Commander C. J. Bullock, H.M.S. *Serpent*, 1866.

† The Japanese manuscript, to which reference is frequently made in the succeeding pages, is a native map of the whole empire, projected on a scale of 6 miles to the inch.

broken in outline, with several deep indentations which may, when examined, prove useful harbours of refuge; four have been mentioned two only of which are described as good harbours.

The COAST of Sikok between Ootzu saki and Ko sima no hana forms a deep bight 3½ miles wide between these points, and 2½ miles in depth. From it two inlets extend farther to the northward and eastward forming the harbours of Susaki and Nomi. The shores of this bight are bold, and high mountain ranges, reaching to upwards of 1,000 feet in elevation, skirt the coast. On the west shore is a landslip which shows conspicuously from seaward; in its vicinity are several rocky patches.

SUSAKI* is a village situated on the west shore of a long inlet which indents the coast of the above-mentioned bight in a northerly direction, and in which is excellent anchorage, completely sheltered and land-locked. The entrance to the inlet, between Kadoya saki and Yama saki is nearly five cables wide, and carries a depth of 7 fathoms. The eastern shore of the inlet is high and steep-to, and should be kept on board; the western shore is low and shoal, but the ground rises on rounding the sandy point on which the village is built, where the spurs from Quada yama (a peak 2,390 feet high) reach the coast in hills of about 450 feet elevation. Immediately north of Kadoya saki the Sinjo kawa, a considerable stream, flows into the bay, and between the above points and Susaki a shoal bank of less than 5 fathoms skirts the coast extending in some places 2¼ cables from the shore.

NOMI HARBOUR in lat. 33° 23′ 18″ N., long. 133° 17′ 48″ E., in the south-east part of the bight above mentioned as lying between Ootzu saki and Ko sima no hana, is formed by the projecting peninsula, of which Yama saki is the extreme on the north, and a long narrow peninsula to the south. This peninsula terminates in a fork, with a chain of islands and rocks extending from its extreme point to the westward, Naka no sima and Hai sima being the largest; this chain protects the anchorage from southerly winds. From the north end of Hai sima a rocky ledge extends 2¼ cables to the northward. A sunken rock lies one cable from the shore on the west side of this island.

Ko sima.—The other prong of the fork above mentioned consists of a chain of islets and rocks which extend to the wooded islet Ko sima in a S.S.E. direction. The islet has a conspicuous clump of trees on its summit.

A rock, which uncovers, lies 1¾ cables to the south-westward of Ko sima.

Wherever tested by comparison with our own surveys, it has been found so accurate that great reliance may be placed on it. The general chart, No. 2,347, of the Japan islands, the Korea strait and Inland sea charts are transcripts of it, but they are being rapidly added to and corrected by our own surveys.

* *See* Plan of Susaki and Nomi, No. 995; scale m=4·0 inches.

Breaker, a small rock, which uncovers at low water, lies S. by W. ¾ W., 1¼ miles from the clump on Ko sima; it may be passed on the south side at one cable. Vessels entering Nomi harbour should keep the northern shore on board.

SOUTH-EAST COAST OF NIPON.—From Siwo misaki, the southern point of Nipon, the coast trends to the north-eastward for 75 miles as far as cape Sima; the whole of this coast is bold and mountainous, the high coast ranges attaining an altitude of 2,000 feet; the hills are thickly wooded and very undulating, those immediately in the vicinity of the coast being steep and conical shaped. Several good harbours of refuge are found, which have been described as follows:—

OÖ-SIMA HARBOUR is formed between Oö sima and the east side of Siwo misaki, the extreme south point of Nipon (page 215) which is connected to the mainland by a low isthmus. The harbour has two anchorages; one in the bay on the south-west side of Oö sima completely sheltered, but the water rather deep; the other in 4 to 6 fathoms, muddy bottom and good holding ground, off the village of Hasingui on the mainland in the northern part of the harbour.*

The latter anchorage is also well sheltered except to the north-east, where it is open from a small arc; it has also some protection from the remarkable chain of rocks, from 20 to 75 feet high, extending in a southerly direction half a mile from the shore eastward of the village, but being detached with deep water between, they do not form a perfect breakwater. The best position is with Itsino sima, the outer rock of the above chain, bearing E.N.E. distant 1½ cables, and Mioga sima, South, or on with Isumo saki, the west entry point.

This very eligible harbour is largely resorted to by windbound junks, and it offers every facility for repairs and replenishing supplies. There are three villages, two on the mainland and one on the island. Water is easily obtained from the latter village, it being led down in bamboo pipes to the rocks, which have deep water alongside them. The large village of Kusimoto on the isthmus, is well supplied with all the essentials usually required by the coasting trade. The country in the neighbourhood is prettily diversified by hill and valley, the former well clothed with wood, the latter well cultivated.

OÖ SIMA.—This island, which forms the eastern shores of the harbour and is about 3½ miles long (east and west), and 1¾ miles at its widest part, is irregular in shape and outline, hilly, and the greater part under cultivation, being only thickly wooded in the ravines. Its summit is 535 feet high.

---

* See Plan of Oö sima and Ura-kami harbours, No. 356; scale, m = 3 inches.

Double rocks above water lie 2 cables to the north-eastward of the east point of Oö sima.

LIGHT.—On the east point of Oö sima is exhibited at an elevation of 130 feet above the sea, a *revolving* white light which shows half a minute, and is eclipsed for half a minute, visible in clear weather from a distance of 18 miles. The position of the lighthouse is lat. 33° 28′ N., long. 135° 52′ E.

Supplies.—The cargoes of the windbound junks consisted of rice, sugar, tobacco, charcoal, salt, sake (spirits), and dried fish. Charcoal of an excellent quality for steaming purposes was obtained from them. The villagers supplied fish and poultry; some deer were brought off, also two or three wild boar, a few bullocks, and a small quantity of vegetables.

DIRECTIONS.—Approaching Oö sima harbour from the westward, a heavy tide race is often met with off Siwo misaki (page 216), which is skirted by uneven masses of rock, most of it showing at low water, with rocks awash 3 or 4 cables off shore. Bottle rock, lying South a quarter of a mile from the point, has some foul ground 1½ cables outside it; a rocky spit extends about a quarter of a mile off Wedge head, and there is broken ground at nearly the same distance off Isumo saki.

To clear these dangers, the right extreme of Oö sima, the most southern point seen, must not be brought eastward of E.N.E. until Mioga sima comes well open of Isumo saki N.N.W., when it may be steered for, taking care not to bring it northward of that bearing until within half a mile of it, or until the east extreme of Isumo saki bears S.S.W. ¼ W. when steer N.W. ¼ N., passing mid-channel between the land and the west side of Mioga sima, which has a small ledge running off its south side; after passing Mioga sima steer for the anchorage of Hasingui.

If compelled to work in, the Oö sima shore is the clearest, but take care to avoid a dangerous rock lying nearly 2 cables westward of the north-west part of Tsuya sima, an island 120 feet high off the south-west point of Oö sima. The south-west bay of Oö sima is clear of danger. In making the starboard board remember the bearing of Mioga sima for clearing the foul ground off the west side of the entrance; to the northward of Mioga the lead will give warning when approaching the mainland, but Oö sima is steep-to.

Approaching the northern entrance of the harbour from the eastward, give the mainland a berth until the Kuro sima rocks are passed, as numerous rocks, only showing at low water, lie scattered along the coast, some nearly a mile off shore, and a shoal has been reported as lying N.E. ½ N. 1¾ miles from the lighthouse on Oö sima. The Kuro sima are two large rocks, with a group of smaller ones off their west side. The south end of the chain of rocks off Hasingui may then be steered for, passing the outer rock at half a cable, and taking up the anchorage off the village.

At 10 miles E.N.E. of the harbour, Oö sima, which is 535 feet high, will be readily distinguished, showing out apparently clear of the land; at night the *revolving* light on the east point will be seen.

KOZA-GAWA is a small but opulent town situated on the east side of entrance of a river, 2¼ miles N.N.E. of the north point of Oö sima. The river has a shifting bar, but a channel is always available for coasting junks. Generally speaking breakers show the position of the shoals, and what to avoid when entering. At high water, which is about 7h. full and change, 10 feet may be looked for on the bar, probably more, but strangers should adopt the precaution of sending a boat ahead to sound.

The entrance bears North half a mile from Katsu sima, which will be readily distinguished, it being a well wooded islet, and the only one of the description in the immediate vicinity. At the north end of the town is an extensive timber yard, in which are spars of considerable dimensions.

Koza-gawa is also the seat of an important whale fishery. The mode of capturing is to entangle the whale in a net made of inch cordage, with small meshes, and then destroy it by blows of harpoons, the spear heads of which weigh 12 to 15 pounds. Poultry, fish, &c., in small quantities can be obtained; also spars, balks of hard wood, and charcoal.

URA-KAMI HARBOUR* is an inlet running 1½ miles in a W.S.W. direction into the land at 8 miles N.E. of Oö-sima harbour, and, although small, affords excellent shelter in 4 to 5 fathoms, over stiff muddy bottom. For steamers it offers an admirable haven, but being only a quarter of a mile wide, sailing vessels might experience a difficulty in getting in or out, particularly entering, as from the direction of the valley at the head of the harbour the wind, which may be free outside, is frequently found inside to be blowing straight out.

In entering take care to avoid a spit of rocks projecting upwards of half a mile in a north-east direction from the south point of entrance. One of them, named Hive, is 36 feet high, and some are covered, but show sufficiently to render them easily to be avoided.

The best anchorage is in 4 to 5 fathoms off the east end of Ura-kami village, which stands on the south shore about half a mile from the head of the harbour. The usual supplies of a few fowls, fish, and small quantities of vegetables and water are to be obtained here.

The COAST.—From Ura-Kami the coast trending N.E. by E. is high and thickly wooded. At a distance of 40 miles is a deep inlet named Kada bay which has not yet been examined, it is however reported to have very deep water, and to be thus unsuitable as an anchorage except for very small vessels and junks.

---

* *See* Plan of Ura-kami harbour on Sheet No. 356.

OWASI BAY* is a deep inlet on the north side of Kuki saki about 5 miles northward of Kada bay. This bay is formed by Kuki saki on the south and Domakura saki on the north, and is 4 miles wide at its entrance and 4½ miles deep, composed of four inlets, two of which are only suitable as anchorages, the remaining two being much smaller are only frequented by junks.

Owasi no minato.—The western inlet, which is the largest and is open to the eastward, shoals gradually towards the village of Owasi situated at the north end of the long sandy beach at the head of the bay.

Yaguchi ura, the western and largest of the remaining three, is on the northern shore of Owasi no minato and lies N.N.E. and S.S.W.; is 3 miles in length and carries deep water up to the head of the inlet where it shoals gradually off the village of Yaguchi.

The Chioshi kawa, a tolerable stream on the western shore of this inlet, is navigable for boats for upwards of half a mile; on its left bank, a little less than half a mile from its mouth is the entrance to a deep lagoon lying at the back of the villages of Hikimoto and Watari mura, which are situated on the left bank of the river; farther up the inlet is the small village of Naga hama. The Chioshi kawa winds through a valley, the foot of which is well cultivated, the hills on each side being steep, lofty, and densely wooded.

The two other inlets, both of which lie on the northern shore of Owasi no minato, are Sugari ura and Moto Sugari ura; both these are deep. At the head of the former, junks moor alongside the wharves off the village of Sugari at the head of the inlet.

The latter inlet though less deep is not a convenient or sheltered anchorage.

DANGERS.—**H'to Te,** (Man's hand) a rocky pinnacle, lies 4 cables S.W. ¾ W. from Hadaka iwa, between which and the southern shore there are several rocky patches.

DIRECTIONS.—In making Owasi bay, Togashira sima, which is 527 feet high and covered with trees, is seen showing out in bold relief against the high land at the back in the shape of a triangle, the dark colour of its foliage causing it to be very conspicuous.

After passing Togashira sima, which on near approach is seen as a steep cone, steer to pass north of Sabaru sima (lying N.N.W. from the former), and to the northward of Hadaka iwa (naked rock) a flat bare rock which lies nearly in mid-channel.

If intending to anchor off Owasi village, having passed Hadaka iwa, steer for the isolated hill Sengin yama in the centre of the sandy beach at the head of the bay, and anchor in 7 fathoms with Benten sima S.W. by S. and Sengin yama W. by S. ¾ S.

---

* See Plan of Owasi bay, on Sheet 356; scale, m = 2·0 inches.

If intending to anchor in Yaguchi ura, when off Hadaka iwa haul up to the north-west and pass to the eastward of Waregami sima at about one cable from it, and keeping in mid-channel pass the point on the eastern shore, on which there is a shrine, at about 1½ cables. This point is surrounded by a reef of sunken rocks, and on the opposite shore a sandy spit extends some distance from the sandy point which forms the south entrance to the river's mouth, contracting the channel to less than 1½ cables. On passing these the channel becomes wider, and the ship should keep the western shore to avoid a rocky patch lying on the eastern shore about East from Nagahama, and anchor as soon as possible after obtaining 8 fathoms, as that depth is carried for some distance and the water then shoals suddenly.*

Supplies.—Fowls, ducks, and vegetables may be obtained in small quantities both at Owasi and Hikimoto, and fish may be had in abundance. Water may be had from the Chioshi kawa.

The COAST for 23 miles trends to the E.N.E., is much indented, and thickly wooded, the mountains, however, are of much less elevation than those to the southward; several islets and rocks skirt the coast, and a near approach is not recommended. At the distance above mentioned from Owasi bay is an extensive inlet named Goza.

MURA HARBOUR, 2½ miles west of Goza harbour, is an extensive inlet which indents the coast in a N.N.E. direction, and is 4 miles deep. At its entrance, which is one mile in width, is 14 fathoms, decreasing gradually up the bay. The bay is divided at the head into two large inlets by a narrow peninsula, which projects to the south-westward nearly 1½ miles, and is terminated by a rocky ledge (some of the rocks on which appear above water) extending 2 cables from the point.

ANCHORAGE may be obtained in either of these arms, that to the westward (Hazama mura) being preferable, abreast a small village, in 10 fathoms. Mura harbour is an excellent and sheltered anchorage.

GOZA HARBOUR.—In lat. 34° 17′ N., long. 136° 46′ E. affords shelter from all but west winds. Its entrance, which is about one mile wide between the two points, has 12 fathoms water. The southern point is a high bluff, and is thickly wooded, and has one or two small rocks lying to the westward of it. From the northern point a ledge of rocks extends some distance. After rounding the south bluff point, keep in mid-channel to avoid some scattered rocks lying 2½ cables off the north shore, and stand in 2 miles to abreast the first inlet on the port hand, and anchor as convenient. The inlet above mentioned affords excellent anchorage for small vessels in from 5 to 7 fathoms, but a bar of sand stretches across the entrance, on which there is only 2 fathoms at low water. Above this inlet the soundings become irregular, and patches of rock appear. The whole of the

---

* Description of Owasi and Matoya by Navigating Lieutenant Jarrad, R.N., 1870.

upper part of Goza harbour is split up into numerous shoal passages and creeks, by innumerable islands, islets, and rocks, the whole covering an area of about 20 square miles. It is high water at full and change, at Hamagema ura (the inlet above-mentioned) at 6h. 15m. Springs rise 6½ feet; neaps, 3½ feet.

CAPE SIMA is a low wooded headland lying 9 miles to the eastward of Goza harbour. East, 3½ cables from the cape, is a conspicuous rock 35 feet in height. At 3 miles S.W. by W. ¾ W. from cape Sima is a projecting point of land with a conspicuous clump of trees on it, and the coast between this point and the cape is skirted to the distance of half a mile with patches of rocks and foul ground; a rocky ledge also extends 2 cables from the point. To the south-westward from the point are the two small islands Ō sima and Ko sima, each having a conspicuous clump of trees. Ō sima the larger and outer is 40 feet in height; Ko sima is 50 feet high; they are 3¼ cables apart. From these islands long reefs extend in all directions, and dangerous detached sunken rocks crop up in various places; on these the sea generally breaks, owing to the constant swell caused by the strong tides off the cape.

Outer reef, on which the sea always breaks, uncovers 3 feet at low water, and lies S.W. ½ W. 7¼ miles from the rock off cape Sima; S. by W. ½ W. 2 miles from Ō sima, and S.S.E. ½ E. 5¼ miles from the wooded entrance to Goza harbour. Numerous tide rips occur outside this reef, but there is no danger. The islands off cape Sima should not be approached within 3 miles, and it would be only prudent to give this dangerous cape a still wider berth.

MATOYA HARBOUR* lies 5 miles north of cape Sima and is open only to the east. Its entrance is 6½ cables wide between Tomio saki on the south and Sungi saki on the north, but a reef of rocks which are nearly all above water situated just within the south point contracts the navigable channel to 3½ cables.

The whole harbour is split up into numerous inlets, narrow channels and bays, and safe anchorage may be obtained in nearly all of them.

Watakano sima, an island nearly three-quarters of a mile long (north and south) of triangular shape and deeply indented, lies in the middle of the south-west arm of the bay which it divides into three narrow channels. A narrow sandy point extends from its southern end and a short distance northward from it is the small village of Watakano.

The town of Matoya is approached by the northern of the above-mentioned channels which is little over a cable wide. The town is small and dirty, and is only resorted to by junks who put in there from stress of weather, often in large numbers, but there is no trade of any sort there. From the town a narrow channel with 4 to 6 fathoms water communicates

---

* See **Plan of Matoya harbour,** No. 107; scale, $m = 3 \cdot 55$ inches.

with an extensive shallow lagoon which extends 3 miles to the westward; this lagoon is the resort of numerous wildfowl.

Another narrow channel opposite the town of Matoya takes a south-east direction and communicates with the southern inlet named Ō ura, and turning to the north-eastward round the east side of Watakano sima, communicates with the main part of the bay.

Haka se, a rocky patch which uncovers at low water, lies $6\frac{1}{2}$ cables within the north point of the entrance, with the outer rock of the reef above water on the southern shore, bearing S.E. $\frac{1}{4}$ S., distant $5\frac{1}{2}$ cables; and the outer rock seen above water off Sungi saki, bearing East, distant 7 cables. Another patch connected with Haka se lies 3 cables to the north-westward from it, the whole surrounding the eastern point at the entrance to the bay on the north shore of Matoya harbour.

Oki-no se, a rocky patch of considerable extent, lies N.E. $\frac{3}{4}$ E. $3\frac{1}{2}$ cables from the outer rock, seen above water off Miya-no saki (at the north entrance to the channel leading to the town), to which it is joined by a reef.

LIGHT.—On the eastern extreme of Tomio saki (Anori saki), the southern head of the entrance to the harbour, at an elevation of 102 feet above the sea, is exhibited a *fixed* white light, visible in clear weather from a distance of 10 miles. The tower is 46 feet high, octagonal shaped, and painted white, and is in lat. 34° 22′ 0″ N., long. 136° 54′ 45″ E.

Supplies are very limited, a few fowls and eggs may be obtained, and also fish. The hills abound in game of various descriptions, especially pheasants, and wild boar may be often purchased.

DIRECTIONS.—On entering Matoya harbour the reef just inside the entrance projecting from Tomio saki, will be avoided by passing from about $1\frac{1}{2}$ to 2 cables from the extreme rock seen above water, after passing which to avoid Haka se, steer West for the opening leading to the town, seen south of the cliffs of Miya no saki; and anchor as convenient.

ANCHORAGE.—With winds from N.E., North, or N.W., good anchorage may be had in the small bay on the northern shore of the harbour off the village of Adako; but with wind from South or East vessels should either anchor off Matoya in from 5 to 6 fathoms, or between the east side of Watakano sima and the reef which extends off the second point from the entrance on the southern shore.

The COAST.—About 8 miles northward of Matoya is the small harbour of Toba, the residence of a daimio. It is said to be available as an anchorage, but is not of any great extent. The harbour is situated at the western entrance to the bay of Owari.

OWARI BAY.—This extensive inlet, the entrance to which is between Momotori (an island north of Toba) on the west and Irako saki on the east, is about 35 miles long (north and south) and divided into three separate arms, that to the westward being the largest. The whole bay is reported to be shallow with a uniform depth of 7 and 8 fathoms, shoaling very gradually at its head in Mia bay to 4 fathoms. Anchorage may be obtained anywhere in Owari bay; in Mia bay in 4½ fathoms, mud. Owari bay is the nearest approach to Nagoya, the capital of the province of Owari, which has several large enamel manufactories.*

MIKAWA BAY and the remaining small inlet have not been examined.

KAMI SIMA is a small island lying in nearly mid-channel at the entrance to Owari bay.

The COAST from Irako saki takes an easterly direction for 60 miles as far as Omae saki, it is fronted by a sandy beach with low sand hills and occasional patches of trees, the whole being steep-to with no known off-lying dangers.

HAMANA.—The entrance to this large inlet was not discerned in passing along this coast, it was therefore concluded to be shallow. An entrance to a river was observed eastward of it, with a breaking bar extending some distance off shore. The water may be seen about here greatly discoloured.

OMAE SAKI, the west point of entrance to Suruga gulf, is a dark wooded bluff 150 feet in height, terminating a very sandy shore with high beaches, backed by wooded hills. It may also be recognised by two remarkable white patches, only one of which is visible from east or west. In a S.W. gale good shelter may be obtained under the lee of Omae saki in 7 to 4 fathoms, but not closer in.

LADY INGLIS ROCKS.†—A reef half a mile in extent, lies 2 miles E. by S. of the southern point of Omae saki, from which it is separated by a 12-fathoms channel, between it and reefs extending 2 cables from the shore. This reef is covered at high water, and does not always break at high tides, but its locality is always marked by tide rips. Vessels may pass between the point and the Lady Inglis rocks by keeping one mile from the shore, in 12 fathoms. The bottom is sand, with shells and stones.

Portsmouth breakers.—Captain Foote, of the U.S. frigate *Portsmouth*, reports ‡ that he nearly lost his vessel on a reef of rocks (not laid down in the charts) about 35 miles in a south-westerly direction from Simoda, and 13 miles from the nearest land.

In steering § for the gulf of Yedo the *Furious* passed inside the above position assigned to these breakers, and although the water changed its

---

* Captain Von Blanc, North German war-vessel *Nymphe*.

† The *Lady Inglis*, Mr. H. Twizell, master, was wrecked on this reef in December 1859, and a few hours afterwards a Japanese junk struck on the same reef outside the wreck, and rolling off into deep water, was lost with all hands.

‡ "Shipping Gazette," 30th March 1858.

§ Stephen Court, Master, R.N., H.M.S. *Furious*, 1858.

colour very decidedly, no indication of danger was seen, nor was any bottom obtained with 13 fathoms. From the mast-head the line of discolouration could be traced from the shore to as far as could be seen seaward. It was from 4 to 6 miles wide in an E.N.E. and W.S.W. direction where the *Furious* crossed, and on emerging from it into blue water, the boundary line was as plainly marked as on entering it from the westward.

Soundings taken near the reputed position of these breakers showed no indication of any shoal, but on approaching Omae saki from the S.E. by E. the depth, which was 71 fathoms at 12 miles distance, and 57 at 9 miles, increased to 129 at 7½ miles, again decreasing to 40 at 5 miles; shelly bottom.*

CAUTION.—As the Portsmouth breakers lie in the direct route of vessels bound to Simoda and Yedo from the westward, a good look out should be kept and more than ordinary care taken when approaching their supposed locality. The position of the reef being doubtful, mariners are requested to obtain information respecting it, which may easily be done by a passing vessel in favourable weather, as parts of it being dry at low water the reef must nearly always show itself by breakers. Although the position assigned on the chart to the Portsmouth breakers has been sailed over by H.M. ships and in all kinds of weather, nothing has been seen since first reported, and it seems highly probable that a shoal of fish or a current overfall † caused the disturbance in the water, which gave birth to the report.

GULF of SURUGA (named Tutomi gulf in former charts), the waters of which wash the western shore of the peninsula of Idsu, is 34 miles deep and 23 miles wide at entrance, and, with the exception of the Lady Inglis rocks, lying E. by S. 2 miles from Omae saki, the low sandy west point of entrance, is, according to present information, free from any impediment to navigation. The water in it is very deep, no bottom at 250 fathoms being found at mid-entrance, none at 160 fathoms midway across near the head of the gulf, and none at 110 fathoms at a little more than a mile from the western shore.

The eastern side of the gulf (the Idsu shore) is generally a belt of cliffs, broken, however, into several deep water havens, which, though small, afford good anchorage, but for sailing vessels with a foul wind are all difficult of access; in fact, even with a free wind outside, it constantly happens, from the numerous gulleys and valleys between the hills eddying the wind out of its course, that vessels are taken aback, and as the entrances of those harbours that are known, Tago, Arari, Heda, and

---

* Commander C. J. Bullock, R.N., 1866.

† These rips have often been mistaken for shoals. *See* description of Japan stream, page 23.

Eno ura bays, on the Idsu shore, are too narrow to admit of much manœuvring, it will be prudent not to hesitate to use the anchors should the vessel make a stern board.

The western side of the gulf is not so well known as the eastern. It appears less precipitous, but, judging from the soundings obtained off Simidzu, is equally steep-to. At the head of the gulf is Fusi yama, the highest mountain in Japan, and although its summit is 15 miles inland, it appears in clear weather to rise nearly abruptly from the beach.

Simidzu and Eno ura are two excellent harbours, one on each side at the head of the gulf. The latter is reported by the Japanese to be a much finer harbour than Simidzu. The high road between Yedo and Miako and the western province forms a tangent to the head of the gulf, so that either of these harbours would appear to be much more eligible for the purposes or traffic than Simoda, almost isolated as it is on the land side by the lofty ranges of Idsu.

SIMIDZU BAY,* surveyed by H.M.S. *Actæon* in 1861, is formed by a low flat tongue of land of considerable width, stretching out in a north-easterly direction from the north-western shore of the gulf. It is most commodious, and affords good shelter in 10 to 15 fathoms soft mud, with an inner anchorage at its head, available for small craft, in which, if required, they could be beached for repairs. A small river flows into the bay, at its head.

This tongue of low land is well covered by sugar plantations and villages. Its extreme north point, of sand and shingle, is steep-to, there being no bottom at 100 fathoms at a little more than a mile off shore, and vessels running for the harbour may safely skirt the beach, and rounding the point at two cables, anchor by the lead or as convenient. With a southerly wind there is ample space for working, the lead giving good warning, and from the flatness of the land the sudden shifts of wind, so very embarrassing to vessels endeavouring to enter either of the four bays on the eastern shore of the gulf, are not so frequently met with. The town is situated at the south end of the harbour, and appears to be one of some little importance. It is the centre of a large and productive sugar growing district; plantations of the cane are to be seen in every direction.

Supplies.—In a timber yard at the north side of the town were some large spars, pine and fir (the latter having a very short grain), numerous small rough spars, and small pieces of particularly hard oak. There were quantities of sugar of a very fair quality in the town, also a little flour, a few fowls, fish, and vegetables. Water was obtained from the authorities.

No coal was seen, but a quantity of charcoal. The latter, when

---

* See Plan of Simidzu bay, No. 270; scale, m = 3·0 inches.

attainable in sufficient quantities, is admirably adapted for steaming purposes, and was extensively used by the gun boats attached to the *Actæon* in 1861. There were several qualities, the softer being little better than Japanese coal; but there is a very hard description (of a blueish black colour) which is better than any Welsh coal for high pressure engines.

ENO URA lies in the north-east angle at the head of Suruga gulf, in lat. 35° 3′ N., long. 138° 53′ E. It is 9 cables long, north and south, and 6 cables deep. Ara sima, a wooded island affording shelter from westerly winds, lies off the south point of entrance, and there is a small monument on the north point. The soundings in the bay are deep, 20 to 30 fathoms, and it is open to the west, but there is good shelter from all winds in a small bay in its northern part, where the depth is 13 fathoms over a bottom of find sand. In steering for this small bay, keep midway between its western shore and the cliffs on the eastern. A town stands on the western shore.*

A small river flows into the bay, but as water is obtained from it with difficulty on account of its shallowness, it is best to procure it from the town wells. There is abundance of fish and vegetables. The rise and fall of tide is about 4 feet.

HEDA BAY, in lat. 34° 58′ 11″ N., long. 138° 46′ E., is 8 cables in extent N.W. and S.E., 4 to 9 cables wide, and carries a depth of 8 to 22 fathoms over a bottom of fine sand. It is sheltered on all sides by high mountains. There is a village in a valley. Six rivers flow into the bay, but it is preferable to obtain water from the wells. Fish and vegetables are abundant.

The entrance to the bay, a quarter of a mile wide and open to the N.W., is to the northward of a low and sandy spit extending half a mile in a northerly direction from the southern shore. The rise of tide is 5½ feet.

ARARI BAY, sheltered also from all winds, is in lat. 34° 50′ N., long. 138° 46′ E. Its extent is 4 cables north and south, and 2 to 6 cables across, but is only 60 feet wide at the entrance, it is therefore only suitable for small craft; the depths are 6 to 12 fathoms over fine sand. The shores of the bay are mountainous. Water may be conveniently obtained from the village on the eastern shore; fish is plentiful.

The entrance is open to the N.W.; in entering keep in mid-channel, and when a small island opens, steer between it and the sandy point to the S.W. After rounding this point the course is South for the middle of the bay, where the depth is 7 fathoms.

---

* The description of Eno ura, Heda, Arari, and Tago bays is by Lieut. Elkin, of the Russian frigate *Diana*, 1853-55. *See* Plans of these bays, scale, m = 1¾ inches, on Chart of Nipon island, No. 2,347, corrected to August 1872.

TAGO BAY, in lat. 34° 47′ 3″ N., long. 138° 44′ 54″ E., is 4 cables in extent, north and south, and half a mile wide. It is sheltered from all winds, and carries a depth of 12 to 20 fathoms, soft mud bottom. There is a small town here, and water can be obtained from the wells. Fish and vegetables can be procured.

In steering for the entrance, which is also open to the N.W., two islands (lying half a mile W.N.W. from the south point of entrance) will be seen, with rocks and breakers extending to the southward from them.

Pass northward of these islands, between them and the mainland. After passing about a cable to the northward of another island, lying off the south point of entrance, steer S.E. for the middle of the bay, where there is anchorage in 13 fathoms.

DIRECTIONS.—These four bays just described will serve as a refuge from S.W. winds, which cause a great swell in Suruga gulf. Their coasts are wooded and mountainous, attaining the height of 1,000 feet. The entrances may be approached fearlessly, for the high coast conceals them, and the bays only open when within a mile.

The whole of the western coast of the Idsu peninsula is shelving, and may be safely approached to 2 miles; islands lie off it, but not beyond the distance of a mile. The current is stronger along the shores than in the middle of the gulf.

IRO-O SAKI (cape Idsu), a fine bold rocky headland which cannot be mistaken, is the southern extremity of the mountainous peninsula of Idsu. It will be recognized by a conspicuous white cliff $3\frac{1}{2}$ miles to the north-west of it, and a conical rocky peak a few miles farther in the same direction, forming the south-western extreme of the peninsula. The white cliff is very remarkable from the S.W. and South. There is an islet 50 feet high a quarter of a mile off the shore, one mile west of the cape. To the E.N.E., the coast for 3 miles is very broken and fronted with numerous sunken rocks.

LIGHT.—On the point, elevated 185 feet above the sea, is exhibited a *fixed red* light of the sixth order, visible in clear weather from a distance of 8 miles. The tower is 20 feet high, octagonal shaped, built of wood, and painted white; its position is lat. 34° 36′ N., long. 138° 51′ E.

MIKOMOTO (Rock island), about 104 feet high and a third of a mile in length, with precipitous shores and an uneven outline, bears E. by S. $\frac{3}{4}$ S. about 5 miles from cape Idsu; it has a thick matting of grass, weeds, moss, &c., on its summit. Between this rock and the main land are the Ucona and four other rocks, among which the junks freely pass; but a vessel should not attempt to run inside Rock island at night unless her distance from it can be accurately estimated, for some of the rocks about Ucona are small ledges and only 2 miles distant from Mikomoto.

TIDES.—Regular tides have been observed, the flood setting W.S.W., 1½ miles an hour, the ebb E.N.E., from 2 to 3 miles per hour; thus with the ebb tide the north-easterly current is considerably augmented in force whilst the flood tide overruns the current close to the shore. To the northwest and north of Mikomoto there are overfalls caused by the tides passing over a very uneven bottom. The Japanese fishermen deny the existence of any danger there.

The channel between Mikomoto and Ucona rocks carries irregular soundings of 14 to 30 fathoms, with the exception of a patch of 9 fathoms 3 cables north of the island. An additional reason for not using this channel at night is, that by crossing on a more southerly course towards cape Sagami the influence of the indraught on the eastern side of Odawara bay is not so likely to be felt.

LIGHT.—On Mikomoto, at an elevation of 164 feet above the sea, is exhibited a *fixed* white light of the first order, visible in clear weather at a distance of 21 miles. A *red* ray is shown between N.W. and N. ¾ E., over all the dangers between Mikomoto and the shore; the eastern edge of the ray leading into Simoda harbour. The tower is 75 feet high, built of white stone, and is in lat. 34° 34′ 20″ N., long. 138° 57′ 10″ E.

Ucona rocks, two in number, though they generally appear as one, bear N. by W., distant 2 miles from Mikomoto; the largest is about 25 feet high. Four other rocks occupy a triangular space of a mile from W.S.W. to N.N.W. of the Ucona. The northern and southern of these are small ledges nearly awash. A reef also extends 3½ cables towards them from Tohadgi point to the north-west of the Ucona. There is deep water between all these rocks.

SIMODA HARBOUR,* is on the eastern side of the peninsula of Idsu, 6 miles N.E. of the cape. To the northward of the harbour a high ridge intersects the peninsula; and south of this, all the way to the cape, it is broken by innumerable peaks of less elevation.

Vandalia bluff, the east point of entrance to the harbour, will be known by a grove of pine trees on the summit of the bluff, and the village of Susaki, which is about a third of the way between it and Sumegi saki.

This cape is 1¼ miles eastward of the entrance, and immediately off it is a rocky islet, and northward of it the bay of Soto ura, which, as it has several sand beaches, may be mistaken for Simoda harbour; but on approaching this, Sumegi saki will shut in cape Idsu, the Ucona rocks, and Mikomoto island to the southward; whilst in Simoda road they are visible from all points. The town of Simoda stands on the west shore of the harbour, and Kaki-saki village on the east. There is good landing for boats in Simoda creek, and also at the village.

---

* See Plan of Simoda harbour, No. 2,665; scale, *m* = 3·8 inches.

CHAP. V.]   S.E. COAST OF NIPON.—SIMODA HARBOUR.   175

Supplies.—Wood, water, fish, fowls, and eggs, also sweet potatoes and other vegetables, may be procured from the authorities at Simoda. It will be necessary to supply them with casks to bring the water off.

Centre island, lying nearly in the middle of Simoda harbour, bears N. ¾ E. 5½ miles from Rock island, and N. by E. ¼ E. 3½ miles from the Ucona rocks. It is high, conical, covered with trees, and a cave passes entirely through it.

Buisaco islet, a quarter of a mile N.N.E. from Centre island, is about 40 feet high, and covered with trees and shrubs.

Southampton and Supply rocks.—There are but two hidden dangers in Simoda harbour; the first is Southampton rock, which is in mid-channel, S. by E. ¾ E. 2 cables from south point of Centre island, and N. ½ W. from Vandalia bluff, about three-fourths of the way between it and Centre; it is about 25 feet in diameter, and has 2 fathoms water on it, and was formerly marked by a *white* spar buoy. The other is the Supply rock, lying S. by W. a short distance from Buisaco or Misana islet; it is a sharp rock, with 11 feet water on it, and is marked by a *red* spar buoy.

Both of these buoys were securely moored and the authorities of Simoda promised to replace them should they by any cause be removed. Should the buoy on the Southampton rock be removed, the east end of Centre island in line with the west end of Buisaco islet will lead to the westward.

ANCHORAGE.—In the outer road, or mouth of the harbour, a disagreeable swell is sometimes experienced; but inside Southampton rock and Centre island vessels are well sheltered, and the water comparatively smooth. Moor with open hawse to the south-west.

When this harbour was surveyed in 1853–54, the bottom throughout was mud; but a few months subsequently the harbour was scoured out to its granite foundations by the back sweep of three huge waves which in succession rose over the tops of the highest trees and left the bay nearly empty. Large junks were thrown some distance inland, and the Russian frigate *Diana*, left all but a total wreck. A great number of Japanese craft were swept away by the retiring masses of water, and their crews perished. It has never since afforded good holding ground in the event of a storm, but it was always an unsafe and exposed bay when the anchorage ground was tolerable, being open to South and S.S.W., the direction from which the heaviest winds blow.

TIDES.—It is high water, full and change, in Simoda harbour at 5h. 0m.; extreme rise of tide, 5¾ feet; mean rise, 3 feet.

DIRECTIONS.—If intending to anchor at Simoda, pass Mikomoto at a mile, when the harbour will be in full view to the northward. Standing in from this island, a vessel will probably pass through a number of tide rips, but no soundings will be obtained with the hand lead until near the entrance, when the depth will be 14 to 27 fathoms. Should the wind be from the northward and fresh, she should anchor at the mouth of the harbour until it lulls or shifts, or until she can conveniently warp in, as the wind is usually flawy and always baffling.

Approaching from the north-east or eastward, a vessel can pass on either side of Vries, island, from the north and south points of which, Sumegi saki, bears respectively W.S.W. and West, distant about 21 miles. Between Vries and Simoda, no dangers are known to exist; but the currents are uncertain, and strong near the coast.

Should Vries be obscured by thick weather, before reaching Sumegi saki, endeavour to sight Mikomoto, for there are no conspicuous objects on the main land by which a stranger can recognize the harbour at a distance, and the shore appears as one unbroken line. To the westward of the harbour there are several sand beaches, and three or four sand banks; these can be plainly discerned when within 6 or 8 miles, and are good landmarks. Off the village of Su saki, at a third of a mile from the shore, is a ledge of rocks upon which the surf is always breaking; give them a berth of 2 cables in passing.

Approaching Simoda from the south-east, pass westward of Kosu sima, from which the harbour bears N. by W. $\frac{1}{2}$ W. distant about 27 miles.

The COAST.—From Iro-o saki the coast rounds in a north-east direction 26 miles to Futo saki, its general features being high, rocky, and even, having near Simoda a few sandy beaches. Between Simoda and Futo saki the coast is bold of approach. Over it, the mountain Amagi yama rises to 4,700 feet, and on the north-east ridge is a conspicuous dome-shaped hill.

From Futo saki the coast trends more to the northward, forming a slight bend to Fuku ura, where it becomes more broken, but maintains its bold features under a lower range, the two highest points of which are elevated 2,970 and 2,460 feet; under the latter is a round hill with a large quarry facing the gulf. From these hills the long low promontory of Manatsuru, bordered by vertical cliffs, stretches to the eastward, and off its extreme point is a rock 20 feet high. On its west side is the open bay of Fuku ura, not yet surveyed. From thence the coast assumes a lower elevation, and gradually bending round to the eastward forms the treacherous bay of Odawara. To the northward of Futo saki are some small islands, the largest of which, Ha sima, 120 feet high, is about $3\frac{1}{2}$ miles off shore. W. by N. from this island is the small bay of Ajiro. The north shore of Odawara bay is low to the east of the wooded bluff 14 miles north-east of Manatsuru, and said to be very shallow in front of the sandy beach.

The bay of Odawara, from the lowness of the land at its head, has been mistaken for the Uraga channel. When past Vries island, however, the channel will be recognized by Su saki, its east point of entrance, being comparatively high (645 feet), whereas cape Sagami, the southern point of the peninsula of that name on the west side of entrance, is not more than 70 feet high, with the exception of a small hill of 354 feet elevation on the centre of its south part, named Tree Saddle, from two conspicuous clumps of large trees on its summit.

From Odawara the coast trends to the eastward for 20 miles as far as Ino saki, and then takes a southerly direction for about 10 miles to Joka sima.

AJIRO BAY* may be distinguished by a small white cliff to the northward; the water in the bay is deep, there being no bottom at 20 fathoms at the entrance. A natural breakwater forms a shelter for small vessels, but the water is deep within it, there being from 13 to 5 fathoms.

ANCHORAGE may be obtained in 7 fathoms, black sand, with the following bearings:—Ha sima, S.E. ½ E.; rock off the south point, S. by E. ⅛ E., and a conspicuous white cottage, W. ⅛ S. The anchorage is open to all winds from south round by east to N.N.E. The deepest water was obtained towards the south bluff, increasing from the anchorage to 9 fathoms, and towards the village and the north point it shoaled gradually to 5 fathoms within a short distance of the shore.

ODAWARA BAY.—Care must be observed when steering for the Uraga channel not to be drawn into this bay, as a considerable indraught has always been experienced, and the low land at the head of the bay contrasted with the high land to the westward of it, looks so distant, that the bay has often been mistaken for the channel, and the error only discovered when deeply embayed and probably close to some of the reefs which skirt the head and east side of the bay, the most dangerous of which is the Macedonian reef.

INO SIMA, 220 feet high, is the eastern extreme of the low shore fronting the plain at the head of Odawara bay, which is said to be very shallow, although there are 56 fathoms at 4 miles distance. A large reef marked by a peaked rock 30 feet high was seen breaking heavily off the beach, 2 miles to the west of Ino sima. Ino sima has bold high cliffs of a light colour which makes it very conspicuous, and a flattish summit with a few large trees. On the south-east it cannot be approached within three-quarters of a mile, as an extensive reef skirts that part of the island. The island is connected with the main, where the Sagami hills terminate, by a narrow ridge of shingle which covers at high water, to the westward of which a small river disembogues. There is generally a heavy ground swell at this part of the bay.

The white pointed cliffs of Kotzbo mura will be seen 2¼ miles east of Ino sima (the coast between being skirted by sunken reefs), and are a guide to the only anchorage on the north side of Odawara bay.

---

* Navigating Lieutenant F. K. Taylor, H.M.S. *Salimis.*

HORINO-UTSI MURA.—The bay directly east of the white cliffs is full of reefs and cannot be approached, but Horino-utsi mura, the bay next south-east, and to the north of Impérieuse bluff, is a fair temporary anchorage, though exposed to W. and S.W. winds.

A reef 3 cables long extends from a low point at the foot of Impérieuse bluff. To the north-west of this, a chain of rocks runs out westward from the low point just north of the bluff; the centre part of these is marked by a large white topped rock 20 feet high; the outer rock is very small but uncovered. At 3 or 4 cables north of this chain there is anchorage in 4 to 8 fathoms. The *Dove* and *Leven* anchored here, the line of rocks quite breaking the heavy swell from the south.

MACEDONIAN REEF lies off the east side of Odawara bay, at 4 miles N.N.W. of the lighthouse on the west end of Joka sima. It dries in many places at low tide, and, except in the smoothest water, always betrays itself by a breaker when covered, and is therefore easily avoided in day time; but if it be not visible do not bring the lighthouse to the southward of S.S.E. ½ E. until the south end of the first range of hills, 700 feet high, north of cape Sagami, bears E. ½ N. The ranges of Sagami peninsula terminate in Impérieuse bluff, 500 feet high, wooded and very conspicuous. By keeping the west slope of the bluff N. by E. a vessel will pass three-quarters of a mile outside the reef in 30 fathoms.

ASINA BAY.—Vessels embarrassed in the vicinity of the Macedonian reef may find an anchorage about 1½ miles north-east of it in Asina bay, in 4 to 8 fathoms good holding ground, and sheltered from all points except westward, in which direction the sea has a clear fetch of 20 miles; but only a case of extreme emergency would justify a stranger in using it.

Entering the bay, when the south end of the above range of hills, 700 feet high, bears E. ½ N., or is in line with the south low projecting point of the bay, the Macedonian reef will have been cleared, and an E. by N. ½ N. course may be steered for the entrance, taking care to avoid a mass of rocky ground extending from the reef to the south extreme of the bay. There are also some rocks off the north side of the bay, but they show, and are easily avoided by keeping mid-channel.

KO-ADJIRO BAY.—There are two or three excellent havens for small craft and junks on the west shore of Sagami peninsula, to the southward of Macedonian reef. Ko-adjiro, the largest of these, is 2 miles north of Joka sima lighthouse, or three-quarters of a mile north-east of the Moroisi, a long reef of rocks, which extend off the point N. by W. ½ W. of the lighthouse. There is no difficulty in entering. There is a reef off the north point of entrance which, with only one fathom water on it, stretches half across the entrance with a 4-fathoms channel on the bold south shore. Farther in a perch marks the end of the shoal from the south shore. Inside this is secure anchorage for a small vessel in 3 fathoms.

JOKA SIMA lies off the S.W. point of cape Sagami, with a channel about 2 cables wide, and encumbered with rocks, between it and the shore. The island is one mile long N.W. and S.E., and about 2 cables in breadth; it is skirted with reefs extending $1\frac{1}{2}$ cables from the shore, and off its southern shore is a rocky patch of 2 fathoms, 2 cables from the island.

LIGHT.—On the west end of the island, elevated 106 feet above the sea, is exhibited a *fixed* white light of the fourth order, visible from between S. by E. $\frac{1}{2}$ E. round by East to N. by W. $\frac{1}{2}$ W., and is visible in clear weather from a distance of 9 miles.

DIRECTIONS.—In navigating the south-eastern coast of Japan, after passing Satano misaki, in Van Diemen strait, if the weather be thick, the vessel's position should be well ascertained before she is hauled to the E.N.E., as her course is parallel to the high land for about 20 miles from the pitch of the cape. It should also be borne in mind that the current on this coast (Kuro siwo) runs to the E.N.E. at the rate of from 40 to 100 miles a day (see page 23).

Vessels therefore bound to the eastward must allow for this current, and should keep more than 30 miles off shore, taking every opportunity of verifying their reckoning;* if working up inshore the north-easterly set will be lost, and the ship will be influenced by the tides. Many vessels have under these circumstances reported the current as setting in various directions in the vicinity of the Kii and Boungo channels, indraughts, and vice versâ, resulting from the ebb or flood tide being experienced at the time. In the summer season the north-easterly current is not to be expected in the vicinity of Iro-o saki (cape Idsu).

Vessels from the gulf of Yedo bound for the Kii channel, after passing Mikomoto (Rock island), should take an inshore passage, steering for Omae saki, and thence for Ō sima, thus avoiding the strength of the Japan stream. Following this course, a vessel may carry a favourable current (on the flood), and it has been often observed that there is a back set to the S.W. in the bights between Rock island and Ō sima. In following this route, take care to avoid the rocks off cape Sima.

In approaching the gulf of Yedo, the remarkable high mountain Fusi yama (page 170), a lofty and symmetrical truncated cone of 12,450 feet elevation, and so different in form from any other land in its vicinity, cannot fail to be of great service in directing vessels either to Simoda or Yedo. In clear weather it is the first distant land seen, and generally to

---

* It is recommended to make the lights at Oö sima (entrance to the Kii channel) whenever it is practicable.

the north-eastward, visible at times upwards of 100 miles. Iro-o saki (cape Idsu) is in line with it when bearing North. When bound from the southward and westward endeavour to make Iro-o saki, and if the weather is at all clear, the chain of islands off the gulf of Yedo will at the same time be plainly visible. Omae saki, the west point of entrance to Suruga gulf, cannot be mistaken for Iro-o saki, the former being low, with a sandy beach and low sand hills, with occasional patches of trees, and the coast is said to preserve this character for 30 or 40 miles to the westward; whereas the cape is high and rocky, has a lighthouse at its foot, its summit being generally hidden in the clouds. Mikomoto (Rock island) being low, unless the weather is clear, or at night when the light is visible, will not be seen until long after this cape and Vries island are made.

Between the Kii channel and Mikomoto, westerly winds are most frequently met with, falling light, when the latter place is passed; and often on rounding cape Sagami a strong N.E. wind is encountered.

The GULF of YEDO,* the entrance to which, named the Uraga channel lies between cape Sagami on the west, and cape King, in the province of Awa, on the east, is 15 miles wide between these points, and 35 miles deep. Situated on the north-west shore at its head is the city of Yedo, now known as Tokei (eastern capital) the commercial as well as political capital of the empire, and on the western shore is the principal seaport and treaty port of Japan, viz. Yokohama.

URAGA CHANNEL, leading into the gulf of Yedo, appears remarkably clear of hidden danger. On its west side are the Ashika sima (Plymouth rocks), which are always uncovered and easily seen; there are some sunken rocks close around them. In their vicinity, off Senda saki and Uraga, are several rocky patches extending some distance from the shore. The mariner should bear this in mind, and as Kaneda bay has also some foul ground in it at nearly a mile from the shore, it would be prudent to give this locality a good berth in passing.

SAGAMI MISAKI,† the western cape at the entrance to the Uraga channel is comparatively low, the hills forming in a table flat about 150 feet in height, and rising, about one mile from the shore, to a saddle peak, having on it two conspicuous clumps of trees elevated 354 feet above the sea. The shore is clear at less than half a mile, except off the eastern part of the cape, where there is a patch of $4\frac{3}{4}$ fathoms at that distance lying S.E., 7 cables from the north extreme of the cape.

---

* See Chart of Yedo bay, No. 2,657; scale, $m = 0{\cdot}95$ inches.

† The directions from Sagami misaki to Yokoska are from the remarks of Navigating Lieutenant W. F. Maxwell, H.M.S. *Sylvia*, 1869.

LIGHT.—On Tsuruga saki, the south-eastern point of cape Sagami, at an elevation of 110 feet above the sea, is exhibited a *flashing* white light of the second order, showing a flash every ten seconds, seen between E. by N., round by South to S.W. ¼ W., and visible in clear weather from a distance of 16 miles. A *red* sector of 16° covers the Ashika sima (Plymouth rocks) extending from S.W. ¼ W. to S.S.W. ¾ W. The tower, 36 feet in height, is in lat. 35° 8′ N., long. 139° 41′ E.

KANEDA BAY, contained between Sagami misaki and Senda saki, having a range of hills sloping down to its north-west shore, the highest, Take yama, being 714 feet above the sea, affords excellent anchorage with winds from south, round by west and north to north-east, in from 10 to 3 fathoms, as convenient; sandy bottom, good holding ground.

Oki-no sima, 3 feet above high water, is a black rock in the south-west portion of the bay, steep-to on the north side, but having foul ground between it and the shore on the south and west sides.

Mits iso form a cluster of rocks in the centre of the bay, that cover at high water. A shoal having 6 feet on it at low water lies W. by S. ¼ S. 7 cables from the southern and highest of these rocks; another shoal of 9 feet lies W. by S. ¾ S. nearly one mile from the same rock.

ASHIKA SIMA (Plymouth rocks) are two dark rocks 5 feet above high water, lying N.E. ½ N. 5½ miles from Sagami misaki, and S. by W. ¼ W. 3¾ miles from the lighthouse on Kanon saki.

Kata sima, a rock awash, lies S.E. by E. ¾ E. nearly one cable from the eastern of the two rocks, and is marked by a *red* beacon, surmounted by a ball about 20 feet above high water.

SENDA SAKI shows in steep white cliffs the termination of the range from Take yama. It has a dismantled fort at the summit of the cliffs, and is surrounded by detached rocks. The eastern portion of these runs out in a spit, the outer edge, of 21 feet, lying E. by S. ¼ S. 6 cables from the point, and leaving only a passage of 3 cables between it and Ashika sima. The outer detached rock awash, steep-to on the south side, lies S.S.W. 9¼ cables from Senda saki.

On entering Kaneda bay from the northward, Ashika sima should not be brought to the eastward of N.E. ½ N. until Take yama bears N.W. by W.

KURIHAMA, the bay north of Senda saki, has a sandy beach at its head, the end of a long plain that is drained by a river running into a lagoon that enters the sea at the north end of the beach. This bay should not be used as an anchorage, the ground being foul in all directions.

KADZUSA SAKI, the north point of this bay, is terminated by a conical mound, Shendōra, 69 feet above high water, from which a ledge of rocks extends S.E. ½ S. 4¼ cables to the outer depth of 5 fathoms. From this to Tomio saki the ground is foul nearly 4 cables from the shore.

URAGA, a thriving village, and clearance port of the junk trade to Yedo, is a capital harbour for vessels drawing less than 9 feet, but should not be entered without a chart.

Tomio saki.—The south point of the entrance to Uraga is a low point with a Japanese lighthouse and a memorial stone near its extreme. These have been erroneously called beacons, when in line they clear Ka yama.

A shoal of 12 feet lies E. ¼ S. 3 cables from the light, and there is less than three fathoms, three-quarters of a cable S.E. from it.

Miojin saki, the north point of entrance to Uraga, is a bold bluff surmounted by a battery. From it to Kanon saki the land is undulating, with villages in sandy bays. The whole of this coast is foul for half a mile from the shore, having depths of 1¾ to 4¾ fathoms on the outer margin.

KA YAMA (Elmstone rock) has only 12 feet on it at low water, with 4 fathoms, 2 cables to the eastward and southward. It lies S. by W. ¾ W., nearly one mile from Kanon saki lighthouse. Ashika sima kept S.S.W. ½ W. until Kanon saki light bears N.N.W. will clear all the foul ground.

KANON SAKI.—Kanon saki is a steep and partially wooded point, within which, one cable from the shore, is a conical hill 272 feet above high water.

LIGHT.—On the slope of the hill above mentioned, at an elevation of 170 feet above high water, is exhibited a *fixed* white light of the fourth order, visible in clear weather from a distance of 14 miles. The tower is square, built of stone, and rises from the centre of the keeper's dwelling; it is in lat. 34° 14′ 45″ N., long. 139° 44′ 17″ E.

The point immediately east of the lighthouse is steep-to, but the south-east extreme of Kanon saki has a reef off it, terminated by a rock awash, steep-to, 1¼ cables from the shore. From this to Rubicon point the coast is slightly indented, having sandy bays between the points. From Rubicon point rocks extend one cable, with deep water close to the outer.

Ó-TSU-NO URA is a deep bay with a sandy beach, having numerous villages, from the largest of which it takes its name. This bay has shallow water in the eastern portion, the outer shoal of 12 feet lying N.W. by W. ½ W. 8¾ cables from Rubicon point. In the centre of the bay is a shoal 4¼ cables long by 3 cables broad, having 9 feet on the north and 13 feet on the south edge, with uneven depths of 2¼ to 4¼ fathoms between. The north edge lies S. ¾ E. 4 cables from the south end of Saru sima, and N.W. by W. ¾ W. nearly 2 miles from Rubicon point.

SARU SIMA (Perry island), 198 feet high, is cliffy, with a wooded flat summit. The south-east point has a conspicuous single tree; and from the south extreme a sandy spit extends half a cable. This island has shoal water all round, except off the north end.

From the south point, E. by S. ¾ S. 3¾ cables, lies Kitsne no se, a rock that covers at high water, and West, 3 cables from the same, lie three rocks awash at high water. Between these and Kitsne no se there is shallow water. No vessel should go between Hana rete and Saru sima.

HANA-RETE, 94 feet high, is a grass covered conical mound, sloping down to dark rugged rocks. Between it and the western end of Ō-tsu-no ura the coast is a series of white cliffs, with shingly beaches intervening.

Immediately south of Hana-rete is a deep bay, off the south point of which there is a conical islet 78 feet high, from which, S.S.E. ½ E. 3½ cables, lies a rock that dries at low water, with foul ground between it and the shore.

A rock, awash at low water, having on it an iron beacon surmounted by a cage, and painted *red*, lies N.E. by E. 3½ cables from Hana rete; East, one mile nearly from Ha sima at the entrance to Yokoska; and N.W. 4 miles from Kanon saki extreme. It may be approached to a quarter of a mile on the north side, but vessels should not attempt to pass inside it.

YOKOSKA HARBOUR,* 11 cables in depth, and with a general breadth of 3½ cables, is the eastern of two inlets, and may be easily recognized by Ha sima, the islet that lies off its north-east point, and by a remarkable clump of trees, 355 feet above the sea, known as Azuma, on the highest hill of the promontory that separates it from Ura-no-go ura, the western bay.

It has a series of cliffs and indentations, the points generally being marked by white stone beacons. At the head of the harbour is a dock, with large smith and boiler factories, and all the necessary works for thoroughly repairing and building ships, with houses for the officials, are built on a plain that joins Ō-tsu-no ura. On one of these factories is a clock tower, that may be seen from that bay. The inner harbour is formed by two breakwaters, and is of considerable width at the entrance.

The dock is 395 feet in length, 82 feet broad, and 26 feet deep. It has no lock, and vessels can pass from the anchorage through the inner harbour direct to the dock.

There are three other slips for building purposes.

Buoy.—Off the eastern points of Yokoska there are spits, having 10 to 12 feet on their outer edges; those off Susu-ga saki extending N.N.E. 2½ cables, and N.W. ½ W. 1½ cables. The outer end of the latter is marked by a small red cask buoy. Vessels should not bring Ha sima to the northward of N.E. by N.

---

* See Plan of Yokoska harbour on Chart of Yedo bay, No. 2,657.

Anchorage may be had in 6 to 8 fathoms in any part of the bay, but large ships should not go inside the red buoy, as there the anchorage space has only 2 cables breadth.

Through the promontory that separates Yokoska from Ura-no-go ura, a canal has been cut, through which boats may go, when the tide has risen one foot above low water. Hako saki, the north-west extreme of this promontory, has rocks that show at low water, and shoals off it for 1½ cables. For the better protection of Yokoska harbour a breakwater is being constructed, which will be about 600 feet in length when completed.

URA-NO-GOURA, 8 cables long, with a general breadth of 4 cables, has excellent anchorage in 7 to 4½ fathoms, mud, as convenient; the water shoaling gradually as the bay is entered. There is no danger in the mid-channel.

Yenokido is a deep inlet on the western shore of this bay, with too narrow an entrance for ships, but a fine harbour for junks, running inland 4 cables, and having a general width of one cable. From its north point, E. by N. ¾ N. 1¼ cables, lies Yabama, a reef that just shows at high water, steep-to on the outer edge.

NATSUI SIMA is a partially wooded island 300 feet high, that stands between Ura-no-go ura, and the entrance to Kanasawa inlet. It has a spit of shoal water with 4 fathoms on its outer edge, extending East 3 cables, and shoaling gradually towards the shore.

Yeboshi yama is a conical rocky islet, joined to the shore near Yenokido at low water, and separated by a channel of one cable from the south-west point of Natsui sima.

The COAST.*—On passing Natsui sima a creek is seen which on entering winds round in a northerly direction, and at about half a mile from the entrance the channel contracts, passing which it opens into a large shallow lagoon. A narrow channel marked by stakes and bushes leads up to the village of Kanasawa, situated in the north-east corner. From this village there is a good road (which lies through a remarkable narrow pass) to the town of Kamakura, celebrated in the history of Japan as being a former opulent town, and also at this time for its ancient temples. Continuing this road for some distance about 2 or 3 miles from Kamakura is the celebrated bronze statue of Daibutsŭ sama, situated in a beautiful grove at the foot of a valley.

From Natsui sima the coast takes a northerly direction for 3 miles to Graham bluff, is shallow for some distance, and at 2 miles off shore is skirted by banks of from 4½ to 5 fathoms, with deep water between them and the coast.

---

* The coast from Natsui sima to Yokohama has not been minutely examined.

MISSISSIPPI BAY* (Nigisi) formed between Graham bluff to the southward and Treaty point on the north, (between which it is 3 miles in width), is well sheltered from the prevailing winds. In anchoring give the shore a wide berth to avoid a shoal which extends half to three-quarters of a mile from it. Between Natsui sima and Treaty point the soundings are irregular, shoaling suddenly from 12 to 5 fathoms on banks of hard sand.

TREATY POINT, the termination of a ridge of low hills extending into the gulf of Yedo, about $10\frac{1}{2}$ miles N.N.W. of Kanon saki, forms the southern point of the bay of Yokohama. The point is formed of a long line of cliffs of a conspicuous yellow colour, the northern bluff of which is called Mandarin bluff.

These bluffs, and a bank which fronts them to the distance of $1\frac{1}{4}$ miles in some places, and which is rather steep-to, protects the anchorage from south-westerly winds, the only ones which blow with sufficient force to send a heavy sea into the bay.

LIGHT VESSEL.—A light vessel, marked "Treaty point" on her sides, with two masts, carrying a ball at her foremost head, is placed at the extremity of the shoal off Treaty point and Mandarin bluff, and lies in 7 fathoms, with the following bearings:—Treaty point, S.W. $\frac{3}{4}$ S.; Mandarin bluff, S.W. by W., and the mouth of the canal (just northward of the English sick quarters), W. $\frac{1}{4}$ N. The vessel exhibits a *fixed red* light elevated 36 feet above the sea, and is visible in clear weather from a distance of 10 miles.

Buoy.—An iron buoy with a cage painted *red* is moored in 4 fathoms on the northern extreme of the shoal off Mandarin bluff, southward of the anchorage off Yokohama, with the following bearings:—Mandarin bluff, S. by E. $\frac{1}{4}$ E.; mouth of the canal, S.W. by S. $\frac{1}{2}$ S.; and the centre of the English hatoba (landing place), W. by S.

YOKOHAMA.†—Yokohama is on a plain surrounded by low hills, and is environed by a canal which entirely isolates it. The only communications are by a bridge and causeway towards Kanagawa from the rear of the town on the west, and with the Yokohama bluffs by another bridge close to the sea. The residences of the foreign community occupy the east, and those of the Japanese merchants the north-west of the town, and the bluff on the south side on which is situated the camp and British Legation is being rapidly built over. Two hatobas or landing places formed of stone piers, the ends of which are protected by a pallisade of wooden piles to break the sea, afford excellent landing; that to the south (the French hatoba) is merely two piers parallel to each other, but the northern (the English hatoba) is a

---

* Named by Commodore Perry's squadron in 1854.

† See Plan of Yokohama bay on Sheet 2,657; scale, $m = 1\cdot9$ inches.

camber in which boats are completely sheltered. Immediately opposite the last landing place is the English consulate, a large building with three peculiar towers. The English sick quarters are on the northern face of the bluff at the southern end of the town ; boats can land there at high water in the canal above mentioned. The position of the square in the sick quarters is lat. 35° 26′ 30″ N., long. 139° 39′ 24″ E. The whole of the settlement or concession is faced by a sea wall of stone, along which there is a broad esplanade. Yokohama exports tea, raw and manufactured silk, lacquered goods, vegetable wax, oil, antlers, cotton, and rice in small quantities. For the Chinese market, paper, camphor, flour, peas, beans, seaweed, isinglass, beche-de-mer, and dried shell fish.

At the head of the bay and on its north side stands the town of Kanagawa, one of the ports opened to foreigners, but this being an inconvenient situation for a settlement it was changed to Yokohama on the south side, it being a more eligible position for business communication. The water also is deeper for anchorage and more convenient for the landing of boats and merchandise than at Kanagawa, where it is so shallow that at low tide the sea retreats to a considerable distance from the shore.

Kanagawa is subject to frequent shocks of earthquakes. It is situated on the Tokaido or imperial highway to Yedo, and British subjects are free to go where they please within the following limits—from Kanagawa, 10 *ri* (21 miles) in any direction except towards Yedo, the boundary in that direction being the river Logo, which flows into the bay of Yedo between Kawa saki and Sinagawa, the southern suburb. A Japanese guard house is situated at the river Logo, and all persons (excepting officers in uniform) passing between Yokohama and Yedo must produce a passport.

Buoy.—A *red* buoy with staff and cage is moored in 4 fathoms at low water springs on the point of the spit extending from Kanagawa fort to the northern side of Yokohama anchorage, and lies S.E. by E. easterly, one mile from Kanagawa fort.

Anchorage.—A good anchorage for large ships is with Kanon saki just open of Mandarin bluff, the latter bearing S. by E., and the British consulate S.W. by W. ½ W., mud bottom. Vessels of lighter draught may, if desirable, take up a position much nearer the town.

Supplies.—All supplies, provisions, water, coal, &c., are to be procured in abundance, and ordinary repairs both to ships and engines can be easily executed.

Tides.—It is high water, full and change, in Yokohama bay at 6h., and springs rise 6½ feet, neaps 4¾ feet ; with southerly winds the tide rises about 2 feet higher.

The streams in this bay are scarcely felt, but they run strong in the middle of Yedo bay, and their velocity is much increased off Saratoga spit,

Saru sima, and Kanon saki, particularly off the latter, round which they sweep with great rapidity.

KAWA SAKI, bearing N.E. ½ N. from the light vessel off Treaty point, is low and wooded, with shoal water extending 1½ miles from the shore, its edge being marked by two buoys. The southernmost, a *red* buoy with cage, is moored in 6 fathoms, with Treaty point S.W. ½ W., Kawa saki, N. ½ W., and Bansu hana, E.S.E. southerly. The northernmost, a *black* buoy with cage, is moored in 6 fathoms with Kawa saki bearing West, Noko gawa entrance N. ¾ E., Bansu hana, S.E. ⅛ E., and the southern buoy S.W. ¾ S.

YEDO,* which has lately been named Tokei, is situated at the northwest angle of Yedo bay, along the shore of which it extends, with its suburbs, for 8 miles. Its aspect is not imposing, as large stacks of timber and elevated ground conceal by far the larger part of the city. Five batteries also interpose between the anchorage and the city. These, with several others on the shore, have green turfed parapets and escarps faced with stone, and are surrounded by a piling of timber which is covered at high water. The suburb of Sinagawa stands on the south of the city, where are seen the low wooded heights of Goten yama, extending 2 miles along the shore. The landing place is on the north side of these and west of the five forts, close to which is the temple occupied by the British legation.

† The small river Sodogawa, which flows through the very centre of Yedo, disembogues at the northernmost part of the bay on which the city stands, thence splitting into two streams it flows S.W. and S.E. for about 3 miles through the extensive mud flats which nearly fill up the head of the bay. The south-western stream flows parallel to the city front at from 5 to 7 cables distance, the channel emerging into the bay by a sharp turn to the S.S.E., between the western of the five water batteries and the forts on and near the shore; its entrance here is about 400 yards wide and from 7 to 8 feet deep at low water springs. The channel itself carries the depth of 3 feet from the entrance nearly up to the mouth of the river, probably then deepening a little. The landing places directly north of the entrance between the forts are also accessible by the same depth of water (3 feet) for 1½ miles along that part of the shore where the Tokaido or high road runs. The above depths apply to low-water springs.

At high-water neaps there would be 6 or 8 feet in this channel, according to the direction of the wind. At high-water springs there would be from 9 to 9½ feet. The ditch at Yedo, according to a large Japanese plan, com-

---

* See Chart, Yedo bay, No. 2,657; scale, $m = 0.95$ inches.

† Commander C. J. Bullock, R.N.

municates on the south with the canal named Kori, which forms an outer circle round the Imperial domain. One end of the canal falls into the Sodogawa a mile above, the other into the sea a mile below its mouth. Two canals also run direct to the sea close to the river's mouth from the ditch. The northern of these runs into the heart of the former Tycoon's castle, and is probably navigable, but the moat itself is not navigable, and is the undisturbed resort of numerous wild fowl."

LIGHT.—On the third fort (commencing with the extreme eastern fort) before the city, at the east entrance to the Tsikiji channel leading to the foreign concession at Tsikiji and the city, elevated 53 feet above high water, is exhibited a *fixed red* light of the fourth order, visible in clear weather from a distance of 9 miles.

ANCHORAGE.—This bay is so shoal all along the shore where the city stands that at low water even a ship's boat cannot approach within a mile. The best anchorage for a large ship is in 5 to 6 fathoms, soft mud, good holding ground, with the south-western of the five forts bearing N.W.; but recollect that on this bearing the water shoals rather suddenly from 4 to 2½ fathoms. It is better, therefore, to anchor a smaller vessel on a N.W. by N. bearing of the fort. H.M.S. *Furious*, in 1858, anchored in 15 feet at low water, with the five forts bearing from N. ½ W. to N.W., Beacon house S. ½ W., and the peak of Fusi yama W. by S.

The COAST* from Tonegawa point round the head of the gulf of Yedo is low, with shoal water extending a considerable distance from the shore forming a deep bay with from 6 to 8 fathoms water between the above point and Bansu hana.

BANSU HANA lies on the eastern shore of the gulf about S.E. by E. 8 miles from Kawa saki; it is very low, and is fronted by shoal water extending 2 miles from the shore in a westerly direction. From Bansu hana the coast takes a southerly and then a south-westerly direction for 12 miles, and is low and shoal from 1½ to 2 miles off shore.

FUTSU SAKI is a low sandy point, having a fort at its high-water line and stretching out in a narrow tongue that forms Saratoga spit.

Buoy.—West from this tongue, in 9 fathoms, is moored a red buoy with staff and cage, 13 feet above the water.

East from the buoy there are only 5 fathoms at 3 cables, and one fathom at three-quarters of a mile. The bank of 5 fathoms trends N.E. ½ N. and S.E. by E., deepening rapidly to 10 fathoms.

The COAST from Futsu saki takes an easterly and southerly direction, forming a deep bay, the northern shore of which is sandy and low but the

---

* The head of Yedo gulf, from Yokohama round the coast to Futsu saki, has not been closely examined.

southern is the termination of the slopes from the high range Noko-gheri yama, and is rocky and steep-to. Shoal water extends from 1½ to 2 miles from the shore in the centre of the bay.

Kanaya point, the south-western extreme of these slopes, is steep-to and bears nearly East of the Tree Saddle on Sagami peninsula; it is at the termination of the sharp well defined ridge of the Miogani yama, a fine dome-shaped mountain elevated 1,096 feet. The coast from this point takes a southerly direction for 7½ miles as far as Daibo saki, between which there are three small bays, the southern of which has several rocky patches.

Chibu isi (Black rock) about 20 feet high, lies three-quarters of a mile west of the latter bay, having several reefs in its vicinity which only uncover at low water. The lofty mountains Miogani yama, Sveno yama, and Double hill are very conspicuous, towering above this coast.

The peninsula of Awa, although mountainous, is less so than Idsu, and possesses much larger tracts of arable land, all of which is carefully cultivated. Its west coast is more sinuous than the opposite shore of the gulf, but only one of the bays, Tati yama, formed in it, affords fair anchorage.

To the northward of these hills the country (Kadsusa) becomes much lower, and a few miles north-eastward of Futsu saki, the point off which runs the Saratoga spit, it becomes an uninteresting dead flat, encircling the head of Yedo bay.

TATI-YAMA BAY.—Formed between Daibo saki and Su saki is the bay of Tati yama, in which shelter and good holding ground may be found in southerly and easterly gales, but it is exposed to the westward.

The best position to anchor is in about 7 fathoms, a quarter of a mile eastward of Taka sima, the easternmost of the two small but well wooded islands on the south side of the bay, with the west extreme of Daibo saki N.N.W. ¼ W., and Siro yama, a hill 290 feet high, S.S.E. ½ E. This hill is remarkable from having a clump on it, and being the north extreme of some rising ground in the south-east corner of the bay. This position is well sheltered from North round East to W. by S., but should there be any appearance of the wind veering westward, an early departure is recommended, as a heavy sea quickly tumbles in.

Supplies.—The *Actæon* obtained fish and fowls in small quantities. Water was brought off in boats by the villagers residing at a hamlet situated at the base of Siro yama.

SU SAKI, the east point of entrance of the gulf of Yedo, when seen from the southward appears as a block of small hills, rather conical in profile, the highest, Hazama, being elevated 650 feet. The point is low, with the exception of a small elevation at the north-west corner on which is an old fort. There is a heavy tide rip off it, but no dangers at a greater distance than half a mile from the shore, and the point may be safely rounded at a mile.

MELA HEAD and LEDGE.—Mela head, S.E. ¼ S. nearly 5 miles from Su saki, forms the eastern point of entrance to the Uraga channel and gulf of Yedo; it is 456 feet above the sea, the general height of the coast range in its vicinity being comparatively low. A small village is situated about half a mile to the northward. No-sima point, 3¼ miles to the eastward, is also low, the shore between them being skirted with rocky patches. An extremely dangerous ledge (Mela ledge) lies 1½ miles off Mela head, about 5 miles S.E. of Su saki. Extending 3 miles from this ledge in a south-westerly direction is a rocky bank in the form of a tongue with 30 fathoms on its outer extreme, gradually shoaling to the ledge; these dangers are steep-to (40 fathoms) on their south side. Heavy breakers occur in rough weather or when a swell rolls home, but in smooth water the rocks are not seen from a distance; the water, however, is so clear that the bottom is visible in a considerable depth.

LIGHT.—On No-sima point, at an elevation of 134 feet above high water, is exhibited a *fixed* white light of the first order, visible in clear weather from a distance of 20 miles. The tower is octagonal shaped and painted white, and is in lat. 34° 53′ 20″ N., long. 139° 51′ 23″ E.

DIRECTIONS.—Approaching the gulf of Yedo from the southward or westward, in clear weather the chain of islands running southward from it are unmistakeable landmarks, and cape Idsu can scarcely be mistaken. Omae saki, the point 25 miles westward of the cape, is low, while the cape, as before stated, is high, bold, and rocky. From 1½ miles eastward of Mikomoto (Rock island) a N.E. ¼ E. course will lead 4 miles north-west of Vries island, from which position the centre of the entrance of the Uraga channel bears N.E. by E., distant 22 miles. Care must, however, be observed when approaching cape Sagami not to be drawn into Odawara bay by the indraught mentioned in page 177. Should Vries island be visible this danger is easily guarded against by not bringing that island southward of S.W. by S.

Vessels approaching the gulf from the eastward are recommended not to hug the shore of the south end of Awa too closely, as dangerous shoals are known to exist in that neighbourhood.

To avoid the Mela ledge and all other *known* danger when rounding from the eastward, do not bring the eastern extreme of land *seen* to bear eastward of E.N.E. until the extreme of Su saki bears N. by W.; and when rounding from the westward do not bring the extreme of Su saki westward of N. by W. until the eastern extreme of land is E.N.E. At night or in thick weather, when the light on No-sima point is not seen, soundings of 40 fathoms may be considered as indicating close proximity to these dangers.

In steering for the Uraga channel the Tree Saddle hill on the south end of Sagami peninsula will be readily recognised; and on nearing the channel the Ashika sima (Plymouth rocks) will be plainly seen on its western side. Give these rocks and the Ka yama a berth of half a mile in passing, or at night keep the white light on cape Sagami in sight, and after rounding Kanon saki at a little less than that distance steer N. by W. ¼ W., which will lead to the westward of the buoy off the Saratoga spit, and continuing this course when the light vessel off Treaty point is seen steer to pass to the eastward of her, taking care not to bring the light to the northward of N. ½ W. The elevated ground above Mandarin bluff, at one mile northward of Treaty point, showing to seaward in brown cliffs well wooded to the summit, will be readily recognised; the bluff being the most eastern.

The light vessel may be passed within a cable's length, after rounding which steer to pass northward of the red buoy with staff and cage moored on the northern edge of the bank off Mandarin bluff, and anchor as convenient.

A sailing ship will have to make short tacks when working into Yokohama bay with a westerly wind, as north of Mandarin bluff the deep water channel is narrowed to 1⅓ miles; the lead here, however, as is the case round nearly the whole shores of Yedo bay, gives fair warning.

WORKING THROUGH the URAGA CHANNEL.—With a northerly wind a vessel after passing cape Sagami may stand across and tack close to the opposite shore, as there are no rocks at any distance off it to the northward of Kanaya point, and to the southward of the point the dangers show. If unable to fetch this point it would not be prudent to stand into the bay between the point and Uki sima, a small rocky island 150 feet high to the southward, as foul ground exists there. This bay will be readily recognised from a distance, as it is the sea shore of a valley between the Miogani yama and Sveno yama ranges, and two small hills are in the centre of it.

In making the western board, the foul ground in Kaneda bay, as well as off Senda saki, and along the shore between it and Kanon saki, must be remembered. The shore of Kadsusa bay, northward of the Miogani yama range, may be approached by the lead, tacking in 5 fathoms.

If unable to fetch Kanon saki on the starboard board, be careful to tack short of the bearing for clearing the Ka yama, page 181. Short tacks should be made when to windward of Kanon saki, not shoaling towards the opposite or Kadsusa shore to less than 9 fathoms. When Saru sima bears W. by S., stand no farther eastward than to bring Kanon saki to bear S. ¼ E. until Saru sima is S.W. ½ W., when the spit will have been weathered. At night do not bring the light off Treaty point to bear west of N. by W. ¼ W. until Kanon saki light bears S. ½ E. Long boards may now be again made, but do not shoal on either tack to less than 5 fathoms, nor off Yokohama bluff to less than 7 fathoms. There are some shoal patches of 3½ to 5 fathoms, sand and mud, off the western side of the bay between Saru sima and Mississippi bay, but none are known at a greater distance off than 2 miles, and they may be avoided by not bringing Saru sima eastward of South.

If proceeding from Yokohama to Yedo anchorage, stand out E. by N. till the house in the tree clump (of which the roof only is generally seen) of Kawa saki bears N.N.E., when haul up N.E. or N.E. ½ E. along the shore, which is skirted by a shallow shelf nearly 1½ miles broad and very steep, passing eastward of the two buoys which mark its edge, and on which three beacons or large posts will be seen, taking care not to decrease the soundings to less than 9 fathoms till the tree clump or house bears W. by N. Then haul up N. by E. if in soundings under 8 fathoms, or North if over 8 fathoms, and anchor in 6 fathoms with the southern part of the wooded heights of Goten yama bearing West, and the southern of the five forts, N.W.; or steer in upon the latter bearing, and anchor in any convenient depth, as above.

The TIDES are much affected by the winds, but both flood and ebb sweep with great velocity round Saratoga spit.

The flood runs N.W. by W. and the ebb S.W. by S., about 3½ knots an hour at springs. Generally the flood stream sets a vessel on to the western shore.

ISLANDS SOUTH of YEDO GULF.*—From the volcanic island Vries, at the middle of the entrance of the gulf of Yedo, extends a chain of islands and rocks some 300 miles in a S. by E. direction, terminated according to present information by the small pinnacle island called Lots Wife, said to be in lat. 29° 47′ N.,† long. 140° 22½′ E. These islands are all bold-to, some appearing to rise like a wall from the depths of the ocean, and they have but few outlying hidden dangers. The lead therefore in foggy weather will give little or no warning, as in some cases no soundings will be obtained with 150 fathoms line within half a mile of the shore.

The currents also in this part of the Japan stream are influenced by the prevailing winds at the different seasons, and capricious, heavy current rips being of very common occurrence and have often been mistaken for *shoals*. These rips are more constantly met with *close* to the islands and rocks than otherwise, and in the event of getting into one at night or in a fog, it may be assumed, when the vessel's position is not accurately known, that danger is near. It may be well to bear in mind that in calms, although the stream may appear to be hurrying the vessel on to an island, if the island be steep, it will always turn to the right or left on approach-

---

* *See* Chart of Japan, No. 2,347.
† U.S.S. *Macedonian*, 1854.

ing within a certain distance of the rocks; not so, however, should shallow water extend any distance, when the anchor must be depended on.

The usual set of the current through these islands is north-easterly, and the rate ranges from 1½ to 3 knots, but the islands frequently deflect it from its course, and the eddies always found on the margin of great currents are here particularly numerous and active, so that it is not unusual, especially among the northernmost of the islands and in the vicinity of the coast of Nipon, to encounter a set precisely in the opposite direction to that anticipated. Close to Fatsizio and Vries islands, at less than a third of a mile off, a regular change of tidal stream was observed, and also between these islands and the coast.

LOTS WIFE or Black rock, in lat. 29° 47′ N., long. 140° 22½′ E., is a tall pinnacle rising about 300 feet above the sea; in clear weather it can be seen at a distance of 25 miles, and bears a remarkable resemblance to a ship under all sail. A cast of the lead within 8 miles of this rock gave no soundings with 160 fathoms of line.

PONAFIDIN or St. Peter island is about 1,328 feet in height, 1¼ miles in length East and West, and visible in clear weather from a distance of 40 miles. The island was discovered in 1820 by Lieutenant Ponafidin of the Russian Navy, and named by him Three Hills island, from its having apparently three hummocks. It was seen by one of the vessels of the United States squadron in 1853, and its position is given as lat. 30° 33′ N., long. 140° 15′ E.

SMITH ISLAND.*—H.M.S. *Tribune* passed this island in 1859, and describes it as a high pinnacle-looking rock, in lat. 31° 15′ 0″ N., long. 139° 52′ E., about 250 feet in height, three-quarters of a mile in circumference, with heavy breakers extending apparently a quarter of a mile from it, and a small rock close to its north side.

BAYONNAISE, in lat. 32° 0′ 40″ N., long. 140° 0′ E., forms a curve a cable long north and south, with several hummocks on it, its northern summit being about 26 feet in height; several rocks extend a quarter of a mile off its north-west and north-east sides.

AOGA SIMA was not visited by H.M.S. *Actæon* in 1861, but the position of its eastern summit was assumed (from a true bearing of it from Fatsizio, and the difference of latitude from a Japanese chart proved very nearly correct in most details) to be in lat. 32° 37½′ N., long. 139° 47½′ E. The island is 3 miles long, and visible 36 miles off in clear weather. Its coasts are steep, and the only landing place is on the east side, where there is a rock level with the water at a little distance from the land. It is inhabited and cultivated on the north and north-west sides.

---

* Capt. Smith, ship *Heber*, 1851.

FATSIZIO ISLAND, the most southern of the islands visited by the *Actæon* in 1861, is 8⅛ miles long, N.W. by N. and S.E. by S., and 4 miles wide at its broadest part. In shape it is nearly an oblong, rounded at the north-west end, while at its south-east end a slight curve forms a bay, the spot of observation which (close to some small huts) is in lat. 33° 4′ 24″ N., long. 139° 50′ 24″ E. Anchorage was obtained off this bay in 16 fathoms, sand and gravel, at less than a mile from the shore, but exposed from S.S.W. to N.N.E., and a vessel would always be liable to experience a heavy swell. There were 30 fathoms, dark sand, at about 2 miles off this shore, but the rest of the coast line appeared to share the bold features and to be as steep-to as the generality of these islands.

This island is a penal settlement of Japan. Its highest part is the northern, where a mountain reaches an elevation of 2,840 feet. At the base of this mountain and creeping up for some distance on its west side, is an extensive settlement, while in several places along both shores, are found little hamlets and villages, so that the island would appear to support a considerable population. A tract of low land in the centre of and extending across the island is well cultivated. To the southward of this the land again assumes a considerable elevation, but does not reach the altitude of the northern part. Approaching from the eastward the island appears as two.

Water.—At the south-east end of Fatsizio are two or three small streams of delicious water falling down the rocks, and in fine weather and smooth water, boats may readily obtain an abundant supply.

KODSINE is a small and nearly oval shaped island 1,820 feet high, 1½ miles long, and nearly one mile broad, lying westward of the highest part of Fatsizio, and separated from that island by a channel about 2 miles wide, which has not yet been sounded. Some small rocks, as is also the case with Fatsizio, are found quite close in shore, but no off-lying dangers are at present known, and the lead gives no soundings at 53 fathoms, a little more than a mile from its western shore. A small population is to be found on the lower part of the island.

BROUGHTON ROCK (Kanawa), in lat. 33° 39′ N., long. 139° 18′ E., is a small inaccessible islet about 60 feet high, flat topped, and so bold that at about a third of a mile from its north-east side no soundings could be obtained with 180 fathoms line.

The north-easterly current in the neighbourhood of this islet was found to be particularly strong, running nearly 4 knots an hour.

MIAKI and MIKURA are two high and bold islands. The highest part of Miaki is in lat. 34° 5′ N., long. 139° 31′ 35″ E., and the highest part of Mikura in 33° 52′ N., 139° 35′ E.; the latter lies about 17 miles to the north-east of Broughton rock. Mikura is called Prince island; and Miaki, Volcano island in former charts.

There is a cluster of rocks about 2½ miles to the south-west of Miaki, and Broughton says, "there are, in addition, some black rocks 2 or 3 miles from the eastern point of the island."

REDFIELD ROCKS (Sanbon-take) are the most western of the chain of islands and rocks south of the gulf of Yedo, and the most dangerous of the whole group. They consist of two patches of black rocks extending nearly 3 miles N.N.E. and S.S.W. The southern rocks, in lat. 33° 56′ N., long. 138° 48¼′ E., are the highest, about 20 feet above high water, while the northern are only about half that height. Nearly midway between the patches is a flat rock, over which the sea breaks heavily, and the heads of two or three small rocks crop up around it. There is said to be deep water between the flat rock and the northern patch, and the channel is reported to be clear, but except in a case of sudden emergency it would not be prudent to attempt passing through.

The hand lead will afford no warning until close upon this dangerous cluster, and in thick weather the islands in the vicinity, the nearest being Kosu sima, N.E. ¼ E. 20 miles distant, would not be seen; in fact, seeing the islands the dangers themselves would be visible, and therefore easily avoided.

As little as 12 fathoms were found when passing along the west side of these rocks, about equidistant from either group. At half a mile from the south and principal cluster are soundings of 30 fathoms, rocky bottom. The flat rock also is connected with the south rocks, and lies close to them.

A depth of 70 fathoms, gravelly bottom, was obtained about 4 miles northward of the rocks, but the soundings increased as they were approached, and at 2 miles west of their centre there was no bottom at 130 fathoms. The current in their vicinity set on one occasion about N. by E., and its rate was from 2 to 3 knots.

ONOHARA is a small islet W.S.W. 5 miles distant from Miaki, composed of a cluster of high detached rocky pinnacles the centre one being perforated in two places.

KOSU SIMA, in lat. 34° 12¼′ N., long. 139° 9¼′ E. (centre), and elevated 2,000 feet above the sea, is 3½ miles long N.E. and S.W., and may be recognized by a remarkable snow white cliff on its western side, and a white patch on its summit, to the northward of the cliff. There is a safe channel 15 miles wide between Kosu sima and Miaki.

Two small rocky islets lie close together about half a mile off the centre of the eastern shore of Kosu sima. About 2 miles southward of the southwest point of Kosu sima are the Onghashi rocks, which should be given a safe berth, as their jagged appearance would lead to the belief that there are many hidden dangers in their immediate neighbourhood.

SIKINE SIMA is low, with a small islet off its north end. It is 1½ miles long N.N.E. and S.S.W., and lies 5 miles north-east of Kosu sima. One of the vessels of the American squadron passed between these islands and saw no danger; there is therefore reason to believe that the channel is safe.

NII SIMA is about 1½ miles north-east of Sikine, and from its broken outline appears from a distance as several islands. Its extent is 5 miles, north and south, and its most elevated part 1,490 feet above the sea. There is a small low islet a short distance off its south-east point.

UTONE is a conical islet, 660 feet high, lying N. ½ E., about 2½ miles from Nii sima; detached rocks lie near its shores.

TO SIMA, bearing N. ½ W. 2 miles from Utone, is one mile in diameter, pyramidal shaped, and its summit 1,730 feet above the sea.

VRIES ISLAND (Ō sima) the largest and most northern of the chain fronting the gulf of Yedo, is 10 miles N.N.E. of To sima, its south-eastern point being in lat. 34° 40′ N., long. 139° 27′ E. The island is oval shaped, about 8 miles in extent N.N.W. ¼ W. and S.S.E. ¼ E., and 5 miles wide, and its summit attains an elevation of 2,550 feet. At its centre is an active volcano, over which a white vapour cloud is generally floating, and frequently, at night, it brightly reflects the glare of the subterranean fires at work in the crater beneath, forming in clear weather a conspicuous landmark visible by night or day for many leagues.

There are several villages on the island, and a considerable population. The coast line is free of all danger, with the exception of a few detached rocks and boulders lying close to it. The principal village is on the north side, off which a narrow bank of soundings affords a precarious anchorage in from 12 to 18 fathoms. Another considerable village, having the advantage of a junk harbour, is situated at the south-east point of the island. Landing may be effected at the north village, or in the junk harbour. The inhabitants were civil and hospitable, but averse to strangers visiting the volcano.

*****MELA HEAD to CAPE ERRATATSI and OHIGASI SAKI** (King and Blanco) is a wild and dangerous coast, skirted by off-lying rocks; the projecting points are generally rugged cliffs of yellow clay or gravel: it is well wooded; the high land ends about Ohigasi saki in a long backed hill terminating in a couple of thumb-shaped pinnacles, and is fronted by a bold chalky cliff.

---

* The description of the coast from Mela head to Yamada harbour is by Commander C. J. Bullock, R.N., 1866.

The coast, when partially obscured by fog, is difficult to identify when coming from the eastward; a ship thus approaching Yedo bay is liable to be set considerably out of her reckoning by the Japan stream. The temperature of the sea is a useful guide, and the soundings will give good warning if attended to. Mela head sometimes shows out in relief when all the coast eastward is obscured by fog.

INABOYE SAKI.—From Ohigasi saki north-eastward to Nakuno saki, a distance of a 100 miles, the coast is low, and for the most part sandy. Inaboye saki is a projecting rocky cape, on which is a smooth, bare, and conspicuous hill, about 200 feet high; reefs extend from the cape fully a mile, but it may be rounded in safety at night in 40 fathoms water. Shipwrecks are frequent on the sandy beach north of the cape, caused, it is believed, by the effects of the currents, which meet here and set a vessel towards the shore (*see* page 24).

ARKOLD REEF, said to be in lat. 36° 4′ N., long. 141° 25′ E., was reported by the Russian frigate *Arkold*, and has been again seen by Russian gun-vessel *Sibole*;* it is described as being about 20 feet above the water with the sea breaking heavily upon it.

CHÖOSI POINT is on the north side of Inaboye promontory. The Tone gawa, a rapid river, flows into the sea on the south side of the point, but owing to the heavy swell from the Pacific its bar can seldom be crossed by ships' boats, and at times native craft cannot attempt it. There is anchorage in 6 fathoms, sand, one mile off the bar, but it is not recommended. The soundings deepen gradually to 20 fathoms at 4 miles from the shore.

The COAST.—North from Chöosi point for 45 miles the shore is wooded, it may be passed along at a distance of a mile, in 9 fathoms. From Machama the shore is bounded by low cliffs and north of Kawajiri, (a populous fishing town,) hill ranges commence.

SENDAI BAY lies on the east coast of Nipon in latitude 38° 20′ N., the land north of it is deeply indented, high, and steep, and apparently thinly populated, fishing boats being seen only off Simidzu. Most of the bays are open to seaward.

At 10 miles from the coast inland, there is a high, easily recognisable mountain, about 4,600 feet high, in lat. 39° 28′ N., long. 141° 41′ E., approximately; unfortunately it is seldom uncovered, and points of recognition on this coast are much wanted.

At the entrance of a bay, in lat. 39° 18′ N., there is a mass of white rocks, that at a distance resembles a town, a little north-east of a wooded isle, half a mile in extent, quite close to the shore. A similar island is seen 5 or 6 miles south of the port of Yamada.

---

* Reported by the Commander of the *Sibole* in 1871.

The bay has moderate depths with mud bottom; at 10 miles south of Matsu sima and 7 miles from the shore the depth is 18 fathoms, and 16 at 2 miles from the entrance.

Care must be taken in rounding Amitsi hama, the east point of the bay, as from beacons being seen nearly a mile distant from the shore, it is believed that they marked rocks.

MATSU SIMA BAY.—The southern entrance of this extensive but shallow harbour, in 38° 20′ N., and 141° 5′ E., appeared completely obstructed by low reefs, and according to the fishermen, no channel exists between the sunken rocks. The northern entrance (4 miles to the northward), is very shallow, there being only 4 feet water over a rocky bar in a narrow channel, but good shelter for two or three vessels may be obtained off it in 5 or 6 fathoms, mud, open only to the east.

ICHINOMAKI.—At the north part of Sendai bay a river of considerable importance falls into the sea after traversing, on a south course, the provinces of Nambu, Mutsu, and Sendai; it is reported to be navigable by junks for 70 miles, and boats can reach Morioka, the capial of Nambu, situated 120 miles from its mouth. The town of Ichinomaki at the entrance was not seen in passing. The anchorage is a roadstead, open to South and S.E., but it is believed that with the wind from those quarters good shelter could be found in the east part of the bay.

KINGKASAN (Goldmine island), dedicated to religious purposes, is resorted to by pilgrims from all parts of Japan; a peak 1,000 feet high and wooded to the summit is conspicuous; the deer on the island are numerous and are considered sacred. Mica in large quantities is found in the soil.

Between this island and the main a depth of 3 fathoms can be carried by passing at one-third the distance from the island; there is anchorage on the south side of the narrows.

It is not recommended to pass inside Hira sima, Asi sima, and their contiguous groups.

KINGKASAN to YAMADA.—The coast between these places is at present totally unknown to navigators; it presents a deeply indented outline, probably concealing some fine harbours. The shores appear bold.

YAMADA HARBOUR* is a large circular basin surrounded by mountains upwards of 1,000 feet in height, and is entered by a broad pass or strait running S.W. between high bold shores, in which there is a depth of from 20 to 50 fathoms; a reef extends nearly one cable south from Miojin saki, the inner north point of the entrance to be avoided by keeping in mid-channel; after rounding this point haul up N.W., and

---

* *See* Plan of Yamada harbour, No. 210; scale, *m* = 3·0 inches.

passing a quarter of a mile north of Ō sima, the larger of the two wooded islands, anchor off the centre of the town of Yamada in 6 fathoms. When standing in for the anchorage the water shoals to 7 fathoms, and then deepens to 10, after which it decreases gradually. The eastern part of the bay is deep, rocky, and exposed, therefore not recommended as an anchorage. It is shallow between the two islands at the head of the harbour. The small island Ko sima is in lat. 39° 27′ 17″ N., long. 141° 59′ E.

The town or village of Yamada is populous and inhabited almost exclusively by fishermen who appear ignorant, uncouth, and dishonest.

The high land on the north may be easily recognized when coming from the northward or southward, in following the coast of which, it forms the most salient point. Outside the port the water changes its colour, but there is no bottom in 38 fathoms at 2 miles from the shore. Yamada is the best anchorage at present known on the north-east coast of Japan.

TIDES.—It is high water, full and change, in Yamada harbour at 6h. 30m.; springs rise 4 feet.

MIYAKO.—The port of Miyako opens at 8 miles north of Yamada, and is a place of considerable trade, situated on the western shore of an inlet about 3 miles deep; junks anchor outside in from 7 to 4 fathoms, mud. The anchorage is open to the eastward. About the time of the equinoxes strong N.E. winds occasionally blow, and in the winter strong westerly winds. The point of Tayomani that forms it is surmounted by a conical hill.

The COAST north of Miyako takes a N.N.E. direction, and is a shelving table land, bordered by broken cliff and backed by high flat ranges, which rise to about 2,000 feet, but the land gradually decreases in elevation towards the north until about Sanemuva point, where it becomes low. Kuro saki stands well out, and may be recognized by its small range of hills about 700 feet high; north of Kuro saki the cliffs get lower, and the long flat slopes run out into fine tapering points.

Two isolated mountains can be seen behind Hon-na-mi. The land is densely wooded.

CAPE DE VRIES is low and flat, about 330 feet high, and is remarkable from the way it stands out between two bays. The *Dupleix* sailed along this coast from cape Kiori to cape Vries, at a distance of from two to four miles, and saw no danger except close to the shore.

SIRIYA SAKI.—The coast rises in the vicinity of Siriya saki to 1,265 feet, and descends again towards the cape in a gentle slope, making at a distance like an island. Off the cape, at the distance of 3 cables, is a small white rock 70 feet high, and at 2 miles to the south-westward is another rather larger than the former, lying one cable from the shore. The coast within 4 miles of the cape is studded with rocks, and very foul.

Rattler rock.—A dangerous rock awash at low water, lies E. by N., distant three-quarters of a mile from the white islet or rock north of Siriya saki, the north-east point of Nipon. As Siriya saki is a salient point off which the Rattler rock lies, vessels are cautioned not to approach it too close.

DIRECTIONS.—Vessels bound from the gulf of Yedo to the eastern entrance of the strait of Tsugar, will, after passing Su saki and cape Erratatsi (C. King) experience the full force of the current setting them to the E.N.E. The land about this cape is high and wooded, and the coast in its locality should be given a good berth, as heavy breakers have been seen some distance off shore.

Caution is requisite in doubling Ohigasi saki (cape Blanco), as the American squadron passed over the edge of a reef in 22 fathoms water S.S.E., distant about 5 miles from this cape, and from the heavy overfalls, in which fishing boats were anchored, there is probably much less water upon its shoalest part. As it was near nightfall it was impossible to examine this reef, but its position is about lat. 35° 8′ N., long. 140° 34′ E., and cape Blanco in lat. 35° 13′ N., long. 140° 32½′ E.*

From this cape to Tsùgar strait no dangers have been seen† excepting the Arkold reef, and as far as is known the coast may be approached within from 2 to 3 miles without danger, excepting in the locality above mentioned. It will be remembered that the Oya Siwo flows to the southward along the north-east coast as far south as Inaboye saki (*see* page 25), and that its average width is from 100 to 200 miles, outside of which the Kuro Siwo flows to the north-eastward. This coast is known to be subject to strong gales and much heavy weather, the only known harbours of refuge being Yamada harbour and perhaps some of the inlets in Sendai bay. On nearing the entrance of Tsugar strait the American squadron experienced a sudden fall in the temperature of the sea of 15° to 20°, as the squadron ran from the north-easterly current into the cold current setting to the southward.

---

* These positions are doubtful, as the unfavourable state of the weather prevented observations being made near the reefs.

† This coast, however, has not as yet been minutely examined.

CHAPTER VI.

THE SETO UCHI, OR INLAND SEA, AND ITS APPROACHES.

VARIATION in 1872 : 4° W.

THE EASTERN ENTRANCES TO THE SETO UCHI.

The BOUNGO CHANNEL,* the western of the two entrances on the east coast to the Seto Uchi, is quite safe to navigate as far as it is at present known,† and the projecting points and islands were found correctly marked on the Admiralty chart by the allied squadron under the command of Vice-Admiral Sir A. L. Kuper, K.C.B., which entered the Seto Uchi by it in Sept. 1864. No dangers were seen in the route they adopted, in addition to those marked on the chart. The western points of the different islands and capes on the eastern shore, from Okino sima on the south to cape Okanaba on the north, are well defined, and apparently steep-to; so is also the land on the western shore in the vicinity of the town of Kitsiku and along the north-east coast of Kiusiu.

OKINO SIMA, forming the eastern point of the south entrance to this channel, is large, of moderate elevation, and may be seen in clear weather from a distance of 35 miles; its south-west point appeared to be steep-to. To the northward of it, also towards Hime sima and towards the main land to the eastward, the space appeared to be rocky foul ground.

EURYALUS ROCK, named after H.M.S. *Euryalus,* is a small rocky islet 50 feet high, lying in the middle of the Boungo channel, 26 miles north-west of Okino sima. It is surrounded by rocky shoals, some above water, to the distance of half a mile. It occupies a most excellent position for a lighthouse.

Soundings in 35 fathoms, sand, were obtained on the parallel of Moko sima, two small islands lying 12 miles N.W. of Euryalus rock.

TAKANABA, the island lying nearly in the middle of the northern entrance of the channel, has two small rocks above water at 2 cables N.W. of it. There appeared to be a good passage on either side of this island, but the eastern one between the island and cape Okanaba was adopted by

---

* *See* Chart of Seto Uchi or Inland sea, No. 2,875, corrected to 1872.

† The whole of the Boungo channel is from the Japanese manuscript, this coast as yet not having been minutely examined. The remarks are by George Williams, Navigating Officer of H.M.S. *Euryalus,* September 1864.

the fleet. This passage appeared free from danger; some tide ripples were noticed whilst passing the island, but the current was not strong.

The **KII CHANNEL**, the eastern and most frequented of the two channels on the east coast of Japan, lying between Sikok and Nipon, is 80 miles across at its entrance from the Pacific, decreasing to 15 miles at 30 or 40 miles within, which width it preserves for 20 miles farther, or up to Awadji sima. The coast of Awa to the west from Muroto saki to Naruto is as yet unknown; but the coast of Kii from Oö sima to Kata, along which vessels pass to and from the Seto Uchi and Yedo, has been surveyed or explored. The fairway from the Kii channel into the Seto Uchi is by Isumi strait, but there is a more direct route, by taking which (if not bound to Ōsaka or Hiogo) a saving of 35 miles is effected, viz., the Naruto passage, west of Awadji, but this channel should not be attempted excepting under the most favourable circumstances, that is, at slack water or within half an hour of it, and at neap tides, and even then it is highly dangerous (*see* page 204). The coast on the western side of the Kii channel from Murato saki to the rocky point Ŏ-iso at the western entrance to the Naruto passage is from the Japanese manuscript.

I SIMA lies nearly in the centre of the western shore of the Kii channel at its narrowest part; its southern peak is visible 30 miles.

The channel between I sima and Kamoda saki (the eastern point of Sikok) is 3 miles broad; in it are several detached groups of rocks, which do not cover at high water, and amongst them (according to the description of the fishermen who acted as pilots) are sunken rocks, over which not more than 24 feet can be carried in any of the channels, excepting the westernmost, which the fishermen stated to be clear of danger and navigable.

This clear channel lies between Misaki (the south-eastern point of Kamoda saki) and the westernmost group of seven low rocks. By rounding the outlying rocks off Misaki at 1½ cables distance, a depth of not less than 7 fathoms may be carried through. The *Serpent* passed through this channel.

Between the reefs the depths are irregular, varying from 7 to 35 fathoms.

The I sima group may be approached on all sides except the west, to a mile.

CAUTION.—These channels between the reefs westward of I sima should not be attempted.

WADA SIMA.*—This harbour, in latitude 34° 0′ N., longitude 134° 39′ E., has a good anchorage in from 4 to 6 fathoms water, just inside a low point with trees on it on the east side of the harbour.†

A patch of rocks, which in some places show about 2 feet above low water, lies N. by E. one and a half miles from the low point; they break heavily when there is any wind or swell, but in calm weather are dangerous. There are 10 fathoms water, mud bottom, close to.

Making the harbour from the eastward, steer in about East for the low point, and round it at a distance of about half a mile; there is deep water close to the point.

The south and west parts of the harbour are very shoal, the harbour banks are here walled in. On the west side there is a conspicuous bluff wooded point, with some large rocks extending off, round which, to the northward, is a landing place; inside the bluff is a small fort built to carry four guns, two to command the entrance to Tatsiye and two to command the landing place, but none appeared to be mounted. The hills inland are high.

The coast from Wada sima takes a northerly direction for 10 miles, several deep inlets, channels, and rivers being delineated on the Japanese manuscript.

SIKOK-NO-AWA.—The north-east coast of Sikok is in the province of Awa, and has high hills, with tufts of trees at their summits, sloping down to wooded spurs near the coast. The islands off this coast form the western shore of the Naruto channel.

Ō-ISO, the projecting sandy point north-east of Sikok, slopes down from a hill named Shiro-muné yama, 290 feet high, ending in a bare conical mound. This hill makes triple generally, the mound and eastern summit being covered with grass, while the western and highest is wooded. The whole shore is fringed with boulders, some of them covered at high water. East, 3 cables from Ō-iso, are some rocks awash, with deep water one cable outside them.

From this point, south, the coast is flat, sand, fronting a large plain, on the southern edge of which stands Toku sima, the capital town of the province of Awa in the island of Sikok, on the banks of a river one of whose mouths flows into the Muya-no seto (from which it takes the name Muya-no kawa) just within the southern entrance. The largest branch of this river, after having passed through a lagoon (Hiro umi) close to the coast, flows into the Kii channel, by the Hiro-do, a few miles south of Ō-iso.

---

* *See* Plan.
† Navigating Lieutenant F. A. Johnstone, H.M.S. *Salimis.*

From Ō-iso to the southward, the water is shallow; only 10 fathoms being found at 4 miles east of the shore, a mile south of Ō-iso; caused probably by the sand brought down by the Hiri kawa, that drains the east of Sikok.

MUYA-NO SETO is a narrow passage, with a general width of one cable, separating Sikok from the islands Oge sima and Simada sima.

At its southern entrance, rocks extend from the north shore, leaving a passage of only half a cable between them and the sandy beach under Shiro-mune yama on the Sikok shore. These dangers, with the strength of the tides (4 to 6 knots), prevent the passage being practicable for any vessel larger than a junk, most of whom take it in preference to the Naruto, and many frequent it, carrying away cargoes of salt, manufactured in large quantities on its banks.

At the north entrance stands the village of Kita-tomari (on the Sikok shore), off which a spit of shingle extends half a cable, and shoal water stretches a short distance off the eastern shore.

OGE SIMA.—The north shore of this island has alternately shingly beaches and bluffs, the latter being the termination of spurs from inland summits, all densely wooded, the highest of this portion, Hori-koshi-no-taka 518 feet, being surmounted by a single tree. Its eastern shore forms the western side of the southern approach to the Naruto passage, and consists of long sandy beaches, between points formed of pinnacle islets, and black sharp rocks. The most conspicuous is a peninsula, wooded at the summit, and cliffy on its sea face, lying S.W. by S. nearly one mile from Hadaka sima. The coast should not be approached south of this peninsula nearer than half a mile, as the depths decrease suddenly. The summit of this island is a conical, flat topped, wooded hill, Kuro yama, 599 feet high.

NARUTO PASSAGE.*—The Naruto (literally, gate of the sea which makes a great roaring) has hitherto been considered to be a whirlpool, and it is not without cause that this dangerous character has been attributed to it, for junks have foundered in its turbulent waves, or been dashed to pieces on its rocks by the impetuosity of the current. This channel lying between Tō saki, the projecting south-west promontory of Awadji, and that of Oge sima, called Mago saki, is only 7¼ cables wide from point to point, and is further narrowed to 3 cables by an extensive reef of rocks off Tō saki, and some reefs and islands off Mago saki.

Through this narrow passage the tide runs, or rather falls, with a velocity of from 7 to 8 knots at within 1 hour to 1½ hours before or after the change of stream, which occurs about every six hours, there being little or no slack water. The junks choose the early and latter parts of

---

* See **Plan of the Naruto passage**, No. 119, scale $m = 2·0$ inches.

the tide, when fair, to pass, but never attempt it when the wind is so strong as to require reduced canvas, for then the sea is so great that vessels are unmanageable.

TŌ SAKI is a long narrow promontory that forms the eastern side of Naruto, and has a clump of trees near its extreme, off which, separated by a channel of $1\frac{1}{4}$ cables that breaks entirely across at spring tides, lies Nagase, a rock about 2 feet above high water, and surrounded by others that cover, the southernmost, lying $1\frac{1}{4}$ cables from it. The channel here is only $2\frac{1}{2}$ cables wide. All these rocks show by breakers at the strength of the tide.

MAGO SAKI, the north-east point of Oge sima and western point of the Naruto, is the extreme of a bluff wooded peninsula, whose western extreme of shingle forms a bay Kame ya in which boats may find shelter. A short distance west of Mago saki, on the north shore, is a granite quarry on the side of the hill.

HADAKA SIMA, lying S.S.E. $\frac{3}{4}$ E. 2 cables from Mago saki, has a double summit, the western, 62 feet high, being wooded, and the eastern, 47 feet high, being bare; it is joined to Oge sima by a chain of rocks that cover at half tide. Off its eastern extreme, three rocks, that cover only at highest water spring tides, terminate in rocks having 10 feet on them, the outer being one cable from the island.

TOBI SIMA, 93 feet high, is a conical wooded islet, lying S.S.E. $3\frac{1}{2}$ cables from Hadaka sima. It has shoal water off its north end for $1\frac{1}{2}$ cables, but may be approached on the eastern side to one cable. A rock, one cable in extent (east and west), with from 4 to 5 fathoms on it, and steep-to, lies S.W. 4 cables from Tobi sima.

UCHI UMI.—Hori koshi is the narrow eastern entrance to Uchi umi, a large expanse of deep water. Boats only can go through, within an hour of slack water. Off this passage there is shoal water for 3 cables, having $2\frac{3}{4}$ fathoms on the outer edge; but the rush of tide prevents it being available as an anchorage.

SIMADA SIMA has a double range of wooded hills, between which two valleys nearly meet. Its highest hill, Kane-kake-matsu, on the north-east side of the island, is 543 feet high, and surmounted by a conspicuous tuft of trees.

Se-no-kata bana.—The north point is steep, having boulders and shoal water extending one cable from it. There is a very strong tide rip off it at spring tides, and it should not be approached within 3 cables, as the bottom is irregular. From this to Hori koshi, shingly beaches and cliffy points alternate, round the bays of Ta-no ura.

HI URA, a bay about 4 miles to the westward of the Naruto channel, is 5 cables deep by 2¾ cables wide, and has good anchorage for a small vessel in 3 fathoms, mud. Shoal water lies off the western point of its entrance, half a cable, and the eastern shore should not be approached within that distance. Large ships can anchor outside in 11 to 13 fathoms, 3 cables from the shore. To the eastward the shore is tolerably steep and densely wooded, sloping to a shingly beach fringed by boulders that cover at high water. It may be approached to one cable's distance.

AWADJI SIMA.—The south-west coast of this island forms the eastern shore of the Naruto channel. From Tō saki the long narrow promontory before mentioned, the coast of Awadji on the south side of the channel takes an easterly direction for about 2 miles to Tsuru sima saki at the entrance to Fuk ura.

ŌSONO SIMA, a wooded island 101 feet high, lying in the bight between Tō saki and Fuk ura, is almost connected to the mainland by a spit of large stones and shingle, and has rocks lying one cable south of the south point; the outer just covers at high water, is steep-to, and resembles a boat.

TSURU-GA SAKI, the north point of the entrance to Fuk ura, is the termination of a grass covered bluff surmounted by three trees, and has rocks stretching from it S.W. nearly one cable, that cover at high water, and are steep-to on the southern side. Kane-kake-matsu, in line with the outer high rock off Tō saki, bearing W. by N., clears both this and the reef off Osono.

FUK URA, a fine bay, having excellent anchorage just within the mouth in 7 fathoms, mud, good holding ground, contains two islands, Keburi sima, conical and densely wooded, and Susaki, flat and covered with a dwarf oak. From the latter, a spit having 6 feet on it continues from the boulders that dry to a shingly tongue, that shelters the entrance of Cha-no-ire, a shallow bight much used by junks in want of repairs. Within this spit the water is deep; this fact, and the want of width in the channels between the islands, prevents any vessel larger than a gunboat from taking advantage of its shelter.

A high range, whose summit is 913 feet above the sea, intersected with numerous valleys, slopes down to the northern shore; the eastern end being a bare granitic hill, Nambeiji, having a remarkable clump of trees 58 feet high, their base being 937 feet above high water. The southern shore has shingly beaches, the base of the gentle slopes of a wooded range, the highest summit of which, 501 feet high, is on the south end of Cha-no-ire.

KO-URA SAKI is the steep bluff at the south entrance of Fuk ura, the western termination of Taziri yama, a double summit, both of which are 418 feet high, and surmounted by a tuft of trees. From this to the southward the coast falls suddenly to the sandy beach of Hama-no hama, fronting an extensive cultivated plain. In the middle of this beach stands an isolated hill, about 200 feet high, topped by a single tree, and sloping down to the beach in three points. The bay off this is shallow, the outer edge of 4 fathoms lying S.S.E. ¼ E. 1⅓ miles from Ko-ura saki.

SHIWO SAKI, the south-west point of Awadji sima, slopes from a wooded hill, 516 feet high, named Gongen yama, and terminates in a conical grass mound 167 feet above the sea. From it shoal water, having 5 fathoms on the outer edge, stretches west half a mile and south a quarter of a mile. The lead will give sufficient warning on approaching it.

The south coast of Awadji sima is bold, having steep slopes from wooded hills, with deep ravines, falling abruptly to the sea, and with several villages scattered about the slopes. No danger is known to exist beyond a quarter of a mile from the shore.

DIRECTIONS.*—The soundings to the northward of the Naruto channel show a flat of sand and shells, with depths ranging from 20 to 13 fathoms, except in the run of the tide, where the water deepens suddenly into a gully, having as much as 65 fathoms.

On going through the Naruto channel with the tide, from the north, Mago saki should be approached to 1½ cables, and from that a course steered in the smooth water, rather nearer Hadaka sima than Nagase, and from mid-channel to 1½ cables from Tobi sima.

On taking the channel with the tide, from the southward, Tobi sima should be closed to 1½ cables, and an opposite course steered.

The passage may be taken at the first and second hour before and after change of stream, with the tide, and for the first three quarters of an hour before or after change, against the tide, in fine weather; but in bad weather it should not be attempted, as the passage then breaks right across, and it is difficult to distinguish the channel.

Vessels must be careful to have the passage well open before approaching it, and at all times great caution must be observed.

TIDES.—The tide sweeps through Naruto in about a N. by W. and S. by E. direction, with a velocity at springs of from 10 to 11 knots, but slacking about an hour before and after change either way to from 7 to 8 knots.

At springs there is scarcely any slack water, but at neaps about a quarter of an hour.

The change of stream after the northerly tide follows the moon's meridian passage at place by intervals ranging from 3h. 25m. at springs to 2h. 8m. at neaps, running on an average 6h. 25m. each way.

---

* The description and directions for the Naruto passage are by Lieutenant C. J. Bullock, 1859, and Navigating Lieutenant W. F. Maxwell, 1869.

With the northerly tide (said by the natives to be a knot stronger than the southerly set) the race extends as far north as Anaga, and breaks with great force, but has no danger for a decked vessel. On either side of the race on this tide the stream sets to the southward, but has scarcely any strength. On the south side of Naruto it takes the line of the shore, converging to the channel as it gets near.

With the southerly tide the race expends itself in whirls about the parallel of Kuro yama, and on either side of it the tides are very variable, though generally close to its margin there are eddies sweeping to the northward.

On the north side of Naruto on this tide the stream rushes with great velocity round Se-no-kata bana and Sozu-no hana in the direction of Mago saki, but there is only a slight stream on the eastern shore, till quite close to the Naruto. The Kii channel, south of Naruto, also shews clearly the run of the tide, 80 fathoms having been obtained about a mile south of Tobi sima.

It is high water, full and change, at Fuk ura at 6h. 17m., springs rise 7 feet, neaps (probably) $4\frac{1}{2}$ feet. The north-western stream makes at $2\frac{1}{4}$ hours before high water at Fuk ura, changing every 6 hours nearly. North of the Naruto passage the tides are anomalous; west of Mago saki in the daytime it was high water, when it was low at Fuk ura; and at Anaga ura in the evening it remained at high water level during the whole of the ebb at Fuk ura, and fell to low water at Anaga ura as it rose to high water at Fuk ura, the rise and fall being only 4 feet above the Naruto; so that at the strength of each stream there must have been a difference of level of 3 to 4 feet on either side. The current set out S.S.E. $\frac{1}{2}$ E.

On approaching from the south with the tide, it appeared to have no great strength until nearing the rocks, through which it sweeps in calm weather in a perfectly smooth stream. At one mile above them on the in going tide, it exceeds 7 knots.

The tide race commences at 2 cables beyond the reefs, where the converging currents meet, forming whirls and eddies for a mile; some of these had a depression of 3 feet, and some junks were turned round and round many times, but they would not much affect the steering of a steamer with attention to the helm. There are strong counter currents on either side the race, where fishermen lie in the smallest boats, guiding them through the passage with great skill.

ANCHORAGE.—If wishing to wait for slack water, or change of stream, anchorage may be found on the Awadji shore, at Maru yama on the north side of the Naruto; and at Fuk ura on the south, in 4 to 8 fathoms. There is also excellent anchorage in Minotoye bay, 5 miles to the westward.

In the bay west of Mago saki the anchorage is bad; there are extensive reefs off the Sikok shore south of Tobi sima.

The SOUTH COAST of AWADJI SIMA, from Shiwo saki, takes an east-north-east direction 12½ miles to Kama saki at the entrance to Isumi strait; it is clear of danger within a mile, and the shore is bold and mountainous, the hills being well wooded.

NOMA SIMA, lying 1¾ from the south-east coast of Awadji, is formed of some very flat-topped hills from 100 to 200 feet high, bordered with low cliffs. It has reefs a cable off its south point, and there is a bay and village on its west side.

YURA* is a town in a curiously sheltered harbour on the south-east side of Awadji, and forms the western shore of Isumi strait. A low island, 1½ miles in length, of sand and shingle and covered with scrub, with a bluff hill on its north point and a large granite fort on its south, lies like a breakwater fronting a bay, and forms the harbour, which has narrow entrances north and south; a little north of the fort where the island is stony, it covers at high water, but a boat can scarcely pass over it. The north entrance has from 10 to 11 feet at low water springs, and is 120 yards wide; the south is a narrow opening with 2 to 3 feet water. The broadest part of the harbour is half a mile, with anchorage in 4 to 6 fathoms, mud. A vessel drawing 16 feet could enter at high water springs, and lie secure in smooth water for repair. The junks anchor somewhere to the northward of this to wait for tide.

Anchorage may also be obtained in 2 to 5 fathoms outside the island on the sand-bank off it, with the outer extreme of the bluff N.W., or of the fort S.S.W., but it is very steep on the edge, and the holding ground is probably not good.

KATA is a town on the eastern side of Isumi strait, on the south side of a bay north of Takura saki, and where there is anchorage in 5 to 8 fathoms. There is a fine landing pier here 200 yards in length for the use of the Daimio, who resides at Wakayama, and to whom Kata belongs. Off Takura saki, and in Kata bay as far as Diyi island, reefs covering at high water, extend about 3 cables off the shore.

TIDES.—It is high water, full and change, at Yura and at Kata at 6h. 5m. Springs rise 6½ feet; neaps, 4½ feet.

TAKURA SAKI, the eastern point of entrance of Isumi strait, is a wooded headland with a small summer house on its summit, the extremity of a mountainous promontory. It is skirted with reefs extending 2 or 3 cables west and south of it. On the north and west the country is high,

---

* See **Plans of Harbours in the Kii channel, No. 357.**

the coast south of it is low and wooded for 5 miles as far as Zoga saki, a rocky point with four small islands off it which are steep-to.

HACHKEN GAWA * is a small river running through a plain 5 miles south-east of Kata. Waka yama, a small isolated wooded hill, is on its left bank 1½ miles from the entrance; on its summit stands the residence of the Prince of Kiisiu, conspicuous from the sea. There are only 3 feet water on the bar, which is a cable wide, and the passage over it is marked by six large posts; at the entrance there are 9 to 12 feet at low water. A detached shoal of 10 feet water lies S.W.byW. 4 cables off the bar. There are forts on both sides of the river.

South of Zoga saki is a bay 4 miles deep, and 3 across its entrance, in which anchorage may be found in 4 to 10 fathoms. There are no dangers more than 1½ cables from the shore, that are known. The southern shores are high, steep, and bold-to, the northern sandy between two ranges, where a small stream disembogues; two hills, one of 410 feet elevation over Zoga saki, and the other, Kamidera, of 710 feet, over the plain to the east, are very conspicuous.

OSAKI BAY† is 1½ miles deep, and open to the W.N.W. The village of Osaki stands on the shore of a narrow inlet on its north side, where small vessels can find good shelter in 5 to 2 fathoms, which they can also obtain in Smotz ura, the innermost bay on the south side of the inlet. The only danger is a rocky patch of one fathom 2 cables S.E. of the north entrance head. The south point of Tree islet should be given a berth of more than one cable. Over the village of Osaki is Takadoösi yama 591 feet high, a smooth-topped hill with two stunted trees on its summit, conspicuous from off shore. The south shore is hilly, the south entrance bluff being about 400 feet high. Fresh water and small supplies can be readily obtained.

OKINO SIMA, W.byS.½S. 2 miles from the entrance of Osaki, has a round hill 275 feet high, and is bare of trees; it may be passed at 2 cables having some rocks awash on the south. Djino sima, 1 mile east of it, is 400 feet high, has high cliffs towards the sea, and is wooded; it may not be passed inside, nor within 2 cables on the west side. A rock awash lies about 2 cables south of it, and two rocky islets about a mile south, the northern of which has a grassy top; these are close off the low shore. A third islet lies half a mile N.E. of them.

MIYA SAKI, 220 feet high and 2 miles south of Okino sima, is an abrupt wooded peninsula at the extremity of a range of small hills of 150 to 200 feet elevation, on which are seen two conspicuous trees. On

---

* See Plan of Hachken river on Plan of Harbours in Kii channel, No. 357.
† See Plan of Osaki bay on the same Plan, No. 357.

its north side, the Arita, a small stream, disembogues, having flowed through the highly cultivated plain at the foot of the hills. It is navigable by small junks for a short distance up. To the eastward, the hills rise in succession to elevations of 1,000 and 2,000 feet. Miya saki may be passed at 3 cables.

TSKAHARA BAY is 5 miles deep and 6 miles across, between Miya saki and Sirasai saki, its north and south points of entrance. Its sides converge somewhat regularly to its head, where there is the bay of Hirowatali, about three-quarters of a mile in length and breadth, with anchorage in 7 to 8 fathoms, even bottom and mud, and well sheltered from all winds except W. by S. A pier at the south end of the sandy beach at its head and off a small town, protects small craft in a shallow inner harbour.

Two islands, Kura sima and Taka sima, lie off the southern shore of Tskahara bay. The former and outer is high, even topped, cliffy and very bold-to, with some islets close off its south-west point, and a run of deep water inside it; Taka sima is undulating, with a conspicuous round hill on its western part, bordered by cliffs. It is 4 cables west of a hilly promontory, on one of the peaks of the outer high double summit of which, is a beacon. Both these islands may be passed at 2 cables, except the south point of Taka sima, off which at nearly that distance there is a rock awash.

The Karamo group of small islands with reefs about their north sides, lie N.N.E. of Taka sima and west of Hirowatali bay, with a cluster of rocks E.N.E. of them half way to the shore, the ground about which has not been examined.*

Golden rock, so named from the large amount of property lost there, is a very small patch, nearly awash at low water, and so steep that the lead gives but little warning, there being 17 fathoms at 100 yards on the outside. It lies 3 miles N.N.E. ¼ E. of Sirasai saki, N.W. ½ W. 1⅓ miles of Taka sima hill, and S. by E. ⅜ E. of Miya saki.

Sung-ami, three-quarters of a mile North of the west point of Karamo, is a sunken rock with 6 feet over it and equally steep-to; it is also 1½ miles N. by E. of Taka sima and S.E. ½ E. 2⅓ miles from the point south-east of Miya saki.

DIRECTIONS.—Unless desiring anchorage or working to windward against tide, Tskahara bay should not be entered within a line joining its

---

* The coast of the Kii channel from Tanabe to Isumi strait, and the south shore of Awadji, were surveyed by Lieut. C. Bullock and James Kerr, Master R.N., in H.M.S. *Dove.*

points, as the two dangerous rocks above mentioned lie in the centre and northern parts of the bay.

Entering Tskahara bay, Taka sima should be steered for, *except* on a bearing between S.E.byS. and E.S.E., and when Shirasai saki is shut in behind Kura sima, stand in for Hirowatali bay passing south of the Karamo group; this mark will lead clear to the eastward of the Golden rock. If working to windward, take care to tack before the western point of Kura sima bears south; if in the vicinity of the rock, this is the best mark to clear it on the outside.

SHIRASAI SAKI or White rock point, derives its name from the large masses of quartz in its cliffs, and which, with the white pinnacle rock 200 feet high 4 cables E.S.E. of it, show very distinctly from the south. The point is not high, but has an abrupt cliff with deep water at its base, and is the end of a range of well defined hills which rise in succession for 1½ miles east to a rock-topped summit, 826 feet high. To the northward is a small bay, the northern point of which is formed by an island, with a large tree on its summit, but which never appears detached. A large round rock lies one cable N.W. of Shirasai saki. Turtle, said to be not known in Japan, were seen here.

FISHERMAN ROCK, a small narrow rock 4 feet above high water and steep-to on the outside, lies 4 cables West of Shirasai saki. Some rocks awash extend a cable's length to the N.E. of it. The passage inside the rock carries 14 fathoms in mid-channel.

OÖBIKI URA is a bay between Shirasai saki and Yura no uchi, where a vessel might anchor for the night with the wind off shore, in 6 fathoms at 2 or 3 cables from the beach. The steep little island Hijiki sima, 120 feet high, off its south point, marks the north point of entrance to Yura no uchi, a wooded hill with a craggy rock on its summit; a large rock lies at the extremity of its low-water reefs.

YURA NO UCHI* is a harbour 4 to 7 cables in breadth and 2 miles deep, and being sheltered by the sharp peaked island Ali sima and the extensive reefs off the south point of entrance, always above water, is only open to two points, viz. W. by S. and S.W. by W. Winds from these directions cause some swell inside in a gale, but it is nevertheless a secure anchorage. The smooth round hill, Kansane yama, on its north side, 860 feet high and surmounted by a clump of trees is conspicuous and well marks its position. To enter, pass 2 cables South of Ali sima and steering N.E. by E. pass the small islet, Tobi sima, under Kasane yama, at a cable, and, bringing it to touch the north point of Ali sima, anchor near the head of the bay in 6 or 7 fathoms, mud, with the hill bearing

---

* *See* Plan of Harbours in the Kii channel, No. 357.

W.N.W., or with the rocky summit, 826 feet high, in line with the west point of Ito ya ura (bay) N.¾ W. The channel north of Ali sima is equally safe, provided a berth of a cable is given to the shore on either side.

HINO MISAKI, being at the turn of the coast, is the most prominent cape in the Kii channel. Its terminal hill, Hino yama, is smooth-sloped, 675 feet high, and the islet off it may be passed at 2 cables. It is steep-to, but the tide sweeping out of the bay south of it, causes an appearance of broken water, especially with a north wind. Thence the coast runs south-eastward for 19 miles to Tanabe, and parallel to the line of the outer capes, but falls back within them from 2 to 4 miles. The shore is hilly with a strip of low land along the beach; the interior is mountainous.

At 2½ miles E.N.E. of Hino yama, on the east of the range extending from it, is a high flat topped saddle of nearly 1,000 feet elevation, and very conspicuous from the south-east. It overlooks a large plain, through which a small river, the Hidaka kawa flows into the sea at the eastern extremity of a long sandy beach. Along this beach anchorage may be obtained in from 4 to 9 fathoms at about half a mile off shore, the water being deeper and the shore steeper on the west than near the river entrance. The best position for anchoring is with the end of the trees on the beach bearing N.W. Small junks enter the river, which has a long sandy spit off its west point of entrance, and there are some reefs off the shore on the east.

The only danger in approaching the above anchorage is a large flat reef, named Nosima, the inner part of which is 15 feet above high water; it lies two-thirds of a mile off the coast, a mile south of the river's mouth, and it is connected with the shore by a shallow ledge of from one to 2 fathoms water with several rocks awash on it. A wooded hill range rises on the coast to the south-east, and on its summits are gravel patches; the eastern summit is most conspicuous, having a single tree on its bare shoulder.

ILIBE SAKI.—The round smooth hill, Kirime yama, rises over this prominent point which has some bushes on its summit, and is the western extremity of a small range. It is bordered by a low cliff with some large rocks off it which are bold of approach. The coast to the south-east of the range has several outlying reefs, the largest of which extends 4 cables off Arari point in detached parts, and its extremity is S.W. by W.½ W. 3½ miles from Ilibe saki.

Eastward of Arari point is a bay affording good anchorage in from 5 to 8 fathoms. It is entered by passing north of the two wooded islands Ichi no sima, lying close together and about 100 feet high, and anchoring at half a mile from the beach. Reefs extend 4 cables from the cliffs on the northern shore of the bay inside Arari point, but the beach at the head of the bay appears clean and shelving. There is a shallow water entrance eastward or inside of the Ichi no 'sima carrying 3 fathoms close to the islands. A chain of detached rocks above water extends 2 or 3 cables to the southward of them.

North of Arari point is a round hill, on the summit of which are three spike-shaped monuments; and 3 and 4 miles inland, north and north-east of this, are two large hill clumps which are very conspicuous from the offing. Off the low point a mile south-east of Ichi no sima are large masses of flat rocks, a little above high water, but which are steep-to. Maruyama point, 1½ miles south-west of this, and which is the north point of entrance to Tanabe bay, is low and wooded, as are the two islets Ebi sima to the north-west of it, around all which are large reefs. The bay north of Maruyama point may probably afford anchorage at its inner part in less than 7 fathoms.

TANABE BAY* is formed in a bight of the coast 22 miles south-west of Hino misaki, its outer parts exposed only to West and N.W. When approaching from the south-eastward, Itsiye misaki, the most projecting point of the coast, will first be made, and being very similar to cape Tanabe, the bay between them, in thick weather, may be mistaken for that of Tanabe. Itsiye misaki is a sloping point with a low terminating cliff, but the hills over it are much higher than those of cape Tanabe, and rise to a sharp peak, the outer of a continuous high range. The summit of cape Tanabe, which has a single conspicuous tree on it, is only 539 feet high, and falls abruptly inland. Outwards a long ridge slopes gently towards the sea, with a dark clump of trees on the brow, from which it falls steeply.

The cliffs which border the cape are bold of approach, but Isaki point, north of the cape, is very dangerous, a reef with two islets on it extending north half a mile from the point, and the Isaki reef of flat rocks above water lying that distance west of it. There are sunken reefs and shoal water between the latter reef and the point, and off both reefs the shoal water extends 2 or 3 cables beyond the outer visible dangers.

In the north-western part of entrance of Tanabe bay are the Saito and North bay reefs, 4 cables apart, with a deep water channel between them. These reefs are low and quite flat. At 2 cables distance S.E. and North of Saito, the southern of them, are sunken rocks, and off North bay reef is a small rock like a boulder. There is also a deep water channel between these reefs and Maruyama point, off which shoal water extends 3 or 4 cables. Within these dangers there is safe approach for a mile, but

---

* See Plan of Tanabe Bay on Plan of Harbours in Kii channel, No. 357.

farther in is a mass of reefs, rocks, and islets, which must be approached with great caution, as in the partial survey of this bay some dangers may have been omitted, although according to the doubtful testimony of the fishermen no others exist than are represented on the chart. In bad weather with the wind in, all the known dangers would break.

The best anchorage is in the south-eastern arm of the bay, south of Anchorage island. This island may be recognized by the dark trees dotted over it, and a tree islet west of it, from which a long uncovered reef extends. The end of this reef may be passed at a cable; then steer to pass the same distance of the north-east point of Anchorage island, between it and the sunken rocks of Passage reef in 6 to 10 fathoms, irregular bottom. Having passed along the east side of the island, stand in S.W. ½ S., anchoring in 10 to 8 fathoms, in a secure and thoroughly sheltered position. There is moderately deep water in the arm to the south, as also in Hosono bay, but they are too contracted for good anchorage.

Binzli reef, lying in the centre of the bay, is an extensive reef with several rocks on it, dry and awash at low water. The north-eastern part of Tanabe bay (only partially surveyed) has many shoals. On the north shore a small river discharges itself, running close under the white loop-holed wall surrounding a residence of the Daimio, the imperial Prince of Kiisiu, hidden among the trees on the left bank at entrance. There is a small turfed earthwork on the west point of entrance, fronting which is an extensive dry reef and a shelving spit running south half a mile into the bay. Avoiding this, anchorage may be obtained in 22 to 24 feet south of the river entrance.

Better shelter in westerly winds would be found N.E. of the Binzli reef. Two sunken rocks have lately been discovered in the fairway to the above anchorage; one of 22 feet water is S. ½ E. 4½ cables from the islet off Maru-yama point; the other with 15 feet is S.S.E. ⅜ E. at the same distance. To anchor stand in for the green earthwork east of the white wall of the Daimio's residence, bearing E.N.E. till Ebisima shuts in with the islet off Maru-yama point; then keep East and anchor in 6 to 4 fathoms. The low rock of Binzli always shows.

The village of Tanabe stands on the shore of the sandy bay to the westward of the river, and to the north is a mountain range, the highest part of which rises to the height of 2,650 feet, the ridge curving round to the range which terminates in Itsiye misaki.

SIWO MISAKI.*—The shore from Itsiye misaki to Siwo misaki, a distance of 21 miles E.S.E., is very bold and under a high mountainous coast terminating in a promontory of table land, which is the extreme south point of Nipon (page 161). There is a great tide race and overfalls

---

* *See* Chart of Japan islands, No. 2,347.

off Siwo misaki, both on the flood and ebb; they are, however, heaviest on the flood. After a south-easterly gale the sea comes in round this point in immense rollers, such as are rarely seen on any coast.

Bottle rock lies $2\frac{1}{2}$ cables South of the cape and foul ground extends $1\frac{1}{2}$ cables further southward.

LIGHT.—On the top of the cape, at an elevation of 155 feet above the sea, is exhibited a *fixed* white light, visible in clear weather from a distance of 20 miles. The lighthouse is a temporary one, and is in lat. 33° 26′ N., long. 135° $46\frac{1}{2}$′ E.

DIRECTIONS.—Passing through the Kii channel it is recommended to steer always for Hino misaki. The course from Isumi strait is South 25 miles, and from Naruto S.E. by S. 30 miles, which latter course, continued for 25 miles farther, passes Itsiye misaki at about 3 miles, from which an E.S.E. course for 25 miles leads on to Siwo misaki.

THE SETO UCHI, OR INLAND SEA OF JAPAN.

GENERAL DESCRIPTION.—The great inland sea of Japan, called by the Japanese Seto Uchi,* is enclosed between the south-west coast of Nipon, which entirely bounds it on the north and east; and the islands of Kiusiu and Sikok, which bound it on the west and south. It extends somewhat in an east and west direction, in length 240 miles, with a breadth varying from 3 to 30 miles. It has six divisions called nadas or seas, taking their names generally from the provinces, the coasts of which they wash; thus, the eastern part of the sea as far as Akashi strait is called the Isumi nada; and proceeding west, we have in succession the Harima nada, Bingo nada, Misima nada, Iyo nada, and, lastly, Suwo nada.

The Seto Uchi was first navigated by H.M.S. *Cruizer* in 1859. It contains upwards of 300 islands and rocks, with numerous shoals and dangers, and has a sea-board of nearly 700 miles, on which are situated numerous large towns and several of the provincial capitals; it abounds also with safe and convenient anchorages. It communicates with the Pacific by the Kii channel on the east, and by the Boungo channel, between Kiusiu and Sikok, on the south; and with the sea of Japan by the strait of Simonoseki on the west. There is a great maritime trade along its populous shores as well as the through traffic to Ōsaka, one of the chief seats of commerce of the empire, and the seaport of its capital, Kioto.

The Seto Uchi can be navigated with safety at all seasons of the year and even under favourable circumstances during the night, the more particularly now that a correct chart† of it has been published from the

---

* Literally, inner strait.
† *See* Chart of Seto Uchi, No. 2875; scale m =0.25 inches.

Japanese manuscript survey, to which has been added the surveys of Commanders Ward, Bullock, Brooker, and St. John, and Navigating Lieut. Maxwell. In the winter months, too, when the westerly gales are so prevalent sailing vessels would probably gain time by tiding through this sea, rather than by endeavouring to beat round Satano misaki (cape Chichakoff), against the Kuro Siwo or Japan stream. As an instance of this, a fine clipper ship was nearly three weeks getting round cape Chichakoff, whilst the *Actæon* sailed through the inland sea in nine days, meeting with one westerly gale, and anchoring every night.

A very destructive species of Mollusk inhabits the Seto Uchi, and might prove very injurious to ships' bottoms. Specimens of new timber were found at Awa sima, the perforations in which were a third of an inch in diameter.*

Supplies.—Water of excellent quality can be procured almost at any anchorage in the Seto Uchi or Kii channel, and is brought off in boats, in buckets, at a very small cost. About 70 tons of charcoal were purchased at the various harbours in the Kii channel, for fuel for steaming, at from 4 to 11 dollars per ton, superior for such purpose to the best Welsh coal.

TIDES.—The tides and currents of the Seto Uchi are as yet but imperfectly known, but are found to be regular at its east entrance: those of the Boungo channel are quite unknown. The tide wave comes from the Pacific ocean by the Kii and Boungo channels; from the latter it branches east and west, meeting the Kii channel tide at about Awa sima, in long. 133° 38′ E., at the eastern entrance of the Bingo nada.

The times of high water having been correctly determined at but few positions in the Seto Uchi between Simonoseki, its western entrance, and Akashi strait, at its eastern end, it has been considered advisable to refer such observations of the currents as have been made to the calculated time of high water at Simonoseki, which is at 8h. 30m., full and change, and the making of the western (flood) stream is here given, the streams having been found as a rule to run six hours each way.

The western (flood) stream along the S.E. coast of Nipon makes the high water in the Naruto passage and Isumi strait. The western stream flowing along the north-east coast of Awadji sima also makes high water in Akashi strait, but the set of the tide on the flood through the strait is to the eastward. That from the Boungo channel also makes the high water at Simonoseki, but east of the Boungo, the eastern stream (probably

---

* The description and directions contained in this chapter are compiled from the surveys and remarks of Commanders Ward, Bullock, Brooker, and St. John, Navigating Lieutenant Maxwell, and of M. Banaré, Lieutenant De Vaisseau, French Navy;—from the remark books of H.M. Ships and various documents in the Hydrographic Office of the Admiralty.

from the Pacific by that channel) makes the high water as far as the Bingo nada. The direction of the streams at Simonoseki are given in page 260.

In the bay on south side of Hime sima, the western stream made at 4h. 30m. after high water at Simonoseki, and ran for six hours; velocity at neaps $2\frac{1}{2}$ knots.

At 2 miles north-east of Simonanba point, this stream made at 3h. 15m. after high water at Simonoseki, and ran six hours each way; velocity at neaps $2\frac{1}{4}$ knots.

Kurusima strait, at 4h. 45m. after high water at Simonoseki; neaps run 4 knots.

Awa sima, at 7h. after Simonoseki. Here the western stream ran for $5\frac{1}{2}$ hours, the eastern for $6\frac{1}{2}$ hours, but there was a westerly gale at the time.

The apparent flood and ebb streams in Akashi strait do not change simultaneously with high and low water; off Maiko point the eastern stream makes at 0h. full and change; the western stream at 5h.: the tide made one hour later on the southern shore.

The maximum strength of both streams on the seventh day of the moon (at which time the observations were made) was $2\frac{1}{2}$ knots, with an interval of slack water of about half an hour.

The southern stream in Isumi strait appeared to be simultaneous with the eastern stream in Akashi strait.*

The tides in the Naruto passage are given in page 207.

The tides run strongly in the narrow channels, especially on the western stream, and whirl about very considerably, so as to render steering difficult.

ISUMI STRAIT, between the south-east point of Awadji and Nipon, is divided into three channels by the islands Tomangai and Diyi. Tomangai, the western island, is wooded, with the exception of its west hill, cleared apparently for military purposes; there is a fort close to the north of the south-western point across a small ravine, and facing the west; Diyi is wooded, but lower. The west or main channel is 2 miles wide, but contracted by a sand-bank which extends half a mile off the large fort of Yura, and by reefs stretching 3 cables off the south-west part of Tomangai. The centre passage is only one cable wide, and full of rocks. The eastern channel is a quarter of a mile wide, and said to be clear and safe, between the reefs which extend $1\frac{1}{2}$ cables off both shore and island.

LIGHT.—On the western extreme of Tomangai sima, at an elevation of 208 feet above the sea, is exhibited a *fixed* white light of the third order,

---

* This is not at all certain.

showing from N. ¼ W. round by east and south to S.W. by W., and is visible in clear weather from a distance of 19 miles. The tower, 21 feet high of granite, is in lat. 34° 16′ 40″ N., long. 135° 0′ 30″ E.

The **ISUMI NADA** at the north-east extreme of the inland sea, and 35 miles in extent N.E. and S.W., is bounded on the south by a promontory of Nipon, and on the west by the large mountainous island of Awadji. Its shores are in general high and thickly wooded; in some places, however, they are low and sandy. It is singular in having neither an island nor a danger. On the east shore of Awadji the water is deep, with no convenient anchorages except in small bays close in. The coast of Nipon, on the contrary, affords good anchorage along its whole extent, reefs only extending off it one or two cables.

ŌSAKA,* the place of greatest commercial importance in Japan, stands on the north-east shore of the sea, on the left bank of the Yodo gawa, which takes its rise in the great inland lake, Biwa, and after flowing on a south-westerly course for 30 miles, enters the Isumi nada by several channels. At the lower or north-western corner of the city the river divides into two branches—the Aji kawa, as the Yodo is here called, continuing directly towards the sea; the other branch, the Kishun gawa, takes a southerly course, and discharges its waters 3 miles lower down the gulf: these two branches are navigable by junks of moderate size, but the heavier classes are compelled to discharge their cargoes in the roadstead. It is the seaport of Kioto, the capital of Japan, which is situate 20 miles to the north-east, on a branch of the Sedo gawa.

Ōsaka is intersected by several canals, which are mostly very shallow and only navigable by the flat boats of the country. The castle of the former Tycoon is on the north-east of the city, overlooking the river.

The Foreign concession, named Ebisu jima or Kawa guchi, occupies the angle formed by the Aji and Kishu branches; its position is indicated by lofty trees; the right of building is confined to this site, but the right of residence extends over the contiguous suburb westward. It is 2¾ miles above Temposan, the fort at the river's mouth, and two miles below the castle. The population of Ōsaka is about 400,000.

THE RIVER AJI is shallow, but may be navigated by ships' boats as far as the castle; it has a bar, which at unusually low tides would be nearly dry; at exceptionally high tides, 7 feet might be carried over. The channel is marked by large piles, the two outer having triangular vanes to distinguish them; the shallowest part is just outside these outer beacons, and the best passage over is at one third the distance from the north beacon, so as to avoid a shoal extending south-west from the other;

---

* See plan of Hiogo and Oōsaka, No. 16; scale $m = 1·0$ inches.

when inside, the deep water is close along the groynes on the south side, which always show. There is generally 3 feet more water in the lower part of the river than on the bar.

The Yodo gawa flows from the southern extremity of the lake Biwa (35 miles in extent), at 30 miles north-east of its mouth. At 20 miles from the sea the river receives the waters of two other streams from the north-west and south-east. At 3 miles above this junction, at the confluence of several small streams or canals, stands Kioto, or as it is commonly called Miako or metropolis. It is situated on a highly cultivated plain. Its walls are said to be 30 miles in circuit, and it is governed by a viceroy appointed by the Mikado, his jurisdiction limited by the canals round the city.

ŌSAKA ROADS.—The roadstead of Ōsaka is open to the west and south. The depths in the roadstead are extremely regular, diminishing gradually over a soft mud bottom; the holding ground is so good that it is considered a vessel could ride out any gale in safety. The shores are everywhere of clean sand (as are the river bars), but it constitutes a fringe only, mud being found at a cable from the low-water line.

ANCHORAGE.—It is not advisable to anchor in less than 4 fathoms, as south-west winds cause much sea. There are 4 fathoms at 7 cables from the lighthouse, and 7 fathoms at $1\frac{1}{3}$ miles. To the southward it is much shoaler. The best anchorage is West of the Temposan or Ōsaka lighthouse.

DIRECTIONS.—From within the bar keep the south bank of the river, which will lead up in a nearly direct course to the Tycoon's castle, (above the first bridge the river is seen to turn off sharp to the south; this is the Kishu branch), keep close past the Concession, but in the same direction, for above this the river has two distinct channels, separated by narrow islands and shallow sand-banks, which can seldom be crossed.

Boats may be obtained just above the fort, or at Ichiokashiuden on the left bank, $2\frac{1}{4}$ miles higher up.

The large fort of Temposan, which stands on the south point, commands the entrance of the river; it is a high turfed earthwork, scarped with masonry, and is a conspicuous landmark, the shores being very low.

LIGHT.—On the parapet of the western salient angle of Temposan fort, 53 feet above the sea, is exhibited a *fixed* white light, shewn seaward between the bearing of N.E by E. $\frac{2}{3}$ E. (round by north and west) to S.W. by W., and is visible in clear weather from a distance of 12 miles. The tower is a square-shaped white wooden building, 30 feet high, and is in lat. 34° 39′ 45″ N., long. 135° 26′ 35″ E.

THE KISHU GAWA.—Two miles S.S.E. of Ōsaka bar is the bar of the Kishu, at the north point of entrance of which river a small star fort is being constructed at low-water mark a mile from the shore. This bar has not been closely examined, but it is probably a little deeper than that of the Aji, as a larger class of junks ascend this branch to Ōsaka.

SAKAI.—LIGHT.—S. by E. 4 miles from Temposan is the mouth of the Sakai river, which enters the sea between two short moles extending from two green batteries; it has no bar, and has two feet at entrance. A light is exhibited from a wooden turret on the north fort.

HIOGO AND KOBE.*—A treaty port, 14 miles west of Ōsaka, is a better and more convenient anchorage than the roadstead of Ōsaka, having slight projection from the south, and being thoroughly sheltered from the westerly or prevailing winds. The shores of Hiogo bay are steep-to, but low, and rise in a gentle slope from the beach to the abrupt range of hills 2 miles inland, which are of 800 to 2,000 feet elevation, running parallel to the coast. The bay has an even depth of 4¼ fathoms, with good holding ground in a very stiff mud. The foreign settlement is situated at the head of the northern bay of Kobe. This bay is somewhat smaller than that of Hiogo, but the shores of it are steep, and there is about the same depth of water as in the former, and if less sheltered in south-west winds it is less exposed to easterly winds.

Several streams flow into Hiogo and Kobe bays, the courses of the two principal being broad sandy beds, the streams in which vary considerably in size according to the seasons. The Minato kawa, separating Hiogo from Kobe, is especially peculiar in this respect, the greater part of the year being only a small stream, whilst at times it fills its broad bed and overflows its banks. During the autumn and winter months small-pox is very prevalent here.

Two inner cambers, where boats and junks of considerable draught are completely sheltered, are situated at the eastern corner of the Concession, opposite which is the Custom house. A pier from the centre of the Concession forms a camber in which boats are sheltered.

British subjects are free to go wherever they please within 10 *ri* (21† miles) of Hiogo in any direction, that of Miako (Kioto) excepted, which city shall not be approached nearer than 10 *ri*. The crews of vessels resorting to Hiogo shall not cross the river Ena gawa, which flows into the bay between Hiogo and Ōsaka.

LIGHT.—On Wada misaki, the south-west point of Hiogo bay elevated 52 feet above the sea, is exhibited a *fixed red* light, shewing seaward between the bearings of N.N.W. (round by west and south) to W. by S. ⅓ S.

---

* *See* plan of Hiogo and Oösaka; No. 16, scale *m* = 1·0 inches.

† The *ri* is 4,275 yards according to treaty.

visible in clear, weather from a distance of 12 miles. The tower is an octagonal-shaped white wooden building, 46 feet in height, and is in lat. 34° 39′ 30″ N., long. 135° 12′ E.

DIRECTIONS.—If entering Hiogo at night from the west, keep the light on Matsu-wo-ga hana (page 224) bearing West, (on which bearing it will be just visible) until the *red* light on Wada misaki bears North, when steer N.N.E. for the anchorage, and when the shipping lights are seen bearing N.N.W. or N.W. steer for them and anchor as convenient. Bound to Kobe from the southward; after passing Isumi strait steer N.N.E. ⅓ E. for Wada misaki light, and when the light on Matsu-wo-ga hana opens out, haul to the eastward until Wada misaki light bears North, when proceed as before mentioned for the anchorage. It must be borne in mind that the ebb tide sets to the westward towards Akashi strait, and the flood to the eastward towards Ōsaka, 2 knots an hour at springs, increasing as Akashi strait is approached.

The coast as far as Tree point, 7 miles eastward of Kobe, is safe of approach, the shore being steep into 4 fathoms, except the bay directly east of Kobe, where there is a sand-bank of less than 2 fathoms extending half mile off shore.

Supplies.—Supplies of all descriptions may be procured in abundance at tolerably cheap rates. Government coal is stored here in charge of a contractor, who also supplies fresh meat, vegetables, and water. Large timber, chiefly cedar (Sungi) is also procurable.

TIDES.—It is high water, full and change at Hiogo at 7h. 15m. Springs rise 5 ft. 8 in.; neaps 4 ft. 3 in.; neap range 2 ft. 6 in. The range of any day seldom exceeds 5 ft. at springs or 1 ft. 6 in. at neaps.

At Ōsaka bar no perceptible differences in the range, from the above, could be observed. At Ōsaka Concession the establishment is 8h. 17m. Spring rise 30 inches, neaps 6. The flood stream does not reach the Concession. At neaps there is only one tide in the 24 hours, and a strong S.W. wind with low barometer may raise the level of the Isumi nada two feet.

The direction of the tidal streams, which are sometimes strong off Hiogo point, are, the flood to the eastward and the ebb to the westward. In Ōsaka roads they are weak and irregular.

ICHI-NO-TANI YAMA (End hill) is a wooded granitic hill 830 feet high, 5 miles to the eastward of Akashi, the end of the range running from Kobe, and falling abruptly to the sea. The land to the westward of this hill is comparatively low, and stretches away like a long table land as far as the borders of the province of Bizen; having high ranges in the background, and two conspicuous hills, with clumps of trees at their summits, north-west of the town of Akashi. The coast line is sandy, with numerous villages along it.

Taka iso, a rock with 9 feet on it at low water, lies nearly a cable off shore, 5½ cables to the westward of the village of Shiwoya.

Hira iso are the highest pinnacles of a bank of rock and shingle, 4 cables from the shore, having 6 feet on them at low water. The eastern lies E. ¾ N. 3¼ miles from Matsu-wo-ga hana (the north point of Awadji sima). South from it, and quite close to, is the wreck of a Satsuma steamer, having two feet on it at low water. To clear them the light on Matsu-wo-ga hana must be kept West, until Ichi-no-tani yama bears N.E. The stone fort at Maiko in sight, N.W.½W., clear of the trees on Kara saki, leads to the westward of Hira iso.

AKASHI NO SETO (Akashi strait),* between the north point of Awadji sima and the coast of Nipon, is nearly 2½ miles wide, the above rocks, Taka iso and Hira iso, being the only known dangers when approaching it.

Akashi.—This town is in the district of Akashi, province of Setsu on the mainland of Nipon; and contains the residence of the Daimio, the four white towers of which show out plainly against the surrounding dark foliage.

In the bay of Yamata ura, between the dark wooded point of Kara saki and the conspicuous granite fort at Maiko to the eastward, and the town of Akashi to the westward, there is good anchorage, with winds from north-west round by north to east, in 9 fathoms, sand, good holding ground.

Yamata iso, a rock in the strait having 2 feet on it at low water, lies N.W. by W. ½ W. 3½ cables from Maiko fort. Care should be taken not to anchor within 5 cables of the fort. The tides take the line of the coast, and have at springs a velocity of 2¾ knots.

SHIKA NO SE, on the northern side of the entrance to Akashi no seto, is a bank of rock, covered by sand and shingle, with depths of from 6 to 12 feet, running W. by S. ½ S. and E. by N. ½ N. 2¾ miles, with an average width of 1½ cables. Its eastern extreme of 12 feet lies W. by S. ½ S. 8 miles from the lighthouse (stone lantern) at Akashi; and W. ¼ S. 8 miles from the fort on Matsu-wo-ga hana. It is steep-to on the southern, but shoals gradually on the northern and western sides.

From the west extreme of the town of Akashi, in the direction of Shika no se, and almost connected to the latter by a series of shoals, is a bank of mud, steep-to on the southern side, but apparently joining the shore on the northern. To avoid this, the lighthouse on Awadji should not be brought to the eastward of E. ¾ N.

The passage between Akashi and Shika no se should not be attempted.

MUROZU NO SE, on the southern side of the entrance to Akashi no seto, has been thoroughly examined both by *Serpent* and *Sylvia,* and nothing less than 5¾ fathoms has been found. The two shoals having that

---

* See Plan of Akashi no seto, No. 93; scale m = 1·5 inches.

depth lie S.W. by W. ¾ W. 8 miles, and W.S.W. 9½ miles from the north extreme of Awadji sima. These patches go by various names among the inhabitants, that in general use being the above, while the name Skenesi (on former charts) was not understood at all by them.

DIRECTIONS.—On approaching Akashi strait from the westward a clear course may be made between the above shoal and Shika no se, by keeping the summit of Ichi-no-tani yama in line with the lighthouse on the north extreme of Awadji sima E. by N. ½ N. or at night by keeping the light on that bearing.

TIDES.—The tides about Akashi no seto are variable, causing heavy tide ripples, particularly off the west end of the town of Akashi where they all meet. About a mile south of the western end of the straits, the tide turns to the eastward at the time of low water at Maiko, and runs through the straits about 7 hours.

The stream turns to the eastward on Shika no se 1½ hours before high water at Maiko.

On Murozu no se it turns to the south-westward at high water, and runs half an hour less than the north-easterly stream.

Close into the shore at Maiko the stream turns with the tide, the flood running to the eastward. The maximum strength of both streams on the seventh day of the moon was 2½ knots, with an interval of slack water of about half an hour.

AWADJI SIMA, the largest island of the inland sea, is 30 miles in length north and south, and 14 miles across at its southern or broadest part, which is between the projecting promontories of Nipon and Sikok, at the eastern entrance of this sea from the Kii channel, which it divides into two passages, the strait of Isumi on the east, and the Naruto passage on the west. Awadji is mountainous, but the hills taper away towards its north cape, which is low and sandy, with batteries on it.

MATSU-WO-GA HANA.—The north point of Awadji sima is terminated by a white stone fort, with seven guns "en barbette," is steep-to, and has a lighthouse erected on it.

LIGHT.—On Matsu-wo-ga hana, the north point of Awadji sima, elevated 158 feet above the sea, is exhibited a *fixed* light of the first order shewn from West round by South and East to N.E. by E. ¾ E., and is visible in clear weather from a distance of 18 miles. The tower is 15 feet high, built of stone, and is in lat. 34° 36′ 40″ N., long. 135° 0′ 30″ E.

YE SIMA, and KO-YE SIMA, 47 feet and 40 feet high respectively, are two cliffy peninsulas on the northern end of Awadji sima, which island forms the southern shore of Akashi no seto; the latter wooded, and apparently detached when seen from north-west or south-east. They lie at the south end of the village of Iwaya, off which there is excellent anchorage, with winds from south round by west to north-west, in 8 fathoms, with Ko-ye sima S.½E. half a mile. The tides are, flood from north-west and ebb from E.S.E., with a velocity at spring of 2½ knots.

The WEST COAST generally is steep, sloping from wooded hills, and bordered by numerous villages. The hills rise to a remarkable wooded and cliffy nob named Rioruji, 1,746 feet high, from which a bare spur runs to the sea, having on its western summit, known as Karuto yama, a remarkable single tree, 1,022 feet above high water.

TSKUYE NO SE, a shoal having 2 feet on it at low water, lies 7 cables from the shore, about 6 miles to the south-west of Matsu-wo-ga hana. From it the water gradually deepens to the westward; 5 fathoms will be found at one mile from the shore. Anchorage with the wind off shore will be found outside this, in convenient depths of 6 to 8 fathoms sand, good holding ground.

To clear this shoal, the north extreme of Awadji sima should not be brought to the northward of N.E. by E.

YE SAKI is a bluff point wooded at the top, and cliffy on the north face. It slopes down to the village of Ye mura, where there is a large camber, available for junks of 50 tons. In the middle of Ye ura is the large village of Gunge mura, at the mouth of a river that drains an extensive and well cultivated plain.

Ye no ura, the bay north of Ye saki, has a bank of sand stretching across it; 3 fathoms being found at 7 cables, and 5 fathoms at one mile from the shore, in the middle of the bay. The bank is steep-to, having less than a half a cable between 6½ and 12 fathoms. Large vessels anchoring here should not let go in less than 8 fathoms. The bottom is of sand, good holding ground.

The COAST from Tsuiji no hana to Maru yama is bold, sloping from a range, the summits of which are Dama yama, 787 feet, and Hichi-ga yama, 800 feet high, interspersed with cliffs, and fronted by a shingly beach. Numerous deep ravines sear the side of this range, the largest, Onagi tani, having at its base a pool of water.

MARU YAMA, 72 feet high, is a flat-topped peninsula, joined to Awadji sima by a neck of sand, on which stands a village. It has a reef off the north end extending 2 cables, most of the rocks showing at high water, the outermost of which must not be approached within 1½ cables.

BEN-TEN SIMA, 99 feet high, is a sharp wooded islet, connected on its north side by shallow water with Maru yama, but may be approached on the south side to one cable. Excellent anchorage will be found, with shelter from off shore winds, in 6 to 8 fathoms, sand, 3 cables from the shore, with Ben-ten sima North 2½ cables. Small vessels may go into a convenient depth, the water shoaling gradually from 12 fathoms to the shore.

URBI SAKI, the next point south, is cliffy, with rocks extending half a cable from it. Between this and Maru yama the coast is bold, with rocks and shoal water stretching a cable off the points.

ANAGA is a small village at the mouth of a large plain. The anchorage off it is not good, as the tide whirls vessels round their anchors continually.

YUBI SIMA, a thinly wooded islet about 130 feet high, stands in the middle of the bay between Anaga and Tō saki, the south-west promontory of Awaji sima. It is separated from the shore by a channel three quarters of a cable wide, has rocks that cover off its south point one cable, and a rock awash lies close to its west point. The bay has projecting ledges off all the points, making it useless as an anchorage.

HARIMA NADA.—Lying between Awadji sima and Sozu sima, is a comparatively shoal expanse, having about 20 fathoms deepest water, the southern portion of the sea being clear of dangers. The northern portion, however, is said to be encumbered with shoals and dangerous covered rocks, extending from Ukado point, the south-east point of Sozu sima to Shika no se, before described. In navigating the Harima nada the dotted track * should be as closely as possible adhered to, as the northern portion of this sea has not been closely examined. Its southern shore from the Naruto passage westward for about 17 miles, as far as Taka sima, is also as yet unsurveyed. Ichi-no-tani yama (end hill) just seen open of the lighthouse on Awadji sima leads between the Shika no se and Murozo-no se, for the south point of Sozu sima.

SOZU SIMA, a large island in the eastern part of the Harima nada, is 10 miles long, 8 miles broad, and 2,560 feet high. On its south side the high promontory of Yosino, terminating in a bluff 980 feet high, stretches to the southward, forming a conspicuous landmark throughout the Harima nada, and the narrow sea to the westward. There are large bays on either side of it, but they are considered not to afford good anchorage.

ANCHORAGE may be found to the north-west of Dyizo bluff, south-east of Si sima, which may be recognized by a high tree on its summit; but the bay is encumbered with shoals. The best anchorage is in Uchi no umi off the village of Sakate to the north-east of Dyizo hana, in 7 fathoms; the shore is bold all round close to. N.W. of Ukado point in the bay between it and Fukube island, there is deep water anchorage in 13 to 20 fathoms; it is however much exposed.

---

* See Chart of the Seto Uchi, No. 2875, corrected to 31st December, 1872; scale m = 0·25 inches.

DANGERS.—Two rocks, that cover at a quarter flood, lie in the harbour of this island. From the outer rock, the steep bluff of Dyizo hana bears S.W., and the west extreme of Fukube S.E. ½ S. The inner, on which are the remains of a Japanese beacon, lies N. by E. ½ E. from the former, and N.N.W. ¼ W. from Higiri point.

HANA MURA, on the Kiusiu shore, S.S.W. 5 miles from Yosino bluff, is said to be the best anchorage in the neighbourhood, and a fine harbour. A bank carrying 19 feet water lies in the middle of the entrance to this bay, with the small islet Taka sima bearing N. by W. On the promontory which forms its west side, the high rugged peak of Gokensan, a sacred mountain, is a very conspicuous object. A large town stands at its head. A bank lies near the entrance to the bay eastward of Kanobe point.

Channels between the HARIMA NADA and BINGO NADA.—Westward of Sozu sima the Seto Uchi is studded with numbers of islands, for miles forming numerous channels, of which the most central and southern only have been examined; these however are sufficiently clear of dangers to be with ordinary caution quite safe of navigation, the surveys of these narrows having rendered the navigation of the Seto Uchi comparatively easy.*

TAKA SIMA, a small island half a mile long, north and south lies 6½ cables from the western point of Hana mura with a deep water channel between. A rocky ledge extend 2 cables from its N.W. point.

Ō SIMA, O KABUTA, KO KABUTA, and INAGHI form a group lying 3 miles to the north-west from Taka sima; they are low and should not be approached closely, as several sand-banks lie between them. Off O Kabuta a shoal extends nearly half a mile from its east side, and 2½ cables from its N.E. point.

OKI SIMA.—2¼ miles to the north-westward from the north point of Ō sima, is about a mile long (N.N.E. and S.S.W.) and less than half a mile in width; it has two summits both of which are about 300 feet high, that to the south being sharp, while the northern is flattened at the top. From its eastern shore a shoal bank extends a considerable distance to the eastward with a patch of 2½ fathoms 7 cables from the shore, between which and it, there is another shoal bank. To the eastward of the former patch the water gradually deepens from 6 and 7 fathoms.

MEKI SIMA lying south of Oki sima, from which it is separated by a narrow channel of less than 4½ cables, is nearly 2 miles long N.N.E. and S.S.W., and half a mile wide. At half a mile from its eastern shore

---

* See Plan, Channels between Bingo nada and Harima nada, No. 128; scale m = 1·5 inches.

a long shoal bank extends nearly parallel with the shore, the northern extreme of which is E. ½ S. 1½ miles from the north point of the island. The western side is also shoal, off its centre extending three-quarters of a mile. From the south point of Meki sima a shoal bank with 1 and 2 fathom patches upon it extends to the westward nearly parallel with the shore, for a distance of 5½ miles to Ohara no hana with 7 and 8 fathoms between it and the shore of Sikok.

ANCHORAGE.—Good anchorage may be had inside the shoal off the large town of Takamatsu, or indeed anywhere between Ya sima and Ohara no hana in 6 and 7 fathoms sand and mud.

DIRECTIONS.—Great caution should be used in approaching this anchorage southward of the islands above described. The best channel is south of Inagi and Ō sima, (taking care to avoid the shoal spit from the southern shore lying between these islands), and passing Ya sima give the shore south of it a berth of one mile to clear the shoal bank which lies S.W. by W. ¼ W. 7 cables from it.

ODE SIMA lies between Sozu sima and Te sima, it is small and from its south-west point a shoal bank extends 7 cables from it towards the south point of Te sima.

AWARI SIMA a rocky islet, lies 6 cables south from the south-west point of Ode sima. Vessels should not pass to the northward of this islet.

TE SIMA.—A large island lies northward of the route recommended and is steep-to along its south shore. A shoal extends nearly one mile from the shore 1½ miles to the westward of its south point.

NAO SIMA.—The next large island to the westward lies 1½ miles from the shores of Nipon, and is surrounded by small islets.

KASIWA.—An islet off the southern point of Nao sima is immediately north of the route through the channels; it is steep-to on its south side.

NAKA SE.—An extensive shoal bank extending from the south-west shore of Oki sima 3½ miles in a W. by S. direction, is to the southward of the route. No-o saki should not be brought open southward of Koduchi in approaching this bank.

THE COAST of Nipon from Nao sima approaches the shores of Sikok to within 3¾ miles, it being the narrowest part of the Seto Uchi. The northern shore westward from the above island about 6½ miles in a direct line to Kusumi no hana has not been examined.

Galatea shoal* (Ozono se) with from 1 to 3 fathoms on it, is 1¾ miles in length, east and west. Its eastern extreme lies 1½ miles W. ½ S. from

---

* H.M.S. *Galatea*, Capt. H.R.H. the Duke of Edinburgh, grounded on this shoal in 1869.

the south point of Kasiwa, and its eastern extreme approaches Odutsi within 11 cables.

ODUTSI (Cone island). This island is very prominent from all directions, it appears perfectly conical with smooth sides which are really covered with dense brushwood, and its summit is 540 feet above the sea.

KODUCHI (Kodutsi), lies 12 cables south of Odutsi having a deep water channel between, through which is the route recommended. A ledge extends one cable from the north shore of Koduchi.

ASSA ROCK, with 15 feet on it at low water, lies E. ¼ N. 9 cables from the northern point of Koduchi.

NO-O SAKI lies 1¾ miles W. by S. from Ohara no hana between which are two bays. The western is shallow, but that to the eastward (Kisawa) is not so shallow. On the eastern side of No-o saki are two very conspicuous landslips.

ANCHORAGE may be obtained in 6½ fathoms in the latter bay, but it is not a particularly good one.

SEI SIMA AND SHAMI SIMA are low, with shallow water between them, and are connected with the shore of Sikok by shoal banks with no passage between. Three-quarters of a mile north of Sei sima is Ko sei sima, a small island with a ledge of rocks extending half a cable from its western point, and a shoal bank extending 3 cables from its eastern side. One and a quarter miles north of Shami sima is a cluster of three small rocky islets.

SANMEN SIMA (three rocks.) The cluster of rocky islets above mentioned lie immediately south of the route through the channels, they are steep-to everywhere but on their western side.

Three Rocks spit.—A narrow bank of gravel extends 6 cables from the three rocky islets towards Siyako. Its spit may be crossed in 10 fathoms by keeping Odutsi, its own breadth open of the small round island, Nube sima off the south point of Yo sima. All these islands from Koduchi lie on the south side of the route through.

YO SIMA to the northward of Sanmen sima between which is a deep channel of 4 cables is cultivated and wooded, with a village on its south-east side.

Ko Yo sima a narrow islet, lies 2 cables from the east shore of Yo sima nearly parallel to it. Between the two islands there are several shoal patches.

Nabe sima lies immediately off the south-east point of Yo sima, it is steep-to on its south side.

LIGHT.—On the summit of Nabe sima at an elevation of 85 feet above the sea is exhibited a *fixed* white light of the third order, seen between

N. ¼ E. round by south to W. ½ N.; visible in clear weather from a distance of 15 miles.

SIYAKO lies one mile west from Yo sima with a deep channel between, it is high and comparatively bare, its ridges which are elevated above 600 feet above the sea being sandy and covered with short grass in patches; there are several villages on its southern shore which is steep-to except off its south point.

Siyako ledge.—A rocky ledge extends 1½ cables off the south point of Siyako, at the outer part of which is a rock of less than 10 feet water. Heavy overfalls are generally seen there.

USI SIMA lies to the southward of Siyako, between which is a deep channel, 5 cables wide. The island is thickly wooded, with two clumps (the northern being 340 feet high) which are very conspicuous when approaching it.

Rocks, which dry towards low water, extend one cable off the north point of Usi sima; they are steep-to.

THE CONQUEROR BANK.* From the south-west point of Usi sima a shoal bank extends 2½ miles in a W.S.W. direction towards Takami. It is a narrow ridge of sand and shingle, with knolls and patches on it of 1¾ and 2 fathoms, and is nowhere more than 3 cables across. Both its northern and southern edges are steep-to, the deeper water being on its northern side.

HIRO SIMA lies to the W.S.W. of Siyako, between which is a channel 1¼ miles wide, which is nearly filled up by an extensive sand-bank. The outline of Hiro sima is very irregular, and its sharp rocky ridges are very conspicuous. The summit of the island, which presents southward the appearance of an almost perpendicular cliff, is 990 feet above the sea. On the south shore is Ino ura, a small bay, on the shores of which are several small villages, the valleys around which are cultivated. The eastern hills are covered with brushwood, but the western ridges are thickly wooded. In the ravines, the sides of which are rocky precipices, numerous deer are found.

ANCHORAGE.—Ino ura is a convenient anchorage for vessels passing through the Seto Uchi, and is generally chosen as a night anchorage, especially when bound from Hiogo to the westward, it being within convenient distance, and can be arrived at before nightfall. Care must be taken not to approach the shore too closely, as the head of the bay shoals very suddenly; the northern end of Takami, just touching or shut in with the south point of Ino ura will avoid this bank, but particular care must be taken only to just close the channel and not to shut in Takami too

---

* H.M.S. *Conqueror* grounded on this bank in 1864, on the occasion of Admiral Kuper's squadron passing through the Seto Uchi.

much. Good holding ground will be found here out of the strength of the tides.

TIDES.—It is high water, full and change, at Hiro sima at 11h. 45m., and springs rise 11 feet, neaps 8 feet. The streams run regularly six hours each way, the flood setting to the westward, and the changes take place about an hour before the end of the tide. The tides, however, are sometimes irregular.

HABUSHI IWA (Ten-feet rock), lies $5\frac{1}{2}$ cables S. by E. $\frac{1}{2}$ E. from the south point of Ino ura, it is 20 feet high and whitened, and may be passed quite safely on either side at one cable distance.

TAKAMI.—A very conspicuous island on the south side of the route, is nearly $1\frac{1}{2}$ miles long (N.W. and S.E.), lofty, and has a sharp ridge through its centre, the whole of which is thickly wooded, forming on its south end a conspicuous clump 990 feet above the sea. Two villages are situated on its south-east side, and it is the undisturbed resort of pigeons, which are to be found in great numbers.

A shoal bank extends from the eastern side of Takami in an E.N.E. direction, and nearly joins the south-west extreme of the Conqueror bank. There is, however, a narrow channel between the two, which may be taken, if necessary, by vessels of moderate draft; this may be done by keeping Habushi iwa (Ten-feet rock) just shut in, or touching the south-west shores of Hiro sima.

SANAGI SIMA lies 3 miles W.S.W. from Hiro sima, is $1\frac{1}{2}$ miles long (north and south), and about half a mile wide; its centre peak, which is wooded, is 815 feet above the sea. On its south-east side is a large village with a camber, affording good shelter for native craft.

Ko sima (Round island), lies half a mile east from the south end of Sanagi, its sides are smooth and steep, and its summit is 480 feet high.

NORTH BANK.—From the eastern shore of Sanagi sima joining Ko sima, and extending 3 miles in an easterly direction from the former island, is an extensive bank of sand, with from $\frac{1}{2}$ to 2 fathoms upon it, its eastern extremity projecting slightly into the St. Vincent channel. In passing this bank, vessels should not shut in the clump on Siyako with the south point of Hiro sima (*see* page 232).

NEZUMI SIMA lies $1\frac{3}{4}$ to the southward of Sanagi sima, between which is the channel recommended, carrying 6 fathoms water. The islet is small, low, and of a brown colour, and is surrounded by rocks, which project on its northern side to nearly 3 cables. It would be advisable, therefore, under any circumstance to give it a berth of half a mile. From the western shore of Takami an extensive bank having patches of 2 and 3 fathoms upon it, extends in a W.S.W. direction to Nezumi sima.

The St. VINCENT CHANNEL, to the northward of the Conqueror bank, lies between the islands above described (commencing from the eastward with Yo sima), and has on its north side the islands of Siyako, Hiro sima, Sanagi sima, and Ko sima, and on its southern side the rocky islets Sanmen sima, Usi sima, the northern edge of the Conqueror bank, and the extensive bank nearly joining it, extending from the east side of Takami and Nezumi sima, together with the shoal between Takami and the latter. In its centre off Hiro sima is Habushi iwa (Ten-feet rock), before described.

DIRECTIONS.—(From the Harima nada to the Bingo nada by the St. Vincent Channel.) Keep as nearly as possible the track on the chart which leads mid-channel between Dyizo hana, the south point of Sozu sima and Kanobe point on the Sikok shore, and keep a N.W. by W. course, paying attention to the set of the tides, pass three-quarters of a mile north of the small island of O Kabuta, and half a mile north of Oki sima, the next island to the westward. On rounding this island the conspicuous cone-shaped island Odutsi will be seen nearly ahead; steer to pass about half a mile southward of it, or mid-channel between it and the small island Koduchi southward of it, taking care to keep the south point of Te sima (immediately north of Oki sima) open southward of Kasiwa (the small island off the south-east point of Nao sima) until Odutsi is passed, by which means the Galatea shoal on the north side of the route is avoided. Care must also be taken not to approach too closely the extensive bank Naka se which lies to the south of the route extending westward from Oki sima. When in mid-channel between Odutsi and Koduchi, the wooded island Usi sima with its two conspicuous clumps will be seen bearing W. by S. ½ S., and in line with it the rocky islets Sanmen sima, the north extreme of which may be brought in line with the northern clump and steered for (passing the small island Ko sei sima), until within 7 cables, when haul up to the northward and, passing in mid-channel between these islets (Sanmen sima) and Yo sima, steer for the clump on Siyako until Habushi iwa (Ten-feet rock) is seen in mid-channel between Siyako and Usi sima, when haul to the southward and bringing its south extreme in line or just open of the north point of Takami W. by S. ¾ S., steer for it. This mark leads clear of the rocks off the north end of Usi sima, and also the ledge off the south point of Siyako. Having passed these dangers Habushi iwa may be passed on either side at one cable, and the north point of Takami at the same distance, after which bring Habushi iwa open its own breadth of the north point of Takami E. by N. ½ N. (northerly), this mark will lead between Sanagi sima and Nezumi sima in 7 fathoms, but care must be taken not to shut in Habushi iwa with Takami. The northernmost clump of trees on Usi sima, in a line with the north point of Takami, also leads in 7 fathoms between

Nezumi sima shoal and the shoal extending from the southward of the island of Sanagi. This route carries the deepest water through the channels connecting the Harima nada with the Bingo nada.

The Channel southward of the Conqueror bank.—This channel was formerly the route used in navigating these narrows previous to our recent surveys, but is now very seldom made use of. If however it be desirable to use this channel, on passing Odutsi steer to pass south of Sanmen sima, the rocky islets before-mentioned, after which bring the summit of Odutsi midway between these islets, and Ko sei sima N.E. by E. ½ E., and with this mark continue on until Nezumi sima is seen open of the south point of Takami, on observing which the least water will be obtained 4¼ fathoms close to which is a patch of 3¾ fathoms. When Nezumi sima is seen well open, haul up for the north peak of Awa sima W. by S. ¼ S. and pass from 2 to 3 cables northward of that island.

The COAST.—From No-o saki the coast of Sikok takes a south-westerly direction for 14 miles to Ko-ya no hana, and is skirted by shoals westward of the islands Sei sima and Shami sima, before-mentioned as connected to the shore by shoals. Eastward of these islands the water is deeper, and westward of them shoal water extends as far off as the two islets Kami-ma sima and Simo-ma sima. The shore is an extensive plain on which are several towns and large villages, the largest of which are Sakaide, Marugame, and Tadotsŭ, the two last being the residence of Daimios. To the eastward of the former are the mouths of the Ahyano kawa, a river of some dimensions, and on the coast fronting the town are extensive salt works. At from 2 to 3 miles inland the mountain ranges attain an altitude of over 1,000 feet, and beyond them are seen the higher ranges of Sikok towering above them to about 10,000 feet above the sea.

TADOTSŬ has a small tidal harbour for junks and small craft. The town is small, clean, and flourishing, and manufactures a great deal of basket work, for which it is famous. About 6½ miles eastward of the town is the mouth of the Makasii gawa. Southward of the town the hills approach and skirt the coast rising to a considerable altitude.

The COAST from Ko-ya no hana takes a north-westerly direction for 6½ miles to Akeno Misaki between which are several shallow bays, the whole forms a narrow promontory the hills in the centre being low and wooded, whilst those toward the cape and those inshore are about 1,000 feet high.

SISI SIMA, a small island on which there are two villages, lies N. by E. 1½ miles from Ko-ya no hana.

AWA SIMA lies between Ko-ya no hana and Akeno misaki on the south side of the southern channel; it is triangular in shape, having bays on its north, south, and west sides, and appears like three islands joined by two narrow, low, sandy isthmuses, the extremes being high and wooded. There is a large village on the south side.

ANCHORAGE may be had in either of the above bays, that to the south having the deeper water, but the northern bay is more convenient for vessels anchoring for the night. Care must be taken not to anchor too near the head of the bay as it shoals a long way out. This may be avoided by keeping Nezumi sima just open of the north point of Awa sima, and the islet Simo-ma sima just open of the eastern point of the bay. The bay on the west side of the island is shoal.

THE BINGO NADA from the channels just described across to the channels leading into the Misima nada is about 30 miles wide, and about 38 miles long in a N.N.E. and S.S.W. direction. It is comparatively clear, having only a chain of 6 islands stretching across it in a N.W. and S.E. direction, and a few others lying near the Kurusima strait.

TOMO is a town on the north shore of the Bingo nada, on the mainland It is famous for its *sake* (native spirits) distilleries. There is a pier and harbour here for small vessels, and anchorage in 5 fathoms in the roadstead sheltered from north and west winds.

MUTSU SIMA is 610 feet high, and cultivated to its summit; two rocks, that show like fishing boats at low water, and cover at a quarter flood, lie nearly half-a-mile to the westward of this island.

UDSI has two peaks 370 feet high, that to the east being double and wooded.

HASIRI is a large island having two peaks, the eastern 400 feet high, the western 200 feet.

The chain of islands above mentioned as lying in a N.W. and S.E. direction 2¼ miles from Akeno Misaki, are,—

TOYO in the fairway from the Wu sima channel, has a double peak on its eastern end, 300 and 250 feet high, falling to a flat on the west of 100 feet elevation.

TAKAIKAMI, OKI, AND YENO, form a conspicuous group. Takaikami has a single peak 800 feet high; Oki, three peaks of 530 feet elevation with a small islet south of it; Yeno, one peak, 200 feet high.

MATA SIMA, MOMO AND IBUKI.—The former is about 100 feet high, small, round, and has a few conspicuous trees on it. Momo appears barren and has three small nobs on it, the highest of which is about 150 feet. The latter island is about 100 feet high and bluff at the east end with a few trees on it, from which it gradually slopes to the west end. The other group above mentioned as lying near the Kurusima strait are,—

KADJI SIMA, 264 feet high, to the eastward of O sima, is a round double-topped island with a red cliff on the hill side north of the summit, and may be approached to 2 cables all round.

MIOJIN SIMA makes in three lumps, the highest having a clump of trees at the summit, 325 feet above high water. The east brow has a single tree. This island has a deep bay on the south side, with a few fishermen's huts, and is steep-to all round.

Nezumi sima is a small round island with detached rocks that just show at high water, one cable off the south point.

SHI-SHAKA SIMA consist of two islands, the higher a grass covered hill 501 feet high, falling steeply on the west side. The north and lower island has a clump of trees near the summit, and is joined to the higher by a shingly beach, at the north end of which is a village.

HIKI SIMA is a group of four islets, lying S.W. by W. ¼ W., 5 miles from Shi-Shaka sima, the eastern being surmounted by a conspicuous chimney-shaped clump 57 feet high and 242 feet above high water. From the east point rocks extend half a cable, the two western being small pinnacle islets, 96 and 30 feet high.

AJIKA, awash at high-water springs, lies E. by N. ¾ N., one mile from the south-east point of Hiki sima, and from it S.W. ½ S. 1½ cables is a rock awash.

HEJI SIMA are two islets, south 2¼ miles from Hiki sima and are three-quarters of a mile in length, the western and higher having a clump of trees at the summit, 309 feet above high water. From the west point S.S.E., three-quarters of a mile, lies a peaked rock, 30 feet above high water, and N.W. ¼ W. 1½ miles there is a sand-bank with 22 feet least water.

Through the BINGO NADA.—On passing Nezumi sima, steer to pass in mid-channel between Mutsu sima and Akeno misaki, from whence, if wishing to take the northern route through the channels between the Bingo nada and the Misima nada, a course W. by N. will lead up to mid-channel between the islands of Hyaku Kuan and Yoko, at the entrance to the Mikari seto.

If intending to take the southern route through the Kurusima strait, a course W.S.W. from Mutsu sima will lead up to Takaikami, the loftiest of the islands above described as lying in the Bingo nada, and, passing in mid-channel between it and Oki sima, continue the same course passing about one mile north of Kadji, the northern island of the next group, and when the islets of the south point of Ō sima are seen, haul up and steer to pass them at about a mile, for the Kurusima strait.

KURUSIMA NO SETO (Kurusima strait).*—The northern shore of the province of Iyo forming the southern coast of the approach to Kurusima no seto, may be known by two curiously shaped hills, one with a double summit; on one of which is a clump of trees 1,202 feet above high water; the other hill has a lower clump, 363 feet above high water, close to the shore, 2¾ miles south of Imabari, the coast being a series of sandy beaches between Imabari and the spurs from the double hill just mentioned. The large town of Imabari is also very conspicuous on this shore, and the islets off the south point of Ōsima on the northern shore of the strait are also easily recognized.

IMABARI is a large town, the residence of a Daimio, whose castle lies behind the trees and pier south of the town. There is a camber, but it dries to the mouth at low water. Anchorage, though in a strong tideway, may be had with off shore winds in from 11 to 13 fathoms, sand, good holding ground, with the pier bearing S.S.W. 2½ cables.

Rocks that cover at high water, and stretch 1½ cables from the shore, lie off this coast N.N.W. ¼ W. 1½ miles from the pier at Imabari.

Tori ishi, a rock with a temple gate, 13 feet above high water, lies nearly four miles south-eastward from Imabari pier, 1½ cables from the shore.

Ōbama is a large village 2¼ miles to the north-west of Imabari, having a bluff point at the north extreme, and a conspicuous temple gate near the centre.

Shiroi iwa 13 feet is a white topped rock, lying 2½ cables N. by E. ½ E. from the rocky point just northward of the village of Ōbama, and may be approached to half a cable on the east side.

Amaze, a rock that dries at low water, lies N. by W. ½ W., 3½ cables from Shiroi iwa; and Hirose, a patch of rocks that dry, lies S. by E. ½ E. 2½ cables from the same place.

Ō SIMA, a large island on the north side of Kurusima no seto, bears evidence of volcanic origin in the remarkable features of its innumerable peaks, deep valleys, and off-lying pinnacle rocks. The highest hill, Nimbutsgata or Tomari yama, is grass covered, and surmounted by two conspicuous trees 1,270 feet above high water. It falls steeply on the north side, and terminates at the north-west point in a conical summit, from which it is separated by a deep valley running from Tomari ura.

The south shore falls steeply from a succession of high sharp peaks: Tate yama, Kiro yama, Takatorisan (surmounted by a clump), and Tōdai yama, granitic, occasionally covered with small trees. The north shore, forming the south side of Kare seto, has no remarkable feature, is cultivated a short distance from the shore, and has several villages scattered along it.

---

* See Plan Kurusima no seto, No. 131, scale m = 6 inches. Also channels between Misima nada and Bingo nada, No. 132, scale m = 1½ inches.

Miya no ura is a large sandy bay with a considerable village along the beach, east of which, and forming the north-east point of Ō sima, is Tōdai no hana, terminated by a cliffy islet, steep-to. On the west side is the deep bay Tsuk ura, shallow to the outside of pinnacle rocks in its entrance, off which rocks awash extend one cable north-west and south-east.

Kamage lies S. by E. ½ E. from Tōdai no hana, a pinnacle rock that may be approached to one cable.

Yoko sima, a bare island, steep-to on the south side, lies S. by W. ¾ W., 1¼ miles from the same point. From this, W.S.W. 1¼ miles, lies Tsukumo no sima, with a round clump of trees at the summit, having a sand-bank extending half a cable off the north point, that dries at low water, and at E.N.E., three-quarters of a mile, is a reef that dries 4 feet at low water, with shoal water for half a cable from the west extreme.

Ōbasan and **Riugon** are two islets lying off the south-west point of Ō sima, the latter and outer being 32 feet high, and having a large tree at the summit.

More no iso.—Two white rocks, which lie East a quarter of a mile from Riugon, are joined at low water, and are 5 and 3 feet above high water. The tide races and whirls round these rocks with great velocity. They should not be approached nearer than 1½ cables.

TSU SIMA, a wooded island, with two summits showing from north or south, has off the west side a small islet joined at low water, and having a tree at its summit; and farther north a bluff peninsula that makes as an islet when seen from a short distance. This island is steep-to, except on the south-east side, from which, separated by a narrow channel, lies a flat cultivated island, having rocks that extend half a cable from the south point. A black rock covered at high water, and joined to the flat island at low water by a sand-bank, lies West two cables from the north point.

UMA SIMA has two summits, the southern and higher 290 feet high, and covered with scattered trees. From the south point, 150 yards, lies a rock awash, over which the tide ripples with great force. The east side of the island is foul for half a cable, and off the islet at the north end, rocks and shoal water extend North, one cable.

NAGATO SIMA is round, wooded and steep-to on the west side, and may be approached to half a cable on the north or south.

O no se, a rock that dries at low water, lies East three-quarters of a cable from the east point.

MUSHI SIMA consist of four wooded islets, the two southern joined at low water, the northern joined to them by rocks awash.

Bushiro, a rock having 13 feet on it, steep-to all round, lies E.S.E. 2 cables from the north point of Mushi sima.

NEZUMI SIMA, to the north-west of Uma sima, is a cultivated island 356 feet high, rising to a wooded summit, and having a clump of trees on the west slope. The east point is steep.

Perseus rock (Ko no se), three granite boulders, having 4 feet on them at low water steep-to all round, lie E. by N. 1½ cables from the north-east point. From the south-west point, two rocks that just cover at high water, stretch out a short distance, and may be approached to a quarter of a cable. A bank of shoal water also extends to the north-west of Nezumi sima for 8⅓ cables, having on its outer edge 4 to 4½ fathoms, and within several patches of rocks awash, and of less than six feet.

Shiroi iwa, a white rock, 25 feet high, lies near the middle of this bank, and a patch of rocks, having 3½ fathoms at low water, lies N.W. ½ W., 7¼ cables from Shiroi iwa.

KURU SIMA, small and wooded, 150 feet high, with a steep fall at the north end, and a village on the east and west sides, lies in the entrance of Hashi hama. Shoal water extends half a cable from the north point, but the mid-channel is clear.

HASHI HAMA is a deep bay, with shallow water 7 cables from its head; a large village is situated on the south-west shore, and a granite lantern on the north-east. Off the north-east point there is a shoal of 6 feet, distant three-quarters of a cable. There is no anchorage here, from the continual whirl of tide, but vessels being swerved in by the tide may round Kurusima at half a cable.

ANCHORAGE.—There is a good anchorage off Hangata in 7 fathoms, with the left extreme of the village bearing W. by S. ¾ S. distant 2½ cables.

There is no really safe anchorage off Ōbama or Imabari, the tides being especially strong there.

From Hashi hama the coast trends to the north west to Ozumi no hana, and about midway between is the village of Hangata near the north end of which is a temple gate, the tide pole datum.

Maru iso lies S.E. ½ S. half a mile from Ozumi no hana and 1½ cables from the shore, and uncovers 5 feet at low water.

Hirose is a ledge of rocks covered at high water, lying off Hangata. Both this and Maru iso are occasionally marked by tree beacons.

OZUMI NO HANA, the north point of Iyo, is a low point falling from a hill with a large clump of trees 419 feet high, and forms the western boundary of the Kurusima strait. Off it, and separated by a channel passable by boats, is a grassy mound 35 feet high, outside which, and joined to it at low water, is a flat rock, 3 feet above high water; and inside two white rocks, 13 feet above high water. The outer flat rock may be approached to 2 cables. The tide ripples are very strong here.

DIRECTIONS — APPROACHING FROM THE EASTWARD. — The channel formerly used between Nezumi sima and Uma sima is the best, that now frequently taken, known as the Kuru sima or Junk channel is not recommended. After rounding Uma sima care should be taken to clear the Perseus rock by keeping in mid-channel, with the eastern point of the entrance to Hashi hama harbour open of Nezumi sima, until a remarkable single tree in the first gap right of the highest sharp hill of Ō sima, is in line with the north extreme of Mushi sima S.E. by E. ½ E. The northerly stream sets on to the south-east point of Nezumi sima, and also towards the Perseus rock.

Approaching from the westward, after passing Kadjitori saki, a course should be steered to pass a quarter of a mile north of the flat rock off Ozumi no hana, when the conspicuous tree in the first gap right of Kiro yama will be seen in line with the north extreme of Mushi sima, S.E. by E. ½ E. This mark should be kept on until the west extreme, of the north-east point of Hashi hama is open east of Nezumi sima S.W. ¼ W.; this clears the Perseus rock (Ko no se). A course may then be steered to pass west of Uma sima, borrowing rather nearer to that island than the mainland, to avoid the Amaze.

Uma sima may be rounded at 2 cables, or continuing the leading mark a little farther on a course may be steered to pass between Uma and Nagato sima, keeping the latter island close on board.

The other channels should not be attempted.

TIDES. — In the Kurusima no seto, from Ozumi no hana the flood runs towards Nezumi sima and Tsu sima, sweeping over the Perseus rock (Ko no se) towards the north point of Uma sima, then taking the direction of the channels, diverging into the Hi-uchi nada. The ebb converges from the last-named place to the channels, running with great velocity from Imabari to the north, so that a vessel leaving that place should guard against being swept on to the More no iso. From the south point of Uma sima it runs for the south-west point of Nezumi sima, and diverges through the channels. The ebb sweeps directly through the channel between Uma and Nagato sima, causing on the north side heavy whirls that must be guarded against, their tendency being to turn the vessel's head towards Ko no se. The velocity at springs is from 4 to 6 knots.

It is high water, full and change, at Hangata at 10h. 36m.; springs range 11½, neaps 5 feet, after superior transit of moon, and at 9h. 52m. springs range 9, neaps 3¼ feet, after inferior transit.

KADJITORI SAKI lies S.W. by W. ¾ W. nearly 3 miles from Ozumi no hana; it is a sharp promontory, steep-to, the northern boundary of a deep bay, with several villages round its shore. In the centre is a bluff point, Nigi no yama, lying E. by N. ½ N., 2 miles from Ka sima.

Idsuye sima are conical rocky islets in this bay S.W. by S., 3 cables from Nigi no yama, and from the same point a rock that never covers lies S.W. by W., 7 cables, and W. by N. ⅓ N., 4¼ cables from Idsuye sima.

There is excellent anchorage in this bay in from 6 to 8 fathoms on a flat of sand and mud not nearer than 2 cables from the shore. The point of Nigi no yama must not be brought northward of East.

A rock that dries at low water, lies in the bay between Kadjitori saki and Ozumi no hana, one cable from the shore.

Ka sima is a round island with reefs extending 1½ cables from the east side.

Adji rock lies W. ¾ S. 1½ miles from Ka sima and 8 cables from the mainland of Sikok, between the villages of Segarta and Kikuma.

Hoso sima is a pinnacle islet close to the shore. From it N. ½ E. nearly a mile distant, lies a shoal of 15 feet.

Kikuma is a large village whence great quantities of fir branches are exported for use in the salt manufactories. A considerable river, spanned by a bridge, runs through it and enters the sea just west of a small hill with cliffy face to seaward, on the summit of which is a temple dedicated to Hachiman. The deposit from this river has formed a sand-bank, the outer edge being 2 cables from the shore.

The COAST.—From this village the coast of Sikok to the westward as far as Mi saki at the entrance to the Boungo channel has not been examined, but from the soundings obtained some distance from the shore it would appear to be shallow of approach.

THE NORTHERN ROUTE through the Mekari seto and Aogi seto is but little greater distance than through Kurusima strait, if when off Mutsu sima a course be at once steered for its entrance through the Mekari seto; and it has the advantage of the Kurusima strait from the fact that the tides are of much less velocity here than in the latter.

DIRECTIONS.—Passing westward of Hyaku kuan at about 7 cables, a course N.W. by W. ¼ W., with the bluff fall of Hachi gaune yama (which will be seen ahead 1,405 feet high), in line with the right extreme of Hoso sima, will lead into the Mekari seto clear of Jarrad bank which lies to the northward off the south-east point of Mukai sima. On passing Hoso sima at about 2 cables distance borrow on the northern shore which is steep-to until abreast Ko saki sima, when keep in mid-channel between Saki sima and the coast of Nipon until within half a mile of Ko-ne sima, when the Aogi seto will open, then haul up S.W. by W. ¼ W. and bring the distant high peak Higashi on Osaki sima in line with the extreme point of Ō-mi sima; this mark will lead in mid-channel between Admiral and

Captain banks. On nearing the dark wooded island Kuno sima a rocky islet will be seen off Ō-mi sima which may be passed at 1½ cables. Keep in mid-channel between Matsu sima and Ō-mi sima, rounding Kodono sima at half a mile, when steer to pass in mid-channel between Yoko sima, Niwatori jima, and the shore of Osaki sima until abreast Noka no hana the south-east point of Osaki, when haul up and pass in mid-channel between Oge and Ko Oge sima into the Misima nada. (For directions from the westward, see page 247).

HYAKU KUAN, an island with a grass-covered conical hill, 237 feet high, has steep cliffs around, except on the north-west side, from which a bank of shingle extends 2 cables, steep-to on the outer edge. From the south-east point half a cable there is a rock awash.

Between this island and Yuge sima there is a bank of mud, shoaling gradually, the least water 5 fathoms, lying W. by N. ½ N., 2 miles from Hyaku kuan. This bank affords excellent anchorage, except off the channel between Yuge and In no sima, where the water is deep and tides strong.

YUGE SIMA consists of two parts, the north-eastern having high wooded ranges faced by cliffs and with steep falls, with three peaks; the eastern being 1,077, the centre 1,030, and the western 954 feet above the sea.

The south-west part is granitic and bare, with a conical summit 463 feet high. Between these parts a bay runs in, where good anchorage may be had in 6 to 9 fathoms, sand, and separating them is a cultivated plain with the village of Ige mura. The south point has rocks and shoal water extending a little more than a cable, and the north point has foul ground for 2 cables.

IN NO SIMA is a high wooded island, forming the south-west side of the channel and having several remarkable hills, the summit 1,268 feet high, being a table land, steep on the south-east side, and falling on the other sides to ridges that run in a north-westerly direction, on each side of a richly cultivated valley.

On each side of the north end of this valley is a bare granitic hill, the eastern, Take yama, 764 feet high, having a fine temple, dedicated to Kanon, at its summit. A large village lies between the bases of these hills, and surrounding a round wooded hill, 452 feet above the sea, that shows out well against the bare ranges in the background.

The south part of this island has a conical hill covered with scrub, from which a spur stretches to the eastward, forming the south side of Mitsu-no-tsu, that affords good anchorage for a small vessel.

The channel between Hoso sima and this island has a bank of shoal water stretching across its eastern entrance to Shi-ziu-jima, (conical islets off the north side of In-no sima). From them the coast runs to the southeast to a point where a fort has been built. From the fort the coast trends into a deep bay, in the centre of which are two conical wooded islets joined together at low water, and at the head of the bay is a wall, the outer margin of reclaimed land. South of this bay the coast is bold and steep, ending in an islet with a tree higher than the rest at its summit. This islet forms the north point of Mitsu-no-tsu. A small bay, Koyo, south of this, terminates at the entrance of Nagasaki no seto.

YOKO SIMA, on the north-east side of the channel, is 856 feet high. There is no beacon off this island, but an islet, Ategi sima, that makes in two lumps from the southward, and is steep-to on the west side. N.W. $\frac{3}{4}$ W. 2 miles from the west point lies a rocky patch, having $2\frac{1}{4}$ fathoms least water. The outer margin of 5 fathoms bears W.N.W. from this point.

MUKAI SIMA has bare granitic hills, the highest a cone of 933 feet, being surmounted by a remarkable single tree. Off its south point is the islet of Sasajima, and N.W. $\frac{1}{4}$ W. 7 cables from this islet is a rock close to the shore, on which is a broken down beacon that just shows at high water.

Jarrad bank, an extensive patch with rocky knolls of $2\frac{1}{2}$ and 3 fathoms, lies to the south and west of Yoko-sima saki, the south-west point of Mukai sima, from which it is separated by a deep channel nearly 3 cables wide. Its outer edge lies S.S.E. 8 cables from the above-mentioned point.

IWASHI SIMA has high granitic ranges, surmounted by dark boulders, the two northern hills showing conspicuously. It is steep-to on its west side. Both Mukai and Iwashi lie on the north side of the channel.

HOSO SIMA is a wooded island running to a sharp bare point, at its north-east extreme a bluff, surmounted by two conspicuous trees, and steep-to. South of this, separated by a channel of $1\frac{1}{2}$ cables, lies Matsu sima, densely wooded with a sandbank that dries, one cable from its west side.

SUKUNE SIMA, a round wooded islet, steep-to all round, lies East half a mile from the east point of Kosaki sima. A sand-bank that dries one foot at low water, nearly 2 cables wide by $5\frac{1}{2}$ cables long, lies east of this island.

Haka no kojima, a rocky islet, peaked with trees, lies to the southward of Sukune sima, and has reefs all round extending one cable.

A rock with a stone beacon on it, 5 feet above high water, and steep-to, lies E. by N. $\frac{1}{4}$ N., a little more than a mile from Sukune sima, and W. by N. $\frac{3}{4}$ N., nearly 4 cables from the north-east point of Hoso sima.

SAKI SIMA shows in contrast to the former island, by having bare granitic ranges, running in sharp spurs to the shore, making in three summits, the two highest of nearly the same elevation, 811 feet, the third and northernmost, an isolated conical hill. A rock with a stone beacon on it, 5 feet above high water, lies three quarters of a cable from the west point, steep-to on its outer sides.

Nearly the whole of the channels between this island, Ko-ne sima, and In-no sima are blocked up by patches of shoal water.

KO SAKI SIMA is north of Saki sima, and separated by a channel of 1½ cables, in the centre of which is a reef. It has a double summit of disintegrated granite, and the north shore must not be approached within half a cable.

KO-NE SIMA, at the entrance of Kuruma no seto, with a high wooded range about 800 feet high, running along its entire length, falls gradually towards the north but steeply to the south, with cultivation extending a considerable distance up the slopes. A remarkable deep ravine runs in from the small bay on the north side, dividing the range into two spurs. The north side of the island is steep-to.

Captain bank, off the west side of this island, having 13 feet shoalest water, lies a quarter of a mile from the shore, the outer extreme of 5 fathoms lying half a mile beyond it.

MAIN-LAND OF NIPON.—From the entrance to Onomichi no seto on the west side of Iwashi sima the shores of Nipon trend W. by S. ¾ S., to a point immediately under Hachi-gaune yama, and then takes a north-westerly direction to the village of Matsu hana, above which is a steep bluff. From this bluff a mud flat that dries at low water, and is nearly steep-to, stretches S.W. by W. ¼ W. to the opposite shore of the large bay of Miwara, the western extreme of which is the steep bluff Kaino.

MIWARA.—On the east shore of this bay, the residence of the Karo, a white castellated building, shows most conspicuously, at the foot of wooded hills, partially cultivated up their slopes. The town of Miwara lies inshore of the castle. There is excellent anchorage in from 10 to 5 fathoms as convenient, but a long vessel (to avoid the extensive mud flat at the head of the bay) should not shut in the north point of Ko-ne sima, with the point west of the bay S.S.W. ¾ W. or the single tree on the summit of Mukai sima, with the point beyond Matsu hama E. by S. ¼ S.

From Kaino bluff the coast trends S.S.W. ¼ W. for 2 miles, when it takes an abrupt turn, and as far as the east point of Tadanomi bay has a general direction, S.W. by W. ½ W. for 3¾ miles.

In the bay of Tadanomi is a rock marked by a stone beacon about 5 feet above high water lying W. by N. 3 cables from the east point. Anchorage may be had off this village in deep water and quite close to the shore, but should only be used in a case of emergency, as the bank is very steep.

From Tadanomi the coast trends W.½N. to the island of Ta-no bashi which is joined to the main-land by a sandbank which dries. From this island the coast trends W.¾S. to the small village of Taka saki situated under the eastern slopes of a conical hill fringed by trees, from which the coast runs along the base to the town of Takewara forming the northern shore of Aogi seto.

ADMIRAL BANK lies on the northern side of the Aogi seto abreast the village Noji ura on the main-land of Nipon above described, its outer edge being about 6 cables from the shore. Its south-east extreme lies S.W. 7 cables from the east end of Uwa sima, a small islet eastward of Noji ura. The bank from this point takes a W. by S. ¾ S. direction for the summit of Kuno sima to which it approaches to within 2½ cables. The largest patch of from 2 to 3 fathoms lies abreast the village above mentioned, and two other patches lie 1½ miles nearer Kuno sima, the whole bank having depths varying from 2 to 6 fathoms upon it.

KUNO SIMA is wooded and wedge-shaped, when seen from east or west, the highest part, about 500 feet, being near the north extreme, which is terminated by a conical islet about 20 feet above high water.

KO KUNO SIMA is a dark wooded islet, with a dome-shaped summit, terminating in a precipitous bluff to the northward, steep-to.

MATSU SIMA makes as a double-topped islet, and is steep-to all round.

The channel between Ō-mi sima, and the islands of Matsu sima, Kuno, and Ko-kuno sima is deep outside one cable from the shore. The south shore of this channel has two conical hills, the west grassy and peaked, the east surmounted by a clump of trees.

ABA SIMA, to the north-west of Matsu sima, makes in two peaks when seen from east or west, the highest a dark wooded hill at the south end about 400 feet, but when seen from the south makes as a wedge, the highest part being to the eastward.

Off the west side of this island are two shoals, the western having 10 feet, lies S.W. ½ W., 5¼ cables from the north-west point of Aba sima, and the eastern with 13 feet, lies S.S.W. ½ W., 3 cables from the same point. Off the east side are two sandbanks; the eastern occupying a space of 2½ by 2 cables, dries at low water, and its outer edge is E. ¼ N. 8 cables from the north-west point of Aba sima. The south side of this island is steep-to.

OSAKI SIMA, forming the western shore of Aogi-seto, is surmounted by a remarkable clump of trees, named Ka-no-mine, 1,524 feet above high water, falling away in grassy slopes towards Noka no hana, the south-east point, terminating in a nearly isolated granitic hill, 590 feet high, that falls with steep cliffs to the sea.

Wooded spurs run both north and south from the summit, the north having on its centre a conical wooded mound (Higashi yama) 2¼ miles from Ka-no-mine, that forms the west end of the leading mark between the Admiral bank and that off Ko-ne sima.

Mebaru saki.—The north-east point has rocks that dry at low water stretching a short distance off the point; and from the north shore of the island a mud bank, having one foot at low water and very steep-to, extends nearly 2 cables.

Sanumi sima lies off the north-west point of Osaki sima, separated by a channel a cable wide, blocked by the mud bank. The island is wooded, and is steep-to on all the other sides. A mud bank a cable square in extent, having 3 feet on it, lies N.N.E. ½ E. 2 cables from the north-east point of this island, and from the same point, N.N.E., nearly 6½ cables, lies Kara sima, a small round islet 30 feet high, steep-to on all sides.

Noka no hana, the south-east point, is bluff and steep-to. At 2 cables N. ½ W. lie rocks that uncover 3 feet at low water. Kinoi-ura lies N. ¾ W. 1⅛ miles from Noka no hana, and dries at low water to the line of the points. It contains a small village, and junks are continually being repaired between the piers.

From this to Mebaru saki the coast is of shingly beaches, with cliffy points, all the valleys being cultivated some distance up the slopes.

The north coast of Osaki sima is deeply indented, principally by three large bays, Haraye no ura, Ōnishi no ura, and Nanami no ura, all shallow a considerable distance from their heads.

IKI or UMA SIMA.—A dark wooded island with a double summit, each surmounted by a conspicuous clump of trees, the south-eastern about 700 feet above high water. It has a deep bay on the north-east side, shallow at the head, and the west side has several deep inlets.

KODONO SIMA, a small granitic island, has off its south-west point at N.W. ¼ W. three quarters of a cable, an islet rock, 4 feet above high water, and at 2 cables north of the island is a rock awash at low water. E. by N. ¼ N., nearly 3 cables from the north-east point of Kodono sima, lies a rock with a stone beacon on it about 5 feet above high water. The shoal continues for 3 cables E. by N. from the beacon.

YOKO SIMA between Ō-mi sima and Osaki sima consists of two islands joined by a sand-bank at low water, the larger having off its north extreme a wooded peninsula, which from a short distance resembles a third island. Off the north end of these islands, anchorage with good holding ground may be had in 10 to 11 fathoms, sand, with the north extreme of Yoko sima N.W. by W. ½ W., and the south extreme S. by W. ½ W., 2½ cables off shore. A rocky patch of 5 fathoms lies W. by S. ¼ S., 3 cables from the north point of this island.

Ō-MI SIMA, 7½ miles long north-east and south-west, with an average breadth of 2½ miles, forms part of the east shore of Aogi seto, the northern of Kare seto, and the western of Kuruma no seto. It has high ranges, the west and north wooded, the south bare and granitic. Along its north and east shores several conical hills make as if detached from the main body of the island. It is apparently divided into three portions by two valleys, the southern running from the south-east part of Ute no ura to the south shore, and the eastern from the village of Osaki to the east shore.

Takashi yama, the summit of Ō-mi sima, a dark wooded hill, 1,465 feet high, lies in the south-west portion of the island, having a ridge running to the north-west, and several deep ravines on its west face.

Ute no ura is a deep bay on the west shore of Ō-mi sima, 1¾ miles across, with indentations at its south and north ends, and in the middle a dry water course of sand. A bank of mud with a grassy surface, having 5 to 12 feet on the outer edge, lies across this bay, 9½ cables from the shore. The point north of this bay has a large sand slip from the north-west face of a granitic hill.

NIWATORI JIMA is a narrow islet about 200 feet high, northward of Kashira, with a small patch of shoal water extending half a cable from the east end.

OGE SIMA is a well cultivated island, having a wooded summit 700 feet above high-water. At its south end is a peninsula 323 feet high, wooded at the summit, with dark basaltic cliffs on the west side, forming a little bay with a village at its head. The island has several off-lying boulders on its south side, and off its south-east point, but may be safely approached to one cable.

The channels between Ō-mi sima and Oge sima have shallow water in them, and should not be taken except in emergency, when the coast of Oge sima must be kept quite close on board.

KASHIRA, 250 feet, lying between Oge sima and Ō-mi sima, has grassy slopes, scattered over with trees.

HI SIMA is an undulating island lying south of Kashira, with steep cliffs on the south-west point, and a small islet close-to off the south-east end. Michi kojima, a chain of islets and rocks extend S.E. by E. ¾ E. 3 cables. The outer of these should not be approached nearer than a quarter of a mile.

KO-OGE SIMA has at the south-west extreme a remarkable conical grass covered hill, 434 feet high, sloping steeply to its southern coast. This shore is fringed with quartz-faced boulders, which from a short distance resemble a wall, and form an excellent object for distinguishing the western entrance to Aogi seto. On its north side is a small bay, where considerable quantities of granite are quarried. The island is steep-to all round.

DIRECTIONS FOR AOGI SETO.—The entrance to Aogi seto from the westward may be readily distinguished by the conical hill and white quartz-faced boulders of Ko-oge sima and the dark wooded Oge sima, care being taken not to mistake the south-west point of Okamura, that has also some white rocks at the base. The mid-channel between these islands being taken, a course should be steered to pass midway between Noka no hana and Niwatori jima, after passing which the vessel must be steered midway between the shore of Osaki sima and Yoko sima until abreast the south point of the latter, when the Osaki shore should be closed, to avoid the foul ground west of Yoko sima.

After passing the small rock off Kodono sima give the north shore of the island a berth of nearly half a mile to avoid the rock awash, which lies 2 cables from the shore, after which a course should be steered to pass in mid-channel between Matsu sima and Kuno sima on the north, and Ō-mi sima on the south, and when east of this channel the round wooded summit of Osaki sima, not the clump, should be brought in line with the north extreme of Ō-mi sima, S.W. by W. ½ W. This will lead between the Admiral and Captain banks, to mid-channel between that island and the main land. The north shore should be kept about half a mile off until abreast Kosaki sima, when that island may be rounded, borrowing rather over to Matsu hama, the village south-east of Miwara, to avoid the sandbank between Sukune sima and the beacon east of it.

Keep in mid-channel between Iwashi sima and Hoso sima, and between Mukai sima and In-no sima, until Sasa jima, the small islet off Mukai sima, bears N. by E., when the fall of Hachi gaune, (the bluff east entrance of Miwara), should be brought in line with the north-east point of Hoso sima, N.W. by W ¼ W., this mark will lead out into the Bingo nada, clear of all dangers.

TIDES.—The tides in the Aogi seto appear to take the line of the channel, running with a velocity of 2½ knots round Noka no hana, 3 to 4 knots in the channel between Kuno sima and Ō-mi sima, and with an average velocity of 3 knots to the narrows between Mukai sima and In-no sima (Mekari no seto), where they increase their rate to 3⅓ knots. The flood runs to the eastward and the ebb to the westward.

It is high water, full and change, at Miwara, at 10h. 37m. Springs range 11 feet, neaps 5 feet. The stream changes to flood at low water, and to ebb three-quarters of an hour after high water.

OKAMURA SIMA presents a varied appearance, from the alternation of cultivation and wood, and has a projecting south point faced by quartz, and a deep bay on the south-east side with a large village at the head. (Care should be taken not to confound this point with Ko-oge sima.) The east and north coasts are of shingle or sand, with no conspicuous feature. The island makes in a double summit when seen from east or west, the highest being 724 feet above high water.

The channel between Mitarai and Okamura is too narrow for ships to take, being nearly blocked up by three islands, Mi ō-to jima, at its north-west end. A shoal of $3\frac{1}{2}$ fathoms steep-to, lies E. by N., $1\frac{1}{4}$ cables from the lighthouse. The anchorage off its south entrance is not good, because of the continual whirl of tide, but vessels wishing to stop for a short time will find good holding ground in from 9 to 13 fathoms sand, with Okamura south point East, and Mitarai lighthouse N.W.

MITARAI SIMA, a high wooded island to the westward of the entrance to the Aogi seto, has a flat-topped summit 1,443 feet above high water, sloping gradually to its west end, when it falls abruptly, has a slightly indented coast line, and an apparently bare double peak at its eastern end, sloping down to a considerable village, with a remarkable white wall at the eastern extreme. South of the village is a Japanese lighthouse, merely a lantern, and rarely lit.

Off the west end of the island is a small rocky islet, 18 feet high, (Tzuzumi sima,) surrounded with rocks, and marking the channel between Mitarai and Toyo sima. This passage has only been partially examined, but has apparently deep water.

The north shore has a deep bay, shallow at its head and deep immediately beyond, affording no anchorage. From this, separated by a channel of 3 cables width, lies the wooded and partially cultivated Mikado sima, 400 feet high, deeply indented, having a sandbank that dries S.E., $1\frac{1}{2}$ cables from its north point; and from its south-west point a reef, steep-to on its south end, stretches out $1\frac{1}{2}$ cables.

KURUMA NO SETO—SETO-DA JIMA, lying southward of Kone sima, and forming with Ō-mi sima part of the Kuruma no seto, has a range of hills, with a conspicuous gap near the middle, running along its entire length, the highest is Ninoge yama, a double summit near its west end, 1,547 feet above the sea, the middle peak being 1,350 feet and the eastern 1,328 feet high. All sides but the east are cultivated some distance from the shores, but the west is wooded from summit to water's edge, and is steep-to. Off the north side some rocks and a sandbank that dries, lie one cable from the shore, and with the strong tides prevent the navigation of the channel between this island and Ko-ne sima. S.E. by S. $\frac{1}{4}$ S. a little more than a mile from the south-west point of this island lies a rock with 4 fathoms on it steep-to all round. Along the north shore a great quantity of salt is manufactured by evaporation from the salt water in the numerous creeks surrounding the mud flats prepared for that purpose.

HIOTAN JIMA, at the entrance of the channel, is a small isolated island, a cable long by half a cable wide surmounted by trees, that make as a remarkable single tree. The spur running to the north has also two trees at its summit.

Ō-MI SIMA.—The east shore of Ō-mi sima has a succession of shingly beaches with villages scattered along their shores, and near the centre a sandy watercourse.

A beacon about five feet above high water is erected on a rock $1\frac{1}{2}$ cables off a steep point in the centre of the east coast, a rock awash lying N.W. 2 cables from it. The beacon must not be approached within a cable, and here the tide ripples with great force at springs. S. by W. $7\frac{1}{2}$ cables from the beacon lie two wooded islets joined to the shore ($1\frac{1}{4}$ cables distant) by a sandbank that dries at low water.

HANAGURI SETO.—The channel between Ō-mi sima and Hakata sima has an average breadth of $1\frac{1}{2}$ cables, and there is no danger in the mid-channel; but the rush of tide is so great, except at slack water, that no vessel should take it except in emergency.

From this channel the coast of Ō-mi sima runs with a general direction of W. by S., having only a slight curve for 5 miles, to the passage between it and Hishima, the background being granitic ranges, to the valley that separates it from the wooded slopes of Takashi yama.

HAKATA SIMA has near its west shore a high range, with three peaks, running north-west and south-east, falling steeply on the south-east side, while a spur of nearly equal height runs off to the northward. The southeast peak, Hokosan, 1,006 feet high, is surmounted by a sharp clump, and the north-west peak, Jiu-no-ka, by an isolated tree.

The north-west point is bluff, having a rock awash one cable off it. From this the coast trends nearly east to the north-east point with shallow bays between. The north-east point is narrow, sloping from a low hill apparently nearly isolated, and steep-to. The east point that forms the west side of the south entrance to Kuruma no seto lies S.E. $\frac{1}{2}$ E. 2 miles from the north-east point, and has off it, joined at low water, a conical islet, steep-to. Between the north-east and east points is a deep bay containing an islet, and having foul ground extending to the line of the points.

The south-west point of Seto-da jima, open of the north-east point of Hakata sima, N.W. $\frac{3}{4}$ W., clears all danger. Hasona, the steep bluff southeast point, forming the northern side of the entrance to Kare seto, has two patches of rocks off it; Mutsu se lying S.E. a quarter of a mile, and Futa ishi nearly one cable South. The latter patch never covers, and may be approached to a quarter of a mile.

The coast west of this forms a deep bay with a village on its shore, and trends to the narrow pass of Wusima no seto, a passage that should never be taken. The south-west coast is the sandy bay of Ka no ura, with shallow water fringing the shore for $3\frac{3}{4}$ cables. From this the coast is wooded and rugged to the entrance of Hanaguri seto.

IWAGI SIMA, on the northern side of Kuruma no seto, is a grass covered island, cultivated round the base, rising to a sharp peak 1,177 feet high, with a line of wood running down the south-east slope. A reef stretches half a cable from the south-west point, the outer rock being generally marked by a tree. Rocks that dry, and foul ground, extend 6 cables W.N.W. from the west point; and N.N.W. $\frac{1}{4}$ W. $7\frac{1}{2}$ cables from the south-west point lies a shoal of 3 feet; and N.W. by W. $1\frac{1}{8}$ miles lies a shoal of $3\frac{1}{2}$ fathoms steep-to on the southern edge with the South extreme of Seto-da jima bearing W. by N. $\frac{1}{4}$ N.

The channels, north, south, and east of this island should not be navigated unaided by the chart, and then only at slack water. Off the north-west point, almost joined to it at low water, lies the wooded islet Tobi sima, 90 feet in height.

HAKO SIMA has smooth grassy slopes and flat summit 536 feet high, surmounted by a clump of trees, and with cliffy faces on the south-west side. Off the west side shoal water extends 3 cables.

MU SIMA has two hummocks joined by a shingly spit, the highest being over the south-west point, cliff-faced and steep-to.

DIRECTIONS FOR KURUMA NO SETO.—The directions for Aogi seto should be followed until clearing the channel between Kuno and Ō-mi sima, when the latter should be rounded at three quarters of a mile, and a south-east course steered to pass a quarter of a mile east of Hiotan jima, and the same distance west of the south-west point of Seto-da jima, bearing in mind that the ebb sweeps strongly towards the beacon on the west side of the channel.

The Seto-da jima shore should be kept about a quarter of a mile off until the islet off the east point of Hakata sima opens of the north-east point S.E. $\frac{1}{4}$ E., when a course should be steered to pass the latter point at a quarter of a mile, and then for mid-channel between the islet off the east point and Mu sima, taking care to keep the south-west point of Seto-da jima open of the north-east point of Hakata sima N.W. $\frac{3}{4}$ W., to avoid the foul ground in the bay between the east and north-east points.

TIDES.—In the Kuruma no seto the flood runs to the south-east and the ebb to north-west, with a velocity of $2\frac{1}{2}$ to 3 knots, in the direction of the channel, except off the south-west point of Seto-da jima, where the ebb sweeps partly across the channel towards the stone beacon on the west side.

TSUBA SIMA has bare granitic ranges, and shews out from the southward against the dark wooded ranges of In-no sima. Off its north end a group of islets and rocks nearly joins it to that island.

IKINA, having hills covered with scrub alternating with bare granitic ranges, makes in a double summit when seen from the southward, and is cultivated in patches round its base.

WU SIMA, to the southward of Hikata sima, rises in gentle wooded slopes to the summit. Off the north point are the Shi-ziu kojima, rocks joined together at low water, having two pinnacles that shew at high water.

Off the eastern side of this island shoal water extends 1½ cables. From its south-west extreme, separated by a narrow channel, are two islets, the north-western and higher surmounted by a single tree.

In this channel are two rocks, the north-eastern with 13 feet on it, and the other awash at low water. These, the strong tides, and the width of the channel, forbid vessels attempting it.

Michi-ga saki is a flat island cultivated along its entire length. It lies off the south point of Hakata sima. Two pinnacle rocks, Niwatori jima, with rocks awash close to, lie off the same point.

YANAGI SETO, the channel between Osaki sima and the mainland of Nipon to the north-west of Aogi seto, contains a large archipelago principally distributed near the coast of Osaki sima, to the north of which there is a safe channel as far as the meridian of Ō-shiba, the western limit of the survey. Between the islands, and from them to Osaki sima, all is foul and shallow.

On entering this channel from the westward, Tsukugawa jima makes as the first island north of Osaki sima, a grass-covered mound steep-to on every side but the north, from which a reef extends 4 cables, steep-to on the outer edge.

TZUZUKI are three remarkably peaked rocks, having reefs that cover off them. They may, however, be safely approached on their north side to 1½ cables.

NAGA SIMA is a wooded island, with red cliffs and granite hills much indented, and having deep ravines.

USU SIMA has a double summit, each surmounted by a tuft of trees. Off the north-east extreme lies Ko-usu sima, a narrow wooded islet, with dark cliffs on the south-west side, and off the south-west point is a wooded island, joined to it at low water.

CHIKIRI SIMA is composed of three hillocks, jointed at their bases by a shingly beach steep-to on its north side.

AKI or GESHIU.—All the south shore of Nipon here spoken of is in the province of Aki or Geshiu.

Ō-SHIBA, a densely wooded island, with a single tree on the summit, forms the west side of the large bay, Akaisaki no ura, across whose mouth a bar of mud, with from one to two fathoms, prevents vessels from making use of the anchorage that the bay would otherwise afford. At the head of the bay stands the large village of Mitzura, and great quantities of salt are made round its shores.

The bay contains four islands. Hira jima, the south-western, cultivated all over its flat mound. Riu jima, the north-western, dark wooded, with red cliffs round its margin. The two eastern, Ō-moro jima and Hanaguri jima, are elongated cliffy islets, surrounded by boulders and shingle that dry at low water. The point at the eastern entrance of the bay, and from which it derives the name Akai saki, is very conspicuous from the red cliffs that fringe it. Off this, separated by a shallow channel of 3½ cables, lies Tō-sen, a wooded islet, from the north-east end of which a shingly spit that dries at low water, extends nearly 2 cables.

MISIMA NADA.—This portion of the Seto uchi is 30 miles long, east and west, about the same distance north and south, and is studded with numerous groups of islands, islets, and rocks, of which as yet little is known At its north extreme is the large town of Hiro sima, on the shore of Nipon. Its southern boundary is an extensive chain of islands stretching across the Seto uchi in an east and west direction, of which Yayo sima, Numa sima, Nuku sima, Mosuki, Nokona, and Kosii sima are the largest. The route recommended lies through the south-eastern part of the Misima Nada, within 2 to 3 miles from the mainland of Sikok.

ISLANDS IN THE MISIMA NADA.—The following, lying in the immediate vicinity of the track usually taken by vessels passing through this sea, only have been noticed :—*

AI SIMA is about one mile in extent and about 200 feet high.

ROUND ISLAND lies about 2 miles S.W. by S. from Ai sima, is about 180 feet high, and is conspicuously round, as its name implies.

NOKONA has a rough appearance from a number of projecting nobs, which are quite barren. A ledge of rocks with 19 feet on its extreme point extends under water from the first cliff West of the eastern point of the island. The ledge is about 2¼ cables long, and projects eastward of

---

* From the remarks of Archibald Miller, Navg. Lieutenant H.M.S. *Perseus,* 1866.

the east point of the island. Vessels should pass 3 cables from this part of Nokona.

KA SIMA is about 400 feet high, conical in form, and has a wooded summit.

MOSUKI is about 400 feet high, forming a conspicuous conical hill with one tree upon it, the north side of the hill being cultivated. Two plateaux of rocks, of which only one is visible at low water, obstruct the passage between Nokono and Mosuki.

The passage between Mosuki and Nuku sima, although practicable, is very narrow, on account of a shingly spit which extends under water from the east point of the latter island.

KOSII SIMA is thickly wooded and but little cultivated, its north point being somewhat sloping and rugged, with some small detached rocks off it, and a rock on which there is 19 feet at low water lies South $3\frac{2}{3}$ cables from the S.E. point of the island. A bank of sand and seaweed, with from 10 to 40 feet water on it, obstructs a part of the central interior bay. The two rocks to the south-east of Nuku sima, and also the three rocks which extend from Futakami towards Tsuri, are high.

Fugusi.—A rock always uncovered lies 5 cables S.W. from the south point of Nuku sima. This rock is steep-to, and is connected to the south point of the island by a flat on which there are from $6\frac{1}{2}$ to 11 fathoms water.

A rock with 10 feet water on it lies S.S.W. about $2\frac{1}{4}$ cables from the small islet named Kutako in the channel between Nuku sima and Numa sima.

An extensive and dangerous plateau of rocks, one of which has only $1\frac{1}{2}$ feet on it at low water, lies S.E. 5 cables from the small island of Mors.

NUMA SIMA.—There are dangers off the N.E. and N.W. points of the island, and they should not be approached nearer than 2 cables.

A rock which uncovers at low water lies about $1\frac{1}{2}$ cables from the western of the two islets which lie S.S.W. from Numa sima, with the two islets in line.

The outer of the chain of islets, $2\frac{1}{4}$ miles south-east of Futakami, on the border of the fairway channel, is small and conical.

TSURI is highest at its southern end, which is a round wooded summit about 150 feet high, partially cultivated. The hills slope down to the northern point of the island, which is low and flat with a clump of trees on it. It appears shoal off the west and south-west points.

CAPE SIMONAMBA is a bluff point of about 200 feet in height, from which the land rises to the eastward or inland in irregular slopes to three conspicuously sharp peaks of about 1,000 feet. The coast eastward to the village of Kikuma takes a north-easterly direction. To the westward the coast takes a southerly direction for 6 or 7 miles, and then taking a sudden turn to the westward approaches Kosii sima within a mile.

ANCHORAGE.—The bay south of Simonamba point affords good anchorage in 6 to 9 fathoms with the north point of Kosii bearing W. by S. ½ S., but one mile south of this position is a sandbank, on which there is only 9 feet water. A sandbank on which there are 14 feet of water lies in the same bay about midway between Ka sima and Kosii sima, with the westernmost of the two largest elevated rocks which are seen west of Ka sima, in line with cape Simonamba.

DIRECTIONS.—After rounding Ōzumi no hana, Itsuki sima, a comparatively low island with bare ridges of a reddish colour should be steered for W. by S. ¼ S., until Kajitori saki bears about S.W. by S., when alter course to S.W. ¼ S. for the south-east point of Nokona, and passing it at about half a mile keep in mid-channel between Mosuki and Kosii sima: cape Simonamba should not be approached nearer than one mile.

IYO NADA.—This portion of the Seto uchi lies westward of the chain of islands above described, between which and Hime sima its western boundary is about 55 miles. The whole of its shores are as yet unsurveyed, but that to the south appears clear, with no off-lying islands or indications of danger; its northern shore, however, is skirted by groups of islands and rocks. Great caution should always be observed when approaching any of the coast which has been inserted in the charts from the Japanese manuscript* only, as the sunken dangers are not often shown on that document. At the south-west of the sea is a deep bight on the north shore of the island of Kiusiu, which from this, westward, forms the southern shore of the Seto uchi. In this bight are several deep indentations, which are probably good anchorages; several large rivers also flow into this part of the Iyo nada. About 20 miles to the eastward is the northern entrance to the Boungo channel (*see* page 201).

ANCHORAGE can be obtained at Oëmura, about E. by S. of the south point of Kosii. There is a large town (Sinhama) in this bay with forts on the shore, and a Japanese man-of-war was seen lying at anchor with a large number of junks; the bay is open to the westward. In passing through between Kosii sima and the main, where not less than 9 fathoms were obtained, there appeared to be good anchorage in the southern bay on the east side of Kosii; junks were lying there. The shore of the mainland opposite Kosii is skirted with rocks and islets.

The islands immediately in the vicinity of the track of vessels passing through the Iyo nada, are,—

YURI, about one mile in length (east and west), has two summits, the eastern being 400 and the western 180 feet high; they are joined by a low sandy isthmus, and appears as two islands when seen from the north-east

---

* This coast is always delineated in hair line.

or south-west. The hills are covered with thicket, in which are numerous deer. Anchorage may be had on its southern side, and the island may be passed either to the north or south at one-third of a mile.

MINASI AND KO MINASI SIMA both lie to the northward of the route; the former is about 300 feet high, and the latter, distant about 8 miles from Yuri, is high, and may be passed on its south side at half a mile.

YA SIMA, a larger island, lies about 13 miles W. by S. from Ko Minasi, is high at its north and south points (from 500 to 600 feet) and low in the centre.

ANCHORAGE may be obtained on the west side of the island in 11 fathoms sand and gravel, midway between the two points, the bottom shoaling gradually up to the beach, which is low and fringed with trees. This bay is open from South to West and N.W.*

UWA SIMA is small, with a cluster of rocks off its south-west side.

IWAMI SIMA has a cone-shaped island eastward of it; it may be passed close to on its south-west side.

HIME SIMA, lies about W. ¼ N. 22 miles from Ya sima, is 3½ miles long (east and west), 1½ miles wide, and its sugar loaf shaped peak, 660 feet high, is a conspicuous object to navigate by, throughout the whole length of the Suwo nada.

There are three bays on the north side of Hime sima,—the north-west bay, the middle or reef bay, and north-east bay. The north-west bay was used as a rendezvous for the fleet in 1864. There is good anchorage in it with the wind from E.S.E. (round south) to W.S.W. in 5 to 14 fathoms, sand. With the peak bearing E.S.E., and the west point S. by E., there are 12 and 13 fathoms, soft sand. There is safe anchorage in 7 fathoms in the middle of the bay, on the line of the east and west points.

The middle or reef bay and the north-east bay are unsafe for large vessels; small vessels, however, wind-bound, will find good anchorage off the middle of either in 5 to 7 fathoms. The middle or reef bay is divided into two parts by a reef, a portion of which is always above water; there are 5 fathoms on each side of the reef, on the line of the points of the bay. There are mineral springs on the N.E. side of the island.

Miname ura, a small bay on the south-west side of Hime sima, affords shelter with winds from W.N.W. (round north) to N.E. in from 4¾ fathoms to 8 fathoms on the bank which surrounds the island. There is sufficient room for several vessels with the eastern bluff bearing East to E.N.E. Strangers anchoring here for the night should be careful not to mistake a line of trees on the isthmus at the head of the bay for junks at anchor.

---

* Navg. Lieut. Adlam, H.M.S. *Juno*, 1869.

TIDES.—The tides, both flood and ebb, set across the bay, but their rate does not exceed 1 to 1½ knots. It is high water, full and change, at about 9h., and springs rise 8 or 9 feet.

DIRECTIONS.—From Nokona a course may be shaped to pass on either side of Yuri, the south side being preferable, from which a course S.W. by W. ¾ W. will lead up to pass about one mile south of Ko Minasi sima, after which alter to W. by S. ¼ S. to pass about 1¼ miles southward of Ya sima. When Ya sima bears north haul up W. by N. ½ N. This course leads about 1¾ miles northward of Hime sima, but according to the tide, vessels are either set to the southward towards the Boungo channel, or to the north-westward, towards Iwami sima. Continuing this course from Hime sima will lead through the Suwo nada up to the entrance to Simonoseki strait.

The SUWO NADA, the western division of the Seto Uchi, is the most open but of no great depth, the soundings varying from 15 to 20 fathoms in the centre. It is bounded on the north by the provinces of Suwo and Nagaton in Nipon, and on the south by the province of Buzen in Kiusiu, and on the east by Hime sima, and is about 40 miles in length (east and west). At its western extreme is the strait of Simonoseki, the western approach to the inland sea.

KOKUMAGE and NISINAKA bays, on the coast of the mainland S.W. of Hime sima, were examined, and found to be convenient for vessels wind-bound through the Boungo channel, the anchorage in each being on the line of their outer points in 5 and 6 fathoms, mud.

MAGASAKA POINT, to the south-west of the above bays, may be known by its outer extremity being perpendicular and having a clump of trees on it, as well as by its having at 40 yards from its base a small rock with a clump of trees on it also, which at a distance has the appearance of a boat under sail. The soundings obtained in this vicinity showed muddy bottom.

Vessels coming from the Boungo channel may round any of these bluff points forming the bays on the north-east coast of Kiusiu at the distance of half a mile.

CAPE IMAGAWA, 10½ miles W.S.W. of Moto yama, terminates in a bluff point, and on a westerly bearing appears in a succession of hills, one rising above the other, stretching away to the northward. All the islands, as well as the points of land (from the Japanese manuscript), on this part of the coast appear to be correctly placed on the chart.

FAYE SIMA is a small oblong-shaped island, which on a S.W. bearing assumes the shape of a haycock.

Ma sima, a small island lying southward of cape Imagawa, when seen from the eastward makes as a low, short island, having a hummock on each end.

Murigawa is a small rocky islet having its summit covered with trees. In thick weather cape Imagawa, with Ma sima and Murigawa, are good leads towards Simonoseki strait.

The small island Mura sima, lying close to the land, about 2 miles north of cape Imagawa, is low, with a slightly rounded top.

ANCHORAGE.—There appears to be good anchorage from 1½ to 2 miles from this shore, between cape Imagawa and I saki, in from 6 to 7 fathoms; indeed in 20 fathoms and under anywhere in the Suwo nada.

MOTO YAMA, the promontory of land stretching to the southward from the north shore of the Suwo nada, about 7 miles eastward of Simonoseki strait, may be known by its long point terminating in a perpendicular bluff having several clumps of trees on it; the land behind, or to the northward of the point, rising in hummocks one above the other, each hummock being crowned with a clump of trees.

DIRECTIONS.—Vessels bound from the Boungo channel or from the eastward for Simonoseki strait, may steer to pass Moto yama at the distance of 3 or 4 miles. Thence a course should be shaped, N.W. ¾ W. for I saki, which is high and bold, as well as steep-to, and may be rounded at the distance of 2 or 3 cables. At night keep I saki *white* light in sight N.W ½ N.

I SAKI is the eastern promontory of the north point of Kiusiu, and south point of east entrance of the strait of Simonoseki; it may be passed at 2 cables.

LIGHT.—On the north-east extreme of I saki, elevated 122 feet above the sea, is exhibited a *fixed* light of the fourth order, showing *red* from E. by S. round by south and west to N.W. ¾ W., and white from the latter bearing to N. ⅓ E., and is visible in clear weather from a distance of 17 miles.

The junction of the red and white lights bearing N.W. ¾ W. clears the shoals off Moto yama.

The tower is of granite 31 feet high, and is in lat. 33° 58′ N., long. 131° 1′ E.

SIMONOSEKI STRAIT,* is 7 miles in length, and has a navigable channel varying from 3 to 7 cables in breadth. Both entrances are encumbered with sandbanks, particularly the western, between which and the off-lying islands extensive reefs project in every direction. The eastern entrance to the strait lies between I saki and Kusi saki, between which it is

---

* *See* Chart of Simonoseki strait, No. 532; scale, $m = 3$ in.

2¼ miles wide, but is divided into three channels by two extensive sand-banks named the Middle ground and Tano bank.

KUSI SAKI, the north point of entrance of the strait, has reefs extending 2 cables off it. There is a large military station here, named Choshiu, or Hagi Chiofu, the fortress of the powerful Daimio, the prince of Daisen or Nagato.

Kanziu and Manziu are two islands E. by N. of Chofu point. They are both covered with trees and should not be passed within 2 cables. Kanziu is low and flat, with some large rocks and a rock awash off its south end; but Manziu is 190 feet high.

Middle Ground.—Midway between Kusi saki and I saki, a shoal bank of sand extends 1½ miles in an east and west direction, being from one half to 3 cables in width, and has depths varying from one to 3 fathoms on it. The eastern extreme is 1¼ miles N.N.E. from I saki lighthouse.

A red buoy with staff and ball is moored in 3 fathoms with Kusi saki bearing N.N.W. ½ W., 4¼ cables from the western extreme of the Middle ground.*

This bank divides the strait into two channels, that to the northward (North Channel) carrying the deepest water.

Tano bank.—The western extreme of this bank, on which is 4 fathoms, lies 4 cables E. ¾ N. from Mozi saki, from which position it extends in an easterly direction for nearly 1¼ miles with depths varying from 2¾ to 4 fathoms on it.

This bank divides the portion of the strait lying southward of the Middle ground into two channels. Neither of them is to be preferred to the North channel (north of the Middle ground), but of the two the channel north of the Tano bank (Middle channel) is the best.

A large clump of trees on Take saki (the south point of Simonoseki town), in line with Mozi saki leads between Kanabuse and Tano bank.

ANCHORAGE in 5 fathoms may be found on the outer part of the Tano bank (which shoals suddenly from 7 to 4 fathoms) well clear of the tide race through the strait.

KANABUSE (Fisherman rock).—This dangerous rock lies 11 cables N.E. by E. ½ E. from Mozi saki. It is 120 yards long (N. by W. and S. by E.), has only 4 feet on its southern end, 12 feet on its northern end, and 5 fathoms between at low-water springs; the south end has the appearance of two large square blocks of stone 10 yards apart. There are 6 fathoms close to its south, east and west sides, and 10 fathoms (sandy bottom) about a boat's length northward of the 12 feet patch.

---

* The buoy in its present position (1872) is of very little use.

Buoy.—A buoy, colored black and white in horizontal stripes and carrying a staff and ball, is moored in 9 fathoms, half a cable south of the southern rock, with Mozi saki bearing S.W. and I saki E.S.E.*

THE NORTH CHANNEL, northward of the Middle ground is, with the exception of the Kanabuse, clear of danger.

The Middle channel, south of the Middle ground, and north of the Tano bank, carries $4\frac{1}{2}$ fathoms at low-water springs. Hino yama kept W. $\frac{1}{2}$ N. until the clump of trees on Take saki comes in line with Mozi saki leads through.

The South channel, southward of the Tano bank, is the narrowest, although the tides here are not so strong as in the North and Middle channels. It carries a depth of not less than $5\frac{1}{3}$ fathoms at low water.

MOZI SAKI.—The strait is narrowed to 3 cables between this point (which is the extreme of a promontory at the north end of Kiusiu), and the eastern end of the town of Simonoseki. The extreme of Mozi saki is a low hill, but there is immediately over it a hill 583 feet high, with some tall trees on its summit.

Hino yama, a peak with three summits, the highest of which is 933 feet above the sea, is conspicuous on the mainland of Nipon, opposite Mozi saki.

Between Mozi saki and the opposite shore of the strait the tide runs with great velocity, but with some interval of slack water between the change of stream.

WHITSHED BAY, on the south side of Mozi saki, affords good anchorage in from 5 to 7 fathoms, with Mozi saki and Observation point in line, or a little open, bearing North; and Mozi village bearing East. Here the heavy ships of the allied fleet anchored after the reduction of the batteries in September 1864; the ships, especially those anchored inshore, rode to an eddy tide during the westerly stream through the strait, and during the run of the eastern stream, the strength of it was entirely avoided.†

An extensive shoal bank, with from 3 to 4 fathoms water on it, fills up the whole of the southern part of Whitshed bay.

SIMONOSEKI is an important town from its position at the entrance of the Inland sea. It is formed of a single principal street running for nearly 2 miles, at the base of some low steep hills, along the shore of Nipon. Its most conspicuous building is the custom-house, recognised by its tall white gables. A small light is exhibited on the shore at the end of a stone balustrade at the eastern quarter of the town.

---

* A white beacon carrying a ball was erected on each of the heads of this shoal in 1867. They had disappeared in 1868, and are probably not replaced.

† George Williams, Master, R.N., H.M.S. *Euryalus*.

Supplies of provisions and coal were obtained by the squadron with difficulty, as it was not a treaty port. The coal, which is much used here in the forging of nails, was of the worst possible description, and gave 75 per cent. of ash and earthy matter. Water of excellent quality was brought off in buckets in large boats.

ANCHORAGE.—If intending to anchor off the town of Simonoseki, take a position well below the custom-house in from 6 to 10 fathoms, out of the tides, which are very rapid through the narrows, with strong eddies along the shore during the western stream, which will cause a vessel to foul and drag her anchors; there is also great risk of collision with the junks, which frequently drift quite unmanageably through the strait.

TIDES.—It is high water, full and change, at Simonoseki, at 8h. 30m.; springs rise 8 feet, neaps 3 feet. The western stream makes at $2\frac{1}{2}$ hours before high water, and the eastern stream $2\frac{1}{2}$ hours after high water, so that the western stream continues 5 hours and the eastern 7 hours.

Off Mozi saki the velocity at springs is from 7 to 8 knots, at neaps 3 to 4 knots; the current is at its full strength for 3 hours of each tide. There are heavy overfalls in the eastern part of the strait at springs.

HIKU SIMA, lying at the western entrance of Simonoseki strait, is 3 miles in extent north and south, and has a smooth green hill 380 feet high on its north point. Its western point, cape Sizikuts, is a ow rocky promontory with an island off it which, from its similar formation, appears connected. Its south-west point, Entrance head, is a wooded bluff 380 feet high, to the north of which is a small harbour called Fuku ura, where junks anchor in from 9 to 10 feet at low water. Its other shores are hilly, but of less elevation.

LIGHT.—A *fixed* white light is shown about two thirds up the hill on the north point of entrance to Fuku ura.

KOSEDO STRAIT is the narrow passage winding round the north end of Hiku sima; it is only half a cable wide at its west entrance, and shoals to 7 feet off the town of Simonoseki.

Ganru island, a small steep island lying north-east of Hiku sima, may be passed at one or 2 cables.

Yodsibi rock lies E.N.E. $4\frac{1}{2}$ cables from Kibune point, and is best avoided by hugging the Hiku sima shore. It uncovers 4 feet at low water springs, and is marked by a *red* conical stone beacon, 20 feet in height and 8 feet in diameter at the base, with a plain rounded top. The rock may be passed on either side, but the western channel is preferable, being twice the width of the other.

Warusi rock is a quarter of a mile S.W. of Kibune point (the south-east point of Hiku sima), and $1\frac{1}{2}$ cables off shore. It uncovers before half ebb and is very dangerous. A white conical beacon, 8 feet in diameter at the base, 20 feet in height, and surmounted by a pear-shaped top, has been erected on this rock. To pass outside it, keep Hino yama, the wooded bluff hill over Simonoseki, open of Kibune point.

Manaita rocks, lying nearly two cables south of Entrance head, uncover towards low water. A conical beacon, coloured black and white in rings, 8 feet in diameter at the base, and 20 feet in height, surmounted by a ball 3 feet in diameter, has been erected on the largest of these rocks.

KOKURA.—The town and fortress of Okasawa, Prince of Sakio, stands on the shore of Kiusiu, south of Hiku sima, at the mouth of a small stream named the Ogawa.

Kokura ledge is a flat of sand and rock, with shoal patches on it, fronting the low shore of Kiusiu south of Hiku sima. The flat extends from one to 2 miles off shore, gradually deepening to 3 fathoms at its outer edge, which is steep-to.

Hiku flat, lying W.N.W. one mile off Entrance head, is a bank of sand-stone rock, 8 cables long and 3 broad, with 13 feet water on it.

The west extreme of Hiku sima (cape Sizikuts), in line with the east extreme of Kanasaki sima, N.N.W. ¼ W. westerly, leads between Hiku flat and a small 3-fathoms bank, 4 cables north-east of it (Hamo bank).

DIRECTIONS—THROUGH SIMONOSEKI STRAIT FROM THE EASTWARD.—Approaching the strait with I saki light N.W. ¾ W., or at night keeping the *white* light in sight, as before mentioned, pass I saki at half a mile, and when the lighthouse bears S.S.W. ½ W., haul to the northward to clear the eastern end of the Middle ground, taking care not to bring I saki lighthouse southward of that bearing until Hino yama bears W. ⅓ S., southerly, when steer for it until I saki lighthouse bears S.E. by E. ¼ E., when a small islet will be seen just open north of Kusi saki, bearing N. by E. ½ E. Alter course to S. by W. ½ W. with the above mark on (which will lead between the western extreme of the Middle ground and Kanabuse rocks) until the clump of trees on the point south of Take saki is in line with Mozi saki W. by S. ¾ S.; keeping this mark on steer for them, rounding Mozi saki at 1½ cables (mid-channel), on passing which haul to the southward, keeping the northern shore on board until Hino yama bears N.N.E. ½ E., when alter course to S.S.W. ½ W., and pass to the westward of the *red* beacon on the Yodsibi rocks. Pass Kibune point at 1½ cables and take care not to shut Hino yama in with the above point until the Narusi rock is passed (at about 1½ cables), when alter course to S.W. by S., keeping the hill over Mozi saki open of Kibune point until Clump hill (1,778 feet high) on the southern shore bears S.E. by E. ¾ E., then alter course to N.W. by W. ¾ W., until the east extreme of Kanasaki sima is in line with cape Sizikuts (the north-west point of Hiku sima) bearing N.N.W. ¼ W.; haul to the northward with this mark on, which leads to the westward of the Manaita rock, and in from 6 to 10 fathoms between the Hiku flat and Hamo bank borrowing to the westward as the Hiku flat is passed, and round cape Sizikuts at about 3 cables; after which, haul up for the lighthouse on the north-east point of Rockuren island, and pass it at from 3 to 4 cables; or at night keep the light in sight, taking care not to bring it to bear eastward of N. by E. ½ E., to clear the shoal extending to the south-east from Wakura sima and Kanasaki sima.

CAUTION.—The mariner is reminded that the tidal streams set through this strait with great velocity (page 260), and that great caution is necessary for the safe navigation of the ship, to avoid the many dangerous rocks and banks with which it is encumbered. It is therefore recommended that vessels should anchor, if the tide be not favourable on arrival at either entrance, and that the strait should be taken at as nearly at the time of slack water as is possible.

ANCHORAGE may be had at the western entrance to the strait, to the eastward of the Hamo bank in from 8 to 10 fathoms, with Wakura sima in line with cape Sizikuts.

The **WESTERN ENTRANCE** to the Seto Uchi is at its outer part 35 miles across, being formed by the west coast of Nipon running south for 25 miles from Kado sima, and the north coast of Kiusiu taking an easterly direction for the same distance, from Kosime no Ōsima, (page 308). At the angle where these coasts meet within 3 miles, is the large island of Hiku sima above described, south of which is the fairway and entrance to the strait of Simonoseki.

IWAYA POINT, low and rocky, with projecting ledges, is at the termination of a sandy bay 5 miles wide. A wooded hill 1,100 feet high, conspicuous from the offing, with a round gap in its summit, rises 5 miles S.W. by W. ½ W. of Iwaya point.

The Kiusiu shore eastward from Iwaya point is generally low and skirted with sandstone ledges, but the back ranges are from 2,000 to 4,000 feet in height. The shore of Nipon is higher, but its hill ranges lower, or from 1,000 to 2,000 feet.

SIRO SIMA.—These two islands, one mile apart, lie W. by N. ½ N. 16 miles from the outer point of Kosime no Ōsima (Wilson island) and nearly 5 miles N.N.E. from Iwaya point. The north-eastern one, 400 feet high, with a wooded summit of rounded outline, has a round rock off its rugged north point and a shoal spit extending 4 cables off its south point. The south island is indented, its eastern sharp peak being 290 feet high; there is shoal water off its south point; but its north point is steep-to.

SIMONOSEKI STRAIT—ROKUREN ISLAND.

A rocky patch of some extent, with less than two fathoms on it, lies from one to 1½ miles S. by E. of the above sharp peak. There are usually heavy overfalls on this patch. Another rocky patch of 2 fathoms water extending half a mile east and west, lies S. by E. nearly 3¼ miles from the same peak, and W. by N. ¾ N. 2¾ miles from Iwaya point.

MASUI SIMA lies N.E. by N. 6 miles of North Siro sima, and 3 miles from the shore of Nipon, off cape Morotzu, the hills over which are 1,000 feet high. The channel between is free from known danger.

The northern part of this island is a triple-topped bluff, 900 feet high; on the west coast (about the middle) there is a very sharp peak; the southern part of the island is lower, and terminates in a bluff. The island is bold-to on all sides, except at its south point, off which reefs extend one cable. One mile E.S.E. of the south bluff is a small black rock, 6 feet high, which should not be approached too closely.

AI SIMA, bearing S. by E., 6 miles from Masui sima, is a low flat island covered with trees, and one mile in length. Reefs, dry or sunken, extend one mile off its north point, and a spit extends S.E. by S. 1¼ miles from the south point; there are also others extending 8 cables east of its south point, and which are marked by a small square rock.

Low reef (Shirasu).—To the south-west of Ai sima is a large detached reef with a sand patch on it; and in the channel, a mile wide between it and Ai sima, the depths are from 3 to 5 fathoms.

LIGHT.—A temporary light has been erected on the southern end of this reef in lat. 33° 59′ 30″ N., long. 130° 48′ 24″ E.

The lighthouse is a square wooden tower and exhibits at an elevation of 42 feet above the sea a *fixed red* light, visible in clear weather from a distance of 10 miles.

ROKUREN ISLAND, 3 miles S.E. by E. of Ai sima, has on its table land a large and conspicuous clump of trees, 390 feet above the sea, which is visible after rounding Kosime no Ōsima (Wilson island), when it will bear about E. ½ N. A spit extends 2 cables from the north point of the island, but the east side is bold.

LIGHT.—On the eastern extreme of Rokuren, elevated 89 feet above the sea, is exhibited a *fixed* white light of the fourth order, seen between the bearings of S.E. ¾ S. round by West and South to N. by E. ½ E., and is visible in clear weather from a distance of 12 miles.

The tower is of granite, 25 feet in height, and is in lat. 33° 59′ 15″ N., long. 130° 52′ 25″ E.

The light when first seen, bearing S.E. ¾ S., leads half a mile from the shoal ground north of Ai sima.

MA SIMA GROUP, consisting of Ma sima, Kanasaki sima, Wakura sima, and several smaller islets and rocks, lies to the south-west of Rokuren.

ANCHORAGE.—There is a small anchorage on the south-east side of Masui sima, with the south bluff bearing S.W. There is anchorage also along the Nipon shore, east of Ai sima and Rokuren, in 7 and 9 fathoms, but the coast should not be approached within half a mile, as it is fringed with reefs; northward of this the reefs extend a mile off shore. If, however, there be sufficient daylight to get round Rokuren, it is recommended to do so instead of anchoring outside for the night, and bring-to on the bank half a mile south of the Ma sima group, in 6 or 7 fathoms.

TIDES.—It is high water, full and change, at the western entrance to Simonoseki strait at 10 p.m., and the rise and fall is scarcely 4 feet. At Kokura, on the south side of entrance, it is high water about 9h. 20m.

DIRECTIONS.—If bound to Simonoseki from the westward, pass about one mile north of Kosime no Ōsima (Wilson island), and steer E by N. ½ N. for the north point of north Siro sima, which pass at half a mile; then steer East, taking care not to bring the north point of north Siro sima to the northward of West, till the lighthouse on the eastern extremity of Rokuren island opens out S.E. ¾ S., or at night until the light is sighted, so as to clear the reefs off the north point of Ai sima. A S.E. course will then lead up to Rokuren, which can be rounded at 3 cables, when steer S. by W. to pass cape Sizikuts, the west point of Hiku sima; or at night keep the light in sight, taking care not to bring it to bear eastward of N. by E. ½ E.

Southern channel.—Should the southern channel be used (which only shortens the distance 4 miles, and is not recommended until better known,) the following directions, if carefully attended to, will *probably* lead through in not less than 17 or 18 feet water.

Rounding Kosime no Ōsima at about one mile, steer E. ½ N., which will lead midway between the coast and south Siro sima and between the two reefs before mentioned S. by E. of the latter. When the Siro simas bear North alter course to East, and having made out Rokuren island the south point of which should then bear East, and be nearly in line with the north extreme of the Ma sima group, keep this point in line with the wooded hill Hino yama, over Simonoseki (933 feet), which is the southern termination of the ranges of Nipon, and when the east point of Ai sima is North, alter course to E.S.E., steering for the smooth green hill of Hiku sima (380 feet), or the rocky eminence (1,193 feet) on the opposite side of Simonoseki strait; the former should be just open, and the latter one cable open of the south islet of the Ma sima group. When the western island of the latter group bears North, haul up S.E. into the strait.

THROUGH SIMONOSEKI STRAIT FROM THE WESTWARD.—After rounding cape Sizikuts at about 3 cables, steer S.E. until the east extreme of Kanasaki sima is in line with the cape bearing N.N.W. ¼ W., when haul to the southward, and with this mark on pass between the Hiku flat and Hamo bank (steering S.S.E. ¼ E.); this mark also leads southward of the Manaita rocks. When Clump hill (the high peak on the Kiusiu shore) bears S.E. by E. ¾ E., steer for it on that bearing until the hill over Mozi saki opens of Kibune point, when haul up, taking care *still to open it* until Hino yama is also open, so as to clear the Narusi rock. Pass Kibune point at 1½ cables, and steer N.N.E. ½ E. for Hino yama, which will lead up to Simonoseki.

After passing Simonoseki, borrow over towards Mozi saki, after rounding which in mid-channel, steer E. by N. ¾ N. with the leading mark on to clear the Tano bank and Kanabuse (page 258).

When I saki lighthouse bears S.E. by E. ¼ E. a small islet will be seen just open of Kusi saki, bearing N. by E. ½ E.; haul to the northward, keeping this mark on (to avoid the western end of the Middle ground) until Manziu island bears E. by N. ¾ N., when alter course to E. ½ N. (keeping Hino yama bearing W. ½ S.) until I saki lighthouse bears S.S.W. ¼ W., then haul to the southward, and when the light bears N.W. ¾ W. (at night the junction of the red and white lights) alter course to S.E. ¾ E., taking care at night to keep the white light in sight to clear the shoal ground off Moto yama.

CHAPTER VII.

JAPAN ISLANDS.—THE GOTO ISLANDS, AND THE WEST COASTS OF KIUSIU AND NIPON.

VARIATION in 1872: 4° to 5° West.

The GOTO ISLANDS.*—This mountainous chain of many islands, lying between the parallels of 32° 37' and 33° 20' N., is 50 miles in extent in a N.E. and S.W. direction, and from 5 to 20 miles in breadth. The chain may be passed through into the Korea strait by six channels, all of which, judging from those parts which have been surveyed and from the nature of the coast, probably carry deep water. The greater portion, however, has not yet been surveyed, so that great caution should be observed when navigating in the vicinity of these islands.†

KOSAKA CHANNEL, the northern of these channels through the group, was entered by H.M. ships *Dove* and *Leven* at dusk, from the eastward, south of the small island Mutz sima, 12 fathoms being the least water obtained in the passage, which is about three-quarters of a mile in breadth. No bottom with 10 fathoms of line was carried through, steering mid-channel, and passing half a mile south of a reef well above water in the centre of the strait. Uku sima or Huko is high, with low land stretching towards its east point, north of which some lumpy islands were seen. There appears to be an anchorage south of its west point and east of Tera sima.

The Hodge rock, the only known danger in this vicinity, is about a mile north of the outermost of several islets which extend 10 miles west of Kosaka.

KA SIMA.—An island about 300 feet high, lies off the east coast of the Goto islands, it is about half a mile long, east and west, and 4 cables broad, and bears from the peak of Hira sima S. 32° W. 5¾ miles. There is also a rocky islet 40 feet high, 1¾ miles S. 32° W. from Hira sima peak.

Several rocks which show above water extend N. 60° E. 3½ miles from Kaba sima, and there are some islets which extend from the south end of Saki-to sima.

KUGA CHANNEL.‡—The *Saracen*, after leaving Nagasaki, stood across to the Goto islands and entering the Naru channel east of Kaba

---

* *See* Chart:—West coasts of Kiusiu and Nipon, No. 358. Corrected to March 1872.

† The description and directions contained in this chapter have been compiled from the remarks of J. Richards, Master commanding H.M.S. *Saracen*, 1855, Commanders E. W. Brooker and C. J. Bullock, 1866–1869, and the remark books of H.M. Ships.

‡ *See* plan, Kuga channel, including Hardy harbour, on sheet of harbours on west coast of Kiusiu and adjacent islands, No. 359.

sima, worked to the westward and anchored in Hardy harbour, a snug anchorage on the south-west side of Naru sima, and in the Kuga channel. This is a small inlet, 6 cables in length, north and south, and 3 to 4 in breadth. There is an islet (Observatory) at its entrance, and one mile south the larger island Mia sima, of two parts connected by a shingle spit, gives protection from that quarter.

Within Observatory islet the water is deep, decreasing from 16 to 5 fathoms close up to the head of the harbour, but the more convenient depth of 6 to 7 fathoms may be obtained by anchoring W.N.W. of the islet and rather nearer to the opposite shore. The Kuga channel was then examined and found to carry deep water, 26 to 32 fathoms, with exceedingly bold shores, and not the least indication of unseen dangers.

FUKUYE, or Fukai, the chief town of the Goto islands and the fortress of the Daimio, Gotjima Saijemma no Djo, is situated on the shore of an open roadstead on the north-eastern side of Fukuye sima, the southern and largest island of the chain, and southward of the Fukuye channel, which separates it from Kuga sima. On either side this channel (which is a mile in breadth, with every probability of carrying deep water throughout) there is an anchorage, also several others surrounding the indented coast of Fukuye sima, but neither channel nor anchorages have yet been explored, with the exception of Tama no ura on the south-west.

OSE SAKI (cape Goto), the south-west point of Fukuye sima, about 500 feet high, is exceedingly bold, having 45 fathoms water at 2 cables distance, its steep rocky shores receding from the cape at a right angle. Behind, or north-eastward of the cape, rise three fine mountains (about N.N.W. of each other), separated by valleys, of which the northern and highest is 1,387 feet above the sea. At the extremity of the coast, which extends E.S.E. 3 miles from the cape, is Otakara point, the highest of the two small hills on which is 330 feet. A quarter of a mile S.E. is the islet Biro sima, 150 feet in height, with a rock 1½ cables off it to the southward.

E. by S. 3 miles from Otakara is Tsutara sima, the eastern of the two hills of which is 320 feet high. Reefs stretch off its east and west points (in which directions both island and reefs extend), especially off the east point from which they dry out in patches for half a mile. To the north of this island and on the south side of Fukuye, is a large rectangular bay 4½ miles in length and a mile deep. At its western part anchorage may be obtained in 9 fathoms, off the village of Daiho, which stands on a sandy bay north of the hill of Otakara point. Situated centrally in the large bay, at 7 cables N.N.W. of Tsutara, are the two islets Hitango sima, with deep water midway between.

One mile west of these islets is a rock 15 feet high near the extremity of a large reef, extending south-westward from the shore nearly a mile, and the greater part of which is awash. The bight at the eastern part of the bay, N.E. from Tsutara, has 7 to 10 fathoms off Hurushe, the eastern of two villages at the base of the southern high peak of Goto.

The coast east of Tsutara has not been explored. Kasayama saki, the southern cape of Fukuye, is low and wooded, and separated by a valley from the mountains.

TAMA no URA,* the name of a large inlet or arm of the sea on the western side of Fukuye sima, is finely situated as a port of refuge, and but for its great depth of water, would be a magnificent harbour. Its only entrance is $4\frac{1}{2}$ miles N.N.E. of Ose saki, and $2\frac{1}{2}$ miles S.E. of the island Saga sima, which is $1\frac{3}{4}$ miles in length, and shows two distinct hills on its north and south parts, which are separated by a valley through the island. In the bay on the east side of Saga there is good anchorage in 7 to 8 fathoms, quite sheltered from all westerly winds.

The entrance to Tama no ura is a mile wide, and must not be mistaken for the blind opening 2 cables wide, only 2 miles north of Ose saki, and which has a reef of rocks extending across its entrance. The steep rocky shore between the blind entrance and the true one is the western face of the island of Sima, the ridge of which rises to its central hill, Sima yama. Off the north point of Sima, which is also the south point of entrance to Tama no ura, there is an islet and some rocks, together extending $1\frac{1}{2}$ cables. The outer point on the north side of entrance to Tama no ura is Algerine bluff, $1\frac{1}{4}$ miles north of Warr point, its inner point; both these lie under the high land of the northern of the three high peaks of Fukuye.

The main inlet of the harbour, which has a varying breadth of from 3 to 7 cables, follows the contour of the coast line for 6 miles, separated from the sea by a belt of land, a mile in average breadth. It first runs S. by W. $3\frac{1}{2}$ miles, then curves to the south-east for $1\frac{1}{2}$ miles to its head, from which an arm branches one mile to the north-east. The depth within the entrance is 32 to 38 fathoms, decreasing gradually to 16 at its head, rendering anchorage inconvenient, except at the following position.

ANCHORAGE.—Directly south-east of the entrance, and on its eastern shore, the harbour branches into three narrow arms about a mile in length; the northern of these has not been examined, the other two are very narrow and the water in them deep. East, 3 cables from the north point of Hallowes island in the centre of this part of the harbour, there are

---

* *See* plan of Tama no ura on sheet of harbours on the west coast of Kiusiu, &c., No. 359.

soundings of 10 and 11 fathoms, which offer anchorage, open only between N.W. and N.N.W.

Off the inner part of the blind entrance there is fair anchorage in from 10 to 13 fathoms, within two cables of the south shore of Sima, but a small vessel may stand farther in west, and anchor in 7 to 10 fathoms in Village bay on the southern part of the blind channel, but where it is only from 2 to 3 cables across. The small arm running to the south-west under the hills of Ose saki has not been explored; there is a sunken rock at its entrance.

The best anchorage for large ships will be found at the south-east part of the harbour, in 16 fathoms, mid-channel, with the peak of Boshi yama, which is seen ahead when standing up the harbour, bearing from S.W. by W. to W.S.W. The arm at the head of the harbour is unexplored. There are many parts of the harbour where ships can make fast to the shore in perfectly tranquil water.

HIME SIMA.—From Tama no ura the coast runs north about 5 miles from Algerine bluff, falling to a low point, the north-western promontory of Fukuye, which is fronted by shelving rocks. Hime sima is separated from this point by a channel a mile wide, in which was seen a rock awash.

PALLAS ROCKS are three in number, two of which lie close together, and one N.E. 1½ cables from the largest, which is the south-western of the group. They lie S.W. 30 miles from Ose saki (cape Goto). The largest rock does not exceed a third of a cable in diameter, and is about 60 feet high; the other two are about one half that elevation. They are steep-to and soundings were obtained at the distance of a mile south from them, in 95 fathoms, sand and shells. The largest rock is in lat. 32° 14′ 17″ N., long. 128° 12′ 30″ E.

MEAC SIMA GROUP.—The relative positions of the Meac sima or Asses Ears group, and Pallas rocks, were determined by H.M.S. *Saracen* in 1855. The Meac sima, consisting of two islands, with intermediate smaller islands and rocks, cover an extent of nearly 4 miles in a N.E. and S.W. direction. The approach* to them from the northward is quite clear. Between the Asses Ears and Pallas rocks the ground is pretty even, and the general depth about 81 fathoms.

Taka sima, the north-east island, is nearly 1¼ miles long, and three-quarters of a mile wide. It is elevated 618 feet above the sea, and is somewhat level at the top, with cliffy precipitous sides, excepting to the

---

* H.M.S. *Furious* passed about 3 miles from these islands, but until they have been more closely examined they should be approached with caution, as the sea has been seen breaking heavily nearly a mile from the shore. S. Court, Master, R.N.

southward, where there appeared to be some shelter for fishing junks, as several were observed at anchor; in clear weather it may be seen upwards of 30 miles.

Kusa-kaki, the south-west island, is less than half the size of the north-east island, but 100 feet higher and very craggy; its remarkable peak probably suggested the name of the group to its first discoverers.

Me sima and Wo sima, the intermediate small islands and rocks, are high and cliffy, the latter partaking generally of the sugar-loaf form.

The only outlying rocks noticed extend south about a third of a mile from the south-west island, and may be almost considered part of the main group.

KOSIKI ISLANDS, consisting of two large and several small islands, extend in a N.E. and S.W. direction from lat. 31° 37' to 31° 53' N., and from long. 129° 41' to 130° 0' E. They are not high, but their appearance is bold in passing. The Nadieda rocks off their west side are considered to be about 4 miles from the shore, and 7 miles North of Haya saki, their westernmost point.

The eastern point of Kamino Kosiki, the northern island, is distant about 13 miles from the coast of Kiusiu. Extending 2½ miles eastward of it, are several islets, the outer two of which are called Futako sima, the easternmost being a pinnacle rock.*

PIONEER ROCKS.—H.M.S. *Pioneer*, in 1861, when passing inside the Kosiki islands, discovered two rocks lying 2½ to 3 miles eastward of the eastern of the two Futako islets, with Dasima saki bearing S.E. ½ E. They are close together, 10 to 12 feet above water, and dangerous from their smallness. No outlying dangers were seen; 46 fathoms, coarse sand and shell, were obtained midway between them and the Futako islets. The Japanese manuscript chart also represents a rock or islet (the Kamome sima) off the coast to the E.S.E., and a danger of some sort farther out; the passage eastward of the Pioneer rocks seems therefore one that should be avoided at night or in bad weather, until more be known of it.

TAKA SIMA.—S. by E. about 11½ miles from Na saki, the south point of the Kosiki group, are the Taka sima or Symplegades. H.M.S. *Highflyer* passed about 2 cables eastward of them in September 1859, and they are described as three rocky islets (which appear to have been originally one) forming a triangle, the sides of which are each not more than a cable in extent; to the southward are two small rocks about 7 feet in height, one a quarter of a mile and the other three-quarters of a mile from Taka

---

* *See* plan, Argus bay, Kosiki islands, on sheet No. 359.

sima; a rock awash was observed lying a quarter of a mile southward of the group.

The TSUKARASE (Retribution rocks) two in number, were discovered by H.M.S. *Retribution*, 6th August 1858. They lie in line north and south, about 2 cables apart in lat. 31° 20′ N. long. 129° 46¼′ E. The two southernmost rocks rise in a needle form about 60 feet above the sea; the northern rock is flat, and only 10 feet high. The vessel passed about a quarter of a mile to the northward of the group, which appeared to be steep-to; no discoloured water was seen, nor bottom obtained with the hand lead.*

UDSI SIMA or Roche Poncié group† consist of one island, with some rocks and islets surrounding it. The island is 2 miles in circumference the western part somewhat flat, but the eastern rising in a precipitous peak to the height of 1,060 feet above the sea. It is in lat. 31° 12′ N. long. 129° 29′ E. Two and a half and one mile respectively to the south west of the island are two small islets; and to the eastward of its peak about a mile, is another islet.‡

THE WEST COAST OF KIUSIU.

From Satano misaki (cape Chichakoff), the south point of Kiusiu, the coast trends to the northward forming a large gulf (Kagosima), the coasts of which have only been partially examined.

ANCHORAGE.—H.M.S. *Furious*, in 1858, experienced a strong breeze from the N.E., and being accompanied with a falling barometer, an anchorage was sought for under and to the westward of cape Chichakoff, where the chart by Siebold appears to point out a small harbour. In searching for this anchorage, soundings were first obtained in 30 fathoms, with the cape bearing S.S.E., and the vessel eventually came to in 13 fathoms, abreast a small village near the centre of the first bay northward of the cape, with the extreme of the cape bearing S.S.W., Horner peak N.W. ½ N., and Oto saki N.N.W.: here she was well sheltered for

---

* H.M.S. *Sampson*, in June 1859, passed some rocks (considered to be the Retribution rocks at the time), the centre one of which bore from the vessel West, distant a third of a mile; and from a good meridian altitude at noon they were found to be in lat. 31° 23′ N., long. 129° 37½′ E. The U.S.S. *Mississippi* also places rocks in this position. Remarks by Captain G. S. Hand, R.N., C.B., H.M.S. *Sampson*. The positions of both Taka sima and Tsukarase are doubtful.

† Thus named (and deservedly so, if an European name is admissible), after the Ingénieur-hydrographe of the French Expedition under Admiral Cecille in 1846.

‡ The Udsi sima are high, and of considerable extent. The easternmost island appeared larger, and its position to be further north than marked in the chart; no foul ground was visible near them. Stephen Court, Master of H.M.S. *Furious*, 1858.

thirty-six hours, with the wind steady between E.N.E. and E.S.E., although it was blowing heavily outside, as evinced by the heavy gusts off the land and low barometer; but on its veering to the southward of S.S.E. the bay became too exposed from that quarter, which rendered it advisable to weigh and proceed to sea.

There was no opportunity of verifying the existence of the above harbour; but there was every appearance of a small but well sheltered inlet in the north-east corner of the gulf in which the *Furious* anchored, (Yama gawa) which has since been examined, and is of great service to small vessels meeting with adverse winds, when bound eastward through Van Diemen strait.

KAGOSIMA GULF is an arm of the sea 35 miles in length and from 5 to 10 in breadth, which runs in a north direction into the southern part of Kiusiu. At 25 miles within its entrance the large island of Sakura nearly fills the head of the gulf, with channels on both sides leading into an inner gulf or spacious harbour, 6 miles by 9, and quite landlocked. The eastern of these channels, (neither of which nor the inner gulf have been explored,) is, according to the Japanese manuscript exceedingly narrow at the south-east point of Sakura. The western channel was surveyed* by the Masters of the fleet under the command of Vice-Admiral Kuper, in August 1862. The extreme depth of the water in the gulf renders anchorage very difficult, as far as at present known; the fleet having only found indifferent anchorage close to the beach on the western shore, near the Seven rocks 4 or 5 miles south of Kagosima.

Tsiring sima lies on the western shore of the gulf about one mile from the shore, to which it is connected by a reef on which the sea sometimes breaks, and is from 150 to 200 feet high. On the eastern shore, opposite, a shoal bank called the Racehorse shoal, extends about $2\frac{1}{4}$ miles from the shore. Between this shoal and Tsiring sima the gulf is narrowed to about 3 miles.

Facing the island of Sakura on the west, the Kiusiu shore projects, narrowing the western channel into the inner gulf to 7 cables at its northern part, its length being 4 miles. On this projecting shore stands the city of Kagosima, the fortress of the Daimio, Prince of Satsuma. Battery Point, to the south of the city, is low, and has a spit extending from and around it to 2 cables, and very steep at its edge: a shoal also fills the bay north of this point. Off the centre of Kagosima in front of the Daimio's castle is an inner harbour or large camber, gained by entrances between five forts of masonry, which have deep water close up to them; this castle cannot be seen from the gulf. There is a cannon shot foundry here, worked by Japanese. Two small rivers disembogue, one on the

---

* *See* plan of Kagosima harbour, No. 372; scale $m = 3$ inches.

north side of the city with long spits off its points of entrance, on one of which H.M.S. *Racehorse* grounded; the other, south of the city, falls into the shallow bay just north of Battery point. North of the city the hills reach the sea.

The western shore of Sakura island is very bold, but anchorage in from 15 to 25 fathoms may be found in Euryalus bay E. ½ N. of the castle of Kago sima, very close in. In an easterly gale there is danger of driving off the bank into very deep water and having to slip the cables.

Kami rock lies in the mid-entrance of Kagosima gulf, 3 miles off the northern shore. The bearings from it are,—Horner point, N.W. by W. ¾ W.; Horner peak, N.W. ¾ W.; Satano misaki, S. ⅞ E.; Oto saki, S. S. E. ⅛ E.; and the East head of Tsiring sima just opening the north and low wooded point of Yama gawa, N.N.E. ⅛ E.

This last serves as a leading mark if Tsiring sima be kept well open. The bottom is very uneven off Yama gawa, a ledge of from 3 to 6 fathoms steep at its edge, extends a mile from the shore. The lead shows black volcanic sand, white sand, and clay, with seldom two casts alike. The well known Seven Stones anchorage is the best on the western side of the bay below Kagosima. The remainder of the western shore of the bay to the southward has been partially examined; some banks and steep ledges were found which render the whole shore generally unsafe for anchorage.

Parker shoal, lying in the southern part of the western channel, has a large fort upon it which forms a good mark, it being about 25 feet above high water. The shoal is nearly circular and about 4 cables in extent, and on its south-west side is a flat of from 3 to 5 fathoms where temporary anchorage may be obtained. Anchorage also may be obtained generally in the southern part of the channel in from 21 to 24 fathoms, but at its northern part it deepens to 70 fathoms.

Oko and Karasuka islands lie close off the south-west and west part of Sakura; the latter has small spits off its north and south points; otherwise both are steep-to.

YAMA GAWA.*—This small harbour, formed on the west side of entrance of Kagosima gulf, is the crater of an extinct volcano. Its north part opens east to the sea by a funnel-shaped passage, a quarter of a mile in length but only one cable wide at its inner part, formed by an extensive shoal bank which extends one mile from the shore, south of the entrance. There are 3¾ to 4½ fathoms over the lip of the crater or bar with one patch of 2 fathoms in the centre. No vessel should attempt to enter in bad weather, although a small vessel may lie there at anchor or moored to the shore. Inside the harbour the water is deep.

---

* *See* plan of Yama gawa harbour, No. 359.

WATERS ROCK.—Two dangerous sunken rocks, on the outer of which is 2½ feet water, and on the inner 9 feet, lie close together, E. ½ N., one mile from the northern point of the entrance to Yama gawa harbour. Between the rocks and the shore is a depth of 6 fathoms.

The COAST.—The whole of the coast from Senda saki northward to Amakusa, together with the Otentosama sea, is as yet comparatively unknown.

AMAKUSA, a large island 23 miles in length, lies S.S.W. of the Simabara peninsula; between them is the western entrance to the gulf, only 2½ miles in width. Two harbours, Tomioka and Sagitsu no ura on the western coast of the island, have been examined.

Kotame bay on the south end of Amakusa is well protected by Kasu sima. A reef lies in the centre of the bay above water with a passage carrying from 13 to 16 fathoms on each side of it, and three other detached reefs which always show above water lie on the eastern shore closer in. The depth in the bay is from 13 to 16 fathoms shoaling to 8 or 9 fathoms at one cable from the shore. In rounding Kasu sima do not approach too near the south-east rock as reefs have been observed on which the sea broke heavily outside this rock.

Koto no ura.—This bay has a series of detached reefs in its centre, and there appears to be no anchorage for anything but native craft.*

SAGITSU NO URA.†—This harbour has been recently surveyed, and the channel leading to the narrow passage found rocky and uneven. There are three rocks north-westward of the entrance the two eastern of which are pinnacles, the western is low. Only 4 fathoms can be carried at low water along the northern shore. Cormorant inlet also is almost closed by the bank of shingle which extends across, and in the channel only one fathom at low water can be obtained. Kami ura is an inlet on the south shore.

TOMIOKA.—About 14 miles from Sagitsu no ura is a lagoon-like harbour on the eastern side of a small peninsula, which forms the north-west point of Amakusa. The harbour is formed by a low tongue of land curving round to the westward and enclosing it, giving complete shelter, the entrance being from the south-east by a channel carrying 5 fathoms water close along the south side of the low tree covered tongue which forms the eastern side of the harbour. The deep part of this channel is only 150 yards broad; a vessel should therefore be steered in at that distance from the shore on a W.N.W. course, with the village of Tomioka ahead, carrying in 4½ to 5 fathoms, and may anchor in the centre of the

---

* J. Elwyn, Lieutenant commanding H.M.S. *Slaney*.
† *See* plan, Sagitsu no ura, No. 135.

harbour in 6 fathoms. It is very shallow off the south shore at entrance, but a flat of 3 fathoms borders the channel, making it for that depth a quarter of a mile in breadth.*

SIMABARA GULF.—Of this large gulf, which extends 70 miles into the heart of Kiusiu, little is known. Simabara is a large and broad peninsula, so situated as to make this gulf an inland sea. On the eastern shore of the peninsula there stands a city of the same name. In the centre of the peninsula is an active volcano, a not high but extended mountain, over which a dark cloud of smoke usually rests. This is the focus of a wide volcanic region, and is associated with some of the severest earthquakes on record, one of which, in 1793, was felt throughout the whole of Kiusiu, and is said to have changed the configuration of the whole coast line of the adjoining province of Higo, and the general form of its territory.

A rock lies at the entrance of the gulf, and uncovers 5 feet at low water. It bears N. 20° W. from the east extreme of Tsuji sima, and N. 64° W. from east extreme of Oösima.†

Another rock 7 feet above low water, lies nearly in the centre of the head of the Simabara gulf. From it Take saki bears S. by W. ¼ W., Siwoda gawa N.W. by W. ½ W. A rocky reef also stretches from Take sima point in a south-east direction for 1½ miles. The head of the Simabara gulf is shallow and full of dangers, and vessels navigating it should avoid the very turbulent chow-chow (or disturbed water).‡

EAST COAST of NAGASAKI PENINSULA.—About 22 miles of the eastern side of the Nagasaki peninsula has been surveyed. It has generally a bold steep coast, but there are several places on it where a vessel blown to leeward of Nomo saki by west winds, will find anchorage and good shelter from them.

MAKI SIMA encloses on the north-east a harbour for small vessels, having from 10 to 12 feet water, accessible by two narrow passages; that on the east towards the sea, has only 9 feet between the reefs at entrance, which is scarcely a cable wide; the western one from Aba bay is about the same breadth, and carries 2 to 5 fathoms for three-quarters of a mile along the north shore of Maki sima. There is a road or bridle path to Nagasaki through the valley, only 3 miles distant from the head of Aba bay.

ABA BAY is rectangular in shape, 1¼ miles deep, and one mile in breadth. There is anchorage in the centre of the bay in 7 fathoms, open

---

* *See* plan, Tomioka harbour on sheet No. 359.
† Mr. Stevens, S.S. *Filepino*.
‡ Master of the Dutch Brig *Wilhelmina Elisa*.

only between South and S.E. The eastern side of the bay is formed by Maki sima, which has some islets on the reefs on its south side, one of which extends 4 cables. There is a boat camber at the village on the western side of the bay.

Mogi bay.—Mogi, another small bay, is 3 miles S.W. from Aba bay. Small craft can anchor in from 3 to 6 fathoms, sheltered except from South to East; and larger vessels in from 9 to 11 fathoms off the entrance.

Tameitsi and Sitziwura bays.—Tameitsi bay is 5½ miles S.W. from Mogi. Steer for the village at its head, and when Kaba sima shuts in behind the southern point of the bay anchor in 10 fathoms or less, about 2 cables off shore. Sitziwura, a small bay 2 miles farther north-east, has anchorage in from 9 to 10 fathoms, at 2 cables off shore. There is an islet or rock on the reef which extends 2 cables off the south point of the bay; it lies directly under and S.E. of the highest peak of Kawara yama.

Between Sitsiwura and Mogi bays, there is an islet and several large reefs which extend 2 or 3 cables from the shore.

MISAKI BAY,* north of Kaba sima and east of the low jutting point and sandy beach where stands the large village of Misaki, affords anchorage in from 7 to 11 fathoms. It is gained from the westward by rounding at 2 cables distance, the south and south-east points of Kaba sima, the latter a steep head, from which steer to pass outside a low reef (East rocks) one mile N. by E. of that head, which being passed steer N.W. ½ W. into Misaki bay and anchor either in 10 fathoms east of the flat rocks, on which are seen a large bamboo erection used by the fishermen, whose nets it will require care to avoid; or, passing north of the flat rocks anchor in 7 or 8 fathoms in the bay. On the north side of the bay, the water deepens to over 10 fathoms. Off the southern point, a low wooded head, are some islets also wooded, and some rocks which form a second bay, but it is too small for anchorage.

Misaki bay can also be approached by a channel less than a cable in breadth, carrying from 6 to 17 fathoms, by passing along the north shore of Kaba sima, and keeping a mid-channel course. The sunken Bay rock is half a mile West of the entrance. Between the East rocks and the reefs of Kaba sima there is only a narrow channel of 4 fathoms.

Fish is plentiful here, and lampreys, and the fishermen eager to sell.

KABA SIMA is covered with steep hills about 400 feet in height, a clump of trees surmounting one of the southern; its sides are mostly bold and abrupt, with rocks a cable off them, a sunken one lying at this distance off the shelving rocks of its south point.

---

* Misaki, Tameitsi, and the coast east from Aba are in the territory of the Prince of Fizen.

Kabasima bay, between Nomo saki and Kaba sima, affords anchorage at its north-western part open only between S.E. and S.W. Here reefs which dry project 1½ cables from the shore; at 2 cables from the shore there are 8 fathoms, and at 4 cables distance 11 fathoms about E.N.E. of the Nomo rock. The eastern part of the bay where a long sandy beach is seen, should be avoided, there being a sunken rock (Bay rock), on which are 6 feet water with 4 and 6 fathoms about it. Its position is E. ¼ N. 1½ miles from the Nomo rock, and N. ¾ W. of the west point of Kaba sima, at half a mile from the shores of island and main.

WEST COAST of NAGASAKI PENINSULA.—From 10 miles outside the islands fronting the west coast of Nagasaki the soundings decrease gradually over a bottom chiefly sand, until 30 fathoms is obtained, which will be at a general distance of a mile from all the outer islands; the only exception is an 18 fathoms spit which extends one mile north-west of the Sotonohirase rock, and the extremity of which is 1⅓ miles W.S.W. of the north-west point of Iwo sima. Within this island, the bottom in the fairway is of mud, gravel, or rock.

IWO SIMA lies in a north-west and south-east direction and is of undulating outline, the eastern summit being 400 feet in height. Signal head, the north-western point of this island is a good guide for entering the harbour of Nagasaki. It is bold and may be rounded at 3 cables distance in 25 fathoms. On its summit, which is cleared of trees, there is a signal staff and look-out house, from which the arrival of vessels is telegraphed to Nagasaki.*

LIGHT.—On the point of Iwo sima above mentioned at the entrance to Nagasaki harbour elevated 205 feet above the sea is exhibited a *fixed* white light of the first order eclipsed from N.E. by N. landward to W. ¾ N. The tower, which is built of iron, is 38 feet high, hexagonal in shape and painted white, and is in lat. 32° 43′ N., long. 129° 46′ E.

OKI SIMA, of much the same height as Iwo, is more wooded, especially its southern summit. There is access to the harbour by the channel east of Oki, between it and Koyaki. Iwo and Oki appear as one long island, although separated by a narrow boat passage.

Hirase rock, which covers at high water only and is marked by a beacon, lies 4 cables from the eastern shore of Iwo sima, and E. by S. ¼ S. 11 cables from Signal head, and although not directly in the fairway, is in the route of vessels beating in and out. There do not appear to be any other dangers near it. If covered, the bluff of Papenburg island, bearing E. ½ S., leads 3 cables north of it.

---

* Literally, Long cape.

Sotonohirase rock, also covering at high water, is 9 cables off the south-west shore of Iwo sima, and S. by W. ¼ W. 1¼ miles from Signal head. It is steep-to in 17 fathoms on the outside, but this depth is continued on a spit running one mile N.W. by W. from the rock, its outer part in 18 fathoms being W.S.W. 1⅓ miles from Signal head, with 37 to 38 fathoms on all sides.

Kutsnose and Kurose rocks.—The Kutsnose, 10 feet above high water, lies inshore of the Sotonohirase, at 1½ cables from Iwo sima.

The Kurose is a large straggling reef of which the southern and highest part is 6 feet above high water. North and north-west of it several reefs dry in parts on the foul rocky ground between it and the south end of Oki, from which it is distant 4 cables.

TAKA SIMA, at 3 miles S. by W. of Signal head, has a precipitous ridge about 900 feet high on its eastern side, and a smaller ridge over the cliffs on its western or sea-face. Its shores are very rugged, with reefs extending 1½ cables off its north and west points. Three small islands, about 120 feet high, Tobi sima to the north, and Futako sima (two islands) on the south, lie in line, north and south of its east face. The latter two are connected and fringed by reefs. There are coal mines in operation on the east side of Taka sima, from which coal of a very fair quality is mined. The only anchorage is on the west side of the island in from 2 to 7 fathoms on a bank of coal and sand, which at 3 cables from the shore deepens suddenly to 15 and 20 fathoms. Small vessels might anchor there in fine weather and smooth water, but the anchorage is neither of sufficient extent or protection to be in any way recommended to H.M.'s ships requiring coal.

Hi sima and Nagano sima, 1½ and 2 miles S. by W. and S.S.W. respectively from the summit of Taka sima, are smooth-topped islands about 120 feet in height, with rocky shores and with reefs extending more than a cable off their southern points. Nagano sima is 4 cables S.W. of Hi sima, there being deep water, about 14 or 16 fathoms, in the passage between them.

Mitzuse rocks, the outermost dangers in the approach to Nagasaki from the south, lie 3¼ miles S.W. of Taka sima, and N.W. ½ W. 2½ miles from the summit of Nomo saki. They spread irregularly over an extent of half a mile, the interior rocks of the group covering with the tide. On the northernmost rocks are two pointed islets, 60 feet in height, with outlying patches on the east and west; the south-eastern of the group is a bare rock about 6 feet above high water. At one cable westward or outside the rocks there are 23 fathoms and no outlying dangers are known, but it would not be prudent to pass between the rocks although the water appeared deep.

CHAP. VII.] WEST COAST OF KIUSIU—NAGASAKI PENINSULA. 279

NOMO SAKI is the south-western extremity of the peninsula of Nagasaki. At a distance it has the appearance of an island, and when nearing, it cannot be mistaken for any other land in its vicinity; from the west or south-west the island Kaba sima will be seen off the low point east of the cape. At 6 cables north of the cape is Nomo yama point, which rises steeply to the wooded summit of a prominent hill, Nomo yama, immediately beneath which on a small bare shoulder towards the sea, stands a look-out house; the hill slopes towards the cape in two gently descending ridges of small hills: the coast between is broken and rocky, and skirted with dangerous reefs which dry out in patches to a quarter of a mile, but it may be passed at the distance of 4 cables in from 12 to 17 fathoms, gravel and rock. At 2 cables off the cape is an inaccessible islet called Nomo rock, which is surrounded by small low detached rocks, most of which cover.

Nomo ura, the entrance of which is one mile north-east of Nomo yama point, is small and perfectly sheltered, 6 cables in length and from 1 to 2 in breadth. Within, there is a depth of 5 fathoms, but it is only accessible to small vessels, having not more than 9 to 10 feet at high water in the deepest part of its narrow entrance, which is only 100 yards across and 2 cables in length. The northern point of entrance is a small, dark, wooded but conspicuous bluff; the southern, the foot of the range of hills next north of Nomo yama. Off the wooded bluff are reefs and uneven ground, so that the harbour should be approached on a S.E. course, taking care to keep rather along the southern shore in entering.

THE COAST.—The coast of the peninsula northward from Nomo yama point is bold with a few outlying rocks, and may be passed at 2 or 3 cables in from 10 to 13 fathoms. To the north-east of Nomo ura, the coast is low as far as a hilly point 2 miles distant. Off it are several long reefs, drying out in patches. On the southern of these reefs, at half a mile N.E. of the entrance of Nomo ura is a tree islet 120 feet high, with shoal water extending 2 cables to the north-west of it. No part of this coast should be approached within half a mile, the ground off it being uneven and rocky.

The coast for 3 miles N.E. by N. of this hilly point is bold, with soundings of from 5 to 9 fathoms near the shore. It lies under a succession of hill ranges, which terminate at a point abreast a group of rocky islets, north of which point the small bay of Ōko mura affords anchorage in from 6 to 8 fathoms. A conspicuous smooth-topped conical islet south of the islet group is very noticeable close off this coast.

Suzume, a bare rock, about 50 feet high, is the north-western of this group of islets. No-sima, the southern, and all the other islets, are wooded and low, and surrounded by large reefs. There is a 5 fathoms channel between No sima and the coast, but the islet must be closed in passing, as a large reef projects from the shore. Suzume may be rounded at 3 cables on its west side in 15 fathoms, rock or gravel, but at that distance N.N.E. there are only 5 fathoms.

KOYAKI.—Koyaki is the largest island off Nagasaki, and is situated directly south-west of the entrance, which may be gained by the channels both east and west of it. This island is not high, but very hilly, its two chief elevations being 362 and 403 feet. Numerous reefs and islets border its broken outline. Of these Joka sima and Hadagase, an islet and a rock, lie about W.S.W. at 5 and 8 cables respectively of Mumenoki, the south point of Koyaki, with from 15 to 18 fathoms inside them.

Hadagase is probably united to Joka sima, as the large reef on which that islet stands stretches far towards the rock, as it also does towards Mumenoki. Hadagase may be passed at 4 cables on its west side in 26 fathoms. The large bay on the northern side of Koyaki has from 17 to 20 fathoms water, and, besides being too deep for convenient anchorage, is open to the north-west swell. On the eastern side of Koyaki there is a mass of reefs in the South channel.

KAGENO.—This island appears part of Koyaki, as it is only separated from its north point by a narrow boat passage. The Naginato or Hungry rock, which covers at high water, lies a cable East of its north-east point, off which is a small islet.

Kamino sima, at 6 cables north of Kageno, is the largest island on the northern side of the fairway to Nagasaki. Its north hill is elevated 330 feet, and on its central hill, which is lower, is a signal staff. On the east side there is a small boat camber; on the south-west the small flat island of Siro sima, on which there is a battery, is connected with a work on Kamino sima by a causeway of masonry. There are other batteries on Kamino sima, all of which command the passage.

North-westward of Siro sima are the two small islands Aino sima and Mats sima. Aino sima, at 1½ cables distance, is a flat table island on a reef, with a conspicuous rock* close off its south point; Mats sima, at 5 cables, is a small hill 90 feet high. There is deep water in the passage between Siro sima and Aino sima.

Barracouta rock.—Off Kabuto saki, the south-east point of Kamino sima, on which there is a battery, are some small islets. One cable from these, S.W. of the Tree rock, and W. by N. of the south bluff of Papenburg, is the Barracouta, a sunken rock, which is the only hidden danger in the entrance, and may be cleared to the southward by keeping the summit of

---

* This rock or islet is the observing place of Belcher, in 1842, from which several meridian distances were measured to Lu-chu, Quelpart, &c.

the coast range (800 feet) over Megami point open of Papenburg, bearing East.

Papenburg, or Takaboko, 2 cables south-east of Kamino sima, is the small precipitous island covered with dark foliage, which so well marks the entrance to the harbour. It may be passed at half a cable in 18 fathoms. To the N.E. of it, and distant one-third of a mile, is a small flat wooded island Nezumi sima,* lying off the small bay of Kibatsu, east of the large village of Kosedo.

The HARBOUR of NAGASAKI,† an arm or inlet running in a north-easterly direction, is large and commodious, thoroughly sheltered from all winds, and available for ships of all classes. From its entrance, which is a quarter of a mile wide between Ogame point on the west and Megami point on the east, it runs N.E. to the city a distance of 2 miles, increasing to a breadth (although irregularly, owing to several bays on its shores,) of three-quarters of a mile. Above the city it narrows again, taking a northerly direction for another mile to its head, which is exceedingly shallow. The depths decrease gradually from 16 fathoms at entrance to 3 fathoms off the city.

Ogame point.—The only danger at the entrance is a sunken rock, lying about 70 yards South of the east extreme of Ogame point. A temple stands on the south extreme of the point.

Megami point is at the foot of a steep ridge, on which are three batteries, one above the other. Within Megami point 1½ cables (a small islet lying between them) is another point, on the extreme of which, in a battery, is a remarkable large tree.

The Hishiwo bank, which fronts the shore from De sima to the foreign settlement, is a good and convenient place for grounding. Its western edge is steep, but off De sima, W. by S. of the Dutch consulate flagstaff, the bank is very flat. This is the spot recommended especially for gunboats and other small vessels.

The harbour has three approaches. The principal one or fairway is directly from the north-west, the entrance of which, 4 miles outside the harbour, is between Fukuda saki and Iwo sima light (*see* page 277), and carries very deep water, 32 fathoms, decreasing to 20 in the passage between Papenburg and Kageno, and again to 15 and 16 fathoms at the entrance of the harbour. Vessels entering Nagasaki harbour should invariably use this channel.

The second approach is by the Oki channel, between Oki sima and Koyaki, but it is only 3 cables in breadth, and further narrowed by the

---

* The observing place of Richards in 1856, from which meridian distances were measured to Hong Kong, Hakodate, &c.

† *See* plan of Nagasaki harbour, No. 2,415; scale $m = 2 \cdot 8$ inches.

reefs which extend into the channel 1½ cables from either shore. There are irregular soundings of 7 to 19 fathoms in it, and the best course through is midway between the reefs which are seen. Neither this channel nor its approaches have been yet thoroughly examined.

The Kurose, a rocky islet with reefs projecting from it (*see* page 278), lies in the fairway to the entrance to this channel from the southward.

The third approach is by the South channel, between Koyaki and the main, and can only be used by steam vessels. Narrow and intricate amongst the reefs, with soundings varying from 4 to 15 fathoms, it cannot be recommended, and can only be taken at the risk of the navigator. The chief danger is a sunken rock in the narrowest part of the channel, where it leads between two large flat-topped rocks, 4 cables north of Fukahori point, and which should be passed at the slowest speed compatible with good steerage way. These rocks, which never cover, are but one cable apart, and the sunken rock is half a cable N.W. by W. of the eastern one. The whole of this channel is so encumbered with rocky patches that instructions for its navigation would not be sufficient; a local pilot would be necessary, and it should never be taken without one.

The CITY of NAGASAKI, a treaty port, at present second only in importance to Yokohama, and the only place of trade open to foreigners between 1623 and 1857, covers a broad valley on the eastern side of the harbour, surrounded by lofty hills. Its population in 1858 amounted to nearly 70,000. Nagasaki is one of the five imperial cities of Japan, and is under the jurisdiction of a governor holding his appointment from the Mikado.

De sima, the historic site of the Dutch factory, projects into the harbour on the south-west side of the city, with which it is only connected by a stone bridge. Shaped like the border of a fan, it is 250 yards in length and 80 in width, and is traversed by a central street. De sima contains the residences and warehouses of the Dutch community, the consulate being situated at its south-west angle. At the broad steps at its west end is the best place for landing at the city.

The Japanese custom house is situate directly east of De sima, but is not accessible to boats before a quarter flood. The exports consist of tea, silk, coal, vegetable wax, gall nuts, copper, gold; also various articles for the Chinese market, as dried fish, sea slugs, seaweed, peas, beans, &c. The imports consist of manufactured goods, metals, and various articles of mixed merchandise, with the exception of munitions of war, which, by the 14th article of the treaty, can only be sold to the Japanese government and to foreigners.

The Chinese community occupy the square secluded block of houses S.E. of De sima, connected with the shore by a bridge. They compose a trading guild and factory, subjected for ages to every kind of restriction. They have three junks annually trading to Chapu in Hang-chu bay.

The Foreign settlement is on the flat south of De sima, having a water frontage of 730 yards; it also stretches up the valley on the Owara creek on the south. The British consulate is upon the bluff south of this creek, where there is a good landing place. There are also two landing places in front of the settlement, but only the lower one can be approached at low water. The American, French, and Portuguese consulates are on the hills at the back of the settlement.

Supplies.—All provisions are plentiful (mutton excepted), cheap, and easily obtained, as also is wood and water; the latter is brought off in boats to the shipping. Coal is abundant, at 9 to 11 dollars a ton, but is of inferior quality for steaming purposes, especially for high pressure boilers. There are numerous mines in the vicinity, one of which is in operation at Taka sima (page 278). There is a Japanese government steam factory at Akunora, on the west side of the harbour, and also a patent slip.

Anchorage.—The best anchorage for men of war is just above the British consulate bluff, large ships anchoring in from 6 to 7 fathoms, rather over towards Minage point,* at this the broadest part of the deep water of the harbour. Merchant vessels usually anchor off the foreign settlement in from 4 to 6 fathoms, or even above De sima in 3 fathoms. In the hot weather of July and August great relief may be experienced from the closeness of the atmosphere, and it will be beneficial to the health of the crews to spring the ship's broadside to the sea breeze, which, in fine weather, is almost constant from the S.W. and generally very fresh.

Pilots, either Japanese or European, can always be had at a charge of 30 dollars,† obtained by requisition through the consul. It is said that they are well acquainted with their business, and that it is their custom to take entire charge of the navigation of the ship; but great caution should be used in this respect, as some of them have only knowledge of particular localities.‡

Tides.—It is high water, full and change, at Nagasaki, at 7h. 15m. Springs rise 9 feet, and neaps about 7½ feet, but they are variable. The current in the harbour is always sluggish. A strong southerly wind is said to raise the level at high water at springs from 10 to 12 feet, or 2 feet above the ordinary level.

---

* The rock on the south side of Minage point, to which all the meridian distances are referred, is a convenient and quiet spot for taking observations.

† J. S. Compton, Master, R.N., H.M.S. *Renard*, 1861.

‡ The same officer remarks, that steaming during the night through the Seto uchi, the pilot in the morning was quite ignorant of the ship's position, "knowing nothing about the sea or the land."

DIRECTIONS.—The entrance of Nagasaki, although safe of approach, is sometimes difficult for a stranger to make out from a distance, especially in clear weather, when the islands blend with the mainland; but on nearer approach or in slightly hazy weather when the islands appear in relief, the uncertainty is removed. It is said that vessels from the south-west are very liable to make the entrance south of Iwo sima.

When making Nagasaki from south-west or west, steer to round Signal head, the north end of Iwo sima, at a quarter of a mile, taking care not to bring the light to bear northward of N.E. by N. (on which bearing it is obscured) on approaching it. By keeping the light in sight or during the day keeping the north point of Iwo sima, bearing eastward of N.E. by N. will clear the shoal water off the dangerous Sotonohirase rock. After rounding the head, steer E. ½ S. for the Papenburg bluff, passing it as closely as convenient, but taking care to avoid the Barracouta rock; then E.N.E. for the entrance. At night do not bring the light to bear northward of W. ¾ N.

Passing in mid-channel between Ogame and Megami points, a N.E. course direct for the Dutch flag on De sima will then lead up in the best water, and when the factory of Akunora, on the west shore, opens of Minage point, N. by W., a large vessel should haul up N.N.E., and anchor in 6 fathoms between it and the British consulate or foreign settlement.

In approaching from the north-westward, the course from 1½ miles S.W. of Hiki sima is S.E. by E. Iwo sima will be made without difficulty (appearing, end on, and under the mountain range Kawara yama, the highest on the Nagasaki peninsula), and should be passed on the north at a mile, when Papenburg will be seen over the three low islands outside Kamino sima.

There is little or no difficulty in getting into Nagasaki at night, if the weather be fine, as the light on Signal head is visible 21 miles in clear weather; but should a vessel, from calms or adverse winds, be unable to enter, every endeavour should be made to get inside Papenburg if it be the intention to anchor, for outside this island the water is inconveniently deep, and it would be preferable to stand off and on till daylight, taking care not to decrease the soundings below 30 fathoms.

Anchorage can, however, be found in 20 to 26 fathoms over a bottom of thick green ooze with fine sand, good holding ground, or possibly rock or sand and shells if near the Hirase rock. A vessel will lie here sheltered from all winds except N.W., but exposed to the swell from that quarter. There is also anchorage east of Papenburg and Kageno, in from 13 to 17 fathoms, or in 11 fathoms on a bank S.W. of Megami point; the bottom here is mud and the shelter good except from West. Towards the eastern shore the ground is irregular and probably rocky.

MIYE NO URA.—The entrance to which is about 5 miles N. by E. from Iwo sima light, is formed between Noöze (3 cables off the north point), and Kagura sima on the south side. It has a shoal of 2½ fathoms in the centre of the entrance, with islets and rocks off its northern shores, and rocks above water off the middle of the head of the bay, the depths are very uneven; but anchorage is said to be good at the head of the bay in 7 and 8 fathoms.

From the western point of the craggy island of Kagura, at 4 cables distance, is a small flat-topped isolated rock, with deep water close-to. Miye no ura runs north-east and south-west, is 2 miles deep, and the navigator should be cautious, as it is much encumbered with dangers.

KASHE, a high square rock, with deep water around, is 1¼ miles E. by S. ½ S. of Hako sima, and one mile off the coast.

HAKO SIMA, a small round island, has off its west side the remarkable perforated rock Tengo, which is of considerable elevation, inaccessible, and has a sharp pointed summit. The perforation takes the shape of an arch, and this conspicuous rock, when seen from the southward, at a distance, resembles a ship under full sail.

HIKI SIMA, the outer and western island, has bluff capes on the south sides, is partially cultivated, and 250 feet high, with a remarkable cone-shaped rounded hummock at its south-east extreme, connected with the main part of the island by a long strip of shore; it is 9 cables long east and west. The channel between it and Ike sima has a rock in the centre, on which the sea generally breaks.

To the north-west of Hiki sima, a long ledge of rocks uncovers at low water, but there are always some heads of the rocks visible. Its north extreme is 7 cables distance from the island, and should therefore not be closed nearer than 4 cables, nor should the passage between this ledge and Ike sima be attempted.

IKE SIMA lies 1½ miles S. by W. of Mats' sima, is flat, with trees on it. At its northern end a shingle beach encloses a salt-water lagoon.

The COAST.—From Miye no ura the coast takes a N.N.W. direction to the east rock (Kashe), with bold points and sandy beaches, and moderately elevated coast range of hills, nearly all the points having off-lying rocks; an isolated rock, with deep water around, lies off the centre of a bay, 6 cables from the shore, and N.W. ½ N. 1½ miles from the outer low flat rock, off the northern point of Miye no ura. Vessels creeping up in shore must be careful of this rock; and nearly 2 miles S. E. ½ E. from Kashe (East rock) are some rocks and islets, 3 cables off the shore.

YUKI NO URA.—This bay is south of Hokimats', and is shallow at its head, with 1½ and 2 fathoms.

MATS' SIMA,* a large and well-cultivated island, with coal mines, is 2 miles long and 1¼ miles broad. Off its north-west shores an islet, 20 to 30 feet above water, lies at 4 cables distance, with deep water around; but from the north point, extending in a N.N.W.½W. direction, are islets and rocks to a distance of 6½ cables, the outer patch of rocks partly uncovering at low water. Vessels should not round into the north-east corner (southward of Oösima) till Takabo cone bears N.E. by E. The summit of the island is flat-topped, and 708 feet above the sea, the ridge running north-east and south-west, with spurs to the several points; the western side more sloping, and the beach of shingle, with moderate depths at 2 cables off the shore.

TAKABO, a conspicuous cone of considerable height on the main land, with a clump of trees on its summit, is immediately over the coast, and overlooks to the northward a narrow inlet of the sea which runs parallel with the coast for 1¼ miles, at the head of which is Nanatsu Gama carrying 5 fathoms in the centre for half a mile, the width of the channel being barely a cable.

The COAST.—Takabo is 3¾ miles southward of Oötawa bay, and thence the coast trends to the northward in bends and indentations. Off Hokimats' is the island of Mats', above mentioned, from the north and eastern sides of which are numerous points, rocks and off-lying dangers. There is also an island immediately off Hokimats', having a very narrow passage of moderately deep water. The whole of the channel between Mats' sima and the main is much encumbered with reefs and obstacles. Its navigation can only be undertaken by those possessing local knowledge.

Ō MURA GULF.—The approaches to Ō mura gulf from the south-westward are faced by chains of islands and rocks lying generally in a north-east and south-west direction.

OÖ SIMA.—The western and largest island, is tortuously indented on its eastern side with numerous ledges and rocks, uncovering at low water.

TERA SIMA lies close to Oö sima (the passage between being crowded with rocks); has also shores of rocky points. The channel between it and the main is 4 cables wide, with depths of 10 and 12 fathoms in the middle, the main coast being steep-to. There are smaller islands to the north-east of Oö sima, but a vessel proceeding by the inside route must have the chart to guide her, and be cautious in looking for rocks just awash north of Oötawa bay, which is situated on the mainland of Kiusiu.

Between Oötawa bay (where there is excellent anchorage) and the entrance to the gulf of Ō mura there are two very deep inlets; the one

---

* See Chart of Mats' sima to Atsusi no Osima, No. 140.

immediately south of the entrance is a harbour called Kuro-kuchi-ya, with a low reef of rocks above water extending from its south shore, with deep water near its outer end.

KAKI-NO-URA SIMA, lying to the south-west and connected at quarter ebb with Oö sima, has a deep inlet, from which it is named, narrow, and only anchorage for small vessels. There are two bluffs on the southeast coast, which are conspicuous when seen from the south.

Mikoto sima, the western of the islands about Oö sima, is faced with cliffs, and can be approached to half a mile. At spring tides the race off its western point is strong.

Imo sima, a low reef, stretches to the southward of the small channel between Mikoto and Kaki-no-ura sima, having two conspicuous trees about 20 feet above high water. From the uneven nature of the bottom, there is no safe anchorage to the southward or eastward of these islands.

KATA SIMA, a sharp wedge-shaped island, 327 feet high, with a perpendicular cliff to southward, and a short spit extending from its north-east point, lies about 1½ miles to the north-west of Oö sima.

To the southward of Kata, three-quarters of a cable, is a small rock above water. The island is steep-to all round.

Gana she.—Three-quarters of a mile north-east from Kata sima is a patch of rocks of about one mile in extent, with some isolated rocks above water.

Shira she.—A similar but smaller patch lies half a mile further to the north-east, the passages between having deep water. The north-eastern rock of Shira she is wedge-shaped, and about 15 feet above water, steep-to on its eastern side, but the reef extends to it westward and southward 5½ cables. Shira she faces the entrance to Ō mura gulf at a distance of a little more than 2 miles, between which are depths of from 10 to 20 fathoms.

DIRECTIONS.—The numerous islands and rocks which lie to the south-west of Ō mura gulf render the navigation near and among them difficult and dangerous; but vessels wishing to go into that gulf (which has not yet been explored), or seeking shelter from northerly, westerly, or southerly winds, will find by keeping outside they will be safe. In clear weather from the northward a course for the bold conspicuous bluff and trees Matsu-yama hana (north cape of the harbour of Kuro-kuchi-ya), taking care to pass to the northward and eastward of the rock Shira she, will take to the entrance of the gulf; or, by closing the mainland to 3 cables, and steering south, can run into Oötawa bay, remembering the rock awash (Hira she), which lies N. by W. 5½ cables, from the south point of Oötawa bay, and which has generally a pole to mark its position.

From the southward (or northward, after rounding the south end of Imo sima), steer for a conspicuous round islet, Bakutchi, passing to the southward of it, when the channel will be open. By keeping the main shore on board, and at a distance of 2 to 2¾ cables, a vessel can pass through and round into Oötawa bay, where anchorage in 5 and 6 fathoms can be obtained. Shoal water extends some distance from the shore in Oötawa bay.

OÖ TATE, N.W. ½ N. from Ko tate, and 9 miles S. by E. ½ E. of Sisiki saki on Hirado sima, is an island with a ridge having two hummocks near its south-east end, 257 feet high. It is 6 cables long, and from its western point, N.W. by N. 8 cables, are 2 sandstone islets above water. Deep water will be found around these islands and between them.

A rock awash has been reported to be at half a mile N. by E. ½ E. from Oö tate. The *Sylvia's* survey failed to find it. It should however be remembered as possibly existing.

KO TATE (Bonnet) is small, with a low rock above water close to its south side, steep-to. It is cone-shaped and easily distinguishable; bears West 4¼ miles from the west point of Mikoto sima; and lies directly in the fairway between Nagasaki and Hirado sima.

YENOI SIMA lies 4 miles West of Oö tate. Its eastern side, which borders on the channel, has some rocks off it; but from south, round west to N.N.W. of the island, are many scattered islets, rocks, and reefs, which renders navigation between it and Hira sima to the westward extremely hazardous.

The island is 1¼ miles long, north-west and south-east, and three-quarters of a mile broad, with a projecting point from the north side, close to which is an islet. The central ridge of the island rises towards the north end with two conspicuous sharp hummocks, the highest of which is 436 feet above the sea, and smooth.

Saracen reefs.—South 2¾ miles of Yenoi sima is the outer or extreme rock, between which and the island's south point are several reefs and rocks, some above water; the most noticeable of them are two islets 150 and 50 feet high, W. ½ S. and S.S.W., 2 miles and 1¼ miles respectively from the south point (a small head) of Yenoi sima. To the N.N.W. and W.N.W. for 1½ miles are reefs and rocks, the extreme northerly rocks are about 70 to 80 feet above water and steep-to. The set of the tides here being N.W. and S.E., much caution is required when navigating in this locality.

HIRA SIMA, 4 miles westward of Yenoi sima, (the channel between has not been examined,) is 2¼ miles long by 1¼ miles broad, with deep bays on the north and south sides. In the latter there is an islet with trees facing a round inlet, in which junks lie securely, and ship a very indifferent coal, obtained from a mine close to. The *Sylvia* took an outside line of soundings half a mile off the west coast, getting 20 to 30 fathoms, and rounded into the southern bay, anchoring in 10 fathoms eastward of the islet. The bay is open to the south-west.

From the south point of the island half a mile S.S.W. is a rocky islet, and further in the same direction for 4 miles is Ka sima.

Fukushe.—A dangerous rock which shows about 4 feet above water at low water springs, and is very small and flat-topped, with deep water immediately around it, lies 4½ miles N. ⅓W. from Ko tate (Bonnet), and 6½ miles from the south cape of Hirado sima; directly in the route of vessels, whether they take the outer or inner passage. The sharp peak over Sisiki (on Hirado) in line with the Ho-age (Sail rock) leads to the eastward, and the wedge-shaped island of Kata bearing East leads to the southward of Fukushe.

Ho-age (Sail rock) lies N.N.W., 3 miles from Fukushe, and may be passed on either side at from 1 to 2 cables.

CAUTION.—As only partial examinations have been made to the westward of Yenoi sima, and known dangers exist off its south end for nearly 3 miles, and also to the N.N.W. of the island, any navigation in these waters must be injudicious and hazardous. The set of the tides too is very strong, and takes a general north-west and south-east direction, right on to the islands and reefs; it is therefore necessary to keep to the eastward of Yenoi sima, the passage between which and Oö tate is safe and clear, or to the northward of Oö tate, remembering that great danger the Fukushe.

The uneven nature of the bottom of the whole sea in the vicinities of Nagasaki, Goto islands, and Hirado, which is clearly shown by the above-named sunken dangers being so isolated, and also by the singular rocks which like the Sail, Bonnet, those near Oö tate, the Tengo (Arch), and Kashe (East) rocks, having deep water immediately around them, renders it necessary that every precaution should be observed and great care taken in navigating this portion of the western coasts of Kiusiu, as the lead is of little, if any, use, and the currents run strong, especially in the strait.

The routes therefore recommended are those, which, from experience, have been found free of danger.

KURO SIMA.—The southern entrance to Hirado no seto is faced by the island of Kuro sima, the southern shore of which is very bold; but from its western end, and separated by a channel of 2¼ cables, is a low flat rock which, it must be remembered, although above water and steep-to, would not be seen at night in calm weather; the bold bluff western end of the island is conspicuous and is connected with the island by a low narrow neck of rocks.

TAKA SIMA, an island 1¾ miles to the north-east of Kuro sima (at the southern entrance to Hirado no seto), and between which vessels steer when taking the eastern route, is a very conspicuous landmark, having a temple near some trees cresting a square-topped hill. The southern point of the island has a sharp overhanging rock, and its southern shores are steep-to.

From the entrance to Oö-mura gulf to abreast Taka sima, the coast of the mainland was not examined, but it takes a north-west direction, having numerous deep bays and indentations, with off-lying rocks and islets.

HIRADO SIMA,* 17¼ miles in length, N.E. and S.W., and, (owing to its deeply indented coast-line,) of an irregular breadth of from 2 cables to 5¼ miles, lies adjacent to the west coast of Kiusiu, from which it is separated by Hirado no seto (commonly known to Europeans as Spex strait). Hirado is high and hilly; the principal ridges running across the island, with sloping spurs encircling the several deep bays. At the northern end, the strait is separated from the harbour of Oösuka on the west side by a narrow neck of land only 2¼ cables in width, whilst the head of the bay of Sisiki in the south is barely 2 cables distant from the sea on the east coast.

Yasman take, the highest hill, is 1,792 feet high, and densely wooded with fine timber to its summit.

Sira take, which crests the long smooth slopes from the North cape, has a double summit, the highest being 880 feet. Here is a small temple to which the people by their frequent visits seem to attach religious importance.

Over Sisiki, the south point of the island, a sharp peak, wooded almost to the top, rises precipitously to a considerable height, and is singularly conspicuous from the southward.

The coasts of Hirado are generally bold, and from the hills being much wooded, the island is extremely picturesque.

NORTH CAPE is bold, and the north-western shores, which rise somewhat abruptly, can be approached quite close, the reef of rocks (about 10 feet above water) off the northern point of Sisiki bay being the only danger. Several deep indentations, with bold rocky points, jut into the sea and can be rounded within a cable; the passage between Kado sima and the coast is clear and deep.

YEBUKURO NO MINATO† forms two deep bays, or rather harbours, on the western side of the north end of Hirado, and under the name of Firando was, previous to 1623, the chief location of Portuguese, British, and other

---

* See Chart, Mats' sima to At susi no Ōsima, including Hirado, No. 140.
† See plan of Yebukuro no minato, No. 139; scale, $m = 6·0$ inches.

foreign trade with Japan, which from that period was restricted to the Dutch and confined to Nagasaki.

The first bay, which runs east and west for two miles, with an average breadth of half a mile, is Oosuka. Two wooded islands are in it, and a peninsula at the east, or upper end of the bay is almost another island. This harbour is clear of dangers with the following exceptions. A rock in the middle near the entrance; and,—

Mina sone, a reef, which uncovers at low water near the head of the harbour on the north side.

Arakabu sone, a rock, with one foot water, lying midway between Hirago sima (the island in the centre) and the north shore.

Kaji-kake (Rudder breaker), is in mid-channel and nearly awash at low water, with deep water around; it is small, and can be avoided by keeping the gap in the hills over the head of the harbour, open to the northward of the centre island (Hirago sima).

The harbour is sheltered from all winds; the depths vary from 18 to 8 fathoms with muddy bottom. A good guide to recognize its position is the small island Kado sima, lying off the north point of entrance, and $2\frac{1}{4}$ miles from the extreme north cape.

ANCHORAGE.—Good anchorage can be found between the Hirago sima and the head of the bay in 12 and 13 fathoms mud.

Feruye, the second arm of Yebukuro no minato,* runs nearly north and south $1\frac{3}{4}$ miles, with a breadth of from $3\frac{1}{2}$ to 7 cables, and is a perfectly land-locked harbour with excellent holding ground everywhere, and deep water close to its shores; its entrance, although barely $1\frac{1}{2}$ cables wide, is easy and clear, and the longest ship could from seaward boldly pass through the narrow passage, and proceeding towards the head of the harbour and anchor as convenient in any depth from 15 to 10 fathoms, mud.

A stream flows into the head of the bay, and there are two or three small villages on its shores. The channel between Hirado and the small islets, Nagai sima, is clear and deep, with the exception of a 6-fathom patch; by passing the islets at a distance of about 3 cables a depth of 17 fathoms will be found.

There is also deep water and a fair passage to the west of the islets Nagai sima, at 2 cables distance.

ITOYA BAY, which is $1\frac{1}{2}$ miles deep and half a mile broad, has apparently good shelter to the eastward of the island at its entrance, except with winds from N.W. to West.

SISIKI BAY is 3 miles deep, and has a general width of one mile, with gradually decreasing depths from 17 fathoms at its entrance to 12, 10, 8, and

---

* Literally Stomach harbour, from its peculiar shape.

5 fathoms. It can be easily distinguished by the Azika sima (erroneously called Sisters), two remarkably bold, rocky, conical islets, having deep water all round, lying off the entrance; the whole of the northern islet kept well open of the southern, leads up the bay.

The bay is open to the N.W. and W.N.W., and the fishermen of the village state that, during the winter, heavy rollers come in; the bay, however, affords perfect protection from all other winds, and to any vessel well found in ground tackle, it would be a welcome haven from a heavy westerly gale, as from 5 to 4 fathoms can be obtained near the head, in the north corner, with the points almost shut in; no heavy sea could reach this position. Ships taking the outer passage could put into Sisiki for the night, or, finding thick weather and southerly winds coming on, to await better weather.

SOUTH CAPE is very bold, its conspicuous feature being the singular sharp peak of Sisiki. Several islets and islands lie on the west side of the cape; the outer one, Taka sima, is a cone-shaped islet with deep water near and can be rounded quite close.

Tide race.—A heavy tide rip is generally to be seen off the south point, extending some distance to the westward.

THE EASTERN SHORE of HIRADO is clear and bold, and can be approached to within 2 or 3 cables without danger as far as the narrowest part of Hirado no seto (Spex strait).

The first deep bay from the South cape on this shore, is Kigatou, which, with the one immediately to the north, Ho-oki, are foul and rocky, and not recommended for anchorages; the small and snug little bay immediately off the village of Kigatsu is an exception, as anchorage in from 4 to 5 fathoms, mud, can be obtained here for one or two vessels, and perfectly sheltered from all winds; to enter this small bay, the southern or left shore must be kept close on board to avoid a shelving reef of rocks on the starboard hand, which extends from the north side.

KAWATCHI BAY.—Four miles further north the spacious bay of Kawatchi opens, in which anchorage can be found as convenient, 7 fathoms being obtained at the head, and off the village.

HIRADO.—The town of Hirado is situated on the east side of the island, and 2¼ miles from the North cape. It is built on the north side of a narrow bay, on the southern shores of which the Prince of Hirado has a residence, which is enclosed towards the sea with a white wall.

KURO KO SIMA lies off the northern entrance to Hirado bay. The bay to the southward of the town of Hirado is rocky and uneven, and subject to much chow-chow water and whirls of tidal streams.

TASKE HARBOUR.—Inside of the north cape Tsuba saki and protected by a rocky islet is the small harbour of Taske, much used by junks, but being only 2½ cables deep and 1½ cables wide scarcely affords anchorage for larger vessels. It has 4, 5, and 6 fathoms in its centre, with steep shores. There is access to this bay by both channels formed by the rocky island which fronts it, but the north one is the best, and carries in mid-channel 4½ fathoms. A rocky patch with 10 or 12 feet at low water lies East 1¾ cables from the north point of the bay: on this point there is a small harbour light.

HIROSE.—A small island 40 feet in height lies in mid-channel at the northern entrance to Hirado no seto; it is steep-to on the east side, and may be passed as close as convenient. Off its north end a bank of 4½ fathoms extends 1¾ cables to the north-eastward.

HIRADO NO SETO, or, as it is generally called, Spex straits, is now much used by steam vessels, being safely navigable with the exercise of due care and judgment.

A sailing vessel cannot, however, be taken through in safety without a commanding breeze, and which to be relied on, must blow directly through the strait.

At its northern part, for 1¾ miles the whole breadth of the strait is only 3 cables and the navigable channel in one place is only 1½ cables wide.

This is the dangerous part of the strait; the great strength of the tides over the uneven bottom, especially to the westward of the Hirose rock causing small whirlpools to be formed, renders it indispensable that a ship should have good steerage way to ensure safety.

After passing the first or northern narrow part, the strait takes a circuitous round for nearly 2 miles to the next narrow passage which is formed by the western coast of Kiusiu and the projecting part of Hirado: from this the channel opens into the spacious waters between the eastern shores of the island and the main, having at its southern end the islands of Kuro sima and the small islets of Kareki, together with the dangerous Costa Rica and Robinett rocks: while the western shore of Kiusiu has numerous indentations fronted by numerous islands, low reefs and rocks, the outer of which, James Rock, is nearly on the route hitherto recommended and generally used.

MIDZU and MI SIMA.—Two islets north of Kuro sima, the eastern of which, called Midzu sima, has from its S.E. point, a reef extending 3 cables S.E. by E. ½ E., most of which dries at low water. The western island, called Mi sima, has from its N.W. point a reef extending W.N.W. 2 cables.

Costa Rica rock.—The first danger in the strait is the Costa Rica rock, which lies 1¼ miles S.W. from south Kareki island, and nearly three miles

N. by W. ¼ W. from Kuro sima bluff. It is small with deep water immediately around, and by keeping the North Kareki island open westward of the south Kareki, the rock is cleared when passing to the westward.

The south extreme of Taka sima, a conspicuous rocky point, in line with the north extreme of Mi sima, E. by S. ⅜ S., leads to the southward of the rock.

Robinett rock, three-quarters of a mile N. by E. ¾ E. of the North Kareki, is nearly awash at low water, with deep water immediately around, and the sea is seldom seen to break on it. The bold bluff of Kuro sima kept in sight half way between the Kareki islands leads to the westward and southward, and the remarkable Table mountain on the east shore, open northward of the dark cape (or island) under the rock, bearing East, leads to the northward of this danger.

James rock, on the eastern shore, 2 feet above low water, is directly in the route generally taken by steam vessels, and lies N.E. ⅛ N. little more than 2¼ miles from North Kareki, and 9 cables N. ⅔ W. from the westernmost island on the Kiusiu shore.

Asama bank with 1¾ fathoms at low water, 9 cables S.W. by S. southerly from Red cliff point (the narrow part of the straits) is composed of shingle and sand—the ebb tide sets across this bank: by closing the eastern shore the bank is avoided.

A small rock with 15 feet at low water lies three-quarters of a cable E. by N. ⅔ N. of the Oötaske rock, which is always above water.

Vineta rock,* or rather bank, the eastern edge of which lies nearly 1½ cables S.W. ½ S. from Hirose, contracts the channel between it and the point on the mainland of Kiusiu (Ushi-ga no kubi) to 1½ cables.

Sylvia rock, at the extremity of a shoal bank extending to the north-east from Ushi ga no kubi, lies nearly 1½ cables S.S.E. ¼ E. from the north extreme of Hirose, and 1¾ cables from the above-mentioned point, leaving a channel 1½ cables wide between it and Hirose.

TIDES.—At Taske it is high water, full and change, at 9h. 44m. At Oösuca it is high water, full and change, at 9h. 16m. Springs rise 8½ feet. Neaps rise 1½ feet.

The tides at full and change run with great strength through the narrow channel at the northern part of the straits. The direction of the flood stream is to the north and parallel to the coast, that of the ebb, to the south, velocity 1½ knots at Springs; in the straits the velocity varies from 2 to 5 knots.

DIRECTIONS.—Entering Spex strait from the north,† vessels of light draught use either passage, but the western, from being full of rocks

---

* So named from the Prussian war steamer *Vineta* striking on it.

† *See* plan, northern entrance to Hirado no seto, No. 139; scale, $m = 6\cdot 0$ inches.

and uneven bottom, with the Vineta rock to the S.W. one cable, and further, subject to much "Chow-chow" water and tidal whirls, is not recommended; the eastern passage, although much narrower, is by far the safest and most easy to navigate.

The north end of Kuro-ko sima kept midway between the rock and the wooded head of Ushi-ga no kubi (a point a little more than 2 cables south of Hirose) leads clear through the passage, passing the rock at little more than half a cable; this course will also pass nearly three-quarters of a cable outside the wooded point.

Vessels of heavy draught when passing through this passage at the springs, when the strength of the tide is great, must remember the shoal patch of 15 feet which extends 1½ cables to the north-eastward of Ushi-ga no kubi point. From the wooded point the Kiusiu shore should be kept at a cable's distance while rounding to Red cliff point, where the passage is narrowed to 2¾ cables.

Due north, nearly 2 cables from Red cliff point, is the Oötaske rock 5 feet above water, and E. by N. ⅔ N., from the latter three-quarters of a cable, is a sunken rock having 15 feet at low water springs; the precipitous fall from the end of a flat-topped ridge on the Kiusiu shore kept open of the Red cliff point will clear the sunken rock.

The Kiusiu shore must be kept on board until abreast Aosa saki which is 1¾ miles S.S.W. from Red cliff point, where a course for the extreme south end of Hirado (S.W. by S.) can be shaped which will lead well outside the Asama bank.

The east coast of Hirado can be kept at from 2 to 3 cables distance.

It has hitherto been the practice to pass down the western shore of Kiusiu to the eastward of Kuro sima, &c., but from the numerous islands, rocks, and outlying dangers off that shore, and from the absence of prominent marks for avoiding the James rock, the above route is recommended; there being no danger along the Hirado east shore.

As soon as the Costa Rica rock has been passed (which may be known when the Kuro sima bluff bears S.S.E. with the North Kareki open of the South Kareki) a course can be shaped to pass between Mikoto and Ko tate (Bonnet); this course passes 2 miles to the eastward of the Fukushe, taking care to keep the peak of Sisiki on with or open to the eastward of Ho-age (Sail rock) until Kata bears East.

Vessels taking the outer passage from Simonoseki, and passing between the Goto islands and Hirado, can round the cone-shaped islet of Take sima off the south end of Hirado quite close, and to avoid the Fukushe, must either take the direct route between the islands of Otate and Yenoi or steer for the Ho-age (Sail rock), in order to run with it and Sisiki peak in line till Kata bears East.

ANCHORAGE.—Vessels passing through this strait will often find it convenient to anchor. The places recommended are Kawatchi, on the east side of Hirado and Taske on the north side, or at Kamada on the Kiusiu shore immediately north of the entrance to the strait from the northward, above mentioned.

IKUTSKI, 5½ miles long, north and south, lies close off the north-west part of Hirado sima, separated from it by the Ikutski no seto or Obree channel. Its northern points, off which is a square-topped rock, have overhanging cliffs of considerable height facing the west, with gentle slopes to the east. There are several hills on the island, the highest, being a prominent truncated cone, as seen on a south-west bearing, 929 feet above the sea. The northern part of the island is narrow, and the water deep along its coast. The south coast is bold and steep-to.

IKUTSKI NO SETO (Obree channel) is quite clear, with a depth of 11 fathoms in the middle: it is advisable to keep the Hirado coast on board when passing through, as the channel is only 2 cables wide, and the south-east point of Ikutski is low and shelving, with a 2-fathoms patch one cable off it. Anchorage inside of the south-east shore of Ikutski can be found in 7 and 8 fathoms, at about 3 cables off a village.

DO SIMA, one mile northward of Hirado, is 2½ miles long, and only 3½ cables wide at its narrowest part, it has some rounded summits of moderate elevation, showing smooth bare rocky sides. There are smaller islands and islets with rocky ledges to the south of Do sima, extending three-quarters of a mile, with one or two sunken rocks, terminating in the small islet Yoko sima, the passage south of which, between it and Hirado, is clear of known danger. There is a prominent cone-shaped islet, Taka sima, close to Do sima, the top of the cone being the highest of the hills near.

There are rocks which show above water to the northward of the east point of Do sima, the channel between Do sima and the next large island northward, Atsusi no Ōsima, being clear.

ATSUSI NO ŌSIMA lies about 5 miles to the northward of Hirado straits. It is 4½ miles long east and west, and 2¼ miles broad, and has two deep bays on its north-east and south-west sides; that on the south-west is the Port Lindesay, of the old charts and China Pilot. Its northern cape is called Nagasaki, and a large rock (Use), with several others near and around it, lies nearly 1¾ miles W. ½ S. from it, at a distance of half a mile from the shore. It is a conspicuous object when entering the Genkai nada from the south. The highest hill of Atsusi no Ōsima, 720 feet above the sea, is situated at the northern end. The island is well cultivated to the summit of the ridges, and its coasts are bold.

PORT LINDSAY, on the south side of the island, is a large bay and but for the inconvenient depth is sheltered from all winds. Anchorage in 16 fathoms can be had at the north-east end of the bay, and light draft vessels could anchor in the small inlet at the head in 5 fathoms, but with scarcely room to swing.

The COAST.—From the northern entrance to Hirado no seto, takes an E. by N. direction to Kamada, which is an excellent harbour, and is far preferable, as an anchorage, to the small and usually crowded harbour of Taske on the opposite shore of Hirado. A little further eastward is the deep bay Kubiki no ura, which would give shelter from all westerly winds. At $2\frac{3}{4}$ miles from Kubiki is Hosika saki, the southern point at the entrance to the Imari gulf.

KAMADA is a bay protected by the island of Yoko which fronts it. It is about one mile east of Hirado straits, and can be entered by steering midway between the south-east point of the island and the opposite shore in 8 fathoms water; inside there are depths of 7 and 5 fathoms. The centre of Yoko sima is connected at low water with the main by a neck of sand and shingle. This anchorage may be found useful to vessels arriving at the straits at dusk, or finding that the current through is too strong.

IMARI GULF, the outer portion of which is protected by the large island of Taka sima and Awasi sima, has three channels leading into it. The north channel is formed by the east coast of Taka sima and the main, and is clear of all dangers. Both shores are tortuously indented, and have from each projecting point ledges of rocks, extending but a short distance, and uncovering at low water. The navigable width of the channel is about 4 cables.

The whole of the channel, as well as the spacious waters inside, almost forms another harbour equal to Kariya, and excellent anchorage will be found off the village of Fuku (which is on the mainland) in depths of 12 and 10 fathoms mud.

KURO SIMA, with a cliffy face to seawards, is $3\frac{1}{2}$ miles south-west of Moko sima, and one mile off the Taka sima north coast. It has a rocky ledge from its south point.

FUKU SIMA, a large island inside of the gulf, is singularly shaped. Between its north-east coast and the main a narrow but deep passage leads to an extensive sheet of water, covered with innumerable islands and rocks, with deep water between, until arrival at its south-east point, when the rocks almost close the passage, except for boats. This portion, with a similar sheet of water and islands immediately south of Fuku sima, has not been examined. The north-west point of Fuku sima is opposite to the south-east point of Taka sima. The passage is half a mile wide. Vessels proceeding up the gulf, round the north-west point of Fuku sima, and keeping the western coast of that island on their port hand, pass the Tobi islands and islets on their starboard hand. This latter group lies off the south coast of Taka sima, at distances of three-quarters and one mile, but between this group and the south coast of Taka sima there is a clear and deep passage.

To the S.S.W. of the north cape of Taka sima, rocks and dangers exist off the shore nearly a mile, and although there is a passage of deep water between them and some rocks extending from the east point of Kuro sima, it is not advisable to take it.

South channel.—A remarkable clump of trees, on a small island, is connected with the south part of Awasi sima by a shingle beach and constructed sea-wall, and is a conspicuous object for entering Imari gulf by the south channel. This island is separated from Hosika saki of the main by a passage of 3 cables, with 13 fathoms water in the centre. There are, however, off the entrance, at 3 and 4 cables distance from the southern shore, depths of 7 and $5\frac{1}{2}$ fathoms; this shore should therefore be avoided, and by keeping rather close to the north side, and near the clump of trees point, greater depths will be obtained, that point being steep-to.

The bay immediately inside the gulf and to the southward is rocky and foul for half a mile off the shore. Vessels wishing to anchor should therefore not shut in Awasi sima, nor in anchoring anywhere along the south coast of the bay should they shut in the clump of trees, as a ledge of rocks, with shoal water, extends from the shore fully a mile.

Middle channel is formed by an island off the south-west cape of Taka sima and a small island 76 feet above the sea, with a single tree on its summit. This latter island lies to the north-east of Awasi sima, at a distance of 4 cables. The channel is $6\frac{1}{2}$ cables wide, but a shoal extends from the single-tree islet in an E.S.E. direction for nearly 2 cables; the middle island must therefore be kept on board. The passage to the southward of the single-tree islet is encumbered by a reef near the centre, and is unsafe.

KANAI SAKI is $5\frac{3}{4}$ miles E. by S. $\frac{3}{4}$ S. from the centre of the entrance of the south channel, and the gulf carries depths of from 29 to 18 fathoms across. Round to the south-west of this cape is a bay of nearly a mile in depth, where good anchorage can be found on muddy bottom.

From Kanai saki the gulf, narrowed by the southern shores of Fuku sima, runs about S. by E. $3\frac{1}{2}$ miles, carrying in the middle, depths varying from 17 to 10, 4 and 3 fathoms, where it is necessary for a vessel to anchor, as the waters shallow from here to the town of Imari.

IMARI is itself situated at the head of the gulf, from which there is a navigable channel for boats, winding amid the extensive sand flats, which

CHAP. VII.] WEST COAST OF KIUSIU—IMARI GULF. 299

uncover at low water, large portions of which, however, are being reclaimed from the sea by substantial walls. The town is small, but it is noted for having in its neighbourhood, about 7 miles distance, the finest porcelain works in Japan.

MOKO SIMA is S.W. 5 miles from Hato saki, shows bluff capes at each end, the higher part, 273 feet, being to the south-east. Off its northern end as well as on the western side a ledge of rocks uncovers at low water for 1½ cables from the shore, and from the south point there is a rock above water, with a passage between of 1½ cables width. S.S.W. about three-quarters of a mile from the south point, is a large rock above water, and from the latter a rock just awash at high water bears E.N.E. 5 cables. These rocks have deep water around and between them, and with Moko sima, face the north entrance to the gulf of Imari.

KARIYA,* the entrance to which is 2 miles east from Moko sima, is a spacious and magnificent harbour, land locked, and without a single danger inside, bottom mostly composed of mud, and depths varying from 17 fathoms at the entrance, to 12, 10, 8, and 7 inside. Its general direction is south-easterly for 1¾ miles, with an average width of three-quarters of a mile. There are several islands in the south part, as well as bays, inlets, and nooks. The village of Kariya, which gives the name to the harbour, is on the north shore. The whole harbour is enclosed by an amphitheatre of hills covered with wood, and is of great picturesque beauty.

DIRECTIONS.—From the westward, by rounding the north end of Moko sima at a distance of 3 cables, steer E. by S. ½ S. until the entrance opens, and then for it.

From the northward the entrance will be seen opening to the right of a smooth green-topped cape (that is 2½ miles S.S.W. from Hato saki), having a square-topped white rock in the foreground, which is 5½ cables outside the harbour. Keeping this on the port hand, steer for the centre of the entrance, that has on its eastern side several large rocks, detached from, but close to the shore.

YOBUKO.†—Yobuko harbour is formed by the deep indentations in the Kiusiu coast, and faced by the island of Kabe (or Kata). Yobuko, a large fishing village, is on the eastern inlet, which is 7¼ cables deep and 1½ cables wide; whilst the western branch runs south for 1½ miles, varying in breadth from one to 2 cables, with deep water. The projecting promontory between, is terminated at its north end by a low flat ledge of rocks, which partly covers at high water, but has isolated red and yellow sandstone

---

* See Chart, Hirado to Simonoseki, No. 127; scale, $m = 1 \cdot 0$ inches.

† See Plan, Yobuko harbour, No. 141; scale, $m = 4 \cdot 5$ inches.

islets, with trees, between the extreme point of which and the southern point of Kabe sima there is a very narrow passage of half a cable wide, with 12 and 16 fathoms water in it, and which is used by the junks in passing from one harbour to the other, and called Ben-ten no seto.

From the western arm the coast trends with rocky points and sandy beaches to the north-west for 2 miles, to Hato saki. The island of Kabe gives protection to these inlets. The eastern is open to the north-east, but the outside islands in a great measure shelter the entrance, which is only $3\frac{1}{2}$ cables wide. The western or southern inlet, although narrow, affords shelter, and has a large village called Nagoya on its western side. This inlet, taking a southerly direction, carries deep water for 8 cables, and then trends to the S.S.E. for half a mile, with shallow waters at its head; the inlet, however, is very narrow.

Taka sima.—Off the eastern entrance is a steep islet covered with trees, 209 feet high.

Me-se, a low flat rock, 20 feet above water, lies half a mile to the north-west of Taka sima.

HATO SAKI, the west point of entrance to Yobuko harbour, is low and rocky, with a remarkable square clump of trees on it, which makes like an islet when first seen from the south-westward. The coast to the southward is much indented with long rocky points extending from the shore into deep water.

KABE SIMA.—The clump of trees on the southern end is 412 feet above the sea, and the highest part of the island. The village is on the south side, where numerous junks collect in bad weather, waiting to round into Karatsu bay for coals. The northern coast of the island is cliffy, black basalt; and all the shores are steep-to.

HIRASE (Passage reef) is $1\frac{1}{4}$ miles N. by E. from Taka sima, and at its north and south end are fish towers, 20 feet above water. The reef is $3\frac{1}{2}$ cables long, and shows at low water. From its south point shoal water extends for 3 cables, with $4\frac{3}{4}$ fathoms on the end. A mid course between any of the islets and reefs is safe and clear.

DIRECTIONS.—Yobuko harbour is easy to enter, the western entrance being bold, broad, and deep. If from the eastward, the prominent object of Taka sima is a good guide to its entrance, and by keeping a mid-channel course vessels can enter and anchor in 14 and 12 fathoms in the centre. There is a remarkable square clump of fir trees on the low rocky point of Hato saki, which makes like an islet when seen from the westward or south-westward. The point and rocks off Hato saki at low water extend some distance out, and must be given a wide berth. The clump or tuft of trees on Kabe sima, bearing S.E. $\frac{1}{4}$ E. will lead clear,

After rounding the point, a mid-channel course leads up to an anchorage as convenient. A long vessel should anchor due south of the tuft of trees on Kabe sima in 10 or 12 fathoms.

TIDES.—It is high water, full and change, in Yobuko harbour at 11h. 16m.; spring ranges 9 feet, neaps, 4 feet.

MADARA SIMA, lying $3\frac{3}{4}$ miles to the westward of Hato saki, is $1\frac{1}{2}$ miles east and west and three-quarters north and south; it is steep-to and bold on all sides. There are two rocks above water, distant from the shore $1\frac{3}{4}$ cables, off its west and south west points. The highest peak, which is round and flat, is 795 feet above the sea, to which is joined by a spur the western peak, 659 feet high, that falls steeply to the sea over a cliff-bound shore. The island is intersected by a valley, fronting which, on the south-east, is a small sandy bay and village, sheltered by a small bold promontory, which forms the south point of the island. The eastern part of the island is a smooth round hill.

All these islands have fishing villages on them. The passages between Madara sima, Mats' sima, and Iki sima are safe and clear, and carry deep-water.

FUTAKAMI.—North $5\frac{1}{2}$ miles from Atsusi no Ōsima, and 9 miles W. by N. from Madara sima, is a saddle-shaped island, 6 cables long and 316 feet high, with steep cliffs.

Ko Futakami.—A wedged-shaped rock 176 feet high lies W. by N. $\frac{1}{4}$ N. $1\frac{3}{4}$ miles, from Futakami.

Kanatōo, lying 6 cables E.N.E. from Futakami, is a small rock above water. Around these islets, and in the channels between them and Iki sima, the depths are 47 to 34 fathoms sand.

KAGARA SIMA is the centre and largest of three islands off the main, immediately north of the entrance to Yobuko. It is $1\frac{3}{4}$ miles long, north and south, and three-quarters of a mile broad, and is steep-to, but off its south point, at $2\frac{1}{2}$ cables, is a low flat rock which nearly covers at high water. Oögawa clump, N.E. by E. $\frac{1}{2}$ E. leads clear to the southward of it.

MATSŬ SIMA lies close off the south-west part of Kagara, the passage between is $2\frac{1}{2}$ cables wide, and carries 5 and 7 fathoms water in it. A rock above water lies at the centre of the passage at its south end, and the south-west point of Mats' sima has rocks off it.

OÖGAWA SIMA, the eastern island of the three, is low, with a clump of trees on its south-east head, 245 feet above the sea; a good object to steer for, in passing through the channel to the eastward of Oögawa. (There is also a high clump of trees on the south end of Kabe sima, at the entrance of Yobuko harbour, which is a conspicuous object on approach.)

The passage between Oögawa and Kagara is quite clear and deep, and is one mile wide. Vessels usually take the passage south of Oögawa, which is the best.

IKI SIMA is the western island of the Genkai nada, and the largest off the north-west coast of Kiusiu; it is 10 miles long north and south, and 6 miles average breadth, and lies 8½ miles north-west from Kagara sima. It is of sandstone and basaltic formation, chiefly table land, the southern part rising to an elevation of 696 feet, and its north-east hill about 500 feet. There are many islands and reefs off its shores, the deep indentations of which afford anchorage in well sheltered harbours. The western and southern coasts have been well examined, but the northern and eastern, with the bays of Moro-yosi, only partially. Reefs, however, were seen to extend a considerable distance off the eastern coast, and shoal water in patches was found in that vicinity, and off the low islands of Na sima; and then still farther out the rocky islets of Idzumi (which are only 14 feet above water).*

GO NO URA, on the south coast, is a deep indentation of the shore, with depths of from 20 to 12 fathoms. Near the centre there is a rock, that covers at high water, opposite to which, on the eastern shore, a ledge of rocks, partly uncovering at low water, extends 2¾ cables. There is also a dangerous ledge of rocks facing a deep inlet, near the southern entrance of the bay on the east side. This bay affords shelter from almost any wind, except from South, when a vessel would find protection by hauling into the north-east corner, from which a narrow and deep inlet winds to the large village. There are five islands and numerous rocks to the south-west of this bay, the southern of which, Hira sima, is steep-to on its south side, but very foul on its north, where a reef of rocks above and under water to the north-west and north-east extends half a mile. The passages between the islands, although having deep water, are nevertheless full of rocks and uneven bottom, and should not be used. The northern island, Oösima, has not been examined on its western side; but between its eastern point and the coast of Iki sima, a narrow channel, having only 3 fathoms in it, is used by the native craft, but cannot be recommended for shipping. The east point of this channel has a large clump of trees, which from the southward makes as a conspicuous object. The south-eastern outline of this bay is rocky, with ledges off the points, and terminated by the bluff point of Ko saki, whose summit is smooth and grassy. W. by N. ¼ N. little more than one mile from Ko saki is a rock above water.

DIRECTIONS.—Vessels from the westward, bound for the inland sea, and finding bad weather coming on from the north or west, will find

---

* Commander E. W. Brooker, R.N., H.M.S. *Sylvia*, 1868.

Go no ura convenient and safe. From the westward, steer for the south point of Hira sima (the outer or southern island, which has a smooth top with black cliffy and rocky shores), giving it a berth of from 2 to 3 cables, then steering E. by N. for the next low rocky islet, giving it a berth of half a mile; haul up N. by E. ½ E., anchoring near the head of the bay in 12 fathoms, remembering the low rock on the port hand, just above water, when passing up the bay. From the eastward, vessels must remember, before making the south coast of Iki sima, the 8-feet rock which lies to the southward of the Idzumi islets, when they can steer for Ko saki (the southern cape), from which the coast should not be approached nearer than half a mile, to avoid the rock above water, and the ledges farther to the northward.

KOÖZE NO URA.—On the west side of Iki sima is a narrow inlet of the coast, 2 miles deep, with numerous indentations, but not to be recommended for shipping, as the swell caused by north-east winds curves round the north end of this island, and rolls into this bay.

YU NO URA, on the north-west coast of Iki sima, is a deep bay, with several islets and rocks in it, but giving shelter when inside, the navigation of which, however, is difficult for the stranger. The anchorage of Katsu-moto no ura on the northern coast of Iki sima cannot be recommended, as the coast is wild and rocky, and the northern islets give but little shelter from the heavy swell which rolls round the coast in north-east winds. The north coast of Iki can be approached to one mile.

NA SIMA.—A cluster of rocks and islets, about 1½ miles long E.N.E. and W.S.W., lies about 3 miles off the east coast of Iki sima; the southern islet is flat-topped, and 60 feet above the sea.

Idzumi islets lie to the eastward of Na sima, at about 2 miles distance, they consist of two low flat rocks only 14 feet above water. Between Na sima and the Idzumi islets, the soundings are uneven, and probably more dangers exist.

A rock, with 8 feet water only, lies at three-quarters of a mile S.S.W. from the outer (Kami) of the Idzumi islets.

TEBOSI SIMA is 25 miles S.W. by W. ¾ W. from Wilson island, and S.E. ¼ E. 4 miles from Kami Idzumi. This islet is situated in the centre of the southern portion of the Genkai nada, and is a most useful guide to avoid its dangers. It is of triangular shape, as seen from the east, but is more lumpy from north and north-west, and formed of basalt, which is extraordinarily contorted; it is 160 feet above the sea, and quite steep-to. The dangers alluded to, which exist in the eastern portion of the Genkai nada, are the Kuri no kami, Nagamo, and Noöze reefs.

GENKAI NADA is the sea comprised between Iki sima, Oro no sima, and Kosime no Oösima, and the mainland of Kiusiu. With the exception of the rock above mentioned, as lying three-quarters of a mile southward of the low flat rocks of Idzumi, off the eastern coast of Iki sima, the western portion of this sea is free from all dangers, the soundings varying from 20 to 30 fathoms with generally a sandy bottom; coral and shells are occasionally obtained, but very little gravel.

In the eastern waters of the Genkai nada, in which a depth of 20 fathoms and under is found, there are three tidal and sunken dangers, viz.: the Noöze, Nagamo, and Kuri no kami reefs, and as they are nearly awash at high water, and steep-to, great care in the navigation is required in thick weather. In ordinary weather the usual route taken by steamers is easy and safe.

TIDES.—The flood streams meet off Hakosaki about the centre of the Genkai nada, and the ebb separate. The velocity at springs is 1½ knots.

KARATSU NO URA.—Keya saki, Hime sima, and Kasira sima are the outer protections of this bay, which is about 7 miles deep, with an eastern arm of 5½ miles; in which are two smaller bays called Shin-matchi no ura and Funa-goshi. In the latter the best anchorage is obtained in 4 and 5 fathoms.

In the south part of the bay are the islands of Oö, Taki, and Tori, lying immediately off the town of Karatsu, affording but little shelter to vessels during northerly winds, when a heavy swell and sea rolls in. Taka sima, 553 feet above the sea, has a square smooth top on its north side, with slopes to the southward, and trees on its south-east point. The native craft, however, being of light draft, can obtain protection immediately south of these islands, while the greater portion get into the estuary of the Matsura kawa, which flows into the bay near the walled-in residence of the Daimio,* the fine trees surrounding the place being a conspicuous feature on the south shore of this bay. Considerable coasting trade is carried on from Karatsu by the junks, which load with coal, brought from the mines, situated on the left bank of the river, about 6 miles distance from the entrance. There are also extensive porcelain manufactories at Karatsu.

Some large sandstone boulders with sand form a barrier to the entrance of the river, and cause a deep channel on the west side, through which the tidal waters rush with great force. The depths in the bay are even and gradual, with mostly sandy bottom.

HIME SIMA, 645 feet in height, is 1¾ miles to the westward of the bluff cape of Keya saki. It is about half a mile in diameter, covered with trees, with a yellow stripe on its north-west side. From the south

---

* Prince of Satou.

point of this island, extending South 8 cables, is a bank of sand and gravel, which uncovers at low water. There is a deep channel between Hime sima and the double capes of the promontory of the mainland.

A reef of rocks, the outer of which is nearly a mile from the shore, lies to the W.N.W. of the cape which forms the northern side of Shin-matchi no ura, and South $8\frac{1}{4}$ cables from Keya saki.

The coast of Karatsu bay is low and sandy, with rocky points, and the ranges of hills inland are extremely bold and picturesque, having a prominent peak with a small square top rising to a height of 2,685 feet, and called Uki take. A considerable stream winds at the foot of this ridge, between which and the Karatsu river is a table-topped mountain, terminating about one mile from the town of Karatsu.

TAKA SIMA, 553 feet in height, has a square smooth top on its north side with slopes to the southward, and trees on the south-east point.

KASIRA SIMA, 281 feet in height, the western island of the bay, lies close to the coast of Kiusiu. The passage between is shallow, and only used by junks; it is nearly one mile long, with a low rounding spit of shingle and sand from the northern end, forming a bay with only one fathom in it. Near the centre of the island a tall tree is conspicuous.

DIRECTIONS.—The depths in Karatsu bay are from 18 to 5 fathoms sand, gradually decreasing; it affords good shelter from all winds, except with those from north-west to north-east, when a heavy sea rolls into the bay. The bay of Funa-goshi then offers the best shelter, and vessels running for that anchorage must bear in mind the low long shingle spit which uncovers at low water, and extends due south from Hime sima 8 cables. The passage between Hime sima and Keya saki is clear in the middle, and the little rocky islet near the western point of Funa-goshi bay can be rounded at $1\frac{1}{2}$ cables. The depths in that bay are from 5 to 3 fathoms and under.

Vessels intending to anchor in Karatsu bay can round the north side of Kasira sima at 6, and the east side of Taka sima at 3 cables, and anchor as convenient. The passages westward of Taka sima are not recommended.

The COAST.—From Keya saki the coast trends N.E. by E. 8 miles to Hakosaki no ura, with some indentations that afford no anchorage. The ridges of hills are of moderate elevation and irregular in shape, having near Keya saki a white sandy soil mixed with red sandstone, with but few trees. The coast is sandy, with a few bold rocky projecting points. There is an islet in one bay to the south, at three-quarters of a mile from the beach.

WOOZE (Dove reef), which shows some round boulder heads, lies off the coast at a distance of $2\frac{1}{2}$ miles nearly. It is $2\frac{1}{2}$ cables in extent, with depths of 4½, 9, and 8 fathoms immediately around; it may be passed at half a mile on the outside, in 18 and 20 fathoms sand.

NAGAMO (Ellis reef), lying 3 miles N.E. by N. from Noöze, is more out of the fairway of vessels making a direct course through the Genkai nada. It bears from Yebosi sima E. ¼ N. 8 miles, and from Toö-dai (the nine-pin rock off Genkai sima) W. by N. 3¼ miles. It never quite uncovers, but in bad weather the heads of the rocks are seen. To the southeast for 2 cables, there are depths of 4 fathoms; and at three-quarters of a mile S.S.E. a patch of rocky ground lies, with 4 and 4¼ fathoms, the least water on it. To the south-west, west, and north-west of this reef, at 2 cables, there are from 15 to 20 fathoms.

HAKOSAKI BAY is a deep inlet with an easterly direction of about 10 miles, and a general width of 3 miles. The outer portion of this bay, carrying in its centre 9, 10, and 11 fathoms, is protected from all westerly winds by Genkai sima and islets in the passage between that island and the southern projecting promontory from the mainland. The entrance between Genkai and Siga sima is about 2 miles wide, and a considerable sea rolls in with northerly winds.

The eastern or inner part of the bay is effectually protected from any sea by the island of Noko no sima, which lies at right angles to the bay. The depth of water, however, in this part of the bay soon shoals after passing Noko no sima to 5 and 4 fathoms, and 3 fathoms off the town, gradually lessening towards the head of the bay. The shores of the inner bay are low and sandy, and on the south side stands the large and straggling city of Fukuoka, the capital and fortress of the Prince of Chikuzen.

Two rapid streams flow into this bay, after wandering through considerable plains, under rich cultivation; the nature of the country at the back, or south of the city, is mountainous with much wood, the upper ridges and peaks attaining an elevation of from 2,000 to 3,000 feet.

SIGA SIMA, the northern island of the bay, is 1¾ miles long and 1¼ in breadth, with a ridge of hills much wooded and irregularly shaped, having a smooth grassy sharp peak near its northern end. The island is connected with the main from its south-east point by a narrow sand bank, which uncovers at low water.

The shores of this island are rocky. W. by N. ½ N. from the north-west point, rocks awash extend 8½ cables. Caution is therefore necessary when entering the bay.

NOKO NO SIMA is a long narrow wooded island, its green summit being 454 feet above the sea; between it and Siga sima there is a clear passage of one mile wide, carrying 9 and 10 fathoms in the middle and deeper towards Noko no sima than Siga sima. The western shore of this island has a prominent rock off it (Hasira sima), and generally shoal water. There is a passage to the south of this island, but having only 3 fathoms in it at low water.

GENKAI SIMA, facing the centre of the outer portion of the bay, is round topped and steep sided; its summit is 740 feet above the sea.

Toŏ-dai, a nine-pin shaped rock, lies 3¾ cables W.N.W. from the island, with rocky and shoal water between, but to seaward and near, deep water. Both Genkai and Siga sima have large fishing villages on them.

Immediately south of Genkai sima are two smooth-topped islets, (the western one being surmounted by a solitary tree,) with bluff coasts. They are small, and have to the south-east a rock nearly always uncovered. A little to the southward of this rock, and surrounding the islets, with a connection from the south point of Genkai sima, is a bank of sand, carrying as little as 3 fathoms near the centre of the northern passage; but the channel to the southward of the islets carries between them and the point Nisi-wura saki of the main, 7, 6, and 5 fathoms, the point being steep-to.

DIRECTIONS.—To enter Hakosaki bay from the southward. The points of the mainland must be kept about half a mile distant, and when the north end of Noko no sima is seen well open of Nisi-wura saki, bearing S.E. by E. ¾ E.; it can be steered for, giving the cape a berth of 1½ or 2 cables.

Most vessels, however, enter the bay by the north channel, and great care is required to avoid the dangerous reef of rocks which lie on the west side of the north point of Siga sima, and also some rocks above water and others awash 3¼ cables immediately north of Genkai sima. A mid course between the islands of Genkai and Siga is the best, and when the northern end of Noko no sima is well open of the southern points of Siga sima bearing S.E. by S., a vessel may haul up for Noko no sima, as she will then be clear of the Siga sima shoals, if seeking shelter from westerly winds. By hauling round the eastern side of Noko no sima, excellent anchorage will be found in convenient depths; but it must be remembered that soon after passing the north end of Noko no sima, and hauling round to the south, 6, 5, and 4 fathoms are obtained.

The COAST.—From Siga sima to Chi-a saki the coast is low and sandy, and, with the exception of one small rocky point, trends in a curve to the S.S.W., having sand hills at the back terminating in the north entrance to Hakosaki bay, which is at low water connected by a sand bank with the island of Siga sima. From Siga sima to Chi-a saki the coast can be approached to a half or three-quarters of a mile, except near the head of Watari bay, when a wider berth must be given; 5 fathoms should be the least water when nearing the coast.

The conspicuous feature in the mountain scenery along this coast is the sharp double-peaked hill Tadchi yama, 1,335 feet above the sea, which overlooks the head of Hakosaki bay.

To the southward of Chi-a saki, a rocky ledge which partly uncovers, extends 2 cables, and gives shelter to the native craft at the head of the bay of Watari mura, from all westerly winds. At the head of this bay an inlet was observed, leading into an inner harbour with numerous junks in it; and the village of Watari, from its size, indicated considerable coasting trade.

Northward of Chi-a saki the coast is moderately low and wooded (but rocky in the immediate vicinity of Chi-a saki) as far as Katsura saki, off which is a small red sandstone islet conspicuous from its having a single tree upon it. Beyond Katsura saki the hills gradually increase in elevation to lofty double peaks, 1,900 and 1,978 feet in height over Kanega saki, high mountains being visible inland.

KOKO SIMA lies off Kanega saki, from the south-east point of the island a long gravel and boulder spit extends to the south-east for 1½ miles towards the mainland leaving a narrow passage between. The spit is usually strongly marked by the tides, which cause heavy overfalls and breakers on it.

ANCHORAGE.—Good anchorage may be obtained in 5 to 7 fathoms, half a mile east of the south point of Koko sima, sheltered from westerly winds by the island and spit; there is also anchorage on its west side.

ROUND ROCK lies 7½ cables from Koko sima with deep water between.

KATSU URA is a bay on the mainland, sheltered on the north-east side by Koko sima, and the spit above mentioned. It is sheltered from all winds except those from N.W. and W.S.W.

KOSIME NO OŌSIMA (Wilson island), lying 5 miles off the northern coast of Kiusiu, and 2 miles W.S.W. from Koko sima, is remarkable from its prominent position off the entrance to the Inland sea; it is flat, 6 miles in circumference, and surmounted by a clump of trees, the highest part being 854 feet above the sea, and visible in clear weather 30 miles. The western side is generally rocky and steep-to. There is a large fishing village on its eastern shore in a small bay between two rocky points, off which rocks and foul ground extend for nearly a mile.

The Serpent rock, with only 6 feet at low water and 6 fathoms on either side, lies immediately off the village on Wilson island. It is nearly one mile from the north point of the island, and vessels, when running through Katsu ura, after passing Round rock, must steer for Katsu sima (which has a conspicuous round cone summit) until about one mile from it, when they will be clear of the rock and also of shoal water off the south point of Wilson island. Coming from the southward, vessels should close Katsu sima, and steer for the north part of Koko sima and Round rock.

Shoal patch.—A patch of 15 feet, rock, lies E. ½ N., northerly, 3⅔ miles from the north point of Koko sima, with the outer high peak of Kiusiu (1,900 feet), bearing S. by W. ¼ W. 3¼ miles. The clump on Kosime no Ōsima, kept open of the north point of Koko sima, leads northward of it.

AI SIMA, lying 8¼ miles S.S.W. from Wilson island, is a table land 240 feet above the sea, with bluffs to seaward, on which a single tree shows conspicuously. The island is about 2 miles round and steep-to, having a bay on the south side which would afford fair shelter to a vessel from almost all winds (the villagers who live on the island, and have their houses close to the beach, say that even in the westerly gales of winter, the bay gives good shelter); the depth, however, is great, and anchorage in 10 fathoms is close to the shore, farther out 15 fathoms. The eastern end of the island has a hummock, which from a distance makes like an island. Off the east point, and 1½ cables distant, is a remarkable arched rock of basaltic formation (Hana-guru), the passage between carrying 6 or 8 fathoms of rocky bottom. Between Ai sima and the mainland there are no dangers, the depths towards the shore being 14 to 7 fathoms.

KURI NO KAMI (Swain reef), is a cluster of rocks, about 3 cables in extent, some of which always show above water, and the depths around vary from 14 to 27 fathoms. It is N.E. 8 miles from Nagamo (Ellis reef), and N.W. by W. ¼ W. 5 miles from Ai sima, and E.S.E. 11½ miles from Oro no sima; this is the principal danger, and lies in the fairway through the Genkai nada.

ORO NO SIMA (Obree island).—Thirty-seven miles W. by S. from Siro sima, at the entrance to the Inland sea, is a double-topped island, the southern of which and the higher is elevated 276 feet. This island is nearly half a mile in breadth and elongated in a N. by W. and S. by E. direction three-quarters of a mile, with its eastern side of bold cliffs; a clump of trees crests the southern hill, and the village is on the south point; the inhabitants are few and wretchedly poor, apparently subsisting on fish and the barest of productions from the island. It is quite steep-to, and can be approached on the southern and eastern sides to within half a mile; two rocks extend from its northern point half a cable.

There are no dangers between this island and Iki sima and Wilson island, and it is believed none exist to the northward between Kotsu sima or Tsu sima, or to the entrance of the Inland sea.

KOTSU SIMA (Colnet island) lies in the Korea strait nearly midway between the east coast of Tsu sima and the western entrance of the

Inland sea. In clear weather it can be seen from Iki sima, Tsu sima, and the coast. It is a mile wide at its broadest part, its sides are steep, with a high cliff at the north-east point, and rise with slight irregularities to a central peak 800 feet high. At a great distance the slopes appear even. Four notched rocks or islets, 80 feet high, and visible 12 miles, lie 4 cables S.E. by S. of the south point.

The COAST from Kanega saki abreast Wilson island trends to the east-north-east, 8½ miles to the Iwaya point, eastward of which the coast forms the southern shore of the approach to Simonoseki strait. Rocky patches exist to the eastward of Koko sima, and as this part has not been very closely examined, the navigator should therefore use great caution in approaching the coast closely between Kanega saki and Iwaya point.*

DIRECTIONS.—From NAGASAKI to SIMONOSEKI.—The coast route is taken by vessels who know the land, and in thick weather prefer to sight it, and feel their way along from point to point; they steer for the square rock Kashe (East rock), and pass between it and the arch rock Tengo, or rather Hako sima, which is to the eastward of the arch rock, making for the south coast of Mats' sima, the western coast of the last island being safe at 2 cables distance off shore, taking care of the rock above water off its north-west shore.

The western cape of Mikoto sima can be approached to 3 cables, and from here, in clear weather, a course may be shaped to the westward of Kata sima, up to Taka sima, passing eastward of Kuro sima, and thence along but outside of the islands which lie off the coast of Kiusiu, and forms the east side of the Hirado straits.

A more direct course from Nagasaki harbour is to steer straight for Ko tate (Bonnet rock), but allowance must be made for the current which is in the vicinity of Oö tate, and to the southward sets north-west and south-east, so that a vessel in thick weather finds herself either to the westward and northward of her reckoning, or to the eastward, and towards the main; but, having sighted the cone-shaped easily distinguished Ko tate (Bonnet), she can steer for the bold bluff of Kuro sima, bearing in mind that great danger the Fukushe, which lies north 4½ miles from Ko tate.

The southern coast of Kuro sima is steep close-to, and the perpendicular cliffs at its western end loom up in thick weather. The mariner, however, must remember that off its western end, and separated by a passage of 2½ cables, is a low flat rock, above water, with deep water close to it. After sighting the bluffs, vessels should steer for the south coast of Hirado, which can be boldly approached to one or 2 cables, and by

---

* For western approach to Inland sea and Simonoseki strait, *see* page 262.

keeping it in sight at 2 cables distance the Costa Rica and Robinett rocks will be avoided. Vessels can run along the east coast of Hirado to the north as far as Kawatchi bay, when it is necessary to steer for the opposite shore, to avoid the Asama, before entering the narrow part of Hirado straits, at the red cliff point, from which the vessel must be guided by the sailing directions. (See directions for Hirado no seto, page 294.)

From Hirado straits to the north there are no difficulties in clear weather. A straight course for Mats' sima, passing eastward of Madara sima, and giving the rocks off Hato saki a good berth; passing to the eastward of Oögawa sima, enter the Genkai nada, having the conspicuous cone islet of Yebosi as a good mark, which can be steered for, and a course shaped to go outside of Wilson Island, taking care to look out for the Kuri no kami (Swain reef).

Another route from Nagasaki is to steer for Oö tate, and take the clear channel between it and Yenoi sima, passing up the west coasts of Hirado and Ikutski, and enter the Genkai nada by the channel south of Iki sima. In this route, the rock south of the Idzumi islets must be remembered.

If proceeding outside Hirado, after leaving Nagasaki steer N.W., unless wishing to pass outside Hiki sima. A run of 16 miles will place a ship abreast that island, and a further run of 13 miles on the same course will lead up mid-channel between Oö tate and Yenoi sima, from which position a N.N.W. course for 11 miles will reach the islets off the south-west point of Hirado. Pass a mile outside these islets, and also of the Aska sima 3 miles north of them, unless intending to take the Obree channel (page 296), in which case the ship may pass between Ko Azika sima and Kasira, and steer N.E. by N. directly for it.

Coasting Hirado and Ikutski on a N.N.E. course, a run of $13\frac{1}{2}$ miles from Oö Azika sima will place a vessel off the north point of Ikutski; then steer N.E. by E. for 7 miles until past Use, the small rocky patch off the north-western face of Atsusi no Ōsima, which, if not seen, may be cleared by keeping the summit of Madara in line with the summit of Mats' sima E. $\frac{1}{2}$ N. Giving Use a berth of $1\frac{1}{2}$ miles a course E. by N. $\frac{3}{4}$ N. leads up in mid-channel between the rock lying to the southward of Kami Idzumi and Yebosi, and when the latter island bears S.E. alter course N.E. by E. $\frac{1}{4}$ E. to clear Kuri no kami and pass northward of Wilson island, being careful lest the eastern tidal stream into the strait of Simonoseki, which sets rather strongly through the channels east of Wilson island, should saddle the vessel on to that reef. (See directions for the Inland sea, page 262.)

Through Hirado Strait.—The inner passage from Nagasaki to the Inland sea by Hirado strait, is 15 miles less in distance than that outside Hirado, but it is seldom that a vessel is not obliged to anchor somewhere for the night. From the entrance of Nagasaki, steer as above directed for the southern entrance to Hirado strait. (See Directions for Hirado no seto, p. 294.)

When clear of the northern entrance of the strait, the course along the land is N.E. by E. to Hato saki, distant 17 miles, steering for the clump beyond it which is on the east bluff of Oögawa sima, the eastern of the three islands north of Hato saki and Yobuko, and passing between the bluff on the south-east point of the island and Hirase (Passage rocks). The same course will lead well outside Nooze and Nagamo reefs (which are 3 miles off shore and may both be covered), and outside but rather close to Kuri no kami (Swain reef).

Another track may be pursued from Hirado strait, steering from it on a N.E. ¼ E. course to pass between Madara and Kagara, and rounding the north-west point of the latter at a mile; from this a N.E. by E. ½ E. course will lead up close to the west point of Wilson island, passing half a mile to the westward of Yebosi, between it and the rock off the Idzumi islets above mentioned.

Should the passage have been made by the Korea strait, after rounding the north point of Iki, an E. ¾ N. course may be steered for the Siro simas at the entrance of the Inland sea, passing well northward of Oro no sima with a clear run of 55 miles. The tidal streams here are not very well known.

THE WEST COAST OF NIPON.

The west coast of Nipon is but little known, and should therefore be navigated with necessary prudence and caution. The only parts at present surveyed are the islands Sado, Awa sima, and Tabu sima, and the strait between Sado and Niëgata, by H.M. ships *Actæon* and *Dove* in 1859. The coast from Tsugar strait (page 325) to cape Noto has been partially explored by the *Bittern* and other of H.M. ships, the Russian gun vessel *Djigit*, and H.M. surveying vessel *Saracen*. The latter vessel has also explored the coast between Simonoseki, the western entrance of the Inland sea, and Taka yama (cape Louisa), lat. 34° 40′ N.

The Coast* between cape Louisa and Sado does not appear ever to have been sighted by European ships; its coast line has been taken from the Japanese manuscript, and may, with the exception of possible dangers off it, be regarded as accurately delineated.

From the entrance to Simonoseki strait the coast trends to the northward as far as Kado sima, and is approached by a very even and

---

* *See* Chart:—Korea Strait and Western Coasts of Kiusiu and Nipon, No. 358; scale, m = 0·15 of an inch.

gradually decreasing depth. The shore should be given a berth as where surveyed or seen it was found to be very rocky.

KADO SIMA is one mile off the south point of entrance to Igama bay. It is 2½ miles long, E.N.E. and W.S.W., and of very peculiar formation as seen from the north, being divided nearly equally into two very flat quoins, the points of the wedges being both to the westward, and their steep falls to the east.

IGAMA BAY is an inlet running in 7 miles in an easterly direction on the south side of Natsungi saki. Some islets or rocks lie off its north entrance point, which is much lower than the land of Natsungi saki, to which it is only joined by a low neck. A double-topped hill is seen on the south shore of the inlet. The north-western corner would appear to afford the best anchorage, but no part of it has been explored.

NATSUNGI SAKI is the northern extremity of the western prolongation of the toe of Nipon; it is 30 miles northward of the western entrance of the Inland sea. It appeared to be about 700 feet high, with a nippled outline, bordered by high cliffs on the north, and slightly tapering towards the sea, where it was about 500 feet in height. It may be easily known by the remarkable square rock or head springing from its base, and which, being entirely detached from the high land of the point gives it the appearance of an island. Seen at the distance of 24 miles from the north-east, it assumes the appearance of gently shelving tableland having three or four large notches, the sharp cone of Aoumi sima and the distant summit of Kabuto yama showing to the eastward. This sharp and remarkable cone of 700 feet elevation marks the eastern point of the deep bay of Fukugawa.

AOUMI SIMA, 4½ miles in length east and west, is 10 miles east of Natsungi saki, its western point being the sharp cone before alluded to. On the Japanese chart there is represented between this island and the coast, a finely sheltered and capacious harbour called Misumi, accessible by a broad channel from the eastward, where lie some islets, and also from the bay of Fukugawa on the west by a narrow channel between the south part of Aoumi sima and a projecting point of the coast.

CAUTION.—Between Ai sima and the east part of Aoumi sima, the *Saracen's* track survey represents four doubtful islets, which do not appear on the Japanese manuscript.

AI SIMA, or Richards island.—Between Natsungi saki and cape Louisa, there is a large bay with many islands in it, generally about 200 feet high and flat-topped with cliffy inaccessible sides. The largest are Ai sima and O sima. Ai sima, the outer, is midway between the above capes and just within the chord of the bay; it is elevated 400 feet, having a flat-topped hill in its centre. O sima, 5 miles east of Ai sima, is also 400 feet high, but longer and flatter. The depth is 40 fathoms, 1½ miles E.N.E. of Ai sima.

TAKA YAMA (cape Louisa) is a remarkable sharp peak, 1,800 feet in height, on a projecting and very prominent point of the coast, 34 miles E. by N. ¾ N. from Natsungi saki. It has a second and lower peak on its north-east slope, and an islet off its north point. This peak appears quite isolated as seen from the vicinity of Natsungi saki.

MINO SIMA is in lat. 34° 47′ N., long. 131° 7′ E., W. by N. ¾ N. distant 24 miles from Taka yama, and 20 miles distant from the northern coast of the province of Nagato which forms the foot of Nipon. Approached from the northward, at 9 miles distance it appears much extended with an undulating outline, its highest part, elevated 492 feet, being in the centre of its west side. On nearer approach, its sides appear steep and cliffy, except on the north-east where there is a sandy bay. A large square rock lies half a cable off its eastern point, and there is an islet on its north-west side.

East 10 miles from Mino sima, soundings of 59 fathoms, sand and shells, were obtained by the *Saracen*, in 1855, from which position an even bottom was carried towards the land with very little decrease in the depths. A bank of 35 to 39 fathoms water extends about 4 miles north and north-east of the island.

MIKU URA, in latitude 35° 32′ N., longitude 133° 24′ E. affords an excellent anchorage in 9 fathoms, mud; shelter (except with winds from the East, which are of little consequence) can be obtained. Rocks are said to lie off the lagoon opening on the south side.

HAKI or HANGI BAY.—The anchorage off the town is bad, being quite open to the west, but good shelter may be found inside the North head (a smooth green head with a conspicuous tree or clump on it) to the north-east of the town, entirely land-locked, in 9 fathoms. The shore between Haki and Se saki has foul ground lying off it.

OKI ISLANDS.—The Oki group, consisting of one large and a group of three smaller islands, and a number of islets and rocks, lie N.E. and S.W. of each other, and occupy an extent of 23 miles in that direction. There is an open and apparently safe channel between the large islands and the group of smaller ones.

Oki sima, the north-east or largest island, about 10 miles in diameter, has a number of detached high rocks close to its northern point, which is steep and cliffy. Its south-west extreme is remarkable from its terminating in a high steep bluff; its south-east point is comparatively low. The highest part of the island was estimated at 3,000 feet elevation, but no indication of a port, nor even the prospect of tolerable anchorage, was observed along its western shore.

The group of three islands is about 9 miles in diameter, and probably good anchorage may be found as there are deeply indented bays. The north point of Nisi sima, the western of the three, rises to a sharp peak of 1,700 feet elevation; the other two are about half that height. They appear to be thickly populated, and the hills are cultivated to their summits. There are three or four islets lying north-eastward of them, separated by channels apparently not exceeding half a mile wide, but they appear rocky and precipitous.

A track survey was made of the western side of this group, and the sun peeping out for a minute the time was obtained, but bad weather setting in soon after prevented Mr. Richards completing what was begun, and for the latitude of the north point of Oki sima he is indebted to Mr. Collingwood, who passed it near noon on two several occasions in the hired steamer *Tartar*. Taking this latitude 36° 30′ N.,* the longitude of the north point of the island was found to be in 133° 23′ E.

MIYADSU,† an excellent harbour, completely land-locked, with good holding ground, situated in about lat. 35° 32′ N., long. 135° 15′ E., is easy of ingress and egress, and free from dangers. The shoalest water is on the western shore, and a rock exists on the eastern side of the entrance between the two inner points.

At the right of the town, and off a sand-bank about 150 yards, there is one fathom water. Outside a line drawn from this spot to the battery, soundings of five fathoms may be found within three ships' lengths from the shore anywhere around the harbour; within this line it is shallow.

A spit, with only 9 feet of water, makes out about one third of a mile from a yellowish clayey bank in the western angle of the harbour.

The town contains about 12,000 inhabitants. Silk is manufactured in the neighbourhood, and this is a great mart for dried fish. A four-gun battery is erected in front of the Damio's residence, but the guns are old and worthless.

DIRECTIONS.—With the southernmost of the Okino islands, bearing N.E. ¾ E., steer S.W. ¾ W. between Whale point and Kata sima; then steer S.W. ¾ S. until at the mouth of the harbour, when steer direct for the battery, keeping in mid-channel up to the anchorage. The soundings from the mouth of the harbour will gradually decrease from 11 to 7 and 6 fathoms to abreast of the town, with bottom of sticky mud.

---

* The Japanese map places it in lat. 36° 20′ N.
† *See* Plan of Miyadsu on sheet No. 61.

ANCHORAGE.—The best place to anchor is on a north line from the battery in about 8 fathoms, with mud bottom and good holding ground.

TIDES.—Rise and fall of the tide barely perceptible.*

The COAST.—The land from sea, as far as the eye can reach, is high and of a uniform appearance.

OKINO SIMA.—The Okino islands are a good landmark; they may be passed on either side, but not between them.

The southernmost of the Okino islands bears N.E. ¾ E., distant about 8 miles from the entrance to Myadsu harbour.

SIRA SAKI has a fine, deep, and safe entrance as far as at present known; the western arm is the better. Keep mid-channel if possible on entering, and run up and anchor in any convenient depth.

OHAMA (OBAMA) BAY.—The entrance to this bay is safe, but the town cannot be approached within half a mile, the depth at that distance being only 2 fathoms. The best anchorage is under the point of the eastern entrance. Both arms of the inlet are shallow.

TSURUGA BAY.—This harbour, in about lat. 35° 40′ N., long. 136° 1′ 20″ E., is very easy of ingress and egress, and, so far as is known, free from rocks; no soundings under 13 fathoms until well in the harbour. Scattered rocks are supposed to exist well in on the western shore, which should be avoided. From the anchorage the point of land forming the western entrance of the bay and a point of land on the east side and to the northward nearly overlap each other. During the autumn and winter months a heavy swell sets in when the wind is from the northward and westward. The land around is high, and numerous villages are situated on the eastern side of the bay.

The town of Tsuruga, at the head of the bay, contains about 15,000 inhabitants, and exports dried fish and rice. Good lime is made in the neighbourhood.

DIRECTIONS.—Approaching Tsuruga bay from the northward, steer so as to be distant 6 miles from the north end of Tamagawa when it is brought in line with Ibo point; then steer S.E. ½ S. until the triangular white cliff seen to the left of the town is opened, when bring it to bear S. ½ E., and then steer for it until the first prominent point on the left of the bay going in is brought to bear E. by N. ¾ N.; then steer S. ½ W. to the anchorage.

ANCHORAGE.—The best anchorage is in Iogo bay, north-west of the town, in 9 or 10 fathoms. There is anchorage at about one third of a mile from the shore, blue sticky mud, shelving bottom, good holding ground.

TIDES.—Rise and fall of the tide, 2 feet.

---

* The description of Miyadsu, Mikuni, and Tsuruga are principally from the remarks of Commodore J. R. Goldsborough, U.S.S. *Shenandoah*.

MIKUNI BAY.*—The approach to Mikuni roads, in about lat. 36° 13′ N., long. 136° 8½′ E., is bold to within half a mile from the shore, when the soundings vary from 9 to 6 fathoms.

The town of Mikuni is said to contain 10,000 inhabitants, and exports silk and dried fish. It is situated on the right bank of the river Ekada (?), about half a mile from its mouth; the bar has only 6 feet at low water. Rise and fall of tide about 9 feet.

There is apparently deep water off the west side of Ajima, and it can be passed at three-quarters of a mile.

ANCHORAGE.—The anchorage in the outer roads is exposed from S.W. round west to north, but completely sheltered from all other winds. Rocks are said to exist inside of the island to the northward of the anchorage: give this island a berth of about half a mile, and haul up for the entrance of the river when the mouth bears E.S.E.

Bring the west end of Ajima to bear north, then steering north or south, as the case may be, until the mouth of the river (which is easily distinguished) bears E.S.E., when 7 fathoms will be found, sand and hard mud bottom, good holding ground. A course E.S.E. then leads up to the entrance, and, as the soundings are gradual, suitable water may be found for an anchorage.

Anchor in 6 fathoms with the centre of the island bearing North, and the bar to the river distant three-quarters of a mile, and borrow a little on the southern shore.

CAPE ROIVEN or NOTO, in lat. 37° 28′ N., long. 137° 22′ E., is elevated about 700 or 800 feet, the land rising 1,200 to 2,000 feet to the westward of it. At 12 miles W. by S. from the cape is a remarkable white cliff that shows well to the westward; from this cliff the coast bends in to the southward and forms Waisima bay. The opposite point of the bay is about 8 miles distant, and immediately above it is the sharp peak of Wasisu yama, elevated 2,000 feet, which is the highest point in the neighbourhood, the land being generally level and of an uniform height of about 800 or 1,000 feet. At 10 miles W. by S. from Waisima, or 30 miles W. by S. from cape Noto, the coast at Isonosu, a prominent projecting hill, 800 feet high, trends away sharply to the southward. None of those rocks and islands were seen which so thickly stud the coast in Krusenstern's chart, although, as the *Saracen* passed at the distance of 19 miles, it is possible that small rocks may exist close in shore. Soundings of 70 fathoms were obtained at 10 miles West of Isonosu, deepening to 232 fathoms at 25 miles southwest.

---

* See Plan, Mikuni bay, on No. 61.

A reef which dries extends eastward 2 miles from the cape, with much uneven ground in the vicinity, and it is reported that a 5-fathoms patch lies at a distance of 3 miles.

A sunken ledge of rocks, with only 3 feet water, is said to exist between the Astrolabe rocks and Waisima, 2¼ miles from the latter place.

AROOSTOOK REEF.*—A dangerous reef lies nearly N.N.W. ¾ W., 10 miles from cape Roiven. From the reef the northern Astrolabe rock bears W. ¾ S., and Isonosu hill S.W. ½ W.

YUTSI SIMA, in lat. 37° 50½′ N., long. 136° 55′ E., is 40 feet high, about two thirds of a mile in diameter, level, and cultivated; there are a few stunted trees on it, and a small village on its southern side. With the island bearing N.N.W. 5 miles, the depth was 46 fathoms, fine sand, and regular both the soundings on approaching and leaving it.

NAWA SIMA (Astrolabe rock), in lat. 37° 35′ N., long. 136° 54′ E., is 200 feet high, about a quarter or a third of a mile in diameter, and is the largest and highest of a group of five rocks, which extend nearly 1½ miles in a N.E. and S.W. direction, and vary from 200 to 70 feet in height.

NANAO HARBOUR,† in lat. 37° 2′ N., long. 136° 58′ E., has two entrances, caused by Noto-jima, an island about 3 miles long, parallel with the coast and between the northern and southern extreme point of land which forms the entrance to this spacious bay.

There are no peculiar features of the coast, or landmarks, to denote these entrances as they are approached from the seaward. They may, however, be readily seen by their open space, which is easily discernible from almost any position. The coast for two miles off appears clear and free from rocks, so far as is known. A sunken rock exists about 5 miles from the southern point, and a reef is said to exist off the northern point of south entrance.

The soundings decrease gradually from 54 fathoms, 20 miles off, until near the land. The best course for standing in either entrance is mid-channel.

The northern entrance is said to be more free from obstructions than the north-eastern.

The entrance to this harbour from the north-east is about half a mile wide; but after passing the projecting point which forms the narrow entrance, a wide and capacious bay opens.

The city of Nanao is situated in the extreme western angle of the bay, and soundings gradually decrease from 14 fathoms at the entrance until the anchorage of the town is reached.

---

* Discovered by U.S.S. *Aroostook*. Another reef has been reported by a master of a merchant vessel as lying 6 miles W.N.W. from the above position.

† *See* Plan, Nanao harbour on No. 61.

The population of Nanao is about 15,000, and its exports very little, if anything—a few dried fish and mats only.

A ship-yard is being built to the eastward of the town.

Ojima and Mejima.—Two small islands, 10 feet above water, lie about 2¼ miles from the town. There is deep water to the eastward of these islands, but W.N.W. from the western one, a shelf with only 16 feet water extends 5¼ cables in that direction, and 4 cables south-west from Ojima. By keeping the starboard hand on board, on entering and passing about a quarter of a mile from the only bluff point on the western side as the harbour is entered, the water will shoal gradually from 7 to 4 fathoms, muddy bottom.

Rocky bank.—In the outer part of the entrance, and mid-channel, is a rocky bank of from 3 to 6 fathoms on which a vessel can temporarily anchor to obtain a pilot; should she proceed without one, a boat should be sent ahead to sound.

Mirjose rock.—A sunken rock of 2 feet, lying north of the centre of the channel, is the principal danger, and this must be left on the port hand on entering; a mark for clearing it (if the mark can be made out) is the north side of Nanatsu-jima in line with low point under Channel bluff W. ¾ S. Two reefs, each one cable long, and with 6 feet water on them, are said to lie 5 miles east of the entrance; therefore the harbour should be made from E.N.E.

The following directions for Nanao harbour are by Commodore Goldsborough, United States Navy:—

"Bring the middle of southern entrance to bear W. by S. ¾ S., and then run for it. After entering the channel, keep close over to the north shore, running parallel to a line passing through Channel bluff and Matsu saki, which will be a course about W. by S. ¾ S.; but do not get inside the bight between the two points, for there is a shoal there with only 3 feet of water on it bearing S. by W. from a small village. In passing through the channel south of Channel bluff, between Fairway bank and Fukura saki, borrow on the northern side, which may be approached quite closely, and steer in towards the harbour S.W. by W. ¾ W.

The southern side of the entrance of Nanao is said to be rocky, with dangerous reefs extending from it in an easterly direction to the distance of 5 miles.

From Channel bluff steer S.W. by W. ¼ W. until north side of square cliff (Ota) is in line with east end of Mejima; then steer S.W. ¾ W. until north end of square cliff is in line with centre of Ojima, when steer S. ½ E. until centre of Ota bears E. ½ N., where a good anchorage will be found in 4½ fathoms water, in about the centre of the harbour.

The danger to be avoided in entering this harbour is a 16-foot spot, which is 850 yards from Ojima, and in range with that island and the north end of Ota cliff."

TOYAMA BAY.—The coast to the south-west of Yafiko yama is very high, especially near this bay, where the three snowy peaks of the Sa yama mountains appear above the clouds. Cape Roiven is the western point of entrance to this extensive bay, which is broadly open to the north and north-east. The *Djigit* passed along its eastern and southern shores, both of which are very populous, as was evident in the number and extent of the villages seen. Some rivers flow into the bay, but having bars like that of Niëgata they are not accessible to ships. All the anchorages off the villages are more or less exposed to winds from the northward. The river Gensiu gawa, on which the town of Toyama stands, has a bar of 7 feet water completely across it.

This bay is in every respect inferior to the roadstead of Niëgata, and with strong northerly winds more difficult to quit. The harbour of Uno ura, on its western side, has not been examined, but according to the Japanese manuscript it is spacious.

YAFIKO YAMA.—At 15 miles S.W. ¼ W. from Niëgata the low shore terminates at Kadota yama head, 4½ miles north of a spur of the fine peaks of Yafiko yama, which has the appearance of a blunt cone sloping on the west. A mile to the south, the peak of Kauriko yama rises to a higher elevation.

PORT NIËGATA.*—The city of Niëgata stands on the left bank of, for Japan, a rather large river, with 4 fathoms water within the entrance; but a bar off the entrance seals it to vessels of greater draught than 7 or 8 feet. In fresh breezes from seaward the sea breaks across the entrance, and at that time not even a boat could cross the bar without risk. The roadstead off the river's mouth is quite exposed, and the holding ground bad.

Niëgata, one of the ports open by treaty to foreign trade, is the most opulent city on the west coast of Nipon, and appears to absorb nearly the whole junk trade of that side of the island. It is said to be more than four times as large as Hakodate, and the population exceeds that comparison. A small battery near the entrance to the river appeared to be unarmed.

The city is situated on an extensive alluvial plain, intersected by many rivers, which fall, near the coast, into the main stream, the Sinano gawa, which takes its rise about 120 miles to the southward. This low coast extends for 42 miles, and presents an even appearance, dotted with trees and houses. When bearing South or S.S.W. it is seen clearly intersected by the river entrance, filled with junks; from other directions their mast-heads are visible over the land, one fleet of them lying just within the

---

* *See* Plan, Sado island and approaches to Niëgata, also Plan of Niëgata harbour on sheet No. 536.

entrance, and another more to the southward, off the city. Farther to the east, on a small elevation, is seen the town of Aosima yama and high mountains rise in the interior.

Soundings reach to a considerable distance off the mainland in the vicinity of Niëgata; vessels, therefore, running between Sado and Nipon at night, or in a fog, should keep the lead quickly hove. Should soundings be obtained and decrease gradually, the mainland is being approached. A run of very deep water will be found on the Sado side of the channel.

During the autumn and winter months no vessel, except a powerful steamer, could anchor off this port, as gales of wind, commencing at S.W. and veering to N.W., rapidly succeed each other, sending in such a heavy sea that no ground tackle could be depended upon.

To the northward of Niëgata the soundings decrease more gradually. In 27 fathoms the water changed to light green, and decreased to 7 fathoms at 3 miles from Niëgata, or half a mile from the bar, over a bottom of black sand, the water being slightly fresh.

The bar, when examined in May 1859 by the officers of the Russian gun-vessel *Djigit*,* was found to be a sand-bank at about a mile from the land, carrying only 6 feet water, with no channel. The depth increased beyond this obstruction. In October, the edge of this bank was scarcely half a mile from the coast, with a small passage over the bar carrying 8 feet at high water, close to the north-west of the west point of entrance.†

The breadth of the embouchure is about 3 cables, the depth at the right bank being 10 feet, and at the left, where some junks where anchored, 6 and 7 feet. The current of the river ran $2\frac{1}{2}$ knots.

The left bank of the river from its mouth is sandy, and first turns S.S.W. and then S.W. up to the city. The right bank is sandy at the entrance, then marshy, but steep; it trends S.E. by S., and then runs parallel to the left bank. The broadest part of the river is 6 cables, opposite the second bend. At this place, on the right bank, it is joined by the waters of the Agano gawa and another stream, which unite in disemboguing. On the east the Sinano gawa receives the waters of another river, which flows into it in a stream of considerable width between rice fields.

Two shoals occur in the centre of the Sinano gawa, with a channel between them carrying 7 feet, and increasing to 12 feet near Niëgata. The second shoal from the mouth is covered with reeds. A clean channel, carrying 4 fathoms over sandy bottom, runs close along the right bank.

The city, which is of great extent, is intersected by canals crossed by bridges, their banks shaded by weeping willows. It is surrounded by

---

* The description that follows is from the officer commanding the *Djigit*.

† In 1867 there were two boat channels, the eastern being the deepest, carrying 8 feet at low water.

gardens of the pear tree, peach, and vine; between the trees are planted turnips, onions, and mustard.

The town of Aosima yama stands near the embouchure of a river, which also has a clear channel carrying only 7 feet. It is said to be 6 miles N.E. of Niëgata, but is but half that distance according to the Japanese manuscript.

TIDES.—For the distance of 4 miles a strong indraught, on the flood tide, is experienced off the entrance of Niëgata, greatly to the inconvenience of sailing vessels seeking an offing. The ebb would, of course, assist them off the land.

SADO ISLAND,‡ lying 25 miles westward of the important trading port of Niëgata, is 33½ miles long, N.N.E. and S.S.W., nearly 17 at its widest part, and is composed of two parallel mountain ranges lying N.W. and S.E. of each other, the neck of land joining them being a plain, on the N.E. and S.W. sides of which are formed two extensive open bays. A remarkable sharp conical hill, 700 feet high, stands on a flat off the north extreme of the island, and from a distance looks like an isolated rock. To the northward of this are a few detached rocks close to the shore, and one off Ya saki or Wa saki, the north-eastern point of the island, which is in lat. 38° 19′ 55″ N., long. 138° 27′ 9″ E.

This latter point rises somewhat abruptly and gains an elevation of 3,800 feet, from which the land, descending slightly, runs in rocky ridges to the south-south-west for 10 miles, and terminates in a sharp nipple of 4,500 feet elevation, whence it descends in a gentle uniform slope to the southward. These ranges rise abruptly from the shore on both sides, which are generally cliffy and steep-to, a berth of three-quarters of a mile clearing all known danger. The west point of the island has a bold, clean shore, whence the coast recedes round Sawa-umi bay to the south-east, and is low. There are numerous fishing villages along the western shores, and a few boat harbours were seen. The shores in the environs of Sawa-umi bay are well peopled, and the land well cultivated, but it is not so populous nor so fertile as the eastern portion of the island, on the southern part of which an extensive undulating plain, stretching from the base of the hills to the sea-shore, offers a more profitable return to the husbandman.

ANCHORAGE.—Although Niëgata is opened to European trade, no vessel except a powerful steamer could, during the autumn or winter months, remain at anchor off that port, as before mentioned. Under these circumstances, the most prudent course to adopt would be to anchor under shelter of Sado, and have the cargo transported from Niëgata in junks or light draught steamers.

---

‡ *See* Plan of Sado island, No. 536.

The bend in the coast-line on the north-east side of the island forms an extensive bay called Minato-mats, which affords anchorage in from 12 to 16 fathoms, sheltered from E. by S. (round south and west) to North. A conspicuous rock, 60 feet high, called Siza, marks Okawa point, the south extreme of this bay, in which no known dangers exist. At the head of the bay is the town of Ibesso or Yebisu.

Another eligible anchorage will be found off Oda village, a quarter of a mile S.S.W. of Matsu saki, a low projecting tongue of shingle, bearing S.S.W. ½ W. distant 10½ miles from Okawa point. The *Actæon* rode out a heavy gale of wind here in 13 fathoms water.

The south part of the east coast possesses several coves and inlets in which small craft will find excellent shelter, but there is no harbour of importance on it.

Supplies.—A few fowls, some fish, and vegetables were obtained by the *Actæon* during her stay at Sado. Several little pack ponies, and a few dogs were met with, but no horned cattle nor pigs. The brushwood, especially in the south-west part of the island, swarmed with pheasants, and a few hares were seen.

Firewood may be obtained, but it is supposed not in sufficient quantities for steaming purposes. Nearly every little valley has its stream of excellent water flowing down to the beach, and when the sea is smooth easily obtainable. Coal is not known.

AWA SIMA, the north-east extreme of which is in lat. 38° 29′ 36″ N., long. 139° 16′ 7″ E., is a narrow strip of land running N.N.E. and S.S.W. and reaching at its southern extreme an elevation of 680 feet. It is 3⅛ miles in length, and nearly a mile in breadth, the widest part being in the centre, where, on the east shore, is a fishing village, while another stands at the south end of the other shore, in a small bay protected by a natural breakwater.

The south-east side of the island is fringed with a narrow bank of soundings, but is clear of rocks, with the exception of one, which shows at all times, and is only one cable from the beach. The remainder of the island is bordered by reefs and rocks, but they do not extend beyond a quarter of a mile from the shore, except at nearly a mile N.N.W. of the north point of the island, where is a dangerous rock which sometimes breaks.

The hand-lead will afford but little warning to vessels approaching the north-west side of this island, as there are 10 fathoms quite alongside the rocks, and no soundings a very short distance outside. Off the north-east point for about 2 miles, soundings on a rocky foul bottom may be carried, but vessels should rather anchor on the narrow belt of soundings on the south-east side. The inhabitants were, as well as at Tabu sima, very civil. Nothing but fish could be obtained.

TABU SIMA, (Observatory rock off the east extreme of which is in lat. 39° 11′ 53″ N., long. 139° 34′ 17″ E.,) is in shape somewhat of a horseshoe, with a club at its north-east end. It is on top nearly a flat, varying from 120 to 150 feet in height. Its greatest length is $1\frac{1}{2}$ miles N.E. and S.W., and its widest part, the north-east end, is not quite a mile across. No supplies could be obtained except a few fish. Springs of excellent water abound.*

The island is covered with a thick vegetation and bordered by cliffs and steep banks, the latter occasionally margined by small beaches, affording space for several fishing villages, the inhabitants of which send large quantities of the dried squid to the main-land. Soundings of 9 fathoms were obtained at nearly a mile off its north-east point, but the lead affords no warning on any other side of the island, as it and the detached rocks are quite steep-to. The *Actæon* anchored in 25 fathoms off the bay on the south-east side, with the south extreme of the island bearing S.W. by W. $\frac{1}{2}$ W., and Observatory rock N.N.E. The Russian gun-vessel *Djigit* anchored in the same bay in 9 fathoms over a coral bottom. It affords shelter from all winds prevalent in the Japan sea.

Except on the south-east side, the island is surrounded by detached rocks; they all show, and are in no instance more than three-quarters of a mile off shore. Some rocks off the west side are remarkable, the largest being higher than the island; these are all inaccessible, but the southern of them is on an extensive flat reef. Those on the north-west are small and low.

BITTERN ROCKS.—This group of three small rocks (page 325), two above water and one awash, was discovered by H.M.S. *Bittern*, 8th July 1855. They lie close together, within the space of 2 cables, steep-to on their western side, having 15 and 17 fathoms at the distance of 2 cables, and no bottom with 140 fathoms at $1\frac{1}{2}$ miles. The face of the rocks was covered with seals, which were with difficulty dislodged, the larger ones barking and snarling in a vicious manner, and carrying off musket balls from within ten yards' distance without any apparent inconvenience.

The south-western or largest rock, in lat. 40° 31′ N., long. 139° 31′ E., and lying W. by S. about 15 or 17 miles from cape Yokoiso, is about 18 feet high, and in size and appearance resembles the hull of a vessel of about 200 tons. The smaller rock, lying rather more than a cable E.N.E. from the larger one, is about 7 feet high, and broken water extends from it about a third of a cable to the northward. The third rock, awash, lies to the S.E. of these two, forming nearly an equilateral triangle with them.

---

* *See* Chart of Japan islands and part of Korea, No. 2,347, corrected to October 1872.

CHAPTER VIII.

JAPAN ISLANDS.—TSUGAR STRAIT, NORTH COAST OF NIPON, YEZO ISLAND; SAGHALIN AND KURIL ISLANDS.

VARIATION { Yezo and Saghalin, 2½° W. to 4½° W.
Kuril islands, 2° W. to 2° E. } in 1872.

TSUGAR STRAIT.

TSUGAR STRAIT,* separating Nipon from Yezo island, is about 40 miles in length in an E.N.E. and W.S.W. direction, and 9½ miles wide at its narrowest part.

NORTH COAST OF NIPON. — CAPE YOKOISO (cape Gamaley).— Approaching the western entrance of Tsugar strait from the south-west, the Bittern rocks (page 324) will be seen lying W. by S. about 16 miles from cape Yokoiso. The land about this cape is moderately elevated and level. The coast between it and Oho saki, to the northward, is low and sandy. Sasagota bay (of Krusenstern's chart), at 6 miles southward of Oho saki, appears to be nothing more than a large shallow lagoon; its entrance is narrow and barred across, with only sufficient depth to admit junks at high water. Between the bay and Oho saki the coast is safe of approach, having regular soundings, and fair anchorage in N.E. winds.

OHO SAKI is remarkable from its peculiar form, and being the commencement of the high land extending to Tatsupi saki, which bears from it N.N.W. ¾ W., 8½ miles. The bay between these points, although containing much foul ground, may be useful to a vessel not able to get through the strait during an easterly gale. The best anchorage is in 12 fathoms and three-quarters of a mile off shore, at one-third the distance from Oho saki to Tatsupi saki. The bottom of the bay is very foul.

TATSUPI SAKI, the south point of western entrance to Tsugar strait, is a bluff, 362 feet high, from whence the land rises to the height of 2,200 feet, at the distance of 4 miles inland. A large rock, 300 feet high, lies 2 cables N.E. of the cape, and is connected with it by a low neck of sand and stones. On a N.W. and S.E. bearing this rock makes like an island. The cape is steep-to, but the strong eddies near it, make it prudent not to approach it nearer than a mile.

---

* See Chart of Strait of Tsugar, No. 2,441; scale, $m = 0.3$ of an inch. The description of this coast is principally from the remarks of Captain John Richards, H.M.S. *Saracen*, who surveyed this strait in 1855.

Taka no saki.—Gun cliff, at 9¼ miles E. by S. ¼ S. from Tatsupi saki, is steep-to, and has a battery of six guns on its apex, which is 200 feet high. There is a remarkable black rocky cliff three-quarters of a mile to the westward.

In the bay between these points, off the town of Memoyah, about half a mile from the shore, there is capital anchorage in 8 fathoms, indeed the best in the strait next to Hakodate. A little southward of the town there is a fine stream of good water, which may easily be obtained. Wood is also abundant.

After passing Taka no saki the shore is less steep, and bottom will be found in from 30 to 40 fathoms right across to the opposite coast of the peninsula of Nambu. From the south point of this coast a steep cliffy shore, with deep water close to, trends 25 miles to the northward, nearly in a straight line to Toriwi saki. The cliffs are coloured with the most brilliant and varied tints, and, like the entire coasts of the strait, are of basaltic formation. Among the most remarkable are the Red cliffs, rising to the height of 1,600 feet, at 17 miles southward of Toriwi saki. At 9 miles farther to the northward are two remarkable pointed cliffs, named Double head. Nearly 2 miles to the S.W. of this head is a rock 42 feet high; and North about 3 cables from this is a rock awash at low water.

AWOMORI BAY.—The bay of Awomori, a vast interior basin at the north end of Nipon, opens on the south side of Tsugar strait. The entrance is 5 miles wide, with high land on both sides. Off the salient part of the west point, some half-tide rocks lie one cable from the shore. The outer coast to cape Kusodomari, the eastern point of entrance, is steep, sharp, and well populated; while after rounding it and entering the bay, creeks more or less deep, sandy beaches, and fishing villages are found. According to the Japanese, no hidden dangers exist. Towards the centre the water is too deep to anchor, but at 2 miles from the shore along the east and west coasts there is generally 19 to 22 fathoms mud, with gravel or sand round Natsu sima, the point on the southern side of the bay. The coast can generally be approached within half a mile, but often the depth decreases suddenly, so that without a pilot or a chart it is not advisable to approach nearer than in 11 fathoms.

WEST COAST.—From Isi saki (about 5 miles south-east from Gun cliff) the coast trends S. ¼ E. to the town of Awomori; a fine cultivated plain, stretching inland from the coast opposite Natsu sima to the above town. The faces of the hills are sometimes close to the sea. At 8 miles south of Isi saki is a river frequented by large fishing junks, with an important village at its mouth. For 10 miles southward of the river to Awomori, there is a uniform sandy beach bordered by villages that nearly join each other, at half a mile from which there are 7½ fathoms mud, decreasing rapidly.

Isi saki.—At the most salient part of the coast there is a little earthwork, apparently dismantled, immediately south of Isi saki, that is surrounded by rocks above water one cable from the shore. Two miles south of them, in a narrow plain, is the small town of Taira-tatte, from which the coast southward becomes rugged.

The TOWN of AWOMORI* stretches along the beach for nearly a mile. It is the most important town in the bay to which it gives the name, and appears to have from 15,000 to 20,000 inhabitants. The shore here is bordered by a fertile plain of rice fields, extending about 10 miles inland to a semicircle of mountains of from 3,000 to 4,000 feet in height, which, in their northern extension, approach the western coast to within a mile and finally reach it at the entrance of the bay. A great quantity of rice is exported to Yezo. Twenty-five large junks were found at anchor.

ANCHORAGE.—This anchorage is open to the north; the soundings decrease gradually, and 9 fathoms will be found at 2 cables from the shore, with good holding ground. A considerable river flows into the sea east of the town, but its entrance is blocked by a bar, the outer edge of which projects 1¾ cables. It is probably more or less changeable, and can be taken only by boats of light draught. There is a Japanese light near the centre of the town, but it is very dim and cannot be relied on. There are no fortifications, but large storehouses are situated to the west of the town.

Supplies.—Beef, rice, timber, and firewood can be obtained, and water may be procured from the river by flat boats, but owing to the fact that it drains the rice fields it cannot be recommended.

MO URA.—A bay, tolerably deep, opens south of Kama ura point, called Mo ura. The country people say there are 10 fathoms of water in it. The best anchorage appeared to be in the northern portion. In the middle and southern, two large isolated cones rise from the sea, and are apparently joined to the shore by a series of banks and rocks awash, that render the passage impassable. Between the two there is an islet and a rugged rock. South of Mo ura there is no remarkable indentation, but at 3 miles from Awomori the heights recede from the shore, and surround a fertile plain, of which that town occupies the centre.

KAMA URA POINT.—From Awomori to Natsu sima the general direction of the coast is N.N.E. for 12 miles. This region is rocky with numerous creeks, and it is thinly populated. The most remarkable point,

---

* *See* plan, Awomori anchorage on, plans of anchorages in Awomori bay, No. 101.

called Kama ura point, is 3½ miles S.S.W. from Natsu sima. At about 1½ cables from its extreme there is an upright rock about 30 feet high, called Kaga sima. In passing at three quarters of a mile there is no bottom at 14 fathoms; shortly after, 27 fathoms gravel is obtained at 1¾ miles W.S.W.

NATSU SIMA.—The point of Natsu sima consists of a series of hillocks that slope gradually. The islet at 2 cables from it is rocky and rugged, and is joined to the shore by a neck of sand and rocks awash. There are some rocks off the coast at 8 cables E.S.E. from the islet.

According to the Japanese, anchorage may be had off the south side of the island. Natsu sima is about 100 feet high. At 8 cables distance there are 20 fathoms, small black gravel.

DEMURA POINT, at 3 miles to the south-eastward, is rugged, and about 246 feet high. At the foot of the cliff there is a low sandy point, that extends 2¼ cables, and is steep-to. At 3 cables from its extreme there are 13½ fathoms gravel and shell.

SHIRANAI.*—The bay of Shiranai, lies 2 miles S.E. from Demura point, and runs in 1½ miles, but there is shoal water in the bay at its southern end. The south-east coast is low, and in 4¼ fathoms the bottom is rocky. There is no mud except in the centre, the rest is sand. In the west part may be seen three small villages. The bay on the south-west is wooded.

This anchorage is tolerably sheltered and has good holding ground, but appears to have few resources. The north point is steep-to, and ends in a hillock surmounted by a clump of trees.

At 7 miles from Shiranai is the bay of Nofitsi. Between which the coast rises gradually, and forms several indentations of little importance. At a mile from the shore there are 13½ fathoms, and the extreme point may be passed at half a mile in 8¾ fathoms.

NOFITSI† lies in the south-east bight of Awomori bay; towards the south the land is tolerably low and uniform. The anchorage may be recognized some distance off by an isolated wood, that stands out against the sky.

The anchorage is in a large semi-circular indentation in front of the town at 6 cables from the shore in 6½ fathoms gravel. The depth decreases rapidly from 11 fathoms, and the holding ground is fair, but a heavy sea comes in with northerly winds. On the north-west side of the bay 2½ miles from the town is a bank of large stones, running out 4 cables, the end of which is nearly awash, and on which the sea often breaks. The east part is composed of little red cliffs with sandy beaches between. The town proper, in the province of Nambu, is half-a-mile from the coast on

---

* *See* plan, Shiranai bay on plans of anchorage in Awomori bay, No. 101.

† *See* plan of Nofitsi on sheet No. 101.

a hillock. At the shore, there is only a large village, on the right of which a river disembogues; junks of 20 tons might go in, but it is barred by a bridge a short distance from its mouth. There is considerable traffic in copper. Nofitsi is one of the stations on the main road to the capital that passes from there to Awomori in the other part of the bay.

The COAST.—From Nofitsi the coast is low and uniform, an isolated hill 1,300 feet in height rising from the middle of the space between Ando bay and the sea.

BAY OF ANDO.*—The bay of Ando is open to the south, and it is shallow at its head. Vessels can go in until the peak over Ando bears W. by N. $\frac{1}{3}$ N., where there is anchorage in $6\frac{1}{4}$ to 8 fathoms, mud. The bottom here rises abruptly.

South-west of the anchorage there is a fine basin, sheltered by a bank of sand running parallel to the coast. It may be entered safely by steering up mid-channel until abreast of the sandy point, when the north-east coast must be kept on board until abreast the second village, where there is good anchorage in $3\frac{3}{4}$ to 6 fathoms, muddy bottom.

The sandy tongue and the south-west shore of the bay have off them banks of mud and muddy sand that reduce the space for vessels of ordinary dimensions to 8 cables by $2\frac{1}{2}$ cables. The entrance is nearly 2 cables wide. The extreme of the sandy point covers a short distance at high water. The large village on the north-east side of the interior basin can be approached within a cable, where anchorage may be had in $5\frac{1}{4}$ fathoms.

The north point of the sandy tongue above mentioned is in lat. 41° 16′ N.

The Japanese villages are poor, their inhabitants subsisting by fishing. Six junks were moored before the principal village (Kanaya), and there was a large one being built.

Supplies.—The slopes of the hills are partly cultivated and partly wooded with a species of pine. The *Dupleix* bought wood here for steam purposes, and also fresh provisions. Water flows down the mountains by many streamlets, and is easily obtained, also at the head of the bay fish is plentiful. The place belongs to the prince of Nambu, and is part of the district of Tanabu.

TIDES.—The tides are felt more at Ando than at any other part of the bay, and have a strength of $1\frac{3}{4}$ knots. It is evidently their action that has formed the bay.

BEN-TEN SIMA.—At 2 miles S.E. $\frac{1}{4}$ E. from Kusodomari, the eastern point of the entrance to Awomori bay, and at $5\frac{1}{2}$ cables from the shore are the two islets of Ben-ten sima, the smallest being nothing more than a

---

* *See* plan, Port Ando, on sheet of anchorages in Awomori bay, No. 101.

mere pinnacle rock about 100 feet high. A rock on which the sea breaks lies one cable S.S.W. from the island. There is a passage for junks between the islets and the shore, but the Japanese say it would be imprudent to take it with a large ship. A depth of 33 fathoms was found one mile south of the islets.

The COAST.—From Ando trends towards S.S.W., then turns towards the west and south-west to Ben-ten sima. In the part of Awomori bay near Ando are long sandy beaches and numerous villages, the largest being Kawa-atchi, at the entrance of a river, off which junks usually anchor. Towards the angle of the bay, a considerable range approaches the coast, the summit nearest to Ando being 3,120 feet high and visible from nearly all the bay. To the eastward of these mountains the land is very low and has the aspect of a uniform plain covered with wood: beyond this the summit of Siriya saki is seen.

TORIWI SAKI is a low tapering point, off which, at the distance of a cable, is Low islet or Omasaki sima, 40 feet high. The ground all around this cape and islet is very foul, except to the N.E., where a vessel may anchor to wait tide in 13 fathoms, with the centre of the islet bearing S.W. by S. distant about a mile. This is a useful anchorage for vessels approaching Hakodate from the eastward, particularly during the light south-westerly winds common to the strait during the summer months. There is a tide race, near the full and change of the moon, 3 miles North of Low islet, and heavy overfalls with a north-east swell. On such occasions care must be taken to avoid this locality. There is no clear channel for large ships between the race and the islet.

SINGAPORE ROCK, with 6 feet on it at low water springs, lies N. by E. ¾ E., 2½ miles from the centre of Low island, and is at the extremity of a sunken ledge, with from 6 to 17 fathoms on it, connecting this rock with Low island, excepting in which direction the soundings round it vary from 13 to 21 fathoms.

CAUTION.—This rock is surrounded to a considerable distance by the most conspicuous of the overfalls existing in the vicinity, all of which should be carefully avoided.

The COAST.—From Low islet the coast to the eastward is foul for about 3 miles, after which it may be approached without fear. At 10½ miles from Low islet is a remarkable red cliff, which shows well to the westward; and at 2 miles westward of this cliff is a high sharp bluff, and a high round bluff 2 miles to the eastward.

From the latter bluff the coast is low to within 4 miles of Siriya saki (see page 199), where it rises to 1,265 feet, and descends again towards the cape in a gentle slope, making at a distance like an island. There is good anchorage in the deep bay between this cape and the red cliff, but the best is on its western side, abreast the coast line where the high and low land meet, in 15 fathoms, with the above round bluff bearing W.N.W. 2 miles.

YEZO ISLAND.

The coast line of Yezo is about 1,000 miles in extent, and its eastern shore appears low from seaward, resembling table-land; its appearance is, however, most deceptive, as the country is a repetition of abrupt hills of a uniform height, interspersed with deep valleys, rivers, swamps, and large lagoons.

The western coast is bold, and ranges of lofty mountains, many of the summits of which are extinct volcanoes, rise in every direction. The highest of these, Shubets, a cone-shaped mountain 30 miles inland, is an active volcano, and from its size and grandeur may well be considered by the Japanese as the Fusi yama of Yezo.

The island is almost entirely covered with wood, the ground being in many places strewn with the trunks of trees in all stages of decay, and covered with moss, lichen, and rank vegetation; and the coarse bamboo grass is found in some places growing to a height of 15 feet.

There are numerous rivers and streams, the largest of which, the Iskarri, is on the west coast, and three or four large lakes are said to exist in the interior. Coal is found in several places, but is principally procured from the village of Kamami, near Iwani, on the west coast. Sulphur abounds, and sulphur springs are numerous.

Yezo is a conquest and colony of Japan, and small settlements of emigrants from the south, and of natives are found scattered along the shores. The Ainos or aborigines of Yezo are a race of stunted growth, and are grossly ignorant, wretchedly poor, and filthy both in person and habits; unlike the Japanese, they allow their hair and beards to grow to a great length.

Little or no agriculture is carried on, both Japanese and Ainos principally subsisting on the produce of the ocean. Salmon and herring fishing on a large scale is their principal occupation, and large quantities of seaweed are collected, dried in the sun, and sent south, finding its way into all parts of Japan and China.

SOUTH COAST.—CAPE SIRAKAMI (Nadiejda), the north point of western entrance to Tsugar strait, is a high bluff similar to cape Siwokubi, but not so safe of approach. The coast, for more than a mile on each side of the cape, is bordered with numerous rocks, generally above water, some of which extend nearly 2 cables from the shore. As it is not known whether the dangers extend under water beyond this distance, it will be prudent to give the cape a good berth in passing.

MATSUMAE.—From cape Sirakami the coast trends W. by N. ¼ N. 5 miles to cape Matsumae, which is low, and off it is a conical islet with a small temple or building on it. The bay between is very rocky, excepting off the east end of the city of Matsumae, where there is good anchorage in 12 fathoms at half a mile off shore; but this anchorage would, of course, be unsafe in southerly winds. H.M.S. *Sybille* in 1855 coasted along this bay at about 2 miles off shore, and had irregular soundings, 16 to 25 fathoms, shoaling suddenly when near the city from 13 to 5 and 7 fathoms.*

CAPE TSIUKA, at 12¼ miles N.E. by E. from cape Sirakami, is a high cliffy point, which may be further known by three rocks extending a quarter of a mile from a point one mile north-eastward of it; the outer rock of the three is of a conical form and 70 feet high. The land to the westward for 4 miles is high and cliffy; about half way between the cape and the end of the cliffs there are two waterfalls.

Vessels can anchor in the bight of the bay, between capes Tsiuka and Sirakami; but as a southerly wind on the western tide sends in a cross swell, it would not be prudent to anchor far in. The best position is in from 15 to 20 fathoms, with the southern white cliff bearing West about one mile.

HAKODADI HARBOUR.—The port of Hakodadi, or more properly Hakodate, on the north side of Tsugar strait, is situated at the foot of the northern slope of a high peninsula which is connected with the mainland of Yezo by a low sandy isthmus. It is an excellent roadstead 4 miles wide and 5 miles deep, and for accessibility and safety is one of the finest in the world. Its entrance is between Hakodadi head and Mussell point, which bear East and West of each other, distant 4⅔ miles. The harbour is in the south-eastern arm of the bay, and is completely sheltered, with regular soundings and excellent holding ground, the best anchorage being over a depth of 5 fathoms, black mud, in a line with the avenue leading to the governor's house. The town of Hakodate stands on the north-east slope of the promontory, facing the harbour, and in 1854 contained about 6,000 inhabitants†. Hakodate exports herring oil; bear, river and sea otter, and deer skins, antlers, and edible seaweed in large quantities; and large junks of from 200 to 300 tons visit the harbour engaged in this trade.

The town and harbour are defended by an imposing pentagonal fort placed on the shoal at the northern extreme of the promontory.‡ It is

---

* The description of Yezo island is principally compiled from the remarks of Commander H. C. St. John, who circumnavigated it in H.M.S. *Sylvia*, 1871.

† *See* plan of Hakodadi harbour, No. 2,672; scale, *m* = 2 inches.

‡ From remarks of Lieutenant Nasimoff, Russian navy, 1859.

constructed for 52 guns, and the walls are faced exteriorly with large uncemented irregular blocks of soft granite, inside of which are smaller stones; the parapet is of earth, turfed. The fort is separated from the town by a moat, always filled with water. Another fortification of earth to mount 60 guns is being erected on the isthmus; it will be a kind of bastioned fort. There are also two 2-gun masked batteries on the western side of the bay.

LIGHT-VESSEL.—A light-vessel painted red, with two masts carrying a ball at the foremast head and exhibiting a *fixed* white light elevated 36 feet above the sea, is moored in $7\frac{1}{2}$ fathoms (at low water spring tides) off the most northern point of the spit which runs out from point Anama (the north-western point of the town), with the mouth of Kamida creek bearing E. by S. $\frac{1}{3}$ S., and white bluff S. by W.

Vessels of large draught entering the harbour should pass north of the light-vessel, as there is a bank of stones directly south of her.

Beacon.—At $2\frac{1}{2}$ cables south from the vessel is a triangular floating beacon moored in $5\frac{1}{2}$ fathoms. The passage between the light and the beacon may be taken by vessels drawing less than 18 feet water.

South of the beacon the bottom is composed of large stones, and is very irregular. The banks on the east side of this bay must be avoided, that extend half a mile from the shore. A vessel can moor at half a mile from the shore in $5\frac{1}{2}$ fathoms mud, good holding ground. In less than that the bottom is gravel, and anchors hold badly.

Supplies.—Water can be easily obtained from Kamida creek, which enters the harbour to the northward and eastward of the town, but the operation is attended with danger to the boats, which have to be dragged over the bar of the river. The Japanese supply fresh water which they bring off in tubs in their own boats at a very moderate rate. A supply of good wood for steam purposes, made up in large bundles, can be procured in considerable quantities at Hakodate and from the Japanese villages in the south of Yezo, and north of Japan. It burns rapidly with a large flame. The proportion required is $2\frac{1}{2}$ times the weight of coal and the price varies from two to four dollars according to localities; and water may also be ordered through the Custom house, at the bazaar, or from the American agents residing at Hakodate.

The seine supplied the American squadron in 1854 with fine salmon and a quantity of other fish, and the shores of the bay abound with excellent shell-fish. Beef, potatoes, sweet potatoes, fowls and eggs, and all necessaries can be procured. For large supplies of provisions, masters of ships should have recourse to the American agents. Vessels, even when seriously damaged, can undergo repairs in the harbour, there being no scarcity of materials for this purpose. Timber of any dimensions can be procured, though not in great quantity: its price is very moderate, and repairs within the scope of intelligent Japanese workmen, and materials can be obtained. There is no want of coopers, but owing to the scarcity of iron they use bamboo for hoops.

There is a brass and iron foundry, though worked on a limited scale. No copper sheathing can be obtained. The native sheet copper is very thin and small in size. Ships' boats can be repaired or constructed by the Japanese in a very skilful manner from drawings.

There is no regular depôt for coal, but cargoes come in from the north The American steamer *Hermann* has procured as much as 300 tons from Junk bay. The bay of Mosyria, 18 leagues to the southward, has coal of good quality and easily worked, but the anchorage is bad, and embarkation difficult, it being necessary to work and transport the coal with the means on board. In the fine season probably less difficulty would be found. Coal can also be obtained in a similar manner from the bay of Iwani, on the west coast of Yezo.

Other depositories of coal are found along the coast of Saghalin.

Merchant vessels entering the port are subject to the Custom house regulations. The laws relating to imports and exports may be learned from the consuls. Japanese tow in a raw state may be purchased at 121*l*. to 140*l*. per ton. Coal of very inferior quality is also procurable.

Pilots.—Vessels entering the bay are boarded by pilots, who charge five Mexican dollars, without any distinction as to the size of the ship. There are no special harbour regulations.

Tides.—It is high water, full and change, in this harbour at 5h. 0m., and the extreme rise and fall of tide is 3 feet.

Directions.—Entering Hakodate harbour, after rounding Hakodate head, and giving it a berth of a mile to avoid the calms under the high land, steer for the sharp peak of Komaga-daki, bearing about North, until the eastern peak of the Saddle mountain, bearing about N.E. by N., opens to the westward of the round knob on the side of the mountain, then haul up to the northward and eastward, keeping them well open until the centre of the sand hills on the isthmus bears S.E. by E. ¾ E. (these may be recognized by the dark knolls upon them). This will clear the spit which runs in a N.N.W. direction two thirds of a mile from Anama saki, the north-western point of the town. Round the light vessel, passing northward of her, and anchor as convenient in from 6 to 8 fathoms, taking care to keep the light-vessel bearing westward of N.W. to avoid the shoal bank off the town. Should the light-vessel be removed, then bring the sand hills a point on the port bow, and stand in until the above point of the town bears S.W. ½ W., when the vessel will be in the best berth, in 5½ or 6 fathoms water.*

If it be desirable to get nearer in, haul up a little eastward of South, for the low rocky peak which will be just visible over the sloping ridge to the southward and eastward of the town. A vessel of moderate draught may approach within a quarter of a mile of Tsuki point, where there is a building yard for junks. This portion of the harbour, however, is generally crowded with vessels of this description, and unless the want of repairs or some other cause renders a close berth necessary, it is better to remain outside.

At night bring the light to bear N.E. ¾ N., and steer for it on that bearing, taking care not to bring it to bear north of that bearing. Round it as before directed, and anchor as convenient. Should the light be removed steer a northerly course on entering Hakadodi bay, to a depth of 7 fathoms, and keeping in that depth on an easterly and south-easterly course the spit will be safely rounded.

Should the wind fall before reaching the harbour, there is good anchorage in the bay, in from 25 to 10 fathoms water.

CAPE SIWOKUBI bears E. by S. 12 miles from Hakodadi head, and N. by E. ¾ E. 9½ miles from Low islet on the Nipon shore; this is the narrowest part of the strait of Tsugar. This cape is steep-to, and the north-east current frequently runs with greater strength close to the rocks than out in the stream. The summit of the bluff immediately above the cape is 1,022 feet high; from thence the high land ranges in towards the Saddle mountain. The coast for about 7 miles to the westward is a level plain of an average elevation of 200 or 300 feet; beyond 7 miles it descends to the low beach connecting the high land of Hakodadi head with the main.

CAPE YESAN, the north point of eastern entrance to Tsugar strait, is the east extreme of a bold promontory, with several remarkable dome-shaped mountains in the rear. The cape itself is a steep cliff about 600 feet high; the volcano immediately above it is 1,935 feet high, and frequently capped with a light cloud of steam, and a jet of steam is constantly seen issuing from a hollow on the west side of the hill, but it is not other-

---

* The north-east the end of fir trees in line with the Joss house clears the eastern side in 5 fathoms water; and the foot of the hill in line with the middle of the sandy point leads along the northern side of the shoal.—Captain K. Stewart, H.M.S. *Nankin*, 1855.

If these leading marks should be in the clouds, as they generally are, keep the western extreme of the promontory of Hakodadi bearing South or S. ¼ W., which will clear the spit, and haul to the eastward when the centre of the sand hills on the isthmus bears S.E. b E. ¾ E.—Commodore the Hon. C. Elliot, H.M.S. *Sybille*, 1855.

wise active. The west side of this mountain is covered with patches of sulphur, having the appearance of snow at a distance. There is anchorage in the bay about 2 miles westward of the cape; a kedge or stream anchor is recommended to be used when unable to make way against the tide.

At 2½ miles E. ⅜ S. from cape Siwokubi is Conical islet, 200 feet high, lying close to the coast, which in its immediate neighbourhood is high and cliffy, and the approach steep and safe. There is, however, a dangerous low point one mile to the westward; and at 2¾ miles to the eastward is Foul point, which is low, and has a dangerous reef extending 2 cables from it.

DIRECTIONS. — TSUGAR STRAIT. — Sailing vessels approaching Tsugar strait from the westward during foggy weather should guard against being carried by the current to the northward past the entrance. Should the weather be clear when nearing cape Yokoiso, it may be as well to sight it; but if doubtful, shape a course (allowing for the probable current) direct for Oho saki. Should a fog come on suddenly when nearing this cape, recollect that the coast is clear and sandy, and the soundings are regular to the southward, but rocky with irregular soundings to the northward of it. The cape is steep-to, and standing out prominently from the coast line, forms a good landmark.

No particular directions are required in passing through the strait from the westward, the only dangers being those off Toriwi saki above described, and the Rattler rock off Siriya saki (*see* page 199), and the north-easterly current will always be found strongest in the middle of the stream. After passing Tatsupi saki, if the weather is thick, and the vessel bound to Hakodate, endeavour to make cape Tsiuka, and proceed from thence to Mussell point; or giving cape Tsiuka a berth, feel the way by the lead into the bay, between it and cape Saraki, and anchor till the weather clears.

Approaching the strait from the eastward, steer for Siriya saki, and endeavour to make it on a N.W. bearing. Pass the cape at not less than 2 miles distant, then haul in to avoid the current and to anchor should it fall calm. In this case, by keeping this shore close aboard, the vessel may probably be drifted up to Low islet, off Toriwi saki, by the western stream, when the north-east current is running like a mill stream in mid-channel.

At the anchorage off Low islet the vessel must wait a favourable opportunity for crossing the strait. During the summer months the winds are generally light from the south-west for a considerable period; the wind, however, generally freshens a little when the western stream makes, and this is the right time to weigh. Pass about half a mile from Low islet, between it and the Singapore rock, and in crossing the current take care not to be set to leeward of Hakodate. If proceeding straight to Hakodate from the eastward, the better course is to cross the strait, and passing about 5 miles off Siriya saki make for cape Yesan, so as to take advantage of the cold westerly set along the south shore of Yezo.

Proceeding from Hakodate to the westward against S.W. winds, keep well inside cape Tsiuka, and if unable to round it, anchor with the stream or kedge about 2 miles to the north-east, weighing again when the next western tide makes. Should the wind be very light, a vessel may not clear the strait in one tide; in this case it will be better to wait a tide to the eastward of cape Sirakami, and take the whole of the following tide to clear the strait, than run any risk of being swept into the strait again by the current. Vessels passing through the strait, particularly to the westward, should have a good kedge and 150 fathoms of hawser ready for immediate use, and must keep the land close on board.

TIDES.—The tide in the stream runs about 12 hours each way near the full and change of the moon, and there are two regular tides by the shore in 24 hours. At full and change the flood or eastern stream makes at Tatsupi saki at 6h. 30m. a.m., at 7h. 0m. at cape Tsiuka, and at 7h. 30m. at Toriwi saki. The western stream begins about 12 hours later. The turn of the stream takes place 1½ hours later every day. With heavy S.W. gales the north-easterly current swells and fills the strait, attaining a velocity of from 5 to 6 knots an hour, and entirely overcomes the ebb tide.

(For winds and currents, *see* page 15.)

WEST COAST OF YEZO.—Of the coast, from cape Sirakami, the southwest point of Yezo to cape Nossyab, the north-west point, very little is known, and there are but few good anchorages, the best being Oterranai in Iskarri bay, between which and Hakodate there are no anchorages, except with an off-shore wind, and then only at Sutsini and Rodgers island.

KO SIMA lies W. ½ S. 16½ miles from cape Sirakami, the north-west point of entrance to the strait of Tsugar. It has a round peak, 974 feet high, and there are two remarkable sugar-loaf islets or rocks lying off its west end, with rocks between them and the island.

O SIMA, 2,800 feet high, bears N.W. by W. ¼ W. 18 miles from Ko sima.

OKOSIRI ISLAND lies off the south-west coast of Yezo, is flat, showing no remarkable summit. On two occasions H.M.S. *Sybille* passed through the channel between it and Yezo. The south extreme of Okosiri is described as low, and detached rocks lie about 2 miles south of it. Some of these rocks are 10 to 15 feet above water, and apparently a reef connects them with the island. There may be anchorage off the south point, but the eastern side of the island is steep-to, and no bottom could be obtained when sailing through the channel, which is about 10 miles wide at its northern entrance. The north-east point of the island appeared from a distance to have a rocky ledge running out a short distance from it. On the Yezo side of the channel the land is high, and the coast apparently bold-to.

IWANI BAY opens at 20 miles north-east of cape Heneko, in lat. 43° 1' N., long. 140° 4' E. An Englishman has opened on Japanese account a mine of coal that is situated in the northern arm of the bay. There is a fair anchorage, and lighters could load easily in a little bay. The materials for working it are complete, with railways to carry the coal to the coast. There are two shafts in operation, that work easily, and when all is in order 100 tons a day will be readily obtained. Off shore 2 miles from the point that divides Iwani bay into two parts, is a rock that cannot have more than 6 feet of water on it. The settlement is in an open bay, and possesses no shelter except with an easterly wind.

OTERRANAI.—This settlement is of great importance, being the port of Iskarri, the greatest salmon fishery in the island. About 6,000 tons annually of this fish is dried and shipped off for the southern ports. Herrings are dried, and boiled down for manure, and sent south; seaweed is also procured.

The bay is well sheltered between N.E. and S.E., open to the eastward, is at all times safe, and might be made an excellent harbour.

When approaching this anchorage a remarkable red patch of cliff, and white sandy spots, mark its position. After rounding cape Skudutro, steer into the bay, bringing the easternmost bluff to bear N.E., or further in for a smaller vessel. The rise and fall of tide is less than 2 feet.

There are huts and houses all round the bay; they also extend more or less for 9 miles east, terminating in a village called Junbako.

Sappro.—The new capital of Yezo at present consists of about 100 wooden huts or houses. It is S.E., 24 miles from Oterranai, and 20 miles south of Iskarri, consequently is about 15 miles from the sea. A new road is being made to Endermo harbour. The country is perfectly wild, and entirely covered with wood, and much of it is fine timber, hard wood, oak.

ISKARRI.—Iskarri is a settlement about 13 miles east from Oterranai by water, and about 20 by land, situated at the mouth of the largest and finest river in Yezo, of the same name. There are about 100 houses at the place, with fishing stations at intervals up the river, for some miles.

On the bar at the river's mouth there is about 10 feet of water, and inside, and along the sandy bank of the river, on which the huts are built, there is 6 and 7 fathoms. The river is 200 to 300 yards in width for a considerable distance, and it is said to be navigable for light-draught vessels a great distance.

A vessel may anchor outside the bar, but with the wind from the westward she would be much exposed.

In the province of Sappro there are 3,000 Japanese. Potatoes, beans, millet, and wheat are grown, but in small quantities on bits of ground cleared by the cottagers close to their doors. The soil is rich and plentiful, and the lower slopes of the hills well adapted for agricultural purposes.

The COAST.—From Oterranai to cape Nossyab, a distance of 135 miles, the coast is bold and rocky, and is without a harbour or sheltered anchorage. A large river flows into the sea about 33 miles south of cape Nossyab, bringing down immense quantities of large timber, which is taken out to sea and through La Pérouse strait.

TARURI ISLANDS.—These two islands are about 300 feet in height.

CAPE NOSSYAB, the north-west point of Yezo island, is the abrupt but rather sloping termination of a remarkable table land, and appears like an island at a distance. Extending a mile northward from the cape is a flat narrow tongue of land, only a few feet above the sea, having upon it a few huts and a fishing station, which are conspicuous objects before the low land, on which they stand, rises to view, at 5 or 6 miles distant. From the extreme point of this low land a shoal rocky spit, partly covered with weed, extends N.N.W. upwards of a mile, with but little water over it in places, and at its extremity a depth of $2\frac{1}{2}$ fathoms, which rapidly deepens to 6 and 7 fathoms. Heavy breakers sometimes disclose this spit, but in smooth water they do not extend to its outer end. No vessel should near it within the depth of 12 or 14 fathoms.

ANCHORAGE.—There is anchorage in a bay 6 or 7 miles to the southward, on the west side of cape Nossyab, with the cape bearing N.N.E., south extreme of land S. by W. $\frac{1}{4}$ W., and the summit of Risiri S.W. by W. $\frac{1}{2}$ W., in 12 fathoms, the soundings decreasing gradually; a little farther north the ground is foul, in a less depth than 10 fathoms, at three-quarters of a mile off shore. The shore abreast this anchorage is low and swampy, covered with long rank grass and weeds, and backed by higher ground terminating in cape Nossyab.

At 6 or 7 miles south of cape Nossyab, there is another point that much resembles it on coming along the coast from the south, and whose continuation is also a sandy spit; cape Nossyab has a few huts at the foot of its hill, while there are none on the false point. Tide rips are very prevalent along that coast, and extend 2 miles from shore.

The bearing of capes Soya and Nossyab in line is E. by N. $\frac{1}{3}$ N. The *Dupleix* rounded these capes, getting 22 fathoms off the extreme of the rocks that terminate them.

CAPE SOYA.—The north extreme of Yezo is wild and barren, it may be easily recognized by a remarkable white rock lying off it to the westward. Reefs extend off the cape to some distance, and continue along the shore of Romanzov bay.*

ROMANZOV BAY.—Between capes Nossyab and Soya is an extensive bay, in which the land, covered with rank verdure slopes to the sea margin and its appearance in the south part or bottom, leads to the supposition of a large river being in that direction. Several huts are distributed along the shores of the bay, and about 5 miles S.W. from cape Soya is a large fishing village having near it on an elevated position an earthwork with embrasures, but no guns were seen. The reefs extend a great distance along the shore of the east side of the bay, but not far off the shore. About 2 miles within the bay, on the cape Soya side, the water shoaled suddenly from $12\frac{1}{2}$ to 8 and 2 fathoms on the outer edge of foul ground, extending nearly 2 miles off shore; a vessel, therefore, intending to take shelter here from a south-east wind, or wait the clearance of fog, should be careful to keep 3 or 4 miles off shore, where there is anchorage for the purpose in 17 or 18 fathoms, but the anchorage is bad in this bay even under favourable circumstances.

THE S.W. AND W. COASTS.—$2\frac{1}{2}$ miles round cape Yesan to the N.W. is a bay which affords good anchorage and shelter during westerly winds, and may often be found of great use and comfort when making for Hakodate, and finding it blowing hard from the westward through the straits; during fog, and when the cape or mountain is obscured, the strong sulphuric steam which descends, and is swept along the water, will frequently be smelt a considerable distance.

VOLCANO BAY and ENDERMO HARBOUR.†—The United States frigate *Southampton* visited both this bay and harbour in 1854, and verified the accuracy of Captain Broughton's survey made in September 1796; cape Yetomo, at the entrance of the harbour, is in lat. 42° 21′ N., long. 140° $56\frac{1}{2}$′ E.

The following description of this bay and harbour is from Broughton's voyages, pp. 102, 104:—He there states, "I have seen few lands that bear a finer aspect than the northern side of Volcano bay. It presents an agreeable diversity of rising ground, and a most pleasing variety of deciduous trees, shedding at this time their summer foliage.

The entrance into this extensive bay is formed by the land marking the harbour, which the natives call Endermo, and the south point, which they call Esarmi; they bear from each other N. by W. $\frac{1}{2}$ W., and S. by E. $\frac{1}{2}$ E.

---

* It was on these reefs H.M.S. *Rattler* was lost.
† *See* plan of Endermo harbour, No. 2,674; scale, $m = 5\cdot 25$ inches.

distant 33 miles. There are no less than three volcanoes in the bay, which induced me to call it by that name. The depth is 50 fathoms in the centre, and the soundings gradually decrease on the approach to either shore. During our stay at the period of the equinoxes we experienced generally very fine weather, with gentle land and sea winds from N.E. and S.E., and no swell to prevent a vessel riding in safety, even in the bay; and the harbour of Endermo is quite sheltered from all but bad weather, and is the best in the island, being exempt from the sudden and fierce gusts of wind which are experienced at Hakodate during a S.W. wind.

A range of hills, 1,800 to 2,000 feet in height, with three remarkable peaks on the highest ridge indicates the situation of this harbour.

Outside the bay the shores are bold, with deep water close up to the rocks. Off the west point of the headland which forms the bay, is a shoal patch extending 2 cables west of the islet.

A vessel may pass in on either side of Daikoku sima, the island in the centre of entrance to the harbour.

A 5-fathoms patch lies N.W. one-eighth of a mile from the N.W. end of this island.

DIRECTIONS.—In running for the harbour, the island must be kept open with the starboard entry point till within half a mile of a small islet (which is only so at half tide), and then steer in to the S.W., when the water will shoal, and any convenient berth taken. The soundings gradually decrease from 10 to 2 fathoms, soft bottom. A few houses are scattered on the south side of the harbour, and towards the head the shores are low and flat, so much so as to prevent boats landing within one hundred yards; in all other parts wood and water are procured with the utmost convenience.

ANCHORAGE.—By bringing the bluff on the extreme part of the isthmus, which forms the starboard point in coming in, to bear N.W.; in this position, in 4 or 5 fathoms water, the port entry point on the north shore is in line with the bluff, and the vessel is in a sheltered position.

TIDES.—It is high water, full and change, at 5h. 30m., rise and fall 6 feet.

UDSUZERI BAY is on the southern shore of Volcano bay S. ¼ E. from Endermo harbour. It is a small indentation having 3 cables of sheltered space, and shut in from the south by a low point from which rise three conical mounds, that serve as good marks for the recognition of the place. The neighbouring land is high and very steep.

ANCHORAGE may be had in 4½ fathoms, muddy sand, with good holding ground. There is a heavy sea, with winds from north-west by the north to east. The bay may be recognised by a large conical hill situated at its head.

TIDES.—The tide rises from 2 to 3 feet.

CAPE YERIMO.—In lat. 41° 55' N., long. 143° 16' E., is a rocky ragged bluff, about 80 feet high, the south extreme of a piece of plateau country, which stretches from the high mountains inland to the sea. There are several remarkable pinnacle rocks close off the cape, about 30 feet in height; and a reef of bold rocks, 10 or 15 feet out of the water, runs off S.E. ⅝ of a mile: 11 fathoms were obtained close off the extreme, and along the S.W. edge of the reef 6 and 8 fathoms; this depth gradually increases to 20 fathoms one mile off the cape. There are several villages containing storehouses for fish and seaweed under the cape.

Numbers of sea lions are found on these rocks; their roaring can be heard a considerable distance. The coast trends N. on east side of cape for some way, gradually hauling to N.E. On west side the trend is N.W.

Immediately behind this cape is a range of mountains, about 3,500 feet in height, and which will be seen from a considerable distance, when approaching this vicinity.

Giving this cape and the extreme S.E. rock half a mile's berth, clears all dangers.

The COAST between cape Yerimo and Akishi, a distance of nearly 90 miles, stretches about N.E. from the cape, slightly curving back, then trending more to the eastward: with not even an indentation along it. Junks anchor during a westerly wind a little to the north of cape Yerimo.

KUSURI, a Japanese settlement 20 miles west of Akishi, is situated at the mouth of a river, and consists of about 500 Japanese and a rather greater number of Ainos; fish and seaweed, being the produce of the place.

ANCHORAGE.—A vessel can anchor off the settlement if the wind is off shore, or between N.W. and N,E., but not otherwise.

AKISHI BAY.*—The land in the vicinity of this bay is (in appearance) perfectly flat and level; in height about 250 feet. Two remarkable high mountains are seen in a N.W. direction, the easternmost one being sugar-loafed, the top broken off; the left is a clump of peaks, with one standing clear by itself from the west end of the clump. Other high mountains are seen in the distance, bearing about N. by E. These are really on cape Sirotoko, which is fully 60 miles off.

Daikoku sima, just at the entrance to Akishi bay, is in lat. 42° 56' N., long. 144° 51' E., and is conspicuous and easily distinguished on approaching from any direction. The island is bold and rocky, and stands out from the land to the southward; the west point has a few rocks studded off it, but within 2 cables.

Between this point of Daikoku sima and cape Tempotze (290 feet high), the western boundary to the bay, a distance of 3½ miles, there is a clear

---

* *See* plan of Akishi bay, No. 992; scale, $m = 2\cdot 0$ inches.

passage of 1½ miles in width, between the west end or point of Daikoku sima and the east end of a reef, which runs out from cape Tempotze in an E. ½ S. direction towards the island, to a distance of 2 miles. There is deep water on either side of this reef, which however ought to be given a wide berth; generally there is a swell rolling in from the S.E. or South, which, breaking over the reef, points out its position and extent.

There is no passage between Daikoku sima and Ko-daikoku sima, neither between the latter and mainland, the whole being connected by reefs on which the sea breaks.

A few rocks are studded half a mile off flat bluff, on east side of the bay.

Rocky shoal.—A reef of rocks which dry at low water, lie 2 miles from the west side of the bay, with a conspicuous bluff bearing West, distant 2 miles. Water is abundant; and wood with the trouble of cutting it. Nothing but fish can be had at this very insignificant settlement, consisting of 40 Japanese and 160 Anios.

DIRECTIONS.—Keep Daikoku sima on the starboard hand half a mile distant, and steer N.N.W. for steep bluff, from abreast the south point of that island.

The water shoals gradually from 14 to 3½ fathoms, which depth will be found due west of furthest-up steep bluff, just over settlement, a distance of 5½ miles.

ANCHORAGE.—A convenient anchorage can be found close off the north end of Daikoku sima, off the flat pebbled point of the island, in 7 fathoms.

During S.W. gales or winds, the best anchorage is in the S.W. bight of the bay near Tempotze saki, where the water shoals gradually.

The Japanese have a settlement at this place, consisting, according to the statement of the head official, of 40 Japanese and 160 Ainos. Fish of numerous kinds, salmon, herring, flat fish, and a very white silvery fresh-water fish, about 10 inches long, abound. The salmon do not come into season until August and September.

Some of the fish are dried, but the greater portion are boiled down for manure, which is sent south. Seaweed cutting and drying commences in July, lasting three months, during which time fishing is almost suspended. Junks bring provisions during the summer, and overland there is a path to Hakodate, which place can be reached in about from 17 to 20 days.

Lagoon and River.—At the head of the bay is a large lagoon, with a good sized river running into it; the lagoon is very shallow, almost dry at low water. The river is pretty rapid, and comes from the N.W. Oysters abound in the lagoon, also other shell-fish, and numerous species of water birds, waders and divers, congregate in great numbers over this well-adapted locality for them.

PINNACLE ROCK.—Approaching Akishi bay, a remarkable pinnacle rock, 7½ miles E.N.E. of Daikoku sima, will very probably be first seen; it stands just clear of a bluff point, and is about 80 feet high, the point being about 160 feet in height.

The COAST.—The country from a little to the westward of Akishi is to all appearance perfectly flat, and in its wildest, most tangled state, and quite impenetrable. Trees of all ages lie heaped on the ground covered with moss and lichen of long growth, and in places there are extensive lagoons and swamps, the latter being overgrown with rank strong reeds and hazel shrubs. From Akishi bay eastward, the land tables gradually down, until it disappears altogether in the eastern horizon: 7½ miles E.N.E. of Daikoku sima, is the above-mentioned pinnacle rock, it is the only remarkable point along this stretch of uniform coast, and is also conspicuous when approaching from the eastward or making Hamanaka anchorage. The trend of the coast from Akishi to Pinnacle rock is E.N.E., and from the latter to Hamanaka or Kiritap is N.E. by E. 6 miles; the shores terminate in broken cliffs (or bluffs), of dark conglomerate rock, with green dips in the land between, backed by (in appearance) table land, which is covered with woods of deciduous trees, intermixed with fir, and where there is no wood, or the country appears open, in patches of bamboo grass. This constitutes the description of the island, from Akishi eastward, and round cape Noyshap to Nemero. No dangers were observed one mile off the shore, neither are there any believed to exist. The colour of the sea is neither blue nor green, such as the hot and cold streams usually are, but has a brownish tint.

HAMANAKA BAY, in lat. 43° 4′ N., long. 143° 8′ E., is a safe anchorage for a small vessel, being shallow. An island named Kiritap gives shelter behind it, and forms the anchorage at this settlement. It is open to the eastward only, and owing to shoal water and reefs, which extend across the eastern part, no sea can possibly be felt from this direction.

The best entrance is between the rocks above water, running off east the point of Kiritap island, and the west extreme of a reef, which is about 10 feet above water; this passage is three-quarters of a mile in width, and has not less than 8 fathoms water, with 12 fathoms in mid-channel; just before entering 7 fathoms will be passed over, probably an extenuation of the rocky island point.

After having entered mid-channel; round the island half a mile off, anchoring three-quarters of a mile off the low flat N.W. point of Kiritap island, in from 3½ to 4 fathoms: houses or huts are built along this flat point, and fishing stations erected. Hamanaka contains a larger population of both Japanese and Ainos than Akishi.

The COAST.—From Hamanaka to cape Usu, 16 miles E. ½ N., the coast slightly trending back from the latter cape, is tabled, unremarkable, and gradually lowering eastward. Reefs and dangers are believed to exist two miles off the coast, probably extending the whole distance from Hamanaka to the cape; it therefore ought not to be approached nearer than 2½ or 3 miles.

URURI SIMA.—Two islands, N.E. from 4 to 5 miles of cape Usu, the largest named Ururi, afford shelter behind them for junks during southerly gales.

CAPE USU is in lat. 43° 10′ N., long. 145° 32′ E. The coast from cape Usu to cape Noyshap, the east extreme of Yezo, trends about N.E. by N. a distance of 18 miles, still gradually lowering most uniformly, terminating in the cape itself, which is about 40 feet high. The aspect of the country between these capes is the same, except that there are larger patches of ground covered only with rank bamboo grass. Where trees are seen they are very much stunted and twisted and weather-beaten in appearance. There are bays and indentations along this stretch of coast.

CAPE NOYSHAP, in lat. 43° 22′ N., long. 145° 48¾′ E., should be approached with the greatest caution, as reefs extend on its south side to a distance of from 2½ to 3 miles, showing only during a southerly swell. There is now a beacon on the cape, 20 feet in height, erected by the Japanese.

From the numerous islands which lie east of the cape, reefs and rocks crop up in every direction towards the cape, narrowing the passage or channel round Noyshap to about 2 miles in width.

ISLANDS OFF CAPE NOYSHAP.—The islands off Noyshap are 11 in number, viz., Skotan, a large high island 50 miles east from the cape, Tarako, Sibutts, and Sisha forming the northern line; Itasiheiso, Mourika, Harukaru, and Akiro, the southern line; with Yurum lying midway between Akiro and Sisha, which are the two nearest to the cape. The remaining two are only rocks.

Of all these 11 islands only Skotan and Sibutts have a few Japanese settlers, and a more barren desolate part of the world to inhabit could scarcely be found.

Numerous reefs and rocks, (with a clear channel between the most western reef and the cape, 1¾ miles in width,) lie off Noyshap, stretching east towards the islands.

Different species of sea gulls and seals are numerous, and doubtless are the most suitable inhabitants.

DIRECTIONS.—If wishing to make cape Noyshap, and proceed through the dangerous pass leading into Yezo strait, the safest course to observe is, firstly, make Akiro sima, the most southern and most western of the group of islands off the cape; it is flat, about 40 feet in height, and except under very favourable circumstances, can be seen at no great distance; no dangers are believed to exist 2 miles off its south side.

If approaching from the south-west, steer N.E. ½ N. from cape Usu, and as soon as Noyshap bears N.N.W., and south point of Akiro sima N.E. by E. ½ E., alter course to N.N.W. to pass the cape not nearer than half a mile. If Kunashir island is seen, a sharp peak near its south-western extreme will now be just open of Noyshap. There are from 20 to 30 fathoms through this channel.

The reefs to the eastward (towards the islands), appear close-to, with strong tide rips and whirls off and around them.

As soon as the cape is passed, keep the coast of Yezo one mile distant. If proceeding to Nemero; a sharp point 8 miles west of Noyshap, which has a rock two cables off it, will be passed.

As soon as this point is abeam, Namow island opens, bearing S.W. by S., distant 5 miles, and can at once be distinguished by a temple and beacon on it.

If proceeding through these straits N.W. ½ W. from cape Noyshap to Notske, a curious sandy hook-shaped spit (running out from the Yezo coast), distant 24 miles from Noyshap, should be passed at one mile, at which distance from the spit is the deepest channel.

The dangers off cape Noyshap, and the group of islands mixed up, as they are, with reefs and rocks, besides those extending some miles off the cape itself (particularly to the southward), cause this narrow pass round the cape to be most dangerous, and fogs coming on suddenly add much to these dangers. If a vessel once gets within the reefs in making for the pass, and becomes entangled in fog and bad weather, she is placed at once in imminent danger. The currents also are strong, and whirl round cape Noyshap and among the reefs. The channel therefore between the islands of Skotan and Tarako, which is apparently clear of danger, is recommended.

The COAST.—From Noyshap the coast trends West 8 miles to the sharp rocky point above mentioned, from which it takes a S.W. by S. direction 5 miles to Nemero, and is unremarkable the whole distance.

From Nemero for 5 miles the trend is the same (S.W. by S.), the coast then dips round a low rocky point to the South, gradually rounding to West, N.W., and North, which is its trend at Nishibets, the next Japanese settlement westward of Nemero, and this on to the curious hook-shaped spit of Notske, situated 8 miles N. by W. from Nishibets.

From cape Noyshap until the coast dips to the South, the country is similar, dark rocky points, low cliffs, and stony beaches, and deciduous trees; bamboo grass covering the ground.

NEMORO, the only place on the north-east coast of Yezo with any pretensions to an anchorage, is in lat. 43° 20⅓′ N., long. 145° 35′ E., and is formed by a small island, Benten sima, running across the bay, which gives fair shelter for one vessel of light draught. In the entrance between the island and point, which is 1½ cables wide, there are 6 fathoms shoaling immediately to 4 fathoms.

The most sheltered part of this bay is shoal, the usual anchorage for junks is close to the island, with hawsers made fast to the rocks.

Wood, water, and fish are plentiful. The land about Nemoro is not more than 100 feet in height; as soon as it dips to the southward the aspect of the country entirely changes; a mass of swamps and shallow lagoons back the stony beach, opening here and there into the sea, fir trees become more thickly mixed with oak, hazel, &c.

The rocky points and cliffs are now replaced by a continuous dark pebbled beach.

NOTSKE SPIT, in lat. 43° 33′ N., long. 145° 18′ E., is low and flat, shaped like a hook, running out from the main land of Yezo about 6 miles. Its north side in a S.E. direction, rounding to the south and running back west; on this side (south) there are open shallow bays where only boats can float. Fir trees and oak appear to flourish on this strange sandy spit; and the Japanese endeavour to do so, as they have established a fishing station on it; a small temple is placed on its extreme S.E. edge. This anchorage affords shelter from winds from the westward, but is open to the east.*

SHIBETS.—The anchorage off this settlement is open to the N.E., and but little wind from that quarter, or East, produces a nasty sea. The country is very low and flat until past Shibets, from whence it rises suddenly into a grand lofty range of mountains, which terminate in cape Sirotoko.

CAPE SIROTOKO.—The N.E. extreme of Yezo is in lat. 44° 18′ N., long. 145° 23′ E. The high range of mountains which run out on this cape terminate abruptly a little back from the extreme point.

There are two projecting and remarkable points on this cape, one forming the eastern extreme, the other the northern. The latter has a rock about 30 feet high 2 cables off it, by which it can be easily distinguished.

---

* *See* plan of Notske anchorage on Chart of anchorages on the east coast of Yezo, No. 991; also plan of Nemoro on same sheet.

YEZO STRAIT, separating the north-east coast of Yezo from the island of Kunashir, is about 20 miles wide at either entrance, narrowing to 9 miles off Notske bay, at which place a shoal ridge having 10 fathoms deepest water extends across the strait to Kunashir. The entrance from the eastward is shoal, 16 fathoms being the deepest water, but the western approach is deep, the coast of Yezo being steep-to. As soon as Shibets is abeam, bearing West, the water deepens quickly, and following the Yezo coast up, it continues to do so, and 40 and 50 fathoms will be found close along the coast; great caution is necessary when proceeding through these straits, sudden patches of shoal water being frequent. The straits between S.W. point of Kunashir island and Notske spit show an irregular bottom, starting with 4 fathoms off the point, deepening to 6, shoaling again to 4, and again deepening to 11 fathoms 1½ miles off Notske spit, at which distance, probably, the best channel runs through the straits.

In December the strait is frozen over to a considerable distance off shore.

The trend of the coast after rounding Sirotoko is S.W. ¼ S. for 37 miles, when it rounds to W. ½ N. for 18 miles further, here it suddenly trends N. by W. for 10 miles, forming a point called cape Notoro. Five miles back from the point, and just behind a curious reef of rocks, with a high mass of light stone and rock at one end of the reef, is the settlement of Abashira. A fair sized river runs into the sea just abreast the village, and there are several large lagoons to the westward of cape Notoro.

ABASHIRA.—Anchorage in 5 fathoms may be had here on either side of the reef. A bank with 1½ fathoms runs from the reef to the entrance of the river.

As long as the wind is off shore the anchorage is safe.

Cape Sirotoko can be distinctly seen from here on a clear day, bearing E.N.E.

The country near Abashira is of moderate height, 500 or 600 feet, but unremarkable. A sudden dip in the hills, and which is the course of the river through them, will be observed when approaching from the East.

MOMBETS.—From cape Notoro the coast trends N.W. by W. ¼ W. for 44 miles; here a low point projects out one mile from the otherwise uniform coast line; just inside the slight protection this point gives, is the settlement of Mombets. With the wind off shore a vessel can anchor one mile off the settlement in 7 fathoms.

The COAST from Mombets to Soya, a distance of 90 miles, trends about N.W. by N. The whole of the N.E. coast from Sirotoko to Soya is low, with higher ground and ranges of hills rising inland. The country is covered with wood and long grass; large lagoons and shallow inlets of the sea are found near Abashira.

CHAP. VIII.]   RISIRI AND REFUNSIRI ISLANDS.   349

Along this stretch of coast, nearly 200 miles in length, there is no shelter for a vessel, or anchorage, except with the wind off shore.

RISIRI ISLAND is about 18 miles to the south-west of cape Nossyab, and the passage between is quite clear of all known danger, and may safely be taken. This island, from its great height, becomes for vessels approaching from the southward, a conspicuous mark for the west entrance of La Pérouse strait. It is nearly circular in shape, with a generally low shore rising abruptly from the sea. No dangers of any importance are known in its vicinity; a few detached rocks exist, but they lie close inshore. It was first seen by La Pérouse, who took it for a mountain on the mainland of Yezo, and named it Pic de Langle. Its summit attains an elevation of 5,900 feet, and may be seen in clear weather from a distance of 70 or 80 miles; it is generally capped with snow, and often peers out most usefully above the harassing fogs.

A bluff point called Nakko head, jutting out on the north-east side of the island, forms a small bay which affords shelter from S.E. round by north to W.N.W. The *Actæon* anchored in 11 fathoms, sand. Gun boats or vessels with steam at command might go farther in, and be more sheltered in 5 fathoms; it is quite open to the other points of the compass.

No supplies, except a small quantity of firewood, could be obtained. There is a small village, with a scanty population, in the bay south of Nakko head. A very small portion of the island is cultivated, the sides of the mountain being wooded to the summit; the inhabitants, like the rest of the Japanese islanders, mainly depending upon the products of the ocean for support.

REFUNSIRI ISLAND, lying off the south side of the western entrance to La Pérouse strait, is in shape an acute-angled triangle 11 miles long, and 3¼ miles wide at the base which is its north end, where there is a shallow bay, with rather a populous village. A large portion of the island is under cultivation, and it is much more thickly inhabited and productive than its near neighbour, Risiri. A few fowls and some fish may be obtained, but no other supplies except water need be looked for. The summit of a range of hills, the highest part of which is nearly in the centre of the island, attains an elevation of 1,300 feet, but it is so close to Pic de Langle on Risiri as to appear to the eye much lower.

The shores of this island appear to be clear of outlying dangers, except the north end, where the ground is foul. At a mile northward of cape Hieber, the north-west point of the island, is an islet called Bomasiri, but the channel between it and the point is blocked up by a reef of rocks. Nearly 2 miles North of the north-east point of the island, and about

East 2½ miles from Bomasiri, is the dangerous rock discovered by H.M.S. *Bittern* in 1855, but it nearly always breaks, and therefore in daylight may be avoided.

In September 1859, H.M.S. *Actæon* anchored in 12 fathoms on the east side of Refunsiri, close to a small rocky islet about 4¾ miles north of cape Karanunai (the south point of the island), with the extremes of the island bearing S.S.W. ¼ W. and N. ⅔ E., fair shelter being thus afforded from S.W. to N.W. the points between which the autumn gales generally blow with the greatest strength.

LA PÉROUSE STRAIT.

This strait is formed between cape Notoro, the southern end of Saghalin, and cape Soya, the north extreme of Yezo. The general soundings in it are from 35 to 40 fathoms and upwards, decreasing to 25 and 20 fathoms as the shores are neared; but as these latter depths will be found in the middle of the strait near the Dangerous rock, and in other places the lead in thick weather cannot always be trusted to ensure safety.*

There are heavy overfalls, giving the appearance of a reef, between cape Notoro and Dangerous rock, but deep water was found on passing through. Neither this cape nor cape Nossyab should be closed by a sailing vessel, without a commanding breeze, on account of the tide race off them. (For winds and currents, *see* page 18.)

SAGHALIN ISLAND, Tarakai of the natives, and Karafuto of the Japanese, extends nearly north and south abreast the coast of Tartary, for a length of 510 miles, by a width varying from 25 to 100 miles. Its northern portion is opposite the entrance of the Amúr river, to which it approaches within 10 miles, while its southern extremes, capes Siretoko and Notoro, are separated from the island of Yezo by La Pérouse strait.

The island is mountainous; two ranges extend respectively N.W. and N.E. from its southern extremes, and meet in Bernizet peak in 47° 33′ N. Its western face is steep and rugged, the cliffs rising to a considerable height, and along the whole of this coast there is not one sheltered anchorage, the Russian ports of Dui, Jonquière bay, &c. being merely open roadsteads; the eastern coast is low and sandy. The middle district of the island is flat and swampy, but to the north hilly and fertile. It is well wooded throughout, and large quantities of timber are exported to Japan for building purposes. The interior of the island consists of a high table land thickly covered with forests of pine. It is not well watered, but the soil is said to be fertile.

---

* The description of La Pérouse strait, the gulf of Tartary, and the sea of Okhotsk is chiefly from the Remark books of Officers of H.M. Ships, 1855–1857. *See* Chart of Kuril Islands, No. 2,405.

There is coal in several parts of this island, and on its west side around Jonquière bay and Dui it rises to the surface, and is of fair quality. Whales are found on the east and south coasts; salmon and herrings abound, and in the deep bay of Aniwa on the south, into which two large streams fall, the Japanese have established an extensive salmon fishery. Saghalin has long been celebrated for its fisheries. The fish taken on the coasts are exported to Hakodate and Matsumae and thence sent to all parts of Japan. The largest fishing station in the island is at the head of Patience bay on the east coast. The fishing season commences in April and closes in August. Besides coal, which crops up in every direction, gold, copper, and iron are found in some quantities. The Russians, notwithstanding the nominal boundary of the parallel of 48° N., claim the whole of the island as also the island of Urup and islands of the Kuril group north of it, but regard Kunashir and Iturup as belonging to the Japanese. Water is abundant at all parts, and drift wood for fuel is found in large quantities along the western coast. The northern portion of the island is inhabited by Ghiliaks, and the southern by Ainos, aborigines of Yezo, a race of small stature.

DANGEROUS ROCK, bearing S.E. ½ S. 8½ miles from the summit of cape Notoro, is a small bare rock about 20 feet high and 60 feet in diameter. It should not be approached nearer than a mile, as dangerous rocky ledges appear to extend from it in three different directions, N.W., E.S.E., and W.S.W. Between the cape and the rock the soundings are irregular, varying from 17 to 32 fathoms, the bottom chiefly of broken coral.

This rock is aptly named, and must always prove a source of great anxiety to the navigator, as it lies nearly in the centre of a channel becoming more frequently used every day, where dense fogs are prevalent, and where the direction and force of the currents are but imperfectly known. The lead here will afford but little warning, but that little should not be despised; less water than 20 fathoms when in its vicinity indicates close proximity. The rock is generally covered with seals, and the noise of their barking and bellowing, if carefully listened for, may in foggy weather warn the seaman of his danger.

CAPE NOTORO, the south point of Saghalin, from a distance of 10 or 12 miles makes like an island. On its summit, 124 feet high, is a small shrine, and 4 miles north of the cape is a conspicuous hill (Quoin hill), which rises abruptly from the shore, but slopes gently towards the cape, and on its north side reaches an elevation of 1,025 feet. A range of hills, varying from 800 to 1,200 feet in height, amongst which is one of sugar-loaf form, stretches along the coast to the N.E. of Quoin hill. These hills are covered with a thick undergrowth of dwarf bamboo, giving them a fresh green appearance, but rendering the country almost impassable, except through the bear tracks, which are numerous. A line of steep earth cliffs, ranging from 80 to 200 feet in height, run along the back of the beach, which is generally a narrow strip of sand.

The Tishia rock, 72 feet high, conspicuously marks the position of the point of the same name, at 8¼ miles N.E. by N. of the summit of cape Notoro. The coast between takes a slight bend, forming an open bay; no rocks exist in it, except quite close inshore; but 2 miles N.N.E. of Tishia point there is a detached reef at three-quarters of a mile off shore. From the Tishia rock the coast trends about N. by E. for some considerable distance, but it has not been examined.

ANCHORAGE may be found in 8 or 12 fathoms anywhere along the coast between cape Notoro and the Tishia rock. The *Actæon* anchored in 15 fathoms, good holding ground, 1½ miles N.E. ½ N. of the summit of the cape, having Tishia rock just open of Tishia point. Good shelter may be obtained here, and also farther to the northward in the bight of the bay, from the prevalent autumnal and winter gales, but it is quite open to the southward and eastward. A few Japanese, with Aino attendants, were communicated with, but they had nothing to dispose of.

Reefs of straggling rocks border cape Notoro at the distance of from 2 to 3 cables. The shore north-west of the cape appears to be fringed with rocks, some of them a considerable distance off shore. On the western side and 3 miles northward of the cape, and near a Japanese fishing station, is an extensive patch of dangerous rocks, covered at high water; they lie about a mile off shore, with irregular soundings of 3 fathoms within them, and 7 fathoms near their outside. No vessel should approach these rocks in less than 12 or 13 fathoms water, as then the ground is broken and foul.

Water was obtained by H.M.S. *Actæon* in 1859 without much difficulty, at a small stream on the east side and 2 miles northward of cape Notoro. On the west side, and 6 or 7 miles northward of the cape, is an excellent watering place, used by H.M. squadron in 1855, at a stream running over a bed of sand and gravel into the sea. Anchorage off it should be taken in 10 to 9 fathoms, sand. The soundings decrease gradually towards the shore.

TOTOMOSIRI, lying N.W. ¾ W., 44 miles from cape Notoro, is 1,400 feet in height, without the volcanic appearance of Refunsiri or of Risiri. There are three rocks awash lying about a mile off its eastern shore, and another about a mile off its N.E. point.

Water.—There is a spring on Totomosiri, from which whalers are in the habit of watering, but with great difficulty and labour.

LA PÉROUSE STRAIT.—ANIWA BAY.

CAPE SIRETOKO (Aniwa), the south extreme of Saghalin, is a remarkable promontory, the more so from a chain of high mountains near it, stretching away to the northward, between which and the cape is a hollow that gives it the appearance of a saddle. The headland itself is a steep abrupt mass of rocks, quite barren, with a deep inlet at its point.

ANIWA BAY is an extensive bight, about 45 miles deep, occupying the southern end of Saghalin between capes Notoro and Siretoko, which bear W. ⅛ S. and E. ⅛ N. of each other, and are distant 55 miles. At its head is Kushankotan, where there is a Japanese settlement, composed of a few wooden houses, also the huts of the natives, which are of the most wretched description. The coast here is moderately high and level, and when first seen has the appearance of chalk cliffs, which continues for about 12 miles to the south-east, when it becomes higher, irregular, and of a dark colour. The Shikawa (salmon river), the largest river in Saghalin, flows into Aniwa bay close to this settlement, and by its numerous tributaries the Ainos keep up a desultory communication with the interior.

The point southward of this settlement runs out shoal, and, until better known, should not be approached within 2 miles. Anchorage may be had in 6 fathoms, sand and mud, at about one mile from the beach, with the village of Kushankotan bearing E. by S. ½ S. and cape Isoja S.S.E. ¾ E.* To the northward of the north point, seen from the anchorage off the village, a shoal flat fronts a low plain covered with trees, and farther back the land rises in an undulating form to high hills. The shore from Shikawa as far as Chebeshani consists of low barren looking hills, and thence to cape Siretoko extends a long sandy beach, forming the south-west boundary of the extensive plain on which the Russian settlement of Boussie stands. About midway between capes Notoro and Siretoko the depth is 58 fathoms, and the soundings decrease gradually to the anchorage. The western shore of Aniwa bay presents good holding ground in soft mud, shoaling gradually from outside 10 fathoms, outside which the bottom is hard.

ANCHORAGE may be had at Ouron in 10 fathoms at about 2½ miles from the shore, where there are a few fishing huts scattered along the coast. Aniwa bay is open to the southward, but the holding ground in it is good.

Supplies.—Water is plentiful in Aniwa bay, but of an inferior quality, and difficult to be procured. Excellent firewood in any quantity can be obtained from the authorities.

---

* The shoal said to lie S.S.W. from this anchorage was searched for in vain, and its existence was ignored by the Japanese inhabitants at this settlement. It would be advisable, however, to avoid its supposed position until the fact of its non-existence is verified.

Fish are abundant; a small kind of salmon weighing about 3 lbs. is taken in large numbers during a few weeks in June and July; herrings earlier in season. Supplies of any other description are not to be obtained.

TOBOOTCHI BAY in Aniwa bay, lat. 46° 29′ N., long. 143° 18′ 18″ W., is a shallow basin having 3 fathoms water in its deepest part. It communicates with Aniwa bay by a narrow channel which is fronted by sandbanks extending a considerable distance from the shore. The depth is 9 feet on the bar at the entrance. Two beacons in line on Klykoff point lead in. The Russians have taken possession of Boussie at the head of this bay, the Japanese having retired to Chibessan 8 miles northward. Vessels at anchor outside, should in the event of bad weather make for Kushan-kotan.*

TIDES.—In and about La Pérouse strait the tides are very irregular and are much influenced by prevailing winds, and are felt mostly inshore, round capes Notoro and Nossyab, where they form heavy tide rips and races. It is high water near these capes, full and change, between 10h. and 11h., and the rise is about 6 feet. The flood stream sets to the northward along the west coasts of Yezo and Saghalin, and to the eastward through La Pérouse strait.

EAST AND WEST COASTS OF SAGHALIN.

KOSOUNAI.—A Russian settlement on the west side of the island in about lat. 48° 0′ N. on the north side of a small river about 50 feet wide and 6 feet deep at its entrance. On the south side of this river is a Japanese post and a settlement of Ainos. The Russians live in large white log houses which can be seen from some distance seaward. There are three beacons of pyramidical form 40 feet in height, one on the north cape, one on the south, and one in the centre of the bay.

DUI.—A Russian settlement in about lat. 50° 50′ N., long. 142° 14′ E., is situated on the shores of a small bay formed by cape Hoidji on the south and cape Otsisi on the north. There are some very valuable coal mines here worked by Russian convicts, who with their guards number about 300. During the summer months steam transports are constantly running between this place and Castries bay with coal. From Castries bay it is shipped off to the Amúr for the use of the Russian squadron. There is a small pier at the settlement to facilitate the shipment of coal, and a small stream runs through the settlement; this has been dammed up to work a saw-mill. The coal is said to be nearly equal to north country coal for steaming purposes, but is not of very prepossessing appearance.

---

* See plan of Tobootchi bay on Chart of Kuril islands, No. 2,405.

A reef extends N.N.W. ½ W. nearly 6 cables from cape Hoidji; it is steep to on the north-west and south, but from the westward the water shoals gradually.

This reef is marked by two beacon buoys 60 feet apart, the outer in 4¾ fathoms, the inner in 4¼ fathoms. From thence to the pier end the water shoals gradually to 3½ fathoms.

LIGHT.—On the slope of a hill between capes Otsisi and Hoidji is exhibited at an elevation of 373 feet above the mean level of the sea a *fixed* white light visible from seaward when bearing from N.E. ¼ E. round by east to S. by W. ¾ W., and is visible in clear weather from a distance of 22 miles.

The illuminating apparatus is catoptric. The tower is square, 40 feet high, white, and surmounted by a gray lantern.

DIRECTIONS.—Owing to the uncertainty of the current and the prevailing foggy weather it is advisable to make the coast south of cape Hoidji and coast it northward. To clear the reefs off the above cape keep cape Otsisi N.E. until the lighthouse bears southward of East, when steer for it.

ANCHORAGE.—Small vessels can lie in 3 fathoms with cape Hoidji bearing S. 30° W., and the lighthouse S. 69° E. off the pier, but larger vessels must anchor farther out. The bottom in some places is covered with large boulders, especially between the 3 fathom line and the shore. It must be remembered that this anchorage is only safe with easterly winds; should the wind shift to the westward it would be advisable to put to sea at once.*

JONQUIÈRE BAY on the west coast of Saghalin island, about 1½ miles north-east of cape Otsisi, is in lat. 50° 54′ N., and may be recognised by three remarkable detached pinnacle rocks, about 50 feet high, off its south point. The coast to the southward is bold, but becomes less so in the bay and to the northward as the high land recedes. This bay should be looked upon only as a fine weather anchorage; it affords shelter from N.E., (round by the east,) to South, but is exposed to all other winds, and the holding ground is mostly bad; there are some good spots, however, for anchorage in 9 to 7 fathoms water. A small river finds an outlet in the bay, and boats can pass over its bar when the tide is in.†

The south end of the cliff in the bay bearing East leads in clear of danger.

The natives are fine handsome people, they wear the front part of the head shaved, the back hair being worn hanging over their shoulders, the

---

* J. Jones, Master, R.N., H.M.S. *Scylla*, 1866.

† *See* plan of Jonquière bay; scale, $m = 2$ inches, on Chart of Kuril islands, No. 2,405.

men also possess large black beards; these natives are inoffensive and obliging.

Coal.—A few huts of the natives will be seen on the south part of the above river entrance, and contain about 30 Ghilyaks, who possess a great number of dogs, which they use for dragging their canoes; they also serve them for food. Between these huts and Pinnacle point are seams of good surface coal, some of which, being close to the water's edge, can be easily worked. The land about the river is cultivated, and some cattle were seen.

Supplies.—Large quantities of fish were taken in Jonquière bay by hauling the seine on the beach to the northward of the huts, and good sized flat fish were caught with hook and line about a quarter of a mile off shore, in 3 or 4 fathoms water. Wild fowl and white hares are numerous. Wood can be got in any quantity up the river.

The watering place is inconvenient. Drift wood is plentiful.

TIDES.—The time of high water, full and change, in Jonquière bay, is at 10h. 0m., and the rise is about 6 feet.

The COAST.—From Jonquière bay the coast trends to the N.N.W., and is bold of approach as far as cape Undy, from which to cape Liak at the entrance to the strait of Tartary it appears as an immense plain, broken only by a few craggy hillocks in the interior (the high land having terminated abruptly at the former cape), and is skirted with a shoal bank, which extends to a considerable distance off shore with from 5 to 6 fathoms at 1½ miles. (For directions for Tartary strait, see p. 107.)

OBMAN BAY, at 22 miles north-east from cape Golovachef, and 44 miles to the southward of cape Mary, has barely sufficient water at its entrance for boats.

For the north entrance of the gulf of Amúr, see p. 106.

NADEIDA BAY, named after Krusenstern's ship, is about 35 miles North of Obman bay, and 10 miles to the south-east of cape Mary. A plentiful supply of wood and water may be easily procured here, but the bay being open, the bottom rocky, and consequently not a safe anchorage, will preclude its ever being much visited.

EAST COAST—CAPE LÖWENHÖRN, in lat. 46° 23' 10" N., long. 143° 40' E.,* is a steep projecting rock, easily to be distinguished from the rest of this coast by its yellow colour. North of it the coast assumes a more westerly direction, and consists of a chain of large lofty mountains, covered with snow in May.

CAPE TONIN, the next headland to the northward, is of moderate height, and entirely overgrown with fir trees. A chain of rocks stretches

---

* The positions on this coast are by Krüsenstern, 1805.

to the northward from it; southward of the cape the bottom is rocky, with small stones; to the northward it is entirely of clay.

MORDVINOF BAY is a large bight in the coast westward of cape Tonin, in which plenty of water was procured and abundance of firewood. On the shores of the bay several dwelling-houses were seen by Krusenstern, but most of them were empty. The natives appeared to be superior to those in Aniwa bay.

CAPE SIENIAVIN is a high point of land in lat. 47° 16½' N. To the northward of it the coast is low, and trends suddenly to the westward; to the southward are lofty mountains covered with snow in May.

Bernizet peak of La Pérouse, is probably the same as mount Spenberg of the Dutch. It is a lofty, rounded mountain, in 47° 33' N., 142° 20' E., near the north-west end of a lofty chain of mountains running through the valley from N.W. to N.E.

CAPE DALRYMPLE, in lat. 48° 21' N., is formed by a high mountain rising close to the beach, in a north and south direction, and is the more easily known from being altogether isolated, except that at 12 or 15 miles to the northward, is another, very unlike this, apparently consisting of four separate mountains; the coast between is, with the exception of a peak of moderate height, quite low.

From this cape the coast trends in a S. by W. direction, and is bounded by lofty mountains, divided by deep valleys, the shore being steep and rocky. In several places are inlets between the rocks which might afford anchorage; one in lat. 48° 10' looked more promising than the rest.

PATIENCE BAY.—Cape Saimonof, in lat. 48° 52½' N., is the western point of entrance to Patience bay, which is limited to the eastward by cape Patience. The former cape is a high promontory, projecting to the eastward, and was taken for an island when it bore North. The north coast of the bay is mountainous, and the beach craggy. Far inland are lofty snow-topped mountains, except in one part, where an even country stretches away to the northward as far as the eye can reach. In the north-west angle of the bay is the mouth of the river Neva.

CAPE PATIENCE, the most prominent and the easternmost cape of Saghalin, is a low promontory, formed by a double hill, terminating abruptly. From this a flat tongue of land projects some distance to the southward; on the north side of the cape the land is likewise low, the flat hill near Flat bay being the first high land in that direction. By this hill, cape Patience, (which, owing to its little elevation, is not easily perceived,) may soon be recognised. The cape is surrounded by a rocky shoal, extending a considerable distance from the land.

ROBBEN ISLAND, the centre of which bears about S.W. ¼ S., 22 miles from cape Patience, is surrounded by a dangerous reef about 35 miles in circumference. Krusenstern examined this reef in 1805. The waves broke violently over it, and to the northward there appeared, as far as the eye could reach, a large field of ice, under which, in all probability, the reef continued. The channel between the cape and the reef was not examined.

FLAT BAY, in lat. 49° 5′ N., is surrounded on all sides by low land. It is a deep opening, in which, even from the mast head, no land could be descried. From this circumstance it was thought by Krusenstern, to be the mouth of a large river.

CAPE BELLINGSHAUSEN, at 30 miles northward of Flat bay has at 7 miles S.S.W. of it, a point which was thought to offer a good harbour. The shore is abrupt, and entirely white. Between two hills that project considerably, the southernmost apparently insulated, is this apparent harbour, and perhaps a small river; it was, however, unexplored. The country about it is regular in appearance.

CAPE RIMNIK, at 40 miles farther northward, has at the back of it, some miles inland, a high flat hill, named mount Tiara, remarkable for having three points on its summit.

CAPE RATMANOF, in lat. 50° 48′ N., terminates in a flat neck of land, stretching a considerable distance into the sea. The coast hereabouts is invariably craggy, and of a yellow colour.

CAPE DELISLE de la CROYÈRE, in lat. 51° 0′ 30″ N., forms the boundary of the mountainous part of Saghalin, for northward of it there is neither high land nor a single mountain, the shore everywhere consisting of sand, of a most dangerous uniformity. This cape is connected with cape Ratmanof by a flat sandy beach, with mountains in the background between them.*

Downs Point, in lat. 51° 53′ N., is rendered remarkable by a round hill. It is not the boundary of the sand coast, for this continues to the northward of the same features as that to the southward, only that behind this point there is a bay of considerable depth.

To the northward of Downs point is a chain of five hills, having the appearance of islands in this extended plain. The whole coast here, like that to the southward, is scarcely raised above the water's edge; it is entirely of sand, and a little way inland is covered with a seemingly impenetrable forest of low shrubs.

---

* See Chart of the Sea of Okhotsk, No. 2,388; scale, $m = 0·03$ of an inch.

CAPE OTMÉLOI (Shoal point), in lat. 52° 32½′ N., so named from its vicinity to the only dangerous shoal Krusenstern met with off this coast, may be easily known by a hill of tolerable height, which on this flat coast almost merits the name of a mountain, and forms a remarkable object.

This shoal might have proved dangerous if great attention had not been paid to the soundings, the depth falling suddenly from 8 to 4½ fathoms. It is in lat. 52° 30′ N., long. 143° 29′ E., and extends, probably, some miles north and south at a distance of 10 miles off shore. The coast, the direction of which from Downs point is north, projects to the eastward nearly on the parallel of this shoal.

CAPE VIRST is in lat. 52° 57½′ N. A long way inland there are several considerable high lands, the coast being, as far as the eye can reach, composed of flat sand.

CAPE KLOKATCHEFF is in lat. 53° 46′ N., and near it appeared to be the mouth of a considerable river, as the land appeared unconnected. The land about it is flat, gradually increasing in height, the shores being flat and sandy.

CAPE LÖWENSTERN, named after Krusenstern's third lieutenant, in 54° 3¼′ N., is a large promontory, from which the coast takes a more westerly direction. To the southward of this cape, the land, which has been hitherto flat and sandy, is high and mountainous, with narrow spaces between the hills, the shore very steep, and in several places consisting of rocks of a chalk like appearance. In front of the cape there is a large rock.

The land between this cape and cape Elizabeth presents a lofty, dreary, and barren appearance; no traces of vegetation are apparent, and the whole coast is iron-bound, consisting of one mass of black granite rock, with here and there a white spot; the depth at 2 miles off shore was 20 fathoms, and at 3 miles, 30 fathoms, rocky bottom. There are four other promontories between these headlands.

CAPE ELIZABETH, the north extreme of Saghalin, is a high mass of rock, forming the extremity of an uninterrupted chain of mountains. It is rendered remarkable from a number of high pointed hills, or rather naked rocks, upon which neither tree nor verdure of any kind is perceptible. It descends gradually to the sea, and at the brink of the precipice is a pinnacle or small peak. From the northward it makes in two rugged points, the western one being divided into peaks. Seen from the west it bears an extraordinary appearance to cape Lopatka, the south end of Kamchatka, except that it is higher. On the west side of the cape a point projects, and between them there is a small bay.

CAPE MARY, about 18 miles W.S.W. of cape Elizabeth, is lower than the latter cape, and consists of a chain of hills all nearly of the same elevation. It slopes gently down to the sea, and terminates in a steep precipice, from whence a dangerous reef appears to project a considerable distance to the north-east.

TIDES.—It is high water, full and change at cape Mary, at 2h., and the rise is about 5 feet.

NORTH BAY (Sévernaia Guba).—Between capes Elizabeth and Mary is a large bay of considerable depth, at the head of which, at the foot of a mountain, is a village in a beautiful valley. The locality is fertile, and the mountains covered with forests of fir trees.

This bay, although open, is said to be safe in the summer when north winds are rare. At 1½ miles off shore the depth is 9 fathoms, fine sand decreasing at half a cable gradually to 3 fathoms over excellent anchoring ground.

The north-west coast of Saghalin is infinitely preferable to the south-west. Between the mountains, which are entirely overgrown with the thickest forests, are valleys which appear capable of cultivation. The shores are broken, and almost everywhere of a yellow colour. The confines of the high and low lands are precisely in the same parallel as on the opposite shore; and beyond the limits, to the S.S.W., as far as the eye could reach, nothing could be seen but the low sandy shore, with here and there a few insulated but picturesque sand hills.

KURIL ISLANDS.

This extensive chain of islands extends nearly in a uniform N.E. and S.W. line of direction from the north-east point of Yezo to the south extreme of Kamchatka. The Boussole channel separates the chain into two portions; that to the northward belonging to Russia, and the southern portion to Japan. The fog in which these islands are constantly enveloped, the violent currents experienced in all the channels separating them, the steepness of their coasts, and the impossibility of anchoring, are such formidable obstacles, that it tries to the utmost the patience and perseverance of the mariner to acquire much knowledge respecting them.*

KUNASHIR, the south-eastern of the Kuril islands, is separated from the north-east end of Yezo by a channel, named by Krusenstern the strait of Yezo, which is about 9 miles wide in the narrowest part. This end of Yezo forms a deep bay, and the south-east part of Kunashir advances very

---

* See Charts:—Kuril islands, No. 2,405; scale, $d = 2\cdot1$ inches: and Pacific Ocean, Sheet 1, No. 2,459; scale, $d = 0\cdot8$ of an inch.

far into it, so that cape Noyshap, the eastern extreme of Yezo, entirely hides the strait, from which cause Kunashir and Yezo are often taken for one island.*

The island of Kunashir is high; the principal summit at the north end in lat. 44° 20′ N., long. 146° 15′ E., being 7,900 feet above the sea; towards the south is another of 3,020, and the farther south is 1,800 feet high. The island is stated to be surrounded with rocks and dangers. Its south-west part forms Itmen bay, the two points of entrance to which bear N.W. by W. ½ W. and S.E. by E. ½ E. from each other, distant 6 miles. The point that terminates the island is a tongue of sand, almost awash, on the west of which is the bay above mentioned. This tongue continues itself with shallow water on which the sea is heavy. At half a mile there are 2⅔ fathoms, and it appears to run to the south-west across to the Yezo shore.

In the bay the depth is uniformly 3¾ fathoms. It is 6 or 7 miles wide, and is open to the south-west. At its head is the village of Tomari, where about fifty Japanese and some Ainos live by fishing, the only produce, the country being bare and uncultivated. Whales frequent the strait, but the natives do not know how to take them.

The depth is generally about 33 fathoms, sand and broken shells, to half way between Skotan and Kunashir, then it decreases irregularly to 8⅙ fathoms at 10 miles east of Kunashir, which must not be approached, the soundings decreasing, to 3¼ fathoms, always irregularly.

The *Dupleix* anchored in 3¾ fathoms 5 miles W. by S. ⅛ S. from the south point of Kunashir. Towards the south the depth appeared to diminish a little to 2 miles south of the point where a hole of 9¼ fathoms was found. The shoalest water was 2⅔ fathoms, the deepest appearing to be close to the shore, where the bottom presented an appearance of a series of ditches having no determinate direction. Cape Rewansi, the north extreme of Kunashir, has a small island off it, as has also cape Moimoto.

SKOTAN is a round island, 12 miles in extent, lying 45 miles N.E. by E. from cape Noyshap, the eastern extreme of Yezo. The southern part is low, and bordered with rocks, and as far as 5 miles from it the water is discoloured and breaks heavily. The north side is rugged and steep-to, indented with several bays that appear to penetrate deeply into the interior. There is a heavy sea near the points, and with fresh breezes from the west it breaks violently in the bays.

---

* The description of the Kuril islands is from the remarks of Captain Du Petit Thours, of the Imperial French Navy, in H.I.M.S. *Dupleix*, of Staff Commanders George L. Carr, and W. H. Drysdale, R.N., and other officers of H.M. Navy.

The *Dupleix* sailed along the coast at 1½ miles, seeking an anchorage, but all these bays appeared bad. The third bay is the largest, but breakers were seen in the middle of the entrance.

She anchored one mile from the shore in 20 fathoms broken shell, the extremes of the island bearing E. by N. ¾ N. and S. by E. ¼ E., and the nearest point E. by S. ¾ S. about a mile. There were 33 fathoms at 1½ miles north of the island. The principal summit of the island is about 1,400 feet high, and the highest north and north-west portions 980 to 820 feet. The aspect is desolate, and no habitation was seen. The space between Yezo and Skotan is much contracted by islands, rocks, and reefs (see page 345), which it will be well to avoid. The only safe channel is between Tarako (the most northern of these islands) and Skotan.

CURRENTS.—At the anchorage of Skotan the sea was high, and during the night a current setting east 2 knots was experienced by the *Dupleix*. At one league from Skotan the strong current felt near that island was lost, and an irregular, scarcely sensible, counter current took its place.

ITURUP or Staten island, separated from Kunashir by the Pico or Catherine channel, about 18 miles wide, is but little known;* but it appears to be about 135 miles in extent, N.E. by E. and S.W. by W., and 25 miles at its broadest part. Cape Okebets, its north-east point, is said to be high and perpendicular, and to be in lat. 45° 38½′ N., long. 149° 14′ E.; its south point, cape Rickord, in 44° 29′ N., 146° 34′ E. H.M.S. *Cormorant* entered a bay on the east side of the island between capes Noneiso and Tosimoinots, it is open but gives shelter from all southerly winds, and is more deeply indented than shown on the chart with apparently deep water throughout. The shores were examined, but no traces of life were observed.

URUP or Companys island, lying on the 46th parallel, is separated from the north-east end of Iturup by Vries strait, 13 miles wide, and free from danger. The island is 58 miles long, N.E. and S.W., and its greatest breadth about 15 miles. Near its centre there is a remarkable peak, in shape like a haycock, which can be seen in clear weather at 50 miles, and is often visible when the other portion of the island is obscured by fog. The south-west point of the island is low and steep, and continues so for about 15 miles in a northerly direction, when it rises to a lofty mountain range; a high and almost perpendicular rock, appearing like a sail when seen at a distance, lies S.E. about one mile from the point.

---

* H.M.S. *Cormorant* made for this channel, but when close-to, observed a line of heavy breakers extending right across; she then stood nearer the island of Iturup, in the hopes of finding a passage, but in vain; night coming on it was not possible to verify the fact of its being shoal, but the sea broke perpendicularly 20 to 25 feet high, and unlike any tide ripple.—Navigating Lieutenant Neville, R.N.

The north-west side of the island is for the most part rugged, steep, and without the least appearance of vegetation, sign of an anchorage, or inlet sufficient to shelter a boat. The north-east point is of a dark colour, moderately high, and slopes towards the sea. A chain of rocks runs off about 5 miles in an E.N.E. direction from this point; and at a distance of a mile from the shore there is a large rock of pyramidal form, with two others smaller.

PORT TAVANO is a small harbour on the eastern side of Urup, but it is open to the eastward, and with the wind from that quarter a heavy swell rolls in, which, with the shallow water and rocks it contains, do not recommend it as a safe anchorage. The entrance has 8 and 10 fathoms water, and is 120 yards across; nearly in the centre of the port there are some rocks just above water, with $4\frac{1}{2}$ and 5 fathoms close to.

Water is procured from two rivers at the head of the harbour. Salmon and rock fish are plentiful.

DIRECTIONS.—The only good mark for port Tavano is a small island lying S.E. by E. one quarter of a mile from the south point of the bay; it is steep-to (except for a few yards on its north side), high, conical-shaped, and of a blackish colour. N. by E. $1\frac{1}{4}$ miles from this island there is a remarkable point with a hole through it near the water, which can be seen at some distance when bearing North. After passing the small island just noticed, the harbour will open, bearing about West, and when the island bears South the soundings will be 27 fathoms, (sand and mud), gradually shoaling as the harbour is approached.

BROUGHTON, REBUNTSIRIBOI, and BRAT CHIRNOEF ISLANDS are between Urup and Simusir, the next large island to the north-east. The northernmost, Broughton or Makanruru island (Round island of Broughton), is of good height, bold, and abrupt, sloping a little to the southward, near which end are some rocks, and apparently the only place where a landing could be effected.

The two other islands, Rebuntsiriboi or Chirnoi, and Brat Chirnoef or Chirnoi Brothers, lie N.N.E. and S.S.W. from each other, distant $1\frac{1}{2}$ miles. Rebuntsiriboi, the northernmost of the two, is volcanic and is remarkable from its having two conspicuous peaks of sugar-loaf form. A reef, which much resembles an artificial breakwater, extends a mile east from its north point, and at its extremity there is a high rock.

SIMUSIR ISLAND is separated from the last-mentioned group by the Boussole channel, which, as before stated, divides the chain into two portions. The island is 27 miles long, N.E. and S.W., and 5 miles in breadth. Its coasts appear safe to approach, no dangers being visible.

It is destitute of any anchorage, except in the northern part, where there is said to be a good harbour, named Broughton bay, which, although spacious, is only navigable for small vessels, on account of a reef lying in the middle of the entrance.

About 10 miles south-west of the north-east point of the island is Prevost peak, which can be seen at a great distance. The south extreme of the island is low, but rises suddenly to a lofty mountain, having a crater on its north-west side.

KETOY ISLAND is separated from the north-east end of Simusir by the Diane strait, about 15 miles wide. The island is high and mountainous, and about 8 miles in circumference. Rocks and islets are said to extend some distance off its north-east and eastern sides.

USHISHIR, 12¼ miles N.E. by N. of Ketoy, is composed of two islands, each about 1½ miles long N.N.E. and S.S.W., which are connected by a reef 2 cables long. A reef of rocks terminated by a small islet extends to the northward from the northernmost of these islands. The channel between Ushishir and Ketoy is safe.

RASHUA, the next island to the north-east, is about 15 miles in circumference, high, uneven, and barren.

MATUA ISLAND is 7 miles in length, north and south, and may be easily known by its lofty peak, which rises near its south-west side. It is separated from Rashua by Nadejda strait, which is 18 miles wide, and free from danger; the currents in it, however, are strong, and must be particularly guarded against, and unless the wind blows right through, a sailing vessel should not attempt to take it.

RAIKOKE ISLAND, lying 5 miles N.N.E. of Matua, from which it is separated by Golovnin strait, is small but hilly, and has a high peak. In using this strait vessels should be prepared for strong gusts of wind.

MUSIR ISLANDS, are four small islets, or rather rocks, one of which is awash, lying 22 miles north-east of Raikoke. They were discovered by Krusenstern in 1805, and named by him the Snares, on account of the great hazard he ran of being drifted on them by the strong current.

SHIASH-KOTAN ISLAND, at 12 miles north-east of the Musir, is 12 miles in extent, N.N.E. and S.S.W., and 5 miles in breadth.

The two islands Ekarma and Chirin-kotan lie respectively N.W. by W. 5 miles, and W. by N. 24 miles from the north-west point of Shiash-kotan.

KHARIM-KOTAN, the next island north-east of Shiash-kotan, is of a round form, 7 miles in diameter, and a peak rises near its centre.

ONEKOTAN ISLAND, 24 miles long N.N.E. and S.S.W., and 5 to 10 miles wide, is separated from Kharim-kotan by Shestoi strait, which is

8 miles wide, and free from danger, but the strong currents in it would make it dangerous to a sailing vessel if overtaken by a calm, or light winds. Onekotan makes in several lofty peaks, two of which are dome-shaped.

MAKANRUSHIR ISLAND lies 15 miles W.N.W. of the north-west end of Onekotan; at 7 miles S.W. of it is Avos island or rock, surrounded by a dangerous reef awash.

PARAMUSHIR ISLAND is among the largest of this archipelago, being 60 miles long N.E. and S.W., and of an average breadth of 14 miles. It is separated from Onekotan by Amphitrite strait, which is 22 miles wide, safe, and generally used by vessels going from Okhotsk to Kamchatka, or to or from the American coast.

Paramushir, from its size and appearance, could not well be mistaken; near its south end is a mountain rising to a high and conspicuous peak, very dark, and unlike the land in its neighbourhood; and to the southward of this are three remarkable peaks. The south-east point of the island is long and low, with apparently a reef extending off it to the southward. A small island about 2 miles in diameter, named Shirinki, lies 9 miles from its south-west point; and Alaid, the most northern island of the chain, 11 miles from its north-west point.

SHUMSHU ISLAND, the last island of this chain, is separated from cape Lopatka, the south extreme of Kamchatka, by Kuril strait, and from the north-east end of Paramushir by another channel, called Little Kuril strait. The south extreme of Shumshu terminates in a tongue of low land; the north end is the same, and is distant 8 miles from cape Lopatka, which is also low.

KURIL STRAIT is about 3 miles wide, but very dangerous, on account of the strong currents and sunken rocks bounding it on either side. Little Kuril strait is also dangerous, owing to the strong tides which set 4½ knots in June; the flood to the southward and the ebb to the northward.*

---

* *See* plan of Little Kuril strait on Chart of Kuril islands, No. 2,405.

TABLE OF POSITIONS

ON THE

COASTS OF KOREA AND TARTARY, AND SEA OF OKHOTSK; ISLANDS IN THE WESTERN PACIFIC LYING SOUTH AND SOUTH-EAST OF JAPAN; AND JAPAN ISLANDS, SAGHALIN AND KURIL ISLANDS.

Place.	Particular Spot.	Latitude, North.	Longitude, East.	Authorities.
WEST AND SOUTH COASTS OF KOREA.				
Choda island	South point	38 27 0	124 34 40	French frigate *Virginie*, 1856.*
Deception bay	Middle of entrance	37 3 0	126 33 0	,,
Caroline bay	West point of entrance	37 1 30	126 25 0	,,
Joachim bay	,, ,,	36 53 30	126 17 50	,,
Chassériau bank	South extreme	36 59 20	126 12 0	French.
Sir James Hall group	North island	37 58 0	124 34 30	Commander Shufeldt, U.S.N., 1867.†
Marjoribanks harbour	-	36 25 0	126 25 0	Horsburgh.
,,	Mauzac islet	36 26 45	126 28 0	French frigate *Virginie*, 1856.
Tas-de-Foin islet	-	36 24 30	126 24 0	,,
Wai-ian-do island	-	36 15 45	126 9 50	,,
Basil bay	South end of curved tongue.	36 7 38	126 42 30	Basil Hall, 1816.
Guérin island	Summit	36 7 0	126 1 9	French frigate *Virginie*, 1856.
Kokoun-Tau group	Camp islet	35 48 8	126 31 0	,,
Barren islands	Centre	35 21 0	125 58 0	Basil Hall, 1816.
Modeste island	Northern peak	34 42 30	125 16 0	,,
Mackau island	Centre	34 40 5	125 28 30	,,
Ross island	Peak	34 6 0	125 7 0	Bullock, 1859.
Maury group	Centre	34 12 0	125 30 0	,,
Craig Harriet	,,	34 12 0	125 51 0	,,
Lyra group	,,	34 8 0	125 56 0	,,
Murray sound	Thistle island	34 22 40	125 57 0	,, 1861.
Virginie island	,,	34 13 0	126 9 0	,,
Washington gulf	Lagravière peak	34 24 0	126 16 0	Wilds.
Bate group	Summit of Thornton island.	33 57 0	126 18 0	,,
Sea rock	Centre	34 42 0	126 19 45	,,
Quelpart island	Observation spot on middle of west side of Beaufort island.	33 29 40	126 58 25	Belcher, 1845.
Montravel island	Centre	33 59 0	126 55 0	Wilds, 1863.‡
Kuper harbour	North-east extreme of Josling island.	34 17 20	126 35 28	,,
Port Hamilton	West point of Observatory island.	34 1 23	127 18 34	Richards, 1855.
Observation island	Point of western arm	34 39 0	128 14 0	Bullock.

* The *Virginie's* positions depend upon Quelpart island (observation spot on middle of west side of Beaufort island) being 126° 58' 25" East from Greenwich. The position of Choda is doubtful.

† Captain Basil Hall places it in long. 124° 44' 0" E., and Nav. Lt. Cole, R.N., in 124° 42' 30" E. The position on the chart is from Commander Shufeldt's survey.

‡ Depending on Richards's Longitude of Port Hamilton, 127° 20' 34".

TABLE OF POSITIONS.

Place.	Particular Spot.	Latitude, North.	Longitude, East.	Authorities.

WEST AND SOUTH COASTS OF KOREA—*continued*.

Place.	Particular Spot.	Latitude, North.	Longitude, East.	Authorities.
Broughton head	-	34 48 0	128 44 0	Wilds.
Sentinel island	-	34 33 0	128 40 0	Bullock, 1861.
Tsau liang-hai harbour	Observation spot	35 6 6	129 1 49	Ward, 1859.

COAST OF TARTARY.

Place.	Particular Spot.	Latitude, North.	Longitude, East.	Authorities.
Tsu sima	Observatory rock (Tsu sima sound).	34 18 55	129 12 0	Ward, 1859.
Matu sima	Peak	37 30 0	130 53 0	,,
Liancourt rocks	-	37 14 0	131 55 0	Forsyth, 1855.
Wayoda rock	-	42 14 30	137 17 0	Russians.
Cape Clonard	-	36 5 45	129 33 30	Russian frigate *Pallas*, 1854.
Ping-hai harbour	-	36 36 0	129 20 0	,,
Tumen ula	Round hill	42 17 38	130 36 2	Grigorief.
Port Lazaref	Observation point (South 1½ miles from south end of Butenef island).	39 19 12	127 32 48	Russian frigate *Pallas*, 1854.
Expedition bay	Tchurkhoda rock (west point of entrance).	42 37 22	130 44 10	H.M.S. *Winchester*, 1855.
Amur bay	Pestchanoi point	43 11 0	131 46 30	,,
America bay	Lisi island	42 41 0	132 56 0	H.M.S. *Hornet*, 1856.
Tcheniya bay	Yakimova point	42 49 30	133 30 0	Russian.
Cape Zamok	-	42 49 0	133 51 0	H.M.S. *Hornet*, 1856.
Vostok bay	Gaidamak harbour	42 53 10	132 38 50	Russian.
Siau Wuhu bay	Observation spot on chart	42 54 14	133 50 32	Ward, 1859.
Olga bay	Observation spot at head of port.	43 46 0	135 19 0	,,
St. Vladimir bay	Orekhova point	43 53 40	135 27 21	Bullock.
Shelter bay	-	44 30 0	136 2 0	H.M.S. *Barracouta*.
Wrangle bay	Observation spot on chart	42 44 18	133 2 3	Russian.
Sybille bay	-	44 43 45	136 22 30	H.M.S. *Barracouta*.
Pique bay	-	44 46 15	136 27 15	,,
Bullock bay	-	45 5 0	136 44 0	,,
Luké point	-	45 19 30	137 10 15	,,
Cape Disappointment	-	45 41 30	137 38 15	,,
Cape Suffren	-	47 20 0	138 58 0	,,
Fish river	-	47 55 0	139 31 0	,,
Low cape	-	48 28 0	140 10 0	,,
Beechy head	-	48 56 0	140 21 0	,,
Barracouta harbour	Tullo island	49 1 50	149 19 0	,,
Castries bay	Quoin point	51 25 0	140 49 30	H.M.S. *Hornet*, 1855.
Amur river	Nikolaevsk cathedral	53 8 5	140 42 58	Russian.

SEA OF OKHOTSK.

Place.	Particular Spot.	Latitude, North.	Longitude, East.	Authorities.
Great Shantar island	North point	55 11 0	137 40 0	H.M.S. *Hornet*, 1855.
St. Jona island	-	56 22 30	143 15 45	,,
Port Aian	Cape Vneshni	56 25 28	138 25 50	Russian chart, 1851.

KAMCHATKA, SOUTH-EAST COAST.

Place.	Particular Spot.	Latitude, North.	Longitude, East.	Authorities.
Mount Villeuchinski	Peak	52 42 0	158 20 0	Beechey, 1827.
Petropaulski	Church	53 0 58	158 43 30	,,

ISLANDS IN THE WESTERN PACIFIC, EAST OF LIU-KIU.

Place.	Particular Spot.	Latitude, North.	Longitude, East.	Authorities.
Borodino islands	Centre of south island	25 52 45	131 12 17	American chart, 1854.
Bishop rocks (doubtful)	Centre	25 20 0	131 15 0	Bishop, 1796.
Rasa island	-	24 27 0	131 6 0	*La Cannonière*, 1807.
Euphrosyne reef	-	21 43 0	140 55 0	Various.
Parece Vela or Douglas reef.	-	20 31 0	136 6 0	Sproule, 1848.
Lindsay island	-	19 20 0	141 15 30	Lindsay, 1848.

Place.	Particular Spot.	Latitude, North.	Longitude, East.	Authorities.

ISLANDS IN THE WESTERN PACIFIC, EAST OF LIU-KIU—continued.

Place.	Particular Spot.	Latitude, North.	Longitude, East.	Authorities.
Santa Rosa shoal (doubtful).	West extreme	12° 30′ 0″	144° 15′ 0″	Raper.
Guam island (Port San Luis d'Apra).	Fort Santa Cruz	·13 26 0	144 39 28	Don E. Sanchez y Zaya, 1865.
Rota island	North-east point	14 12 0	145 23 0	,,
Aguijan island	Centre	14 54 0	145 38 0	,,
Tinian island	Sunharon village	14 59 0	145 36 0	,,
Saipan island	Peak	15 13 0	145 49 0	,,
,,	Magicienne bay	15 8 30	145 44 0	H.M.S. *Magicienne*, 1858.
Farallon de Medinilla	South point	15 59 30	146 0 30	Don E. Sanchez y Zaya.
Anatajan island	East point	16 20 0	145 47 0	,,
Sariguan island	Centre	16 40 0	145 52 0	,,
Zealandia breakers	-	16 50 0	145 50 0	Ship *Zelandia*.
Guguan island	East point	17 20 0	145 53 0	Don E. Sanchez y Zaya.
Alamagan island	North-east point	17 38 0	145 52 0	,,
Pagan island	North point	18 10 0	145 51 0	,,
Agrigan island	,,	18 53 0	145 40 0	,,
Assumption island	Peak	19 41 0	145 27 0	Beechey, 1827.
Urracas islands	Centre	20 7 0	145 20 0	Don E. Sanchez y Zaya.
Farallon de Pajaros	,,	20 30 0	145 32 0	Douglas, 1789.
Weeks island	-	24 5 0	154 2 0	Gelett.
Los Jardines or Marshall islands.	Centre	21 40 0	151 35 0	Marshall, 1788.
Sebastian Lobos or Grampus islands.	South-west island	25 10 0	146 40 0	Raper.
Forfana island (doubtful).	Centre	25 35 0	143 0 0	,,
San Augustino island	Peak	24 14 0	141 20 0	King, 1805.
Sulphur island	,,	24 48 0	141 13 0	,,
San Alessandro island	,,	25 14 0	141 11 0	,, 1799.
Malabrigos or Margaret islands.	Centre	27 20 0	145 45 0	Magee, 1773.
Bonin islands (Peel island).	Port Lloyd (Ten-fathom hole).	27 5 35	142 11 30*	Beechey, 1827.
,, ,,	Newport in Hillsborough island.	26 36 0	142 9 0	American Chart, 1854.
Rosario or Disappointment island.	-	27 16 0	140 51 0	Raper.

MEIACO SIMA, LIU-KIU, AND LINSCHOTEN ISLANDS.

Place.	Particular Spot.	Latitude, North.	Longitude, East.	Authorities.
Ti-a-usu island	Centre	25 58 30	123 40 0	—
Raleigh rock	,,	25 55 0	124 34 0	Bullock.
Hoa-pin-su island	North face	25 47 7	123 30 31	Belcher, 1845.
Meiaco sima group	Kumi island (north beach).	24 26 0	122 56 0	,,
,,	Port Broughton (landing place).	24 21 30	124 17 40	,,
,,	Port Haddington (Hamilton point).	24 25 0	124 6 40	,,
,,	Tai-pin-san (south-west bay).	24 43 35	125 17 49	,,
Liu-kiu group	Nafa kiang (Abbey point)	26 12 25	127 40 10	American Chart.
,,	Deep bay (observatory spot at the head).	26 35 35	127 59 42	American Chart, 1854.
,,	Port Oonting (village)	26 40 42	128 0 0	Basil Hall, 1816.
Yori sima	Centre	27 2 0	128 25 24	Cécille.
Yerabu sima	South peak	27 21 0	128 33 10	Basil Hall, 1816.
Kakirouma	Highest peak	27 44 0	128 59 0	French Chart, 1846.

* Is possibly farther to the eastward (*see* page 182).

TABLE OF POSITIONS. 369

Place.	Particular Spot.	Latitude, North.	Longitude. East.	Authorities.

MEIACO SIMA, LIU-KIU, AND LINSCHOTEN ISLANDS—continued.

Place.	Particular Spot.	Latitude, North.	Longitude. East.	Authorities.
Iwo sima	-	27 53 0	128 14 30	Collinson, 1845.
Oho sima	North extreme	28 31 40	129 42 30	American Chart, 1854.
Kikai sima	Summit	28 18 0	129 59 0	,,
Yoko sima	,,	28 47 30	129 1 30	Various authorities.
Tokara sima	-	29 8 0	129 13 30	,,
Simago islands	Highest	29 13 0	129 21 0	,,
Akuisi sima	-	29 27 0	129 37 0	,,
Suwa sima	-	29 38 0	129 43 0	,,
Fira sima	-	29 41 0	129 32 30	,,
Naka sima	Peak	29 52 0	129 52 30	,,
Hebi sima	,,	29 54 0	129 33 0	,,
Kohebi sima	-	29 53 0	129 38 0	,,
Kutsino sima	Summit	29 59 0	129 55 0	,,
Firase (Blake reef)	Highest rock	30 5 0	130 3 0	,,
Yakuno sima	Mount Motomi	30 21 0	130 29 0	,,
Nagarobe	Highest peak	30 27 0	130 13 0	,,
Take sima	Centre	30 49 0	130 26 30	,,
Iwoga sima	Highest peak	30 48 0	130 19 0	,,
Kowose (Powhattan reef).	-	30 43 0	130 22 0	U.S. frigate *Powhattan*, 1860.
Use (Trio rocks)	Centre rock	30 44 0	130 7 0	Various authorities.
Kuro sima	Centre	30 50 0	129 57 0	,,
Kusakaki sima (Ingersoll rocks).	Highest	30 51 0	129 28 0	,,

JAPAN.—S.E. AND E. COAST OF NIPON.

Place.	Particular Spot.	Latitude, North.	Longitude. East.	Authorities.
Yura no uchi	Observation pier	33 57 34	135 7 33	Bullock.
Osaki bay	Tree islet	34 7 42	135 8 31	,,
Yura harbour	North end of fort	34 16 46	134 58 45	,,
Tanabe	Fossil point	33 41 14	135 23 16	,,
Siwo misaki	Lighthouse	33 26 0	135 46 30	Japanese lighthouse board.
Oö sima harbour	Pisayama rock	33 29 8	135 48 55	Ward, 1861.
Ura-kami harbour	Village point	33 33 37	135 55 11	,,
Owasi bay	South point at entrance to Chioshi kawa.	34 6 10	136 14 47	St. John, 1870.
Matoya harbour	South point of Watakano sima.	34 21 28	136 52 37	,,
Gulf of Suruga (Simidzu harbour).	Miosaki	35 0 51	138 32 4	Ward, 1861.
,, Eno-ura bay	Centre	35 3 0	138 53 0	Russian frigate *Diana*, 1853-55.
,, Heda bay	,,	34 58 11	138 46 0	,,
,, Arari bay	,,	34 50 0	138 46 0	,,
,, Tago bay	,,	34 47 3	138 44 54	,,
Iro-o saki (Cape Idsu)	Lighthouse	34 36 0	138 51 0	Japanese lighthouse board.
Mikomoto (Rock island).	,,	34 34 20	138 57 10	,,
Simoda harbour	Centre island	34 39 49	138 57 30	American Chart.
Cape Sagami	Lighthouse	35 8 0	139 41 0	Japanese lighthouse board.
Kanon saki	,,	34 14 45	139 44 17	Ward, 1861.
Yokohama	Naval sick quarters (square).	35 26 30	139 39 24	Various authorities.
Mela head	Lighthouse on Nosima point.	34 53 20	139 51 23	Japanese lighthouse board.
Yamada harbour	Ko sima	39 27 17	141 59 0	St. John, 1871.

ISLANDS OFF SOUTH COAST OF NIPON.

Place.	Particular Spot.	Latitude, North.	Longitude. East.	Authorities.
Lot's Wife rock	-	29 47 0	140 22 30	American Chart, 1854.
Ponafidin island	-	30 33 0	140 15 0	,,

30495.

A A

Place.	Particular Spot.	Latitude, North.	Longitude, East.	Authorities.

ISLANDS OFF SOUTH COAST OF NIPON—continued.

Place.	Particular Spot.	Latitude, North.	Longitude, East.	Authorities.
Smith island	-	31 18 0	139 52 0	H.M.S. *Tribune*, 1859.
Bayonnaise island	-	32 0 40	140 0 0	American Chart, 1854.
Aoga sima	Eastern summit	32 37 30	139 47 30	Ward, 1860.
Fatsizio island	Observation spot	33 4 24	139 50 24	,,
Broughton rock	Centre	33 39 0	139 17 45	,,
Redfield rocks	Southern	33 56 50	138 48 15	,,
Mikura island	Highest part	33 52 0	139 34 0	,,
Miaki sima	,,	34 5 0	139 31 0	,,
Kosu sima	,,	34 13 15	139 8 0	,,
Oö sima or Vries island	South-east point	34 39 30	139 28 0	,,

JAPAN.—WEST COAST OF KIUSIU AND ADJACENT ISLANDS.

Place.	Particular Spot.	Latitude, North.	Longitude, East.	Authorities.
Simonoseki	Mozi saki (south part)	33 58 0	130 58 24	Ward, 1861.
Western entrance to Simonoseki strait.	Lighthouse on Low Reef (Shirasu).	33 59 30	130 48 24	Japanese lighthouse board.
,, ,,	Rokuren island	33 58 15	130 52 25	,,
Kosime no Ōsima (Wilson island).	Summit	33 53 50	130 25 20	Ward, 1861.
Kuri no Kami (Swain reef),	-	33 48 15	130 15 40	Brooker, 1868.
Yebosi island	Centre	33 41 30	129 58 50	,,
Oro no sima	Highest part	33 52 10	130 2 0	,,
Idzumi islets	Kami Idzumi	33 44 0	129 55 0	,,
Iki sima	Summit at south end of island.	33 44 30	129 42 30	,,
Yobuko harbour	Observation spot on chart	33 32 30	129 52 55	Brooker.
Hirado	,, ,, ,,	33 23 0	129 28 0	,,
Taske (Hirado sima)	Lighthouse	33 23 31	129 33 33	,,
Rock in north part of Obree channel.	Summit	33 21 30	129 26 11	Richards, 1855.
Yenoi sima	South side of	32 59 44	129 19 24	,,
Hardy harbour (Goto islands).	Observation islet	32 49 0	128 56 39	,,
Tama no ura	Observation spot on chart	32 36 35	128 38 50	Brooker, 1868.
Ose saki (Cape Goto)	Extreme	32 39 30	128 35 30	,,
Sagitsu no ura	Oonska saki (Observation spot).	32 17 42	130 2 26	,,
Yama gawa harbour (Kagosima gulf).	Observation spot on chart	31 12 40	130 38 43	Blundell.
Nagasaki	Minage point	32 44 28	129 51 30	Brooker, 1868.
,,	Lighthouse on Iwo sima	32 43 0	129 46 0	Japanese lighthouse board.
Pallas rocks	South rock	32 14 17	128 12 30	Richards, 1855.
Meac sima	Ears peak	32 3 0	128 25 0	,,
Tsukarase Retribution rocks).	Centre	31 20 0	129 46 20	H.M.S. *Retribution*, 1858.
Udsi sima	High peak	31 12 0	129 29 0	French Chart, 1846, corrected.

JAPAN.—WEST COAST OF NIPON.

Place.	Particular Spot.	Latitude, North.	Longitude, East.	Authorities.
Bittern rocks	South-west rock	40 31 0	139 31 0	Richards, 1855.
Tabu sima	East extreme	39 11 53	139 34 17	Ward, 1859.
Awa sima	N.E. extreme	38 29 36	139 16 7	,,
Sado island	Ya saki	38 19 55	138 27 9	Richards, 1855.
Port Niegata	Lighthouse	37 56 30	139 4 0	Ward.
Yútsi sima	-	37 50 30	136 55 0	Richards, 1855.
Nana sima (Astrolabe rock).	-	37 35 0	136 54 0	,,

TABLE OF POSITIONS. 371

Place.	Particular Spot.	Latitude, North.	Longitude, East.	Authorities.

JAPAN.—WEST COAST OF NIPON—continued.

Place.	Particular Spot.	Latitude, North.	Longitude, East.	Authorities.
Cape Roiven or Noto	- - - -	37 28 0	137 22 0	Richards, 1855.
Tsuruga - - -	Town - - -	35 40 24	136 1 22	Goldsborough.
Mikuni roads - -	Observation spot on point north of river's mouth.	36 13 0	136 8 30	Bullock.
Nanao harbour - -	Sorengo point - -	37 2 37	136 58 24	,,
Oki islands - -	North point - -	36 30 0	133 23 0	Richards, 1855.
Mino sima - -	Centre - - -	34 48 0	131 9 0	,,
Taka yama (Cape Louisa).	- - - -	34 40 0	131 36 0	,,
Ai sima (Richards island).	- - - -	34 32 0	131 18 0	,,

JAPAN.—INLAND SEA.

Place.	Particular Spot.	Latitude, North.	Longitude, East.	Authorities.
Naruto passage, Fukura.	Su saki - - -	34 14 56	134 42 51	Maxwell.
Isumi strait - -	Lighthouse on Tomangai sima.	34 16 40	135 0 30	Japanese lighthouse board.
Ōsaka - - -	Lighthouse on Tomposan fort.	34 39 45	135 26 35	,,
Kobe - - -	Landing place at E. end of Concession.	34 41 3	135 12 15	St. John.
Akashi strait - -	Maiko fort - -	34 38 29	135 1 59	Maxwell.
Channels between Harima and Bingo nada.	Lighthouse on Nabe sima.	34 23 15	133 48 45	Japanese lighthouse board.
Kurusima strait -	South point of Kuru sima.	34 7 0	132 58 5	Brooker.
Suwo nada - -	Lighthouse on I saki -	33 58 0	131 1 0	Japanese lighthouse board.

JAPAN.—STRAIT OF TSUGAR.

Place.	Particular Spot.	Latitude, North.	Longitude, East.	Authorities.
Hakodadi harbour -	Entrance to Kamida creek.	41 47 8	140 43 44	St. John, 1872.
Cape Matsumae -	Islet off - -	41 24 54	140 7 20	Richards, 1855.
Siriya saki - -	Small islet on west side.	41 25 24	141 28 32	,,
Red Cliff point -	Extreme - -	41 28 7	141 9 0	,,
Toriwi saki - -	Centre of Low island off	41 33 34	140 56 36	,,
Tatsupi saki - -	North side - -	41 16 17	140 22 37	,,
Oho saki - -	Small rock off south side	41 5 39	140 20 19	,,

LA PÉROUSE STRAIT AND YEZO ISLAND.

Place.	Particular Spot.	Latitude, North.	Longitude, East.	Authorities.
Risiri - - -	Pic de Langle - -	45 11 0	141 19 0	Krusenstern, 1805.
Refunsiri - -	Cape Hieber - -	45 27 45	141 3 0	,,
Saghalin island -	Cape Notoro - -	45 54 15	142 9 30	Ward, 1859.
Yezo island - -	Cape Nossyab - -	45 25 50	141 39 50	,,
,,	Dangerous rock - -	45 48 15	142 15 0	Ward, 1855.
Saghalin island -	Cape Siretoko - -	46 1 20	143 26 30	Krusenstern, 1805.
Akishi bay (Yezo) -	Observation spot at entrance to shallow lagoon.	43 2 22	144 51 50	St. John, 1871.
Nemoro (Yezo) -	Benten sima - -	43 20 24	145 34 57	,,
Iwani bay (Yezo) -	- - - -	43 1 0	140 4 0	,,

SAGHALIN ISLAND.

Place.	Particular Spot.	Latitude, North.	Longitude, East.	Authorities.
Cape Löwenhörn -	- - - -	46 20 0	143 41 0	Krusenstern, 1805.
Cape Tonin - -	- - - -	46 50 0	143 33 0	,,
Cape Seniavin -	- - - -	47 16 30	142 59 30	,,
Bernizet peak -	- - - -	47 33 0	142 20 0	,,

TABLE OF POSITIONS.

Place.	Particular Spot.	Latitude, North.	Longitude, East.	Authorities.
SAGHALIN ISLAND—*continued.*				
Cape Moulovskoi	-	47° 57′ 45″	142° 44′ 0″	Krusenstern, 1805.
Cape Dalrymple	-	48 21 0	142 50 0	,,
Cape Soimonof	-	48 52 30	143 1 30	,,
Cape Otsisi	-	50 52 30	142 12 0	,,
Robben island	Centre	48 32 15	144 23 0	,,
,,	N.E. edge of reef	48 36 0	144 33 0	,,
,,	S.W. edge of reef	48 28 0	144 10 0	,,
Cape Bellingshausen	-	49 35 0	144 25 45	,,
Cape Rimnik	-	50 12 30	144 5 0	,,
Mount Tiara	-	50 3 0	143 37 0	,,
Cape Ratmanof	-	50 48 0	143 53 15	,,
Cape Delisle de la Croyère.	-	51 0 30	143 43 0	,,
Downs point	-	51 53 0	143 13 30	,,
Cape Otméloi	-	52 32 30	143 14 30	,,
Cape Virst	-	52 57 30	143 17 30	,,
Cape Klokatcheff	-	53 46 0	143 7 0	,,
Cape Löwenstern	-	54 3 15	143 12 30	,,
Cape Elizabeth	-	54 24 30	142 46 30	,,
Cape Maria	-	54 17 30	142 17 45	,,
KURIL ISLANDS.				
Kunashir	St. Anthony peak	44 20 0	146 15 0	Admiralty Chart.
Chikotan	Centre	43 48 0	146 40 0	,,
Iturup	Cape Okebets	45 38 30	149 14 0	,,
,,	Cape Rickord	44 23 0	147 0 0	,,
Urup	Cape Kastrikum	46 16 0	150 27 0	,,
,,	Cape Vanderlind	45 37 0	149 34 0	,,
Brat Chirnoef	-	46 29 15	150 33 30	Golownin, 1811.
Rebuntsiriboi	-	46 32 45	150 37 10	,,
Broughton	-	46 42 30	150 28 30	,,
Simusir	Prevost peak	47 2 50	151 52 50	,,
Ketoy	South point	47 17 30	152 24 0	,,
Matua	Peak	48 6 0	153 12 30	Krusenstern, 1805.
Raiokoke	,,	48 16 20	153 15 0	,,
Musir	-	48 35 0	153 44 0	,,
Shiash-kotan	Centre	48 52 0	154 8 0	,,
Kharim-kotan	Peak	49 8 0	154 39 0	,,
One-kotan	South-west point	49 19 0	154 44 0	,,
Makanrushi	Centre	49 51 0	154 32 0	,,
Shumshu	,,	50 46 0	156 26 0	,,
Alaid	,,	50 54 0	155 32 0	,,

TIDE TABLE for the COASTS of JAPAN, KOREA and RUSSIAN TARTARY, the GULF of TARTARY, SEA of OKHOTSK and KAMCHATKA.

Place.	High Water, Full and Change.	Rise. Springs.	Rise. Neaps.	Place.	High Water, Full and Change.	Rise. Springs.	Rise. Neaps.
	h. m.	ft.	ft.		h. m.	ft.	ft.
Japan.				*Korea.*			
Yama gawa harbour, Kagosima gulf	7 15	8¼	3	Ping Yang inlet	7 45	21	14
Sagitsu no ura	8 0	9		Choda island	6 20	12	
Nagasaki harbour	7 15	9	7½	Ta-Tong river	6 30	13	
Taske (Hirado)	9 44	8¼	5	Séoul river, Boisee island	5 20	36¼	16 to 27
Oōsuka	9 16	8¼	5	Séoul	9 30	6½	
Tama no ura, Goto islands	8 40	6 to 8	4-6	Kam-pai-oul	7 50	—	
Yobuko harbour	11 16	9	4	Marjoribanks harbour	3 30	29	
Iki island		8		Basil bay	4 15	17	10
Simonoseki	8 30	8¼	3	Kokoun-Tau group, Camp islet	2 25	20	10
Mikuni		2		Nimrod islands	8 30	—	
Tsuruga	1 30	2		Washington gulf, Green islands	11 0	12	8¼
Sado (Yebisu)	5 0	2		Nan How group, Port Hamilton	8 30	11	
Hakodate (Tsugar strait)	5 0	3		Kuper harbour	9 28	11½	8¼
Yezo island, Notske	4 50	4½	1½	Crichton harbour	9 50	11½	8¼
„ Nemoro	5 0	4	2½	Tracy island	9 10	11¼	8¼
„ Akishi	4 30	5		Tsau-liang-hai harbour	7 45	7	5
Endermo harbour	4 35	5		Tsu sima, Korea strait	8 30	8	6
Yamada harbour	6 30	4					
Yokohama*	6 0	6¼	4½				
Uraga	5 55	4¼	½-1				
Tatiyama bay	5 50	5					
Fatsizio island	6 0	5					
Simoda harbour	5 0	3 to 5					
Heda bay (Suruga gulf)	—	—					
Eno ura „		4		*Russian Tartary.*			
Simidsu „	7 30	7		St. Vladmir bay	1 0	2	
Matoya harbour	6 50	6	1½	Expedition bay	2 30	2¼	
Goza harbour	6 15	6	1½	Nov-gorod harbour	2 30	2¼	
Owasi bay	7 0	5½	2	Olga bay	5 30	3	
Ura-kami	7 30	6	5				
Osima harbour	6 50	5	4				
Tanabe, Kii channel	6 0	6	5¼	*Gulf of Tartary.*			
Yura no uchi	6 0	5½	4½	Barracouta harbour	10 0	3¼	
Osaki	5 55	6¼		Castries bay	10 30	6 to 8¼	
Hachken river	6 4	6¼		Jonquiere bay, Saghalin	10 0	6	
Naruto passage	6 14	6¼	2	Amúr strait	11 40	5 to 6	
Isumi strait	6 5	6¼	4½				
Inland Sea.							
Ōsaka roads	7 30	5¾	4½				
„ city	8 17	2½	½	*Sea of Okhotsk.*			
Hiogo and Kobe	7 15	5½	4½				
Akashi strait	6 27	3¼	1	Cape Mary (Saghalin island)	2 0	5	
Ananga (Awadji)	11 27	2 to 4	4½				
Hi-ide	11 25	2 to 4	4½				
Awa sima	0 7	10¼	6				
Hiro sima	11 45	11	8				
Siyako	0 16	9½	4	*Kamchatka.*			
Yuge sima	11 25	11¼	6¼				
Miwara	10 37	11	5	Avatcha† bay	3 30	6¼	4½
Kurusima strait	10 36	11¼	5				
Hime sima	9 0	8	0				

* With southerly winds the tide rises about 2 feet higher.
† The tides in Avatcha bay are affected by diurnal inequality.

INDEX.

	Page		Page
Aba bay	275	Aniwa bay	353
—— sima	244	Annenkof island	80
Abashira	348	Aoga sima	193
Abbey point	143	Aogi seto	247
Abreojos shoal	134	Aosima yama	321
Admiral bank	244	Aoumi sima	313
Adolphe island	39	Apapa island	118
Agfayan bay	117	Apra village	118
Aghesinak	151	Arakabu sone	291
Agincourt island	141	Arari bay	172
Agrigan island	126	—— point	172
Aguijan island	121	Arevief islands	85
Agunyeh island	145	Argun river	106
Ai sima	252, 263, 309, 313	Arita river	211
Aian, Port	110	Arkold reef	197
Ajayan point	120	Aroostook reef	318
Aji river	219	Arzobispo islands	130
—— rock	240	Asama bank	294
Ajika	235	Ashby inlet	67
Akashi strait	223	Ashika sima	181
Aki	252	Asina bay	178
Akishi bay	342	Assa island	151
Akuisi sima	155	—— rock	229
Akunora	283	Assumption island	127
Alaid island	365	Atsusi no Osima	296
Alamagan island	126	Auckland island	59
Alceste island	47	Auguste island	35
Alexandrovski	105	Aunt islets	72
Alfred peninsula	40	Avakum river	97
Algerine bluff	269	Avatcha bay	111
Aliman point	81	Avvakum islets	85
Amagi yama	176	Awa sima	233, 323
Amakirima group	150	Awadji sima	206, 224
Amakusa	274	——, south coast	209
Amaze	236	——, west coast	225
America bay	92	Awari sima	228
Amúr bay	90	Awomori	327
—— gulf	105	—— bay	326
—— river	106		
Anaga ura	208, 226	Baikal lake	106
Anatajan island	125	Bailey group	130
Anbian village	79	Balbi point	88
Ando bay	329	Bald rock	63

INDEX. 375

	Page		Page
Bansu hana	188	Broughton head	67
Barlow island	54	——— island	363
Barnpool anchorage	147	——— bay	78
Barracouta harbour	102	——— port	137
——— rock	280	Brown channel	97
Barren island	46	Bruat, Cape	84
——— bluff	104	Brydone island	96
Barrow bay	150	Buckland island	175
——— island	53	Buisaco islet	175
Basil bay	44	Bullock bay	100
Bate group	51	Buoy rock	88
Baugh island	137	Bushiro	237
Bayonnaise	193	Byki, Cape	104
Beaufort island	53		
Bedwell island	65	Camp islet	45
Beechey group	131	Captain bank	243
Belaya Skala	85	Caroline bay	40
Bellinghausen, Cape	358	Carr bank	102
Beltzova islet	94	Castle island	63
Ben-ten sima	225, 329	——— point	95
Bingo nada	234	Castries bay	104
Binzli reef	215	Catherine, Cape	108
Bishop rocks	135	——— channel	362
Bittern rocks	324	Cecille archipelago	155
Black rocks	69	Centre island	175
Blakeney island	71	Chapeau, Le	36
Blossom reef	144	Chasseriau bank	37
Bluff cliff island	51	Chichachef, Cape	101
Bochet island	38	Chichakoff, Cape	160
Bodisko peninsula	88	Chikiri sima	252
Boisée island	38	Chioshi kawa	165
Bonin islands	130	Choda island	31
——— winds and currents	10	Chööshi point	197
Borodino islands	135	Chung-chi island	136
Bott rock	52	Chwang-shan, promontory	32
Bottle rock	163, 216	Cliff island	59
Boudrouet rocks	136	Clonard, Cape	77
Boungo channel	201	Cocks comb rocks	85
Boussole channel	363	Codrika point	79
Bowker island	58	Coin island	58
Boyarin bay	91	Colnett strait	156
Brat Chirnoef island	363	Cone island	62
Breaker	162	Congress island	128
Brisant du Chat	37	Conqueror bank	230
Britomart reef	129	Coromandière rock	40
Broken islands	66	Costa Rica rock	293
——— head	95	Cove, The	71
Brother, Big and Little	58	Craig island	141
Brothers' rock	113	———, Harriet	48
Brook islands	60	Cragie islet	71
Broughton rock	194	Creasy, Cape	95

Crichton group	55
——— harbour	56
Currents, The Japan stream (Kuro Siwo)	23, 25
———, The Kamchatka current	25
———, The Oya Siwo	25, 26
———, Kuril islands	19
———, La Pérouse strait	18
———, Tsugar strait	16
———, Liu-Kiu islands	12
———, Mariana and Bonin islands	10, 11
———, S.E. coast of Kamchatka	9
———, Sea of Okhotsk	8
———, Korea strait and Japan sea	6, 7
Currie channel	91
Daikoku sima	342
Dalrymple, Cape	357
Dangerous rock	351
De sima	282
—— Vries, Cape	199
Deception bay	39
Deep bay	147
Delisle de la Croyere, Cape	358
Demura point	328
Dent, Cape	104
Deserted islands	50
Destitution, Cape	104
Direction, Mount	88
Dirt islands	59
Do sima	296
Dolores island	134
Dot groups	58
Double rocks	163
Douglas inlet	67
Downs point	358
Dui	354
Dun-gan river	82
Duroch, Cape	78
Eastern Bosphorus	91
Elizabeth, Cape	359
——— reef	152
Endermo harbour	340
Eno ura	172
Erratasi, Cape	196
Eugenie archipelago	91
——— island	85
Euphrosyne reef	128

Euryalus rock	201
Expedition bay	89
False Sentinel island	66
Family group	50
Farallon de Medinilla	124
——— de Pajaros	127
Farmer island	60
Fatsizio island	194
Faye sima	256
Feleney point	79
Ferrieres, Isles	35
Feruye	291
Fira sima	155
Firase	156
Fish river	102
Fisherman rock	58, 212
Fitton bay	133
Flat bay	358
Flower island	52
Forfana island	130
Fugusi	253
Fuhuye	267
Fuk ura	206
Fuku sima	297
Fukushe	289
Futakami	301
Futsu saki	188
Galatea shoal	228
Galvez bank	120
Gana she	287
Ganru island	260
Garapan	123
Genkai sima	306
——— nada	304
Germantown reef	154
Ghibu isi	189
Giffard island	54
Goalen island	57
Goat island	133
——— Little, island	133
Golden rock	211
Go no ura	302
Goshkevich bay	85
Goto islands	266
Goza harbour	166
Green islands	50
Guam	116
Guerriere island	39
Guguan island	125

INDEX.

	Page
Habushi iwa	231
Hachken gawa	210
Hadagase	280
Hadaka sima	205
——— iwa	165
Haddington, Port	138
Haka se	168
Haka no Kojima	242
Hakata sima	249
Haki bay	314
Hako sima	250, 285
Hakosaki bay	306
Hakodate harbour	322
——— through Korea strait	28
Halls reef	150
Hamana	169
Hamanaka bay	344
Hamilton, Point	139
———, Port	61
Hana mura	227
——— rete	183
Hanaguri seto	249
Harima nada	226
Hashi hama	238
Hasiri	234
Hasyokan	137
Hato saki	300
Haycock island	60
Heber reef	150
Hebi sima	156
Heda bay	172
Heji sima	235
Henty reef	156
Herschel island	62
Heso sima	240
Hesper island	154
Heto, Cape	150
Hi sima	246, 278
— ura	206
Hiki sima	235, 285
Hiku flat	261
——— sima	260
Hillsborough island	130
Hime sima	255, 269, 304
Hino misaki	213
——— yama	259
Hiogo	221
Hiotan jima	249
Hira sima	288
Hirado sima	290
——— no seto	293

	Page
Hirado no seto, directions	294–5
Hirase	300
——— rock	277
Hiro sima	230
Hirose	238, 293
Hishiwo bank	281
Ho-age	289
Hoa-pin-su island	141
Hodge rock	266
Hodo island	83
Hong-Kong to Yedo	26, 29
Hooper islands	59
——— island	53
Hope promontory	62
Horino utsi	178
Hoso sima	242
Hounlodgna bay	117
H'to te	165
Humann island	36
Hyaku Kuan	241
Hydrographers group	47
I saki	257
I sima	202
Ibuki	234
Ichinomaki	198
Ichi no tani yama	222
Idsu, Cape	173
Idsuye sima	240
Idzumi islets	303
Igama bay	318
Ike sima	285
Iki sima	245, 302
Ikina	251
Ikutski	296
——— no seto	296
Ilibe saki	213
Imabari	236
Imagawa, Cape	256
Imari gulf	297
Imo sima	287
In no sima	241
Inaboye saki	197
Inaghi	227
Ingersoll patches	145
Inglefield island	137
Inland sea	216
Ino sima	177
Insult island	57
Iro-o saki	173
Isena sima	152

Isi saki	327
Iskarri	338
Isumi nada	219
—— strait	218
Itoya bay	291
Iturup	362
Iwagi sima	250
Iwami sima	255
Iwashi sima	242
Iwani bay	338
Iwaya point	262
Iwo sima	153, 277
Iwoga sima	157
Iye island	148
Iyo nada	254
James rock	294
Japan islands	159
—— —— winds and currents	12
Japan sea, winds and currents	2
Japan stream	23
Japanese strait	91
Jarrad bank	242
Jardines, Los	128
Joachim bay	40
Joka sima	179
Jonquière bay	355
Junk islets, Inner and Outer	66
Ka sima	240, 253, 266
—— yama	182
Kaba sima bay	277
Kabe sima	300
Kadgi sima	235
Kadgitori saki	239
Kado sima	313
Kadzusa saki	181
Kagara sima	301
Kageno	280
Kagosima gulf	272
Kaji kake	291
Kaki no ura sima	287
Kakirouma	152
Kalavala bay	88
Kamada	297
Kamage	287
Kama ura point	327
Kamchatka, South-east coast	111
—— —— current	25
Kami sima	169
—— rock	273
Kamino sima	280
Kaminone	155
Kanabuse	258
Kanagawa	186
Kanai saki	298
Kanatöo	301
Kanaya point	189
Kaneda bay	181
Kanon saki	182
Kanziu island	258
Karasuka islands	273
Karatsu no ura	304
Kariya	299
Kashe	285
Kashira	246
Kasira sima	305
Kasiwa	228
Kata	209
—— sima	287
Kater island	134
Katona sima	153
Katsu ura	308
Kawa saki	187
Kawatchi bay	292
Keppel island	59
Ketoy island	364
Kharim-kotan	364
Kien-chan island	36
Kii channel	202
Kikai sima	154
Kikuma	240
Kingkasan	198
Kishu gawa	221
Klokatcheff, Cape	359
Knorr island	131
Ko sima	161, 231, 337
—— Adjiro bay	178
—— Futakami	301
—— Kabuta	227
—— Kuno sima	244
—— Saki sima	243
—— Oge sima	246
—— Tate	288
—— Ura saki	206
—— Ye sima	224
—— Yo sima	229
Kobe	221
Kodono sima	245
Kodsine	194
Koduchi	229
Koko sima	308

INDEX.

	Page
Kokoun-tau group	44
Kokumage	256
Kokura	261
——— ledge	261
Kolokozev point	85
Komisang	152
Koo-kien-san island	136
Koöze no ura	303
Kone sima	243
Korea, east coast	76
——————— winds and currents	2
———, south coast	55
———, south-west coast	49
——— strait	74
Korean archipelago	44
Kosaka channel	266
Kosedo strait	260
Kosii sima	253
Kosiki islands	270
Kosime no Oösima	308
Kosu sima	195
Kosunai	354
Kotame bay	274
Koto no ura	274
Kotsu sima	309
Koubah island	137
Koumi island	135
Kowose	157
Koyaki	280
Koza gawa	164
Kozakof, Cape	85
Kozu sima	150
Kuga channel	266
Kunashir island	360
Kuno sima	244
Kupa sima	151
Kuper harbour	55
Kuri no kami	309
Kuri hama	181
Kuril islands	360
——— winds and currents	18
——— strait	365
——— Little, strait	365
Kurose rock	78
Kuro sima	159, 297
——— Ko sima	292
Kuro Siwo	23
Kuru sima	238, 289
Kuru sima strait	236
——————— directions	239
Kuruma no seto	248

	Page
Kuruma no seto, directions	250
Kusa-kaki	270
Kusaki sima	158
Kusikawa	152
Kusi saki	258
Kusuri	342
Kutsino sima	156
Kutsnose rock	278
Lady Inglis rocks	169
Laguerre group	371
La Pérouse strait	350
——————, winds and currents	18
Lazaref, Port	81
Leven reef	49
Lexington reef	146
Liancourt rocks	75
Lindsay, Port	297
——— island	129
Linschoten islands	155
——————, winds and currents	11
Liu-Kiu group	142
——————, winds and currents	11
Lloyd, Port	131–133
Loney island	137
Long island group	51
Lot's wife	192
Low cape	102
——— reef	263
——— Table point	96
Löwenhorn, Cape	356
Löwenstern, Cape	359
Lyra group	48
Ma sima	257
——— group	263
Macedonian reef	178
Mackau island	46
Madara sima	301
Magasaka point	256
Magicienne bay	123
Magnetic head	70
Mago saki	205
Maisonneuve	57
Makanrushir island	365
Makirima islands	150
Maki sima	275
Malabrigos	130
Manaita rocks	261
Mandarin island	56

Manziu island — 258	Misima nada — 252
Margaret islands — 130	Mississippi bay — 185
Mariana islands — 116	Mitarai — 248
Marjoribanks harbour — 40	Mitre rock — 60
Maru iso — 238	Mito iso — 181
—— yama — 225	Mitsuna island — 139
Mary, Cape — 360	Mitsuse rocks — 278
Masui sima — 263	Miwara — 243
Mata sima — 234	Miya no ura — 237
Mathews bay — 150	Miya saki — 210
Matoya harbour — 167	Miyadsu — 315
Matsu sima — 244, 286, 301	Miyako — 199
—— bay — 198	Miye no ura — 285
—— wo ga hana — 225	Mo ura — 327
Matsumae — 332	Modeste island — 46
Matu sima — 75	Mogi bay — 276
Matua island — 364	Moko sima — 299
Maury group — 47	Mole reef — 151
Me sima — 270	Mombets — 348
Me-se — 300	Momo — 234
Meac sima group — 269	Montgomery group — 152
Mears islands — 128	Montravel — 57
—— reef — 128	Montressor island — 57
Mebaru saki — 245	Mordvenof bay — 357
Medusa reef — 156	More no iso — 237
Megami point — 281	Mosuki — 253
Meiaco sima group — 135	Mosquito island — 62
——, winds and currents — 11	—— river — 95
Mejima — 319	Moto yama — 257
Meki sima — 227	Mouse islands — 59
Mela head — 190	Mozi saki — 259
—— ledge — 190	Mu sima — 250
Mequet island — 39	Mukai sima — 242
Mi sima — 293	Mura harbour — 166
Miaki — 194	Murigawa — 257
Michi-ga saki — 251	Murozu no se — 223
Midzu sima — 293	Murray sound — 48
Mikawa bay — 169	Mushi sima — 237
Mikomoto — 173	Musir islands — 364
Mikoto sima — 287	Mutsu sima — 234
Miku ura — 314	Muya-no seto — 204
Mikura — 194	
Mikuni bay — 317	Na sima — 303
Miname ura — 256	Nabe sima — 229
Minase sima — 255	Naboska rock — 54
Mina sone — 291	Nadeida bay — 356
Mino sima — 314	Naga sima — 251
Miojin saki — 182	Nagamo — 306
—— sima — 235	Nagano sima — 278
Mirjose rock — 319	Nagarobe — 156
Misaki bay — 276	Nagasaki — 282

INDEX.

	Page		Page
Nagasaki harbour	281	Noyshap, Cape, islands off	345
———, directions	284	Numa sima	253
Nagato sima	237		
Naka se	228	Ō-iso	203
—— sima	156	O no se	237
Nakhodka bay	92	Ō-shiba	252
Nana sima	318	Ō sima	236
Nanao harbour	318	O sima	227, 337
Nan How group	61	Obama	236
Nao sima	228	Ōbasan	237
Napha-kiang	143	O Kabuta	227
Narusi rock	260	Oar channel	146
Naruto passage	204	Obman bay	356
———, directions	207	Observation island	65
Natsu sima	328	Odawara bay	177
Natsui sima	184	Ode sima	228
Natsungi saki	313	Odutsi	229
Nelly rock	160	Ogame point	281
Nemoro	347	Oge sima	204, 246
New-port	130	Ohama bay	316
Nezumi sima	231, 235, 238	Ohigasi saki	196
Niegata, Port	320	Oho saki	325
Nii sima	196	—— sima	153
Nine-pin rock	51	Ojima	319
Niofa, Cape	148	Okamura sima	248
Nipon island, east coast	196–200	Okhotsk harbour	111
———, south-east coast	162–192	———, Sea of	108
———, west coast	312–324	———, winds and currents	7
———, north coast	325–331	Oki	234
Nishinaka	256	Oki islands	314
Niwatori jima	246	—— sima	227, 277
Nofitsi	328	Okinawa sima	143
Noka no hana	245	Oki-no se	168
—— sima	306	—— sima	181
Nokona	252	Okino sima	201, 210, 316
Noma sima	209	Oko islands	273
Nomi harbour	161	Okosiri island	337
Nomo saki	279	Olga bay	96
—— ura	279	Olivier group	35
No-o saki	229	Omae saki	169
Noöze	305	Ō mi sima	246, 249
North bay	360	Omura gulf	286
—— bank	231	Onekotan island	364
—— cape	290	Onohara	195
Northern route	240	Oöbiki ura	212
Nossyab	339	Oögawa sima	301
Notoro, Cape	351	Oonting, Port	149
Notske spit	347	Oö sima	162, 286
Nov-gorod harbour	89	Oö sima harbour	162
Noyshap, Cape	345	Oö tate	288

382 INDEX.

	Page
Opposite island	66
Oro no sima	309
Ō saka	219
——— roads	220
Osaki bay	210
——— sima	244
Osono sima	206
Ostrano point	88
Oterranai	338
Otméloi, Cape	359
Ō-tsu-no ura	182
Ousouri bay	92
Outer reef	167
Owari bay	168
Owasi bay	165
Oya Siwo	26
Ozumi no hana	238
Pagan island	126
Pago harbour	117
Pallada road	88
Pallas rocks	269
Papenburg	281
Paramushir island	365
Parece vela	128
Parker shoal	273
Parry group	134
Passages in S.W. monsoon	29, 30
——— N.E. monsoon	26–28
Pat-chung-san group	136
——— island	137
Patience bay	357
———, Cape	357
Peel group	62
——— island	131
Peh Leng Tao	33
Perseus rock	238
Pestchanoi point	91
Petit Thouars, Cape	84
Petropaulski	112
Petrova islet	94
——— rock	97
Pico channel	362
Ping-hai harbour	77
——— yang inlet	31
Pinnacle group	142
——— island	63, 141
——— rock	344
Pioneer rocks	270
Pique bay	100

	Page
Ponafidin island	192
Portsmouth breakers	169
Posiette bay	87
Pretty islands	59
Prince Imperial archipelago	34
Pylades shoal	31
Quelpart island	53
Raikoku island	364
Raleigh rock	142
Rasa island	134
Rashua	364
Ratmanof, Cape	358
Rattler rock	209
Rebuntsiriboi island	363
Redfield rocks	195
Reef islands	151
Refunsiri island	349
Reille rock	47
Rimnik, Cape	358
Ripple island	52
Risiri island	349
Ritidian point	119
Riugon	237
Robben island	358
Roberton island	137
Robinett rock	294
Roche conique	36
Roiven, Cape	317
Rokuren island	263
Romanzov bay	340
Rosario island	134
Ross island	47
Rota	120
Round island	252
——— rock	308
Roze island	38
——— roads	37
Saddle island	45, 60
Sado island	322
Sagami misaki	180
Saghalin island	350
Sagitsu no ura	274
Sail rock	131
Saint Eustaphia bay	96
——— Jona island	110
——— Valentine bay	95
——— Vincent channel	232
——— Vladmir bay	98

INDEX.

	Page		Page
Sakai	221	Siga sima	306
Saki sima	242	Sikine sima	196
Saipan island	122	Sikok, south coast	160
Samarang rock	62	—— no Awa	203
San Alessandro	130	Sima, Cape	167
—— Augustino	129	Simabara gulf	275
—— Luis d'Apra, Port	118	Simada sima	205
Sanagi sima	231	Simago	155
Sandon rocks	154	Simidzu bay	171
San-men sima	229	Simoda harbour	174
Sanumi sima	245	Simonamba, Cape	253
Santa Rosa shoal	120	Simonoseki	259
Sappro	338	—————— strait	257
Saracen reefs	288	——————, directions	257, 264
Sariguan island	125	Simusir island	363
Saru sima	182	Singapore rock	330
Satano misaki	160	Sira saki	316
Se no kata bana	205	—— take	290
Sea rock	52, 66	Sirakami, Cape	331
Sebastian Lobos	130	Siretoko, Cape	353
Seen island	65	Sir James Hall group	32
Sei sima	229	Siro sima	262
Selby island	56	Siriya saki	199
Senda saki	181	Sirotoko, Cape	347
Sendai bay	197	Sisi sima	233
Sentinel island	66	Sisiki bay	291
Seriphos	157	Sisuro point	86
Serpent rock	308	Sitziwura bay	276
Serrated island	56	Siwo misaki	215
Seto-da jima	248	Siwokubi, Cape	335
—— Uchi	216	Siyako	230
Shah bay	149	—— ledge	230
Shami sima	229	Skeen islands	65
Shanghae to Nagasaki	27, 30	Sketch island	66
Shape island	60	Skotan	361
Shantarski islands	109	Slavianski bay	90
Shelter bay	100	Small group	58
Shiash-Kotan islands	364	Smith island	193
Shibets	347	Sober island	51
Shika no se	223	Son Tsik group	60
Shirasai saki	212	Sosanjaya bay	121
Shira she	287	Sotonohirase rock	278
Shiranai	328	Southampton rock	175
Shi-shaku sima	235	South Black rock	52
Shiwo saki	207	—— cape	292
Sho Cheng Tao	33	—— Double island	50
Shoal gulf	42	Soya, Cape	340
—— patch	309	Sozu sima	226
Shumshu island	365	Split island	66
Siau Wuhu bay	94	Spindle islet	65
Seiniavin, Cape	357	Stapleton island	134

INDEX.

	Page
Stevens island	151
Su saki	189
——— harbour	161
——— sima	152
Suco island	148
Suffren bay	102
Sukune sima	242
Sulphur island	129
Sung-ami	211
Sunharon roads	122
Supply rock	175
Surley island	60
Suruga gulf	170
Suwa sima	155
Suwo nada	256
Suzume	279
Swallow rock	52
Sybille bay	100
Sydney to Yedo, passage	30
Sylvia rock	294
Tabu sima	324
Ta Cheng Tao	33
Tache blanche, La	37
Tadotsŭ	233
Tago bay	173
Taka sima	227, 270, 278, 290, 300, 305
Takabo	286
Takaikami	234
Takami island	231
Takanaba	201
Taka no saki	326
——— yama	246
Takashi yama	246
Take sima	157
Takura saki	209
Tama no ura	268
Tameitsi bay	276
Tanabe bay	214
Tanapag harbour	123
Tanega sima	157
Tano bank	258
Tarara island	189
Tarofofo harbour	117
Tartary, Gulf	100
———————, winds and currents	5
Taruri islands	239
Tas de Foin, Les	87
Taske harbour	293
Tate mura	72
Tati-yama bay	189

	Page
Ta-Tong river	32
Tatsupi saki	325
Tavano, Port	363
Tcheniya bay	93
Te sima	228
Tengo	285
Tera sima	286
Three rocks spit	229
Ti-a-usu island	142
Tinian island	121
Tishia rock	352
Tō saki	205
To sima	196
Tobi sima	205
Tobootchi bay	354
Toka-shee	151
Tokara sima	155
Tomio saki	182
Tomioka	274
Tomo	234
Toö-dai	306
Tori	36
Tori ishi	236
Toriwi saki	330
Totomosiri	352
Toyama bay	320
Toyo	234
Tracey island	59
Treaty point	185
——— ports	159
Tree island	130
Triangle island	60
Tsau-liang-hai harbour	68
Tsiring sima	272
Tskhara bay	211
Tskuye no se	225
Tsu sima	72, 237
Tsuba sima	251
Tsugar strait	325
———————, winds and currents	15
———————, directions	336
Tsuika, Cape	332
Tsukarase	271
Tsuri	253
Tsuruga bay	316
Tsuru-ga saki	206
Tubootch harbour	148
Tumen river	86
Tunashee island	151
Twins, The	51
Typhoons	19

INDEX.   385

	Page		Page
Ty-pin-san group	139	Webster island	58
Tzuzuki	251	Whale island	52
		——— reef	151
Uchi umi	205	——— rock	88
Ucona rocks	174	White cliff bay	90
Udsi	234	Whitshed bay	259
——— sima	271	Winds: West coast of Korea	1–2
Udsuzeri bay	341	——— East coast and Sea of Japan	2–5
Uma sima	237	——— Gulf of Tartary	5–6
Umata bay	117	——— Sea of Okhotsk	7–8
Unkofsky bay	77	——— S.E. coast of Kamchatka	9
Uraga	182	——— Mariana islands	10
——— channel	180	——— Bonin islands	10–11
———, directions	191	——— Meiaco sima group	11
Ura-kami harbour	164	——— Liu-kiu and Linschoten islands	11–12
——— -no-go ura	184		
——— no-utsi	161	——— Japan, south and east coasts	14–16
Urei saki	226	——— Tsugar strait	16
Urracas islands	127	——— Yezo island	17–18
Uru sima	153	——— La Pérouse strait	18
Urup	362	——— Kuril islands	19
Ururi sima	345	Wo sima	270
Use	158	Wrangle bay	92
Usi sima	230	Wu sima	251
Ushishir	364		
Usu, Cape	345	Ya sima	255
——— sima	251	Yafiko yama	320
Ute no ura	246	Yaguchi ura	165
Utone	196	Yakang island	151
Uwa sima	255	Yakimu, Cape	150
		Yakuno sima	156
Van Diemen strait	150	Yama gawa harbour	273
Vandalia bluff	174	Yamada harbour	198
Vashon, Cape	68	Yamata iso	223
Venancourt rock	47	Yanagi islet	152
Villeuchinski, Mount	113	——— seto	251
Vincennes strait	157	Yasman take	290
Vineta rock	294	Ye sima	224
Virst, Cape	359	— saki	225
Vladivostok, Port	92	— no ura	225
Volcano bay	340	Yebeya sima	152
——— islands	129	Yebosi sima	303
Vostok bank	104	Yeboshi yama	184
Vries island	196	Yebukuro no minato	290
Wada sima harbour	203	Yedo	187
Walker bay	133	——— anchorage	186
——— island	63	——— gulf	180
Washington gulf	50	———, directions	190
Watakano sima	167	——— to Hong Kong	27, 29
Waters rock	274	Yeno	234
Wayoda rock	76	Yenoi sima	288

	Page		Page
Yenokido	184	Yokoiso, Cape	325
Yerabu sima	152	Yokoska harbour	183
Yerimo, Cape	342	Yori sima	153
Yesan, Cape	335	Yu no ura	303
Yezo island	331	Yubi sima	226
—— west coast	337	Yuki no ura	285
—— strait	348	Yung-Hing bay	80
—— winds and currents	17	Yura	209
Ykimah island	141	—— no uchi	212
Ynarajan bay	117	Yutsi sima	318
Yo sima	229		
Yobuko harbour	299	Zamok, Cape	93
Yodsibi rock	260	Zealandia breakers	125
Yoko sima	155, 237, 242, 245	Zeyts-por	62
Yokohama	185	Zoga saki	210